AquaPisces
reach for the balance

Dev Bhattacharyya

Disclaimer – The author or the book AquaPisces does not guarantee the accuracy or reliability of any information, content or advertisements contained in, resulting from, or linked to the text or affiliated website. The author reserves the right, at his sole discretion and without any obligation, to make improvements to, or correct any error or omissions in any portion of the service or the materials. By utilizing and accessing the contents of AquaPisces book or website and/or by requesting and/or receiving astrological or Ayurvedic interpretations and/or advice, you agree to release the author from any and all liability with regard to the contents of the book, site and/or advice received. All services, materials and products at AquaPisces are provided for entertainment purposes only. Potential benefits from herbals, music, aroma or astrology are recommended based upon traditional uses and may not be generally recognized as substantiated by competent and reliable scientific evidence. No warranties are made as to the correctness of the service, materials or products. The author, AquaPisces or any affiliated site expressly disclaim any and all warranties, expressed or implied. In no event, shall the author or AquaPisces be liable for any direct, indirect, incidental, punitive or consequential damages of any kind whatsoever with respect to its service, materials and products. If for political, cultural or social reasons astrology or Ayurveda is not accepted in your locality or community, by accessing, reading contents of AquaPisces or affiliate site and/or by receiving astrological or Ayurvedic information and the associated services or products from AquaPisces, you agree that you do so of your own free will and that you will not hold the author or AquaPisces responsible in any way.

DevbInc

Copyright © 2016 Dev Bhattacharyya
All Rights Reserved

Library of Congress Cataloging. LCCN: 2017906327

Published by Devb Inc. https://www.devb.com

ISBN: 0997888717
ISBN-13: 978-0997888713

DEDICATION

*** To the lord ***

To Mithoo, Dea, Sonne, Kamryn, My Mother, My Mother-in-law, Sha
And to everyone else I know
No names missed or forgotten

To the fallen, who need to rise
to the risen, who want to pause
to the paused, who seek the lord
a small helping hand

in the memory of fallen heroes
veterans, belated fathers
grandsires
to a family that goes back 33 generations
who have inspired me all along

CONTENTS

Dedication iii
Contents iv
Acknowledgments ix
Introduction 1
Beginning of time 7
Different Shores 23
King and Us 26
Wellness Axioms and corollaries 34
    Dosha Axioms 41
Personal Wellness 54
    Vayu streams 57
    Dhatu systems or tissues 67
    Secondary tissues - Upadhatu 72
    Waste from tissues 72
    Seven kala-s 78
    Mull excretions, waste produced internally 79
    Erroneous flow 94
Basic Constitution 101
    Proportions of dosha types 102
    Basic body structure 103
    Effects of guna vectors on dosha mental makeups 118
    Seasonal changes in temperate regions 122
    Aggravation times for dosha 123
    Dosha modes in the disease process 128
    Other factors in dosha aggravation 128
    Six stages of disease 130
    Diseases traverse three different pathways 133
    Disease as a state model 135
    Symptoms of aggravated dosha types 139

Vata in the dhatu-s 144
Pitta in the dhatu-s 146
Kapha in the dhatu-s 148
Three methods of pinpointing the problem...149
Disease busters 150
Pulse reading 151
Pulse and organ correspondences...155
Synthesis..156
Tongue diagnosis...157
Abdominal diagnosis 158
Six tastes 159
Dosha and the six tastes 160
Six tastes as they occur in nature 164
Combining tastes 166
Protective elements 171
Diet..172
Diet for dosha types...175
Incorrect food combinations..190
Digestive, eliminative disorders..191
High dosha levels in the digestive system 193
Elimination..195
Laxatives and constipation..196
Preparing herbs 198
Therapy..203
Reduce first, supply next..204
Refreshing oil..210
Tonics for dosha types...211
Rehabilitation 212
Rejuvenating the mind 214
Treat Vikruti safeguard Prakruti...215
Key Treatment Principles...216
Subtle therapy 219
Perfumery..226
Treating tissues and channels 227
Ojas...235
Herbs and channels 235
Sub-dosha treatment...241

- Vata dosha and sub-dosha treatment 241
- Pitta dosha and sub-dosha treatment 244
- Kapha dosha and sub-dosha treatment 246
- Treating five prana airs, tissues and channels 249
- Prana diagnosis and therapy 251
- Prana absorption 252
- Prana in digestive system 256
- Prana healing 260
- Massage and touch 269
- Marma therapy 272
- Stimulating Marma regions 275

Co-Creating Wellness 276
- Attributes of Signs 292
- Graha friendship and enmity 295
- Astrology and Ayurveda 305
- Astrology and yoga 307
- Graha-s and signs 372
- Weak ascendants 375
- Aspects 376
- House and sign positions 376
- Graha forte 377
- From graha-s to the stars 382
- Nakshatra-s 383
- What the Nakshatra-s mean? 389
- Nakshatra-s and guna vectors 397
- Nakshatra gender 400
- Nakshatra and Purushartha 400
- Nakshatra Pairs 401
- Nakshatra-s and Lunar Months 402
- Retrogression and hidden traits 403
- Quality of time 404
- Favorable and unfavorable Nakshatra-s 406
- Siddha Yoga 406
- Nakshatra-s transits 408
- Nakshatra daily transits 412
- Favorable birth Nakshatra 413
- Tithi-s for activities 416

  Lords of Tithi-s 419
  Karana 422
  Panchanga yogas 424
  Unfavorable yogas 426
  Karana and yoga 426
  Siddha favorable tithi-s 427
  Dagdha unfavorable tithi-s 427
  Krakacha favorable tithi-s 427
  Sun's travel into new signs 428
  Equinoctial and Solstice Points 428
  Northern and Southern Courses of the Sun 428
  Music therapy 429
  Dasa system 436
  The way forward 445

Piecing It All Together 450
  Music Making 460
  Gemstones and Colors 460
  Herbals 461

Index 474

Reference 483

About The Author 484

ACKNOWLEDGMENTS

Salutations to *Parasara* and *Agnivesa* who pioneered the work on *Vedanga Jyotish* and *Ayurveda*. It is so easy to stand over their shoulders and seek beyond what they found. Had they not commenced the composition, we would still be taking baby steps.

This book will be a work in progress for the next several years. There cannot be a true rendition of the ancient documents, this text is no exception, but in all its imperfections, I hope it nurtures an awakening.

While I realize the purpose in life is much more than personal fulfillment, peace or mere happiness, I have yet to discern what that objective truly is.

> of what use is this wealth
> when it will not buy an ounce of health
> ...

INTRODUCTION

he name AquaPisces comes from the changeover to Aquarius era from Pisces, the cusped move from the benign Jupiter ruled Pisces into aerial, mind-persuading Saturnine Aquarius. AquaPisces provides a deep insight into the workings of Western and Vedic Astrology, Ayurveda and Chinese Medicine. Astrological findings and insight, coupled with herbal supplements, transitory influences, dietary supplements, seasonal cleansing appear interspersed in the text.

We are all here on this land on a mission - a divine mission - to better our lives and the lives of many other planetary dwellers. The 'fundamental being' or 'the Cosmic Man' is an archetypal figure symbolizing existence, consciousness and bliss. We clothe this principle in different ways.

Traditional medicine has observed nature and natural phenomena over thousands of years, it views humans as a microcosmic representation of the universe that surrounds them. Humans and all life forms are inseparable from natural cosmic laws. Even Native Americans were a 'part of the total living universe,' wrote anthropologist Frederick Turner, 'they achieved spiritual health only by accepting the condition and by attempting to live under it.'

Simplifying the above principles, AquaPisces is many-thousands of years' journey across two astrological phenomena of Aquarius and Pisces. While we are at the threshold of Aquarius, the oceanic secrets revealed in the era of Pisces escape us. Astrology is at the mainstay of this transformation of era, what we were to what has changed. Ayurveda is at the center stage of all advents of the current era, it is a known fact that man enjoyed better health before the Iron Age. All systems stem from the principles that define our role in the ecosystem.

AquaPisces addresses astrology, herbal wellness and others with the belief it can narrow down the predictions accurately, confirm a diagnosis and offer supplements to a cure prescribed by a registered-practitioner on a multitude of mind and health problems. The ancestors believed in detailed analysis of an astrological chart with health as a prime focus. They understood that health came first, immortality later.

- AquaPisces standardizes on a wellness approach[1]
- Provides approximate timing of disease onset, outcome, cure and rehabilitation
- Offers hints on possible sites of disease and the nature
- Information provided in this book or the website https://www.aquapisces.com is not a substitute for advice from a physician or doctor. Please consult a licensed doctor or physician before starting any diet or exercise; especially if you have a medical condition.

Agnivesa's Charaka Samhita affirms the 'fundamental being' or the 'Cosmic Man' was the one who propounded Ayurveda and later sub divided under three branches of etiology, symptomatology and therapeutics. According to the ancient *Puranas*[2], the progenitor *Daksha Prajapati* first learned the Veda, Jyotish and Ayurveda, and he transferred his knowledge to the deities, *Ashvini-Kumaras* and *Indra*, and Sage *Bharadwaj*. His devotee, Atria learnt from Bharadwaj and distributed the entire education to his six disciples, *Agnivesa, Bhela, Jatukrana, Parasara, Harita* and *Sharapani*.

---

[1] As described in ancient, somewhat forgotten scriptures. These scriptures in no way refutes modern medicine, pharmacology and related health matters as studied in the schools, colleges and universities.
[2] Puranas are ancient Vedic mythologies and legends which were narrated in a story like manner.

The popular term Ayurveda comes from the *Samhita*[3] composed by *Agnivesa* along with several chapters narrated from *Charaka*. Jyotish, known as Vedic Astrology or *Hora Sastra* comes from *Parasara's* composition. Other sages such as *Brighu* and *Jaimini* contributed to such subjects that dealt with wellness. They devised multiple systems to realize the pervasive karma influencing our mind and body function and their external interactions and relationships. Vedic systems balance psychology with the physical, dealing with life, character and achievements and not just the metaphysical or the physical phenomena. The usefulness of Vedic Astrology is more in timing the disease onset and its outcome, determining when disease can occur and how it is likely to progress. Vedic Astrology is a great aid to Ayurvedic health matters, it is useful with other systems of wellness, besides it shows a native's physical prowess and possible weaknesses.

Ayurveda, Vedanga Jyotish also referred to as Vedic Astrology, Yoga and Classical music have a common connection through the Pancha-Bhutas - five elements of earth, water, fire, air and etheric space. The beauty of these systems and their integration is that their study, analysis and interpretations come from a few empirical principles. There is no need to dissect or break apart a substance to understand its core, both the systems emphasize on mapping the elements, the vectors to traits and attributes and reconciling thereof. To understand these methods, we must first examine the background, the philosophy and worldview that constructed them. Study of Ayurveda emphasizes certain cosmological axioms and philosophies, a special understanding of cosmic evolution and the purpose of life we find in the system of Yoga. Ayurveda came about within the context of the Yoga system, which provides the broader ideas and principles by which one can comprehend Ayurveda. Ayurveda is the health aspect of the 'Vedic System'. It is the 'Veda,' the knowledge and wisdom of 'Ayu,' life or longevity. Ayurveda comes from the great stream of Vedic spiritual knowledge. It also has much in common with older Greek thought. Ayurveda is supplementary Veda or Upaveda. Other important branches of the Vedas include Vedanga, limb of the Vedas, which are closer to the Vedas, Vedic practices than the Upaveda, the most important of which is Vedic astrology frequently used along with Ayurveda.

---

[3] Samhita is a compilation of text from different sources, times and authors

The practical side of Vedic system is the scheme of Yoga. Yoga develops the ideas of Vedic philosophy into tools that helps uplift the consciousness. Yoga is not just asana or yoga postures but a part of the stirring, inspiring uplifting it provides. As a custom, Ayurveda is the healing branch of the scheme of yoga, devised by yogis and seers in maximizing longevity for the pursuit of Yoga and the other legitimate aims of life. 'Ayu' or 'life' in Ayurveda is the harmony of the body, mind and spirit.

All forms of ancient eastern and western philosophy share similar principles, which spreads into Astrology and Ayurveda scriptures. Summarizing the hermetic principles, the fundamental truth or reality dawns on us that there is without a shred of doubt, a state of pure consciousness or pure awareness, beyond word and thought, where there is peace, bliss, compassion and liberation. The goal of all life is in achieving that. Being caught in a state of suffering or unhappiness comes from ego or principle of selfishness. The ego sets in motion a stream of action or karma, which keeps us in shackles. To break free from this chain of suffering, one must negate that ego, and silence the mind. Breaking out of the confines implies going beyond dread, longing and anger; beyond the emotions that terrorize the mind, by adopting the ideals of honesty, modesty and passivity. To a great degree, yoga and meditation can speed up the progress; however, this goal is not a personal one but a part of a greater liberation involving all life. A practitioner must observe the systems of astrology and Ayurveda, and Vedas for the unity and good of all. The challenge is how do you initiate a collective start. To strengthen a community, you must get strong first. Those disturbances or imbalances of the dosha types in the body need correction first before expanding the ecosystem to include others.

Ayurveda has deep roots in the Vedas. An esoteric view suggests Vedas existed even before creation and Vedas' principles make up the cosmos. The four primary celestial Vedic texts are the Rig, Yajur, Sama and Atharva Vedas. Rig Veda or the knowledge of 'Riks' deals with essential principles that the ancient seers heard while engrossed in their normal ascetic methods. The celestial sound revealed showed the keys to the vibratory structure of the universe, which became the secret science of mantra or sacred chants; essentially defining a book of cosmic law. The aspirant who wishes to know more on this subject, who finds enlightenment in the Rik-sounds, becomes a Rishi. Vedas are the basis of Cosmic Speech or the Divine Word. Sama Veda gives a deeper meaning to Rig Veda mantras through the vibrational melodies and musical forms in transforming the mind and emotions. It is the basis of Cosmic Prana. Yajur Veda or science of action develops them into outer and inner rituals or transformative actions like the practice of Yoga forming the basis of Cosmic Mind.

Atharva Veda adds supplementary mantras for diverse conditions, including health and psychic protection, describing mantras that treat diseases along with names of plants that can be used for healing. Traditional texts often relate Ayurveda to Atharva Veda. Indus culture grew into a dominant way of life on the periphery of Sarasvati river of Vedic fame. When the river dried around 1900 BCE it brought about a sudden upheaval to cultural advancements, and life and civilization migrated to the plains of the rivers of Yamuna and Ganga. Ayurveda borrows a lot from the Indus or Sarasvati values, which witnessed a tremendous rise in knowledge and culture. It continued to develop in different increments to what remains in the present-day state. Rishis and seers who taught the art were often doctors and apothecaries. A Rishi of the Rig Veda, Bharadwaj transmitted the science of Ayurveda from the realms of the gods or higher cosmic intelligences to his disciples. Rig Veda Samhita[4] text speaks on three main Ayurvedic forces Vayu[5], Agni and Apah. Mantras mention the secret depths where medicines are found in the oceans. Metaphor of knowledge as ocean is a common occurrence in the Vedas. Yajur Veda acquaints us with specific rituals empowered to supplement health and longevity. Sama Veda institutes music and harmonics to streamline the mind with its cosmic counterpart. Atharva Veda suggests specific mantras with plant offerings in curing disorders. The works of the seers found a new meaning with Dhanvantari of Varanasi, circa 1500 BCE, who extended Ayurveda. Considered a pioneer, he brought several texts under one compilation. Thereon, Ayurveda continued to mature in rapid acceleration and took on a focused form and arose as a distinct school of thought and practice. The classic texts of the Charaka Samhita and Sushruta Samhita, named after the two great Ayurvedic physicians, Charaka and Sushruta acknowledges this fact. Charaka represents internal medicine or herbal school while Sushruta represents surgery. At the time of the Buddha circa 500 BCE, Ayurveda was already an established form of healing. Ayurveda spread throughout the orient into Tibet, China, Indonesia and Cambodia with different degrees of adoption. Ayurvedic influences reached as far as Greece, cohabiting with traditional Greek medicine. Vagabhatta of Sindh renewed the Ayurvedic approach in his classic, the third of the main Ayurvedic texts, Astanga Hridayam c. 500 CE. Vagabhatta rewrote the original Charaka and Sushruta texts into a concise form for easy learning.

---

[4] Rig Veda has no date. The compilation of Rig Veda Samhita – many Mantras into a single compilation happened around 3000 BCE.

[5] The cosmic power Vayu is related to Prana or Vata. Agni related to Pitta, and Apah related to Kapha.

Soma, as it appears in Rig Veda is described as a potent herbal preparation whose knowledge became extinct in the passage of time. Many alchemic preparations appear in texts later, which attempt to take the place of Soma. Practice of Ayurveda declined after 1000 CE when Persian invaders and Huns destroyed many libraries and colleges. In spite of the despotism, the wise painstakingly prepared several Ayurvedic classics in that period. Ayurveda suffered under British rule after 1750 CE, where the new government tried to suppress it, shutting down all the Ayurvedic colleges. Ayurveda survived in smaller settings and private schools.

Why this book? The questions that haunt most people on why they are on this planet is not an easy one to answer. Then there is this unresolved question on the 'how's' and 'whys' of creation. The ancient texts offered several solutions and hypothesis that were lost in incorrect interpretations and biased religious dogmas. I chose the subject to present the works without dragging religion and ownership into the midst. The ancient seers had worked out some of the answers; this was a better way of enlightening the reader on what they found. The ancestors enjoyed a deep spiritual appreciation of life, and it can become yours too.

It takes several years to get a handle on how you want to organize your experiences, learning and readings into a compiled version. I do not recall when I started, some of my notes are not even dated; but yes, it has been a few years since I undertook the work. Dr. R.L. Kashyap's course on Rig-Veda was a tremendous help. Dr. Kashyap, former professor of Purdue University runs SAKSHI with one aim to bring out the intelligent flavor of the Vedas.

The chapters cover many scriptures. Sometimes transliterated text appears in italics; sometimes, Sanskrit words are used to improve their understanding. Not all stanzas are transliterated. The stanzas sometimes contain sentences from other scriptures just to keep the relevance.

BEGINNING OF TIME
1741 CE

Night covered the red, alluvial grounds with a drenched, shroud of darkness. The tall grass swayed with the incessant rain. Distant music cooed from a Murali[6], accompanied by the jingles of cowbells of returning cattle. A Rudravina[7] played a lone, haunting tone. As soon as it had started, the voice of the instrument ceased. The night was still as the abandoned string instrument; just the motionless full moon festooned the land with incessant silhouettes. Even the Damodar River that ran along the village lines awaited in tepid stillness as it tugged higher, closer to the tides of moon. The only signs of agitation were that of the temple architect, who had lost his air of easy assurance. He was perspiring freely, looking every bit anxious, mopping his face constantly with his bandana, while he spoke incessantly. Dharanidhar, who preferred men call him Dhar, glanced at his neighbor in distaste. It was a little unfair to let this architect suffer such prolonged discomfort; at the same time, he felt he was not particularly sorry for him. He reminded himself, he had other things to worry about.

Assembled were twenty-seven people from different professions in the village under the thatched, terracotta cabin, where roughly hewn planks covered the floor, the monsoon weather turning it slippery and damp. Several cots lay in seeming confusion around the wide floor with piles of shawls, carpets and jute cushions offering a quiet comfort to the large gathering.

---

[6] Murali is a bamboo flute, one of the musical instruments associated with Lord Krishna
[7] A Rudravina is a predecessor to other stringed instruments like the Sitar and Sarod.

Some of them stood, while the rest reclined, the glow of the earthen lamps and lanterns tendered their beams on a pile of curious parchments and hand drawings that had everyone's attention. Purists would have contended without sentiment that the drawings were pathetic, almost childlike in their appearance, but it held everyone's gaze and attention at that snapshot in time. Dhar had carefully stressed to the assembled folks that the contents in the parchments were more important than the presentation, especially to the village chieftain who shared the wooden cot with the temple architect. A dull pain found its way towards his throat and grew in intensity. Far above him, the late autumn rain battered the disappearing greenery, and the colored leaves of the nearest maple came down harsh on the makeshift room through the gloom. Dhar was a fine, upstanding, tall, young, promising master of the scriptures, whose acumen and sharp intelligence complimented his rich black, fierce moustache.

As the temple architect rambled on what the Malla kings had architected for centuries in that region, Dhar's mind turned to inner recesses as he sought Pancharatha design. Pancha, 'five', ratha, facets or a five-faceted design with a repeatable structure using squares and cubes would define the architecture. He counted in his mind the squares he would need to finish the structure and he reassured himself that 54 was the exact number he had counted earlier. He had never in his life advertised his architectural skills; this was perhaps his only opportunity to influence the people on how he wanted to construct the building. The reigning king had extended the budget to build three temples over the next two decades. While two of the elaborate temples awaited architecture, their design decisions were already in place. His was still in works though in his mind he had a clear picture of what he wanted built, the question that lingered was, would these influential people let him? It was difficult to express the augmented reality of his virtual play-place to the men around; his mind and brain were different, and he knew it. Fifty-four squares would complete the internal design. The extruded floor would resemble three-dimensional mosaic floors he had thought of designing.

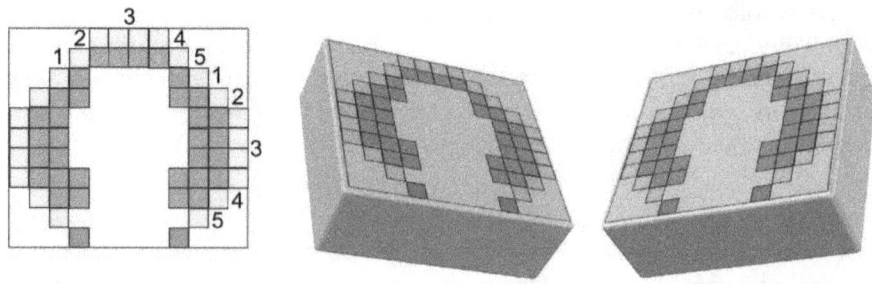

To speak against the earlier designs of Terracotta and use stone, bricks and stucco would not be an easy idea to convince the elite gathered under the makeshift hall. Design of the other two temples accommodated more people, offered more room and ambience, this was a strange design compared to them. Worst, it needed the approval of the village chieftain and all his merry-men gathered there. The base of the building was just 12 feet by 12 feet. It had a small stairway leading into the inner sanctum. A Pancha Ratha design in bricks and stucco, just 33 feet from the ground to the finial. Five tiger-statues made in stone would adorn the building facets at the curving docks at nearly 30 feet above ground. Facets on the Ratha would have minimum decorations. The entrance, with high stairs; where the first set of stairs was 2 feet high leading to an arched doorway scarcely 6 feet high. A large bodied person would barely get through the doorway. He was proposing a design that coerced the surrounding energy to navigate to the subtle in the core.

"O' Dhar," cried the temple architect, "Why build a temple this cramped and insipid in a land where our eyes seek nothing but the ornate temples. These are our churches to the community, to hold sermons of scriptures, to train our men and women on matters of peace and war, on family and lineage, on faith and learning. Besides, think of how much time it will take to finish this church."

"I understand your feelings Ajay," Dhar spoke in earnest, his voice slow and curt. "Unlike a shrine with traditional design, the design here is of an open-door church. This is our only opportunity to transfer the scriptures from Vedagarbha to the insides of the proposed building. When we reinstate the deities within, under their surveillance would stay the scriptures they themselves have propounded." His voice was a whisper as he fought the emotions.

"Young Dhar, wise you are for your age. I had known your father for many years, he was a brilliant scholar, he must have taught you many things we know little of," the village chieftain spoke sending a spiral of tobacco smoke towards the ceiling. "The scriptures, privy to your family have remained in safety for twenty generations. Our kings have withstood the attacks of the men of Persia many times. No one has dared to even step into the sacred libraries, why then do you worry about the scriptures and the deities so much Dhar? They are in very safe hands."

"Sire, call it a premonition, call it advanced warning, but I have in my subconscious mind witnessed Vedagarbha[8] destroyed by men who are different. They wear coats of red, invade our lands in pursuit of gold, silk and spices. Unlike the Persian raiders, they destroy our key scriptures; our scriptures that have no equal."

"I will grant you the permit to build this temple, son. But you will have to tell us what those scriptures contain, tell us the secrets young Dhar. We wish to know."

"Thank you, Sire. Thank you all for hearing my plea. I am honored to speak on the scriptures. It had waited many thousands of years for this night, this moment. In fact, the architectural approach to the building stems from self-manifestation concepts, where the proposed design appears channeled and not imposed, which becomes plain as I speak of the scriptures and their pragmatic side. Today is the full-moon when we make the five-year correction of the leap year. I am surrounded by the wise and rain streaked winds that howl. Vayu be my witness, Varuna be thou my reveler and benefactor; in this Aquarian-Pisces hour, let me tell you from where the universe began."

"In the midst of nothing did it all begin. I use the word nothing, for whatever it is, it lies beyond perception, a logical indication of 'nothing'; it would be similar to sailing the Damodar river in winter on a moonless night. As a speck in the vast, surrounded by the tepid water, it is the imagery of nothingness. As you scan the surroundings, you spot this eddy on your starboard. Abruptly, the subtle monotony is fractured, and a whirlpool becomes visible, crested by waves and force in an otherwise lukewarm world. This entity has qualities; it has attributes; yet it is the same river. The housefly that set sail with you, now startled by the eddy, hovers near your face. He tries to focus his vision on your eye. At first, he sees a huge rounded mass, the size of this village; he is unlikely to see even the zenith of your eyeball or its nadir. Then he witnesses the skin, the mountainous nose; it would take much more to imagine that he is looking at another organic creature, but outside his dimensional world. Constrained by space and time, pertinent to his physical world, how can he even stray his imagination to boundaries and constrains which are unfathomable?"

---

[8] Vedagarbha – the Womb of the Vedas was a place in eastern India, which was named as Buxar.

"As you move your face, the fly turns away, some uncanny vibrations warn him. Unexpectedly the rounded mass is no longer there; he settles on his leaf-ferry that leads him to a mountain of food," he let the laughter and mirth settle, before he continued, "However, we see this fly, the leaf and the sugar crystal about the fly's size in a corner on the wooden raft. The fly enjoys the nourishing sugar crystal unaware of a towering creature standing above him; one who can play with him, offer more sugar crystals or swat him to his death."

"So are we my friends - under a playful, wrathful, benign and malefic yet alien influence of someone or something we cannot grasp from the limitations of the dimensions that surround us."

"While we can see the housefly, and watch over where it keeps travelling; the fly perceives nothing. His sixth sense; if he has five normal senses, tell him when it is no longer safe near the sugar mound. Likewise, we sense in our time frame and space when safe it is to do our work and when it is prudent we seek shelter elsewhere. Someone or something we cannot grasp, who bears no limits and constraints as we do, is watching us. For all you know that someone or something faces inhibitions by dimensions that limit his comprehension to what lies beyond him."

"There are so many explanations on how the universe could have begun its journey. Samkhya offers a more definite, common, palatable theory which is not blatantly esoteric."

"In a nutshell, there are many such dimensional worlds that defy our sense of logic, but through the lens of mathematics and metaphysics, they become comprehensible. Our ancestors drew upon the principles and arrived at certain axioms. There is this someone or something beyond all understanding, who may have taken part in our creation, but has nothing more to do with us. He, the cosmic man is a phenomenon and force that exists; active in his world, inactive from our perspective. The creative force approaches him, for the creative force has three vectors in sublimation the Cosmic man can activate. Passion of their meeting ignites the three vectors of Sattva, Rajas and Tamas to a state of readiness. Cosmic man presents to Creative-force - Prana, the life-force that escapes into the abyss of the Purity- Activity- Stability equilibrium state. As Cosmic man moves away, the three vectors and the life-force multiple into different units of mass and matter and the resulting universe is but a product of the Guna vectors and the life-force."

"Anu or atom is likely the smallest form of matter. The future, I am sure will reveal its constructive and destructive usage. However, a trillionth of an Anu or Atom is the dimension of the three vectors. Smaller therefore is the size of the life force. Threaded, it can combine and recombine many such thread-units of Purity-Activity-Stability complexes to form different sub-units, which on further combination form the micro, macro and the celestial universes. The gods or someone or something beyond our dimensional universe consist mainly of these same guna vectors, making them and the life-force the main unit of permeability."

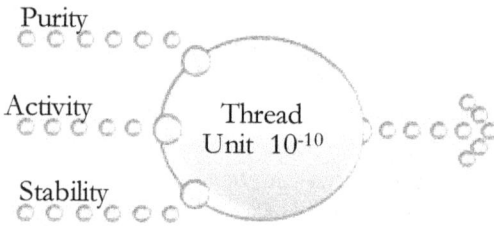

"In the process of creating, many patterns evolve; patterns, cyclical and repeatable. Patterns like the season of spring where life blossoms and autumn, where life faces decline. But, like the prior years, repeated are such phenomena. Such patterns lead themselves to predictability. The pattern, once revealed, becomes unconsciously a routine to us. When something falls outside the norms of the predictability; where the probability of repeated occurrence fails; challenged are we with catastrophes, mass deaths, mental anguish and headaches. The patterns are our key to harmony."

"Creative-force is the baseline comprising matter and antimatter that makes and breaks this universe. There is a gross side to her and a subtle side. Why do I keep referring to Creative-force as feminine? It is because someone or something beyond our comprehension, in his time frame and dimensional world feels the urge to begin the act of creation. Creative-force provides the womb for it. When he offers the seeds of life-force to her, she accepts it and continues to nourish her creation; Cosmic man, however declines to partake in any more activities. So, she devises a calendar of events; events that encompass all matter including the macro and micro, as she is the original form of matter or objectivity, the actual essence that will eventually manifest, the undifferentiated potential seed that will one-day stage an arrival, identified by name, form and action. Name and form are transient; action on the other hand is the qualifier for the calendar of events. She is not 'matter' in the material sense; Creative-force is essentially the capacity for the mind to experience, not limited to the visible objects in the outer world. Creative-force contains the prime attributes needed by all perceptible things."

"Think of Creative-force as the 'prime mover', 'the first power of action', closest resemblance to primal form of nature. As the prime material of creation, at the start of the process of creation, she is 'primal matter' or the first substance, where the three-guna vectors of Purity, Activity and Stability, are in a state of equilibrium. Creative-force provides the ground for multiplicity."

"All manifestation occurs through an underlying organic cosmic intelligence called the Mahat. It is a repository of all laws and principles that gets executed in the manifestation process; it also contains the mold from where the archetypal forms get seeded. Mahat is the 'vast', 'the great' and refers to the great principles behind life. Our ancestors knew for certain, even a fleeting glimpse of what is in the Vast would reveal to them the greatest knowledge. They sought through incredible means to access a fraction of this 'Kumbha'[9] of knowledge and found some in the celestial sounds of the 'Riks'[10]. They who heard these incredible, cosmic sounds; who became Rishis thereafter, spoke of them to their students and disciples and devised the mantras of Rig Veda to replicate the repository of the Vast on terrestrial earth. While the Vast is the Divine Mind, the mortal mind in its purity is its repository among us. From the complexity of the Vast, come the dimensions of space and time, the propagation of Divine Word and the seeds of differentiation. In the individual, The Vast becomes 'Buddhi,' the power of intelligence through which we discern truth from falsehood, right from wrong, the eternal from the transient."

"Once past the Vast phase, all other manifestations result from the process of differentiation. A generalized vastness of knowledge expresses the great cosmic knowledge. The analogy of the clay and its product, the vase that came from the potter's wheel is very relevant here. Imagine the clay to be the Vast, it engulfs the earth, extending to places we have not visited and perhaps never will. The vase resembles not the clay to the beholder; it has a specific shape with limited dimensions. When finished is the vase, stored it is carefully, lest it break. When it breaks, it returns to clay. Unlike the clay, which suffers no such breakages; it lives on, undaunted. Creation works through various separate, individual identities, which are the basis for the ego. 'Ahamkara' in a literal sense means 'towards individuality' or the 'I' factor."

---

[9] Kumbha – the pot. Namely the pot held in Aquarius. Kumbha is also the Sanskrit name of Aquarius
[10] Riks are the divine, celestial words heard by seers who eventually assembled all of them in the form of Mantras in the Vedas. He who heard a Rik became a Rishi.

"Though the word 'Ahamkara' is a noun, it describes the process of specialization. The process of 'I'-ness is built on a series of divisive thoughts; and not a real separate entity that exists within itself. It is a necessary power of division inherently found in nature, occurring as a stage in the process of evolution, but not representing the underlying truth or identity of creatures. Through it, the basic energies latent in Creative-force, working with the fundamental laws found in Cosmic Intelligence can take on specific forms. Under the sharp focus of ego, the basic qualities of Nature diversify as three groups of five, the senses, organs of action and the five elements."

"Every manifestation takes place through several individual, conditioned mentalities - consciousness. Ego automatically projects the mind. Even 'Anu', the atom has a 'mind', an underlying mind that coordinates atomic and subatomic activity and energy at an inorganic level. 'Manas' is the principle of emotion and imagination. It connects us with the outer world through the senses."

"Just a quick recap, Creative-force, in its primal state has three prime quality binding vectors, Sattva, Rajas[11] and Tamas. The guna-s, subtler than the five elements, which arise from their activity, precedes the appearance of 'Tanmatra'[12] or sensory potentials. All this happens within the realms of Creative-force, and becomes her champions for diversification. Thereby, every object takes birth, and every one of them has different combinations of the three vectors. Three vectors give us the key to different forms and life processes. While guna vectors are the causal factors in creation, the sensory potentials are the subtle factors, and the elements, the effects. Understanding the science of three guna vectors, like the science of the five elements, is an important pillar of Vedic methods. The foremost vector, Purity reflects quality of stability, harmony, virtue, being 'sat'. It is light or laghu[13] in nature and luminous. It has inward and upward motion and brings about the awakening and development of the soul. Purity gives happiness. It is the principle of intelligence."

---

[11] सत्त्व, रजस्, तमस् (Sattva, Rajas and Tamas)

[12] Tanmatra transliterated from the word तन्मात्र, means subtle element, mere essence

[13] Laghu means 'brilliance', Ursa Minor, the little bear constellation is called laghu saptarshi - लघु सप्तर्षि

"Rajas portrays the quality of distraction, turbulence and passion. It is mobile and deemed motivated. It possesses outward motion; its self-motivation and self-seeking actions lead to disintegration. A principle of energy, directed outwards, Rajas subjects us to pain and suffering. Tamas projects the quality of inertia. Heavy, stable, obstructing, its flow downward causes decay, degeneration and death. Stability is the principle of materialism. When the three-guna vectors are back in balance, Creative-force returns to the un-manifest state in which all her potentials get cognized at once. Then withdrawn is the creation. When not in balance, three guna vectors continue with the process of cosmic manifestation."

"Relative to Cosmic man, who is the sole seer in a state of seeing and the only true conscious entity, the entire creation is seen as something within the realms of observation, something objective in nature. As we evolve, we learn to discriminate between the seer and the seen, between subject and object, and cease to identify ourselves with other forms and functions of the external world. Yes, the I-factor slowly creeps in. In our normal ignorant consciousness, we identify ourselves with things like the body or emotional states as 'I am this,' 'this is mine,' 'I am delighted,' 'I am sad.' In this process of thought, we superimpose various qualities on the consciousness that transcends the guna qualities. All these are wrong, nothing short of an identity crisis of the seer and the seen. They place us under the influence of the external world where we suffer by its changes; when the body dies, we feel we are dying. Consciousness is not anything material or observable; what is noticeable is Creative-force with her attributes of matter. Just this mere knowledge sets us free from all sorrow and disturbances that the outer world promises. As we evolve, we gradually learn to detach our consciousness from the external world. First, we learn to detach ourselves from physical matter, then from emotions, thoughts, and the ego itself, which are all forms of subtle matter. It is only when we stop to identify with our thoughts, we get rewarded with a perception of the entire realm of Creative-force, we then return to our nature as Cosmic man or pure consciousness, to a state of nothing but self-realization and liberation."

"This balance of the three guna vectors define the homeostasis where pure Sattvic play is at its foremost. Preponderance and refinement of Purity empowers the balance. Purity as it develops, is the basis of practices in the higher plane. Stability throws in the power of ignorance that veils our true nature. The world gets projected when the Activity vector jumpstarts the power of imagination. It puts us in bondage where we believe in the multiplicity of the external. Sattva sets the clarity or peace through which we can perceive the truth."

"Three guna vectors working through Ahamkara-ego on the five Tanmatra sensory potentials produce three groups with five objects. Sattva invokes changes in Tanmatra to harvest five sense organs. Rajas adjusts them into the five organs of action. From Tamas comes their alteration into the five elements. Rajas' energy turns into the five vital breaths or Prana, enabling coordination between the five sense organs and five action organs. Rajas even ensures transference of sensory information into capacity for action, establishing relationships with the motor organs. All this is possible because the vectors possess deeper and broader actions as cosmic energy."

"I am sure you are wondering what then are the Sensory-Potential entries? These are the root vivacities of sound, touch, sight, taste and smell. Such prime energies are necessary in coordinating sense organs with sense objects. Emitted they are on a subtle level by all things in the world. They are the subtle forms of the five elements before they get differentiated into different gross objects. Tanmatra objects get named after their sensory qualities, Shabda Sensory-Potential is from sound, Rupa Sensory-Potential is after sight, a pleasing sight; Sparsha Sensory-Potential from touch, Rasa Sensory-Potential after taste, Gandha Sensory-Potential from smell and olfactory. The word 'Tanmatra' or Sensory-Potential means 'primal measure' from the root words 'tat' and 'matra', not to be confused with sensory potentials as they are subtler and the root of all sensory and elemental potentials. Sensory-Potential forces show the basic fivefold structure of the cosmos."

"Then there are five sense organs or Pancha Jnanendriyani[14], which have the potential for mental experience of the outer world. They become differentiated and sensitized through the process of evolution. Ears as organs of sound senses the objects of etheric origin, skin experiences the aerial, eyes, organs of sight sense fire, while tongue, an organ of taste, experiences water, and nose, organ of smell experiences the earthy. Subtle or inner forms of these organs also exist beyond the limitations of the physical body enabling extrasensory perception. Sense organs as journals of knowledge are receptive only, not expressive."

"Sense organs run their activities through their corresponding organs of action, which are five organs or Pancha Karmendriyani[15]. These are the five organs of action that correspond to the five sense organs and five elements. Mouth provides expression, covering ether and sound. Hands do the grasping, comprising air and touch."

---

[14] Pancha is five. Jnana means knowledge. Indriya is an organ.
[15] Pancha is five, Karma is action, Indriya constitutes the sensory organs.

"Feet provide motion, embracing fire and sight. The genitals provide emission, involving water and taste. Anus offers elimination, covering earth and smell. Five organs of action materialize the internal ideas by moving and grasping. Physical organs as structures let these ideas of action occur. Body as a vehicle, lives up to its design, executing actions that enable the mind to gain experience. When you look at nature, you will find such potentials in everything, they just manifest in different ways. Subtle or inner forms of these organs open subtle conduits in enabling direct action with the mind and psyche. Different from the sense organs, the organs of action are expressive only, not receptive. Their ability to receive is through the sense organs."

"Five great elements are earth, water, fire, air and ether, which represent the solid, liquid, radiant, gaseous and etheric forms of matter defining the outer world of experience, the physical body and matter. Sense organs operate on them through receptive means, while organs of action act on them actively. While the elements participate at physical and subtle levels, we experience only their gross forms in a world made of matter. Subtle elements or tanmatra objects affect the mind in dream-state. They are principles of density that apply to all manifest mediums, basically the domain of the mind. Earth, on one hand, is a dense medium that permits no action; ether, contrary to that is a subtle, receptive medium granting complete freedom of action. Between these two polarities are all possible densities affording the complete range of experience and fulfillment of all ideas. Elements also represent how ideas manifest. Different densities or fields express different ideas, like earth for instance, conveys solidity or stability offering resistance in action. Water shows liquidity, flow and movement consenting the propagation of life. Fire symbolizes light, sanctioning perception and movement from place to place. Air is symbolic of subtle movement, managing the mindset for direction, velocity and change; supplying the basis for thought. Ether is about connections; communication and self-expression that interchange between material mediums. Ether is symbolic of space, air, time, fire of light, water of life and earth of form. With a palette of mediums, brushes and different strokes, the creative cosmic intelligence expresses herself."

"Did they always exist? Where the elements known to the ancestors? How did the elements originate?", asked Ajay, the temple architect.

"Ether is the original, immutable, untarnished bhuta-element, represented as 'void', 'space' and 'vast'." Dharanidhar continued, "It derives from mind, which is kind of subtle space. Ether from movement becomes 'air', motion innate in space. Air through repeated movement generates friction that kindles fire, symbolizing illumination essential in movement."

"Fire leads to condensation, energy turning into water or liquid as life inherent in illumination. Water coagulates to become earth as a form, which is integral to life. Five elements have different densities of one key element, ether, and one focused idea of space and location. Other elements derive from basic etheric substance. A tenth of each transform into another - that is the order of degradation. Tenth of ether becomes air, a tenth of which becomes fire. One tenth of fire becomes water, whose one tenth becomes earth. Five elements are nothing but recast from ether. It is easy to observe that solids are nothing but a simple illusion, an energy field; there is plenty of space in between. Derivative of the subtle elements are the gross elements by a process of reduplication. Each gross element contains all five of the subtle elements, plus itself as another gross element. Hence gross or physical ether contains all five subtle or astral elements - ether, air, fire, water and earth at a subtle level. Behind the subtle forms of the five elements or Tanmatra objects are their causal or seed forms."

"Logic of the Samkhya suggests that the established intelligence is the same as the universe, the intellect gradually encasing itself into matter to explore all the different ideas of action and extend its experience to places inherent to itself. The expectation of a native to experience all possibilities of life and understanding is within the realms of the principle. As the mind evolves, we become capable of greater and wider experiences, going beyond the boundaries of our body to a direct experience through the mind, until we can eventually understand the entire universe within ourselves. Practice of yoga facilitates this knowledge. Bhuta-s, the five elements mirror all these fivefold correspondences of the Tattva-s including the five Chakra-s. Let me show you by drawing a table that explains the correspondence." Dharanidhar stopped and on the black slate he drew the table with his makeshift chalk.

Chakra	Element	Tanmatra	Sense Organ	Motor Organ
Root Chakra	Earth	Fragrance	Nose	Anus
Sex Chakra	Water	Taste	Tongue	Urogenital
Navel Chakra	Fire	Sight	Eyes	Feet
Heart Chakra	Air	Touch	Skin	Hands
Throat Chakra	Ether	Hearing	Ears	Voice

The men peered over his shoulder to look at the drawing. In the dim light, they strained their eyes to look at the table crafted with his nimble hands.

"In this way, the Tattva-s define our three bodies." Dharanidhar continued while the slate went around. "The physical body has the five elements along with 'gross' forms of the sense organs, motor organs and mind, keeping the body operational while awake."

"Subtle body has the five-tanmatra objects, along with the subtle forms of the sense organs, motor organs and mind; all of which ensure the subtle body operates during the inspirational dream state. Causal body has the buddhi, ego and mind, along with the causal form of the tanmatra objects; it operates in deep sleep and in states of Samadhi, enabling the mind to unite with higher consciousness."

"That's the analogy of the meta-system, the way our forefathers looked at the universal laws that lend them a definition. The laws, axioms and principles came from what they observed. They did not have to break a plant to study the insides or visit the planets to know their functioning. Observation was the key to dissecting the knowledge. They understood quickly that nature works coherently as long as the forces and systems adhere to the basic principles. The smallest aberration in their functioning, or when the forces and vectors get out of synchronization from their normal behavior spells trouble."

"At the mortal level, three dosha types[16], or disease potentials, vata, pitta and kapha develop from the Rajas, which symbolizes the mobile or vital energies."

"Vata, the biological air humor is a direct manifestation of Prana[17] and Rajas. Pitta, the biological fire humor, and Kapha, the water humor, also have five forms. Three dosha types give a physiological structure, permitting the interplay of the organs and elements in the physical body. Different Pitta forms evolve from Prana as relating to the sense organs because fire arouses perception. This gives pitta many sattvic properties. Different forms of Kapha evolve from Prana, the life-force related to the five elements, giving bulk to the body, therein Kapha earns some Stability."

"Under the predominance of the Stability vector, the five elements evolve diversified, the three guna vectors recombining. Ether comes from clarity that Sattva represents, fire comes from energy or Rajas, and earth comes from inertia of Tamas. Air has the lightness of Sattva and movement of Rajas. Water emulates Rajas' movements and inertia of Tamas."

"Though all the different guna vectors have their suitable place in nature, like Tamas or the lethargy-vector's dominance in the mineral kingdom or Rajas as aggression in the animal kingdom become the factors of disharmony in the mind."

---

[16] Astanga Hridayam, 1.6 to 1.7
[17] Prana – the closest definition in English implies it is the life-force.

"The mind appropriately is the domain of Sattva that provides clarity, mind itself being Sattvic. Evident is one's quality of Sattva reflected in the clarity of perception and peace of mind. When in balance in the mind, the three-guna vectors suggest the perception of truth, when out of balance, they advocate ignorance as in Tamas and desire or false imagination as seen in Rajas, leading to distorted perception. Sattva attempts to restore the balance of Rajas and Tamas."

"Simply increasing the level of Sattva in the mind, one returns to peace and harmony where one can merge back into nature and spirit. Yet, be warned that attachment to Sattva, like clinging to virtue, can also bind the mind. What is required is pure Sattva, which in essence is the detached form of it. The mind like the guna vectors is the causal or creative principle in existence. But only when we switch the mind to being Sattvic can we understand its temperament and the features of reality."

"Activity and Stability vectors trigger pain, grief and disease, not Purity, whose effect is harmonizing. While Rajas and Tamas are psychological disease factors, they also have physical ramifications. Rajas dissipates the energy, Tamas brings about decay and death. Both usually work together. Activity, as the principle of force, in its outward direction of energy causes loss of energy that destabilizes Tamas through decay, just as excess stimulation leads to depression."

"Spice, alcohol, meat, indulgence and excess movement are Active. They eventually lead to fatigue and collapse, where Stability reigns. Pure principles and living upholds the delicate fabric of health. Activity and Stability are more useful in the healing process. Purity does not always have the power to destroy either Activity or Stability. Though it does not cause disease, Purity is not always effective in curing it. It is too harmonizing and accepts everything. One can defuse hyperactive Activity with an equal amount of Stable inactivity. Similarly, one can bring vector Tamas from a downward spiral with Rajas. This applies particularly to acute or extraordinary conditions where the usual Pure methods fail to work."

"A return to spirit by yielding to nature's beckoning is the key to restoring the lost balance. As is the cause, so are its effects; which further defined becomes 'from a real cause can only occur a real effect resembling the cause', principle of 'Satkaryavada,' or the law of real effects. The classical example is the clay and pot where from the qualities inherent in earth as the cause gets to build a pot as the effect. Just water or air cannot make a pot, as these do not have the inherent qualities or causative potential. A clear indication there is a definite and understandable order to every event in the universe."

"This doctrine of cause and effect is the basis of the law of karma, the basic universal law of action. Whatever we do produces an effect, an effect similar to the character of the act. From violence comes unhappiness, as violence in its own nature is essentially a state of distress. From nonaggression comes peace, as nonviolence is itself a state of peace. Whatever be our situation, there is a reason for the state, a disease or a disorder cannot arise without a cause, which is unlike the disorder."

"A kapha phlegmatic disease like the common cold comes from a weather like the one you are experiencing tonight. The kapha increase is plainly the result from exposure to cold or damp, eating damp or mucus laden food, excessive sleeping and other kapha-increasing actions. Everything has a reason and if we can narrow down that reason, we can correct the chain of happenings that lead to pain, disease or sorrow."

"Nothing happens that is uncaused or unmerited, or not produced by our own actions. This doctrine of causation is easy to understand, we bring upon our own problems, our own condition in life results from our doing, whether it is physical or mental. It also means we possess the power to correct it. Correct it by remedies that advocate adopting the opposite of what caused the problem. As we have made ourselves, we can also unmake it. However complicated be the cause of such things, having come from the distant past, even from previous lives, the myth can be broken, the problems unfolded."

"Having understood them, we can correct the source and result, thereby preventing their reoccurrence and the negativity they harbor. Nature is quite 'just' by which we can experience the forces we individually and collectively, have previously set in motion. This doctrine of responsibility gives us the basis for correcting any wrong actions. The very thought that one is being oppressed by some external fate or room for self-pity or resignation is preposterous."

"What has become rotten is in our capacity to become better. There is only freedom through which we can arrive at self-mastery."

"This brings us back to the knowledge of the cosmic spirit or Cosmic man. From its viewpoint, health is part of right action that arises when we learn to observe things as they are and use them according to their own potentials. This knowledge of the inner self is truly the subject of psychology. Even the scriptures teach that we are not the body; the body is a tool or vehicle for consciousness to express itself. In this way, we cease to indulge in the body and give it the objective care it requires for health."

"We treat it like a vehicle or like a plant in the garden but not as a means of self-gratification, which acts like a force of destruction both to the body and to our inner purpose in life. Apart from that inner self or higher nature all other things are but a deviation, a Vikruti, a disturbance, a disease. Until we learn to take proper respite in our true nature, we are prone to rapid decay and degeneration. Real cure for disease is the right knowledge of the self." Dharanidhar sat on the traditional woven bed. He must have spoken well over three hours and his feet and back hurt.

"My proposal with the conceptual church is to conceal many such scriptures held at risk in Vedagarbha. The sanctuary will be much safer with the Damodar Jehu construct. So far, the invaders from the north were not familiar with the value these documents provide, all they cared about was some of the gold in the temples left as decoy. Next time, we may not be so lucky."

"I think your intentions are very convincing. I will speak with the prince to sanction the money and other resources to get the work started on this." The village head nodded his head in conformation. "I cannot speak for everyone, but I learned a lot in today's discussions."

The men slowly stood up as the clearing sky and dense fog reminded everyone it was past midnight. Dharanidhar watched the assembly disperse and sat in solemn silence with the temple architect. Finally, when everyone else had left, they stood up and doused the candles. In the glow of the cooling wicks, an occasional moth flew swiftly past the hut onto the thinning clouds of the night. The rain had thinned to a trickle; there was no arguments, no emotions, no excitement. There was courage in their hearts, faith fired their souls, the land they knew, they were born in, would see another day.

DIFFERENT SHORES
1785 CE

Sheets of rainwater smashed against his body almost tearing through the skin as Padmalochan[18] took a final look at the submerged room and splashed out of the waterlogged doorway. His eyes met the intense expression on Radha Mani's face and he nodded his head in the negative. His wife Radha Mani knew better than to argue as she held their nephew close to her. He knew he had to act fast, for the water was rising. Damodar River, dubbed 'the sorrow of Bengal' rose in ferocity, challenging the monsoons in battering the earth; combined with the nor'easter cyclonic weather bearing down on the unfortunate land-dwellers - a menacing, perfect storm. Lochan heaved his bosom as the realization occurred to him that their home where they had lived for generations would crumble under wind and water any moment. Several walls, groaning under tremendous water pressure were damaged beyond repairs. He beckoned his family to move. A messenger had run through the rising waters informing him that his brother who lived a few blocks away had taken another boat and deserted their house.

"Our only recourse is in crossing the river to the other bank." Lochan spoke over the banshee of the winds swishing the banana leaves that protested the barrage of pouring waters. "The land yonder is at a much higher elevation, likely above the flooded river. In such a weather, chances of encountering any stray crocodile is low, let's not worry about them, rather use our strength against the water-current." He turned to Radha, "We will use the boat as a float while we swim. We will use the rope to stay together. I would suggest all of us tie it around our waist and I will secure it to the boat. Grab the sides of the boat and let the rope be tension free, it is our only hope if we lose the grip on the boat. Do you see the sun up there, behind the clouds? That is our only compass in the deep."

---

[18] Padmalochan nicknamed Lochan

"What do you think are our chances of making it alive?" Radha slipped the safety harness over the child and then herself.

"When I was younger, I could swim the length without pausing. I hope that stamina and strength is still alive. Let's not give up hope, Radha. The almighty has plans for us, this is his way of setting the course."

Lochan tugged the small raft behind him as he waded through the waist deep water. It was difficult to see in the muddy water, he recognized he would soon fumble down the steps that led to the banks. His toes felt the change in the underwater current and he swiftly signaled his wife and the child to hold on to the ropes and the boat. In a second, the swollen river pulled them in. The waves hit them hard, tossing the little canoe. Lochan flexed every muscle he could to push themselves deeper into the river. They gasped for air as they surfaced at a distance from the shore. Letting the boat drift, tugging on to the sides, they floated on the rapidly flowing water. He knew his way through the river. There were no eddies, and the river ran deep. The current was strong and erratic, but they pushed their way against it with steady strokes. Every now and then Lochan cast a glance at the sky to spot the veiled sun in ensuring they were in the right direction. For over two hours they swam in a never-ending crossing, it was then his feet struck ground. Lochan was aware it would still be a while before they could wriggle out of the river; at least for then there was a sliver of hope, the loose alluvial soil meant they were getting close to the opposite bank. While they progressed through the occasional waves and heavy rain in a slow, unwieldy way to the high grounds, they held on to the raft that had a few essential belongings tied up in whatever sheets of cloth he could find in the last minute.

Lochan finally thrust his nephew and Radha on to the grassy bank. The soil was wobbly and volatile. He let himself up on the bank and using their last ounce of strength, they hauled the raft out from the brown waters. Guiding the raft through the wet grass was not difficult, but he knew he had to reach at least another six feet to safe grounds. For a moment, he focused at the shore from where he had swum away. All he saw was a large expanse of water. Their home must have long yielded to the swirling river.

Uncovering the ground till it reached about six feet above the rising waters, they stopped and fell on the wet grass. The rain came down heavily, but the thick undergrowth assured them of a brief, fleeting safety.

As his hands went to his neckband, he sat upright in disbelief. 'Damodar Jehu' tied to the band across his neck when they had left the former house was no longer found on the belt. His hands in reflex felt the grass and the ground near him, expecting it to have fallen next to him. Despondent, he beckoned his wife to look after the child and headed back to the river. His heart thumping wild with every step he took, he tried to recollect the spot where he had climbed the beach. His mind in a whirl was of no help; he closed his eyes and fought back his apprehensions with techniques he had learnt from his childhood. The mind under control, the hands steady, he remembered the rock ledge on which he had last rested his weary hands. Finding the ledge, he dived back into the turgid river. His hands fumbled the sides of the rock and almost as quickly as he had started, his hands struck a clothed metal. Even in the murky water, he could see the distinct, rick colored sheet struck on the rock ledge. With trembling hands, his head and torso still underwater, he secured the lost idol in his left hand, climbed up and collapsed. He pushed his body upwards towards the higher grounds, but his eyes closed, his strength resisting the unconsciousness engulfing his mortal mind, he remembered what he had read in the Vedas that every hymn to the mystic fire was a reminder that the aerial Aquarius and Piscean water he had encountered twice that day were just a mere representation of tremendous power; all mortals were a small exemplary of the almighty.

KING AND US

When Lochan regained consciousness, it was bright. He gradually opened his pupils to an incredible brightness; a limited glow of the fugitive sun brightened the dismal surroundings. As his eyes focused, he could make out Radha and the child; there were other people around him. His face covered in warm sweat, his cotton shirt drenched in perspiration mingled with rainwater, he closed his eyes again as they hurt from the dull glare. He caught the voices distinctly and allowed his eyes to turn towards the sound source, realizing the voices were no longer distant. Lochan felt a gentle hand move under his shoulders to raise his torso. He sputtered grass and mud as a numbing pain hit him hard. Clasping his head, he pushed his stiff legs out into the cold of a wet and drenched ground.

"I think I will be all right", he choked, his face covered in grass and leaves. "I sensed I had a bout of fever, my body shook and shivered, but I don't feel that now." Lochan overheard a cheer as the small crowd heard him speak. The sharp, numbing pain was receding, several hands helped him to his feet. He rapped out something indistinguishable directed his vision and thoughts away to a distant land nowhere discernable. Whatever it was, the thought seemed to convince him; he turned towards the hill assisted by many hands; hugging Radha and the child closer, they walked towards the warmth and comfort of the hills that loomed before them. He demurely touched the 'Damodar Jehu' tied to his waistband and reassured he was by the cold touch of the metal. The torpid waters behind them gradually plunged into a world of absolute gray. Shapes, sprays and angles, heights and depressions resolved themselves into many nebulous outlines.

As they went up the incline, he thought of the early Vedic ancestors and their obsession to cut out disease, deformity and weakness they considered depraved and vicious. He sensed them appear all around him with their concern, his health. Health, first and greatest boon, a gift supplicated from the heavens. Only health could reverse mortality. They reached the top of the incline where the land stretched flat for several miles.

While they proceeded in silence, he pictured the town on a busy day with the birds playing hide and seek in the tall, banana plants, rushing to the mango groves, picking on the unripe fruit, much to the amusement of the children racing to pick the green mango that accidentally fell to the shaded grounds below. Walking past the tree, through an area of vacant, high-walled, terraced garden stalls in need of repairs, the group stopped at a flight of abandoned white stone steps that cleared nowhere.

A young person in his early twenties ran towards the seated citizen band "The king would like to meet the family that swam the river. His highness sends his concerns to the family who must be tired and exhausted from this unnerving feat, he has therefore sent his palanquin to transport the family to his palace. He has expressed his wish to meet them as quick as possible."

There was a flurry of movement as three palanquins followed the youth and the carriers put them down gently on the wet paving. The king's representative met the gathering and greeted Lochan. "With all due respects, Sir Padmalochan, the king would like to meet you. His medic who lived on the other side of the river has not shown up since the storm started. He has heard of the vast knowledge you have on health and treatment. His highness welcomes you to stay with him and find a cure for his sons who are suffering something strange, occult disease that no one knows of."

"I can only help as a mortal, for I am no miracle worker." Lochan offered little resistance to the offer, but he also wanted to make it clear, he was no sorcerer. "I will do my best, but I need to get out of these drenched and filthy clothes first."

"The king has sent fresh clothes for you, your wife and the child. Please use this abandoned hut on this side of the road to clean up and change into fresh clothes. My team will assist you in every possible way. He has also sent his collection of balm and herbs for you to anoint. I am sure you agree that the swim across the river was not a hygienic one."

The attending team helped Lochan and the family to shed their wet and muddy outfits, rub the herbs all over and clean themselves before climbing into the godsend fresh clothes. As they climbed the palanquin, the representative welcomed them with light sweets and beverages.

The ride to the palace was uneventful and short. Relieved and grateful for a ride on the palanquin, Lochan closed his eyes savoring the moment and turn of events.

No one spoke except the palanquin bearers who zipped through the drenched roads into the colossal marbled walls of the palace, where they dismounted rapidly and moved into a parlor where lay two children covered in sheets attended by several women.

Lochan carefully examined their faces, the skin, and the body pallor. He gingerly touched their wrist for the pulse and examined the tongue, his multitasking brain rapidly calculating, and eliminating options. He at once discarded the possibility of yellow fever or malaria. He turned to the person attired in regal clothes, "Your sons' run a high fever and their pulse is high, your highness." Then turning to the attendants, he spoke in a brisk voice, "Can you also, please bring ginger, tea and astragalus? Also pluck about five fresh leaves of Pipal tree and boil it in milk, add a little amount of honey, once cooled. Put that Cinchona bark in the broth. If you have pepper, capsicum, dogwood tree bark and garlic, please bring them here. And, onions too! The children need to sip hot water in regular intervals besides the rest. I am quite certain they will recover tomorrow. Incidentally, I noticed an Agaru plant near the entrance. Can you look for a few dried barks? Bring them along with the other herbs. I will add them to the incense[19]."

"I believe you could benefit from a cup of ginger tea," he turned to the king. "It is amazing how ginger and tea work better than tobacco or alcohol for relief from stress."

"I am so relieved you are here, Sir Padmalochan. Is it true that the children will get better tomorrow? My medic could not figure out what was wrong." The king asked in despair.

"I can assure your highness; your children will be better tomorrow. I will not speak negative of your medic, but I am sure like any other mortal, sometimes the most obvious deludes us." As he rolled up his sleeves to prepare the herbal concoctions, he felt the numb and tiredness return. He slumped on a high stool, his thoughts and acts contained within like a cocoon, his hands strayed away from the mortar and pestle. In his heart, he reasoned, this was his chance to prove himself in a different turf; Lochan's grandfather had said his astrological birth chart had showed success in foreign places. He wondered, if the neighboring riverbank was a stretch in redefining the word 'foreign'. Wrecked was the house where he had spent his infancy and youth, and where he and Radha had shared their moments.

---

[19] Astanga Hridayam, 1.42. Jvara Chikitsa and others.

All his inherited books, writings, almanacs that his ancestry had preserved for many decades were now in a Piscean trove. Lochan had this premonition, this feeling, his predecessors who surrounded him, repeatedly reminded him, he had to re-establish what Dhar and other forefathers had left him as heritage.

Lochan turned to the caretaker, "Here, can you please grind the leaves. I need to re-check their pulses and fever." Lochan handed the mortar to the caretaker and strolled back to the patients. He examined their pulses and stopped to check their tongue. "From the pulse kickback, seems more a kapha problem than a vata one," he turned to the king. "We can get this under control shortly," he sipped the tea and took a bite of the savories. Lochan took the small jar containing the paste the attendant had just finished grinding, he fed them to the two children. He offered them warm water to relieve the taste.

"Your highness," he turned to the king, "I suspect the medic did the right things in the beginning, he just did not follow it through to a closure." he turned to the king. "I'd give them some time for respite, I was planning to take a stroll; I was wondering if you are up to it."

"Why! Certainly! It is such a big relief you are here. I am sure it comes more than a relief in knowing you are still alive swimming the riven in that menacing storm. The storm and the flooding are unbelievable. What happened to other members in the family? What made you think you could swim across the river?"

"Your highness, my other family relations left the shores before I did. I do not know my brother's whereabouts, all I learned was he took the other boat. I pray, he made it to safety. I had this forewarning about this storm; I realized beforehand that everything downstream would get inundated for miles. My only course was to defy the odds and cross the flooded river."

They strolled into the gardens surrounded by a large brick wall. The rain though lighter, remained an incessant downpour accompanied by winds. Together they howled an eerie tune.

"Your father and I were an acquaintance. I remember your family as traditional, conservative and scholarly." The king spoke over the noise and the shrieking wind.

"Yes, we learnt grammar when other kids climbed trees and played ball. My uncle taught me more about methods in health and wellness. It remained my signature study as I moved the ancient scriptures one after another to a single compilation. If you recall, our sages were the real 'go to' persons in matters about health. The wellness approach they taught us starts with identifying the underlying malfunction, restoring the afflicted part through cleansing and revitalizing the system, ensuring there is no recurrence."

"Tell me about them Lochan, I always wanted to be a medicine man, I guess the lord had different plans for me."

"In Wellness, we deal with two steps, the first identifies the Prakruti and the dual state of Vikruti[20]. For complete wellness, it is wise to narrow the different procedures down to a program that tunes the lifestyle to the cosmic order, thus ensuring a sustained protection. Sometimes, your highness, we become so obsessed with our disease, we fail to switch-on our natural healing power, which alone can correct the malfunction. In any treatment, I therefore insist on setting a method, which comes as natural, intrinsic and spontaneous. Nothing complex or clinical can offer a cure; the cure must come from within; from the depths of our return to simplicity. Perhaps a return to the innocence of our inner self." They reluctantly turned away from the corridors and headed back to the room. As they entered the room, they were both astounded to see the children sitting.

"I was just about to get you, your highness," cried the attendant "the princes have fever no more. I guess the herbal mixture you game them sir, was perfect." He turned with a smile towards Lochan. "I showed your wife and son the guest room. They really needed the rest."

"Thank you. He's actually my nephew; Radha and I never had a child. He's more than a son to us."

"Yes Lochan, please be our guest for the next few days. I am sure in a few days or months; this flood and dreadful day will be a thing of the past. You can reinstate your life in this small empire of mine. I would need scholarly people like you to counsel me."

---

[20] Creative-force is Nature. Prakruti is natural constitution. Vikriti is manifested nature. Vikruti is original along with the altered state of constitution. 'Pra' means 'progression', 'kri' means an 'outward manifestation'. Our originality is the progressive external manifestation of the original cause. 'Vi' means 'to be divided into two' or to be 'set in a different direction'.

"Thank you, your highness, I am honored by your hospitality and the offer. Let me attend to the princes first. I'd rather not have anything fall through the cracks on their treatment."

"How do you feel son?" Lochan turned to the younger of the princes. "I will give you more of this awful antidote to reduce the fever and the ache. Do you know how it works?"

"No. How does it work?"

"For one, it's so awful that even the germs run away from it. That's a secret between us, don't tell your Dad about it." Lochan had the boy's promise. "We will repeat this again tomorrow. Let's see who can swallow the great tasting medicine first? You or your brother? I bet your brother will beat you to you it."

The weariness from the fever and aches, the trauma and fatigue crept on their strength. In no time, the two princes were deep asleep. The king and Lochan stepped out into the corridors.

"I brought with me the Damodar Jehu, instituted by Dhar, one of my forefathers, a few generations back in a brick-laid temple to ensure the scriptures never fell into the wrong hands. When Radha, the kid and I were on the hilltop all by ourselves, tired and hungry, alone and scared, I sensed a revelation. I realized, knowledge comes when good and evil are exposed through something common - something they share. That thread of knowledge helps us develop an insight; helps us weigh one against the other in a positive way. However, that which epitomizes good and the powerful can also become abominably evil by turning it into collective knowledge. The scriptures therefore must stay a secret, taught to the discerning, spoken to the believer."

"Ayurveda and medicines of Tibet have different types of herbal preparations. Several suggestions of these preparations apply precisely to a condition of error or a disorder. The strategic old saying is still so correct in the way it suggests to 'try what sounds good and see what works'. Like any other alternate healing process, such a regimen gets prescribed until the symptoms disappear. A few treatments take months, while others take days; the native's constitution determines how long would be the combat. Other than that, the depth of the dosha types and how much the disease has matured also can deter the time it takes to get well."

"Traditionally, this wellness technique had eight different branches covering many topics. From the ancient days, the study of wellness has become an important factor in preserving the health of the planet. While one branch analyzes the body, its psychology part of study is equally intense. Rasayana[21] and Vajikarana[22] present a theme of rejuvenation and revitalization, as necessary to deal with chronic diseases and degenerative conditions that result from the breakdown of the immune system. Study in pediatrics is endured as a special branch, so goes specializations in gynecology and techniques in treating the disabled and the elderly. There is never one or limited number of prescribed treatment methods, every treatment ranges different for individuals spanning herbal therapies, massage, yoga and corrective actions of colors, gemstones, fragrance, music and sound of mantras, or just silence. Wellness is universal, but to get there is specific to an individual, his unique constitution. The pathways to treatment are many, but all such roads end in one wellness highway."

"I consider the big challenge in care giving and wellness is the level of involvement for both the native and the practitioner. It is not about a passive ask for a medicine, wherein the practitioner pours a handful of herbs, powders or pills in their hands. The native has to take an active part in becoming well as only he can alter and change the chain of cause and effect. The practitioner can at best prepare the native on how to combat the resistive forces of disease and equip him with the tools that speed up the process. Such powerful is this principle that on reversing the process that caused the deficiency, we return to the origin of things, all the way back to primal-nature and even the true self."

"I know we are getting late, but I am sure, your highness would like to know more about the way the program deals with deficiencies in physical, mental and spiritual health. How about we spend some time tomorrow and go through the lessons?"

"Absolutely Lochan. What you say sounds very fascinating. I would also like the queen and your wife, Radha to join in the conversation. We can enjoy beverages prepared by my chef and served in the gardens next to the river Damodar. My chef believes his preparations rival the Soma served to the gods." The king chuckled. Lochan realized the normally humorous person had gone through a big crisis with both princes in deathbed.

---

[21] Rasayana transliterated from रसायन implies an elixir or toxic substance

[22] Vajikaran transliterated from वाजीकरण means an aphrodisiac

"My attendant will show you to the guest room, if there is anything you need, please let the attendant know. I have briefed him that there should be no shortcomings in your stay in the palace."

"Thank you, your highness. I will retire for the night; it has been a tumultuous day. We shall meet at the strike of dawn."

WELLNESS AXIOMS AND COROLLARIES

The next morning dawned a dreary overcast with frequent cloudbursts and prominent thunderclaps; a lifeless, ravaged landscape greeted the sleep-deprived eyes. In the palace, rainwater seeped into the tapestry and exquisite carpets within the halls and guest rooms. Volatile was the weather, sheets of torrential rain sang the ballads of cacophony through the silken drapes, lifting the drapery and slapping them against the stucco walls of the guest room, making it near impossible to even step into the patio. Speechless, Lochan and Radha stood in their sheltered room in the palace, next to the ornate woodcarvings of the large bed and looked into the distant, angry river. Visibility was down to a few yards and the river seemed only to be swelling. They were both aware that the moment it reached the highlands, it would spell a catastrophe. The river named after the lord was their main source of water, but in the seasons of summer and monsoon, there was no telling when it went ballistic.

They heard footsteps outside their door. The king, barefoot, holding an umbrella stood in a state of despair. "The tower by the wall, where lies the sacred altar collapsed in the storm just now. This storm is out to destroy us all." He lamented.

"I feel sorry about the altar. We have the Damodar Jehu right here with us. Allow me to reinstate that. River Damodar is named after Vishnu, who goes by several names. Yashoda tied Lord Krishna when he was a child with a lasso or 'daama' around his waist 'udara' to keep the divine incarnation from mischief. A divine pastime in which Krishna's mother Yashoda thought she could keep the Lord shackled. My intuition tells me to reinstate the lord."

"I agree, Lochan. Indeed, by 'udara' or a mind purified and by 'daama' - self-control is the lord perceptible. I am with you. He must find his rightful place."

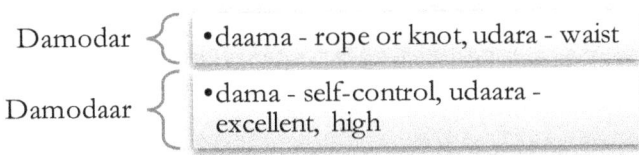

Wading in neck deep waters, they crossed the courtyard to the room that had collapsed. The water had risen to a point where the courtyard was just a pool and the fallen brick and stucco lay in disarrayed heap. While one room had collapsed, the remaining walls held firm. The adjoining room beckoned to them, an empty hall with no doors. They climbed the porch and carried the deity into the room.

"We used this room to store rice and dried lentils. We moved the grains to a higher mezzanine from fear of rodents." The king's eyes rolled in surprise as the barren white washed walls with intricate wood latticework running up to the ceiling, greeted him. Even a predestined mantle stood against the wall facing west. Lochan wasted no time and removed the small brass deity from this neckband and placed it on the dais. For a moment, the cosmic clock stood still as Lochan closed his eyes. An eternity must have passed before his eyelids opened again. When the senses turned towards the doorway, all he could hear was the soft patter of the water as it ran down the gutters. He stood up to face the king. The king was beaming, "I cannot believe it."

Lochan smiled, "What a surprise. I guess Damodar has his own ways of expressing discontent. Look, even the floodwaters are receding. The aquatic forces, which a moment before bulldozed all this destruction, is getting ready to irrigate the paddy—what a turnaround? The same forces capable of moving the mighty river are the ones that move us too. As ebbs the mighty river, so will peace surround us when the negative forces recede. Each of us possesses a basic nature or constitution, called Prakruti[23], a configuration, which came about when we were first introduced to the ecosystem. Think of it like this, we are in a secure pre-birth harness first. Then some forces propelled us into a universe expediently congenial to our birth. This snapshot, this moment when we stepped into this terrestrial world contains our signature Prakruti."

---

[23] Astanga Hridayam, 1.10

"Composed it is of two words, 'Pra' meaning 'progression' 'kri' implying 'outward manifestation'. If you ponder on it, you realize our originality is a progressive manifestation of the original cause. Which means 'we are necessarily good; our lives are divine'. Disorders arise from a differentiation or degeneration from this basic state of health, leading to a state of Vikruti. 'Vi' means 'divided into two' or 'set in a different direction'. Vikruti shows the directional split in the constitution from the original signature. Some authors have reasoned Vikruti as bad, which is a common misunderstanding. The River Damodar wreaks devastation and yet irrigates the land working through a split personality. Is that bad? No, definitely not. It is nature's way of provisioning an obverse side to our original constitution, and like the flip of a coin, the head-side or the tail is always active."

"Parts of Vikruti are reliable as they contain the original signature. Our progenitors and forefathers also spoke of Vikruti in a different sense, a mutation necessary to become biologically adaptable."

"The untarnished ego, the I-factor holds the key to our signature constitution, which may become divided both on a personal and at a cosmic level. Tarnished, the ego causes us to act in a deviated and different way."

"The wellness program aims at restoring our basic nature; reinstating to a known state which is in harmony with the laws of nature."

"We must first verify a person's Prakruti to come to any conclusions. There are several tools that do the work, what is important is that the verification must be base lined and mutually accepted by both the practitioner and the native. It also means that practitioner stays away from the traps where real inner desires of the native get subdued, and what gets satisfied are a few conditioned or artificial wants."

"Since I raised the topic on 'ego', let me take you back a notch. Every scripture that has withstood the test of time has stipulated the simple order of cosmic principles, where four primary levels outline the cosmos. First comes the principle of Cosmic man, or pure Spirit that is eternal, conscious, and inactive; clearly outside the realms of creation."

"Such a phenomenon is beyond our reasoning; a far cry from this dimensional world where space and time are nothing but specialization of cause and effect. No one in his right mind can explain in spoken or written language what this wonder is, it has always been the privilege of mathematicians to lend the right shades in explaining."

"Next, we have Creative-force or primal nature, characterized as eternal, insentient, active and the source of creation. She is the indicator of the creative power of the Cosmic man[24], but in a dimension not comprehensible to us mortals. Cosmic man can through recursive powers see the creative potential inherent within himself, which manifests as Creative-force. Creative-force is inconceivable; however, her existence can be surmised as a foundation for the observable. She causes all things but is herself not the effect of anything."

"Think of Creative-force as the material cause of the universe, just as clay is that of an earthen pot."

"At the third level appears Mahat or cosmic intelligence, which gets released as individuality or Ahamkara and the five Tanmatra or sensory potentials comprising a group of seven. They are both causes and effects namely Prakruti and Vikruti. They are the effects of Creative-force and the mind, where the organs and elements are its products. Then we have cosmic Vikriti, stipulated as transient and differentiated products of creation, which arise through the 'I'-ness of Ahamkara. These add up to sixteen different objects, comprising the mind, the five organs of sense and action and the five elements. They are 'finished' effects and no longer the cause of anything further. Bonded to cause and effect is time, having risen through the individuality of ego, by which differentiation proceeds. The ego is the knot in creation. The moment we resolve that, we gain mastery over it." Padmalochan paused, "Blame it all on ego to cause both physical disorders and psychological sorrow."

"There are no less than twenty-four tattva[25] essences, factors that drive the wellness programs. Life finds a meaning when Cosmic man and Creative-force make contact, where Cosmic man gives Prana to inert Creative-force. This interchange produces the different dosha types or biological humors. Five Prana or life forces work as active energies and interconnect all tattva essences. The tattva essences set the foundation for a wellness practitioner's dissected interpretation of the physical, subtle and causal bodies."

---

[24] Like the fact, Eve was a part of Adam

[25] Sanskrit word तत्त्व (tattva)

"Creative-force or primal nature is composed of three prime qualities or guna vectors. The word 'Guna' literally means 'what binds'. At the sub-atomic level, they bind the threads that can pervade all dimensions. I will return to this sentence again. Guna types are three - Sattva, Rajas and Tamas. Not just small, they are extra subtle than the five elements resulting from their activity. They come even before the Tanmatra or sensory potentials. All of them are inherent in Creative-force and are the potentials for diversification. Every object formed in the world uses different combinations of the three-guna types; our forefathers understood many of the combinations and deciphered what worked and what did not. Three-guna vectors are our clue to different structures and behaviors in this universe. Guna vectors are the causal vectors in the creation process, Tanmatra are subtle factors and Bhuta-Elements comprise the gross effects."

Creative-force → Sat-Raj-Tam → Mahat → Ahamkara → Tanmatra Prakruti → Vikruti

"Living things have four targets in life as pointed out in the Purushartha definition, Kama or enjoyment, Artha or prosperity, Dharma or our duties culminating in Moksha or liberation."

Dharma → Kama → Artha → Moksha

"Constantly engaged are all creatures in the pursuit of the four objectives, the extent and sequence may differ from person to person, or from species to species. Kama or enjoyment is the basic, primitive goal of life. It is but natural for all living things to live in joy and not suffer the pangs of misery. We all love the joy or beauty that a sensory experience brings. Even the bee cannot resist the gorgeous spring blossoms. Our emotional mind namely Manas pursues the Kama goal where a strong form of pleasure comes from sex."

"Next comes Artha, which defines the need for prosperity or wealth, seeking exterior objects as possessions. We come to this planet without a shred and leave with none, but in our stay here, we collect enormous number of things, labeling them our own. It is natural to possess things as we are all but one and reaching out to other things is intrinsic to our Prakruti. The ecosystem promises us coexistence to maintain equilibrium; therefore, our need for clothing, shelter and other external objects for proper functioning in life, a goal that comes from the ego principle or Ahamkara, is nowhere unnatural. What is unnatural are the excesses, the craving, the coveting."

"Dharma relates to intrinsic-duties, career or vocation, in attaining inner objects or status in life, fulfilling particular capacities for self-expression and self-realization. A child who has no career or professional plans cares for a sibling, not just out of seeing others doing it, but more from an intrinsic feeling. The sun gives us light and energy, returning to its place in the zodiacal sky diligently after the night has passed. It follows its solemn-duties to the best of its ability. Who knows what other dharma-s it needs to support, we mortals can only guess a few. As mortals, the need for recognition, for giving and receiving gifts, in building skills or talents is inherent in us. This is the inner goal of the I-factor inherent in us. As you notice, your highness, these three goals have an outwardly and secondary character."

"Prime goal in life is Moksha. Some call it liberation. The question that comes to the mind is, liberation of what? The other three aims in life bless them all; can have a binding effect once they cross the thresholds. We get shackled to our homes, our family, friends, and food and garden. We believe in the absurdity of imaginary associations! We came from ashes, to ashes we must return, O' king; how did we ever get into this trap then? Moksha is that liberation. Moksha is more than freedom from life; it promises the freedom to express the inner. Freedom comes from knowledge, it is nothing but knowledge."

"When nothing else matters, just the three lower goals, life becomes a trailblazer of many errors, many disorders, physical and mental. Where pleasure, Kama turns out to be the primary goal, all you have is self-indulgence and dissipated energy. Wealth, Artha, as the main goal leads to greed and meaningless accumulation. Dharma, status, as the main goal leads to the pursuit of power, domination and violence. The reminder that one came alone with nothing but a handful of knowledge and will return with nothing, but perhaps better knowledge is the best thing that can happen to one in the early phases of life. We must inculcate a way in leading life by staying in harmony with spirit and nature and pursuing the right goals that become evident on a dharmic pursuit. Once the alignment ensues with nature, a majority of problems disappear. What remains, blends into the natural course of Moksha."

"The three lesser goals come from Rajas quality. Conceivably, all goal seeking desires, actions and provocations are Rajasic, reflecting an essential commotion or perhaps shortage of harmony, a tremendous desire to be somewhere or get something. Somewhere below is a Tamasik plane of negation where one seeks nothing and life is a mere drift."

"Somewhere above is a Sattvic plane also passive, but acts to cancel the three goals by attaining them and concluding the search. The lower Tamasik plane seeks no means to meet any of the goals, an anti-thesis of the higher plane of Sattva."

"The original degenerated caste system today provided a link to the Purushartha system. Four different social statuses are mnemonics of how the profession and skill of man became his destined professional-Varna. The scriptures provided the freedom and flexibility to move up and down the professional scale if a person failed to perform the duties. The foremost of the professionals were the ones who pursued knowledge. They chose the roles of gurus and teachers, key role models in the social fabric. They studied and taught a wide variety of subjects from the scriptures, archery and weaponry, wellness and health, art, music and culture and were counsels to the kings. This class of teachers and priests were not permitted to own any land. Their work involved teaching and general welfare of the community. The next class comprised kings and knights, who provided defense, law and justice to the people. Farmer-merchants provided wares, merchandise and farm-produce to the society. The fourth rung provided all other services. Those who had no positive goals in life and were not within the four classes did not belong to the Vedic system. Four levels of society have existed in all human cultures at all times; they reflect the goals inherent to human existence. Strata come not from mere birth but values and behavior."

Money	• spend, donate, enjoy
Service	• serve, duties, labor
Defense	• arm, defend, treatment
Education	• learn, teach, give back

"Where was I, O' King! Yes, the principles that form 'wellness' is that system, its practitioners and natives accept the fact that all life unifies into one. This unity is evident in the various connections between things that reveal the interdependence of all life. Within many interdependent lives comes common intelligence. Take us as an example; composed we are of many microcosmic elements, which likely have their own intelligence. But we have a centralized intelligence, Buddhi that governs the million parts, resembling not many, but one. Taking this analogy to the celestial world, the centralized intelligence becomes the cosmic Mahat, the storehouse of stellar intelligence, unified as one."

"Wellness runs on a few principles. Concepts in 'samanya and vishesha' tell us of a simple axiom of how similar things add up, and dissimilar things reduce. Ancient text states 'Great sages grasped knowledge of samanya or similarity, vishesha or dissimilarity, guna or properties, dravya or substance, karma or action and samavaya or inherence; which they followed firmly the tenets of the compendium and attained the highest well-being and nonperishable life-span[26].' Factors having similar attributes as health, like adequate rest, happiness, laughter, good food and meditation supplicate health. Those that are contrary like overwork, bad diet, stress and worry; detract health. To arrive at the optimum, promoting the 'like' factors and reducing the 'unlike' one's becomes essential. Without this precursor, we cannot expect our condition to improve." Padmalochan sipped his beverage and let the sentence sink.

"This concept further develops into the idea that in enforcing opposite conditions, the situation gets corrected; summarized as 'like increases like, and opposites cure each other[27]'. Applying cold corrects a condition of excess heat in the body. Using opposites to balance disorderly conditions is an age-old technique."

Dosha Axioms

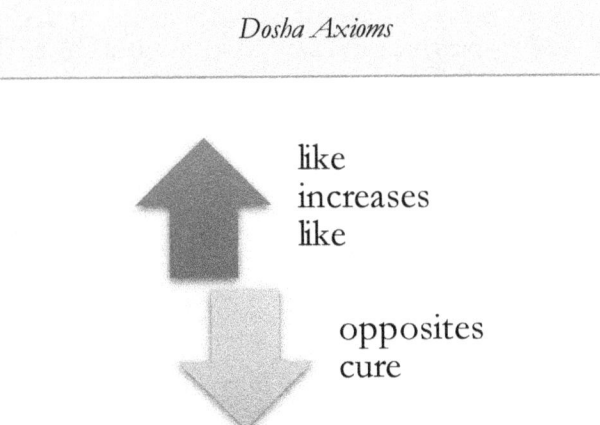

like increases like

opposites cure

---

[26] Charaka Samhita, Chapter 1, Slokas 27-29
[27] Astanga Hridayam, 1.13. Dosha, dhatu and mull-s witness vriddhi (increase) through use of samana-similar and its opposite (decrease) by viparita-dissimilar.

"Let us examine the case of your sons, first I ascertained the qualities in excess, like cold and humidity. Both princes were suffering, therefore the environmental was likely adding to the children's constitution using the similarity principle. Once I knew the disorder, I applied substances or actions that acted in contrary. It may sound simple, in fact, it is nothing but simple, and as we get deeper into the topic, these principles become our masonry tools."

"We can extend this principle to a psychological level. Violence cannot end when pitted with violence. Only peace can correct it, its opposite. If you are suffering from a bout of anger, which has the nature of violence, eating food that has violence in its history will only add to the anger. As a start, eliminate anything that comes from the butcher's shop or the fishmonger, as they are a product of violence. The gently picked fruit and leaves, fresh green vegetables are what you need to pacify the anger."

"Vedic literature has unique perspective of the human body. It teaches us the basic language of life energy and its functioning in the organic body. Three primary life forces or 'dosha' are present in the body. Concepts that bring them together are 'Tridosha'. Dosha types are primary forces and subtle substances affecting all physiological and psychological functions. They sustain and grow the body and disrupt its functioning. Dosha comes from the root word 'dush,' which means 'stain', 'fault', 'twilight', to spoil or darken, or what causes decay. Dosha types have a positive effect in the body when in balance as they support all tissues and organic functions."

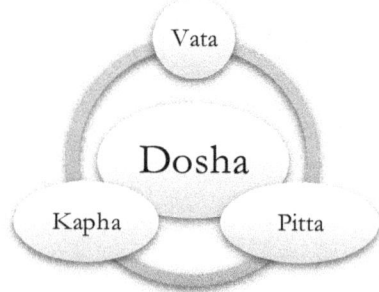

"Dosha types, vata, pitta and kapha correspond to the elements of air, fire and water. As the active, mobile, Rajasic side of the five elements their involvement in the life processes of growth and decay is strategic. They develop the biological potentials inherent in the elements. The sense organs, organs of action base their workings on the three elements, which are shaped and ready to be worked on."

"Vata, pitta and kapha originate from the Rajas vector as mobile, vital energies. Vata, the biological air humor, owes it to Prana and Rajas; pitta is the fire humor, and kapha, the water humor. They provide a physiological structure for the interplay of the organs and elements, which makes up the physical body. Numerous forms of pitta evolve from Prana related to the sense organs because fire provides perception, giving pitta a few Sattvic properties. Many forms of kapha evolve from the vital-forces related to the five elements as they offer structure and bulk to the body, suggesting Kapha's Tamasik role."

"In the celestial, etheric world, under Tamas' predominance, the five elements turn into many diverse types with help of dysbalanced guna orientation. The vastness of ether comes from Sattva and is symbol of clarity, fire is from Rajas that characterizes energy, and earth comes from Tamas denoting inertia and stability. Both Sattva and Rajas compose the element 'air' and it is the symbol of buoyancy and movement. Water has both Rajas and Tamas and implies movement and inertia."

"From their iconic representation, it comes as no surprise that inert Tamas signifies the mineral or material kingdom, aggressive Rajas with movement is more about the animal kingdom, and they incubate as factors of disharmony in the mind[28]. For Sattva with clarity, the mind is its domain. One can measure the degree of Sattvic influence by the clarity of perception and peace the mind exhibits. When the three-guna vectors stay balanced in the mind, they unlock the powers of perception needed in comprehending the truth. When out of balance, Tamasik ignorance settles in, shadowed by surge in Rajasic desire and distorted imagination. Perception and knowledge flow come to a halt, because Sattva can stay active no longer; its activity dependent on the Rajas-Tamas balance. Through an increase in the Sattva content, one achieves peace and harmony, one can merge into nature and spirit. It has to be pure Sattva content, just its detached side to reach the heightened accord. The wellness program puts to use the three-guna vectors in determining the mental nature of a native. Guna we absorb from the external environment helps to build the mind; mind like guna is the causal or creative principle. With Sattvic influence used in orienting the mind, our understanding of the mind's nature and the nature of reality gets unfolded."

---

[28] Astanga Hridayam, 1.21. Manasikah Dosah. Rajas and Tamas cause doshas of the mind.

"Triggered are many disorders by the Rajas and Tamas vectors. Sattva attempts to harmonize and correct the disorder. Working at physical and mental levels, besides working in concert, Rajas causes dissipation of energy and Tamas brings about decay and death. Rajas, as the principle of force, in its outward direction of energy causes loss of energy through over indulgence that culminates in Tamas, fatigue and decay, just as excess stimulation leads to depression."

"Sattva upholds health, it causes no disease, and is moderately effective in curing ailments. Its balancing character is prone to accept everything. Sattva does not always have the power to administer Rajas or Tamas. Entrusted is the healing process to the actions of Rajas and Tamas, which have several opposite attributes. The 'hyper' Rajas stays pacified by some amount of 'hypo' Tamas; and so, does Rajas neutralize Tamas. While Sattvic principles have long-term effects, the above principle helps in immediate needs. When I sensed your children suffering from intense fever, I realized I had to calm the hyper activities of fever first, before the incense could become effective."

"Disease or Roga[29] is when dosha-s are no longer in equilibrium, health is in contrary. Disease arises out of Nija, from the body itself or from traumatic agantu owed to external causes. The disease 'adisthana' gets seated in the mind and body. Rajas and Tamas get enumerated as mental dosha-s[30]."

"The school of medicine that my predecessors taught me aims at restoring balance with return to nature, which provides the ammunition to return to the spirit. The style and methods in this school of thought are largely Sattvic. Sattvic healing employs natural laws and the power of the life force, supported by herbs, Sattvic diet and yoga."

"Vayu, pitta and kapha are three-dosha-s. They maintain the body when it is normal and destroy it when things are abnormal[31]. The air humor is 'Vata', the wind; originated from the root 'va' meaning to blow, to flow, to direct or command; in a nutshell, it means 'the force that moves things'."

---

[29] Astanga Hridayam, 1.19. Roga and Arogya
[30] Astanga Hridayam 1.20-21. rogestu doshavaishyamyam doshsamyamarogata | nija gantuvibhogen tattra roga dwigha smrita || tesham
kaya manobheddaddadhishtnmpi dwidha | Rajastamacha manso dwau ch doshavudahaitto ||
[31] Tridosha definition in Astanga Hridayam 1.6 – vayuh pittam kaphashroti trayo doshah | vikrita vikrita deham dhananti tai vartayanti ch |

"Motivating other two lame dosha types, incapable of movement without it, vata acts as the prime force on the nervous system, governs the sensory and mental balance, sensory and motor orientation and offers mental adaptability and comprehension. Vata is the basic vital or life force deriving primarily from the breath.[32]"

"The fire humor is pitta or 'bile', meaning 'the digester'. It comes from the root word 'taap', or 'the heat-sensation'. Pitta handles chemical and metabolic changes in the body. It oversees 'mental digestion', our capacity to perceive reality and understand things as they are. It draws on our ability to facilitate digestion of food."

"The water humor is 'Kapha,' 'phlegm' etymologically means 'what holds things together,' signposts the qualities of stickiness and adhesion. Kapha gives nourishment, provides substance and gives support. Kapha makes up the bulk of our body's tissues, supporting us emotionally, governing emotional traits as love, compassion, modesty, patience and forgiveness. It obliges as a vehicle, container and substratum for the other two forces."

"The dosha types have a second element that serves as medium for manifestation, acting as its container. Vata's force is air and field of operation is ether; Pitta uses the fire force and field is water and Kapha uses the water force with its field being earth."

"The container for Vata is ether; the attributes of ether rub into Vata. Ether dwells in the empty spaces in the body, like the colon or the pores of the bones, and fills up the subtle channels of the nervous system. The mind represents space in the body. Vata is the life force that moves about in the mind."

"Pitta or fire exists in the body as energy absorbed in liquid such as water or oil, giving it the traits of water. It subsides in an acidic form, a befitting analogy that fire cannot exist directly in the body without destroying it. Such fluids in the body signify the digestive system and the blood."

"Kapha or water humor occurs in the medium of earth-element, which provides a container for kapha making it an earth-composition. Our main physical composition is water and thrives within various boundaries of our skin and other tissue linings that define the 'earth' boundaries."

---

[32] Charaka Samhita - Three-body dosha-s are Vata, Pitta, and Kapha Chp 1, Sloka 57. Vata, Pitta and Kapha are eternally present in the body of living beings either as normal or abnormal. The wise should know. Chp, 18 Sloka 48

"Pure earth, however, acts damaging; earth's rigidity blocks organic functions. Only in a soluble and sedimentary form in liquid does it operate as a useful nutrient. Earth and ether as the physical, mental and conceptual borders of our vital energy contain the three dosha types within."

"The scriptures define Vata as dry, light, cold, rough, subtle, mobile and restless[33]. Pitta is little greasy, sharp or penetrating, hot, light, unpleasant odor, mobile and liquid[34]. Kapha is wet, cold, heavy, dull, sticky, soft, fixed[35]. Vata exhibits the drying, cooling, lifting and agitated properties of the wind. The heat of Pitta is evident in blood's character and in acid secretions in the stomach and intestines. Kapha exhibits its nature of phlegm or that of water confined in a small area where it stagnates and congeals. Dosha types share one major quality with another, and act opposite in two others."

"Vata and pitta are light or subtle by nature, vata and kapha are cold; pitta and kapha are moist or damp. Vata and Pitta share a light or subtle nature in providing perception and power of movement. Dosha types, vata and Kapha act cooling by which they retard body heat. Vata dosha disperses the heat and Kapha conserves in tissue form. Pitta and Kapha by their common humid-quality supply body fluids. Pitta provides the heat, the energizing force present in the blood and its circulation. Kapha delivers the nurturing force as evident in plasma containing the body-nutrients."

"One can distinguish dosha types from their attributes. An excess or deficiency of these qualities shows a similar excess or deficiency of the dosha. A change in such threshold brings about various pathological changes in the body. Excessive dryness shows an excess of vata and a deficiency of kapha, resulting in vata pathological changes like constipation, dry skin or emaciation that specify a decrease in kapha within body tissues, like plasma or fat."

"Actions or functions of vata on the body and mind are many. Vata is the root of all dosha types, tissues and waste within the body."

---

[33] Astanga Hridayam, 1.11. Vata attributes - ruksha - dry, laghu or light and incandescent, shita - cold, khara, rough and abrasive; sukshma - subtle, chala - mobile.
[34] Astanga Hridayam, 1.11. Pitta attributes - sasneha or oily, tikshna – sharp, ushna – hot, laghu – incandescent, visrama - a kind of sour, unpleasant, fleshy smell; sara; mobile, but not agitated; drava - liquid
[35] Astanga Hridayam, 1.11. Kapha attributes - snigdha: wet, unctuous or oily; shita – cold, guru-heavy; manda – dull, average, slow; slakshna: sticky and gelatinous; mritsna – soft; sthira: steady and fixed.

"In its natural state it sustains effort, enables exhalation and inhalation, stimulates the movement and the discharge of impulses, sets the equilibrium of the tissues and the coordination of the senses; making it more prominent among the other two dosha types. It oversees the other two and owns the responsibility of all physiological processes and organic functions. Vata manages energy, breath, nerves and sensory systems. It is answerable in maintaining the right balance of functioning in tissues and organs. Disturbances in Vata have worse implications than the other two-dosha types. Vata affects the mind and the entire body through the nervous system."

"Pitta operates on the body and mind in a different way. It partakes in controlling digestion, generation of heat, visual perception, hunger, thirst, luster, complexion, intelligence, courage and pliability. Pitta administers light and heat in the body and mind, combusting materials to create warmth and color. While vata governs mental power and coordination, and capacity for mental movement and adaptability; pitta administers mental perception, judgment and discrimination, develops the penetrating nature of thought."

"Kapha provides solidity, lubrication, binds the joints and inculcates qualities such as patience. Kapha is the material substratum and support for the other two-dosha types, offering stability to the body functions. It serves as a conserving and restraining force on the other two-dosha types, putting a check on their active and devouring acts. Without kapha, the other two-dosha types disperse and disintegrate our energy. Kapha lubricates the mucus membranes and the joints and cushions the entire body. It promises emotional calm and endurance and promotes the capacity to feel and sympathize."

"Vata flourishes in the colon, thighs, hips, ears, bones and organs related to hearing and touch. The colon is its primary site, where gas, a product of air accumulates. Thighs and hips are the main site of muscular and skeletal movement in the body, of which vata assumes full responsibility. Vata governs the organs of hearing and touch, having close association with the elements ether and air. Bones as tissue belong to vata. Pitta monopolizes the small intestine, stomach, sweat, the sebaceous glands, blood, lymph and eyes. The small intestine is its primary site, the main seat of digestive fire - digestive acids have a fiery nature. Sweat and sebaceous glands store and produce heat. Blood and lymph contain heat and color. Eyes as sense organs belong to the element of fire. Kapha occupies the chest, throat, head, pancreas, sides, stomach, lymph, fat, nose and tongue."

"The stomach is Kapha's primary site. Chest and lungs produce phlegm, and so do throat, head, sinuses and the nasal passages. Mouth and tongue produce saliva, another Kapha fluid. Tongue as the organ of taste belongs to the water element. Fat tissues store water. Kapha fills our sides surrounding the abdominal cavity as peritoneal fluid."

"Dosha types 'accumulate' at their primary sites instigating the disease process. Vata accumulates in the large intestine, pitta in the small intestine and kapha in the stomach. Treating them at these locations stops the disease process at the root. Deranged vata gets produced in lower regions as gas from the colon. Unbalanced pitta uses the liver, grows in the middle as bile and as acids in small intestine. Disturbed kapha gets produced in upper regions as phlegm in the lungs and stomach."

"Their locations are quite different when dosha types are in normal state. Vata as nervous and mental force prefers the central part of the brain, traversing the nervous system. Kapha resides below in the kidneys and reproductive organs and gives us energy reserve to rely on. Pitta remains in the middle. Earth element surrounds the region below, from the knees section to the feet in managing the body's firmness. It enables us to stand and sit, besides offering other stability functions. Water element is traceable to the lower abdomen and the region of the hips and buttocks where most of the water and fat in the body accumulates, anchoring the urinary and the genital system. Fire element prefers the mid-abdomen region starting from its center in the navel, closely resembling the complete digestive system. Air element occupies the heart and chest, the center of circulatory and respiratory systems. The borders include the arms. Ether resides in the head, governing the mind, senses and the nervous system. The senses are the main spaces or orifices in the body."

"The scriptures state that the elements water, fire and air elements oversee similar aspects of the body as kapha, pitta and vata. Besides them, earth element relates to the bones, particularly the skull, the intestines, muscles, skin, hair, nails and the solid bodily tissues. Water remains analogous to plasma, blood, urine, sweat, saliva and mucus. Weightless fire element is comparable to urges of hunger and thirst, delirium from excess heat, fever and sexual activity, passion in surplus. Air corresponds to every movement such as effort, breath and cellular respiration. Ether relates to emotions like desire, anger, fear and delusion, our want of mental space or environment."

"In their state of aggravation dosha types become the factors that cause disorders giving rise to different symptoms. Diseases by definition are nothing but expressions of aggravated dosha types. O' king, we need to understand these excess conditions of the dosha types carefully, along with their effects."

"Vata in excess produces symptoms of emaciation, debility, hypothermia where the body in desperation seeks warmth, but suffers tremors, distention and constipation, insomnia, sensory disorientation, incoherent speech, dizziness, confusion and depression. High vata dosha compels the life force and the mind to loosen their connection with the body resulting in decay and loss of coordination. Hyperactivity occurs at the expense of loss of vital fluids, and the physical body thereby withers. The life force disconnects from the body resulting in high extent of mental disassociation; prana separating from body, the body begins to decay. You will notice such symptoms in natives suffering pain, trauma and disorientation."

"Pitta in excess, colors the stool, urine, eyes and skin in yellow; it brings about hunger, thirst, burning sensation and insomnia. High pitta dosha progresses as internal heat stockpile resulting in high fever along with inflammation. The native literally starts to burn. Numerous acid and bile accumulate in the tissues producing fermentation and infection. Bleeding and excessive discharges of sweat and urine occur often. Kapha as water and phlegm indents the digestive fire, instigating nausea, lethargy, heaviness, much pallor, chills, and looseness of the limbs, cough, difficult breathing and unwarranted sleeping. High kapha dosha results in accumulated weight and mass in the body, which inhibits normal operation and lowers the normal activity, and excess tissue accumulation. The native caught in a force of inertia, heaviness, congestion and stagnation, gradually loses the power of movement."

"Kapha is phlegm, pitta is bile; phlegmatic diseases belong to Kapha, choleric disorders to Pitta. Vata, when deranged leads to melancholy; born of cold and the dry, dark discoloration in the body especially around the eyes; vata is behind a majority of chronic and debilitating diseases. Dosha types offer a key in understanding the body's vital forces, balance and imbalance. The program gives the practitioner the ability to personalize the wellness to the uniqueness of the loss of balance."

"Three guna vectors, the prime qualities of primal nature emerge in the long run as twenty attributes, ten opposing pairs. In the opposing pairs, each has an obverse like two sides of the coin. These attributes are present in all objects we perceive in the material and mental world."

"The pairs are (1) cold and hot, (2) wet and dry, (3) heavy and light, (4) gross and subtle, (5) dense and flowing, (6) static and mobile, (7) dull and sharp, (8) soft and hard, (9) smooth and rough and (10) hazy and clear[36]. Cold, wet, heavy, gross qualities come together to form a syndicate, while the hot, dry, light, subtle qualities form another. Former group descends and contracts in constructing the body; latter group ascends, expands and produces the vitality and mind. Former group has similarity to Soma, the aquatic, enjoyment principle, the latter is similar to Agni, the fiery, perceiving principle."

"In analyzing the twenty attributes, certain corollaries emerge. 'Hot' relates to fire and to pitta. Whatever is 'hot' increases pitta, decreases kapha and vata. Colder objects decrease pitta and increase kapha and vata. Heavier elements, earth and water retain heat; the lighter elements like air and ether disperse it."

"Wet state relates to water and to kapha; wetness it fuels kapha, shrinks vata, offers a delta increase on pitta. Dry state relates to air and vata and stays as its primary attribute. Dryness augments vata, decreases kapha and gives a mild cut to pitta. Besides water, other elements stay dry; though earth absorbs and secures water. Fire, air and ether evaporate and disperse the water element, ether showing the traits of a subtle fluid. Wet is analogous to oil, acting 'unctuous,' as thickening and condensation escorts dampness."

"Dry acts as reverse of unctuous. Heavy is a strong attribute of earth and water. Heaviness shows increased precipitation of kapha, intense decline in vata and moderate drop in pitta. Light relates to fire, air and ether; influencing vata's increase; discrete increase of pitta and weakening of kapha."

"Blatantly does 'grossness' attribute relate to earth and water, much like 'heavy'. It increases kapha and offers rapid drop in vata, besides a moderate lessening in pitta. Subtleness attribute is similar to 'light' involving fire, air and ether; bringing forth a strong increase of vata effect, moderate increase in pitta and decrease in kapha."

---

[36] Astanga Hridayam, 1.18. (1) Cold/Hot - Shita/Ushna, (2) Wet/Dry - Snigdha/Ruksha, (3) Heavy/Light - Guru/Laghu, (4) Gross/Subtle - Sthula/Sukshma, (5) Dense/Flowing - Sandra/Drava, (6) Static/Mobile - Sthira/Chala, (7) Dull/Sharp - Manda/Tikshna, (8) Soft/Hard - Mridu/Kathina, (9) Smooth/Rough - Slakshna/Khara and (10) Cloudy/Clear - Picchila/Vishada.

"Denseness is earth's primary attribute. Water along with earth as in kapha is oriented towards densification. It increases kapha and shrinks vata and pitta. 'Flow' sometimes rendered as 'liquidity' relates to water and fire. It increases pitta and decreases vata. It helps remove kapha. Turning kapha into liquid is necessary before discharging from the body."

"What is mobile and nimble relates to air and fire, resulting in strong proliferation of vata effect and moderate upsurge in pitta, while decreasing kapha. Static or slow relates to earth and water, increasing kapha effect and potently decreasing vata and moderately lessening pitta. Ether though impassive, it does not slow things down. What is meant by mobile can be thought of as 'active', and what is static is related to 'passive' states."

"Dull or 'resistant' relates to earth and water, denoting sharp increase in kapha and strong decrease in vata and moderate decrease in pitta. Sharp or 'penetrating' relates to fire, air and ether. Fire is the sharpest of them. 'Sharp' shows a strong increase in pitta, moderate increase of vata and cut in kapha. Soft for the most part relates to water, resulting in a strong increase in kapha, moderate increase in pitta and strong decrease in vata. Ether is also soft but in a very subtle way."

"Hard relates to air and earth, the constricting effect of the wind, which accounts for the hardness inherent in earth. It warrants increase in vata and mild decrease of pitta and strong decrease in kapha. Smooth relates primarily to water, ensuring a strong increase in kapha, mild increase in pitta and decrease in Vata. Ether's smoothness is expressive more in the subtle world. Rough relates to air and earth, with increase in Vata, mild decrease of pitta and strong decrease in kapha."

"Clear, light or 'transparent' relates to fire, air and ether, with strong increase in vata, moderate increase in pitta and decrease in kapha. Murky, dark or 'opaque' relates to water and earth. It increases kapha and decreases pitta and vata. Sometimes 'murky' gets rendered as 'sticky' or 'slimy' and clear as 'not sticky'. Kapha is sticky whereas vata and pitta are not."

"In a nutshell, vata has the traits of cold, dry, light, subtle, mobile, sharp, hard, rough and clear. Pitta is hot, somewhat wet, light, subtle, flowing, mobile, sharp, soft, smooth and clear. Kapha is cold, wet, heavy, gross, dense, static, dull, soft, smooth and cloudy. On observing the attributes that get exhibited, the dosha types become recognizable and differentiated."

"When someone complains of cold in the body, it may be either vata or kapha as both incline towards cold. When sensing them as cold and dry, you can clearly pinpoint to vata, and cold and wet to kapha. These qualities exist to different degrees in the dosha types. Vata and pitta share many properties in common, like both being light, subtle, mobile, sharp and clear. The way to distinguish them is that vata expresses the attributes powerfully, where in pitta, the attributes are mild. Pitta presents a continuous motion like a flow whereas vata is a jerky motion like a series of jolts and shocks. Pitta moves while vata shakes. Kapha and pitta have much in common in that they are wet, liquid, soft and smooth; kapha exhibits the attributes intensely, pitta is milder. In case of pitta, all qualities other than heat stay moderate. The extent or the intensity of the characteristics exhibited varies between vata-pitta or kapha-pitta."

"These qualities may appear contradictory. How can pitta be soft and smooth as well as sharp? Its soft and smooth attributes come from its secondary water element. The 'fire' component makes it sharp. Heated oil exhibits similar qualities. Ether is soft and smooth, as it shows characteristics of subtle liquid, which the scriptures described as the ethereal or celestial ocean, but is furthermore sharp or penetrating as it goes through everything. Sattva is neither hot nor cold, neither damp nor dry; it is light, subtle, mobile, sharp, soft, smooth and clear. Rajas is hot, showing marginal humidity, a tad heavy, gross, mobile, sharp, hard, rough and cloudy. Tamas is cold, wet, heavy, gross, solid, static, dull, hard, rough, cloudy and dark."

"Guna vectors contribute to the attributes, Sattva being subtle, light and balanced in qualities, Rajas remaining imbalanced, agitated and aggressive and Tamas being heavy, gross and stagnant. Tamas attributes are the same as the earth element; Rajas attributes are like the fire that does not burn clean thereby producing a lot of smoke. Sattva resembles ether."

"Using the same principles, we can arrive at the attributes of the five elements. Earth is cold, dry, heavy, unrefined, solid, static, dull, hard, rough and murky. Water is cold, wet, heavy, gross, liquid, static, dull, soft, smooth and unclear. Fire is hot, dry, light, subtle, mobile, sharp, rough, hard and clear. Air is cold, dry, light, subtle, mobile, sharp, rough, hard and clear. Ether is cold, dry, light, subtle, liquid, mobile, sharp, soft, smooth and clear. Many attributes get shared between the elements. Earth appears more gross, heavy, static, dull and darker in opacity than water. Air and ether bespeak of more light, the elements are subtle and clearer than fire. Air shows added roughness and rigidity than earth because it produces these qualities in earth. Water shows signs of added smoothness and softness over ether."

"Though similar, the qualities of elements differ in magnitude from dosha types. Pitta and fire are not analogous because pitta contains additional water, but both act on same primary attribute of heat. Qualities of vata are similar to those of air and kapha qualities match those of water. Yet we can find conditions when the ether element is higher in vata or the earth element is higher in kapha, in which case these added attributes become more noticeable and the treatment method becomes different. From their qualities, it comes to our observation earth is to a large extent kapha with minor traits of vata. All of water-elements are kapha, though it shares many features with pitta. Fire is predominantly pitta, with partial traits of vata. Air is totally vata. Ether is chiefly vata, with secondary connections to kapha. Ether as the root of the other elements is the most balanced form among them."

"The twenty attributes work at all levels of energies, objects and situations. Through them, we can discern their long-term effects. This brings back the general axiom of 'like increasing like', like a cold, dry wind or a cold, dry emotional relationship hastens to aggravate vata. An increase of 'like' or comparable attributes initiates the buildup of similar dosha types. Applying opposite powers, like heat in cold weather reduces any tendencies towards imbalance and disease. Around us at all times are factors increasing and decreasing the twenty attributes. It is important that we use these to factor what can bring about the balance in such situations."

"Dosha types when aggravated show an increase in their symptoms and attributes. It is not always the same attribute that shows signs of aggravation in diseases of a particular dosha, nor do all the attributes of the dosha become uniformly perturbed. When the cold property of vata witnesses more aggravation, we can without harm use hot, dry spicy herbs like ginger or trikatu, however, when the dry attribute goes up, such herbs would need extra diligence in their usage as they could easily aggravate the condition by their drying nature. In such a situation, a more demulcent or oil based herb, like Licorice[37], Shatavari or sesame oil, would serve the purpose. Treating the dosha types by gauging individual attributes, leads to personalized medication."

---

[37] Licorice, Liquorice, Yashtimadhu, Mulethi (Glycyrrhiza glabra) is an herb found in several parts of the world.

PERSONAL WELLNESS

None protested the avalanche of concentrated textual study. The king had the room overlooking east with Damodar Jehu reinstated, turned into a central classroom for the princes, their cousins and Padmalochan's nephew. A community college in the making, the news spread about Padmalochan's teachings and the room saw many curious visitors and aspirant learners. Padmalochan leafed through his well-bound palm leaf notebook as the crowded classroom slowly settled down for another day of intense learning. He had chosen the subjects and words with much care for admonition was something he demanded least from his audience. Having successfully completed a preliminary session on Samkhya, Dosha and Bhuta, the eager apprentices approached with relish a bigger bite into the fruits of wellness and terrestrial health.

"Allow me to do a quick recap on what we discussed in the last few sessions. In a nutshell, the basis for all creation is the agitation of three guna vectors that places us in a limited dimensional world. While the guna-qualities are the vectors that make up everything perceptible in the universe, they give rise to three forces internally, vata, pitta and kapha. Vata is aerial and represents movement, pitta is energy and kapha is structure. There are many attributes exhibited by the three-dosha types. The attributes stand out when one or many dosha types are imbalanced. It is by observing the attributes we can decide the state of disorder and what measures we can take to bring the system back to a state of equilibrium. The wellness program offers a vantage in keeping the analysis simple; the course maintains the brevity using a skillful hand. Brief it is, but exact; there lies its virtue. Such accurate is the system that a practitioner can with ease personalize a wellness program by a correct assessment of the attributes."

"As wellness programs became personalized, our forefathers dug deeper into the dosha types and determined how each dosha had different target areas and came up with five different sub-dosha types for every dosha. We will now study five sub-types of vata, pitta and kapha, which live in diverse sites in the body and do dissimilar functions. Judging the sub-types, the practitioner can offer more specific treatments for dosha imbalances and understand their dysfunction better. Of these, the five forms of vata or the five Prana energies rank as important, Prana being the life force, the underlying force support all our activities. Five sub-types in vata dosha are (1) Prana (2) Udana (3) Vyana (4) Samana and (5) Apana[38], collectively grouped as 'Vayu' in other words 'the wind'. Vayu is a Rig-Veda deity[39], in plural represents different movements of the life force."

"Starting with Prana Vayu, which comprises the rootwords 'pra' and 'ana' meaning the 'forward, primary air' or nervous force. Pervading the head, centered in the locus of the brain, Prana descends to the chest and throat. Prana administers the acts of inhaling and swallowing, in addition to sneezing, spitting and belching, and overseeing impressions, while the five senses in the head ingest them. At the inner plane, it controls the mind, heart and consciousness, supplying them with energy, coordination and adaptability. Prana is like a slice of cosmic life energy tagged to us that directs all other vata gusts in the body. It is our inspiration, connecting us with our inner self or pure consciousness. Prana's movement is inward; external food, air and water are pulled inward, impressions captured and sensory impulses grasped. Prana allows us to express feelings, grasp knowledge, making us accessible to external sources of nourishment and supports our connection to the cosmic life force. We become free of diseases when Prana is adequate; diseases strike when it finds the Prana weak. Such weakness and susceptibility can be overcome through methods like Pranayama, breathing exercises, aroma and music therapy."

---

[38] Vayu has five forms, operates in 5 sectors in the body - Prana, Udana, Samana, Vyana and Apana. Charaka Samhita Chp 12, Sloka 8

[39] Vayu is also referenced in Charaka Samhita as Vayu is all powerful, producer and indestructible; causes negation of the positive factors in creatures and brings about happiness and misery; he is Death, Yama, god of death, regulator, Prajapati, master of creatures, Aditi, Visvakarma, taking all sorts of forms, penetrates into all, executes all the systems, is most subtle, pervasive, Vishnu (protector), moves in the entire nature, what else Vayu himself is the Lord (all powerful). Chp 12, Sloka 8

"'Udana' owes its name to the root words 'uda' and 'ana' implying the 'upward moving air' or nervous force. Placed in the chest and centered in the throat, Udana oversees exhalation and speech, both of which occur through the outgoing breath. Damaged Udana makes us cough, belch and vomit. On an inner level, Udana assumes the responsibility of memory, strength, will and effort; suggesting how our energy can ascend in life. It administers how the energy of life and our work get expressed, even governing our self-expression through word, thought and effort. Udana regulates the aspirations in life and at the hour of death, it leaves the body, rising and directing us to the predestined subtle world. When developed in full, Udana gives us the power to transcend the outer world by affording us many psychic powers. Udana remains poised towards upward movement; it brings the air up and out in the act of exhalation. It brings our energy up in our strivings in life. Udana causes our minds and spirits to ascend. Udana points us to the higher values and deeper powers of discrimination."

"The name 'Samana Vayu' originates from root words 'sama' and 'ana' meaning the 'equalizing or balancing air'. Samana stays lodged in the small intestines and is the nervous force supporting the digestive system, overseeing the process of digestion and assimilation of nutrients. When impaired, it affects the appetite negatively, leading to nervous indigestion. It is a predominant Vayu acting on internal organs such as liver, spleen, pancreas, stomach, and upper part of the large intestine. Within the organs, it assists by helping in absorption, in this regard, Samana works in the lungs to help absorb air. Samana largely has an equalizing or balancing action and a contracting movement. It balances the higher and lower body portions and stabilizes their energies. Samana balances inner, outer, upper and lower body parts as regards digestion. Its aid in integration and energy increase is a clear sign of ascending action."

"Vyana Vayu composed of root words 'vi' and 'ana' is the 'diffusive, separative or pervasive air'. Centered in the heart region is the Vayu, from where it gets distributed throughout the entire body. It administers the circulatory system and through it influences the joints, muscle movement, and carries out impulses and secretions within these systems. Vyana tends towards outward and expanding movement. As such, its action occurs chiefly around the active motor organs, the legs and arms, main sites of movement in the body. When lessened, it makes us suffer from lack of coordination, difficulty while walking; our motor impulses suffer large damages. When Vyana is strong, we have good powers of movement and physical articulation. Vyana motivates physical work, however, it also diffuses and disperses our energy."

"Apana Vayu composed of words 'apa' and 'ana' implies the 'downward, flowing or moving air'. Centered in the colon, Apana orchestrates all downward impulses such as elimination, urination, menstruation, parturition and sex. Its impairment manifests as difficulty or abnormality in these discharges. Managing water absorption in the large intestine, it gives us the power to ingest maximum nourishment from food in the final stages of digestion, which also occurs in the large intestine. It aids in the nourishment of the fetus, and it supports the immune system shielding us from toxic substances. Apana has a predominant downward movement."

"As Udana, the ascending air, carries with it the life force upward and helps evolve the consciousness, Apana, the descending air, pushes the life force down and brings about the devolution of the consciousness. In excess, Apana accelerates decay leading to death. It drains the energy forcing the life force to slip away. Interestingly, Apana supports and controls all the other forms of Vata because it rules the large intestine, which is the main site of accumulation for Vata. Instabilities of Apana trigger maximum of Vata disorders. As a downward moving force, when aggravated, it increases production of waste and toxins. Treating of Apana becomes the first consideration in Vata handling. Prana, Udana and the other Vayu airstreams, even Vata extremes revert to normal when Apana gets reduced. Vata disorders being the root of most diseases, they usually accompany the other two-dosha types. Apana's descending force imposes decay that manifests whenever there is loss of strength or toxin accumulation. Apana is the disease power inherent in the body itself, our natural tendency to decay as part of our connection to the earth."

Vayu streams
Prana — • Pra - forward, Ana - moving air
Udana — • Uda - upward, Ana - moving air
Samana — • Sama - equalizing, Ana - moving air
Vyana — • Vi - seperatative, Ana - moving air
Apana — • Apa - moving away, fluid, Ana - moving air

"Unique are the movements of the five prana forces. While Prana and Apana administer the intake and elimination of vital energy, Samana and Vyana operate at a deeper physical level. Samana chaperons Prana to the tissues, and from the tissues, Vyana circulates prana throughout the body. Four prana forces culminate into Udana in motivating life. We comprehend oneness of prana life force in all, though represented in five forms, each with different powers and directions of movement."

"Think of them as cluster of five in a Celtic cross with Prana in the center as the regulating factor. Udana, which rises, stays on top; Apana, which sinks, stays at the bottom. Samana in the left side moves from Apana to Udana balancing the two in an upward direction. Vyana on the right side moves from Udana to Apana, balancing the two in a downward direction. It is our prerogative to ensure the five forces stay balanced."

"Samana exhibits a leveling, centripetal force that converges towards the center, as in the power of digestion. Vyana has an equalizing and centrifugal force that spreads from the center to the periphery, denoting the power of movement. Vyana is the inherent capacity to circulate the absorbed Prana among other parts. Udana is the positive side of exhalation, the capacity to extract energy following inhalation of breath."

"Five Prana potencies reach their thresholds in different stages of breathing. (1) Prana, the primary air snaps in at the act of inhalation. (2) Samana, the equalizing air stems at the point of retention, between inhalation and exhalation. (3) Vyana, the outward moving air trails Samana, acts at exhaling the breath as second part of retention. (4) Udana, the upward moving air occurs at the first part of the act of exhalation. (5) Apana, the downward moving air occurs at the second and final part of exhalation. The yoga of pranayama breath control works to heighten these different points, we as the learned and the learner get to know on how to better regulate and strengthen the Prana forces."

"Five Prana potencies occupy their specific boundaries of space. Prana stays housed in the area formed from openings of sense in the head and space in mouth. Apana fills the space generated by the lower orifices. Samana and Vyana do not have specific openings. Samana relates to the vacant space within the internal organs covering the digestive system and also the heart. Vyana prefers the space within the joints and vessels. Udana, like Prana fills the space created by the mouth. It becomes evident that the upper part of the body has a strong correlation with Prana and Udana while the lower part with Apana. Vyana dominates the limbs while Samana controls the trunk."

"Prana governs the intake of energy from food, drink, breath, impressions, emotions, thoughts and consciousness. Dwelling in the head and moving inward and downwards, Prana allows for acceptance of every energy source. Breath is the key source of action for Prana. In breathing we not only take in energy from the air, we also connect with other subtle sources of energy through consciousness. Conscious breathing feeds the vigor and consciousness. Being receptive to the right things, openness to divine and cosmic life-forces has a positive effect on Prana."

"Udana administers the energy that is output through speech, song, chants, physical effort, emotional outbursts and mental activities. It assumes responsibility of the creative use of energy. It is the definite result of nutrition, the positive energy created from intake of nutrients. Right aspiration in life and right values come from Udana."

"Samana oversees energy absorption in digestive and other systems. When our minds and emotions are not in Sama-balance, we cannot absorb nutrients at any level. Positive Samana comes from peace and balance, harmony and equilibrium within, and with our natural environment."

"Vyana manages energy distribution using the circulatory system of the physical body along with the breath, senses, emotions, thoughts and consciousness. It transports the absorbed Prana to the places where it can work and express itself. Vyana is positive, expanding thought, emotion, perception and consciousness when stimulated by our right action and when we are in harmony with our values and aspirations."

"Apana administers elimination of waste energy using all energy sources. These include urination, defecation, and exhalation. Apana is like an energy valve, when opened, drains out just the right amount of unused or waste energy."

"In the process, Apana eliminates toxins, supporting the other Prana-s, and continues propagation of life through reproduction. Apana functions right when we shake off negativity and stop responding to pessimism. Apana once set in the right motion stops the degeneration by eliminating the forces of decay from the body."

"Five Vayu types are more complex than their simple physical presentation. Besides their sites, their feats on the physical body, they act on the many subtle aspects of our being using the senses, breath, emotions, thought and consciousness. They enact their activities on the skin, senses and breath. Sustaining all five Vayu gusts and keeping them in balance, besides ensuring their proper functioning is the key to real health."

"Prana plays host to the life-force, enabling us with means to receive life-force on different levels. Prana is the thin line of separation between the material world, mind and spirit. It offers possibility of life formation and its continuum on the material level. It also provides means to connecting with the primary life-force or spirit, a representation of Cosmic man, empowering us to vitalize all the energies that enter us. Udana assists the life-force in its ascent and positive extraction of the energy at different levels. Our life-force has a natural tendency to ascend and Prana reinforces it. More of consciousness gets revealed with every upward movement. When our faith in life is positive, Prana takes us upwards and guides us through the transformation process. Blocking this natural ascent of the life-force are the forces of descent that originates through thought and material attachment. Apana accounts for the life-force's descent and how it promotes negative energy. In its correct functioning, Apana removes the negative life-energy, while in its erroneous functioning it opens to forces of destruction."

"Udana and Apana represent two forces of evolution and involution, two contradictory forces which normally join hands and balance the outcome. One of them is a positive current, which herald's growth, enabling evolution of consciousness. Udana is this positive life-force. There exists the negative current that speeds up decay and involution of consciousness. Apana is that negative life-force. Udana is the force through which the soul rises in consciousness and moves to higher dimensions of consciousness, taking the soul up into the higher worlds after terrestrial life is complete. Apana is the force through which the soul descends in consciousness and permeates into lower states of consciousness."

"Wellness aims towards balancing the opposite forces of Udana and Prana. Our food, breath, senses and mind need a pure dose of Prana to achieve that. Anything Sattvic increases the power of Udana whereas Rajasic and Tamasik regimens intensify Apana. Udana is also the power of speech, which in its higher form is the power of the word, knowing and speaking the right, in all honesty is harmonic to the forces."

"The scriptures often give details of many other prana forces, of which I spoke on five major ones. Texts tell us also on five minor Prana strengths 'Upavayu', which I will cover in brief. Five minor Prana forces are Naga, Koorma, Krichara, Devadatta and Dhananjaya. Naga is the most important and the leader of the minor forces. Devadatta dwells in the nostrils and the mouth, governing the actions of yawning and sneezing. Krichara resides in the throat, administering hunger, thirst and digestion. Koorma stays located in the eyelids, overseeing the opening and closing of eyes, including winking and blinking. Naga finds a seat in the crevices of the mouth, supporting the actions of belching and hiccups. Dhananjaya pervades the entire body, causing swelling and inflammation, including abdominal distention. After death, it takes responsibility when the body swells. It aids in bodily movements and helps absorb what comes to us as nourishing."

"Next come the five sub-types of Pitta Dosha. They are Sadhaka, Alochaka, Pachaka, Bhrajaka and Ranjaka. As Agni forms, they provide and promote heat on some level. Sadhaka Pitta is the fire that assists us in gauging truth and reality, derived from the root word 'sadh' meaning 'to accomplish or to realize'. It resides in the regions of brain and heart, facilitating our needs of accomplishing the goals of intellect, intelligence and ego. On a material level, the goals manifest as worldly pleasure, wealth and respect; on a higher level, they offer the means to salvation. Sadhaka Pitta acts through the nervous system and senses. Sadhaka imparts the sharpness and warmth of fire and the capacity to ingest information to the organs of brain and senses. When weakened, the person suffers from lack of clarity, he stands confused, even delusional, soon the native becomes incapable of distinguishing between fantasy and real. Sadhaka Pitta administers mental energy and digestion, suggesting the mechanism by which impressions, ideas and beliefs get ingested, while developing the power to discriminate. Only true knowledge can enable us to differentiate between eternal and transient, real and apparent. As with Prana, Sadhaka denotes an inward movement, facilitating an inner combustion and releasing energy from our impressions and life experiences in empowering the mind. It is the force of introspection."

"Alochaka Pitta represents the fire that oversees visual perception. It resides in the eyes and takes accountability of reception and digestion of light energy from the external world. Centered in the pupil of the eyes, Alochaka grants us vision. When lessened, we suffer from vision malfunction and eye diseases. Like Udana Vayu, Alochaka has an upward drift, pushing us to seek light, clarity and understanding. On receiving the light, it feeds the mind and soul. The quality of the soul is always visible through the light of the eyes. Through it we can read the condition of the liver organ in the body. Lucidity in the eyes denotes a good digestive power and a deeper understanding of Sattva principles."

"Pachaka Pitta is the sub-type of pitta that digests things through 'pach[40]'. Placed in the small intestine, it oversees the process of digesting food. It is the driving force for bile salts and acids production useful in digesting our food. In addition, Pachaka regulates body temperature and helps support the circulatory rhythm. When impaired, Pachaka makes us suffer from food indigestion, even leading to hyperacidity and ulceration when acute and high. When the fire runs low, we suffer poor absorption, dearth of body heat and diminutively low Agni, the digestive fire[41]. Pachaka is the foundation pitta, supporting other types of pitta. Pitta sub-types use the small intestine as their prime location, their main work is digestion. Pachaka pitta is often the first consideration when it gets to treatment of pitta conditions, the primary source of heat being the digestive fire - Agni, with which this form of pitta is intimately bound. Similar to Samana Vayu, Pachaka has an equalizing, balancing action, and discriminates nutrient parts from non-nutrient parts of food. Pachaka assumes responsibility in building tissues and destroying any pathogens that have entered through food."

"Bhrajaka[42] Pitta is the fire that covers luster and complexion. A skin tenant, it maintains complexion and skin pigmentation. When aggravated, it may cause skin rashes and discolorations. Bhrajaka administers our ingestion of warmth, heat and sunlight, which occurs through the skin. Bhrajaka provides us with metrics by which we can read the heat and warmth of the body and the glow of our aura. Like Vyana Vayu, it promotes circulation and has an outward moving energy. Bhrajaka is like the warmth of our peripheral circulation. This Pitta diffuses and disperses our heat. Perspiration results from its increase."

---

[40] Pach is the act of cooking
[41] Astanga Hridayam, 1.8 – Agni-Bheda. Charaka Samhita, Chp 27, Sloka 342, Chp 6, Sloka 12
[42] Bhrajaka means 'making bright', 'causing something to shine'

"Ranjaka pitta is the fire that reveals color. Posited in the liver, spleen, stomach and small intestine, Ranjaka lends color to the blood, bile and stool. Its association with several liver disorders is apparent. Ranjaka imparts warmth to the blood and the circulatory system. Like Apana Vayu, its energy moves downward and sponsors the toxins. With Ranjaka accumulated, it lends color or rather discolor to other secretions and waste from the body, such as urine and feces."

"Finally, we arrive at five sub-types of kapha dosha. They are Tarpaka, Bodhaka, Kledaka, Sleshaka and Avalambaka. Think of them as different mucous secretions and lubrications. Tarpaka kapha has the construct of water that makes us content, 'tripti[43]'. Found in the brain and heart, it supports the cerebrospinal fluid; imparting strength, nourishment and lubrication to the nerves. Internally, it calms the emotions, ushering stability, and happiness and enhancing memory capacity. Its impairment manifests as discontent, malaise, nervousness and insomnia. Practice of Yoga increases this mental form of kapha in a positive way leading to contentment and bliss. As with prana, it has an inward motion, speeding the ability to enjoy happiness with our own nature. Meditation promotes its secretion, orienting us towards inner forms of joy."

"Bodhaka kapha is an aquatic sub-dosha that enables perception. Posited in the mouth and tongue as the saliva, it helps to savor the food. Like Kledaka, there exists a distinct association with the first stage of digestion. Its impairment manifests as loss of palate or deranged sense of taste, which often precedes kapha disorders. As with Udana, its movement is upward, helping us in gaining knowledge. Residing in the head like Alochaka pitta, it clears the perception, governing our sense of taste and its refinements as we seek subtler forms of enjoyment in the course of our evolving. Kledaka kapha implies the form of water that moistens. It dwells in the stomach as alkaline secretions of mucous lining and as mucous lining of the digestive tract. Kledaka assumes responsibility for the liquefaction of food and enabling the first stage of digestion, making it easy for the acids to work on liquefied food. Any weakening in Kledaka manifests as irregular secretion of stomach fluids and excess phlegm. Like the dosha Samana, it suggests a balancing action and mediates between the contents of the gastro-intestinal tract and internal tissues, regulating the moisture content in the digestive process. Kledaka works in harmony with Pachaka pitta to protect the mucous lining of the digestive tract from being damaged by the heat of Pachaka pitta and Agni, the digestive fire."

---

[43] Tripti is the satisfaction that comes from sipping water when thirsty

"Sleshaka Kapha is the liquid lubricant. Formed from the root word 'slish', it means 'moist or sticky'. While located in the joints as the synovial fluid, Sleshaka manages in holding them together and permeating ease of movement. Its deficiency leads to arthritic conditions. Like Vyana Vayu, its movement is outward; it provides us strength and stability in external movement. Looseness, heaviness and difficulty in movement come from Sleshaka, besides many arthritic disorders. Too little of it triggers dry, cracking joints and difficult movement. Sleshaka in excess will force the joints to swell."

"Avalambaka Kapha implies 'support that comes from water'. It is located in the heart and lungs, lubricating large portions of the chest. A storehouse for Kapha-phlegm, the actions of other Kapha types depend heavily on it. Avalambaka not only helps the lungs with mucus and fluid lining, but also the heart and throat. Avalambaka corresponds to the basic plasma or rasa of the body, the body's primary watery constituent; plasma formation occurs from lung and heart action, from which produced are all Kapha sub-types as byproducts. Just like Apana, its action is downward, offering overall support, especially in extending stability to the chest and heart region. However, on the downside Avalambaka brings heaviness and attachment. Most types of emotional attachment and clinging increase with higher levels of Avalambaka sub-dosha. Avalambaka Kapha facilitates obesity and most pulmonary disorders as evidenced from congestion in the lungs and swollen glands. Most accumulations of phlegm in the body are from Avalambaka's dysfunction. Clearing the chest of phlegm removes excess water from all over the body; even water retention or edema is often better treated by dispelling phlegm in the chest; in fact, a lot better than using diuretics. Much like Apana Vayu and Pachaka Pitta, Avalambaka is key sub-dosha in the disease process."

"Sub-dosha systems enjoy an internal relationship, forming five sub-dosha triads from each set. The first set comprises Prana Vayu, Sadhaka pitta and Tarpaka kapha. Second set is Udana Vayu, Alochaka pitta and Bodhaka kapha. Third comprises Samana Vayu, Pachaka pitta and Kledaka kapha. Fourth set is Vyana Vayu, Bhrajaka pitta and Sleshaka kapha. Finally, the fifth consisting of Apana Vayu, Ranjaka pitta and Avalambaka kapha."

"First three, Prana, Sadhaka and Tarpaka encompasses the brain-heart-spine-nervous system functioning in turn controlling the other triads. Second three, Udana, Alochaka, and Bodhaka occupy the head, face, mouth and neck and relate to sensory activity. They improve sensory perception, increase the will power and aspiration, and improve operational capabilities of other forms of same dosha type."

"Third group comprising Samana, Pachaka and Kledaka help in the digestive process and dwell in the stomach and small intestine region. Fourth group comprising Vyana, Bhrajaka and Sleshaka have close relationship to the limbs, the skin, the joints and the surface of the body and enjoy connections to the circulation system. Fifth group made of Apana, Ranjaka and Avalambaka play a supportive role for the other dosha types and stay associated with the internal organs like kidney, liver and heart. They govern the dosha waste products. Apana manages the intestinal gas, Ranjaka takes care of excess blood and bile, and Avalambaka manages excess mucus in the chest and lungs."

"These internal sub-dosha relationships provide useful clues when treating any sub-dosha escalations. When dealing with Sleshaka Kapha as evident in arthritis, the role of Vyana Vayu, which helps in peripheral energy flow, and Bhrajaka Pitta, which comprises surface heat all come under consideration."

"Prana strengthens from pranayama practice and adopting a lifestyle with positive attitude and will. Sadhaka pitta improves from practice of good-and-evil discrimination and clarity of perception. Contentment and faith enhance Tarpaka Kapha. Prana Vayu, Sadhaka pitta and Tarpaka kapha as related to Prana, Tejas and Ojas increases through factors that augment Prana, Tejas and Ojas."

"Yes, in addition to sub-dosha, there subsists three other subtle-dosha types essential in managing the life engine's upkeep and maintenance. The subtle types are Prana, Tejas and Ojas, definitely more advanced than their five counterparts in the physical body. These have a tremendous influence on the mind, prana, and the subtle and causal bodies. Consider them as sub-dosha types working on higher dimension corresponding to Prana Vayu, Sadhaka Pitta and Tarpaka Kapha. It is wise to think of them as the subtle kinds of Vata, Pitta and Kapha."

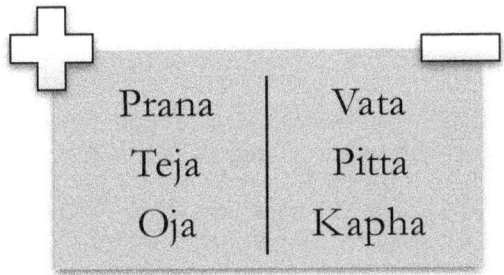

"We referred to the subtle form of Vata as Prana[44], though it carries a different meaning, working through Vayu-Prana. Pitta in its subtle form is Tejas formed by the root word 'tij' which suggests 'giving heat', working through Sadhaka Pitta on a gross level. Kapha has its subtle form in Ojas and works through Tarpaka Kapha on a gross level. Ojas is the essential vital fluid of the body in subtle form in the brain. These three vital essences regulate our mental and vital nature, and the work endocrine system. They, being the higher evolved types, get to control vata, pitta and kapha in the body. Vata, pitta and kapha are the particles of anti-particles Prana, Tejas and Ojas[45]."

"Subtle Prana enhances mental adaptability, the capacity to communicate, coordination of ideas and comprehension. It is the basic life force, the vitality of the mind. On a prana level, it builds enthusiasm, adaptability, creativity and strength. It nourishes the will to live, to grow and to get well. It governs overall growth, and the evolution of body and mind."

"Tejas infuses intelligence, reason, zeal, self-discipline, passion to learn, to discover, and the capacity to perceive. It is the basic clarity present in the nascent mind. On a prana level, it signifies courage, fearlessness, daring, boldness and valor."

"Ojas imparts mental strength, contentment, patience, fortitude, peace, memory-power and sustained concentration. It is our basic mental and psychological stability and endurance. In essence, Ojas is our peace of mind. On the life-force level, Ojas grants a strong immune system, physical endurance and the capacity to achieve sustained work and exertion."

"The human body has seven Dhatu covers or tissue layers[46]. Dhatu gets derived from the root word 'dha' meaning 'to support'. This concept of layers parallels the logical universe, which has seven dimensions of existence. While dosha types are the contributory factors in disease, the tissues are the sites where diseases occur, hence the word 'dushya,' meaning 'what can get spoiled'."

---

[44] The word Prana is overused in the Ayurvedic and Vedic Astrology context.

[45] Photon, which is of type Boson in particle physics, interacts with target photon to produce lepton-antilepton or a quark-antiquark. The Vata, Pitta and Kapha act in similar manners being anti-Guna particles of their positive polarity. These are not particle-antiparticle as such, but represent a similar structure.

[46] Astanga Hridayam, 1.13. Dhatu-s are also known as Dusyas, vitiated by three dosha-s. 'Disease is disequilibrium of the Dhatu-s. Health is equilibrium of Dhatu-s'. Charaka Samhita Chp 9, Sloka 3.

"Dhatu 'covers' owe their production to the digested food mass, devoid of any waste. The layers form a concentric circle of covers, ranging from the perimeter of gross to the subtle center."

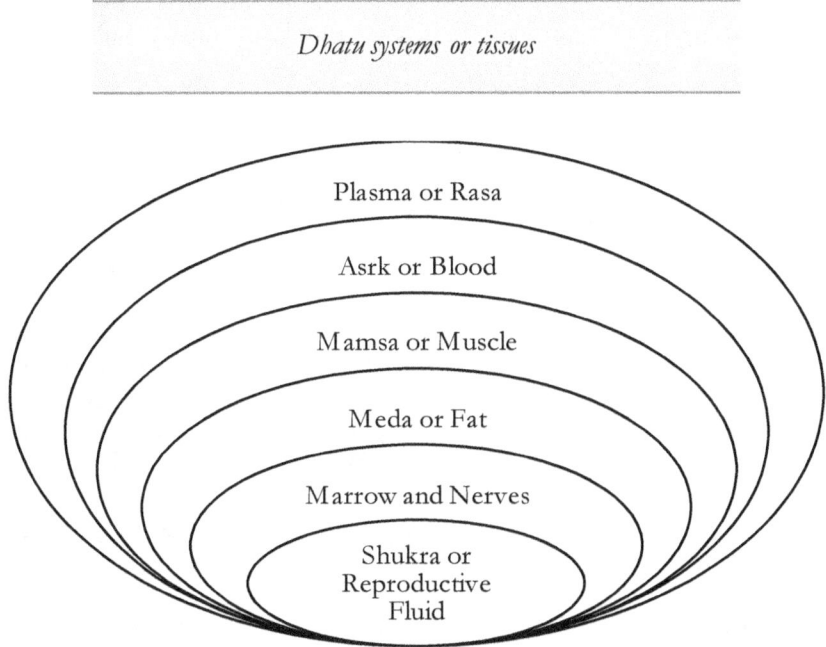

Dhatu systems or tissues

"Regarding dhatu covers and dosha types, Kapha manages all the tissues in general. It specifically supervises top five of the seven tissues, being the basic substance of the body. The top five are plasma, muscle, fat, marrow, and reproductive fluid. Both Pitta and Vata produce one tissue each. Pitta generates blood and Vata produces the bone."

"Plasma or Rasa dhatu is composed mainly of water; it is the fundamental liquid-mass in which suspended are the other tissues. It provides nutrition to all the five elements in the body. Fire and water forms Blood or Asrk dhatu, which upon becoming a fluid and enables the mechanism to convey heat. Muscle or Mamsa dhatu is composed of the earth-element along with water and fire as secondary. It is thick and heavy and defines the bulk of the body. Fatty tissue or Meda dhatu borrows its composition from water, but is more refined than plasma. Cartilage, ligaments and connective tissue also belong to this group. Bone is an earth composition, inheriting the mineral constituents, and from air, its porosity. Airs drying action congeals the bone tissues."

"Marrow and nerve is a subtler form of water that has the power to convey nerve impulses, something the less evolved forms of water as plasma and fat cannot. It also has certain earth composition being heavy. Reproductive fluid is the essential or causal form of water that has the power to create new life. It is the essence derived from all the tissues, particularly the nerve tissue. Ojas is the eighth tissue, subtle essence of all Kapha within, the crux of reproductive fluid. It is the crucial product of nutrition and digestion and the prime energy kept in reserve for the entire body. Though not a structurally defined like the other tissues, its subtleness plays an important role in their functioning."

"The tissue of plasma or rasa gives nourishment or pleasure. Plasma provides nutrition to all the tissues. It fills them up and affords us a sense of fullness. It assumes responsibility for hydration of the tissues and for maintaining the electrolytic balance. When the plasma or rasa is enough, our sense of happiness and contentment goes up several notches. We bounce with juice and vitality, and enjoy moving and acting. A zest for life and a sense of beauty and joy comes from the plasma. The term 'rasa' itself means 'essence' or 'sap' and 'to circulate', as experienced in the delight of dancing. Plasma pervades the entire body but its main sites are the heart, blood vessels, lymphatic system, skin and mucous membranes. Rasa shares a close relationship with kapha. Think of plasma as the container and kapha as contained.[47]"

"Critical is blood or Rakta dhatu to life and vitality. On a physical level, revealed is the dhatu's capacity to oxygenate the cells, which otherwise would decay. Many diseases like cancer spread when the cells lack oxygen. When the blood production is enough, our life energy flourishes; we have faith, love and ardor. 'Rakta' means 'a colored object' or 'what is red'. The blood imparts color and as a circulating fluid like the plasma eases our movement. Blood draws a parallel to pitta in qualities and functions where blood is the container and pitta is the contained."

"Muscle or mamsa dhatu functions to plaster and lapel the insides. The muscles, like a gelatinous covering act as a cover and give strength to our basic body frame. Muscle defines the capacity to work and act. When muscle tissue is deficient, we lack cohesion and our structure suffers from absence of integration. When adequately formed, mamsa promises courage, confidence and strength, openness, forgiveness and happiness. Derived is the term 'mamsa' from the root word 'mam' meaning to hold firm."

---

[47] Charaka Samhita - Dhatu-s are Rasa, Rakta, Mamsa, Meda, Asthi, Majja, Shukra/Artava. Chp 28

"Fat or meda dhatu lubricates the internal engines, mainly the muscles, tendons and other tissues. When it promises to lubricate the throat, the person gets a melodious voice. Fat gives a sense of smoothness, ease, and on a psychological level imparts the compassion of being cared. Many people turn obese to counter any feelings of not being loved. 'Meda' means 'greasy'."

"Bone or asthi dhatu leads the critical role of overall support. The bones sustain all tissues, making them firm and providing a strong foundation. When well-formed with enough mass, Asthi promises stability, confidence, security, certainty and good stamina. 'Asthi' owes is derivation to the root word 'stha,' meaning 'to stand or endure'. Bone stores vata within the body, where bone is the container, contained is vata. Vata resides in the spaces in the bone system."

"Marrow or Majja dhatu provides the attribute of permeation and contentment. Marrow serves to fill the empty spaces in the body, as in the nerve channels, bones and brain cavity. It helps in the secretion of synovial fluid and in lubrication of the eyes, stool and skin. There are two types of Majja, first one consists of fillers in the spinal cord and the second as bone marrow[48]. Marrow imparts a sense of fullness and sufficiency. When short in quantity, feelings of emptiness and anxiety prevail. Majja promises affection, love and compassion as is evident in its lubricating nature. 'Majja' gets derived from the root word 'maj,' meaning 'to sink', implying the nerve tissues sunk deep in the bones."

"Reproductive fluid or Shukra dhatu involves the critical machinery of reproduction or 'garbha utpadana'. It enables reproduction of life and is the harbinger of human life continuity. Shukra here stands for the seed - the ovum in women and all fluids enmeshed in reproduction. When insufficient, the ambience lacks creativity and reeks of impotence and infertility. It provides strength, energy and stamina for the entire body and sustains the immune function. The dhatu of Shukra restores light to the eyes, inspiration to the soul, though there are several differences between women and men. Shukra has reproductive components like semen and ovum, an enjoyment component of pleasurable fluids and hormones released during sexual activity. It is the enjoyment aspect of the reproductive tissue for a woman that serves as sublimation for spiritual practices."

---

[48] bone marrow is also capable of producing red blood cells

"Tissues need suitable nutrition. Rasa, the basic plasma originates from Agni's digestion of food. The rasa produced, helps develop other tissues by providing them nutrition. Rasa, plasma is the core ocean in which other tissues thrive. Each tissue owes its development to its predecessor. Every individual tissue is produced from digestion of another; the producer becomes food for the produced. Plasma when digested becomes blood, blood develops into muscle, muscle converts to fat, fat becomes bone, bone develops marrow, and marrow converts to reproductive fluid. There really is only one tissue in the human body, which undergoes seven levels of transformation or metamorphosis. As is expected, any problem in any one tissue spreads like wildfire on to the rest as defects or problems."

"Dhatu-tissues are either in a stable or 'sthayi' state or in unstable or 'asthayi' state. Developmental part of the tissue stays stable while a specific 'agni' or digestive fire acts on that tissue. In the tissue digestion, secondary tissues known as 'upadhatu' are produced like menstrual fluid for rasa dhatu, besides waste byproducts like kapha for plasma. Think of the formation as analogous to the digestion of food where produced are both, nutrients and feces. The evolutionary process continues with production of a pure portion of the formative tissue serving as the formative tissue for the next tissue layer."

"The plasma-in-the-making produces stable plasma and secondary tissues along with its kapha waste. It leaves behind a subtler form of substance, which becomes the constructive tissue for blood or 'asthayi rakta', the next tissue level. Such is the process with ongoing flow of nutrition and metamorphosis occurring at the seven tissues."

"Improper nutrition to one tissue is reflected in those further down the line. Proper formation of tissues depends on previous tissue's proper formation and the normalcy of the digestive fire or Agni of the tissue. The tissue with low Agni[49] will produce surplus and low-quality tissues. Tissue with excess Agni digesting it, inadequate and burnt tissue will be produced. It is like a machine, you feed bad yarn, you get bad clothes."

"Produced tissues support their predecessors, storing their accumulated energy. Blood keeps thickened plasma, muscle stockpiles concentrated blood, fat stores condensed muscle, bone contains collected fat, marrow keeps concentrated bone, and reproductive fluid has clustered marrow. The reproductive fluid is the concentrated essence and energy reserve of the entire body."

---

[49] Dhatu Agni – the digestive fire within the dhatu-tissues.

"Coarser tissues are more in quantity. Only a part of plasma becomes blood, of which only a portion becomes muscle until only a relatively small amount of reproductive fluid gets produced."

"Subtler tissues are more concentrated and enduring, developed through a long-drawn process. While food intake generates plasma regularly, it takes five days for it to transform into blood. Reproductive fluid needs a month for its full formation, once built; it supports all the other tissues from the core, as plasma does from the outside. Just as inadequate nutrition from plasma weakens the tissues, so does low-energy reserve in deficient reproductive fluid lead to a collapse of the tissues within."

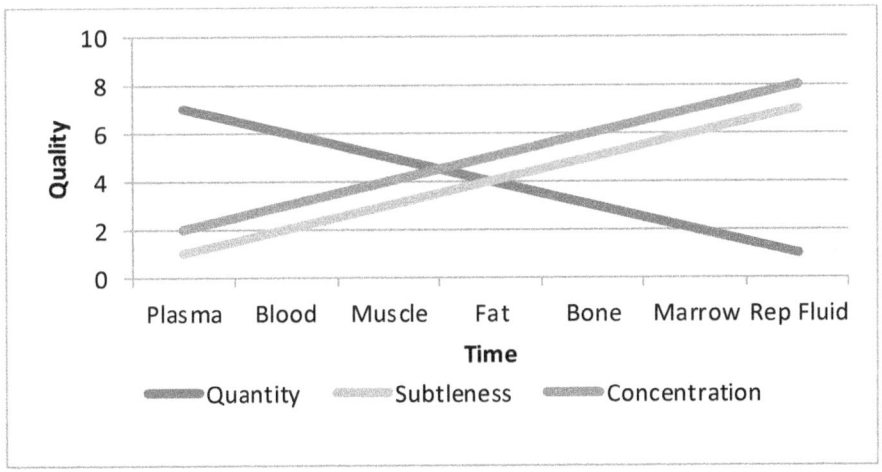

"A basic tissue has seven layers of thickness with different densities, much like the five elements calibrating as diverse densities of matter. Tissues develop concentric group of densities; they also form a ring where the concentric circle turns back upon itself. The act of recursion is a reminder of the cosmic phenomena turning back on itself. Plasma as the first tissue stays connected with the reproductive fluid, the last in the chain of formation. Plasma can directly nourish reproductive fluid, and the reproductive fluid in turn, can nourish or support plasma. Many substances that increase plasma production, like milk, increase the reproductive fluid formation. Deficiency of plasma and that of reproductive fluid go together and the reverse is equally applicable".

"Dhatu-tissue produces a secondary tissue or 'Upadhatu' and waste material or 'mull'. Adequate dhatu-tissue formation gets faithfully echoed in secondary tissue production. Excess or impurity of a tissue gets reflected in its waste products."

Secondary tissues - Upadhatu

Plasma dhatu produces breast milk, menstrual flow as upadhatu
Blood dhatu generates secondary blood vessels and tendons
Muscle produces ligaments and skin as upadhatu
Fat generates peritoneal fat in the abdomen
Bone brings forth teeth as upadhatu
Marrow gets Sclerotic fluid in the eyes
Reproductive dhatu gets Ojas as upadhatu

Waste from tissues

Plasma produces the waste Kapha in phlegm format
Blood produces Pitta in the form of bile
Muscle creates waste-material in the outer cavities of the body like the ear and navel, such as earwax
Fat generates sweat as waste
Bone produces nails and hair
Marrow and nerves produce tears and eye secretions
Reproductive dhatu produces *Smegma*, a waste material secreted by the genitals

Dosha, dhatu and waste

"Like the clay that makes a pretty vase, and on breaking, goes back to clay, Kapha and Pitta not only produce plasma and blood, but also are their waste byproducts. They produce the two tissues, and in turn, they generate some waste. As Kapha or Pitta gets generated in excess, they create a significant amount of waste that becomes toxic to the tissues. When the production of the two tissues, plasma and blood are in excess, their corresponding two dosha types get amplified. Many Kapha diseases tend to involve the plasma, and similarly, Pitta diseases engage the blood. A large number of toxic blood diseases are related to Pitta and most excess mucus conditions are closely associated with Kapha."

"Vata is a trifle different from the other two in this matter. While vata is not a waste of the bone tissue, it remains in close association with it, besides being held in it, in the spaces in the bones or between the bones namely the joints. Most vata diseases include the bones, like in arthritis. Vata dosha is actually waste gas produced in the digestive process. Excess gas and distention in the lower abdomen are signs of high vata dosha."

"Overdeveloped and even underdeveloped tissues create situations leading to diseases. When the digestive fire of the tissue is low, it produces excessive amount of tissues, but of inferior quality. With the fire set to high, it burns the tissue, besides breeding shortfalls in production."

"When plasma thrives in excess, saliva and phlegm accumulate, blocking the channels, leading to loss of appetite and nausea. Kapha level increases with such congestion and triggers the formation of cysts and benign tumors all over the body."

"Blood found in surplus brings skin diseases, abscesses, liver and spleen enlargement, hypertension, tumors, jaundiced-state, digestive weakness, delirium, burning sensations, and redness, and sometimes bleeding in the skin, eyes and urine. It can give rise to many pitta problems like fever, inflammation and bleeding disorders."

"Excess muscle tissue triggers muscular swelling and tumors, heavy and swollen glands, obesity, liver enlargement, irritability and aggression. In women, fibroid conditions and miscarriage may occur, often inhibiting vitality in sex."

"When in excess, fat dhatu leads to obesity, fatigue, immobility, asthma, sexual debility, thirst, hypertension, diabetes, impaired longevity, sagging of the thighs, breast and belly, emotional outbreaks of fear and attachment. These are well known Kapha problems. Bone in excess creates extra bones, bone-spurs and superfluous teeth, excessive large frame, joint pain, accompanied by fear, anxiety and poor stamina. Such individuals tend towards arthritis."

"When in surplus, marrow and nerve tissue produces heaviness in the eyes, the limbs, and in the origins of the joints, deep sores that do not heal, turbidity and infections in the eyes. When in excess, reproductive tissue generates undue sexual passion, leading to anger, surplus quantity of reproductive fluid, stones in the semen and swelling of prostate in men, ovarian and uterine cysts in women."

"It becomes evident that excess states of the tissues reveal themselves as dosha overloads of the corresponding type. Surplus production of plasma, muscle, fat, marrow and reproductive fluid comes from different degrees of high kapha. Extra blood is high pitta, not high kapha; high or low blood pressure symptoms result from extreme pitta levels. Majority of excess conditions is kapha in nature as kapha represents the constructive aspect of dosha types."

"From affluence to deficiency."

"Deficit plasma results in rough skin, dry lips, dehydration, weariness, intolerance to sound, tremors, palpitations, pain and sense of emptiness in the heart, feeling exhausted after little exertion. Weakened nutrition to the body, in deficit state, the blood creates pallor, low blood pressure, shock, longing for sour and cold food, looseness and dryness of the head, loss of skin luster, collapse of the blood vessels, dryness, roughness and cracks in the skin."

"When under-provided, muscle produces emaciation of the hips, abdomen and back of the neck, fatigue and looseness of the limbs, lack of coordination, fear, insecurity and sorrow. Shortages in fatty tissues induces tiredness, cracking of the joints, weary eyes, spleen enlargement, emaciated limbs and thin abdomen, along with brittle hair, nails, teeth and bones."

"Bone in an inadequate state makes the native complain of weariness, pain or looseness in joints and falling of the teeth, hair and nails. Bone and teeth are poorly formed, often leading to periodontal diseases and weak bones. Dwarfism occurs in extreme cases. When deficient, marrow and nerve produce weak and porous bones, pain in small joints, dizziness, seeing spots before the eyes, darkness around eyes, sexual debility and feelings of emptiness and fear. Vata diseases result in shortcomings in the nervous system."

"When deficient, reproductive tissue instigates lack of vigor and sexual interest, sterility, impotence, dryness of the mouth, lassitude, weariness, lower back pain, difficulty and slowness in ejaculation, blood in semen in men, lack of lubricating fluids during sexual activity in women. Fear, anxiety and lack of love cloud the emotions. Most deficient states of the tissues display high vata symptoms. An under-provided tissue fails to nourish the next tissue and symptoms of its shortage may re-occur."

"What you said was very interesting. How do the tissues grow in a person afflicted with a high dosha or even just people stereotyped by having a particular dosha?" The intrigued students felt lost in the labyrinth of words and wellness verbiages.

"That's a great question." Padmalochan was relentless, "Anyone with high kapha gets rewarded with the best development of tissues but shows tendencies to over-develop, and probably grow excess fat tissue or produce plasma in excess like water and mucus. Blood and bone, representing the pitta and vata tissues in the body remain less developed or get mixed with mucus and water."

"Pitta prone people tend toward average tissue development. They retain large quantities of blood but of poor quality often mixed with bile. On the contrary, their muscles are good and strong."

"Vata people tend toward substandard tissues development. Vata people often have good bones but other tissues show inadequacy. Over development of one tissue may instigate under development of others. Surplus of plasma and production of excess phlegm may prohibit blood development. Surplus growth of muscle may affect deeper tissues, like fat and reproductive tissue. Unnecessary production of fat tissue may block other tissue advancement, chiefly bone, marrow and reproductive fluid. Obese people live with more pressure on their bones and usually have a low libido. Poor growth of any tissue blocks the other's expansion, failing to nourish subtler and extra gross tissues. Shortage of fat fails in nourishing the bones, it also comes short in lubricating the muscles. Few individuals are fortunate to have near-perfect tissues, a remarkable condition known as 'Dhatu Sara', which promises strong constitution and good health."

"An optimal amount of rasa dhatu shows up as good complexion; soft, smooth, greasy and glowing skin and hair; good stamina, compassion and happy disposition. Blood in optimal state nourishes the color of hands and feet, cheeks, lips and tongue, conjunctiva of the eyes and ear pinna; promising the native warm skin, good vitality, sensitivity to sun and heat; good vitality and much passion in life."

"Muscle in an optimal state reveals as good physical strength, capacity to do physical workouts, adaptability in movement and strong muscles in the neck, shoulders and thighs. Person's character is strong; he has courage, resilience and integrity. An optimal state of fat shows as adequate fat in the body, good lubrication of tissues, natural oil in the hair, eyes and feces; a melodious voice; emotional - exhibiting love, affection, joy and humor."

"Optimal state of bone shows a person with tall frame, large joints, and prominent and straight bones; where flexible are the movements. They have white, large and strong teeth and their foot size is large. Endowed are such natives with long lasting patience, consistency, stability and capacity for hard work. Optimal state of marrow and nerve tissue results in large clear eyes, strong joints, good sensory perception, power of speech and eloquence and the ability to handle agonizing pain. Mind stays sharp, clear, sensitive and responsive. Person has a good memory. The individual will be open, receptive and compassionate. Optimal state of reproductive tissue shows as glow in the eyes, ample hair growth, well-formed sexual organs like the scrotum or the breasts, an attractive body, charming personality and exhibition of love, empathy and compassion."

"On one hand, the body can construct tissues by consuming meat - muscle tissue from red meat, fat tissue from animal fat, bone from eating bone or cartilage. The person can build marrow by having marrow soup; reproductive fluid from eggs; blood from animal blood. However, there are many herbivores like elephants, rhinoceros, bear and bison that have strong muscles, bones and blood and are not meat eaters. There must be another way."

"Many herbals with homologous attributes strengthen the tissues. One can build plasma through adequate water and liquids, with sour fruit juices, such as lemon or lime. Dairy milk can also construct them[50]. Proper intake of minerals is important. Building blood through food containing iron and molasses, black grapes and vegetables like carrots and beets are an age-old tradition. One can assemble muscle from grains like wheat and oats, beans, nuts and other protein containing foods. Building fat from vegetable fat such as sesame oil, butter and ghee, cheese and animal fat is a standard practice. Person can build bone by mineral supplements like calcium, iron and zinc or mineral-containing food and from bone. Marrow and nerve tissue owes its construct to butter and ghee or clarified butter, by seeds and nuts containing oils, almonds, animal fat and marrow. Reproductive tissue owes its construct to milk, raw sugars, and ghee and by seeds and nuts like almonds, sesame seeds, lotus seeds and different eggs. Milk itself is a product of the reproductive system and supplements it. Animal tissues rapidly construct human tissues. They are also likely to clog the tissues, overdevelop them, or build up an inferior form of tissue contaminated with toxins."

---

[50] Astanga Hridayam, Chapter 5 Dravadravya Vijnana – Knowledge of liquids

"Diseases belong to different dosha types as they appear on tissues the dosha's govern. Kapha diseases usually involve plasma; pitta diseases implicate the blood and vata diseases the bones. However, this is not a hard and fast rule as any of the dosha types can penetrate any tissue and start a disease. The dosha type does not classify diseases only, but also the tissue from where the dosha type invaded the body. A severe muscular infection becomes termed as 'Pitta in the muscles' or Mamsagata Pitta."[51]

"The ancient scriptures spoke of a correlation between the tissues and the five Prana streams. Prana is linked to the nerves, which govern the life-force in the body. Apana is associated with the bones, which relate to the large intestine, the theatrical seat of Apana. Udana corresponds to the muscles, the seat of strength and exertion. Vyana associated with the ligaments and connective tissues that shape the body. Samana relates to the fat tissue, which cushions and nourishes the entire body. The relationship between Prana and the nerves and Apana and the bones is a concept to remember."

"Recall my discussion on Ojas. I want you to think of them as eighth tissue. Remember, Ojas is the essential energy reserve of the body. It means 'vigor', being the subtle essence of the reproductive fluid and all other vital secretions. It is a conceptual source fluid that invigorates our psychophysical capacities. Ojas is not a physical ingredient; it is but the sap of our life energy, which exists on a subtle level in the region of the heart chakra. Sufficient Ojas ensures health, deficient Ojas, disease follows. Disease strikes at locations where weakness prevails. In modern terms, we could say Ojas is the essential energy of the immune system."

"Ojas in brief is the final essence of the reproductive fluids and the heat of the tissues. Tenanting the heart, it pervades the entire body, offering stability and support. Ojas is moist like Soma, almost transparent, tinged by colors of red and yellow. Its destruction leads to death. Anger, hunger, worry, sorrow and overwork decrease Ojas. When these factors become dominant, fear and weakness join the pack. Lacking in luster, weak in mind, the person wastes away and qualities such as patience and faith dissolve."

"Other factors that decrease Ojas are excessive or unnatural sex, and abuse of substances and stimulants. Stress, anxiety, food made of dead products, pollution, unnatural environment and unrighteous lifestyle are other grounds of its decline."

---

[51] Similarly, Osteoarthritis can be termed as "Vata in the bones" or Asthigata Vata.

"Milk, ghee and honey replenishes Ojas, along with special tonic herbs like Ashwagandha, Kapikacchu and Shatavari[52]. Practices like meditation, pranayama and overall moderation strengthen the Ojas. Purity of the heart and positive attitudes of faith, peace, love, compassion and contentment strengthen it. Proper rest, time spent in natural surroundings and unlocking the cosmic life forces are time-tested techniques in increasing the Ojas force. When low, Ojas causes chronic, degenerative diseases, which are mysterious and hard to treat infectious, even nervous disorders. Ojas' level gets lowered with age. Diseases of old age reflect low Ojas, just as low Ojas causes premature aging. Low level of Ojas weakens the emotions and spawns negative attitude and emotion, anxiety, depression, apathy and self-pity. Self-destructive and suicidal tendencies are clearly evident, which are in fact, the qualities exhibited in extreme vata."

"Each of the seven tissues and their channels equipped with a special membrane, Kala facilitates absorption and diffusion of nutrients. Membranes demarcate the underlying tissue from its channels. They also seal and protect the tissues. Membranes are the main site of the 'Dhatu Agni', where the tissue's digestive fire operates, allowing basic food substance for the tissue sieved from the waste. Their dysfunction occurs in most diseases."

Seven kala-s

1. Sleshma Dhara Kala	Membrane that holds Kapha
2. Pitta Dhara Kala	Membrane that holds Pitta
3. Mamsa Dhara Kala	Membrane that holds muscle
4. Medo Dhara Kala	Membrane that holds fat
5. Purisha Dhara Kala	Membrane that holds feces
6. Majja Dhara Kala	Membrane that holds marrow
7. Shukra Dhara Kala	Membrane that holds reproductive fluid

"Most of them earn their name from their corresponding tissue, like Mamsa Dhara Kala, the membrane that holds 'muscle'. Derived are names of others from their particular waste. The membranes not only feed the tissue, but also filter out the waste, the naming is consistent for both systems."

---

[52] Astanga Hridayam, Chapter 5 Dravadravya Vijnana – Knowledge of liquids. See the rear of the book for notes on herbals. Ashwagandha is Withania somnifera, kapikacchu is Mucuna pruriens and Shatavari is Asparagus racemosus.

Kapha, 'Sleshma' or phlegm, is the waste from rasa, and pitta is a waste of blood. Pitta Dhara Kala is also the membrane of the gastro-intestinal tract and assumes responsibility for much of the digestive processes in the body. The membrane of the bone takes the name of the lining of the colon as this points to its site in the body. Vata discerns its absorption through the colon and the nutrients to feed the bones and become absorbed at this site. The bones absorb positive portions of vata or prana as vital energy, transporting them to the deeper tissues. The negative side of vata becomes the gas dispelled from the colon. When the membrane malfunctions, this gas finds its way into the bone tissue and sources various derangements."

"In a very unique way, abnormalities in colon become evident in bone damage. This is an added reason that colon treatment becomes essential for most vata and bone disorders, like arthritis. On the flip side, the colon is also the site where assimilated are many positive aspects like nutrition for the bones."

Mull excretions, waste produced internally

Three 'Mull' excretions are 1. Feces or Purisha, 2. Urine or Mutra and 3. Sweat or Sveda[53]

"Waste produced inside the body are three 'mull' excretions or 'mal', a term derived from the root word 'mul' meaning to darken, stain or harm. Unlike dosha types, they have no constructive role in the body, but like them they support the process of discharge. Waste themselves can become damaged and vitiated, turning their locus into disease sites. Excess dosha levels affect the waste products negatively, so do abnormal dhatu-tissues. Dosha in excess can even co-mingle with them, increasing the complications."

"Waste plays an important role in the body upkeep. Feces offer support through 'avasthamabhana'; they upkeep the colon-tone and save the digestive and lower abdominal organs like the uterus from prolapse. In addition, they maintain the colon warmth and its mucous membranes. Urine carries away wastewater as in 'kleda vahanam'. Sweat eliminates waste water 'kleda vidhruti'. Both flush wastewater from the system."

---

[53] Astanga Hridayam, 1.13. Also read Charaka Samhita Chp 17, Slokas 63-72

"We perspire more in the summer and urinate more in the winter, as hot weather promotes perspiration to cool us down and cold weather fuels urine production by its sinking and contracting action. Feces derive from colon action abetting to throw out excess earth from the body. Excess air or vata also gets discharged from the colon, both being byproducts of the digestive process. Urine comes from bladder action discharging excess water, solid wastes and acids. Sweat comes from lungs action discharging excess water and toxins. Sweat dispels heat or fire, cools the body and moistens the skin and surrounding hair. Excess fat from the body also gets removed."

"Three different waste types remove excess heat from the body, the discharge of waste materials brings about an effective cooling. Urine also expels acids from the pitta blood; sweat eliminates acids also, helping in blood purification. Apana Vayu, the downward moving aerial force oversees the three mull excretions, specifically feces and urine. Vyana, the outward moving air, administers perspiration. Both forms of Prana when functioning correct, throw out the waste. When obstructed, they let the waste accumulate. Surface disorders like cold and influenza block Vyana. Internal disorders of the digestive tract usually vitiate Apana."

"Excess production of waste can aggravate the disease process. When their discharge is improper, they accumulate, invade and damage the surrounding tissue. Deficient waste also aggravates the disease. In the case of excess feces, the aberration shows up as abdominal pain and distention, constipation, feeling of heaviness and pain while excreting. It retains too much earth in the body and increases the toxins, as indicated by bad breath and body odor. It causes indigestion, headaches, dullness and damages to movement. Surplus urine instigates pain in the bladder and the urge to urinate even after having just finished urination. It involves excess water, water retention, frequent urination and thirst."

"More sweat production results in profuse perspiration, unpleasant body odor and oozing skin diseases. Often excess fire or pitta accompanies skin diseases like urticaria, eczema, boil, and fungus infections. Too much perspiration in a person who is thin with vata constitution can result in dehydration, fatigue and convulsions. Such vata perspiration can occur even when the body is dry. As with excess, deficiency in waste production is a big concern."

"Shortage of feces causes gas and dryness in the intestines, abdominal distention, abnormal and painful movements of vata heading upwards and to the side."

"The lack of earth in the body causes low energy, an ungrounded feeling, nervousness and wrong movement of vata in the body, pain, palpitations, lower back ache, as well as prolapse of the organs showing the symptoms of vata disorders. Difficult urination, thirst, discoloration of urine, blood in the urine comes from dearth of urine. Such indications are from lack of fluids in the body, pitta and vata disorders may include fever and dehydration."

"Deficit sweat inhibits perspiration, the hairs stiffen along the skin and fissures appear. Dry skin, wrinkles, dandruff, skin diseases, susceptibility to common cold and influenza, other surface conditions and vata disorders get indicated; all a result of poor peripheral circulation."

"In most cases, normal production of waste is expected, however, many other factors hinder adequate waste production. Feces production and quality undergo damage from excess use of purgatives or colonics, even by food too heavy or too light, bad food combinations, excessive travel, sleeping late, coffee and drugs, antibiotics, dysentery, inadequate physical exercise and emotional factors such as worry and fear. Any low energy condition can weaken the colon, which incidentally is the support site of Prana, the life-force."

"Diuretic substances can damage urine, even if they are herbs or food. Drinking fluids in excess, drinking too little, alcohol, overindulgence in sex and emotional trauma and fright add to the damage. Unnatural use of diaphoretic substances spoils the sweat, besides perspiration methods like saunas, hot tubs, or consuming excessive dry food, lack of salt in the diet and by abnormal workouts[54]. One of the ways to control waste as such is by different food substances."

"Many substances produce healthy feces, such as bulk laxatives, bran, grains like barley, most beans, root vegetables like potatoes and most leafy vegetables[55]. Meat also increases feces production. Feces production suffers from fasting, using purgatives and laxatives, eating light food and drinking fruit juices."

"Drinking more water produces more urine. Even drinking sugar water, fruit juices and other liquids augments its production. When water intake is lowered, or when taking light or dry food, and exposure to heat throttles the production."

---

[54] Astanga Hridayam, 2.14. Unnatural workouts.
[55] Astanga Hridayam, Chapter 6.72-6.73 Leafy vegetables

"There are several ways to generate healthy sweat - taking sour fruit juices, hot peppers that increase plasma or rasa and exposure to heat. Reduced intake of water, dry food, exposure to cold brings down the perspiration."

"The texts describe nine excretory orifices like the two eyes, two ears, two nostrils, mouth, urethra and anus, where elimination is a part of their normal functioning. Seven are in the head and two are below the waist. Eyes produce tears, the ears generate earwax, the nostrils produce nasal phlegm, the mouth generates phlegm and saliva, the urethra manages urine and the anus has feces. Orifices also are important sites for Prana invigorated with special 'nadi-s' or energy channels. At such locations, treatment of Prana occurs along with body cleansing. Health of the body depends upon the proper functioning, lubrication and elimination these sites promise. Remember, sweat glands cover the entire body; the waste products not only discharge toxins from the tissues, they also aid in the sites' lubrication and cleansing. It is natural for the body to decay, decompose back to its main constituent elements of earth. What becomes necessary, as part of healthy living is the continual cleansing of the body to prevent any internal build-up of waste. It is equally important to keep these orifices unobstructed and functioning well."

"Incidentally dosha types are also the waste produced by the body, an extension to their functions as dosha types and supportive energies. Kapha is the mucus produced as waste, a byproduct of the plasma or rasa dhatu. Pitta is the bile, acids and excess blood piled into waste, a derivative of the blood dhatu. Vata is the air and gas produced as waste, a spinoff from the digestive process. The mouth, nose and sweat glands, the urine and feces discharge waste kapha. Removal of waste pitta happens through urine, sweat and feces, which cleanses the blood. Removal of vata as gas takes place through the rectum but may come out also by belching. In addition, the lungs expel vata waste through the exhaled air. The real difference between Dosha and Mull is that the former has more complex functions; the mull is simple waste material. When looking into waste, one must analyze the role of the dosha types and see to what extent the Dosha and Mull are mixed into mucus in the urine, or as blood in stool."

"In the midst of the scriptures is the principle of Agni.[56] Rig Veda begins with nine mantras to Agni, even ending with Agni's mantras; the human being is alleged to be fire, representing the element of fire on earth as a mechanism to perceive consciousness."

---

[56] Astanga Hridayam 1.8 Agnibhedah. Agni is the metaphorical fire.

"Vedic term 'Agni' means 'burning, transforming, communicating and perceiving' derived from the root word 'ang', which implies 'to burst or flame forth'. Seated are the universe and the body on the principles of energy. We are an organism devised to produce and harvest energy to enable perception, action and expression. Iconic fire symbolically is this central energy. Its main form in the body is the digestive fire. Digestive fire carries the name of 'Jatharagni' or the 'fire in the belly' as Agni shares the attributes of fire."

"Agni, the digestive fire is hot, dry, light, fragrant, subtle, mobile and penetrating, augmented by ginger, black pepper and cayenne which have a similar nature to it. Unlike external fire that requires dry wood as fuel, Agni is a force that dwells within and energizes body fluids and tissues. Sage Angirasa describes Agni in Rig Veda."

> O fire of the first, exceptional in the Angirasa
> Seer, the endeavors of the gods
> festooned they are, covering all sides
> While you are expressed in so many ways
> for the earthlings
> You are wise, you span the two worlds
> It's a wonder, in how many ways you dwell in man
>
> *Rig Veda Book 1, chapter 32, mantra 2*

"It is more like lightning whose energy exists in the aerial-aquatic base. Food by this principle gets broken down to a homogenous, liquid, greasy mass for the digestive fire to work upon it. Agni is an oil lamp; oil provides the greasiness and the fuel to set the digestive ignition."

> Ornate and brilliant
> you sail over the swelling waters of the ocean
> and allotting the waters
> you flow instantly to the seeker
>
> *Rig Veda Book 1, chapter 27, mantra 6*

"Fiery Agni is crucial for health, life and life beyond; at a more foundational level than even the three-dosha types. I quote the Rig Veda again, the very first three mantra-s by Rishi Vaiswamitra."

> Agni ignites, heralds the order of truth
> O sacrificial lord,
> the bejeweled ecstasies come to life in your glow

Fire befriended by the ancient seers
The sages of the new adore you
bring with you the gods

> From the mighty flame, come to light many treasures
> becoming more visible day upon day,
> glory be your valor
>
> Rig Veda. Book 1, Chapter 1, Mantras 1-3

"When Agni is sufficient, toxins do not build up, the mind and senses stay clear and acute. With Agni perturbed, the person suffers tedium, weight problems, inactivity and obfuscated emotions and perceptions."

"In the scriptures, documented are four settings of the digestive fire as high, mediocre, variable and balanced[57]. Pitta type persons exhibit high Agni; they have intense appetites and can digest well, without fear of gaining excessive weight. They have the proverbial craving of a goat, a Pitta animal. Agni stays low in kapha types of persons, who have little but constant appetites and slow metabolism, end up retaining weight even when they do not eat a lot. Agni is usually variable and cardinal in vata types, with their fluctuating nature and nervous digestion. Vata types are alternatively ravenous or not hungry at all. Agni remains balanced when the dosha types and emotions are in a state of equilibrium. Regular and moderate appetite with good power of digestion is a good health indication."

"Agni has many forms spread into every conceivable part of our body. Translating that to the universe, yes, Agni as energy is everywhere, from the Sun to the Moon, to the tunnel in the ground to the bottom of the river Damodar."

> Far and near is your protection
> fed constantly by deific, vivacious forte
> serving us in times of ill health
>
> Rig Veda Book 1 Chapter 27 Mantra 3

"Digestive fire of 'Jatharagni' is the Agni in the belly, constituting main form of gross fire and the core power of digestion in the body. The Agni distributes its energy to all the secretions and enzymes involved in the digestion process in stomach and intestines."

---

[57] Tikshna means 'High', Manda defined as Low or Mediocre, Vishama or and Sama or Balanced or Sama

"Five elemental fire energies make up the 'Bhutagni'. The energies dwell in the liver section and assume responsibility in turning the digested food material into groups of five elemental types necessary for building the corresponding tissues in the body. When the energies are insufficient, the respective element in the body does not form correctly. Such substances as ghee or aloe gel help regulate the elemental digestive fires. Some consider that these Agni fires produce the tissues and energies for the five senses development."

> You dwell within
> within the seeker and his gods
> O Agni, your grace
> is a vast luminous cradle of energy
>
> *Rig Veda Book 1 chapter 74, mantra 9*

"Fire energy in the seven-tissue system is 'Dhatuagni'. Every one of the seven tissues get their own digestive power from Agni; responsibility for Agni also is in proper formation of the tissue. When the fiery energy is extremely low, produced is a lot of inferior tissue; when the energy is uncontrollably high, not enough tissue gets formed. Wellness thinkers often consider the five forms of Pitta to be five additional forms of Agni. They also count an extra Agni type for each of the three waste materials, taking the count to twenty-one. Counted are additional Agni fire types for the five sense organs and the five kosha types or sheaths. Agni is a universal principle and represents the cosmic energy at work on all levels. Agni is not only the digestive fire, but also the flame of the individual soul and ultimately the flame of pure consciousness at the highest level."

"Let me tell you what I have learnt from the scriptures on the process of digestion, where there are two opposing theories; both have their merits. The wellness program recognizes three dosha stages of digestion. First stage is the kapha stage of digestion occurring in the mouth and stomach, dominated by sweet taste and kapha secretions of saliva and alkaline fluids. Earth and water elements get digested in this preliminary stage rendering the food liquid homogenous and capable of being worked upon by the digestive fire. Most kapha problems occur at this stage of digestion, like nausea, lack of appetite and vomiting of phlegm owed to our intake of heavy, greasy, sweet, saline, mucus forming food."

"Second stage of digestion influenced by pitta occurs in the stomach and small intestine, where there is dominance of sour substances and acids which are typically pitta secretions of the liver, pancreas and small intestine, helping in digesting the fire element from food."

"Food, in this process releases heat and energy, imparting strength to the body, completing the main stage of digestion. Pitta problems occur at this stage of digestion, like hyperacidity, heartburn and ulcers caused by food that is too hot, sour or spicy, and alcoholic drinks."

"Third stage of digestion influenced by vata takes place in the large intestine, highlighted by pungency and gas release in the colon. At this juncture, the body absorbs all air and ether elements in the food. Thrown out as waste is the indigestible part of earth as feces. Absorption and subsequent elimination of undigested water occurs through urination. Purer air released in the process of digestion in the colon feeds the five forms of vata in the body. Impure or foul-smelling air or gas is let out as waste. In this latter stage of digestion, the process of elimination and assimilation of subtle nutrients play a dominant role. Most vata problems occur at this stage of digestion, like gas, distention and constipation. Food that is too light, dry or astringent resembling vata instigates such problems."

"Digestive fire operates on the swallowed and liquefied food mass. It separates the pure or nutritive part of the food from the unwanted material[58], breaking it down into groups of five elements. These move to the liver organ where the elemental Agni fires break them down for supplying to the corresponding elemental tissues. Fire digests and transforms the earth elements to fabricate the basic bulk or protein of the body, like the muscles and the fat. Water components build up the vital fluids, plasma and blood. Fire elements build up the enzymes and hemoglobin. Air elements shape the bone and nerve plexuses. Etheric elements develop the mind and senses."

"When the digestive fire is out of commission, the food mass conversion occurs not in any approved way, it leaves a residue of undigested or partially digested food that can accumulate, stagnate, ferment and start a disease. This badly semi-digested toxic food mass is 'Ama' derived from the root word 'am' meaning 'to harm or to weaken'. Deposition of Ama is the precursor to many disease processes. Feeble digestive fire along with accumulation of the undigested food mass deteriorates our defense system."

"No disease can affect us when the digestive fire is normal. State of Agni is an important key to good health. Any wellness treatment always emphasizes on ways to improve Agni and reduce Ama for all dosha types."

---

[58] Digestive portion of food is 'sara' and unwanted material is 'kitta'

"Ancient texts describe the human body as composed of innumerable channels, conduits of supply to the many tissues of the body. Channels are 'Srota' derived from the root word 'sru' meaning to flow. Body is like a system of canals or rivers where Srota channels nourish the different tissues and organs of the body. They also keep the tissues clean, forming a network of sustainable forces. In fact, the channel networks contain the tissues within their drapery. Channels have a similar color to the tissue or substance they encompass. They are of both large and small sizes, tubular in shape and while the larger ones are straight, the smaller ones' form lattice like capillary networks. Proper flow through these channels ensues good health. When unobstructed, they enable proper intake of nutrients and elimination of waste, besides maintaining communication between different tissues and organs. Think of improper flow through the channels as disease."

"What exactly is proper and improper flow in the channels? I can't imagine consequence of improper flow." The student in the front row was quite attentive.

"There are four definitions of different defective flow in the channels. Excessive flow, deficient flow, blocked flow or flow away from the proper channel. This town is a living example of what happens when the Damodar river flow runs erratic. Excessive is the flow when the movement through the channels is copious and nimble. Tissues get flooded, resulting in them functioning on hyper-mode or becoming over-developed. Deficient is the flow when feeble or sluggish. Tissues begin to under-perform, dry up or collect waste. Blocked is the flow when the dosha types, waste materials or Ama accrue, stagnate and congeal in the channels, hindering supply to the tissues, which causes the tissues to store waste, besides being deprived of nutrition. Flow blockage may sometimes occur from deficient flow that speeds up stagnation and accrual. Flow out of the correct channel results from a choked channel. When not allowed to flow in the normal way, a substance like water, will try to flow abnormally, causing movement of improper substances into tissues or piercing the channel walls, directly invading the tissues. An un-metabolized fluid in such circumstances can be very damaging to the underlying tissues."

"Inappropriate material amassing in the channels brings about an erroneous flow. Dosha types in surplus along with waste materials invading the channels result in these erratic flows. Vata presides over all impulses and energy flows regulating the flow in the channels. The dryness vata brings can also block the channels. Clearing the channels and reducing the vata content is an important notion in the wellness and healing process."

"A textual reading from the ancient scriptures tells us that three channels connect with the outside environment to bring in nourishment to the body using breath, food and water. Pranavaha Srota channels carry Prana, the breath or vital force[59]. Channels originate in the heart and gastrointestinal tract, primarily the colon. Prana owes its absorption through the lungs and colon with blood and plasma distributing through the heart. This aspect of Prana connects with Pranamaya Kosha, the breath sheath, which envelops the food sheath or physical body."

"Next come the Annavaha Srota channels[60] that transport food or 'anna'. Originating in the stomach and left side of the body, this channel arrangement also goes by the name 'Maha Srota' or the 'great channel', owning the main canal in the body, the gastrointestinal tract. Ambhuvaha Srota channels carry water or 'ambu' and regulate water metabolism[61] along with substances like sugar dissolved or found in it. It is no surprise that Diabetes[62] is a disease of this system. The channels originate at the palate and pancreas, intimately involved in sugar metabolism."

"Seven intricate channel systems make up a set of dedicated suppliers to seven tissues of the body. They are like the channels or aqueducts carved from the Damodar River to irrigate the farms and provide drinking water to the cattle. Rasavaha Srota channels carry plasma[63]. This plasma is the solution in which all the tissues of the body live, like a river speckled with many islands. The channels originate in the heart and blood vessels, forming a primary network of channels in the complete body."

"Raktavaha Srota channels transport blood[64]. Its origin is the liver and spleen, which stores and demolishes the red blood cells. Mamsavaha Srota channels are suppliers to the muscles[65] or the muscular system. Channels originate at the ligaments and skin and connect to the muscle tissue."

---

[59] Primarily the respiratory system though aspects of the circulatory and digestive system are contained in this idea of Pranavaha Srota.
[60] Annavaha Srota channels make the digestive system.
[61] It is like the fluid absorbing aspect of the digestive system.
[62] Diabetes is not a recent definition, even in Vedic times, early Chinese and Roman civilization, excess sugar was a major concern.
[63] Rasa – Plasma. Rasava Srota is similar to the lymphatic system and circulatory system.
[64] Rakta – Blood. Raktavaha Srota is related to the circulatory system, particularly the hemoglobin containing part of the blood namely the red blood cells.
[65] Mamsa मांस – muscles.

"Medovaha Srota channels are suppliers to the fat system or adipose tissue[66], having their origin in the kidneys and omentum[67]."

"Asthivaha Srota channels are suppliers to the bones[68] forming the skeletal system, originating from the adipose tissue and the large bones of the hips. Majjavaha Srota channels finish the supply to the marrow and nerve tissue[69], mainly the nervous system or the cerebrospinal fluid originating at the bones and joints."

"Shukravaha Srota channels are suppliers to the reproductive tissue[70] leading to the reproductive system. The channels originate at the testes and uterus, where semen and ovum get manufactured, connecting to prostate in men and to pleasure and reproductive parts in women that produce secretions during sexual activity."

"Three more channels connect to the outside world, eliminating unwanted substances from the body with ease. Waste product of breath is sweat, food waste is feces and wastewater is urine[71], which together with their channels can undergo damage or obstruction from surplus buildups of the dosha types or their own products."

"Svedavaha Srota channels transport sweat[72], its network consists of the sebaceous system. The channels originate at the adipose tissue and the hair follicles leading to the sebaceous glands. It is of no surprise that increased fat leads to added perspiration."

"Purishavaha Srota channels move feces[73], its network spanning the excretory system. Colon and rectum, organs of excretion are the tissues of origin. Mutravaha Srota channels carry urine[74] through the urinary system. Urinary channels originate from the bladder and kidneys, the organs of urination."

---

[66] Meda मेद – fat tissue
[67] Omentum is the abdominal fat
[68] Asthi are the bones (Sanskrit - अस्थि - मज्जा)
[69] Majja – Nervous tissues
[70] Shukra – reproductive system
[71] Mull मल, (some authors incorrectly transliterate as Mala) are waste materials or toxins.
[72] Sveda – Perspiration system, sebaceous glands.
[73] Purisha – feces.
[74] Mutra – urine.

"Mind exists as an exclusive system where Manovaha Srota channels carry 'thought', outlining a complex network of the mental structure. It is not a physical channel per se; it is a thin line that separates the perceivable world and the unperceivable, subtle one. The system originates in the 'nerve tissue' on a physical level, and in the 'emotions' at a mental level. Mind connects to the nervous system[75] using it to motivate the entire body, especially the reproductive system[76], the physical site of desire, fetters us to the body. It is only that part of the mind that connects with the physical body and facilitates activation of sensory and motor systems. Subtle aspect of mind is not in this scope. Mind in the higher sense transcends the physical body and makes up the subtle body, principally the mental sheath[77]."

"Women have complex systems enabling reproduction and child rearing. When the breast milk is at flow, menstruation stops; channels act mutually exclusive like two aspects of one system. Products like menstrual fluid and breast milk are secondary tissues[78] of the plasma[79] though connected with Shukra. Artavavaha Srota channels carry menstrual fluid[80] and the other secretions of the female reproductive system. Shukravaha Srota channels in women are closer to reproductive and hormonal functioning, including growth hormones, which exists both before and after the time of life in which menstruation can occur having its source in the uterus. Stanyavaha Srota channels carry the breast milk, enabling the system of lactation[81] as subsystem of the previous with channel origination in the uterus. Sexual activity provokes the system to act different from lactation."

"The theme of 'mind and channel functioning' is an abstract matter. Let me introduce you to a reasoning hypothesized by our forefathers. Thought is 'matter' capable of producing several biochemical reactions in the brain resulting in measurable brain waves. Our thoughts and energy also visit the part of the body that has our attention. Distribution of energy to different channels depends on the mind stimuli, which then gets transferred rapidly by the windy vata. Mental disturbance can quickly set disorders in any channel. Emotional obstructions turn into energy stagnation that results in jamming the flow in the channels."

---

[75] Majjavaha srotas मज्जा – Nervous system channel
[76] Shukravaha srotas – Reproductive fluid channels
[77] Manomaya Kosha – the mental sheath
[78] Upadhatus – secondary tissues
[79] Rasa - Plasma
[80] Artava - Menstruation
[81] Stanya – place of lactation

"It is essential to clear out the bottled-up emotions in the mind for the proper circulation of energy in the body. Emotional outbursts or lack of mental control are like irregular flow out of the channels in the physical body and can produce heart failure. Excessive or deficient mental activity can cause excess or deficient flow in the channels of the body. Too much flow in the mind may cause deficient flow in the body. It is also true with inadequate flow in the mind, there begins excess flow in the body. Worry, which is undue mental activity, is one of the major causes of disease in the body. Any disproportionate mental activity, like excess flow through any of the channels can deplete one's energy. Meditation, which aims at keeping the mind calm or silent is important in preventing excess mental activity and depletion of energy."

"Several reasons disrupt proper running of the channels, many of them relate to eating habits, flawed physical workouts, bad use of organs or systems, besides the play of emotions. Channels transporting the breath or life force specifically the Pranavaha Srota channels face the prospect of damages that come from malnutrition, inhibition of natural urges, extreme dryness and physical exertion without proper nourishment."

"What weakens Prana movement aggravates Vata. Fraught is Prana from smoking tobacco, air pollution, loud talking, cacophony, disproportionate singing and strenuous physical workout."

"Overeating, eating at the wrong time, unwholesome food and derangement of the digestive fire harms the Annavaha Srota channels that carry food. Incorrect food quantity, untimely or irregular eating habits, food made of poor nutritional quality, such as dead, old, stale, preserved, artificial or junk food has an unfavorable effect on the digestive system. Any abnormal functioning of the digestive fire will add to the damage. Ambhuvaha Srota channels bringing in water suffer damages resulting from exposure to heat, from improperly digested food, Ama, fear, alcohol, excessive dry food and extreme thirst."

"These are mainly vata and pitta increasing factors and operate by dropping the water level in our body, which makes it tough for the channels to do their jobs, subjecting the body to the trauma of dehydration."

"Rasavaha Srota channels carrying plasma are prone to injuries from eating food unbearably heavy, cold, mucus forming, besides from overeating and excessive worry. Issues that hurt the plasma and lymphatic system aggravate Kapha and increase mucus, like sweets and dairy goods."

"Raktavaha Srota ducts transporting blood are subject to harm by food and drink disproportionately stimulating[82], oily, hot and liquid; from overexposure to heat and sun. Items that damage the circulatory system aggravate Pitta, like hot, spicy, sour, oily and salted food; sweet, heavy, greasy and oily food, meat and others. Mamsavaha Srota channels that supply the muscles face damages by food that is unduly oily and liquid[83], gross or heavy; from sleeping at odd hours. Factors that harm the muscular system are mainly those that increase Kapha, particularly its attribute of heaviness. Incorrect physical exercise can also add to the problem. Medovaha Srota channels that carry fat face destruction from lack of exercise, sleeping at odd hours, eating too much greasy food and alcohol abuse. Factors that increase fat tissue and cause obesity also increase Kapha, especially heavy, oily and liquid food."

"Asthivaha Srota channels that supply the bones are harmed by excessive exertion that jars and strains the bones and by vata increasing regimens. Factors that damage the bones are mainly those that increase vata, like light, dry or insufficient diet. Any activity that is erratic and rough will eventually damage the bones. Majjavaha Srota channels that supply the nerves and marrow suffer damages from crushing, dislocation or fracture of the bones, extreme pain and unhealthy food combinations. Nervous system sustains damages from trauma, physical or emotional, including overly harsh sensations like violence or noise, though a disruptive diet can also imbalance it in time. Intestinal gas can aggravate the nerves. Shukravaha Srota channels that carry the reproductive fluids face damages from incorrectly timed sexual indulgence, suppression of sexual urge, promiscuity and surgery. Improper sexual activity deranges the reproductive system. Surgery, though sometimes necessary, by its strong nature damages the highly sensitive tissue. Svedavaha Srota channels carrying sweat suffer damages from physical workout in excess, exposure to heat, taking food that is too hot or too cold and by emotional outbursts of anger, grief and fear."

"Purishavaha Srota channels that carry the feces face impairments from suppressing the urge to defecate; from overeating, eating when an earlier meal is still undergoing digestion and weak digestive fire. Factors that derange the excretory system are similar to those of the digestive system. The irregularity in attending to the urge is an added source of destruction. Mutravaha Srota channels that carry urine suffer harm from inordinate intake of food and drink, too much sex, withholding the urge to urinate, from debilitating diseases and trauma."

---

[82] Vidahi - Stimulating
[83] Abhisyandi – oily and liquid

"Damage to the urinary system can be quite extensive by wrong use of the urogenital organs and by any trauma or weakness, including prolonged travels; the kidneys being a sensitive organ[84]. Manovaha Srota channels carrying thought suffer harm by excess emotion, suppression of emotion, drugs and strong sensory stimuli like loud music or noise. Emotional factors can impair the channels of the mental system."

"Channels face blockages from heavy and sticky food. Such food is slow in movement and can inhibit flow through the channels. These food substances also increase Kapha and Ama. Food from dairy, particularly cheese, yogurt, butter and ice cream; heavy and fatty meat like pork, greasy lard, animal fat, sticky and sweet bread, pastries, candies and bananas come under this category. Such food aggravates channel blockage conditions prevalent in diseases such as arthritis and gout."

"Any overeating, especially heavy, sweet or saline food impedes the channels, more so when the person leads a sedentary lifestyle. On the other hand, a light spicy diet keeps the channels clear though may not properly nourish the heavier tissues like muscle."

"Common spices like ginger, cinnamon, peppermint or sage and specifically turmeric, cardamom, calamus and camphor taken internally in small amounts are effective in clearing the channels. Other methods that keep the channels clear include breathing practices[85], proper physical exercise, fresh air and water, creative mental activity and meditational exercises for clearing the mind. Perspiration therapy[86], including the use of saunas and steam baths, is helpful."

"Vata accounts for all movements in the channels, pitta and kapha are influencers only. Blockage of flow is often agonizing, accompanied by tumors, leading to infection and inflammation. Sometimes the flow is incorrect, where it exits the channel abruptly or reverses its direction. Reversal as in vomiting can be less harmful than flowing out of the channel as happens in an injury. Besides, blockage of flow can result from unhealed injuries and clots. Scarred tissue can block the flow of blood and nerve impulses."

---

[84] These statements have been taken from Charaka Samhita 5.10.22 scriptures.
[85] Pranayama – breathing practices as prescribed in Yoga.
[86] Svedana – a therapy that involves perspiration

"Surplus flow can involve abnormal movement of tissue or increase in their rate of movement; deficient flow occurs from poor movement or decreased rate. Excess flow in blood channels results in palpitations and rapid pulse; blockage of flow may hinder movement of the tissue, like severe muscular cramps. Erroneous flow may instigate just the opposite. Sometimes deficient flow may lead to excess, or excess flow in one tissue may lead to deficient flow in another as the body attempts to normalize its circulation."

Erroneous flow

Pranavaha Srota or the Respiratory System.

Incorrect flow type	Indication
Excess Flow	Rapid breathing, hyperventilation
Flow hampered	Slow or shallow breathing, shortness of breath
Flow blocked	Difficult breathing or dyspnea, cough, wheezing, asthma, hiatal hernia
Deviated flow - away from destined route	Perforation of the lungs

Annavaha Srota or Digestive System

Incorrect flow type	Indication
Excess Flow	Excess appetite, hyperacidity or excess digestive secretions, diarrhea
Flow hampered	Deficient appetite, hypoacidity or deficient digestive secretions, anorexia, constipation
Flow blocked	Intestinal obstruction, tumors
Deviated flow - away from destined route	Puking, perforation of the stomach or intestines like perforated ulcer

Ambhuvaha Srotas or Water Intake System

Incorrect flow type	Indication
Excess Flow	Excess thirst, Sharp sense of taste, Hyperglycemia
Flow hampered	Nausea, Lack of taste, Hypoglycemia
Flow blocked	Diabetes, Pancreatic Cancer
Deviated flow - away from destined route	Vomit mostly watery type, Anorexia

Rasavaha Srotas or Plasma or Lymphatic System

Incorrect flow type	Indication
Excess Flow	Edema like excessive hydration of tissues, swollen glands and lymphatic
Flow hampered	Dehydration, emaciation
Flow blocked	Severely swollen glands, lymphatic obstruction, lymphatic cancer
Deviated flow - away from destined route	Bleeding, coughing of blood

Raktavaha Srotas or Circulatory System

Incorrect flow type	Indication
Excess Flow	Rapid pulse, palpitations, hypertension
Flow hampered	Slow pulse, hypotension, varicose veins
Flow blocked	Arrhythmia or irregular heartbeat, enlargement of liver and spleen, blood clots as in phlebitis, tumors, heart attack
Deviated flow - away from destined route	Bleeding disorders generally

Mamsavaha Srota or Muscular System

Incorrect flow type	Indication
Excess Flow	Muscular hyperactivity, tremors
Flow hampered	Muscular hypo-activity, spasms, lack of muscle tone
Flow blocked	Muscle tumors, chronic inflammation of muscle tissue
Deviated flow - away from destined route	Tearing of muscle tissue

Medovaha Srotas or Adipose System

Incorrect flow type	Indication
Excess Flow	Edema, obesity
Flow hampered	Emaciation, dry skin
Flow blocked	Fat tumors (usually subcutaneous and benign)
Deviated flow - away from destined route	Tearing of adipose tissue

Asthivaha Srotas or Skeletal System

Incorrect flow type	Indication
Excess Flow	Excess bone tissue
Flow hampered	Weak bones, deficient bone tissue, osteoporosis
Flow blocked	Calcification of bones, bone spurs, bone cancer
Deviated flow - away from destined route	Occurs with breaking of bones

Majjavaha Srotas or Nervous System

Incorrect flow type	Indication
Excess Flow	Hypersensitivity, pain, insomnia, tremors, overly sharp perception
Flow hampered	Hyposensitivity, numbness, dullness, cloudy perception
Flow blocked	Convulsions, coma, multiple sclerosis
Deviated flow - away from destined route	Damage to nerve tissue

Shukravaha Srotas or Reproductive System

Incorrect flow type	Indication
Excess Flow	Spermatorrhea, nocturnal emission, premature ejaculation, leucorrhea
Flow hampered	Delayed ejaculation, lack of lubrication
Flow blocked	Inability to ejaculate, swelling of the testes, stones in the prostate, uterine tumors
Deviated flow - away from destined route	Discharge of sperm into the bladder

Svedavaha Srota or Sebaceous System

Incorrect flow type	Indication
Excess Flow	Excess or oily Perspiration
Flow hampered	Deficient Perspiration, temporary stoppage of perspiration
Flow blocked	Inability to sweat
Deviated flow - away from destined route	Discharge of sweat into the plasma

Purishavaha Srota or Excretory System

Incorrect flow type	Indication
Excess Flow	Diarrhea
Flow hampered	Constipation
Flow blocked	Intestinal obstruction, diverticulitis, tumors in the colon
Deviated flow - away from destined route	Perforation of the large intestine

Mutravaha Srota or Urinary System

Incorrect flow type	Indication
Excess Flow	Excess or frequent urination
Flow hampered	Scanty urination
Flow blocked	Difficult or painful urination, urinary obstruction, stones
Deviated flow - away from destined route	Bursting of the bladder

Manovaha Srota involving the Mind

Incorrect flow type	Indication
Excess Flow	Hyperactivity of senses, worry, gossip, anger
Flow hampered	Dullness of senses, depression, grief
Flow blocked	Blocked emotions
Deviated flow - away from destined route	Delirium, schizophrenia

Artavavaha Srota or the Menstrual System

Incorrect flow type	Indication
Excess Flow	Excess menstruation (menorrhagia)
Flow hampered	Scanty or delayed menstruation
Flow blocked	Painful menstruation like dysmenorrhea, absence of menstruation like amenorrhea, chlorosis, tumors
Deviated flow - away from destined route	Discharge of the menses into the urine or stool

Stanyavaha Srota or the Lactation System

Incorrect flow type	Indication
Excess Flow	Excess flow of breast milk
Flow hampered	Deficient flow of breast milk
Flow blocked	Inability to discharge breast milk, pain and swelling of breasts, mastitis, breast cysts, tumors and cancer
Deviated flow - away from destined route	Injury to the breast

"Ten sites in the body are important to good health, wellness, body-defense and protection. The two temples, three main vital organs - heart, bladder and head, throat, blood, reproductive fluid, Ojas and rectum are the members of this group. Crucial are many of them to life. Even small injuries can result in death. Even loss of sensitive tissues such as blood, reproductive fluid or Ojas may trigger lassitude and death. Some of the important organs like head, heart, bladder and rectum when in dysfunction, lead to sluggishness and low mortality. When the bladder or the colon fails to function, other tissues get swamped by toxins. Such problems can result in long-term problems. The ten sites hold significant amount of prana in a delicate state, and any harm can result in losing the prana."

"When channel flow stays blocked, they are disrupted triggering the propagation of a disease, especially when normal functions of the channels suffer suppression or inhibition[87]. Channels have their purpose; no flow in any of them is incorrect or meant to undergo clampdown. Suppressing any flow has an unbalancing effect on everything, unhinging the life force. Forced are the products that were meant for discharge to stay in the body and suppressed is the natural urge to expel them. This not only weakens the curbed function more, but also disturbs the entire nervous system. Such weakened functioning may force the flow in the wrong direction or out of the channel. Suppression of natural urges disturbs the vata levels, such as the urge to urinate, excrete, ejaculate, fart, vomit, sneeze, belch, yawn, eat, drink, cry, sleep and breathe."

"Defeating the impulse to urinate disturbs the kidneys and the urinary system. Difficult or painful urination, besides pain in the bladder, lower backache and headache results from the failed urge. Withholding the urge to defecate impacts negatively the colon, the excretory and digestive systems. Constipation, abdominal pain and distention, headache and muscle cramps accompany the problem."

---

[87] Astanga Hridayam, Chapter 4 Roganutpadaniya

"Suppressing the need to ejaculate hurts the reproductive and urinary systems. As a result, the person experiences pain in the penis and testes, swelling of the prostate, difficult urination, cardiac pain, malaise and insomnia. Withholding the itch to fart produces constipation, difficult urination, abdominal pain and distention and various vata disorders. The waste air held back finally gets absorbed into the bone and marrow, where it can aggravate arthritic and nervous disorders. It harms the digestive system and augments the vata levels all over in the body. Defeating the urge to vomit stimulates nausea, anorexia, edema, anemia, fever and skin diseases. The water intake system[88] faces damages. Restraining the urge to sneeze triggers headache, facial nerve pain, numbness on the face and weaknesses in the sense organs. It injures the lungs, respiratory system and intensifies allergic reactions. Suppressing the impulse to belch or cough produces hiccups, anorexia, difficulty in breathing and palpitations. Both respiratory and digestive systems can feel deranged in a significant way. Withholding the need to yawn produces tremors, numbness, convulsions and insomnia. It worsens vata levels and irritates the nervous system. Restraining the impulse to eat kills the appetite, accompanied by poor digestion, abnormal absorption and light-headedness. It upsets the body and mind. It has a severe impact in the digestive system and may quench the digestive fire. Withholding the urge to drink produces dryness, deafness, fatigue and heart pain. It wrecks the water distribution system and upsets the vitality, resulting in dry skin and dehydration. Suppressing the need to cry triggers eye diseases, allergies, light-headedness and even heart disease. Such a withholding involves suppression of emotions. Restraining the urge to sleep promptly causes insomnia, fatigue, headache and heaviness in the eyes. It upsets the nervous system and defocuses the mind, shooting up the Vata levels. Suppressing the need to breathe produces cough, asthma, arduous and shallow breathing, collapse of strength and heart disease. It often happens when disturbed or fearful without even noticing the symptoms. Conscious breathing can easily correct many temporary emotional disorders."

"Vata gets impacted most when channels suffer from such inhibition. Withholding excretion, urination or ejaculation upsets Apana Vayu, the downward advancing air. Restraining the activities of normal eating and drinking disturbs Agni and Samana Vayu. Depriving the body of sleep, inhalation, sneezing or yawning disrupts Prana, the primary vital force. Withholding the act of exhalation, belching, vomiting and coughing upsets the Udana action. With the cry restrained, Vyana stays unhinged."

---

[88] Ambhuvaha srotas – water intake system

"It nowhere suggests that we indulge in the urges as a routine, but follow the needs as they occur. Overly promoting the urges through factors like excess eating, drinking or sex, is equally unbalancing. To force a function when there is no natural urge, to eat when not hungry, can be very disturbing for vata levels. What is natural is never extreme! To attend to an urge is not the same as to cater to it. Once our tastes and senses are over stimulated, it is hard to restore them to a state of balance. Worse, we come to crave the same things that aggravate our condition more."

"Emotions represent different impulses in the mind. Suppressing them imbalances the mind. Their energy soars inwards and promotes a greater unconsciousness in us by accumulating in the subconscious, causing anxiety, malaise and lack of peace. Inhibited emotions block the channels of the physical body, disrupting circulation, promoting pain, letting toxins build up and encouraging tumors. Blocked emotional energy needs an outlet. When emotions are not expressed, they appear distorted at a physical level. Repressed emotions provoke many diseases and endorse poor immune function. Fear and anger are part of immune responses when in danger, it is the natural thing to avoid and resist the situation. Subjugated, the immune function undergoes depression. Withholding the emotions also weakens the digestive fire, wherein toxins crowd the tissues."

"Immune system disorders such as allergies, arthritis and cancer are born of bottled-up emotions. Insomnia, unpleasant dreams, irritability, fear, depression and shifting of moods come from emotional blockage. Even at the physical level, there are telltale signs of lack of appetite, nausea, indigestion, pain, and tension in the liver region. Incidentally the organ, liver oversees expression of emotion. For women, suppressed emotions show in premenstrual stage."

"I will stop now."

Padmalochan stopped at the corridors, Radha was asleep; he sat in the bench at the courtyard, his eyes strayed beyond the trees and palace walls to distant mountains lost in the clouds. The mountains once had power of flight and often flitted from one place to another. They obstructed the sunlight; Indra with his thunderbolt cleft their wings and robbed them of any further movement. The quiet moon greeted him from behind a stray cloud; he did not remember when he drifted off to sleep.

BASIC CONSTITUTION

Signs of learning were evident, the wellness message imparted, though many obscure texts in the confines of secrecy would likely not see another day. As Dharanidhar had prophesied, the redcoats now occupied the land; their alien language and strange food habits had already cast their influence on the people. Padmalochan had one mission, teach as many so they could bear the flag. The old school would eventually die; health and wellness in the future would develop as program for the masses. There would be no room for personal medicine; personal care would be a forgotten art. The future perhaps had no room for his program, for man would believe they owned and controlled nature. While he discarded idealism, he shrugged at the possibility of one apothecary formula for the hundreds of reasons that force a headache. If such a possibility would become real, headaches would never go away and a possibility of reviving the ancient wellness thinking would re-emerge. He scribbled feverishly on the large slates of granite, drawing tables and other illustrations, the sessions beginning that day held a lot of statistical content.

"One of the key suppositions in a wellness program is that a person's constitution reveals dosha states[89]. We went through earlier lessons on how to judge anatomy and physiology. Having completed the study on constitution, we have enough ammunition to recognize the different dosha conditions in diverse individuals. Our aim as wellness educators is in providing the guidelines to better health. We must never forget our role as a guide and not an authority and expert on diagnosis and diseases. The skills we gain today are a tool, a means to a much higher end."

---

[89] Creative-force Pariksha is the term for constitution examination

"According to the program, the superior practitioner is one who can recognize the dosha types in their various states, not necessarily one who knows how to diagnose many diseases. While the former knowledge gives us the knowledge of the life force and how to balance it, the latter remains trapped in just the disease and ceases to be holistic. It defeats the wellness aim at understanding the life force behind the workings of a human body and learning to work with it."

"By way of combinations, the ancient texts list seven primary dosha types - Vata, Pitta, Kapha, Vata-Pitta, Vata-Kapha, Pitta-Kapha, and Vata-Pitta-Kapha. Some individuals are strong in one dosha level or another. These we might call pure vata, pure pitta and pure kapha types. Dual types are more common when two or more dosha types stand in relatively equal proportion. Few balanced types with triple dosha also exists, making seven major constitutional variations."

"Mixed types do not necessarily suggest better or worse health. They just complicate the practitioner's treatment by hinting high presence of more than one dosha, where efforts to balance one dosha may often aggravate another. A simple method for mixed dosha types is to treat the dosha types using the factor of time, season[90] and astrological dasa, trying to lower the dosha that dominates during that period. Astrology steps in here with greater accuracy in managing time-boxed events. For dual types, it is often better to raise the level of the third dosha, the one that is too low. This is a trifle contrary to usual Ayurvedic rules of lowering levels of dosha types that are too high. In this wellness program, I encourage the practitioner to increase kapha in vata-pitta types and vata in pitta-kapha types. We must reassure vata-kapha type natives in developing pitta. For triple types, treatment is symptomatic, time and dasa-bound, and seasonal, as no basic imbalance needs treatment. Triple types show tendencies of good health."

Proportions of dosha types

"Dosha types have double standards. Different degrees of aggravation exist in the dosha types. There is much difference between high vata as insomnia and high vata as dementia; the former, temporary and mild vata increase; latter, long-term and severe."

---

[90] Astanga Hridayam, 3.1 Seasons

"In addition, the dosha types become unbalanced in different ways, relative to their different attributes. High vata, excess air, for example, can manifest as excess dryness, causing rigidity or reduced motion. It can also manifest under one of its other qualities as excess mobility, body tremors, conditions very different from the former. Though the dosha types give us a simple background in understanding conditions, one must complete a specific analysis to reckon the qualities out of balance."

"The dosha types provide a general background for specific diagnosis. While this background gives someone an effective means of treatment, it suggests more fine-tuning to arrive at specific results. Outer circumstances can aggravate the dosha types not predominant in the nature. These include climate, environment, lifestyle and culture. When assigning scores or weights to the dosha, one must be careful of where it applies as just numbers may be misleading"

"Weights denote the proportion of the three-dosha types in the body. Commonly, the number 1 indicates a low state of the dosha, 2 indicates moderate state, 3 high, 4 very high and 5 extremes. A person with vata 4, pitta 2, kapha 1 scores, would show a high vata, low kapha person. However, we should carefully note that there is no fixed or standard way of using numbers to denote the dosha types."

"Different practitioners may give them different values according to their own standards of measurement. This method can be very convenient but can also act misleading if we do not know the standard being applied, especially need to know what those numbers are for high or low dosha thresholds."

"In examining the constitution, the natural makeup is most easily revealed by the attributes of the physical body. These include frame, weight and complexion. The general state of the metabolism and digestion through time is also a good indicator."

"Lifelong habits and proclivities, and lifelong disease tendency are important. Though the inherent constitution retains its signature throughout life, exceptional factors like a long-term illness can alter it. Sometimes it may change with the stages of life."

Basic body structure

Structure	Vata	Pitta	Kapha
Frame	Unusually tall or short, thin; poorly developed physique	Medium; moderately developed physique	Stout, stocky, short, big; well-developed physique

Vata people are usually taller or shorter than the average. Most extreme types in height are characteristically vata. But they will show tendencies of a thin build. Kapha people are sometimes tall but stocky or big in build and hold weight. Other factors like appetite reveal pitta types as they fall in between the two.

Weight	Low, hard to hold weight, prominent veins and bones	Moderate, good muscles	Heavy, tends towards obesity

Vata people can be obese but will usually have variable weight gain and weight loss, with spongy tissues. Generally, they hold little weight even if they eat in excess. Kapha types may not be heavy but will have to struggle to keep their weight down as they easily accumulate fat and water. Pitta types usually stay at an even weight even if they are heavy eaters though too much red meat or greasy food can make them overweight.

Complexion	Dull, brown, darkish	Red, ruddy, flushed, glowing	White, pale

Complexion needs adjustment for race, region and lifestyle. Vata types lack in luster and have a darkish or dull tinge to the complexion. Pitta types flush with ease and their complexion stays hot. Light appears to come forth from their skin. Kapha types have a white or pearly type complexion. Skin discoloration, even when it turns white as in vitiligo or in an albino, indicates pitta, which burns out the pigmentation of the skin.

Skin texture and temperature	Thin, dry, cold, rough, cracked, prominent veins	Warm, moist, pink, with moles, freckles, acne	Thick, white, moist, cold, soft, smooth

Skin texture is a more reliable factor than complexion. Pitta types sunburn easily; commonly suffer from skin rashes or sores, including acne; though these may arise temporarily from impure blood in any of the dosha types. Their skin is warm to the touch. Vata types stay plagued with chronic dry skin and hair, wrinkles, cracks or fissures. Their skin is cold, dry and not thick. Kapha types have oily skin and hair and much subcutaneous fat or edema. To the touch, their skin is cool, damp or soggy.

Hair	Scanty, coarse, dry, brown, slightly wavy	Moderate, fine, soft, early gray or bald	Abundant, greasy, thick, very wavy, lustrous

Again, color of hair varies according to racial and regional characteristics. It is more the luster, texture and quality of the hair that is significant. Pitta types tend to baldness or gray early but the head is ruddy, sensitive to sun. But vata types, with their poor nutrition may bald early and often have dandruff. There is sensitivity to wind, and the head has a dull tinge in color. Kapha types have attractive, abundant, thick hair but sometimes may have excessive body hair.

Head	Small, thin, long, unsteady	Moderate, angular	Large, stocky, steady, square, rounded

Head size echoes mental nature as Sattva, Rajas and Tamas. A larger head may show better intelligence. The movements of the head may be more important than the size. Vata types tend onwards stiff neck and rigidity of the head or excess mobility on the other hand. Their head movements are not necessarily more frequent but are more erratic. Kapha types have the least head movements and usually have more square heads. Pitta falls in-between.

Forehead	Small, wrinkled	With folds	Large, broad

Structure	Vata	Pitta	Kapha
\multicolumn{4}{l}{The forehead also reflects mental nature. Those with good minds and memories will often have prominent foreheads even if Vata constitution. Otherwise, forehead is much like the head in its characteristics. A large and prominent forehead shows an elephant type. Such types have powerful minds and good memories though they may be any of the three-dosha types.}			
Face	Thin, small, long, wrinkled, dusky, dull	Moderate, ruddy, sharp contours	Large, round, fat, white or pale, soft contours
\multicolumn{4}{l}{Kapha people, particularly women, often have a typical large, round or moon face. Pitta types have more angular features and a penetrating look. Vata types look more gaunt or weathered. One can judge color and complexion of the face by the same factors as that of the body. Practitioner can usually determine the constitution by face alone with a fair amount of accuracy.}			
Neck	Thin, long	Medium	Large, thick
\multicolumn{4}{l}{Kapha types have large, square, thick necks, which are not long. Vata types have long necks and develop neck problems, with loose tendons in the neck. They may crane or bend the neck.}			
Eyebrows	Small, thin, unsteady	Moderate, fine	Thick, bushy, many hairs
Eyelashes	Small, dry, firm	Small, thin, fine	Large, thick, greasy, firm
Eyes	Small, dry, thin, brown, dull, unsteady	Medium, thin, red and inflamed easily, green, piercing	Wide, prominent, thick, greasy, white, attractive
\multicolumn{4}{l}{The eyes are another important indicator. Pitta types have piercing and penetrating eyes, but develop sensitivity to light, develop photophobic headaches and commonly need glasses and sunglasses. Kapha types have big, wide, pearly attractive eyes and big lashes and brows. They also cry easily and may have mucus discharges in the eye. Their eye movements are steady but not sharp. Vata types may suffer from blinking, usually from dryness of the eyes or feel tremors in the eyes with excessive or erratic eye movement. It is hard for them to concentrate their eyes on any point for long.}			
Nose	Thin, small, long, dry, crooked	Medium	Thick, big, firm, greasy
\multicolumn{4}{l}{The nose varies according to racial characteristics, but can still be of some help in determining constitution. Size and breadth is the main thing, along with complexion. Pitta has a sharp or pointed nose; a long, narrow and pointed nose is vata. A kapha nose has wide nostrils.}			
Lips	Thin, small, darkish, dry, unsteady	Medium, soft, red	Thick, large, greasy, smooth, firm
\multicolumn{4}{l}{Kapha types commonly have big and attractive lips. Pitta will usually have ruddy lips and face. Vata types will have thin lips, which they may bite into with their teeth, and the lips are often dry or chapped.}			
Teeth and gums	Thin, dry, small, rough, crooked, receding gums	Medium, soft, pink, gums bleed easily	Large, thick, soft, pink, greasy
\multicolumn{4}{l}{The state of the mouth is variable according to diet and dental hygiene and so may not always be significant but form and color are the main things here, and the general structure of the teeth. Vata types may have spaces between teeth. Kapha has large, white, attractive teeth. Pitta types suffer more from inflammatory diseases of the mouth as elsewhere.}			

Structure	Vata	Pitta	Kapha
Shoulders	Thin, small, flat, hunched	Medium	Broad, thick, firm, greasy
Vata types dominated by fear, develop hunched shoulders and tight muscles. Pitta folks have the best build, as they do not tend towards over or underweight.			
Chest	Thin, small, narrow, poorly developed	Medium	Broad, large, well or overly developed
Vata types have a narrow epigastria angle. Kapha types usually possess a broad one. Pitta types have a medium size epigastria angle.			
Arms	Thin, overly small or long, poorly developed	Medium	Large, thick, round, well developed
Vata may have thin, long or spindly arms with pronounced elbows. Kapha has round and fleshy arms and forearms. Pitta has wiry arms.			
Hands	Small, thin, dry, cold, rough, fissured, unsteady	Medium, warm, pink	Large, thick, greasy, cool, firm
Kapha types have big, square or round hands without many lines. Vata tends towards narrow hands with many lines and with pronounced knuckles or irregularity in the shape of the fingers. Veins will also be prominent on the hands in Vata types. Pitta types have warm hands even in cold weather. The hands also reveal the state of the mind or Sattva. Refined hands show an evolved character. Long and elegant hands show more sensitivity than short, stocky hands with stubby fingers.			
Nails	Small, thin, dry, rough, fissured, cracked, darkish	Medium, soft, pink	Large, thick, smooth, white, firm, greasy
The nails show the general state of our nutrition, our mineral absorption and bone metabolism. This is usually lowliest in Vata types. The nails become rougher and more Vata like as we age or after debilitating diseases.			
Thighs	Thin, narrow	Medium	Well developed, round, fat
Big, plump thighs are common in Kapha types, along with possible cellulite. Women have more body fat and larger thighs than men, who are more developed in the shoulder region.			
Legs	Thin, excessively long or short, prominent knees	Medium	Large, stocky
Vata people like to walk and run but may suffer from lack of coordination in walking. Kapha people can stand for long periods of time.			
Calves	Small, hard, tight	Loose, soft	Shapely, firm
Feet	Small, thin, long, dry, rough, fissured, unsteady	Medium, soft, pink	Large, thick, hard, firm
The dryness of Vata often manifests through the feet, which need oil massage regularly. Pitta types will have good skin tone and circulation even in the feet. Kapha types have a thick skin on their soles and large feet.			
Joints	Small, thin, dry, unsteady, cracking	Medium, soft, loose	Large, thick, well built
Vata people have prominent joints that project. This is because their lack of weight allows the joints to stay exposed. Kapha types have larger joints, but surrounding tissues			

AQUAPISCES

Structure	Vata	Pitta	Kapha
	may obscure them. The greasy nature of pitta affords them softness of the joints, which may also be loose.		
Urine	Scanty, difficult, colorless	Profuse, yellow, red, burning	Moderate, whitish, milky
	Urine analysis is an important diagnostic tool in Ayurveda. Vata has frothy urine, which may be difficult to discharge. Pitta has more urinary tract infections. Kapha has thick urine with possible mucus in it.		
Feces	Scanty, dry, hard, difficult or painful, gas, tends towards constipation	Abundant, loose, sometimes yellowish, tends towards diarrhea, with burning sensation	Moderate, solid, sometimes pale in color, mucus in stool
	This is another of the main factors in constitutional determination. Kapha people may have constipation from slow metabolism, but the stool when it comes out is soft. It will be abundant and soft. Pitta types may get constipated during fevers, but otherwise suffer from loose stool. Chronic constipation, especially in the elderly is a vata symptom.		
Sweat and body odor	Scanty, no smell	Profuse, hot, strong smell	Moderate, cold, pleasant smell
	Many factors like region, temperature and diet influence perspiration. Meat eaters will sweat more than vegetarians will. Take such factors into consideration. Vata people seldom sweat. Pitta types sweat a lot, particularly when exposed to heat. Kapha types will sweat a lot when they exercise, but not otherwise. Emotional distress causes more perspiration to occur. Spontaneous perspiration or autonomic perspiration in conditions of emotional distress is usually Vata in nature.		
Appetite	Variable, erratic	Strong, sharp	Constant, low
	Appetite is one of the best long-term indicators of constitution. Vata types have extremes of appetite, either no appetite or extreme hunger. When they are hungry, they become light headed and fearful. Kapha types have a consistent, but not high appetite and like to be around or working with food. They suffer from attachment to food. Pitta types can often digest almost anything and can eat large amounts of food without gaining weight. They have very strong appetites and get angry when they have not eaten. Most diseases weaken or lower our appetite, including colds and fevers.		
Taste	Prefers sweet, sour or saline food, cooked with oil and spiced	Favors sweet, bitter or astringent food, raw, lightly cooked without oil or spices	Desires pungent, bitter or astringent food, cooked with spices, but not a lot of oil
	This reflects the taste preferences of the dosha types when relatively in balance. When toxins like Mull or Ama invades the body, the sense of taste turns perverted and opposite of what they should be. Culture and conditioning also have their effect here. Most people prefer sweet food. This is better judged not as the tastes that people like, but the ones that make them feel better and healthier.		
Circulation	Poor, variable, erratic	Good, warm	Slow, steady
	Vata people have poor circulation and may be prone to palpitations. They have cold and dry extremities and abdomen. Pitta people have excellent circulation and may be prone to flushing, their face turning red. Kapha people have low but consistent circulation. When overweight, their peripheral circulation will be poor with cold limbs, but their abdomen stays warm.		
Activity	Quick, fast, unsteady, erratic, hyperactive	Medium, motivated, purposeful, goal seeking	Slow, steady, stately

Structure	Vata	Pitta	Kapha
Vata types exhibit extreme of activity. Their hyperactivity may however bring them to a state of exhaustion, withdrawal or paralysis. Or their extreme mental activity may reduce outer activity. Pitta types are only active towards a particular aim. They stay focused, but not necessarily obvious in what they attempt. Kapha types are steady, but not always adaptable in action and may get caught in a pattern. They may not want to act very much or often.			
Strength and exertion	Low, poor endurance, starts and stops quickly	Medium, intolerant of heat	Strong, good endurance, but slow in starting
Often vata types are good runners and can develop a good deal of physical adaptability. They are poor at lifting or carrying weight and tire easily. Pitta people like to show their power and domination, but may not possess as much endurance as they think they have. Kapha types have good endurance, but not necessarily high performance.			
Sexuality	Variable, erratic, strong desire but low energy, few children	Moderate, passionate, quarrelsome, dominating	Low but constant sexual desire, good sexual energy, devoted, many children
Vata types can be extreme in their sexual behavior. They are more promiscuous and deviant on one hand, but also more capable of becoming celibate. Kapha types are seldom promiscuous, but cannot give up sex either, unless compelled by some traditional or monastic faith. They like the constancy of touch and affection. Pitta types are more involved in the drama of sex and like to dominate. When they become preoccupied with other goals, their sex urge takes a nosedive.			
Sensitivity	Fear of cold, wind, sensitive to dryness	Dread of heat, dislike of sun, fire	Fear of cold, damp, but native likes wind and sun
Vata types have the greatest sensitivity to the elements and must protect themselves from them. Kapha types do well outdoors, but prefer to sunbathe or relax rather than work or exercise. Pitta types are most tolerant of cold.			
Immunity	Poor, variable, weak immune system	Medium, prone to infections	Good, consistent, strong immune system
Vata types come down with whatever diseases are around and may develop chronic conditions. Pitta types have trouble with infections, bleeding and febrile diseases. Kapha types can resist most diseases, but those of a damp or phlegmatic nature can strike them hard.			
Tendency to disease	Nervous system disorders, pain, arthritis, mental disorders	Febrile diseases, infections, inflammatory diseases	Respiratory system diseases, mucus, edema
Vata types are prone to suffer from pain. Their diseases involve the bones and nerves, mainly through the large intestine. Pitta types suffer from fever, inflammation, burning sensations, and diseases of the blood and liver. Kapha types are susceptible to congestive disorders and diseases of the lungs.			
Reaction to medications	Quick, low dosage needed, unexpected side effects or nervous reactions	Medium	Slow, high dosage required, effects slow to manifest
Vata types are hypersensitive and may overreact to things. Often their reaction to herbs or drugs is extreme or erratic. Practitioner should give them medications in small dosages			

Structure	Vata	Pitta	Kapha
\multicolumn{4}{l}{first and increase gradually. Subtle medications like aromas, spices or gemstones can affect them strongly. Kapha types may need strong dosages or therapies for any effect to occur.}			
Pulse	Threaded, rapid, superficial, irregular, weak; like a snake	Wiry, bounding, moderate; like a frog	Deep, slow, steady, rolling, slippery; like a swan
\multicolumn{4}{l}{The quality of the pulse is the most important thing. For Vata, it is thin and erratic. With pitta, it is wiry and bounding. For Kapha, it is slow, broad or deep.}			
Voice	Low, weak, hoarse	High pitch, sharp	Pleasant, deep, good tone
\multicolumn{4}{l}{Tone of voice faces influence from body strength or weakness and other transient factors. Kapha people have beautiful voices and make good singers, like opera singers. Yet they may lack in energy and motivation. Pitta people make good orators and make strong singers, like rock singers. Vata people have a monotonous tone of voice and not much strength to it.}			
Speech	Quick, inconsistent, erratic, talkative	Moderate, argumentative, convincing	Slow, definite, not talkative
\multicolumn{4}{l}{Speech is another important indicator. Speech is the main Prana expression in physical existence. Our main intake in life is food we swallow through the mouth. Our main output is speech we express through the mouth. Vata people are hyperactive in speech and may digress. They may become silent though they may still talk in their minds. Kapha people are hypoactive in speech, but like to draw out the state of communication. They like to be with people without saying much. Pitta people like to talk more than others, trying to prove a point or criticizing something.}			
Mental nature	Quick, adaptable, indecisive	Intelligent, penetrating, critical, logical	Slow, steady, deep, dull
\multicolumn{4}{l}{Mental nature does not entirely equate with physical nature, but there are many correlations. One dosha type is not more intelligent than another but each has a different sort of mentality. Vata people have quick, but often superficial minds. They are better at information or abstract thought and look at numerous points of view. Pitta people manifest their intelligence through a questioning nature and often have a probing or scientific bent. They are better at setting goals or values. Kapha people are clever with broad principles, strong sentiments and much consistency in their views. Yet they may be poor at details, their feelings dominate their mental makeup.}			
Memory	Poor, notices things easily but easily forgets	Sharp, clear	Slow to take notice but will not forget
\multicolumn{4}{l}{Memory may reflect a more mental than physical nature. Good intellect often leads to better memory. The quality or nature of the memory is more important than its strength. Kapha people remember personal feelings, love and sentiments, and intimate human interchanges. Emotion colors their memory. Pitta people remember hurts and insults, but also victories and achievements. Pitta person's will-power colors his memory. Vata people remember ideas, information, or trivia; personal remarks occupy priority storage.}			
Emotions	Fearful, anxious, nervous	Angry, irritable, contentious	Calm, content, attached, sentimental

This factor is of great importance. Vata types suffering from ungrounded sense always breeds fear. Vata people are not always highly emotional, but are nervously sensitive and so may show shifting reactions, either thoughts or emotions. Pittas vehemence causes

Structure	Vata	Pitta	Kapha
anger and a strong display of emotions. Kapha types having a settled nature breeds attachment and sentimentality. However, we each possess all these emotions, and each of them can turn into the other. So again, we must discriminate which are characteristic and which may be of a transient or secondary nature.			
Neurotic tendencies	Hysteria, trembling, anxiety attacks	Extreme temper, rage, tantrums	Depression, unresponsiveness, sorrow
Vata tends toward extreme emotional expressions, often along with loss of sensory or motor control, to the extreme of tremors or convulsions. Yet these emotions are transient and superficial. Pitta types have anger attacks or temper tantrums. Kapha types become chronically depressed, lethargic or sorrowful.			
Emotional strengths	Flexibility, adaptability	Fearless, courage, daring	Calm, contentment
Each dosha types emotional potential has its positive side. Emphasized it is less because the negative side is more likely to cause disease, but we should understand the strength of each dosha.			
Faith	Erratic, changeable, rebel	Determined, fanatic, leader	Constant, loyal, conservative
Faith is an important indicator of psychological nature. Good faith in life and truth shows Sattva, inner virtue. Vata people are unsteady and easily go contrary in their faith, which may be constantly changing. Or they may have faith in many things. Pitta people may apply their faith in a strong manner that may become aggressive. Kapha people like to stick to their faith whether it means good or bad and often have an unquestioned sense of loyalty. They can stay attached to the status quo.			
Sleep Patterns	Light, tends towards insomnia	Moderate, may wake up but will fall asleep again	Heavy, difficulty in waking up
Sleep is an important physical and mental indicator. Vata types with more air and ether have a hard time sleeping. Almost anything disturbs their sleep or wakes them up. Pitta types often have dream-disturbed sleep. Kapha types with more earth and water sleep easily and may sleep during the day as well. Vata type sleeps less than four hours at a stretch; Pitta four to seven; Kapha types can sleep for eight to ten hours.			
Dreams	Flying, moving, restless, nightmares	Colorful, passionate, conflict	Romantic, sentimental, watery, few dreams
Dreams are an important factor in constitution, the practitioner must be wary of stress and psychological problems which can disturb sleep in any of the dosha types and yield incorrect results. Vata types have the most dreams, which are often erratic or disturbed. Pitta types have the most colorful or dramatic dreams, but they may disturb their sleep, particularly when they are violent. Kapha types are least able to remember their dreams, but may have a vague sense of pleasure from them.			
Habits	Likes moving, travelling, parks, plays, jokes, stories, artistic activities, dancing	Enjoys competitive sports, politics, debates, hunting	Adores water, sailing, flowers, cosmetics, cooking
Habits can be more indicative of personal traits or mental nature. They should not be taken too seriously for determining constitution. Vata types are diverse, curious and erratic in their habits, sometimes eccentric. Pitta types are purposeful and competitive and seek results and achievements. Kapha types like to luxuriate, relax and be lazy.			

"Traditional text considered Kapha as the preferred dosha type over the other two. That was the Piscean age, where kapha types enjoyed dominance. Pitta types better fitted for military and political roles belonged to the earlier epoch. The Aquarian age vata types, regarded as mavericks carry the seeds of social change and renovation. The Vata-Pitta type is lean with active body, expressive and competitive mind. This type is more communicative, reactive, changing and outgoing, yet having more volatility, is likely to burn himself out."

"Every character and constitution has its strengths and weaknesses. Persons with vata constitution are more prone to disease but also are more open to treatment and better able to manage changes. Persons with high levels of vata like to do new things and take on new activities, including acts of wellness and healing. Kapha people have lower disease tendency, but are slower to adopt any treatment. They find it difficult to initiate positive changes when they are sick. Pitta type is the most engaging and interested in healing, but easily becomes hostile. Their flexibility in treatment and ability to change negative habits balances the disease tendency of each type. Even two persons with identical dosha constitution differ vastly in terms of treatment."

"Some level of three dosha types is evident in all people, of which one or more are dominant. When the more visible and physical factors, like frame, complexion or digestion, differ from habits or emotional factors, it is wise to go with the former."

"Unfortunately, bias, a product of ahamkara along with Maya deters us from firm judgment. Often as practitioners, we judge the native based just on our experience, as it is difficult to understand those radically different. We realize in the process we have not experienced enough to judge firm. Imagine an elephant approaching you with a physical problem, you could only treat it if you knew its diet, the herbs it can tolerate and the organs that need fixing, not the symptoms. Same is the case with a person you have never met."

"Dosha types are more obvious when out of balance, but how about those who take good care of their health? It is always safe to assume all cases are hard to judge and start at the very beginning, for vata person having indulged in a strong kapha diet would show the kapha signs of imbalance. The diet, season and other factors dominate the person's actual constitution, often misleading the practitioner. Judge after you have eliminated through proper analysis, the native will cherish your treatment."

"Analysis by astrology plays a key role here. Moreover, a person may momentarily suffer from an excess of a dosha not predominant in his nature. An obese person may have temporarily high kapha from circumstantial factors but has generally been thin most of her life. Wherever time comes into the picture, and the constitution dosha is not obvious, it is wise to use astrology as an extra pair of eyes. Apart from the dominant dosha in the constitution one must also note the general strength of the person. It helps the practitioner to decide whether to apply strong or moderate methods to reduce the aggravated dosha. Sturdy dosha types can take strong therapies; not-so-strong types may need milder and longer therapies."

"Usually, kapha types have the strength but tend not to display it. Pitta types show aggression but do not always have patience or endurance to back it. Vata types suffer weakness being deficient and emaciated. But these are general abstractions. Generally, men have more physical energy, however, women have greater endurance than men. Strong types usually have better health, capable of stronger exertion but can suffer from extreme and acute conditions like heart attacks or high fevers that may cause quick or early death. Weak types have poor health and chronic diseases but may still live a longer life."

"When such doubts cloud the judgment, the use of astrology and pulse reading yield better, unbiased results on the analysis of constitution."

"A strong kapha person has a robust, broad and wavy pulse, good energy, health, and capacity for work, good muscle tone, excellent resistance to disease and a good immune system. They exhibit faith, confidence and integrity; the constitution is solid, steady, sturdy and yet capable of action and response."

"A weak kapha type has a fragile, slow or wavy pulse, low energy, shortness of breath, flabby or flaccid skin and muscles, very slow metabolism and quick to fatigue. They are shy, dependent, passive, sentimental and easily hurt. Strong pitta person has a resilient, wiry pulse, good energy, health and capacity for work. Such a type shows signs of aggression; they make a dynamic and expressive leader. They possess sharp, clear mind and strong will."

"A weak pitta type has a feeble, wiry pulse, low energy, suffering from anemia or chronic liver disorders, hidden anger and frustrated emotions. They act in defense as if they are under attack."

"Strong vata type has a sturdy but narrow pulse, good energy, good physical adaptability and mobility, good health and good healing energy or prana. The mind is strong, quick and inquisitive. They talk a lot and they are strong in communication. A weak vata type has a frail, threaded pulse, low energy, poor circulation, suffering from emaciation, chronic diseases and debility. The mind wavers, acts erratic, with signs of fear, anxiety and negativity. They may become secretive and fearful, showing little faith."

"It is easy to spot the constitution for people who are in thirties. Childhood kapha shades the constitution of children under fifteen, particularly under five becoming quite dominant at twenty. There is also a youthful vata apparent in thinner builds and more active people that show along with childhood kapha. This usually comes out after the age of five and manifests more in the ten to fifteen-year age group, just before they enter puberty. Even Kapha types may be thin when young from such trend."

"After the age of forty, midlife kapha sets in, stirring an increase in body weight. Sometimes a midlife Ama of accumulated of toxins also develops from years of unhealthy living, overeating and insufficient exercise. It may well be a product of slowing metabolism or more comfortable life-situation. This mid-life Kapha may continue to develop into an older age Kapha, which we often see in post-menopausal women, though old age vata is more known in men and women. It is most characteristic after the age of seventy where memory loss, insomnia, constipation, anxiety and other vata traits appear even in non-vata types."

"Among the different constitutional types, eight such groups pose a major problem in their treatment or remedy[91]. Such conditions show deep-seated disorders, often congenital or hormonal and usually signify poor longevity. The eight conditions make prognosis uncertain, the types being (1) very tall person, a vata condition, (2) unusually short, also a vata condition, (3) excessive body hair, kapha, (4) devoid of body hair, pitta, (5) excessive dark complexion, vata, (6) excessive pale complexion, pitta, (7) highly obese, kapha, (8) excessive thin, vata."

"Extremes of height show vata disorders, especially when parents are of normal height. If an oddly tall or short person comes from a family without such extremes, it shows possibility of constitutional imbalances. These conditions of high vata brings upon lack of coordination, poor circulation and nervous disorders."

---

[91] Ashta Nindita or eight difficult type of constitutions

"Hirsute folks with excess body hair indicate high kapha levels with too much earth in the body, leading to obstruction of organic functions and possible blockage of channels. Absence of body hair occurs from high pitta destroying the hair follicles. Even high vata with tissue deficiency can bring about a similar condition. Very dark complexion is owed to high vata levels, and abnormal pale complexion to high pitta levels. Kapha people may be pale or white but not to such extremes."

"Severe obesity is more common in persons with high kapha levels, whereas high emaciation owes it to high vata. Obesity usually involves excess fat, where other tissues suffer insufficient development, especially the reproductive fluid and Ojas. Surplus weight instigates stagnation and accumulation of toxins that breed diseases like arthritis, gout and asthma. Overweight folks suffer from poor longevity, difficulty in movement, low libido, lack of strength, bad body and breath odor, excess perspiration, hunger and thirst. Emaciated types may suffer from digestive power so low or suppressed that they are left with little appetite, along with unusual absorption of food, and cannot take heavy food or food in large quantities. Their endurance and stamina are low, their tolerance to heat and cold is remarkably low and they suffer from common cold, influenza and cough, often developing hemorrhoids and prolapse of the organs. When the weight is over its threshold, it continues to accumulate and poses a challenge in slowing. When the weight is below its lower threshold, it stays low and requires substantial effort to increase it. These conditions are very difficult to treat. These extreme and difficult conditions occur when metabolism crosses the limits."

"The three dosha types impact body and mind, creating a stoic mix of physical, psychological and emotional challenges. Each dosha suggests a certain physiological and psychological set of problems. Individuals harboring physical vata tendencies usually have aerial mental leanings, emotional bends of fear, anxiety and insecurity, which are quite ungrounded. They are mentally changeable, excitable and indecisive with quickly fluctuating and unpredictable moods and interests. A powerful Saturn in a birth-chart shows such vata mental make-up. They have highly sensitive but unsteady minds and senses. Vata types have good but erratic mental powers; they are quick to perceive and react, but are not always consistent in their judgments and opinions. Comprehensive in their views, sometimes incredibly superficial, they have many ideas and speculations but lack pragmatism. Threats or promises easily influence them. Their intellect is often well developed with abundant information. They cultivate the abstract and philosophical part of the mind once they have reined their wandering thoughts."

"Vata minds are great at grasping and forgetting; they are quick at attachment and detachment, fast at getting emotional and expressing emotions and quickly forgetting them. They have little courage or daring, but seldom become vindictive and usually blame themselves. They are awful at forming long lasting relationships. Their love for solitude results in having many transient friends. However, they are quick at becoming friends with people outside their social sphere, age group and build many such acquaintances. Vata folks do not make good leaders, they are not great as followers either; they are not very materialistic and are not so concerned with amassing possessions or money. They spend money quick and easy, they also make money quick and easy."

"Folks having pitta physical nature tend towards fiery passions of irritability, rage and hatred. Their minds are sharp, penetrating and aggressive; they are logical, critical, perceptive and intelligent. They are quick to get emotional though they think themselves to be otherwise; in this regard, they are seldom sentimental and have no trouble expressing their anger. They simply cannot rein in their anger and outbursts."

"Pittas types make a determined, articulate and convincing individual who gets his point across by dominating others with his ideas. Pitta folks often become self-righteous, sometimes fanatical; with their strong will power, they make good, dignified leaders. Ambitious they are, with high goals in life, working hard to achieve them. While very helpful and kind to friends and followers, pitta types are cruel and unforgiving to opponents. When studying astrology, you can see how Mars and Sun in certain pitta positions control and influence their opponents. Yes, they act bold; they are adventurous, daring and reckless and like the smell of danger and challenges. Pitta folks are inventive, ingenious and possess good mechanical skills, enjoying the use and expression of energy and technology. Their memory is sharp, not sentimental; they have much clarity but lack compassion. For them is all about power, not money; money is just a means to that end."

"Those gifted with kapha constitution tend towards soggy emotions. Love and desire, romance and sentimentality, greed and lust are common in them along with a strong Moon or Venus in their birth-chart. They act out of kindness, they act considerate and loyal, but adjust poorly to change and are slow to adapt; just as they are slow to respond, acting conservative, shy and obedient. Kapha types usually have many friends and love the family closeness or being knit with community, culture and country. Anything outside this, they become close-minded. They act suspicious of strangers; they travel less and are happier at home."

"Kapha folks easily get attached and find it hard to let go of the past. While they can display affections easily, they are slow to express anger. Mentally, kapha types are steady with good forethought, but need extra time to consider things, they find it difficult to work with abstract ideas and learn better through something practical. Not sensitive, or perceptive, rare are the moments when they turn negative, rude or critical. The tendency to throw their weight around comes naturally to kapha people; however, they like to expropriate things for themselves. They accumulate possessions and value material resources."

"As you can imagine, it is not uncommon to find exceptions to this correspondence of physical and psychological traits in different dosha types. A heavy, thickset kapha person may have a vata or light mind - a contradiction, where treating psychological conditions and physical dosha alike may be far from accurate."

"The physical body reflects not the mental nature, but tries to balance it. Mental makeup being more subdued, more malleable than the physical one, offers greater variations, accepting, even reacting to disturbances of a type different from the physical constitution."

"Mental disturbances can be quite different to the disorders physical constitution can bring and may show different symptoms. Judging the mental setup from the guna vectors[92] is much more accurate, as the vectors denote the mental traits - Sattva shows clarity, Rajas shows distraction and Tamas specifies dullness."

"Dosha types take a back seat in this approach to mental health and cognitive wellness. The guna qualities also reflect the level of development of the inner being. They are not simple intellectual proclivities or emotional types, they express the mind's sensitivity, its capacity to perceive truth and act accordingly."

"Mind is naturally sattvic, clear and pure, darkened by negative thoughts and emotions. Mind, when pure, under Sattva's divine influence, becomes a source of enlightenment and self-realization, unifying the head and the heart. Rajas sets the mind to a state of distraction and turbulence, instigating an easy turn to the external world to seek fulfillment. Mind agitated by desire, unable to quench the craving, the frustration turns to anger."

---

[92] Guna - prime attributes of Creative-force-nature as the vectors Sattva, Rajas and Tamas.

"Fueled by disturbed thoughts and ideas, it paves the making of a willful, manipulative and egoistic person, who constantly seeks power, stimulation and entertainment. When the search becomes excess, the personality turns negative. Tamas directs the mind to dullness, darkness, lacking the ability to perceive, a mind clouded by ignorance and fear. Promoting sloth, sleep and inattention, Tamas decreases mental activity, increases insensitivity and allows external or subconscious forces to dominate. In excess, the personality turns servile and beastly."

"While the wellness program advocates treating the physical disorders by determining the dosha levels and mental ailments from guna levels, we are left with a burning question – how do dosha-s relate to guna-s? It is a question that has perplexed us for thousands of years and there are no straight answers. I have propounded a suggestive correlation, though it may vary in content with other traditional works."

"Sattva as a vector offers its services to Prana, it needs the aerial movement of vata, the agni of pitta and the steadiness of kapha. From a few earlier definitions, Sattva is immutable and so is the Tridosha state of vata-pitta-kapha. Rajas is movement and excitability, which the vata-pitta combination manages. Tamas is inertia, darkness; whose stability kapha fulfills."

"All of us have different degrees of variations in the three guna vectors, as distinct as dosha levels. Without Sattva, our perception becomes zero; our aim therefore is to ensure Sattva has no closure and can open the true doors to learning. Variation in guna types is what is needed to find out different mental types. Seven generic mental types are (1) Sattva, (2) Rajas, (3) Tamas, (4) Sattva Rajas, (5) Sattva Tamas, (6) Rajas Tamas, (7) Sattva-Rajas-Tamas. Pure Sattva[93] gives enlightenment. In the first case, it does not mean Sattva is by itself, alone; it implies Sattva is the most active ingredient in the makeup, the remaining are inactive, not absent."

"Mental traits may not always agree with a person's physical nature and behavior. The central theme in wellness is to align them to the cosmic forces. Therefore, remedial measures such as meditation reduce the negative and disease-causing habits."

---

[93] Shuddha Sattva or pure Sattva

Effects of guna vectors on dosha mental makeups

Vata Mental Nature	
Sattvic - Harmonious	Energetic, adaptable, flexible, quick in comprehension, good in communication, strong sense of human unity, strong healing energy, good enthusiasm, positive spirit, ability to start things, good capacity for positive change and movement
Rajasic - Disturbed	Indecisive, unreliable, hyperactive, agitated, volatile, restless, disturbed, distracted, nervous, anxious, overly talkative, superficial, noisy, disruptive, false enthusiasm, excitable
Tamasik - Darkened	Fearful, servile, dishonest, secretive, depressed, self-destructive, drug addict, prone to sexual perversions, mentally disturbed, suicidal
Pitta Mental Nature	
Sattvic - Harmonious	Intelligent, clear, perceptive, enlightened, discriminating, good will, independent, warm, friendly, courageous, good guide and leader
Rajasic - Disturbed	Willful, impulsive, ambitious, aggressive, controlling, critical, dominating, manipulating, angry, wrathful, reckless, proud, vain
Tamasik - Darkened	Hateful, vile, vindictive, violent, destructive, psychopath, criminal, drug dealer, underworld figure
Kapha Mental Nature	
Sattvic - Harmonious	Calm, peaceful, content, stable, consistent, loyal, loving, compassionate, forgiving, native, devoted, receptive, nurturing, supportive, strong faith
Rajasic - Disturbed	Controlling, attached, greedy, lustful, materialistic, sentimental, needing security, seeking of comfort and luxury
Tamasik - Darkened	Dull, gross, lethargic, depressed, apathetic, slothful, coarse, slow comprehension, insensitive, a thief

"Sattva dwells in pitta as knowledge, in vata as simplicity and lightness, in kapha as mercy and love. Tamas in kapha acts as heavy, dull and sloth, and as aggression and competitiveness in pitta, and perhaps as confusion in vata. Rajas gets promoted as active and hyper in vata and pitta, none in kapha."

"A dosha undergoes three basic stages of development - (1) Increase or accumulation or Sanchaya, (2) Aggravation or provoked state or Prakopa and (3) Decrease or alleviation or Prashama[94]. The dosha sorts are constantly changing, rising and falling like waves with the natural movement of time, with one dosha dominant at one time, another dosha at another time. It is important not to allow them to increase to the point of aggravation and to keep their fluctuations mild. Once you know how and when they tide and ebb, it becomes relatively easy to avoid them going awry."

"In case of vata, qualities such as dryness connected with heat can cause vata to start its accumulation. With the same qualities connected with cold, vata just gets provoked. In an environment, where opposite qualities are dominant like dampness connected with heat, vata undergoes alleviation. Heat along with dryness and other vata promoting qualities allow it to increase. Such qualities are roughness, hardness, lightness, mobility and all other vata or wind-like attributes. They accelerate vata's accumulation, because the heat prevents them from manifesting the negative powers."

"Cold along with these vata qualities provokes vata's negative manifestation as disorders, like constipation, insomnia and arthritis. Heat, wetness, smoothness, softness, slowness and even application of warm oil such as sesame eases and alleviate vata."

"Pitta undergoes accumulation with sharpness associated with cold. When the condition changes to heat from cold, pitta gets provoked. Using opposite qualities such as dullness connected with cold, pitta gets pacified into a state of alleviation. Cold along with pitta's bilious qualities, like sharpness, lightness and oiliness, pushes pitta levels to increase. Cold keeps the other pitta qualities from becoming provoked, letting them accumulate. Heat provokes the negative manifestation of these qualities as pitta disorders, like hyperacidity, fever or infection. Opposite attributes, like slowness or dullness, along with cold, alleviates and eases pitta, as with cold, bitter and alterative herbs in cleansing the blood and bile."

---

[94] Astanga Hridayam. Charaka Samhita - Triple movements of the Dosha-s are Diminution, Normalcy and Aggravation. Chp 17, Sloka 112-113

"Kapha undergoes accumulation from dampness connected with cold. Involving heat instead of the cold, kapha still gets provoked. Opposite qualities like dryness along with heat, eases it.[95] Cold and kapha based phlegmatic attributes like dampness, heaviness and dullness, increases kapha levels. Kapha-like attributes speeds up kapha intensities to become dominant. Heat and kapha qualities of dampness provoke kapha. This is because heat has the power to stir up the heavy kapha attributes, thereby allowing the negative effects to grow. Such are the qualities of water. Cold as in ice increases kapha levels. Heat by melting it causes it to flood and bring about damage. Anti-kapha qualities like heat, dryness, lightness and sharpness alleviate kapha levels. Fasting along with taking hot spices like ginger can quickly ease high levels of kapha. Dosha types increase from an increase in 'like' attributes. Heat or cold provokes the dosha types, especially the stronger of the attributes. The levels decrease when 'opposite' qualities are applied."

"Sinusoidal and cyclic processes build and develop the dosha types. In one such process, Kapha marks the first stage, pitta the middle and vata the end. The other process starts with vata, followed by pitta and kapha. Such cycles may repeat. The middle stage always involves energy of pitta. Dosha modes are dominant at certain stages of life, even in the hours of the day."

"The early stage could well be dominated by kapha or vata, marking the physical age of youth, from conception to late puberty about age 15. This period reveals a person still in field of the water, nourished the kapha way; or a carefree, vata attitude. The person undergoes conception and growth, but there is always the notion of restlessness and instability. While tissues keep growing and the native adds weight, expands and increases in density; many grow tall for their age or stay short. Emotionally the native is dependent, receptive, fearful, seeking protection. The diet forced on a child is more kapha dominated by dairy products and rich foods to provide the nutrients for growth. Many childhood diseases are of a kapha nature, with mucus, phlegm, colds and influenza and swollen glands and most mental problems have a high vata level of inattentiveness, irrelevant fears, carefree attitude. While in terms of the tissues or bodily substance childhood is the age of kapha, in terms of body function, childhood is the age of vata. Children appear more vata-like mentally because their energy remains unstable and restless. Some children grow fat when young only to become skinny when they grow up, other children are skinny when young and become heavier as they age."

---

[95] Astanga Hridayam 1.12.19.21 scriptures

"Pitta solemnizes the middle age, from puberty to the onset of old age likely about ages 15 to 50. The growth process slows down and comes to a grind. Most people set their targets on accomplishing their goals in this period of their life. Aggressive and ambitious, their motivation directs them to do things for themselves. Late teen rebels show this uprising of Pitta, where even the diet turns towards more pitta foods like spices, alcohol and meat. Pitta disorders are more common, starting with acne and ending up with heart attacks and other manifestations of extreme energy."

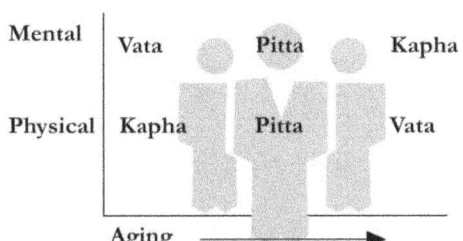

"Vata and kapha commemorate old age gradually setting in after 50 and specifically after 65. The forces of decay and degeneration move into motion. Gradually the vital fluids dry out, the vigor starts to fail, hair and teeth fall, senses, sight and hearing are diminished, and memory fails. High vata continues to attack the life force to break the connection with the physical body. Since youth marks the time the life energy from the soul enters the body, middle age marks the time in which it creates a vehicle through which it can act. Old age marks the time in which the life force is compelled to return to its origin because its connection with physical matter is but artificial and temporary."

"On the positive side, the old-age time of life serves to enhance wisdom and detachment. It gives the opportunity to the elderly to become the main teachers and guides in the life of others. Some elderly people become more kapha, sluggish, putting on weight and being less active. Old age is functionally a kapha time though the age is a time when the tissues undergo vata vitiation. Kapha women, for example, are often thin when young, but easily put on weight, particularly after her first child."

"Process of increase and decrease of the dosha levels work closely with the cycle of time, particularly the seasons. In equatorial regions, there are six natural seasons of two months each. These are spring, summer, monsoon, autumn, winter and the dewy season, marking the months of March–April, May–June, July–August, September–October, November–December and January–February.[96]"

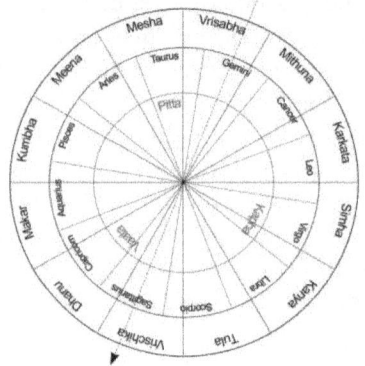

"In this system, Vata increases in the summer periods of May–June, when the climate is dry and hot. Pitta sees increase in the rainy season of July–August, which is a hot and damp season, and kapha in the dewy season Jan–Feb, where the climate is cold and damp. Vata undergoes provocation in the rainy season of July–August by the cooler weather that follows the dry heat of summer, and the wind and frequent storms in monsoon. Also in this season light and dry food plants grow in abundance, linking climate to diet. Pitta encounters provocation in autumn in Sep–Oct, which in tropical zones brings renewed heat after the rains. Spring in March–April period provokes Kapha from the heat that liquefies it. Vata sees alleviation in autumn in Sep–Oct period by the return of heat. Pitta gets alleviated in winter months of Nov–Dec, which brings cold. Kapha eases in the summer months May–June which has opposite qualities to it."

Seasonal changes in temperate regions

Applying them to other climate zones like the four seasons in North America: **Vata** *relates to late autumn when cold, dry and declining energy prevails.* **Pitta** *levels see increase in midsummer when heat is predominant.* **Kapha** *reaches its levels in early spring when water turns into liquid, from the melting of the winter snow. Dating them according to our four–season climate:* **Vata** *is strongest in November–December,* **Kapha** *is strongest in March–April and* **Pitta** *is strongest in July–August. Irrespective of latitude, here is a general rule that dosha types follow.*

---

[96] Astanga Hridayam, Chapter 3 Seasons. Charaka Samhita, Chp 17, Sloka 114

	Provoked	**Accumulating**	**Eased**
Feb. 1–June 1	Kapha	Pitta	Vata
June 1–Oct. 1	Pitta	Vata	Kapha
Oct. 1–Feb. 1	Vata	Kapha	Pitta

"Vata accumulates in summer and fall, and early winter provokes it. Late winter and spring eases it with return of moisture and heat. Care during summer is necessary to avoid becoming exceedingly dry or adopting a diet that is light or cold with much fruit and salad as it may aggravate vata in the fall. Preparing for the declining season with supply of tonics or supplementation therapy in early fall, taking more rich and nutritive foods, as nuts, grains[97], oils and dairy products is an age-old technique to combat the cold[98]."

"Pitta accumulates in the late winter and spring, and summer provokes it. Autumn and early winter eases it with the return of cold and the shortening of the days. During spring, food that is hot, spicy, greasy or fried must be avoided. A blood-cleansing regimen comprising green herbs, sprouts and vegetables in the spring will help stop pitta from becoming aggravated in the summer. Kapha accumulates in the fall and early winter. Late winter and spring provokes it. Summer lessens it with the heat and sun. In the winter, it is prudent to not eat excess sweet, heavy, fatty or mucus-forming foods, for when they liquefy in the spring, they bring many kapha disorders. In late winter, more spices, light diet, occasional fasting, saunas and physical exercise prevent kapha diseases in the spring."

"Confluences of the seasons provoke the dosha types. Move from spring to summer worsens pitta. Change from fall to winter intensifies vata. Transferal from winter to spring heightens kapha. Sudden alterations in weather intensify the dosha types, particularly vata."

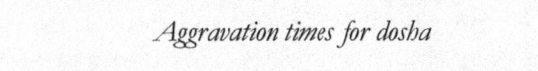

Aggravation times for dosha

"The ancient texts state vayu gradually settles in the night after day, in the last stages from middle age and in digestion. Pitta and kapha do not appear in the texts and are likely variables in the three processes.[99]"

---

[97] Astanga Hridayam, Chapter 6 Annasvarupa Vijnana – Knowledge of food
[98] Astanga Hridayam, Chapter 5 Dravadravya Vijnana – Knowledge of liquids
[99] Astanga Hridayam 1.6 'vayohoratribhuktanam te antmadhyadiga: karmat' vayo (vayu)

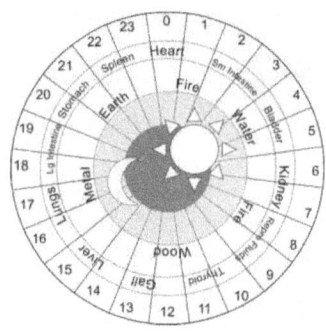

"Wellness clock divides the day into two, day and night, starting at sunrise and sunset. Daytime belongs to pitta, night to kapha. In general, Pitta is stronger or more pronounced during the day and kapha at night. To vata belongs the transition points of dawn and dusk,[100] points of great change that agitate and derange vata. To pitta belong the zenith points of noon and midnight, arriving at power points. Flanked is Kapha, which falls in the middle. Each half of the day is further divided into three; the first part belongs to kapha, the second to pitta and the third to vata, as the three dosha types always relate to beginning, middle and end in all time processes. These times are only approximate, more organic rather than clock time and adjustments must be made accordingly[101]. Vata time ends just after sunrise or sunset. Pitta time begins soon before noon and midnight. In summer, when the days are longer, the times belonging to the dosha modes will be longer during the day and shorter at night. The reverse is true during the winter."

	Day	Night
Kapha	7 am–11 am	7 pm–11 pm
Pitta	11 am–3 pm	11 pm–3 am
Vata	3 pm–7 pm	3 am–7 am

"During the day, morning hours provoke kapha, noon eases it and afternoon accumulates the dosha type. Morning assists in pitta accumulation, provoking it at noon and easing pitta in the afternoon; morning eases vata, noon accumulates it and afternoon, especially sunset provokes it. During the night, the evening hours provoke kapha, midnight eases it and the early morning accumulates it. Pitta accumulates in the evening, gets provoked at midnight and eased in the early morning. The evening eases vata, which accumulates at midnight and the early morning dawn, provokes it. Commonly, the morning provokes kapha, liquefying after accumulation at night. Hence, hot beverages and spicy herbs is a great wake-up mechanism first thing in the morning to relieve excess kapha."

---

a horatri (day and night) bhukta (digestion) a nt (end) Madhya (middle) karmat (gradually)
[100] Sandhis are the transition times of dawn and dusk
[101] Adjustments because of calendar fluctuations and daylight savings time in summer

"Largely, the day provokes pitta at a superficial level for example with skin rashes. Night provokes it at a deeper level with ulcers. Normally, early morning before dawn provokes Vata with insomnia but also manifests as sleep deprivation in the late afternoon."

"Diverse climate types impact dosha types differently. Climate and geographical locations of the same nature show tendencies of aggravating them. Examination and diagnostics adds one more factor to the list including the individual, stage in life, time of day, season and the place in which he lives. The scriptures call it 'examination of place'[102], which comes after 'examination of time'[103], similar to observations of different stages of life and the seasons. Wellness system recognizes three baseline climate types, Vata climate region[104], and kapha[105] and pitta climate region[106]. Vata climate is short on water and vegetation; they have many hills and elevations catering to the wild. Human population is low and less civilized. Kapha climate has controlled water and vegetation, flattened lands, often marshy, large population as in settlements along rivers or sea. Pitta climate falls somewhere in the middle of the other two. Vata climate boasts of the lowest disease as fewer bacteria survive in such arid conditions. Kapha climate accounts for occurrence of most ailments. Pitta climate again hovers between the two."

"In this method, Desha or habitat is of two types, the region of land and the borough of Deha, the body. Bhumi, land is three types, arid regions predominantly vata, Anupam catering more to kapha and Sadharana which suffers from maximum mulls[107]."

---

[102] Desha Pariksha – Place examination
[103] Kala Pariksha – Time examination
[104] Jangala or forest, wild region
[105] Anupa or a moderate, wet region
[106] Sadharana or ordinary, warm region
[107] Astanga Hridayam – 1.23, bhumi-deha-prabheden desha-mahurahi dwidha | jaangalam (arid) dhatbhyushtham-anupam tu kapho-lvanam || sadharanam sam-mullum trigha bhudeshmadishet | Jaangala is arid, desert like. Anupam is marshy land and Sadharana is moderate type.

"Vata levels are higher in climatic regions that are cold, dry, clear, light and windy, and at higher elevations[108]. Pitta levels are elevated in climate regions that are hot and damp and at a moderate elevation[109]. Heat and sunny days prevail with a fair amount of moisture. Hot tropical locations favor the pitta dosha. Kapha gets elevated in climate types that are cold, damp, and cloudy and at low elevations, near the sea or large bodies of water[110]."

"Dual climate zones exist everywhere[111]. Far northern places, which spell cold with 'brrr!', less precipitation and high winds, vata and kapha prosper well. High mountain forests where the air is thin show similar traits. Tropical islands and coasts comprise of pitta along with kapha. The climate inland in continental zones face the brunt of hotter summers and colder winters than their coastal brothers whose temperature gets moderated by the ocean. Such climatic zones with extreme temperature variations aggravate the dosha modes rapidly[112]."

---

[108] Vata Climate in the US - A typical Vata climate in this country would be the high desert of the southwest like Santa Fe, New Mexico, where all these factors exist. Most of the year is cool, rainfall is slight, days are mainly sunny, windy and the elevation is high. The high plains region from New Mexico to Montana and North Dakota and northwards into Canada has a similar climate, as does most of the great basin region and submontane regions in the Rocky Mountain area from northern Arizona to eastern Washington state and eastern British Columbia.
[109] Pitta climate in the US - Eastern Texas away from the ocean, like the climate of Dallas, is typical of this except in the winter.
[110] Kapha Climate types in the US - Such climate regions are typically found in the northeast, like New England. Rain and dampness are prevalent the entire year, winters are cold, most days are cloudy, and the elevation is low and near the ocean with its fog. Much of the Great Lakes region has a similar climate, including most of eastern Canada, also the Pacific Northwest. Even a wet tropical climate, like that on the wet side of the Hawaiian Islands, is still predominately Kapha.
[111] Dual Type Climate types - The low desert of the southwest like Phoenix, Arizona and most of the inland areas of California with heat and dryness combine both Pitta and Vata qualities. Pitta and Kapha climatic factors combine in Florida, the Gulf Coast region and the southeastern United States generally, which are both hot and damp.
[112] Extreme Climate Variations - Chicago, Illinois in the central part of this country, for example, is very hot in the summer and very cold in the winter. This will be a more unbalancing type climate than Portland, Oregon, which has both milder summers and milder winters, though both are predominately Kapha climate types.

"It is not that the moderate climate regions are free of diseases, it is more likely that in such moderate weather the dosha types increase gradually and predictably without outside influence. Other climatic zones have different type of seasonal changes."

"Living in a similar climate as one's constitution needs careful adjustments. Using astrology and dosha levels, one can fine-tune a place that is congenial to one's health[113]. Dietary or herbal methods are also effective, like in elevated vata climate; moist food products like dairy products, oil massages, and nasal oil intakes can ease the drying effect. While pitta climate gives the freedom to eat raw food and fruit juices, herbal bitters, cooling powers of coconut and sandalwood also help ease pitta. Kapha climate permits use of hot spices and more physical workouts."

"The home is an excellent place to monitor dosha modes and control their proliferation. High house heat can aggravate pitta; low can aggravate vata and kapha. Excess dampness in the house can aggravate kapha and pitta, too little can damage vata. Chances of dosha accumulation in the home environment are lower than the outside. Outside the home, climatic changes are sudden and dramatic; the likelihood of provoking diseases is much higher. The important thing is to be wary of the environment the bodies are subject to - outdoors, the home, place of work and others. The qualities that dwell in these places instigate diseases of like nature unless we compensate for them. If we live in a hot and dry climate, often expose ourselves to the sun and heat, work in a hot room and do a lot of jogging, accumulating factors that derange pitta. Factors that strain our system, like a long run on a miserable hot summer day, or experiencing uncontrollable anger that may provoke pitta and cause a fever or other pitta manifestation."

"Changes occur in dosha levels during food digestion. Dosha types increase and decrease depending on the stage of digestion they control. Vata increases when food enters the small intestine. The levels are provoked with the food in the colon, its stage of digestion and place of ultimate accumulation."

---

[113] In modern society, it is different. As we largely live indoors in a controlled climate, some of geographical challenges are easy to counter. We may use a humidifier to counter the dryness of a Vata climate, an air conditioner to balance the heat of a Pitta climate and dry heat, like a wood stove to counter Kapha locations.

"It stays in a low level of alleviation while the food is in the stomach. Pitta increases with food in the stomach. Provoked it gets while in the small intestine, its stage of digestion and place of ultimate accumulation. Pitta gets eased when food enters the colon. Kapha increases with food in colon. It gets sufficiently provoked when in the stomach, its stage of digestion and place of ultimate accumulation. Eased it stays in the small intestine. Kapha problems appear almost immediately after eating, like nausea and vomiting. Pitta problems occur two hours later manifesting as heartburn. Vata problems occur four hours or more afterward as intestinal gas."

Dosha modes in the disease process

"Dosha types undergo accumulation at their respective primary sites. Vata accumulates in the colon, pitta in the small intestine and kapha in the stomach. With this, there arises aversion to the qualities that made them increase. In the case of vata, there comes dislike of dry, rough, light and agitated qualities with sensitivity to the wind, aversion to cold and dry food. With change in pitta come dislike of sharp, light and greasy things accompanied by aversion to sunlight or fried food. For kapha the aversion to greasy, slimy and the dull increases along with aversion to cold dairy products or fatty foods. At the same time comes desire for substances and conditions of opposite quality to the dosha, like in vata, desire for moist, soft and heavy food and longing for heat. In case of pitta there comes the wish for cool shower, cool drinks and raw food. Elevated kapha may bring about cravings for hot drinks and spices. When provoked, the dosha modes move out of their site of accumulation and invade other tissues and organs of the body causing various diseases, their return to their site of accumulation is the only way to end the vitiation. In order to alleviate the dosha types it becomes important to reverse their movement to the place that provoked it in the first place. Dosha modes accumulate like rain as it fills the Damodar River, then with all its ferocity pour over the land causing great damage. Little by little, like the receding of flood waters, the dosha levels diminish."

Other factors in dosha aggravation

"Our constitutional dosha, Prakruti outweighs the environmental factors that come from Vikriti in causing diseases. Vata people are more prone to vata diseases even if they live in a kapha climate, though the nature of the climate may regulate the disorder. Vata people tend towards vata diseases even in summer, a pitta time of the year, though the pitta nature of the season offers some moderation."

"Lifestyle and social factors being different, they outweigh environmental factors. A person who is overly active, travels a lot, does not get enough sleep, eats irregularly and otherwise follows a strict vata regimen, will tend toward vata disorders. This applies even if they are outside a vata climate and season; though these factors moderate the disorders, which may worsen in a vata season or climate. What we take internally outweighs what we expose ourselves to externally as disease causing factors. Diet is a more important factor in the increase and decrease of the dosha types than climate or season[114]."

"Mental and emotional dynamics outweigh the physical factors in producing disease. Excess of anger aggravate pitta even if the native is not pitta dominant or in a pitta climate or season. A pitta person with much anger is prone to pitta diseases when all other physical pitta factors remain passive. As human beings are primarily creatures of the mind, the body acts like a vehicle for manifesting the thoughts. Though the body does not respond to immediate thoughts, its condition is still the product of the deeper and long-term mental class. If someone went missing in wilderness for several days, with long exposure to cold and lack of food, there will come a severe vata whiplash. The duration plays an important part; whatever gets done consistently with regularity has a strong effect and influence. However strong the influence is, the original dosha still retains dominance."

"In a nutshell, the greater the mix of constitution, lifestyle, season and environment, the higher is the impact upon the dosha types. For example, a vata person living a vata lifestyle and diet, in a vata time, season and climate, and with an anxious, vata frame of mind, the stage gets set for a severe vata disorder."

---

[114] This is particularly true in the modern world where we are more insulated from environmental changes than in traditional cultures of the orient.

Six stages of disease

"One can summarize the disease process in a simple way. Dosha levels increase by aggravating factors like diet, climate, seasons, lifestyle and emotions, similar in nature to the dosha. High dosha levels weaken the digestive agni-fire. Excess kapha blocks the digestive fire by its cold and damp personality, excess vata by its cold and variable character, and excess pitta by its greasy temperament. As a result, from the weakened digestion, undigested Ama-food mass develops rapidly. Ama along with the increased dosha accumulates at the dosha's site. When provoked, it moves out and blocks the channels and becomes deposited in any weakened site in the body, from which the disease manifests."

"Vata accumulates while the food is in the small intestine, provoked while the food is in the colon, its stage of digestion and eased while the food is in the stomach. Pitta accumulates while the food is in the stomach, provoked in the small intestine, its stage of digestion and eased when it enters the colon. Kapha increases while the food is in the colon, provoked in the stomach, its stage of digestion and eased in the small intestine."

"I have heard there are six stages in a disease process. Please tell us what those stages are, and how does a disease propagate?" The student in the front row interrupted Padmalochan.

"Why, certainly! The wellness system recognizes six stages in the disease process from the point the dosha types develop to the time they move when aggravated. Dosha types accumulate, aggravate, overflow, relocate, manifest and diversify[115] to form diseases. You are familiar with first two stages where the dosha levels increase while resident in their sites. The remaining four stages transpire when they spread to other parts of the body and morph into specific diseases."

"In the first process of accumulation, the dosha level intensifies in a specific locale. It could come from bad diet, seasonal confusions, incorrect lifestyle, emotional disruption or any of the usual factors that boost the dosha's level."

---

[115] Disease Stages - Accumulation (Sanchaya), (2) Aggravation (Prakopa), (3) Overflow (Prasara), (4) Relocation (Sthana samsraya), (5) Manifestation (Vyakti) and (6) Diversification (Bheda)

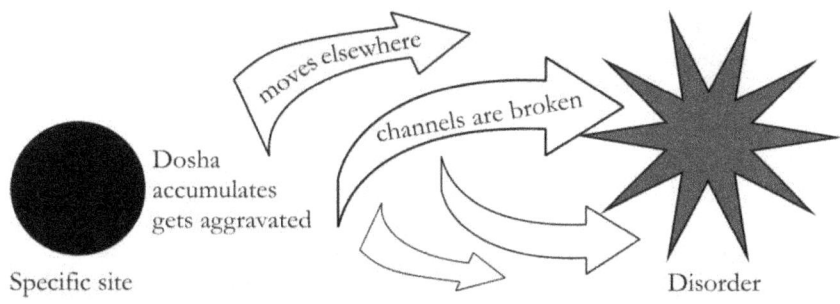

"Symptoms are mild at this stage. Level of vata grows in the colon to a point where distention, gas, constipation, insomnia, fear, fatigue, dryness and seeking of warmth show up as symptoms. Accumulation of pitta in the small intestine produces a burning sensation, fever, hyperacidity, and bitter taste in the mouth, yellow urine and stool, intense craving for cooling beverages, irritability and anger. Kapha's increase in the stomach results in feelings of lassitude, heaviness, pallor, bloating, indigestion and longing for light food. In the next activity, resulting in aggravation, dosha levels continue to intensify in their own sites, forcing the symptom levels to increase. Pressured by this accumulation, symptoms show up elsewhere in the body. Vata augments light-headedness, increased constipation, abdominal pain, spasms, further accumulation of gas, gurgling, and rumbling, squeaking noise from the abdomen, along with upper abdominal distention. Pitta boosts increased acidity, acid regurgitation, burning pain across the abdomen, too much thirst, loss of strength and insomnia. Kapha amplifies loss of appetite, indigestion, nausea and increased salivation, heaviness in the head and heart followed by oversleep."

"In the third step instigating overflow, the dosha levels reach their tipping point and overflow into other parts of the body. Dosha types enter the plasma and blood, spreading out from the gastrointestinal tract. No longer localized, the dosha types and can now penetrate organs and tissues in a damaging way. The breach, the damage is the beginning of a disease. Symptoms remain broad-spectrum and show no signs of localization. Worse, the dosha comes into close contact with tissues and waste, comingle with them, worsening the symptoms at their specific sites."

"Vata symptoms show as dry skin, pain or stiffness of the joints, lower back pain, convulsions, spasm, headache, dry cough, intermittent fever, continued abdominal pain with constipation and painful bowel movements and overall general fatigue."

"Pitta augments inflammatory skin diseases, conjunctivitis, gingivitis, dizziness, headache, high fever, bilious vomiting, and diarrhea with burning sensation. Kapha amplifies cough, difficulty in breathing, gasping for air, swollen glands, low-grade fever, vomiting, swelling of the joints and mucus in the stools."

"In the fourth phase of relocation, dosha types reposition to explicit sites in the body. Through the bloodstream, having entered the tissues, they form a new 'diseased' site with specific symptoms. Usually weak and vulnerable sites are their victims. In arthritis, dosha types redeposit themselves inside the joints and accumulate there. While the symptoms show in specific locations, however in their overflow state, the dosha types move around and fluctuate and so do their symptoms."

"In the fifth phase of disease manifestation, the dosha types demonstrate specific symptoms at certain sites. Diseases become recognizable as asthma, diabetes, arthritis, heart attack, jaundice or the medical name they go by. Symptoms of such diseases are still preliminary but more specific, and no longer just that of the dosha types moving around."

"In the last phase of diversification, at these sites, dosha types exhibit their special characteristics. The manifested disease carries the dosha signature. A native with vata-instigated arthritis evidences severe pain, cold, stiffness, dry skin and constipation. Pitta induced arthritis shows as fever, burning sensation, red swelling of the joints and loose stool. Kapha exhibits swelling, edema, phlegm and congestion. The disease undergoes its own characteristic development and indication of symptoms, like arthritis advances to bone and joints degeneration. Dosha buildup is like over seeding the backyard. A seed once deposited at a weak location in the body grows into a rogue tree."

"Is there something we can use in treating them at each stage?"

"Yes, one can tackle the problem at earlier stages or even after the damage is done. Undoing the damage at later stages is a behemoth task. As with the six stages of disease, so can one devise its treatment at each stage. While treating, it is always easier to treat the dosha types while they are resident in their sites. Disease stages of accumulation and aggravation are easier to detect and cure. The stage of overflow is the transitional stage. Even at the relocation phase, the disease is still preliminary, the vitality is still there, so treatment is not that difficult but needs perseverance."

"The last two stages present a completely developed disease. A mature disease takes much time and effort to rectify. Once it becomes part of the person's nature and life, it requires a major change of lifestyle to bring things back to normal. Developed diseases take months, often years of natural therapy to ease or cure, the life force disrupted by the disease, may harbor it."

"Yes, all diseases are easy to treat at the dosha site of accumulation, even if we cannot measure the stage, degree and diversification of the disease, we can still treat the dosha levels in an effective way. Dosha accumulation phase in the whole process is the root of all diseases, something medical astrology can predict. The practitioner can forewarn a native when he sees an overdose of the elements in the Dasa, pinpointed by transits in the person's chart. An old aphorism, 'to be forewarned is being forearmed' is so true here. Knowing a dosha-bearing planet or combinations of planets, signs and houses are around the corner is a big blessing. The longer the dosha gets to accumulate, it will just keep getting worse. Stopping its accumulation is the key. Knowing when it begins to accumulate beforehand is the silver-weapon."

Diseases traverse three different pathways[116]

"An inner disease pathway formed from an otherwise normal digestive tract starts from the mouth to the anus. This pathway referred to as inner is not because it occurs inside the tissues and organs, but because the digestive tract forms a channel inside the body. Diseases here are easy to treat from the ease in dispelling them directly out of the body through the digestive tract, the main route for eliminating all toxins. Besides, dosha types live in the digestive tract in their states of accumulation and provocation."

"Outer disease pathway includes the plasma, skin and blood, and the superficial tissues. These are closer to the body exterior. Diseases here are more difficult to treat, as they are deep rooted in the tissues, like skin diseases, lymphatic problems and toxic blood conditions. Dosha types enter this pathway in their overflow state and remain deposited here."

---

[116] Disease Pathways - (1) Outer (Bahya marga), (2) Inner (Antar marga) and (3) Central (Madhyama marga)

"Central disease pathway comprises the deeper tissues of muscle, fat, bone, bone marrow, nerves and reproductive network. The texts refer to it as the 'middle disease pathway' because it lies between the outer and the inner pathway. Sensitive points and organs of the body such as the head, heart, bladder, genitals, joints and bones lie in this pathway. Diseases here are extremely deep-seated and the painfully difficult to treat. Most severe, chronic and degenerative diseases come from this area - everything from cancer, heart attacks, and asthma to arthritis. Dosha types occupy this area only after spreading through the superficial tissues. Diseases that occur in this pathway feature toxins that have embedded themselves into the deepest recesses of the body-tissues."

"Outer and central disease pathways capture seven important tissues of the body; skin and blood as outer, and muscle, fat, bone, marrow and reproductive fluid in the middle. A majority of milder kapha diseases, affecting mainly the inner pathway of the digestive tract, some invading the plasma are known and catalogued. Also known are Pitta-diseases, moderate in effect, which damage the outer pathway that of the blood. The list of vata diseases is long, they are severe and damage the deeper tissues, particularly bones and nerves."

"How do the diseases move through these pathways? Can they be stopped or their progress reversed?"

"Several factors instigate diseases to move from the digestive tract to the tissues. Strenuous workout, high temperature or sharp food, bad life-regimen and transportation provided by vata are the major causes. These conditions provide easy transportation for heightened dosha types to enter the tissues as they open the channels. There are techniques to reverse their progress. The diseases can be moved back from the inner tissues to the digestive tract by cleansing the channel-openings with oil and perspiration therapies, and controlling vata through breath-control, pranayama and adopting the right life-regimen. They provide the necessary means to drain the disease factors from the channels."

"One important thing to remember that disorders occur at two levels, physical and mental. The mental occurrence of disease outweighs and triggers the physical, the physical in-turn influences the mental. Besides, ailments are under constant influence of external factors like exposure to heat and cold, and internal factors such as dosha imbalances, or Rajas and Tamas play on the mind. External factors trigger most diseases and internal imbalances make the person vulnerable to the external factors."

"Twofold are diseases, some caused by others and remaining self-caused. Those caused by others are largely external additionally incorporating elements like sex and violence. The diseases owed to the self, include those coming from the dosha types and guna vectors. Twofold are diseases in their formation from physiological and spiritual factors. Physiological factors are the three-dosha types and spiritual factors come from negative karma, which may stem from an earlier incarnation not usually amenable to purely physical remedies. Many diseases combine the two factors."

Disease as a state model

1. Diseases have a cause, *Hetu*
2. Diseases show preliminary signs, *Purva Rupa*
3. Diseases show primary signs, *Rupa*
4. Diseases come through pathogenesis, *Samprapti*
5. Diseases can be relieved when symptoms are unbearable, *Upasaya*
6. Diseases get aggravated, and exception to relief, *Anupasaya*

"Disease is four-footed, rather four-factored, which yield two possible results. The cause of disease lies in the factors that increase the dosha types. Preliminary signs manifest between the stages of overflow and deposition, likely the signs of the excess dosha types trying to relocate to a specific site. The primary signs become obvious at the manifestation stage. After this, the disease may get better or worse."

"There are five ways of knowing a disease[117], from the cause, the preliminary signs, primary signs, pathological changes and the means to relief. Treatment sometimes can become a part of diagnosis, if we try a remedy to ease a condition and it fails, it narrows the possibility of the condition. Such preliminary or exploratory treatments are part of all systems of medicine. The important thing is that it leads us to a greater understanding of the disease. When beginning the treatment, it is always beneficial to try exploratory treatments, giving tentatively, in a short term, reduced manner or lower dosage, what you as practitioner think may improve the condition. With such a limited application, only enough of the therapy gets endeavored to see if it helps the native, but not enough to harm the native if it turns out to be wrong. The important thing is to ascertain the degree and attributes of the aggravating dosha."

---

[117] These five phases relate to the five ways of knowing a disease (pancha nidana).

"Texts tell us that treatment like disease is four-limbed[118], comprising the practitioner, practitioner's assistant, the remedy and the native or the person. If flawed are any of the limbs, the treatment will not see success. Practitioner must be knowledgeable, experienced and practical in approach. Remedy must be appropriate to the disease, taken in the right manner, in the right dosage and for the right duration. Assistant must be competent and compassionate. Native must have faith in the treatment and the means to carry it out which may require money to pay for the treatment."

"We arrive at four possible prognoses of a disease. Disease may be (1) easy to cure, (2) difficult to cure, (3) not curable, where there is possibility of relief and reduction of symptoms and (4) simply incurable[119]. Diseases are easy to cure if they comprise a different class from the predominant constitutional dosha of the native, like a kapha disease in a pitta constitution. Such diseases are easy to cure if they do not involve tissues and waste materials of the same type as the dosha, not influenced by climate, season, work or other environmental factors. Mild symptoms, new condition, not a reoccurrence, and a resourceful native motivated to follow the therapy to the end complete the picture. Even better if the disease gets confined to one dosha, one channel and one disease pathway, preferably the inner pathway or digestive tract. Diseases are difficult to cure if their type turns out to be the same as the native's constitution, like a vata condition of arthritis in a vata person."

"If outer conditions are at play, the symptoms severe, the condition recurring and disease involves more than one dosha or channel and found to have invaded the outer or middle disease pathways, it poses big challenges in curing the disease. Such complications are seen in diseases of pregnant women, young children, elderly people or those in convalescence from another disease. Their vitality to combat virulent attacks is missing. Lack of resources or motivation from the native also makes a condition difficult to treat. Symptomatic relief is available for congenital, chronic and degenerative diseases like rheumatoid arthritis in an aged person, Diseases requiring major surgery, even those that have suffered severe tissue damage like loss of an organ or deformation of the bones come under this category. Often the vitality or Ojas of the native defies any attempts to rebuild, wherein a symptomatic relief goes a long way to decrease the trauma[120]."

---

[118] Astanga Hridayam 1.27 bhisagh dravya nyupsthata rogi padchatushtyam | chikitsitasya nirdishtinam pratyekam ta ccgrunam ||

[119] Astanga Hridayam 1.30-1.31 Susadhya (easily curable), krichasadhya (curable, with some difficulty), Sadhya (curable), Asadhya (incurable), yapya (controllable) and anupahrama (no response to any therapy, fatal).

[120] Astanga Hridayam, 1.32-1.33. Surgery and terminal diseases.

"Incurable diseases involve almost every conceivable dosha type, where the deeper tissues are affected in an irreversible way, where vitality and Ojas have near collapsed, and in which there are signs of imminent death, or the native has given up the will to live."

"Claiming cures for every disease is walking the vanity lane. Such claims are useless as many disorders are not curable, until divine intervention proves otherwise. The body made of mutable material, produced by time is vulnerable to disease and decay. Once the structure undergoes radical damages, once the cumulative effect of time, destiny and karma reaches a certain threshold, destruction becomes inevitable. In most cases, we get to work with situations that show some signs of responding to treatment. To be an effective practitioner does not warrant treating the most impossible disorder, but rather to know how to prevent the disease from happening."

"Does it mean the disease is the same as the dosha? By knowing the dosha, can we determine the disease?" The student asked as Padmalochan paused for a break.

"Diseases are not always the same as a dosha out of balance. Dosha in many diseases is an adjective to the disease, like a pitta-heart-problem, a vata-dementia, and kapha-arthritis. Just as we learn to determine an individual's constitution, so we must be able to ascertain the specific nature and type of the diseases they suffer, in other words an 'examination of disease'[121]. In treating diseases, we must learn to discover their location, stage and strength."

"Dosha types, as the underlying forces and factors of the body are a dual miscreant. Not only are they the factors that cause disease, they also hand out the sites where diseases can occur, especially the tissues, organs and systems they rule. Dosha levels of three types when their levels run too high begin to damage one another and they all become imbalanced eventually. We must be careful as practitioners in incriminating dosha types, as a dosha type may just be an innocent bystander at the disease scene. Like a disease involving the nervous system may have vata dosha at the site. Such a disease is commonly vata, but in this case, may be a pitta or kapha type. Vata may not be the miscreant, may be just present in a pitta or kapha disorder site. We must still record the vata presence in nervous disease case, even though pitta and kapha cause the problem, there may be aspects of vata involved."

---

[121] Vikriti Pariksha or examination of the disease

"Usually, a dosha aggravates the factors it rules; it owns the site and acts the causative agent in the disease process. High kapha may damage the lungs, a kapha organ. An excess dosha may use a disease site belonging to another dosha, representing a nasty condition where the dosha having damaged its own sites, is at the stage of spreading and overflowing. Like the high kapha after damaging the lungs, may damage the nervous system in the aftermath, resulting in asthmatic wheezing or epilepsy with phlegm, blocking the subtle channels and affecting vata. Other dosha types tend to damage vata, producing diseases of the bones, nervous system and the mind, since vata rules the deeper tissues and energies. Dosha types affect each other and in severe diseases, all three dosha types may become out of balance, rendering the treatment extremely difficult."

"To identify the diseases of the dosha types, the practitioner must recognize their attributes. Dosha types exhibit many symptoms when aggravated or elevated. Vata when aggravated, shows signs of collapse, spasms, piercing pain, numbness, depression, breaking, striking and biting pain, constipation, cracking of the joints, contraction, retention of waste materials in the body, excitability, thirst, trembling, roughness of skin, porosity of tissues, dehydration, agitated movement, stiffness, astringent taste in mouth, and dark or reddish brown discolorations. The symptoms exhibit the drying, disruptive and agitating powers of the wind, the derangement of nerve impulses, and tissue deficiency combined with excess movement and hypersensitivity."

"Pitta when aggravated comes with burning sensation, redness, heat, boils, perspiration, pus, bleeding, necrosis, exhaustion, fainting, inebriation, pungency, sour taste in the mouth, display all colors but white and brown. It exhibits symptoms of burning, boiling, fermenting action, and colors of fire."

"Aggravated kapha brings about phlegm, tissue hardening, itching, cold sensation on the skin, heaviness, congestion, obesity, edema, indigestion, excessive sleep, white color, sweet and saline tastes in the mouth which emerge slowly. All these reflect the symptomatic heaviness, torpor, pallor and stagnation of water."

"Low dosha level is not so significant in accelerating a disease. The practitioner may want to know their signs to identify the nature of conditions. Low vata causes lassitude of the limbs, speech deficiency, lack of enthusiasm, sensory confusion as well as an increase in phlegm along with production of toxins. Low vata resembles high Kapha, restricting the native's movement, making him dull, heavy and desensitized."

"Insufficient pitta weakens the digestive fire, carrying in cold and lack of luster. Low pitta resembles both high vata and kapha levels. Pronounced are the symptoms of severe coldness with poor metabolism, appetite and reduced circulation."

"Low kapha level creates empty feelings in the stomach, palpitations and loosening of the joints. Insufficient kapha level resembles high vata. Stability and firmness in the tissues get reduced, the mind and emotions become ungrounded."

"Only high dosha levels spur a disease, at low levels they become powerless to begin the disease process. This is an important observation. If the skin is dry and cold, but no cough or fever, chances are pitta is low, and it is not a high vata case. I present you this table which in a nutshell gives the symptoms that each of the three dosha types contribute towards. You may add these to constitutional examination enabling better elucidation."

Symptoms of aggravated dosha types

	Vata	Pitta	Kapha
Pain and trauma	Most severe; throbbing, biting, churning, beating, tearing, variable, migratory, colicky, intermittent	Medium; burning, steaming	Least; heavy, dull, constant
	Pain is perhaps the unbearable characteristic of all diseases. As vata ailments are more severe, they involve more trauma. Strong, sharp, shocking and disruptive appear in vata disorders. For pitta, pain is accompanied with swelling, bleeding and burning; for kapha pain with feelings of dullness, heaviness, congestion and stagnation dominate. Pain gets severe when channels are blocked and there are clear signs of wrong movement in the channels.		
Fever	Moderate temperature, variable or irregular fever, thirst, anxiety, restlessness	Highest temperature, burning sensation, thirst, perspiration, irritability, delirium	Low grade fever, dullness, heaviness, constant temperature
	Fever is the feared the most in all diseases and in traditional cultures the main killer. Fever is more significant in Pitta disorders and is their main characteristic, along with other heat sensations like inflammation, infection and burning sensation. Acute fever is more pitta like. Constant fever at low temperature is more kapha. Irregular, intermittent or variable fever is more vata.		
Discharges	Gas, sound	Bleeding, yellow pus, bile	Mucus, whitish pus, water, salivation

	Vata	Pitta	Kapha
The main characteristic of Kapha disorders is excess discharges particularly phlegm, water as in watery skin sores or rashes and pus, mainly white in color. Pitta also causes an increase of discharges, including Perspiration, bile in the system, bleeding and pus with toxins in the blood. Vata has the least discharges as it is subtler in nature, mainly intestinal gas or other noises, cracking of the joints, or moaning and sighing, which are all discharges of Vata.			
Color (as in complexion, discharges and discolorations)	Black, brown, blue black, blue, pink, decrease or absence of normal color	Red, purple, yellow, green, black, smoky	White, pale
Pitta causes bright discolorations, Vata dark discolorations and Kapha pale discolorations. The color of pitta usually reflects excess bile or blood. Color of kapha reflects excess water or phlegm; that of Vata reflects excess gas or decay of tissues. Discolorations are more typical of pitta disorders.			
Mouth Taste	Astringent taste, dry	Bitter or pungent taste, increased salivation	Sweet or saline taste, profuse salivation, mucous discharges
High Vata dries out the mouth and causes cracked lips. Pitta causes thirst and burning sensation with possible greasiness in the mouth. Kapha causes increased salivation or mucous in the mouth.			
Throat	Dry, rough, pain and constriction of esophagus	Sore throat, inflammation, burning sensation	Swelling, dilation, edema
Vata causes dry throat and difficulty swallowing, with possible chronic dry cough. Pitta causes swelling and sore throat. Kapha causes accumulation of mucus in the throat.			
Stomach	Decreased secretions, irregular appetite, frequent eructation like belching, hiccup, sense of constriction	Excessive appetite, sour or pungent eructation, burning sensation, ulcers, cancer	Slow digestion, sweet or mucoid eructation
Heartburn, hyperacidity or burning stomach pain relates primarily to pitta. Nausea, feeling of heaviness and vomiting are characteristic of kapha, or eating too much kapha food. Vata causes irregular peristalsis, and dryness in the stomach.			
Liver and Gall Bladder	Dry, rough, scanty secretions, irregular activity	Soft, excessive bile production, gall stones, inflammation, abscesses, increased activity	Enlarged, heavy, firm, scanty bile, decreased activity
Most pain in the liver and gall bladder area is due to high pitta. Kapha causes heaviness and stagnation in the area. Vata causes dryness and atrophy.			
Intestines	Dry, peristalsis disorders, distention, gas, constipation	Profuse secretions, quick peristalsis, inflammation, ulceration, abscess, tumors, cancer, bleeding, perforation	Mucus coating, slow peristalsis, obstruction, distention, edema, tumors
Intestinal gas and irregular movements relate to vata. Inflammation and bleeding relates to pitta. Heaviness, congestion and phlegm relates to kapha.			

	Vata	Pitta	Kapha
Feces	Constipation, painful and difficult bowel movements, dry, small in quantity	Diarrhea, watery stools, quick or uncontrollable evacuation, burning sensation, increased frequency, moderate amount	Solid, decreased frequency, large amount, containing mucus, with itching

In vata diseases, constipation and gas occur along with nervousness, dryness and lack of vitality. While in pitta diseases, diarrhea is common, often with burning sensations. Under kapha conditions, mucus discharges increase, along with slower and more difficult elimination.

	Vata	Pitta	Kapha
Urine	Scanty, difficult to discharge, increased frequency or absence of urination, colorless	Profuse, with burning sensation, increased frequency, yellow, turbid, brown or red colored	Profuse, increased frequency, mucoid, white or pale

Pitta diseases usually bring on increased urination along with thirst. Vata diseases have scanty, difficult urination accompanied by thirst. Kapha ailments indicate thickened urine.

	Vata	Pitta	Kapha
Sweat	Scanty, irregular, inability	Profuse, hot	Moderate, constant

Vata diseases cause poor peripheral circulation and lack of lubrication to the skin. Pitta diseases bring about Perspiration to relieve heat. Kapha diseases may increase Perspiration as water overflowing the tissues.

	Vata	Pitta	Kapha
Mind And Senses	Delusion, fear, apathy, sorrow, loss of consciousness, insomnia, desire for hot and dislike of cold things	Weakness of senses, intoxication, restlessness, violent emotions, delirium, loss of sleep, dizziness, fainting, desire for cold things	Slow perception, lack of desire, lethargy, stupor, excessive sleeping, desire for hot things

Vata type persons lose coordination of the senses and calm of mind, along with restlessness, feelings of being ungrounded, disorientation and anxiety. Pitta types feel agitated, with heat in the head, dizziness, and difficult or painful vision. Kapha types become dull, unresponsive and inert.

	Vata	Pitta	Kapha
Onset Rate of Disease	Rapid, variable, irregular	Medium, with fever	Slow, constant

Persons with vata dosha can quickly come down with diseases or quickly experience changes in their condition. Pitta diseases start with high fevers. Kapha diseases develop slowly out of congestion and stagnation.

"Ama accumulations influence the toxic condition of dosha types. Undigested food mass, Ama collects in the digestive tract where it shows its symptoms from absence of taste and appetite, indigestion, bad breath, thick tongue coating, expectoration of sticky phlegm or saliva, distention of the chest or abdomen with pain on palpation, general feeling of heaviness, tiredness or scarcity of strength, and dullness of the mind and senses. Other symptoms include buildup of waste, constipation, shortage of sweat, difficulty urinating, channel blockage along with a deep, dull or slippery 'nadi' pulse reading."

"Ama has similar tendencies of kapha. Cold, damp, heavy, thick and sticky, Ama is also turbid and fermentative. Diet and some external factors aggravate Ama. Meat, heavy food, mucus-laden food, oil massage, application of pressure and overcast weather instigates Ama. It combines with the dosha types, altering their attributes. Ama suppresses the digestive fire; lack of digestion increases Ama, leading to a vicious accumulation. Upon increasing Agni, Ama gets counteracted. Ama gets involved with the dosha buildups at their specific sites, commencing the disease process. Diseases owe to Ama production. However, as the dosha types enter deeper tissues, Ama formation becomes a lesser problem. To extract the dosha types from the deeper tissues, eliminating Ama becomes a priority. The rule of treatment is to turn Ama to non-Ama state and then discharge the excess dosha from the body. Wherever dosha types go along with Ama, the phenomenon gets termed as 'Sama' from 'sa' prefixed to 'ama', meaning 'with Ama'. In situations where dosha types persist without Ama is termed 'Nirama' from the word 'nir' meaning 'without'."

"There are many diseases featuring Nirama and Sama. Nirama settings are simpler to treat than Sama, there being no Ama to remove. Ama combines with vata to augment dullness, heaviness and fullness, along with regular vata syndromes, while Ama combines with pitta to create heaviness and dullness, with more dampness and less heat than regular pitta symptoms. Combining Ama with kapha increases the attributes and makes the combination toxic."

"Sama vata, where vata conditions have Ama toxins present, shows as brown coatings on the tongue, particularly in the back of the tongue, bad breath, abdominal pain, distention, gas formation and constipation. Strong are the feelings of heaviness, dullness and fatigue, along with disorientation. Nirama vata symptoms include no tongue coating, but dry or cracked tongue, normal appetite, no constipation, dry mouth with astringent aftertaste, thirst, dehydration, the body light and dry with emaciation, less heaviness and fatigue."

"Sama pitta shows as yellow and greasy coatings on the tongue, bad breath, little thirst, loss of appetite, bitter or sour taste in the mouth, tightness in the abdomen region, mild burning sensations, yellow urine and feces, and clouded perception. Nirama pitta indications are increased appetite and thirst, red or inflamed tongue, clear tongue, strong burning sensations, normal urine and feces, clear, acute perception and tissue depletion."

"Sama kapha shows as thick white tongue coating covered in mucus, mucus in the saliva, and saline or sour taste in the mouth. Throat and sinuses may experience blockages or congestion. Other symptoms include congested tight and painful chest, mucus in the stool and urine, chest mucus is thick, sticky, white and difficult to expectorate. Nirama Kapha does not affect the appetite or tongue coating, but exhibits sweet taste in the mouth, no mucus in the stool or urine, and no pain on palpation. The mucus is clear, watery and easy to discharge."

"When Ama ferments, it spawns heat and fever[122], exhibiting symptoms of greasy tongue coat, heaviness and fatigue, combined with elevated body temperature, inflammation, infections and pus. Many chronic diseases exhibit symptoms of rheumatoid arthritis. The Ama sustains a low-grade fever. When we observe someone with signs of debility plus Ama, we must first clear the Ama before trying to restore their strength. Ama needs reduction before any tonic-invigoration or nutritive therapy can proceed."

"Ama's qualities are contrary to Agni, the digestive fire. Reinstating and balancing the Agni, Ama ceases to occur. Main treatment for Ama is increasing or balancing Agni with different herbs and spices, light diet or fasting."

"Ama while opposing Agni associates with Apana Vayu increasing waste and Ama production when aggravated. Reducing Ama often involves reducing Apana Vayu and removing the excess waste with laxative herbs. Along with Apana's connection to the bones, Ama easily invades the bone tissue punishing them with arthritis, which gets experienced as Ama in Vata. Anti-arthritic herbs and practices, induced perspiration involving Svedana decrease Ama. Increasing prana is another method that can not only cut Apana but also lessen Ama. Breathing using pranayama techniques is a great tool for Ama-reduction. People having high Ama suffer from obstructed breath and poor circulation."

"From another viewpoint, we could say Ama and Ojas have opposing natures. Ojas is the source and repository of life and healing. It sustains the organic integrity of the body and prevents foreign matter aggregation whether as waste or undigested food particles. Ama is the source and repository of decay and death. It represents the build-up of foreign matter in the body outside the control of the life force. Ama decreases Ojas, low Ojas allows Ama to accumulate. It becomes essential to remove Ama in the cleanup process before rebuilding Ojas."

---

[122] Ama jvara or Ama fever

"Using the thumb rule of 80-40-20, eighty vata, forty pitta types and twenty kapha diseases totaling one hundred forty appear in the wellness catalog. Vata accounts for the highest number and majority severe diseases, kapha the least, with pitta in the median. The key to classifying diseases is to observe not only the dosha, but also the tissue affected by it."

"While the dosha in excess takes active part in the disease process, damage to the dhatu-s[123] becomes the next effect of disease. This mixing of dosha types and dhatu-s is the secret sauce to diagnosis and treatment. Deeper into the seven tissues, the dosha types penetrate, greater the damage they bring. Remember, accumulation of dosha occurs in the inner disease pathway or digestive tract[124]. From there dosha types move into the outer disease pathway[125], the plasma and blood. This gives them access to the central disease pathway[126] where they can enter the deep tissues and vital organs and trigger debilitating and life-threatening disorders."

"Now you understand why diseases in deeper tissues like bone, marrow or reproductive fluid are so difficult to treat. In the reproductive tissue, they often involve the collapse of Ojas and the immune system."

Vata in the dhatu-s

"Vata moves from its site of accumulation in the large intestine and enters the seven tissues using the bloodstream. Having vata in the plasma[127] vitiates the skin. It causes dry skin, along with roughness or cracking and black and brown skin discoloration."

"Vata also prevents perspiration; it tightens and constricts the skin turning it cold besides weakening the peripheral circulation. Apparent become the signs of prickly pain, itchiness and numbness of the skin. Dry skin diseases, psoriasis, eczema, and dry scabies, influenza, dry cough and vata type fevers are the result."

---

[123] Damage to the dhatus - dushya.
[124] Inner disease pathway is the 'antar marga'.
[125] Outer disease pathway is 'bahya marga'.
[126] Central disease pathway is 'madhyama marga'
[127] Vata in the plasma or Rasagata Vata.

"Vata in the blood[128] damages and dries out blood and its vessels, affecting the circulation and making the varicose veins bulge. The body suffers easy bruising, palpitations become noticeable along with blood clots and hardening of the arteries. Additional symptoms involve cold extremities and slow healing of sores, wounds and slow ripening of boils. Disease conditions involving varicose veins, gout, heart diseases and hypertension transpire in such circumstances."

"Vata entering muscles[129] dries and depletes them resulting in emaciation, muscle weakness and deterioration. It also produces muscle rigidity, spasms, tremors, twitching, and cramps in the muscles, sometimes paralysis. The extremities feel heavy with lack of coordination and flexibility in movement. Diseases such as muscle paralysis, dry, hard tumors in the muscles occur."

"Vata in the fat or adipose tissue[130] dries and depletes them, resulting in emaciation, dry skin, inability to sweat, sinking of the eyes, thirst and lower back pain. The spleen or kidneys may become enlarged. Diabetes of vata type may occur; other deteriorating diseases like tuberculosis may also strike. Fatty tumors like small, dry or hard lipoma may manifest."

"Vata in the bone[131] weakens and wastes the bone tissue, making bones brittle, enabling easy and spontaneous fractures, imposing osteoporosis and pain infiltrating the bones. Pain and sensitivity of the teeth, cavities in the teeth, brittle nails and hair with teeth and hair falling are common. Dominant diseases are arthritis, osteoarthritis, rheumatoid arthritis, osteoporosis and bone tumors."

"Vata invading the marrow[132] dries and depletes it, weakening the nerves, triggering nerve pain, tremors, convulsions, coma and paralysis. Pain or cracking of the joints, dizziness, and blurred vision and ringing in the ears, along with nervousness, insomnia, and feelings of emptiness, fear and anxiety. Diseases include neurasthenia, neuralgia, sciatica, epilepsy, multiple sclerosis or tumors in the nerve tissue."

---

[128] Vata in the blood or Raktagata Vata.
[129] Vata in the muscles namely Mamsagata Vata.
[130] Vata in the fat or adipose tissue namely Medogata Vata.
[131] Vata in the bone namely Asthigata Vata.
[132] Vata in the marrow namely Majjagata Vata.

"Vata entering the reproductive fluid[133] causes it to wither, bringing about sexual debility, impotence, infertility and sterility. Difficult or painful sexual intercourse results from shortages in proper secretions. In women, it deranges the hormonal cycle, triggering difficult periods, scanty flow, sometimes ceasing menstruation altogether. For men, the sperm count gets low and amount of sperm produced is deficient. It has a tremendous psychological impact pushing the native to the brink of nervousness, fear, anxiety, lack of love and suicidal feelings. Other diseases involve swollen prostate and testes in men, breast or uterine cysts and tumors in women, usually the hard and dry kind. The immune system shows signs of collapse along with failure in vitality."

Pitta in the dhatu-s

"Pitta, from its site of accumulation in the small intestine, or from the liver and gall bladder, enters the bloodstream and invades the tissues. With pitta in plasma[134], skin foregoes damages, instigating searing sensations on the skin and promoting red, blue or yellow skin pigmentation. It produces many inflammatory skin diseases and rashes including acne, dermatitis, urticaria, psoriasis, eczema and others where the skin turns red, hot and greasy. Besides, it fuels high fever, accompanied with thirst and perspiration, and conditions such as influenza, bronchitis, measles, mumps, chicken pox and herpes, with swollen, inflamed lymph glands."

"Pitta entering the blood[135] heats it up and propels it to flow faster, producing burning sensations in hands and feet, along with flushing and hot flashes. It decreases the ability for blood to clot; body sores heal slowly from blood soaked pitta. It promotes bleeding involving epistaxis, hematemesis, hemoptysis and even hemophilia. Liver spleen disorders such as jaundice and hepatitis can strike. Inflammatory skin diseases involving plasma appear with redness, bleeding and pus. Boils, carbuncles, abscesses result with toxic blood conditions in the body accompanied by high fever."

---

[133] Vata in the reproductive fluid namely Shukragata Vata.
[134] Pitta in the plasma namely Rasagata Pitta.
[135] Pitta in the blood namely Raktagata Pitta.

"Pitta invading the muscle[136] produces inflammation and abscesses in the muscle tissue. Symptoms of bursitis and tendonitis in the voluntary muscles are rampant. In the smooth muscles, as in the gastrointestinal tract, pitta causes ulcerations, gastritis, stomach inflammation, enteritis, intestinal inflammation, colitis, colon inflammation, appendicitis, gingivitis and inflammation of the gums. In cardiac muscles, symptoms of myocarditis and coronary heart disease appear. There are clear signs of fever, swelling and pain."

"Pitta in the fat or adipose tissue[137] burns and infects the fat tissue, producing abscesses and tumors in the fat tissue and sebaceous glands. Profuse perspiration, thirst, excess urination and dehydration accompany such situation. Kidney infections whether acute or severe with blood in the urine can strike along with pitta induced diabetes and other degenerative diseases."

"Pitta entering the bone[138] infects and inflames the bone tissue. Such pitta conditions of damp heat with much redness and pain, arthritis, periostitis, osteomyelitis with burning pain strike the bones and joints. Deep abscesses appear in the bones. Greying or balding of the hair are possible along with deep nail infections."

"Pitta in the marrow[139] propels many inflammatory diseases of the nerve and bone marrow. These involve neuritis, encephalitis, meningitis and sciatica. Bone marrow suffers burns and depletion resulting in anemia. Nerve tissue may face burns triggering neurasthenia. Heat moves to the head and eyes, setting off dizziness, headache, anger and irritability. In such conditions, perception may become overly sharp and painful."

"Pitta in the reproductive fluid[140] produces inflammation and burning of the reproductive fluid. Uterine bleeding, infections, tumors, even cancer are seen in women, accompanied by hot, excess, painful menstruation, excessively frequent periods, sometimes bleeding in between. In men, the conditions show up as infected, swollen testes and prostate, along with fever and blood in the sperm. Just about everything needed for the immune system to collapse."

---

[136] Pitta in the muscle namely Mamsagata Pitta.
[137] Pitta in the fat or adipose tissue namely Medogata Pitta.
[138] Pitta in the bone namely Asthigata Pitta.
[139] Pitta in the marrow namely Majjagata Pitta.
[140] Pitta in the reproductive fluid namely Shukragata Pitta.

Kapha in the dhatu-s

"Kapha travels from its site of accumulation in the stomach and enters the bloodstream and tissues from there. Kapha in the plasma[141] triggers many phlegmatic diseases of the skin and lungs. The skin gets pale, white, cold, damp and thick. Several skin diseases with dampness can strike along with fungus infections, warts, cysts and damp kind of eczema. Edema, facial or subcutaneous, is possible, besides congested lungs accompanied by fever, cough and swollen glands. Such conditions include influenza, bronchitis and asthma. Nausea, scarcity of appetite and feelings of heaviness of the body and heart ensue."

"Kapha in the blood[142] triggers phlegmatic diseases of the blood and heart, resulting in poor circulation, cold extremities, thickened veins and pale, sticky, viscous and stagnant blood. Cholesterol levels run high along with arteriosclerosis and hypertension. Blood begins to clot along with narrowing of the coronary artery, leading to heart attacks; besides anemia, enlargement of the liver and spleen, jaundice, congestion of the bile and soft type gallstones episodes."

"Kapha invading the muscles[143] produces various congestive diseases of the muscle tissue, accompanied by swelling of the muscles, difficulty in movement, heaviness, rigidity, lethargy and lack of muscle tone. Tumors and chronic ulcers run rampant along with uterine tumors. Possibility of enlarged heart along with cardiac edema runs high. Earwax occurs in plenty."

"Kapha in the fat tissue[144] produces an excess of fat as in obesity, edema and fatty tumors, heaviness and fatigue. Kidney disorders, chronic infections, albuminuria and diabetes are possible. Spleen-pancreas action may be weakened. The sweat stays cold, sticky and slimy. Kapha in the bone[145] produces excess and congestion of the bone tissue. Bones are heavy, joints swollen remain damp escorted by watery or kapha type arthritis with chronic low-grade bone infections. Extra bones, bone spurs or extra teeth may occur, along with bone tumors. Nails and hair have stubbed and thick growth."

---

[141] Kapha in the plasma namely Rasagata Kapha.
[142] Kapha in the blood implying Raktagata Kapha.
[143] Kapha in the muscles implying Mamsagata Kapha.
[144] Kapha in the fat tissue namely Medogata Kapha.
[145] Kapha in the bone namely Asthigata Kapha.

"Kapha in the marrow[146] results in congestive disorders of the marrow and nerve tissue supplemented by swelling and painful loosening of the joints. There is lack of nerve sensitivity, dullness of the senses, numbness and lethargy, along with low-grade nerve infections. Other possible manifestations are tumors in the nerve tissue like neuroma, hydrocephalus with excess water in the brain and many nervous system disorders like multiple sclerosis, along with the blocking of the nerve channels."

"Kapha in the reproductive fluid[147] disrupts the reproductive system, signifying sexual debility, infertility and impotence. In women with such kapha disorders, common are uterine tumors, cysts or polyps, possibly ectopic pregnancy or endometriosis, with thick leucorrhea or a cold, damp uterus. For men, it shows as swollen prostate and testes. The semen produced is cold, thick and in excess. Fortunately, the possibility of cancer is low, as tumors are benign. The immune system stays unresponsive with poor resistance to common cold and influenza. Energy runs low, prominently showing lack of motivation and degenerated metabolism."

Three methods of pinpointing the problem

"Diagnostic approaches are three, observation and visitation[148], touch and feel,[149] and query[150]. In most cases, the practitioner can arrive at a diagnosis with the three. A quick examination of the tongue, eyes, skin and nails reveals the dosha imbalances providing many a clue to the diagnosis. Observing their movement and talk, body posture, facial expressions reveal the state of disorder. Pulse reading and palpation of the abdomen confirm the state of the insides. The query can extend to medical history once the native conveys the immediate problems. Specific questions on appetite, digestion, elimination, urination, sweat, menstruation, sexual function, general energy level, susceptibility to disease like immune system function and others play an important role in personalizing the wellness. A word of caution, we cannot entirely trust the person to know what their condition is or to report properly on how their body is functioning. Querying requires facts from the native, not his interpretation.[151]"

---

[146] Kapha in the marrow namely Majjagata Kapha.
[147] Kapha in the reproductive fluid namely Shukragata Kapha.
[148] Observation and visitation – Darshana
[149] Touch and feel - Sparshana
[150] Query – Prashnana
[151] Astanga Hridayam, 2.25-2.28

"General examination comprises the anatomical and mental constitution. Complete examination hovers around dosha types, tissues, waste materials, systems and organs of the body, and the state of the mind and prana. It is a better practice to profile each organ, tissue and system as strong or weak, balanced or imbalanced relative to which dosha types are affecting it the most."

Disease busters

"All examinations begin with the inherent constitution or Prakruti. The body frame of the native, conditions of limbs, complexion, general strength and activity, tendency to heat and cold are the easiest to observe. The appetite tells a lot about the state of digestive fire, circulation and condition of waste, so does diet and eating habits show the long-term metabolic tendencies and potential imbalances. The pulse, tongue, abdomen, speech, memory, sleep, dreams reveal the state of Prana, Tejas and Ojas. A more extensive examination involves checking each of the dosha types, tissues, waste materials, channel systems, vital organs, sense organs, organs of action and emotion, ego and reason, mental faculties. Whenever someone gets treated, a clear diagnosis needs to be its outcome. The diagnosis may extend to show all other problems, though it is preferable to treat one thing at a time, unless they are all related."

"Narrowing down the inherent, primary constitution, the practitioner must rapidly start examining the present situation, diseased, altered state of Vikriti. The focus shifts to the just the disease condition, not the underlying constitution. All questioning converges on the disease nature and onset, its symptoms, sensitivities and development; the condition unique to this disease, in contrast to what is usual or normal for the individual. Changes in appetite, thirst, elimination, urination, temperature sensitivity and energy level shows the disease progress. Astrology can time the onset of the disease, whether chronic or acute and narrow down the recovery. Underlying dosha imbalance must be ascertained, and if reinforced by the predominant dosha of the individual. Main symptom in the disease such as pain, fever, infection or fatigue must also be noted. The conditions, whether Sama or Nirama, whether toxins need removal from the digestive tract must be determined. The stage the disease is in from one to six, along with the disease pathway and what tissues, waste materials, systems and organs involved, and anxiety and fear form the basis of prognosis."

"It is always good to remember that examination is the basis for a strategy of treatment. Diagnosis is an art; though there are guidelines to it, there is no absolute right way of doing it and several possibilities exist. A native may have several problems or imbalances, so we may have to focus on one and let the results of our treatment dictate further modifications. Our skill in diagnosis should go hand in hand with skill in the modalities of treatment. The best diagnosis in the world is not of much value if it comes with no treatment. Unable to arrive at a complete diagnosis, if you can at least find the dosha level imbalance, it opens a line of treatment."

Pulse reading

"Pulse examination or *Nadi Pariksha* is one of the most important factors for determining the inherent constitution of the individual and the nature of the particular disease. Pulse readings are based on constitutional influences of Prakruti and the disease aspects. The two conditions are not the same and hopefully not add to any confusion. To find the constitution, take the pulse reading when not under disease's influence or adjust the pulse to the impact of the disease. Medications, food and drugs alter the pulse. When a kapha like slow, broad pulse occurs in a thin, dry, and nervous vata person, one should expect certain stagnation, Ama or superficial kapha, and not a person with kapha constitution. One must verify pulse diagnosis with other forms of diagnosis to make sure. There is much in pulse diagnosis that only practice can divulge. There are obvious pulse differences easy to work with, such as the rate of the pulse, which can give us important information in diagnosis and treatment, even if it does not show us everything."

"Pulse readings yield better results when free of physiological activities, on an empty stomach, in between meals, in a state of rest and when free of mental or emotional agitation. Readings taken after meals or when hungry are often incorrect, since the influence of the digestive fire affects the pulse. After a physical workout, the pulse rate changes from the increased circulation. One may use three fingers for pulse diagnosis. Index finger gets placed at the base of the wrist and the other two fingers behind it. Few practitioners take the pulse with the index finger at the first crease of the wrist, others a finger below that, at the prominence of the wrist bone. Flex the native's wrist a little; apply pressure gradually noting the strength, nature of the pulse and kickbacks. Pulse reading has a high certainty with Kapha and Ama problems, other dosha types may not reveal themselves."

"If the pulse is perceptible and strong, it shows good health. A large number of factors determine the pulse nature and quality. Learning to synthesize them for the right judgment, while we have arranged these according to the three-dosha types, it becomes evident that for dual dosha types, combination of factors denoting two types of pulses surface in the readings. It is the predominance of factors that matters. No one factor calls for a decision. Some have more weight than others."

1. Quality of Pulse	2. Site of the Pulse
3. Rate of Pulse	4. Depth of Pulse
5. Strength of Pulse	6. Regularity or Rhythm of Pulse

"Dosha constitution or Prakruti is one among many factors in the pulse reading. Disease condition Vikruti, dietary and seasonal factors are others. In general, vata, pitta and kapha constitutions exhibit similar dosha based pulses[152]. However, a diet consisting of kapha with sweet food may influence a kapha pulse, similarly, a diet prevalent in pitta especially if it tastes pungent may read as a pitta pulse. Likewise, a vata aggravating diet in the same way brings a vata pulse. During kapha season of late winter and spring, kapha will appear strong in the pulse reading and in pitta season of summer and early fall, pitta will show in the pulse. Vata season of fall and early winter will make vata appear strong in the pulse. Similarly, exposure to kapha-environmental factors like cold and damp will increase kapha in the pulse. Pitta-environmental factors like heat will raise pitta levels in the pulse. Vata-environmental factors like dryness and wind will increase vata. Exercise and life-style factors affect the pulse in a similar way. One must treat the variability of pulse types exactly like the dosha types and not consider them fixed for life."

"Quality of the pulse gives a good perspective in judging the constitution. Quality refers to the movement called 'gati' of the pulse. It may be hard to grasp at first, as it is influenced by the strength of the individual. In healthy types, it shows up much more easily. Vata types have a pulse resembling a serpent's movement - 'Sarpagati'. The pulse slithers in an irregular, horizontal movement, sometimes it thumps narrow and threaded, more so in vata women. Even when broad and easy to locate on the wrist, it is still irregular. Low volume and tension of the pulse are observed. Pulse may be difficult to palpate from its tenuous and fluctuating manner, it behaves changeable and subtle as the wind."

---

[152] Person with vata constitution will have a vata pulse normally. Under influence of seasons, diet and the environment, the pulse may become colored and show a different dosha.

"Pitta pulse has a spring like movement, 'Manduka Gati' resembling a frog leap. It is wiry and tight with recoil, appearing excited and dancing while in motion, resembling the flickering of a flame. Kapha pulse is uniform and wavy, possessing 'Hamsa Gati' or swan's grace. It runs wide, broad, rolls in grace like the flow of a river in late spring. Volume and rhythm stay balanced. In kapha women with thick skin, the pulse site may be hard to locate."

"The disease process speeds up accumulation of phlegm, rendering the pulse slippery, rolling almost kapha-like. Consuming dairy or mucus-forming foods also gives this effect. Such pulse appears in Ama conditions when the undigested food mass makes the energy stagnate, breeding congestion. Weak spleen, pancreas and poor sugar metabolism makes the pulse appear more kapha. Liver disorders, like hepatitis, turn the pulse stiff with a frog like motion. Trauma renders it tight and wiry. Fever makes the pulse larger, broader and quicker. Kidney disorders, weakness and general debility turns the pulse into threaded, snake-like weak movement, which is hard to detect."

"In determining the site of the pulse, the index finger placed in a position closer to the base of the wrist marks the vata reading. Middle finger position is a measure of pitta. Ring finger position shows kapha. Sometimes the little finger marks a fourth position, offering metrics on the blood. These positions link to three layers of the body. Index position measures energy in the chest and upper body, and organs in that region. Middle finger reads the energy in the middle section between the navel and the breast, and organs in that region. Ring position measures the energy below the navel, in the lower body, and the organs in that region. Right-hand pulse echoes the state of organs on right side of the body and left-hand pulse echoes the organs on the left side. As vata with air and ether components move upwards, kapha with earth and water components show downward movement and pitta or fire stay in the middle, the energy in these different parts of the body reflects state of the three dosha types."

"Many vata people have a more pronounced pulse in the first position as measured by the index figure and several pitta persons have a stronger pulse in the second position. It becomes prudent in not giving too much emphasis to the site of the pulse; the quality of the pulse is more important in determining the constitution. Few people, including most kapha types have a stronger pulse in the third position."

"When disease prevails, biased becomes the pulse reading towards its sites; acute lung disorders show as a stronger first position pulse, acute digestive disorders in the second position and acute kidney problems in the third. Moreover, chronic diseases that accelerate the de-vitalization of the organs and tissues of the body weaken the pulse reading of their site. Hence, chronic kidney diseases and low Ojas and sexual debility disorders get reflected in a weaker third position reading."

"Pulse rate is one of the easiest to observe and most reliable. Vata pulse runs the fastest, pitta moderate and kapha slow. Vata runs from 80 to 100 beats per minute or about 5 beats per breath. Pitta pulse runs 65 to 80 beats per minute or 4 beats per breath. Kapha pulse runs less than 65 beats per minute or 3 beats per breath."

"Pulse rate changes with disease. Fever makes the pulse rate more rapid, higher the fever, faster the pulse. Pulse can only offer clues on constitutions when no overriding disease factors like fever are present. Other factors like physical exercise and eating spicy foods can increase the pulse rate, anything that increases or stimulates circulation. Cold weather slows the pulse as does any stagnation or Ama in the system. In addition, children have a faster pulse and the rate of the pulse decreases with age, with the elderly having a slower pulse."

"Depth of the pulse relates to the level at which the pulse is found, or level of pressure exerted to feel the beat. Vata pulse is perceptible more at a superficial or surface level. Pitta pulse occurs at a moderate level and Kapha at a deeper level. However, when a disease like common cold or influenza occurs, the body's energy rushes to the surface. The pulse acts superficial when such diseases are just starting. In deep seated, chronic or degenerative diseases, where weak energy has been drawn into the interior, the pulse location shies away from the skin surface. Ama makes the pulse deep and heavy, as do congestive or stagnation conditions."

"Strength of the pulse is the power it has at the level it is detected. It is easy to determine once the pulse site is found. Vata types, with poor circulation, chronic low energy and tendency towards deficiency, have the weakest pulse. Pitta types, with their more aggressive nature, have the strongest pulse. Kapha types, with their even-flowing pulse, fall in between. Their pulse has more consistent strength than pitta, but is often harder to find and more diffused by its broader volume. However, a vata pulse is often superficial and easy to find, while a kapha pulse may be buried deep. A vata pulse may seem stronger than usual, while a kapha pulse may appear weaker."

"Any long-term, chronic or debilitating-disease, or any condition of old age or convalescence shows a weaker pulse. Weak or debilitated kapha types, who are still overweight, often run a feeble, deep and slow pulse. In acute diseases, the influence of high fever or severe pain makes the pulse stronger. Men have a stronger pulse than women, strength of the pulse may tell us more about the strength or weakness of the native than about their constitution."

"Regularity of the pulse is the rhythm constancy of the pulse. Irregularity of the pulse is when a beat gets skipped. Pulse rate may slow down or speed up in an irregular manner, skipping a beat. Normal pulse in three dosha types should be regular; vata pulse is little more irregular than the others. Kapha pulse is highly regular and Pitta pulse falls in between. Vata pulse may be regular or irregular; it may not only skip a beat, it may do so in an erratic manner. Pitta pulse is more regular or irregular, it may skip a beat, but not break the rhythm."

"Transient irregularity of the pulse comes from emotional and nervous factors. These involve stress, anxiety, worry and insomnia; where overuse of alcohol, drugs, and stimulants like coffee can induce the effect. Transient conditions are not indicative of any heart weakness, but show a straining of the heart and nerves. Irregularity of pulse usually points to heart disease more than a constitutional nature where problems like angina, hypertension, arteriosclerosis or heart weakness may manifest."

Pulse and organ correspondences

"The pulse corresponds to the different organs of the body, just as the three sites relate to the three levels of the body. At a superficial level, the pulse reveals what the 'bowels' or hollow organs are up to. At a deeper level, it reveals the corresponding internal or solid organ. Hence, the organs come in pairs from the exchange of energy between them along their channels. The body's right side is solar and left side lunar, where the pulses reflect the two sides of the body; the liver organ is a right-side organ, and the pancreas is on the left. Yoga sees a secondary solar chakra on the right side of the body near the liver and a secondary lunar chakra on the left side of the body near the stomach."

Left Hand	Superficial Pulse	Deep Pulse
First Position	Small Intestine	Heart
Second Position	Stomach	Spleen
Third Position	Urinary Bladder	Kidney

Right Hand	Superficial Pulse	Deep Pulse
First Position	Large Intestine	Lungs
Second Position	Gall Bladder	Liver
Third Position	Pericardium	Triple Warmer; Vata-Pitta-Kapha

"Sometimes a simpler method of reading is used in which each site corresponds to one organ, and the hollow organs get skipped."

Right Hand	
First position	Lungs
Second position	Liver
Third position	Right Kidney
Left Hand	
First position	Heart
Second position	Spleen
Third position	Left Kidney

Synthesis

"For determining the constitution through the pulse, the most important factor is the general quality of the pulse. Second comes the rate of the pulse. Strength of the pulse may give misleading results, as it measures the energy quantity, not quality. Site where the pulse is strongest is a secondary factor, however, the depth of the pulse is of help, besides noting the skin's condition, whether thick or kapha, thin or vata, or in between as pitta. Other skin indicators can hover between pitta, which is warm, vata signifying cold and dry, or kapha cold and damp. Skin complexion may enumerate between pitta showing a ruddy color, vata displaying dusky and kapha as white."

Tongue diagnosis

"The tongue is another significant site, which reveals the condition of the body and the digestive system in particular. It is important for sensing the dosha types, their Sama and Nirama states. It becomes prudent in considering other factors like the body, size, shape and movement of the tongue, its color, coating and amount of fluids on it. Vata types have a thin, small or long tongue, which trembles often. Pitta types possess medium sized tongues, which are sharp and pointed. Kapha types have large, round, thick or fatty tongues with big lips. Weak spleen, pancreas functioning and excess eating of sugar shows up as a thick or swollen tongue. Scallops, tooth prints or indentations around the margin of the tongue show chronic low Agni, suggesting a weak digestive power. Such are more common with large or flabby tongues."

"Normal tongue color is pink. Red tongue shows heat or fever. Pale tongue, lips and complexion demonstrate anemic condition. Blue or purple tongue shows stagnation of blood and often shows liver disorders, especially purple spots on the tongue. Vata presents a tongue that is pale or dull in color. A red tongue verifies Pitta's presence; blue, purple and other pronounced colors of yellow, green also belong to it. Kapha shows up as a pale or white tongue. Tip of the tongue as red shows heat in the heart, stress and anxiety. Tongue tip and borders as red shows superficial heat or the early stage of a febrile disorder. Redness of the whole tongue shows a severe, long-standing heat ailment."

"Normal and healthy tongue has no significant coating. There may be a slight white coating. Tongue coating shows Ama, the by-products of indigestion. It also confirms the dosha types may be accumulating. Thick white coating discloses strong presence of Ama. Thick or greasy yellow coating shows fever or inflammation from Ama fermentation. No coating on the tongue indicates a Nirama disorder. Vata shows a brown, sometimes black coating, more pronounced at the back. Pitta presents a yellow coating. Kapha confirms a white coating with mucus layer. Black tongue coating may occur following a febrile disease from burning out-of-body fluids. Moist tongue exposes fluids, phlegm or Ama accumulation in the system. Dry tongue confirms dehydration or fever. Vata shows a dry tongue, cracked or with a dry coating. Pitta exhibits a moist tongue in Sama conditions but a red and dry tongue in Nirama conditions. Kapha exposes a moist or wet tongue with possible mucus and excess salivation. Froth, foamy saliva or bubbles reveals Kapha and weakness in the lungs."

"Cracks in the tongue indicate high vata or a Nirama pitta condition when red. A central crack discloses pain and distress in the spine. Deviations in the crack point to the problem sites. With cracks in the front of the tongue, upper back or neck problems are indicated. When cracks appear towards the back of the tongue, it is a sign of lower back problems. Sores in the mouth and tongue, like cold sores or fever blisters, prove pitta or poor liver function, a febrile disease that may need purgation. Such indication may result from ulcers in the digestive tract left by hyperacidity. Raised papilla or small mounds at the back of the tongue proves hemorrhoids or prolapse of the organs in stomach or uterus."

Abdominal diagnosis

"Palpation of the abdomen is another important diagnostic tool. As the method has more variances than the pulse or tongue, we outline it only in brief. Abdomen check is not always necessary, but can be useful when abdominal pain or distention accompanies. The examination extends to the heart, the respiratory system and marma points."

"The abdomen's lower, middle and higher areas reveal to the inquiring hand a good deal of important information on the dosha-s. Warm or ruddy abdomen confirms pitta. Cool, moist and thick abdomen proves the presence Kapha. Cold, dry and thin abdomen gives evidence of Vata. Hot and sweaty abdomen denotes fever. Kapha types have more fat, and a flaccid abdomen that is not so resistant to pressure. Pitta types often have tight abdominal muscles that offer resistance to touch. Pitta folks store tension and emotion in the abdominal region as part of their dominant nature. Vata types often have abdominal tension but mixed with weakness, with more tightness in the lower abdomen or region of the colon where vata dosha accumulates."

"Pain felt during palpation shows Ama presence. Sama vata person experiences pain and distention in the lower abdomen; Sama Pitta person feels more pain and burning sensation in the middle region of the abdomen. Sama Kapha person receives more pain and congestion in the upper abdomen and chest."

"Kapha people are more tolerant to touch, as they can bear a good deal of pressure on the abdomen. Vata people respond negatively to cold fingers, but find a warm, gentle touch soothing. Pitta types exhibit higher intolerance to touch. Lower abdominal distention, tenderness, pain on palpation shows high vata accumulation in the large intestine. A hollow sound when tapped may imply gas formation, besides audible sounds from the intestines or peristalsis. Liver disorders and suppressed emotions show up as pain along the margin of the ribs and hypochondria. Often bile accumulates and congeals, marking a pitta or kapha situation. Pain and tension beneath the sternum in the sub-cardiac position indicates weak digestion. When such symptoms are accompanied by gurgling sounds, it signifies trouble with the water metabolism, excess sugar consumption, or perhaps poor spleen, pancreas role. Ama gets exposed when there is malabsorption. When it happens along with burning sensations, it exposes Sama Pitta levels with signs of hyperacidity."

Six tastes

"The six tastes or 'shad rasas[153]' and their energetics baseline the treatment process. Just as diagnosis of disease uses three dosha types, disease treatment is according to the six tastes and flavors. Six tastes owe themselves to the actual taste of herbs in the mouth and reveal an intricate dynamism of therapeutic properties. They apply not only to herbs, but also food and minerals, even to gemstones and emotions. Tastes are a measure of all possible therapeutic substances and actions in the world of nature. Tastes show the potential of energies abundant in nature in raising, lowering or balancing the affected dosha types [154]. They confirm the healing powers inherent in all substances and forces in the natural world. The six tastes start with sweet, saline, and move to sour, pungent, bitter and astringent."

---

[153] Astanga Hridayam, 1.14. Swadu or Madhura (Charaka Samhita) (sweet), Amla (sour), Lavana (salted), tikta (bitter), usana (pungent) and kasaya (astringent). Charaka Samhita Sutra 26.9.
[154] Astanga Hridayam, 1.15

Taste	Herbs or food	Elements
1. Sweet	Sugars and starches	Earth and water
2. Saline	Table salt, seaweed	Water and fire
3. Sour	Fermented food, acid fruit	Earth and fire
4. Pungent	Hot spices like cayenne, ginger	Fire and air
5. Bitter	Bitter herbs like golden seal, gentian	Air and ether
6. Astringent	Herbs containing tannins, like alum, Witch hazel	Earth and air

"Most herbs and food are classified from the dominant taste, secondary aftertaste and potential tertiary taste. Three tastes increase and remaining three tastes decrease the dosha types by direct action on the plasma dhatu, from the elements that compose them. Sweet, sour and saline tastes increase kapha and decrease vata levels. Pungent, bitter and astringent tastes increase vata and decrease kapha levels. Sweet, bitter and astringent tastes decrease pitta level, while pungent, sour and saline raise pitta level."

Dosha and the six tastes

"Salted taste works better at reducing vata levels, sour and sweet does it to a lesser extent as these tastes contain no vata elements. Vata level reaches its maximum with bitter taste, made of air and ether, then astringent and pungent, made of air. Astringent increases vata instantly, while bitter works slowly. Pungent taste can help reduce it by its warming nature. Sour taste or pungent, sweet with warm and added moistness is best for vata. Vata persons may avoid bitter, pungent and astringent substances. Food that is saline flavored, sweet and sour work best for vata folks."

"Sour taste quickly raises the pitta levels. Pungent and salty taste containing the element of fire comes next. Individuals with pitta constitution must learn to avoid pungent, sour and salted., even though it is to their liking. Sweet, bitter and astringent tasting food agrees better with them. Pitta drops to its lowest from bitter taste, trailed by astringent and sweet, none of which have any fire component. Sour taste, as in acrid fruit juices, relieves pitta temporarily by its moist and thirst-relieving powers. Salt also induces this effect through sweat. Their long-term accumulations only intensify pitta's growth. Bitter is the best taste in controlling pitta at a therapeutic level, as it decongests and cleanses the bile and blood, but sweet is quite useful in its cooling and nutritive features."

"Kapha reaches its peak while indulging in sweet taste, closely followed by saline and sour food, which are made of moist earth element. Kapha folks can avoid sweet, sour and salted and can embrace pungent, bitter and astringent. Pungent taste lowers kapha the most, then come bitter and astringent, made of dry air element. Saline taste helps soften and decongest kapha; makes it easier to expel phlegm. Expectorant herbs like Licorice also achieve this. Sour taste cuts fat though it increases kapha and plasma. Pungent is the best taste for kapha possessing contrasting properties."

"The six tastes range from heating to cooling[155]. The hotter the taste, the more pungent the food is, little less hot is sour and then saline. Bitter tasting food wins the coldest title and then comes astringent and sweet. Sweet and saline are between cold and hot."

"Six tastes also range between heavy and light. Heaviest are the food types that taste sweet, trailed by saline and astringent. The lightest are bitter tasting, followed by pungent and sour."

"Six tastes come under a different range between moist and dry. Wettest are food that taste sweet, followed by saline and sour. Driest is pungent, followed by bitter and astringent. The three characteristics define their long-term effects. In terms of immediate action, sour is most thirst relieving, pungent moistens the skin by promoting perspiration and sweet is also emollient and thirst relieving. Astringent dries directly out of the mouth and on the skin. Saline taste aggravates thirst though it promotes water retention. Bitter taste promotes salivation though it is internally drying. Moist and dry features vary by the liquid content of a substance. Apples and plums, though sweet, differ in that apples have less water than plums."

"Six tastes result in three long-term post-digestive effects[156], different from a secondary taste or aftertaste left in the mouth. It refers to their long-term effect on the digestive process. Sweet and saline have a sweet post-digestive effect, increasing saliva and the alkaline secretions of the stomach, and helping build all body tissues. Sour taste has a sour post-digestive effect by increasing acid and bile secretions in the digestive process, mainly in the small intestine. It builds all body tissues except the reproductive. Pungent, bitter and astringent have a pungent post-digestive effect in increasing gas production and being involved in the final stage of digestion in the colon. They have a long-term astringent-like drying and contracting effect on the tissues."

---

[155] Virya – heat or cool.
[156] Vipaka Taste (Rasa)

"Pungent post-digestive effect is easier to understand if we refer to such as astringent. Sometimes herbs have a post-digestive effect quite different from their taste, which gives them special features. It is more a reason of Prabhava[157] or special effects. Moreover, when we refer to a taste, we must distinguish between an herb's taste, aftertaste and post-digestive effect, as the term is applied in a generic manner."

"Beyond their basic energetics relative to taste, heat and heaviness[158], herbs have powers to initiate other specific actions, from their complex chemical composition. Some herbs are antitussive, purgative, diuretic, blood-thinners or possess other features not necessarily revealed from their taste and energy. Others may have special actions on the mind or emotions or on other subtle systems of the body. All these exceptions come under Prabhava."

"To every taste, associated is a healing action. Food that is sweet builds and strengthens all body tissues, harmonizes the mind and promotes a sense of contentment. It is demulcent and soothing to the mucus membranes, acts as an expectorant and is mildly laxative. It counters any burning sensation. Food with saline taste is often a softener, a laxative and sedative. When taken in lower doses, saline food stimulates digestion; in moderate amounts, it acts as purgative and in very large doses it induces vomiting. It helps soften hard tumors and defuse hard phlegm masses, calming the nerves and relieving anxiety."

"Sour tasting food is stimulant and carminative, helps in dispelling gas, it is nourishing and thirst-relieving. It awakens the mind and senses, promotes circulation and strengthens the heart and nurtures most tissues except the reproductive ones."

"Pungent tasting food is a stimulant, it is carminative and diaphoretic, promoting perspiration, improving metabolism and sponsoring all organic functions. It promotes heat and digestion, countering cold sensations. Pungency improves circulation, dissolving stagnant blood and blood clots. It opens the mind and senses, clears the channels, relieving nerve pain and muscle tension. Bitter taste is an alterative, it also purifies blood, cleansing and detoxifying it. It reduces the mass of all tissues and feverishly works to lighten the mind. Its antibiotic and antiseptic features are useful in clearing and cleansing the mind and emotions. In small quantities, it acts as a digestive stimulant, mainly digesting sugar and fat."

---

[157] Special Action or Prabhava
[158] Taste, heat and heaviness are Rasa, Virya and Vipaka

"Astringent taste stops bleeding and excess discharges such as uncontrolled perspiration and diarrhea, and it accelerates the healing of skin and mucus membranes. It acts as an expectorant and a diuretic. It squeezes the tissues and treats conditions of prolapse."

"In a way, even the stellar plasma forms from an expression of the six tastes. Tastes are imbued with traditional, cosmic memory that goes back in time to when creation began. The guna activations that happened at the hour of creation were instigated by the forces of taste."

"Food substances that have taste, when consumed in excess, damages the body, starting with the dosha it aggravates naturally. It even intensifies the dosha it is otherwise supposed to alleviate. Different food tastes differ in their power in aggravating the few dosha types. Bitter ranks the highest as an aggravator among the five. Saline taste comes next then sour, pungent, astringent and sweet. Different tastes owe their association to the water element. No water, no taste. Taste is learning; taste therefore finds a deep association with Tarpaka water related memory."

"Bland food with little taste, if taken in large quantities aggravates the pacified dosha types. For example, when sugar is low in a sweet substance, vata and pitta get aggravated first, followed by lightheadedness. When the deficiency reaches the point of malnutrition, low sweet can even weaken a person of kapha constitution. On the contrary, excess of sweet taste damages the spleen and pancreas leading to hyperglycemic conditions like diabetes. While food low on sweetness consumed constantly and in large quantity is extremely dangerous where shortage of sugar may damage the internal organs such as kidney and pancreas permanently. Food when excessively salted starts to damage the kidneys, inciting edema, hypertension and kidney stones. Highly pungent substance damages and dries the lungs, and may cause dry cough and bleeding in the lungs. Excess of bitter damages the heart and may instigate anemia, low blood pressure or insomnia, whereas right measure of bitter taste is a tonic for the heart and liver. Extra astringent taste damages the colon and may cause gas, distention and constipation."

"Any food with dominant taste consumed in excess damages the body. Sweet taste builds toxins and increases mucus; saline taste produces looseness in the tissues; sour taste stimulates acidity, burning sensation and bleeding; pungent taste triggers burning sensation, dryness and tissue depletion; bitter taste produces cold, vertigo and emaciation; astringent instigates contractions, muscle tension, blood-clotting, constipation and nerve pain."

"In the voluminous Charaka Samhita, our ancient predecessors mention a few food types such as rice, barley, amalaki, rainwater, rock salt, honey, milk and ghee. Not a wide variety that we eat today. Taste historically evolved from these food flavors. Let us for a moment consider them as constitutional tastes. Among them, strong tastes come from amalaki and rock salt. Ignoring salt, whose potency leaves it a condiment level, the main taste mainly comes from gooseberry or amalaki, one of the few primal fruits that cater to all dosha types. Sour, pungent with a sweet aftertaste, amalaki is the princess of herbs."

"Six tastes add flavor to our emotions. Their effect is the same as diet and herbs. Hot emotions as comes through hot taste are expressed as anger, hatred and envy; cold emotions through fear, grief and sorrow. Sweet taste exhibits love and attachment, saline expresses greed, sour comes out as envy and resentment, pungent taste expresses enmity and hatred, bitter is an expression of grief and sorrow, and astringent expresses fear and fright."

"Emotions portray a similar effect like food or herbs. Such psychological factors far outweigh the anatomical ones. Anger can damage the liver and the kidney as much as alcohol. So, in any treatment, herbs and diet are just not enough if the mind's taste is not aligned to the cause. Our emotional body has a taste for certain emotions and can become addicted or accustomed to them exactly the way physiological body does with certain food and substances. We must be careful not to let its sense of taste become perverted, for it can bring the same disease consequences. Sweet emotions increase kapha and phlegm and may trigger stagnation. Saline emotions increase kapha and make it easy to put on weight. Sour emotions instigate heartburn and hyperacidity. Pungent emotions make us hot and hyperactive. Bitter emotions have a depleting and reducing effect. Astringent emotions produce constipation and muscle tension."

"Tastes compete with one another to prove which one turns the strongest. As a taste, 'bitter' dominates, followed by salted, pungent, sour, astringent and sweet. Smaller amounts of the stronger taste counteract and nullify large amounts of food with tastes that are less dominant. Sweet taste possesses certain neutrality and can serve as a vehicle for the other tastes. Bitter just overcomes all other tastes, while saline nullifies all other tastes."

Six tastes as they occur in nature

Salted taste

Mineral salts: Sea salt, rock salt, kelp, laxative salts, alkalis; rock salt is preferable as a digestive stimulant; laxative salts draw water from the tissues and can aggravate vata in excess.

Sea products: Sea food, shell fish, ocean fish, sea weeds, sea shells; their properties are milder, less heating, helping them combine with other tastes; sea shells are expectorant, antacid and sedative.

Sour taste

Acidic fruits are refrigerant and thirst relieving, sometimes cooling; citrus fruit, lemon, most berries though they are sub-acidic, sour plums, sour cherries, sour grapes, sour apples, sour pineapple, passion fruit, hawthorn berries.

Acidic Vegetables occur rare, mainly as tomatoes or of nightshade family, but spinach, chard of oxalis family, or rhubarb stems in excess can build acidity.

Alcoholic ferments are manmade.

Other fermented foods – Sour cream, yogurt, cheese and kefir are heavier and invigorating and increase Shukra; pickled vegetables work great for digestion, but pickled cucumbers may be too heavy, particularly when joined with excess salt. Fermented food comes in this group along with vinegar.

Sweet taste

Simple sugars: Fruit sugars, milk sugar lactose, cane and beet sugar, honey, maple sugar, dates, rice and others. These derive from fruit, dairy and sugar producing plants.

Starches and carbohydrates - Starches from grains such as rice, wheat, barley is more balanced, occasionally diuretic, sometimes heating, but neutral. Vegetable starches like potatoes are similar. Unfermented dairy product is heavier and damper, more nourishing, but more mucous-forming.

Lipoids, oils and fats - These are fatty oils from seeds, nuts and animal products. They are usually heating and aggravate pitta.

Pungent taste

Essential oils, aromatics, spices - Typical aromatic plants and spices like onions, radishes, garlic, mustard, ginger, cayenne, cardamom, mint and others.

Acrid, pungent, bitter alkaloids, poisons, narcotics - In small doses these are stimulants, sedative, antispasmodic, perhaps expectorant, emetic, purgative and powerfully cleansing, but in large dosages they are narcotic, paralyzing and deranging to all dosha types. Milder alkaloid herbs and beverages include tea.

Bitter taste	
Simple bitters – Bitter melon, Coffee, Yellow dock, Turmeric root and Sandalwood typically bitter in their properties.	
Astringent bitters like bitters and tannins, where examples are Uva-Ursi, Pipsissewa, dandelion root that combine the effects of pungent taste.	
Bitter aromatics like bitters and aromatic oils - wormwood, mug wort, tansy, rue, and vetiver. Combine the effects of pungent taste; stronger action on the mind, good digestive stimulants, may be anthelmintic, occasionally warming, and some are toxic.	
Astringent taste	
Barks, resins and sap - Many resins like coniferous or myrrh-like resins combine astringent, bitter, pungent and even sweet tastes. They are slightly warming and have rejuvenating properties, like myrrh, frankincense. Most resins are astringent, helping plants in healing. Most saps are astringent.	
Astringent herbs and vegetables - Beans are often astringent and sweet, but heating; Many starches like potatoes, have astringent secondary taste. Some fruits exhibit astringent flavor when unripe. Many green herbaceous plants are astringent, like lettuce, alfalfa, comfrey leaves, dandelion, and plantain along with tree leaves and grasses are astringent.	

Plant compounds that are heating	Most alkaloids Essential oils Aromatics Lipoids or fats Resins, where most are flammable Acids, salts and alkalis having a caustic effect
Plant compounds that are cooling	Sugars and starches or mucilage Tannins Bitter principles Proteins, almost neutral

Combining tastes

Bitter-Sweet	Light and heavy
Pungent–Astringent	Expanding and contracting
Sour–Salty	Acidic and alkaline

"Tastes may counter other tastes and neutralize each other, having reverse actions. One can treat an excess of one with another. Bitter taste reduces our craving for sweet taste and helps improve the digestion of sweet and fat. Pungent taste promotes excess discharges like perspiration, bleeding and diarrhea. Astringent taste reduces the discharges and stops perspiration, bleeding and diarrhea. Sour taste increases acidity while salted counters acidity and promotes alkalinity."

"Tastes reinforce the actions and vitalities they have in common. Bitter and astringent do most of the cooling, detoxifying and acting as diuretic and potentially anti-pitta. Tastes such as pungent and astringent while acting as a drying agent and expectorant works well as anti-kapha. Pungent and bitter tasting food used in detoxification and clearing action, becomes useful in cleansing Ama and the digestive system, acting anti-kapha. Pungent, sour and salty tasting food stimulates digestion and acts anti-vata. Few tastes trigger side effects when used together. Sweet and Salty aggravate each other from their opposite hot and cold properties. Many tastes aid in relieving the side effects of each other. Sweet counters heat, pungent relieves heaviness, like taking cloves with sugar, or spices with sweet food. Herbs that contain multiple tastes are good candidates for multiple disorders."

Multiple tastes	Usage
Bitter and astringent	Common in herbaceous and green plants, uva-ursi, pipsissewa, dandelion, violet
Bitter and sweet	Rare herbs like licorice, aloe
Pungent and bitter	Bitter aromatics like mug-wort, wormwood, citrus peels, prickly ash, bay leaves
Pungent and astringent	Spices as sage, hyssop, bayberry, cinnamon
Sweet and astringent	Common in many food types, lotus seeds, fox nuts, potatoes, most beans, fresh apples
Sweet, sour and astringent	Common in fruit. Astringency usually is more common when unripe, particularly with berries, like hawthorn, raspberry, also aduki beans.
Sweet, pungent and astringent	Honey, herbs like cinnamon, dill
Astringent, bitter, pungent, sweet	Resins like myrrh and guggul, usually slightly heating
Pungent and sweet	Garlic, onions, cinnamon, ginger, fennel, leeks, cardamom, cloves and sweet spices
Sweet and salty	Fish

Multiple tastes	Usage
Salty, sweet and astringent	Seaweeds
Salty and bitter	Rare, found only in few seaweeds

"Minerals that own the six tastes, transmit them on a more subtle and direct level than plants, not using the digestive system route, but to the brain and nervous system directly. Plants offer their taste through the tongue and the medium of water. Minerals, on the other hand, work straight on the brain. Powerful is their action; most are toxic unless defused using the right preparation. For minerals, the heating and cooling action is stronger and more important than the taste."

"Let me take you beyond the six tastes to balancing the five elements[159] on which are founded the six tastes and other healing approaches. Conscious use of elements in energizing health and awareness is an important aspect as the five elements exhibit important therapeutic properties. The general rule is that the extra subtle element purifies the extra gross element. In this way, water purifies earth, fire cleanses water, air distills fire and ether cleans air. This axiom pertains to the external usage of elements, like water and heat therapies which extend to many internal applications."

"The elements adhere to a certain sequence of purification, (1) water purifies earth, then (2) fire purifies water, (3) air purifies fire and (4) ether purifies air. The first thing is to keep the elements pure. This includes the elements within our body and mind, within our anatomical and psychic spaces. This works both on the individual and groups of people. When the elements are pure, they function harmoniously to promote health and awareness, and when they are impure, they propagate disease and disharmony. The elements naturally become impure, like all matter, they decay; impurity comes from them becoming extra gross. Impurity in the elements causes too much of the gross elements to accumulate. This manifest physically as waste and socially as pollution."

"In nature's dominion, rain cleanses the earth. When the body is dirty, a bath or a shower cleans and re-energizes it. Water cleans the earth and waste from the body internals. It keeps the channels clean and clear. External use of oil with sesame or coconut, oil therapy or 'snehana' belongs to this domain."

---

[159] Pancha Bhuta Vidya – study of five elements

"With majority diseases having earth-element accumulation as excess waste, hydrotherapy becomes one of the main ways of treatment along with therapeutic baths. When excess earth and toxins are detected in the body, water therapy becomes the choice of treatment. Water therapy has its use in Ama, kapha and vata diseases involving accumulated earth with heaviness, weight, inertia and dullness. Let me recite you the mantras on water that Sage Kanva reveals in the Rig Veda."

> In the middle of waters swims immortality
> waters empowered to heal
> O Gods, your offer be generous
> Perfect role model, the waters are

Soma remarked to me
all medicines are in the waters
while the fire confers happiness in us
waters lug the cure for all

> O waters, inoculate the healing into my body
> surround it with an armor
> let me see the Sun through the waters
> uninterrupted

Rig Veda Book 1, Chapter 23, Mantras 18-20

"When water turns impure, heat cleanses it. Herbs cooked lightly in boiling water are a valuable recommendation. Heat makes the water pure and neutral absorbing better the qualities of the herbs. Through perspiration therapy, the element of fire purifies the water in our body. Hot and diaphoretic herbs also come under this category. In the body, adequate Agni or digestive fire is needed to purify the body waters and tissues, otherwise water stagnates, ferments and causes various kapha diseases. Heat therapy is primary, with methods included to induce perspiration and spices for raising the digestive and mental fires. It is refreshing to recall the Rig Veda on the elements, when Sage Saunaka turns his attention to Agni and all definitions suddenly become clear."

> O' Fire, born bathed in glowing light
> born you are from the waters and stone
> born you are from the forests, from the terrestrial plants
> pure is your birth, Master of human race

Rig Veda Book Two, Chapter 1, Mantra 1

"When fire turns impure, air rekindles it and reduces the smoke. With fresh air, fire burns better. In the body, adequate flow of breath keeps the digestive and mental fires pure. Otherwise they burn low, form toxins and diseases. Pranayama comes to the rescue as an important therapy. Other air therapies involve aromatic oils, fragrances, incense and music and bitter. They are immensely helpful in pitta and kapha disorders. The practice of pranayama for purifying the fire in the body has been taught for thousands of years. Herbs like mint, basil and cardamom; their aromas dispersed in the air purify and energize the digestive fire. They work like camphor and sage to energize the perceptual fires and make the senses more acute."

"Stagnant air soon turns impure. It returns to purity by exposure to space. The breath becomes impure through stagnation. If the air we are in is not open to the outside space, it becomes impure. Similarly, if the breath in our body is stagnant in some area of the lungs or elsewhere, it causes disease. Hence, it becomes important that we have adequate and clear space in the body and mind. This requires keeping our orifices and channels free of blockages caused by earth and water. Above all, it involves having space for our minds and senses to move and be active. Such mental and sensory treatments are useful in managing vata disorders. These methods of purifying the elements are useful for everyone and regular usage helps general health maintenance."

"We need to maintain our right connection and interchange with the five great elements of earth, water, fire, air and ether. Often, when one element gets imbalanced, so become the others. Normally elements that are more subdued cleanse the highly gross elements. Element earth restores its purity from water, fire, air and ether. Water owes its purification to fire, air and ether; air and ether purify the element of fire."

"Looking at it from an element's view, water sanitizes earth, fire cleans water and earth, air purifies fire, water and earth and ether cleanses them all. The heat of fire cleanses earth and water. Air's movement cleans water, earth and fire. Ether purifies all the elements as it gives them the space in which to release their impurities. The purity of fire depends much on what is fueling it. Air becomes impure only when rendered stagnant. Earth and other gross elements can block and languish the subtle elements, and render them impure. At the level of the mind, we must attempt to purify the elements, the mind being the subtle part of our nature and all the elements have their psychic counterparts. At the mental level, such cleanup and restoration is easier to fulfill as the results flow to the external world of senses."

"Earth's impurity is revealed as attachment to the body and senses, or to our property, which triggers greed. Water's impurity manifests as emotional and personal relationship liking and bonding, which breeds desire. Fire's contamination expresses as attachment to our will and ambition, which farms anger. Air's impurity reveals as connection to our ideas and expectations, which generates frustration. Ether's impurity manifests as utmost belief in our idea of reality, which breeds delusion."

Protective elements

"Earth offers protection from the water element, Water shields from fire, Fire safeguards from air, and Air protects from ether. Such security by the elements within us gives each element its proper sphere and boundary in which it can work unimpeded. Elements that tend to be more gross offer protection over those that are extra subtle. Earth shelters us from water, fire, air and ether. Water protects us from fire, air and ether. Fire safeguards us from air and ether. Water protects us from drying out by the influence of air and from spacing out from the influence of ether. Fire protects from the cold and dispersing nature of air and ether. Such protective action is necessary when an element is in excess. Particular element in excess will damage the others, particularly those elements more gross."

"Security function of the elements applies to the physical body in a similar way. If we over expose ourselves to the external elements, they manifest as disease as well as psychological challenges. Contact with water expresses as impressionability, where the person is vulnerable to the feelings of others. Experience with fire makes the person as defenseless against others' will and domination. Exposure to air turns the person susceptible to others' ideas and stimulation. Introduction to ether makes the person give in to the judgments and discriminations of others, believing in their concepts of reality."

"Five elements belong to 'matter' or Evolved-Creative-force. This is not just gross matter or solid stuff but the essence of experiencing anything that stands out as an object. As such, it includes the body, senses and mind, thought, emotion and ego, which is essentially a self-image. Matter and its elements become hallowed when they reflect the spirit's presence and consciousness we observe in the natural world. They become profane or impure when they become charged with want and outward seeking, as we witness in the social and commercial world."

Diet

"In the treatment process, the practitioner at some point must suggest a diet that is in line with the native's constitution, taste, season and the problems he is experiencing. People with dual or triple dosha makeups may modify their diet based on season and when an imbalanced dosha troubles them, others can follow the anti-dosha diet. Diet is a simple way to treat the physical body, which is a derivative of food. Then again, it is not about just handing out a food list; the practitioner must coach the native on how to use the diet principle suitably, knowing it is not easy to introduce or change diet quickly and radically. Many humans are creatures of habit, habituated with the food they have taken for years and it takes a while to adjust to something new or different."

"Satmya is the principle of adapting to habit. Yes, we being creatures of 'habit', become what our health, diet and diseases suggest, finding ways to adapt to such a routine in the long run. We are what we eat; our life becomes what our health and disease have to offer. Our learning defines us. When we learn the skills of woodworking, we become a carpenter, once we acquire a taste, like a Rajasic dietary flavor, we turn Rajasic. Once our system adjusts to disharmony, there may be severe side effects in reestablishing harmony. Imagine the people who have grown up eating hot spices, who have thick stomach mucosa. For them a bland diet would be a real torture. For someone used to meat, introducing him to fruit and vegetable could bring about laxative indigestion and severe gas problems."

"Healing through diet is a slow process, which can run into many months to produce any positive results. Dealing with the body, a product of time and habit, dietary therapy requires not just patience, but constant reinforcement. Often changing an item or two in the diet brings better results than a radical change in menu. While there is no substitute to pure starch in such healing, a diet may begin with rice and lentils[160], and gradually introduce other food."

"Sometimes the whole digestive system needs re-education, a food though healthy for a person may not exactly be palatable for him. There is always the question of taste, rather acquired taste in this case."

---

[160] Astanga Hridayam, Chapter 6.9-6.10 rice and paddy. Sastika (the paddy, which matures in two months) is best for such digestion

"We learnt about food that tastes sweet, neutral in energy and sweet in post digestive effect[161] decreases vata and pitta, raising kapha levels. Food nourishes and maintains the dosha types, tissues and wastes. It is the basis and support of the body and physical existence. Its subtle portion feeds and supports the mind. Even the Bible smiles on food, 'Stolen water is sweet; and bread eaten in secret is pleasant'. While elucidations on the above phrase are many, yes, all food when they taste sweet and pleasant can just about nourish every tissue. To re-educate the digestive system, starch and sweets are a good beginning."

"Astringent flavor is an ancillary taste owed to legumes, green vegetables, beans and raw fruits. Astringent taste provides a good deal of earth-element minerals, not intended for strength, more for building the tissues. Sour flavor found in sour fruit, tomato and some parts of dairy is comparatively lower in nutritional value than sweet; sour nourishes every other tissue except the reproductive tissue. Yogurt, which is sour, is quite an exception as it nurtures all the tissues. Pungent flavor found in spices and spicy vegetables do not boast of much food value either. They stimulate the digestive process, but provide little nutrition. Gardens do not produce salted flavor; saline flavor is found in seafood and remains a condiment in the diet menu. It does, however, strengthen all the tissues when dosage stays moderate, however, too much salt depletes the tissues. Any food with bitter flavor has little value. It clears and cleanses the digestive organs. Taking bitters before a meal stimulates the digestion."

"Most food in state of 'Virya[162]', where its internal thermal energy stays neither too hot nor too cold. In this state, the best nutritive properties are retained and promoted. This inherent energy, if not agitated ensures the best of nutrients gets to nourish kapha and the tissues[163]. Anything hot, such as ginger or pepper, or cold like bitter herbs of golden seal, gentian have little food value. Large quantities can tell if heating or cooling attributes really work. Spices, salt, vinegar and warm oil makes the food hotter, they stay cooler when taken cold, raw, uncooked, un-spiced and without oil. Food attributes also vary from heavy to light, though most food tends towards heaviness providing bulk to the body."

---

[161] Astanga Hridayam, 1.17. Vipaka – post digestive effects are three - sweet, sour and pungent
[162] Astanga Hridayam, 1.16. Virya or potency is either usna, heat or sita, cold. Charaka Samhita deals with Virya in several chapters like Chapter 3, Sruti 4. Chapter 26, Sruti 82.
[163] The inherent energy of food is not the external temperature, at which it gets served and eaten.

"Food stays light when taken with spices in low quantity or when taken raw. Heavy becomes the food by applying oil, sauces and cheese. Remember, food may also have properties of being dry or moist, where most are moistening, supplying body tissues with fluids. They turn drier by preparing them as such, like toasting, dry frying, popping them or adding spices. Moistening food comes from cooking them with liquids and oil; even salt and sugar moisten food."

"It is prudent that the existing diet of the native is examined to see what factors in the diet aggravate dosha types, the person suffers from. The food eaten, its quantity and quality, regularity and frequency of eating, food preparation and combinations give a complete picture of the diet. Some food types are specific to certain diseases, as with rich, greasy and acidic foods that are known to cause gout. We can steer the diet to target certain attributes, like making the diet 'dry' to offset any 'dampness'. This requires an exact knowledge of the specific attributes of foods and diseases. It also becomes important to consider not just what gets eaten, but the way in which it is eaten. Questions around right quantity and quality of food are important in the diet. Quantity ensures optimal production of Ama-toxins whereas quantity depends upon the individual's power of the digestive fire. Usually those who need heavier food have weaker digestive fires. Heavy food may require herbs for the person to consume it."

"Food should be of the proper quality, fresh or cooked fresh and rich in the life force or prana. Quality food involves organic, homegrown vegetables, locally produced, picked from the wild, and raw dairy. Poor quality is recooked, burned, overcooked, stored, spoiled, rancid, junk and any prepared food with artificial ingredients. Additives, preservatives and artificial coloring reduce the food's quality. The texts caution against food 'prepared in haste, in a wrong, disharmonious frame of mind' as an added measure on its quality."

"Some food combinations make no sense, like mixing food hot with too cold, or too light with too heavy. Vata folks tolerate the fewest food combinations though they feel inclined to eat many things at once. Pitta people tolerate most food combinations with their good digestive fire. Kapha folks fall in between with a steady, but slow digestive power."

"Tasty food increases Rajas and aggravates the blood, while un-spiced food increases Tamas and suppresses the digestive fire. Vata types tolerate rich food and moderate spices. Pitta types endure moderately rich food and light spicing. Kapha types need light food with strong and hot spices."

"Time, environment, diet, seasons, astrological dasa period, planetary transits, age are several variables in wellness. None of them are constant. Some are cyclical. Starting with seasons that cycle through time, one may consider anti vata diet in the fall and early winter. Even colors of red, gold or silver can please the vata and help ease the levels in this period. Anti-pitta diet may be considered in the summer and Anti kapha diet in the late winter and in early spring. Individuals whose constitutions may have two dominant dosha types may vary their diet by season. Vata-Pitta types can follow an anti-vata diet more in the fall and winter and anti-pitta in the spring and summer. Vata-Kapha types may follow anti-vata diet in the summer and fall and anti-kapha in the winter and spring. Pitta-Kapha types should follow an anti-pitta diet in summer and fall and anti kapha in winter and spring. Diet can be adjusted for climate, more anti-vata food consumed in a dry, cool or high altitude vata climate: more anti-pitta food in a hot climate; more anti-kapha food in a wet climate. In a noncyclical phase as in old age, an anti-vata and anti-kapha diet is more appropriate. In the middle age, an anti-pitta diet makes better sense. Men should consider more of an anti-pitta diet; women should consider more anti-kapha diet. Such general rules and factors must never interfere with disease or any treatment. Where Ama is prevalent, a spicy, light and cleansing diet may be adopted to clear out undigested food mass first."

Diet for dosha types

"Let me outline a few basic diets for different dosha types. These are general guidelines and by no means exhaustive. Whenever possible one should choose the diet from locally available food, as nature provides vegetation appropriate to environment, climate and season. If the native is under duress, different medication, it is better to check the history of what was prescribed."

General diet for vata types

	Suggested	Optional	Avoid
Fruits	Fresh fruits are acceptable for vata like apples, apricots, avocado, bananas, berries, cherries, fresh dates, fresh figs, grapes, grapefruit, lemon, lime, mango, papaya, peaches, pears, pineapple, plums, oranges, raspberries, strawberries, tangerines, tamarind	In moderation, fruits need to be soaked in fluids like yogurt or vinegar if they are too dry	Avoid dry fruit generally, raw apples, melons, cranberries, dry dates, dry figs, pears, pomegranates, dry prunes, dry raisins.

	Suggested	Optional	Avoid
Vegetables	Beet, bell pepper, carrots, cilantro, hot peppers, Jerusalem artichoke, mustard greens, okra, black olives, pumpkin, cooked onions, parsley, radish, sweet potatoes, winter squash, yams	Boiled or perhaps cooked. Alfalfa sprouts, artichokes, asparagus, broccoli, Brussels sprouts, cauliflower, cucumber, eggplant, green beans, peas, potato, spinach, squash, tomato, turnips, zucchini	Excess raw vegetables like mushrooms, lettuce, bitter lemon, burdock root, dried corn, green olives, dandelion greens, kale, dried raw peas,
Grains	Paddy rice[164], oats, wheat	Barley, buckwheat, corn, millet, rye	Dry grains, granola, corn chips
Legumes	Red lentils, Mung, soy products	Aduki beans, black gram, chick peas, lima beans, peanuts, tofu	Fava beans, kidney beans, navy beans, pinto beans, lentils, split peas
Nuts and Seeds	Nuts and seeds are acceptable except in excess – brazil nuts, cashews, coconut, filberts, hazelnut, peanuts, pine nuts, pistachio, walnut, chia, flax, pumpkin seeds, sesame seeds, sunflower seeds	Almonds and sesame seeds	Popcorn, psyllium
Oils	Oils are generally good, particularly olive, coconut, sesame, almond and Ghee		Flaxseed
Dairy Products	Dairy products are good, particularly those that are sour, buttermilk and kefir		
Sweeteners	Sweeteners are acceptable in moderation and in the right food combinations		
Condiments	All condiments are good including spices, salt, pickles and vinegar		
Animal products	Animal products are acceptable for vata, but can interfere with the mind. Fish and eggs are better than meat in this regard, and chicken is better than red meat.		

---

[164] Astanga Hridayam, Chapter 6.9-6.10. Paddy rice that matures quickly in two months.

General diet for pitta types

	Suggested	Optional	Avoid
Fruits	Sweet and astringent fruit like apples, avocado, cranberries, dates, figs, grapes, mango, and melons. pears, papaya, persimmons, pineapple, plums, pomegranate, prunes, raisins, watermelon	Sour fruit like apricot, bananas, cherries, lemon, lime, oranges, papaya, plums, peaches, strawberries	Sour fruit. Sour apples, sour berries, sour cherries, sour grapes, green mango, sour pineapple, tamarind
Vegetables	Artichoke, alfalfa sprouts, asparagus, bell peppers, broccoli, black olives, cabbage, cauliflower, celery, cilantro, cucumber, dandelion green, fennel, leafy greens, green beans, lettuce, mushrooms, okra, peas, potatoes, winter and summer squash, turnips, zucchini	Beets, carrots, chard, eggplant, mustard greens, parsley, spinach, sweet potatoes, sweet pepper, tomatoes	Chilies or hot peppers, garlic, pickles, radish, raw beet, burdock root, fresh corn, eggplant, mustard green, green olive, raw onion, turnip green, turnip
Grains	Paddy rice, oats, wheat, corn, granola	Brown rice, buckwheat, millet, rye, corn chips	
Legumes	A pitta person tolerates most beans. However, most are Rajasic, except Aduki beans, mung beans, tofu which are sattvic		Lentils, especially red
Nuts and Seeds	Coconut, sunflower seeds, flax seeds, psyllium	Pine nuts, pumpkin seeds, soaked almonds	All other nuts, particularly roasted and salted. Seeds chia, sesame and tahini
Oils	Canola, coconut, Ghee, corn, sunflower, flax seed, olive in moderation	Soy, flaxseed, primrose, walnut	All other oils – avocado, apricot, corn, safflower, sesame
Dairy products	Sweet dairy, especially milk, cream cheese, cottage cheese	Buttermilk, kefir, yogurt	Sour cream, salty cheese
Sweeteners	All sweeteners are good except honey, Jaggery and molasses		
Condiments	Fennel, mint	Black pepper, caraway, cardamom, cinnamon, coriander, cumin, curry leaves, dill,	Condiments can be avoided including spices, salt and vinegar. Exceptions are coriander, cumin, fennel, mint, turmeric and soy

	Suggested	Optional	Avoid
		ginger, neem	sauce in moderation
Animal products		Animal products are acceptable better avoided except egg whites or the white meat of chicken, if one wants to take them.	

General diet for kapha types

	Suggested	Optional	Avoid
Fruits	Dry fruit, apples, berries, cranberries, raisins, prunes, dry figs, pears, prunes, raisins	Apricots, grapefruit, grapes, lemon, lime, mango, papaya, pomegranate	Sweet fruit: bananas, cherries, dates, figs, grapes, melons, oranges, pears, peaches, persimmons, pineapple, plums, raspberry, strawberry
Vegetables	Astringent and pungent vegetables like alfalfa sprouts, asparagus, artichokes, beans, beets, bitter melon, bell peppers, broccoli, Brussels sprouts, cabbage, carrots, hot pepper, cooked tomato, cauliflower, corn, celery, chilies, cilantro, dandelion green, fennel, lettuce, garlic, mushrooms, mustard greens, parsley, peas, potatoes, radish, spinach, turnips, watercress, wheatgrass	Cauliflower, cucumber, eggplant, squash, spinach, tomatoes	Okra, sweet potatoes
Grains	Barley, buckwheat, corn, rye, dry grains	Millet, rice, granola from sugar	Oat, wheat
Legumes	All beans are generally good, particularly soybean products	Tofu can aggravate very high kapha conditions	
Nuts and Seeds	Only pumpkin seeds and sunflower seeds, charole.		All nuts and seeds avoided

	Suggested	Optional	Avoid
Oils	Oils should be taken in small quantity: only corn, Safflower, soy, sunflower or a little ghee	Flaxseed	Avocado, apricot, coconut, olive, primrose, safflower, sesame, sunflower, ghee, almond
Dairy Products	Goats milk or a small amount of buttermilk		Dairy products should be generally avoided.
Sweeteners	Small amounts of honey		All other sweeteners should be avoided
Condiments	All spices are acceptable, particularly Cayenne, black pepper, Garlic and Ginger		Salt, vinegar and pickles should be avoided
Animal Products	Chicken and turkey are acceptable, if one wants to eat meat.		Animal products should generally be avoided, particularly pork and beef.

"Fruits taste sweet, sour and astringent, their energy stays cool and sweet in post-digestion. They reduce vata and pitta, and increase kapha. Fruits lessen Agni, weakening the digestive fire. Fruit is thirst relieving, refrigerant, alterative and laxative. Fruit is a little cleansing and nurturing and only in excess will increase Ama-toxins in the system. The texts state, Draksa or grapes are best among fruits, as they are an aphrodisiac, great for eyes, can relieve excess urine and feces and others[165]. Large portions of fruits are made of water and ether elements, more of the latter than any other food group. While building plasma, it cleanses the blood and can have a reducing effect on the other tissues in excess. It sets an ambience of lightness and purity in the body. Fruits demonstrate ample sattvic or spiritual behavior, perhaps the most sattvic promoting lightness, clarity, harmony and contentment. It increases intelligence and a sense of harmony and aids in meditation."

"Moreover, fruits fail to stimulate mental work. It does not help in any studious pursuit either. By its light and cooling effect, fruit may instigate a dispersing effect. It may not be strengthening enough for those who do heavy physical work or have to take a strong role in social action or interaction."

---

[165] Astanga Hridayam, 6.115 onwards is about fruits and their groups.

"Fruits can diffuse our aura when consumed in excess, making us more sensitive and subliminally vulnerable, if living in congested cities or leading a hectic lifestyle. In addition, it may not be heavy enough for those with high vata condition to ground them. For kapha types, it may be too cooling and may promote edema, mucus formation and fatigue."

"Grapes have their usage in many disorders. Mango is great for strength and skin. Many abdominal-disorders, cough and blood deficiencies benefit from mango. Banana is 'cold' and good for controlling pitta, and so do oranges. Sapato is used more in convalescence to restore strength. Lichi is extremely nourishing; it purifies the blood, regulates the heartbeat and improve the immune system."

"Figs have their use in heart problems, besides helping the liver sand urinary tract function better. Watermelon works as anti-pitta. Pineapple can help join broken bones, benefit the heart, decrease fever and heat, and cut the excessive thirst and weakness. Dates enrich the blood and douse the nausea, fever, urinary obstructions, constipation and headaches."

"Dry fruit is more suitable for kapha, but it aggravates vata, increasing intestinal gas and causing distention. Fruit juices are more likely to aggravate kapha; they are cooling and laxative and can aggravate vata and cut Agni, more so if incorrectly together with other food. Baked or boiled fruit is better for vata and kapha. They become easier to digest taken with sweet spices like cinnamon, ginger, cardamom and cloves. Taken with salt, sour fruit like lemon and lime controls vata. Sour fruit taken with sugar keeps pitta levels down."

"Fruit does not go well when eaten along with other types of food. Most fruits do not go with meals and is often taken alone though any sour fruit is an exception. Fruits like lemon, pineapple, papaya or cranberries are better taken with meals. Sweet fruit like apple family, works fine with yogurt. Fruit can be had along with grains or dairy, but other food items may not be added to the mix."

"Vegetables[166] carry a pleasant taste, harboring a mild flavor, reasonable energy and a sweet post digestive outcome. They are more diverse than fruits and have division. Veggies are sattvic, perhaps a little less than fruit, they grow more on the ground and are a less evolved than fruit as food. Root vegetables are heavier and more nutritive in energy. They are better for vata, but more likely to aggravate kapha."

---

[166] Astanga Hridayam, 6.72 onwards is about leafy vegetables and others.

"Leafy or green vegetables are lighter and drying and better for kapha and pitta, but more likely to aggravate vata. They are well equipped with blood-cleansing properties. Cabbage family plants also fall in this category."

"Pungent vegetables like onions or chilies are better for vata and kapha, but aggravate pitta. They are Rajasic, with properties that make them irritant. Nightshades, like tomatoes and potatoes provoke food allergies in vata and pitta types if consumed raw. Few vegetables, diuretic or drying, act healthier for kapha, like carrots, celery, lettuce, mustard greens, parsley, cilantro, watercress, asparagus, broccoli and potatoes."

"Leafy and astringent take less part in building the body being light and porous, so do sprouts like alfalfa or sunflower. Root vegetables are the most nutritive in bulk food value. Nutritive vegetables, such as potato, sweet potato, yam, onion and artichoke mainly boiled or cooked are far better in conditions that suggest deficiency."

"Consuming raw vegetables in moderation works well for pitta, unless their Agni is low. Cooked, boiled or baked are better for vata and kapha. One thing to remember is that vegetables contain sensitive nutrients in small amounts. Cooking, storing even pickling them may destroy these valuable nutrients. Some vegetable juices endowed with cooling effect are lighter and may aggravate vata, however, vegetables cooked in oil and spices made into a curry are better for vata. Deep fried vegetables are more likely to aggravate pitta and kapha. Use of salt in vegetables is better for Vata. Grilled vegetables help lower kapha and vata elevated conditions. Pickled vegetables improve vata conditions, but may aggravate pitta and kapha. Vegetables are often bland and neutral in flavor, combining well with other foods like grains and beans. Light vegetables, like cabbage family plants do well with whole grain like rice or pasta."

"Vegetables offer their best value in seasons, they ripen and mature. Green, leafy vegetables appear in spring, early summer and fall. Root vegetables develop in fall and winter."

"Cereal crops or grains are reckoned as an important part of any healthy diet. They are a balanced food that supports digestion and tissue growth. Sweet tasting, grains are neutral energy with sweet post digestive effect. They are sattvic and provision the tri-dosha balancing, as all year-round staple food. They contain significant amounts of the earth element, necessary to build the tissues and give bulk to the stool. Protecting their properties well, grains do not deteriorate easily as other food. Easy to digest, few grains are diuretic with water dispelling properties."

"Cereals are nutritive and great for kapha. Barley, pearled barley, corn, rye, amaranth and buckwheat also help discharge phlegm and cut the water retention. Many grains such as wheat, oats, brown rice, and barley are very strengthening, perfect for vata conditions, debility, convalescence and physical exertion."

"Steamed cereals put forward a balanced, easier way to digest food. For vata folks, bread is more challenging to digest as the dryness and yeast intensify vata levels in them. Pitta types handle them much better. Bread is better toasted, which dries it and alleviates its stickiness. Breads are a strengthening food, easier and quicker to take, as they take less time to prepare. Pastas or noodles are a good way to take grains like wheat."

"Dried grains, like granola aggravate vata, but are better for kapha as morning cereals. By the same token, corn chips are difficult to digest, their greasy content aggravates pitta and kapha and their dryness irritates vata. Since grains are balanced, there is seldom a need for anything to counteract them. In fact, spices ease their digestion. Grains are neutral and mix with vegetables, fruit, nuts, dairy and animal products. They retain their potency within the seed and work well any time of the year. They are useful in the winter, being quick in energizing the body."

"Beans offer a sweet and astringent taste, neutral energy and sweet post digestive effect. They decrease kapha and pitta, but may aggravate vata. Beans contain large amounts of earth or protein mass, but also a fair amount of air. Beans yield protein together with grains; make for the main staple food for nearly all diets. They yield the energy needed for physical work. Paddy rice cooked with split mung beans as Kitcheree is excellent in this respect."

"Beans normally require strong cooking and spices, those prepared in heavier oils are harder to digest and more likely to aggravate pitta and kapha; vata shows more tolerance to them. Beans are edible all year round; mostly useful in winter when energy is short when it comes to combating cold. Beans are difficult to mix; they do well with grains or vegetables, but mix poor with sugar, fruit or dairy."

"When parboiled, soy or kidney beans become more palatable. Parboiling involves with them being boiled first and then the water discarded. Spices are also helpful antidotes, including onions, cumin, cayenne and asafetida and salt. However, these can cause elevate pitta."

"Nuts are a secondary food source, sattvic to the subtle body and nourishing to the external body. Many nuts offer a sweet taste, heavy with strong oils, slightly warm in energy and sweet in post digestive effect. They decrease vata, but increase kapha and pitta. In roasting them, their oil gets released and light roasting renders them better for vata. Blended with milk, cream and turned into a drink, they are better. Nuts are a nutritive and strengthening tonic. Nuts help increase fat, marrow, nerve and reproductive tissue along with the Ojas. They also help build healthy blood and muscles, strengthening the memory and creativity. Edible seeds are similar in properties to nuts but lighter, less nourishing and easier to digest. Because of their light nature, they can aggravate vata when taken in excess. Nuts persist well over time, best taken in fall and winter. Their oil may aggravate kapha more in the spring, and elevate pitta in the summer."

"Milk products are basically sweet in taste, cool in energy and sweet in post digestion. They decrease pitta and vata, and increase kapha levels. When sour, their energy exudes warmth, increasing pitta. Dairy products build all the seven tissues, in particular plasma, fat and reproductive tissue. In addition, they calm the mind, nerves and emotions. Products from milk are sattvic, good for the practice of yoga and meditation; great in case of emaciation, debility and convalescence, particularly bleeding disorders, wasting diseases or sexual debility. Being damp, heavy and sticky, dairy can increase mucus and Ama when taken cold. They are not so great for kapha and Ama conditions as indicated in arthritis and gout."

"Most milk products do not mix well with other food and condiments. Milk is incompatible with meat, fish, yeast breads which cause it to ferment; sour fruit, which curdles it; nuts, pickles, pickled vegetables and green leafy vegetables. It works better with whole grains and raw sugar. Yogurt also does not mix well with sour fruit, nuts, meat or fish. Ginger, cardamom and cinnamon antidote milk, while mustard, cumin and cayenne antidote cheese and yogurt."

"When used in short term, meat[167] nourishes and strengthens well. It is excellent in cases of debility, convalescence and one of the best substances for lowering high vata. It offers a sweet flavor, slightly warm and sweet in post digestive effect, decreasing vata and increases pitta and kapha. Meat is highly Tamasik; it potentially deranges the system breeding Ama-toxins and feeding infections, fevers and tumors. It dulls the mind and senses, and negatively impacts love and compassion. Raw or incompletely cooked meat is very aggravating and turns into toxic Ama."

---

[167] Astanga Hridayam, 6.43 mentions meat and it consumption, the right way

"Meat soup or stew is easier to take[168]. Meat when fried deep is more aggravating to the dosha-s. Besides, meat mixes poorly with other foods. Mixed with milk, it turns toxic. Raw vegetables, leafy greens and vegetable juices especially papaya cut the toxicity of meat. Bitter herbs like aloe gel also help. Spices are a big help, but aggravate pitta."

"Edible oils derived from nuts, seeds, beans, vegetables taste sweet, sometimes bland, slightly warm in energy and sweet in post digestive effect, carrying the taste and flavor of the source. They decrease vata, but increase pitta and kapha. When used in frying, their heat attribute reaches new levels, none of which are good for pitta. They do not come under the definition of food as such, but as an adjunct to cooking or flavoring. Extracted oil is necessary for maintaining fat tissue, marrow and nerve tissues. They ease secretions and discharges. Oil finds a new use in body massage. They soothe and soften the skin and muscles, and dissolve toxins and congestion that get absorbed from the skin. They lubricate the lungs, the large intestine and nourish the deeper tissues of the body. Such nourishment from the skin is very rewarding in conditions of debility and convalescence."

"Oil is used in many treatments[169], which involves internal consumption as well as external application, besides being used as demulcents and laxatives. Medical usages of these oils come with simple rules, where barred are heavy oils when Ama conditions become evident or when the blood turns toxic. When the skin is red, oozing skin diseases are noticeable, or severe pain occurs on palpation, oil massage is held back."

"Food with sweet flavor is what the tissues' welcome. Sugar, being refined, needs no further digestion and gets directly absorbed. They instigate allergies and immune system disorders, eventually enter the tissues as Ama."

"Sweet flavor and sugar in particular, decreases pitta and vata, while increasing kapha, but in excess, sugars can derange all the dosha types. Sugar as such, works as a tonic, demulcent, diuretic, calmative, refrigerant, laxative, antiseptic and preservative, forming the basis for many tonic herbal preparations like confections and jellies where raw sugar is mixed with milk, fruit or nuts and given to natives in conditions of debility and rejuvenation. Sugar applied to skin sores, burns, wounds, rashes or inflamed eyes soothes the infected area."

---

[168] Astanga Hridayam, Chapter 6.32 Meat soup
[169] Snehana - The rubbing or kneading of parts of the body specially to aid circulation, relax the muscles, or provide sensual stimulation.

"Sweet taste, especially sugar plays an important part in Nirama states of pitta and vata, when the digestive system is faced with no clogging. If there is any significant tongue coating, or evidence of a Sama state, one should avoid sugar. Honey, however, may be used in moderation when conditions are Sama."

"While every substance has specific traits, actions, karma-influence, they offer a unique application in wellness matters. There is nothing in nature that does not have healing value when applied correctly; on the contrary, anything can act destructive when inappropriately applied. Fire that cooks the food can burn the food and the kitchen. Exposure to different energies and their effects is an ongoing activity, often unconsciously. Some of the effects can improve the well-being, or detract from staying well. Key to healing comes from maximizing the positive influences and minimizing the negative ones."

"Herbal alternatives to any medicinal system is about applying the energies of nature, it is a big mistake to keep them stove-piped and isolated, and away from the total picture that wellness provides. Laboratories cannot explain the Bengal tiger's elegance when it pounces on a prey, an herbal laboratory cannot be an answer to the complex process of wellness. The wellness program works with diet, life style, love and work. Food builds the body, and herbs correct the imbalances – it is that simple. The point to remember is food and herbal remedy goes together. Astrology comes in as a savior, it points to the nourishment, and time, events and the positive energy one can take advantage of. Before herbs are prescribed, the house must be set in order, the diet must undergo correction before the homeostasis can be established."

"Five elements and twenty qualities inherent in herbs enable many therapeutic actions. Any hot substance has a stimulating, expanding and diffusive effect of Svedana. Hot substances make us sweat, open our pores, clear the head, stimulate digestion, circulation and perception and promote all body functions. On the contrary, cold substances endorse a contracting, astringent effect of Stambhana and cut perspiration, stop bleeding, allow muscle spasms, lower digestion and decrease all body functions."

"There are a couple of ways to apply remedial substances, first through external, environmental means, exposure to heat, water promoting hydrotherapy, wind and cold and second, by using substances internally as food and herb, sent down the digestive tract and other permissible body openings."

"Three basic types of substances can go into the body - food, herbs and poisons[170]; food builds body tissues, herbs catalyze various organic functions and quits the body once the work is complete, and poison fastens to the tissues and instigates diseases."

"Food substances are often embroidered with herbal character, notably tonics like Rasayana-*s* and Vajikarana-*s* exhibit strong food value, though  some herbs are toxic and some drugs flaunt herbal effects along with unwanted side effects. To have a long-term positive effect on the body, the life-force needs to stay sustained at increased levels. Study of herbs comes from biochemical, bioenergetic and biodiversity models. Biochemical model analyzes the chemical constituents of herbs and plants to extract their active ingredients. It judges herbs by their chemical components and considers them of little medicinal value if discovered is no strongly active chemical compounds in the herb. The biochemical model views the human body as a storehouse of chemicals whose adjustments by the intake of the right chemicals only keeps the machinery running. There is no room for life-force or consciousness in the biochemistry model. Herbs proposed by the biochemical model have stronger potency and a more immediate effect on the body."

"Biochemical approach manipulates natural substances to achieve dramatic results, where its results are not always wholesome in the long run. Such chemical substances have been around the block for too short a period to make any judgments about its safety in the long run. The biochemical model works fairly well with aromatic herbs containing strong active oils, like camphor or mint, or toxic herbs that have powerful effects in low dosages, such as digitalis or aconite. Complex herbs, like the tonics of oriental medicine like ashwagandha and shatavari, seldom have a simple active ingredient and are of little biochemical value."

"Bio-energetic model is the preferred model in studying herbs. Energetic approach is rather naïve and simplistic. It has no complex chemical analysis of substances and often uses intuitive methods like the doctrine of signatures; flavor and taste, texture or color of herbs to figure properties and usage, which may not reflect any chemical components. Biochemical medicine is also naïve because it misses the main thing in healing, the effect of herbs and drugs on the life-force in the body, it being shy of any complex analysis of the life-force and its different functions."

---

[170] Astanga Hridayam, 1.16. Dravya are of three types.

"The bioenergetic model approaches the subject from a different dimension, it does not distinguish herbs by their chemical makeup, no doubt, such knowledge is very helpful. The life-force present in herbs and body is not a topic of chemical analysis, but is certainly the subject of the bio-energetic system of analysis. Herbs, as complex organic substances are just not made of simple, active and inert ingredients. Much of their action may not depend on the whole herb, nor can one understand the herbs' action outside the human body. Herbs may catalyze certain effects within the body that has no correlation to chemical constituents. Herbs when working synergistically in large formulas may have effects outside our scope of understanding in terms of their chemistry. In addition, herbs may not work apart from the right environmental support factors, including diet and lifestyle. Practitioner must coax the native to understand he cannot expect to get well through natural healing methods if his life is out of harmony with nature."

"Not only are herbs mixed, but also processed in different ways and taken with different mediums or vehicles. Bhallatak or marking nut has toxic oil, much like poison oak, or Arnica Montana that fires up allergic reactions if we applied directly on the skin. Yet taken internally, or applied with the right medium, like in a little ghee, or almond oil it can be useful for many disorders. Herbs work more slowly than drugs, but have a more lasting effect in improving the quality of the life-force. In contrast drugs act to palliate or suppress disease symptoms, in turn, drive the disease deeper into the body."

"Biodiversity model classifies herbs according the three divine qualities of nature, Sattva the clarity vector, Rajas the restlessness attribute and Tamas the dullness vector. This approach examines the effect of herbs upon the mind and consciousness and their ability to either increase or decrease awareness. Sattvic substances improve perception and discrimination, Rajasic substances substantiate imagination and mental agitation, and Tamasik substances dull the mind and senses. According to the biodiversity model, all drugs are Tamasik or have a long-term dulling effect, as they are heavy and inorganic. Herbs may be of any of the three qualities depending upon their nature and application. Biodiversity attitude to life treats life as divine."

"Herbs enhance or retard our development towards the divine. Sattvic substances lessen violence while Rajasic and Tamasik substances increase it. Biodiversity attributes of substances are key to long-term human health and harmony."

"All three models, the biochemical, bioenergetic and biodiversity are expedient and cohesive. However, this requires subordinating the biochemical to the latter two approaches. Herbalism, like wellness packs two levels of care and usage. The first usage attempts to balance individual constitution or Prakruti, meaning the inherent vata, pitta and kapha and their variations dominant in us. It is part of a program of health enhancement, disease prevention, and promotion of longevity and rejuvenation. Second usage lies in treating particular diseases, as they manifest through Vikruti, which does not deviate one bit from the model of the three-dosha types. This second usage intends to relieve particular diseases and their symptoms."

"First level of treatment requires us to become familiar with the dosha-constitution. It comprises mild remedies to keep our constitution in balance and to supplement the deeper tissues and energies of the body upon which vitality depends. In this respect, herbs find usage as digestive aids or as food supplements. Such constitutional measures along with daily 'dinacharya' and seasonal 'ritucharya' health regimens could define a personalized wellness program[171]."

"Kapha people benefit using Trikatu comprising dry ginger, black pepper and long pepper taken before meals since it raises their metabolism and reduces kapha. This is true even if they have no particular health problems because Trikatu maintains right organic function in the body. Similarly, most vata people if they do not eat heavy foods, benefit using Ashwagandha, a tonic and rejuvenating Rasayana for vata."

"Ashwagandha nourishes the deeper tissues deficient among vata folks. Such herbs, administered in lower dosages, are safe and effective as long as native stays healthy. 'Constitutional' treatment is the fundamental principle. It is the first stage in the wellness process and foundational. While constitutional treatment may not be strong or specific enough to treat severe diseases or acute symptoms, in the long run can drop the cause of disease or dosha imbalances."

"Hence, over long periods of time constitutional treatment become effective in countering chronic diseases even without specifically addressing them. Underestimate not its importance, even though its effects are not immediate. As part of a nutritional approach, its effects may take a month or so to be discernible, equaling the time needed to build deeper tissues."

---

[171] Astanga Hridayam, chapter 3 – Ritucharya Adhyaya.

"Second level of treatment requires knowledge of the disease process and the ways to treat specific conditions. It also proceeds on two levels. First level of disease treatment focuses on common and mild diseases. These are things like the common cold, sore throat, headaches, constipation and insomnia - conditions that occur often in the ordinary course of life, which are often not complex or life-threatening and do not force medical consultation or clinical treatment. These are largely conditions that can many-a-times be self-treated. A tea of fresh ginger with honey is a good home remedy for the common cold, so is the formula *Sitopaladi Churna*. At this level, treatment can be effective even if we do not know the dosha-constitution. Such conditions are transient and superficial whose symptomatic treatment has high degree of efficacy. There are similar remedies for many common conditions in all herbal traditions."

"The dosha-constitution, once revealed, opens up new avenues in all related treatments. Even herbal home remedies can be customized to long-term constitutional needs. Say, a pitta person susceptible to common cold may use a less hot diaphoretic than ginger, like mint or yarrow, as these would be less likely to aggravate the pitta levels in the long run. If the person has vata dominance, he might want to balance out hot diaphoretics like ginger with soothing demulcents like licorice, so he does not dry out from surplus perspiration. Common cold has all the symptoms of kapha – the phlegm, the surplus fluids, the congested nose. Any anti-kapha diet that can dry out the excess kapha helps the kapha person recover quickly."

"Second level of disease treatment puts the spotlight on complex and severe diseases that can be life threatening such as high fever, infection, heart disease, convulsion, bleeding and severe trauma. They need specific medical and clinical treatment and it is not safe to treat them on one's own or without considerable training. Owing to the fact, these two levels of common or severe diseases come under the category of chronic diseases, often as complex as arthritis, multi sclerosis or chronic low-grade fevers, there sometimes is little that biochemical medicine can do for them. Clinical therapies of the Pancha Karma legend on the other hand, come in very helpful, especially when symptoms are not severe by applying home and self-care measures to restore the immune function with tonic herbs such as Ashwagandha, Shatavari, and Guduchi."

"Some severe diseases, like cancer, are not amenable to biochemical treatment and herbal treatment can be helpful for them[172]. We may try self-care measures, but accessible clinical methods, if we can get them, are preferable when the disease is so advanced and degenerative."

"Before we apply herbs, we should know the nature of the condition we are treating and what our qualifications and law of the land allow us to treat. As long as we understand these different parameters, we can safely embark on those treatments and not put anyone at risk. Most of us can determine our own constitution or have it determined by a qualified practitioner, so we can apply herbs for known dosha-constitution. In the same way, we can apply remedies for common and superficial disorders, as most of these conditions do not need medical treatment unless they fail to respond in normal time."

"Just as animals live a life, healthy, in harmony with nature and require few medical checkups or take medications, so can human beings not be hostage to a complex and artificial medical system to live a healthy life. Scriptures tell us that only when we live in disharmony with nature, complex treatment methods become necessary."

Incorrect food combinations

"Food and herbs are generally taken in through combinations, though there are few exceptions where a single source serves as food. This imposes quite a challenge in determining combinations that work better and those that can be avoided. Again, some people have high tolerance of certain combinations; therefore, these suggestions must be looked upon as general guidelines and not gospels. There are combinations in food and very common at that, which may turn them into toxins or unserviceable as food. In the wellness program, they are termed as 'Viruddha Ahar' or antagonistic diet. Like milk and fish don't go well, but some folks tolerate them. Honey and ghee in equal quantities is not great for health. Honey and hot water or even roasting honey renders it useless, as heat can damage the nutrients in honey."

---

[172] Author's note - It does, however, require much caution in application of herbals in cancer like conditions as many of its most effective medicines and therapies again may not be legal.

"It's the same if honey is used in cooking or roasting. Milk is not a great companion to radish, garlic, menthol, barli, raw mango, lemon, banana, jambool, plum, pineapple, tamarind, peanuts, yogurt, watermelon, salt, sesame and jaggery. Wine does not go well with the kheer rice pudding."

Digestive, eliminative disorders

"The central aim in this wellness program is to visit the cause of the disorder and fix it at the root; not just ease any symptoms and indications. The treatment methods therefore involve the forces that drive our daily lives. What we do every day determine who we are and how we feel and the most prevalent among these factors is diet. The physical body is a direct product of the food we eat. Gross portion of the food substance converts to feces, the intermediate part is harnessed as body tissues and the subtle portion supplies energy and nutrition to the mind. Physical and mental ailments are accompanied with irrelevant digestive disorders. While such digestive maladies may appear insignificant compared to other symptoms, we experience through a disease, even mild digestive system disorders over time can instigate severe health problems."

"Upon eating excess kapha-forming substances like dairy, sugar, oils or animal fats, polluted air, improper posture or grief - kapha eventually accumulates in the system triggering problems such as bronchospasms or heart disease. Digestive tract symptoms that accompany this condition may be mere heaviness and occasional nausea after meals, though the disease from such dietary indiscretion can prove fatal in time, even with no major digestive system symptoms."

"Some food deteriorates and accumulates as toxins, especially when those portions fail to undergo proper transformation as body tissues. Over time the toxic mass gets bigger, large enough to damage the organs and clog the channels. Correcting such poor eating habits can cut off the root of many health disorders and even cure severe diseases in the passage of time. By no means does the disorder or its correction by diet happen overnight, it may require anywhere from several months to a year or more for the diet alone to cure the diseases. The cure comes gradually from the same process that produced the condition. However, if the diet does not agree with the herbs and medicines, then it is futile to think that they may work."

"Dosha-s accumulate at prescribed sites within the digestive system. The large intestine for vata, the small intestine for pitta and the stomach for kapha are the three major sites. These are the places in the gastrointestinal tract where the three-dosha types remain predominant and on sensing food intake begin their main activity in the process of digestion. Earth and water elements from food substance get digested in the stomach at the kapha phase of digestion. The pitta phase absorbs fire elements in the small intestine and vata ingests air and ether elements in the large intestine."

"When something goes wrong in the digestion process at any of these stages, the dosha controlling the site starts to accumulate and become disease-causing factors. Aggravated dosha suppresses the digestive fire, Agni worsening the food absorption process. From these sites in the digestive system, the dosha infiltrates the blood and lymph system, which transport it to other parts of the body propagating a disease. They deposit themselves at weak sites in the body places earlier damaged by disease, injury and misuse. Aggregate kapha levels move from the stomach into the lymphatic system and lungs spreading diseases like common cold, asthma, pneumonia and heart disease. Pitta accumulated in the small intestine moves into the blood and liver triggering fever, infections, toxic blood conditions, and liver disorders like hepatitis and jaundice. Accumulated Vata moves from the large intestine by the blood stream into the bone tissue where it spreads nervous and arthritic disorders."

"Incorrect diet often contributes to increase in dosha level to a point of accumulation. While emotional, environmental and lifestyle factors also fund it, accentuating this deteriorating process, imbalances also are indicated at a diet level. High vata targets the mind making us anxious, in turn deranges the appetite and causes vata to accumulate in the digestive system from irregular eating."

"First phase of correction that brings long-term benefit comes from diet. Next phase may require the use of herbs to fix the disorderly process of digestion. Some practices advocate taking herbs along with food as, I do not support mixing herbs and food and would recommend herbs taken before or after. Spices are an exception; almost everyone stands to benefit from eating spiced food as digestive corrective. Not only are such herbs and spices useful in preventing dosha levels from reaching alarming numbers and accumulating, they also compensate for the dosha aggravation that some food types instigate."

"Every food mix requires delicate balancing, it is almost like adulterating the natural essence to reduce the inherent dosha toxicity."

"To compensate kapha-increase that may result from food like dairy, use of anti-kapha spices like cardamom and ginger prevents any ballistic increase of kapha, regardless of the persons constitution. Pitta-increasing substances like chilies are compensated by celery, coriander and cilantro. Vata gas producing beans are compensated by anti-vata spice like Asafetida or the *Hingashtak* preparation."

"Agni, the digestive fire has four states - high, low, variable, and balanced. It runs high in pitta types evidenced by strong appetite and metabolism. It stays low in kapha types evidenced by low, constant appetite and slow metabolism. It remains variable in vata types shown by alternating strong and low appetites. Right herbs help to correct and balance the digestive fire. Hot spices like dry ginger, cayenne pepper raise the digestive fire and counter its low state. Demulcent or astringent herbs like licorice, raspberry leaf thwart its high state. Carminative spices like cardamom, fennel neutralize its variable state by normalizing Samana Vayu, the vata governing digestion. Treatment of Agni is analogous to the treatment of different dosha types."

High dosha levels in the digestive system

"High vata level in the digestive system results into gas, distention, bloating, and constipation along with nervousness, anxiety and insomnia. Tongue turns brownish and gets a dry coating, pulse reading is rapid, erratic and slithery, the appetite stays unpredictable and soon becomes erratic, and the eating discipline turns into a mess. Vata symptoms show up three to five hours after eating, sometime during the vata phase of digestion. Eating a light diet or vata-aggravating foods such as beans, raw salads, cabbage-family plants and mushrooms intensify the condition."

"Most spices work better for vata just as they do for kapha. In vata conditions, spices spread on any sweet, demulcent substance such as licorice or honey act more efficient. Spices by themselves are drying and can aggravate vata, taken with honey reduces the risk. For very thin people who are suffering from dryness as evidenced by dry or cracked tongue or skin, and insomnia, hot spices can aggravate and over-stimulate vata. Vata types tolerate milder spices like cardamom, basil, fresh ginger and fennel better than hotter spices such as cayenne or dry ginger. Many vata people endure hot spices well and find them effective in improving blood circulation and for relief in vata-caused arthritis."

"Hot herbs like cayenne, dry ginger and cinnamon are useful for such conditions and taken during the vata season starting late fall into early winter. The formula of choice for high vata in the digestive system is Hingashtak or Asafetida with eight other ingredients. Hingashtak counters gas and bloating. It eases constipation and intestinal cramps, besides being effective against food allergies and mouth diseases. Hingashtak also addresses high kapha levels. The formula Trikatu is beneficent for kapha and vata though trikatu is not as carminative and gas dispelling as Hingashtak. Hingashtak along with laxative Triphala works efficiently in reducing vata and kapha disturbances. Triphala works to correct high Vata in the large intestine."

"As a cautionary note on spices, people can only adjust to herbal and spicy substances over time, where habitual use of hot spices builds a tolerance for them, the mucus lining in the stomach thickens and protects the insides. To the uninitiated, spices are a new kind of food with alien taste that may disrupt the system. Sometimes even vata or kapha people may experience discomfort from having strong spices. Only time and patience can ensure success. The practitioner must also remember that many spices are turned into gasses within, the spices used must be untreated and wildly grown otherwise they may not have enough Prana or life-energy to do the work. Remember the laboratory dilemma on Bengal tiger. Harvested herbs like fenced poultry do not yield sufficient Prana when consumed as food. The wilder the sunflower variety of Arnica is, the stronger is its potency in stopping pain."

"High pitta levels in the digestive system lead to hyperacidity, chest pain, and burning sensation in the mouth along with irritability and emotional distress. A yellow, greasy coating builds on the tongue, though the tongue color remains red. Pulse reading is wiry, abrupt like leapfrog. Elimination is loose, yellowish in color. Symptoms while localized in the small intestine and liver region, have their onset an hour or two after eating. The conditions worsen pitta-increasing food, where sour, salty and spicy flavor are dominant. Many spices deteriorate the pitta levels bringing about pitta-instigated indigestion. Cooler spices, like coriander, turmeric, fennel, cumin, and mint are an exception as they rectify such disorders. When Pitta levels run very high affecting the nervous system, even these spices become intolerable. Avipattikar Churna is the herbal formula of choice in fixing pitta-caused indigestion. Amalaki, shatavari, licorice and dry ginger, with the first three items added in equal parts and the last item just one-quarter part serves to correct hyperacidity. Demulcent herbs, like licorice, shatavari and milk reduce typical pitta problems such as hyperacidity and ulcers. Herbal bitters like Aloe Gel reduce pitta-induced indigestion."

"Strong bitters like barberry or gentian are of tremendous help in Pitta elevated conditions. Bitters have powerful mechanism in countering craving for sugar and help treat the initial stages of diabetes in adults. Cilantro or coriander leaf, and parsley are good antacid green that can accompany the meals to counter such problems of hyperacidity and stomach ulceration."

"High levels of kapha in the digestive system are detected from white, greasy, damp tongue coating, with possible mucus on the tongue. Congestion and mucus flare up in the morning hours or right after eating. Pulse stays heavy, soft and slow. The native tires easily, feeling heavy and groggy, slightly nauseous. Symptoms appear prominently in the stomach region shortly after eating, especially kapha-increasing sweet, salty, and sour food that just aggravate the situation."

"Kapha herbal treatments with hot spicy herbs yield the best results. Spicy or pungent tasting food having high fire and air elements easily counters the earth-water dominance of kapha. Formula of choice is trikatu, which literally implies 'three spices', formed by mixing three herbs, dry ginger, black pepper and long pepper or pippali, the last being the key ingredient in this formula. Taking small quantity of the formula before a meal balances the kapha, besides supporting digestion and countering the effects of overeating. Cardamom, fresh ginger, mustard, horseradish and fennel work like a charm in treating nausea that arise from high kapha. Cardamom defies the kapha-increasing effects of milk and sugar. Cayenne and mustard oppose the kapha-increasing effects of cheese. For countering deranged sugar metabolism, turmeric is most effective. Turmeric accelerates the digestion of fat and sugar, and keeps the liver from becoming sluggish and congested. Turmeric being a fat digester, it must be taken with fat, cooked in curry or taken with milk or ghee to be effective."

Elimination

"A good digestion needs an equally good finesse through proper elimination of waste. Elimination mirrors the entire process of digestion, gauging how well was the digestion. Even the stool's condition measures the state of the whole digestive tract. When stool formation is poor with a pronounced unpleasant smell and does not float, this shows Ama presence with improper digestion. Other indications are bad breath, tongue coating, erratic appetite, flatulence, feelings of heaviness, body ache and headache."

"It is often necessary to add herbs to support the process of elimination. While many spices counter gas and bloating, they also act as mild laxatives[173], like ginger and asafetida, though no spice in isolation can function as an effective purgative. When taking strong, bitter laxatives, it is helpful to add spicy herbs. Ginger, cardamom and fennel in about one-quarter proportion added to the bitter herb counters the cramping or griping that strong laxatives bring. Chronic constipation is without a doubt a vata problem. Often, diet cures the problem by adding more oil and roughage. Regarding roughage, grains are more efficient than greens. Salads and greens irritate vata, instigating constipation. Whole grains, bran, oil of sesame and ghee are committed to vata reduction."

"Colon earns special importance for its role in digestion and elimination. Large intestine is the site in which air and ether elements from the food are absorbed to reinforce the nervous system. Ether elements shape the senses and assist in reproductive tissue formation. These elements bring with them prana, the life-force through the medium of food. While quick intake of prana takes place in the lungs from the breath, deeper prana absorption happens in the large intestine during the final process of digestion. Low energy and weak vitality can come from poor colon function; very similar to symptoms indicated in shortness of breath. As a site where the life-force is absorbed from food, the large intestine earns an important position in the activities that comprise digestion."

"When the colon malfunctions, gas problems become discernable from the resulting intensified vata. Instead of the pure prana being absorbed from the food, waste gases pour in, almost as bad as breathing polluted air, except the air intake is from the colon. Normally, from the colon membrane, prana from the food moves into the bone tissue and sustains all the Vayus in the body. Vata being the primary disrupter dosha, it is easy to see how malabsorption in the colon can cause many deep-seated, systemic disorders. When proper digestion fails in earlier stages, it continues to fail in the large intestine."

Laxatives and constipation

---

[173] Laxatives or "anuloman" in Sanskrit

"While many herbal laxatives help in waste elimination, Triphala is among a small number which also corrects prana absorption from the colon. Triphala comprises three tropical fruits of the myrobalan family, haritaki, amalaki and bibhitaki. Triphala swallowed with warm water before sleep works wonders. Main laxative ingredient in Triphala is the herb haritaki, which one can take without the other two when stronger laxative action becomes necessary. Triphala is a rejuvenating Rasayana for the large intestine and for the life force. In normalizing prana absorption, it can strengthen the life-force wherein lie most health problems. Bitter laxatives are also quite effective. They are better for pitta and kapha types and used more in acute conditions. Triphala remains tridoshic and can be used without fear of drying the system like the bitters."

"Laxative salts are effective in promoting elimination, but have plenty of side effects. They draw water through the walls of the colon by osmosis. Hence, they can have a drying or vata aggravating effect. Adequate fluids along with laxative salts can correct the dryness."

"While pitta types rarely suffer from constipation, when they do, a mild laxative such as Triphala, 'Chyavana Prash' jelly, and psyllium work quite well for them. When the 'hot' quality of pitta starts to dominate over the 'wet' quality, dryness is the outcome, invariably leading to constipation. In severe conditions, when constipation results from a febrile disease, bitters tend to be more effective. Though purgative therapy is quite effective in dropping high pitta levels, such therapy needs proper preparation. The preparation consists of toxins being forced out of their hiding within organs and tissues into their dosha site in the digestive tract. Only then can the elimination begin. It is futile to administer laxatives if the toxins are not in the digestive tract."

"Kapha folks suffer constipation from sluggishness. Triphala is adequate for them though bitter laxatives may help in the short term. Bitter laxatives are best administered with spices like Trikatu. In themselves, bitters are frigid and can further lower the metabolism, besides weakening the digestive capabilities of kapha and vata types; the intake of other spicy herbs helps rebalance this condition. Bitters can ease the flow of bile, supporting both pitta and kapha types, and preventing gallstones formation. Kapha must be treated with hot spices, the root of kapha disorders being in the stomach. For kapha though, the large intestine is just an overflow and drainage site, not the origin of the problem. While bitters appear to work short term in shedding weight, their long-term effects are not always beneficial."

"The primary therapy for weight reduction in kapha types is not to promote elimination, but to raise the metabolism - rekindle the Agni embers! For this, one benefits using Trikatu, which raises the metabolism in the stomach, along with Triphala, which normalizes absorption in the colon. In addition, one can add guggul, which clears plaque and fat, and a bitter herb such as gentian or katuka, which clears the liver and pancreas and supports sugar and fat metabolism."

Preparing herbs

"As we embark into the amazing world of herbs, let me caution you that we will not unravel a Materia-medica of herbs and plants. Our intent is to know the major players that can span a majority of dosha disorders. What I am also about to suggest are some therapeutic methods that use these herbals extensively. No doubt, the remedies involve herbal methods, but it is far from merely giving away a fistful of herbs. It's about the lifestyle, the graha combinations and First, we try to understand the causes of disease, which may be psychological, dietary or life-style in nature. Our aim stands undaunted in getting to the root of these causes and correcting them. Herbs help support a broad-based treatment, they are an important adjunct treatment, but herbs cannot treat diseases alone. However, among substance based healing, herbs offer the most powerful and safest usage in the place of drugs."

"Herbal preparation has its own bag of rules. One such guideline is in grouping one or two herbs that work together on a dosha condition. In the mix, an herb may counter the heating-cooling properties, lower or increase the energy or enhance the taste of another herb. Likewise, some herbs are targeted for specific disorders like Arjuna for liver-organ and heart, Vasa for cough and many others. In formulating a mix of such herbs, it is generally a specific mix pursuing the dosha type, changing the herbs potency and a generic tridoshic mix targeting the disorder. Formulation offers more leeway in setting the right energetics of the formula by changing the weightage of different herbs. Arjuna and Ashwagandha act better for vata instigated heart problems, Arjuna and brahmi for pitta and Arjuna and Guggul or Calamus for the kapha heart. Arjuna targets the organ and the other herbs are dosha specific. Herbs can be used symptomatically in transient or surface diseases. Great are basil and ginger for common cold or aloe for the skin as they refrain from aggravating pitta unless the native continues to consume the preparation beyond the disease."

"Herbs are often shared with other herbs, each playing a different role. Some herbs may share the main qualities of the primary herb; other herbs may work to counter the side effects of the primary herbs, while a few herbs may take part in special actions. Some herbs may occur in a formula to speed up the preparation's digestive process. A practitioner may prepare herbs on a base substance like honey, ghee, guggul or amla paste and serve with different substances like hot or cold water, sugar, honey, ghee or aloe gel to moderate the effects."

"Fresh neem leaves or dried neem leaves in warm water with sugar soothes the irritated skin itch. Garlic oil reduces ear pain. Turmeric along with equal parts honey stops a cough at its onset. Tea prepared with ginger, black pepper, clove and bay leaves can stop the running nose. Neem, tulsi and belpatra taken early in the morning on an empty stomach controls the blood sugar. Tulsi or holy basil or even wild basil taken over a long period reduces body ache. Eucalyptus oil can reduce backache."

"Honey comes with a big bag of features, besides being a vehicle for numerous other herbs. Being a predigested food, it assists in the digestion of the herbs and transports them to deeper tissues. Honey colors the herbs with its properties, turning the compound into expectorant, laxative, tonic and rejuvenating mix. Many herbs for colds, cough, congestion and sore throat, like dry ginger, calamus and bayberry use honey as their base. Honey added to herbal tea along with powdered herbs enable the mix to reach target organs quicker. Herbal powders stay in storage longer with honey added. Such 'honey forte' reinforces the effect of the herbs, makes them edible by countering the bad taste, besides providing the means for longer storage. Honey can enhance the herbs' properties, counter any possible side effects, moderate the herbs' potencies making it easier for the body to assimilate."

"Honey forte prepared to combat debility, reduced immunity and low vitality is a terrific starting point in implementing such combinations. To prepare this herbal combination, one can spread five parts of honey on clean surface covered with light almond oil, to which gets added one part of ashwagandha, shatavari, small amount of pippali, brahmi and dry ginger powder. A small mortar and pestle would easily grind the roots and herbs into powder for a homogeneous mix. Fresh brahmi leaves make it even more potent. It is a good way to start the day with the tonic."

"As the days grow shorter and the chill settles, honey has its use in treating cold and cough. The herb preparation uses five parts of honey on clean surface covered with light almond oil, into which is mixed small amounts of dry ginger, cinnamon, cloves, bayberry, thyme and echinacea. This preparation is an excellent 'SOS' against cough and cold."

"Many herbal ingredients feed the brain. One such herbal preparation suggests spreading five parts of honey on clean surface covered with light almond oil and mixing into it one part of shankha pushpi, brahmi, licorice, little less of cardamom and nutmeg. It works wonders in conditions of stress, anxiety, irritability and insomnia. Another similar formula entails mixing calamus, brahmi, pippali, tulsi and cardamom in equal proportions. It is an awesome herbal formula for depression, loss of sensory perception, sinus congestion, while promoting mental acuity."

"Aloe Vera is another such herb as honey that acts as vehicle or anupana to ease the uptake of other herbs. It is a strong medium for taking anti-pitta herbs, equally useful for kapha and vata herbs. Aloe, in the gel or liquid form becomes a base for other herbal preparations. In such fortified aloe gel, herbal powders are added, thoroughly mixed and allowed to settle for a day or two. Spices find a usage when dipped in such mixtures. Taken with aloe, spices like ginger and coriander counter the cold nature of aloe. For eight parts of the gel, one part of powdered herbs is added. Different in approach from honey forte, any preparation using aloe remains in a liquid form. Such aloe forte in dosages of one or two teaspoons in the morning and evening as digestive formula taken before meals is a potent herbal concoction."

"Turmeric in aloe gel base is a known preparation, imparting it Tridosha capability. The mix stimulates the liver, promotes circulation of blood, cleanses the blood, eases menstruation, stops excess bleeding and promotes healing of sores or wounds. Sandalwood added to aloe gel is used in cleansing the blood, easing urination for urinary tract infections, stimulating digestion, and calming the mind and emotions. Brahmi alongside aloe gel works in calming the mind, cleansing the blood, coagulating it, easing urination, calming excess sexual desire, making more blood and promoting hair growth."

"Ginger powder added to aloe gel stimulates digestion, regulates sugar metabolism, normalizes pancreas and dispels mucus. Coriander powder taken in aloe cleanses the blood, stimulates liver and counters allergies like skin allergies, sinus and food allergies. Cardamom taken along with aloe gel manages the pancreas and sugar balance."

"Any raw or natural powdered sugar added to aloe gel preparation, improves the taste. It helps increase the tonic properties of the formulae."

"Let me tell you about a few more aloe-vera combinations. They are mild in their action and quite unsuited for acute conditions. Neither strong in reducing nor sturdy in fortifying, these combinations have an all-purpose balancing effect. Base lining aloe as a blood purifier and liver tonic, many combinations are possible."

"The aloe combination for liver organ is an important one. The preparation requires eight parts of aloe gel, added to which are turmeric, sandalwood, gotu kola and coriander in equal parts. Though the mixture is neutral to all dosha, it can aggravate vata where dry ginger powder comes to the rescue. Such a mix works well with sluggish liver, impure blood as in acne, diabetes, allergies also helps in many post menstrual disorders."

"Aloe blended with herbs can also sustain the female reproductive system. In making the aloe concoction, eight parts of aloe gel are mixed with turmeric, manjishta, brahmi and shatavari in equal parts up to one part. As such, it is neutral to three dosha types, but can aggravate vata. The combination is useful when pronounced are symptoms of dysmenorrhea, menopause with hot flushes, menorrhagia, venereal diseases like herpes and post menstrual disorders."

"Aloe combinations accelerate the digestion process when organs like spleen, pancreas and stomach turn sluggish. Eight parts of aloe gel are added to a mix of ginger, turmeric, cardamom and cloves in equal parts up to one part. The mixture works for kapha and vata, but aggravates pitta; excellent for sugar addiction, hypoglycemia, cold, influenza, cough and allergies."

"Aloe recipes for the urinary system are yet another way the herb gets used for other problems. Eight parts of aloe gel are added to brahmi, gokshura, lemon grass and coriander in equal parts up to one part. Pitta and kapha persons are quite tolerant to the herbal concoction, but vata folks are not so tolerant. When dealing with vata aggravation, it is easy to replace coriander and lemon grass with ginger and cinnamon. The mixture is great for difficult, burning or painful urination, urinary tract infections, bleeding, venereal diseases, genital herpes and uncontrolled sex urge."

"Like Aloe and Honey, Ashwagandha is another tonic that has a number of uses combined with other herbs or just by its own merit. Ashwagandha usage varies from reducing anxiety and depression, combating the effects of stress, increasing stamina and endurance, reducing brain cell degeneration, stabilizing blood sugar, lower cholesterol, improve the immune system, and thyroid function, improving bone health, fighting osteoporosis and inflammation and treating adrenal fatigue. The list runs quite long with Ashwagandha. The herb is often mixed with Shatavari and Brahmi to address many such problems."

"Whenever an herbal formula is introduced to a person, it becomes more palatable with a few spices added. Amount of spice can vary by dosha type. In high kapha, one may use cayenne and ginger; for pitta, one can use turmeric and coriander; for vata, ginger and fennel. Pippali or long pepper is effective in buttressing the lungs and reproductive system."

"Natural sugar present in honey along with herbs provides the tonic a pleasant taste. Herbal spices along with sugar can easily battle cold and cough. Combination of one-part sugar with one-half part spices like dry ginger, cloves, cinnamon, cardamom or pippali effectively combats the early symptoms of common cold. Not-so-tasty tonics like ashwagandha and shatavari can turn pleasant when taken with equal parts of a raw sugar. Other tonic such as vidari, bala, amalaki, kapikacchu, black or white musali are also sugar based, where sugar acts as a preservative. Herbs such as licorice root and stevia are excellent flavoring agents. They require smaller dosages than raw sugar."

"Starch based herbs made with lotus seeds, vidari, gokshura, comfrey root, marshmallow root or slippery elm improve their taste. Ground into powders and taken with herbs, they work well with tonic like ashwagandha and shatavari. Tonic starch with ashwagandha and vidari are useful to people who suffer from very weak digestion and have difficulty handling either sugar or spices."

Therapy

"Practitioners have prescribed three ways of managing wellness - 'aahar, vihar and aushdhi'[174]. Allow me to introduce the general types of therapies or aushdhi. As with any treatment, total wellness requires two major activities of supplementing and reducing[175]. Part of the overall process, they may vary in their implementation. Reduction aims at decreasing the toxicity and supplementation feeds the undernourished body. They do not occur in any sequence and different therapies use them differently."

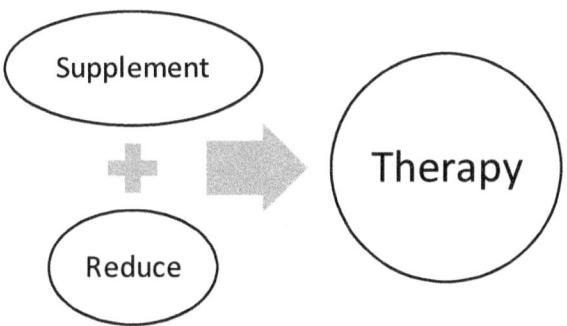

"Reduction therapy lowers excess toxins and dosha types, eliminates surplus tissues and other waste from the body. Supplying the body with nutrients is supplementation therapy when insufficiency of tissues[176], debility and low dose of Ojas are indicated. 'Reducing Methods' aim at eliminating the factors that cause disease. Supplementing through tonics acts to reinforce lost energy and other shortages in the body that instigate a disease or may be its result. In acute stages of disease, reducing works well, when disease strikes in all its fury. Prevention by reducing helps to eliminate deep-seated toxins, enabling disease prevention and internal cleansing[177]. Tonics that invigorate are best for chronic illness, convalescence and lessening the side effects of reduction methods. Employed in reduction are herbal means of eliminating toxins."

---

[174] Aahar is diet, vihar are deeds and aushdhi is treatment.
[175] Reduction, "langhana," literally means "to lighten". Supplementation, "Brimhana" from the root "bri" meaning "to expand" means "to make heavy".
[176] Insufficiency of tissues or "dhatu-kshaya"
[177] Such a program is well known as "*Pancha Karma*"

"Diaphoresis or elimination through sweat, purgation and elimination through the feces, diuresis or elimination through the urine, emesis or elimination through vomiting, expectoration or discharge of phlegm, carminative herbs in discharge of gas, and direct pathogen destroying action of blood, lymph and bile by cleansing herbs such as bitters, febrifuges and alterative are all used. Tonic-invigoration method is simpler and comprises one main approach of using herbs to increase strength and nutrition, like ashwagandha, licorice or ginseng."

Reduce first, supply next

"Reducing the toxins first, then supplying tissues with tonics is a common sequence. Sometimes, the need for tonics may come first. Almost all of us profit from some reduction methods, if only to make our systems purer so we can enjoy tonics. Such things as fasting or blood-cleansing programs are useful in this way. However, conditions can be such where an individual is too weak for any reduction methods. This is where tonics take precedence over reduction to manage an individual who may not have the strength for purification. Combining the two methods into one yield a milder and long-term therapy."

"The nourishment that tonics provide is elating[178] as it comprises complimentary care, relaxation, ease and enjoyment along with the dietary sustenance. Tonic aims at making the individual feel better about themselves. It encourages faith, love and positive attitude. Reduction therapy is a lot gloomier[179], as it includes practices of discipline, hard living and relinquishing things. It involves self-examination, rectification and atonement."

"Reduction works best for people who have dominant kapha, while tonic-supplements are paramount for vata type persons. This is because the main attribute of kapha is heaviness and vata lightness. Pitta requires a mix of reduction and supplementation remedies. Preferable for kapha are strong reduction methods, like fasting or rapid elimination. For vata folks, the techniques are milder, and for pitta, elimination methods are moderate, like purgation."

---

[178] Elating, gladdening or 'santarpana' therapy
[179] Discontenting or 'asantarpana'

"Conversely, tonic methods for vata are strong, with powerful tonic herbs like ashwagandha or ginseng. Tonics for kapha are milder using herbs like elecampane or long pepper that are not too heavy. In contrast, tonics for pitta are moderately strong with shatavari and aloe gel. Tonic supplementary method works better if the native has chronic low energy, a weak pulse, emaciation, lack of muscle tone, flaccid and weak type obesity. Reduction method applies when the individual has more definite energy and pulse, good muscle tone and a pronounced tongue coating. None of these are an indication of good health, it just implies the person can endure the pains of reduction."

"Pancha Karma with a stronger practice base replaces any reduction therapy initiated with palliative techniques[180] when the former fails to suffice. Palliative technique induces calming by strongly cutting through Ama, the undigested food mass, and sedating the dosha types. The technique has both Dosha and Ama quelled in the second part of the therapy. Dosha may inhabit along with improperly digested toxic accumulations, which irritate and make the symptoms complex. The palliative part of the wellness separates the dosha from any extra baggage of Ama, enabling the course to work on them separately. Being a milder reducing therapy, it can self-manage and needs no proctoring like the complete Pancha Karma."

"There are seven parts to a palliative herbal therapy. The first step to a palliative beginning is from consuming herbs to burn the toxins; such herbs include spices like ginger or bitters like gentian. Then the person can switch to herbs for stimulating the digestion, again spices and bitters but much milder like fennel, followed by light eating and less fluids. Physical workout is a must after this. Exposure to sunlight and brisk stroll outdoors in natural surroundings completes the palliative therapy. These methods strengthen the digestive fire, Agni and burn up toxins. They clean the digestive tract and allow the toxins in the deeper tissues to drain into it to be eliminated. Such methods apply to Sama conditions."

"For those endowed with vata constitution, the palliative techniques commence with massage using oil in abundance. Sesame oil works the best inlaid with herbs like ashwagandha, bala-powder and shatavari along with spices like cinnamon, ginger and calamus. Almond or apricot oil with warm, gentle and firm touch goes a long way to ease the elevated dosha."

---

[180] Astanga Hridayam, 1.24. Palliative or Shamana - relieving pain or alleviating a problem without dealing with the underlying cause from the root "sham" meaning "to calm".

"Any practitioner worth his salt will refrain from applying oil until hot spices have removed most Ama. Mild perspiration therapies with sweat baths, steam baths or hot tubs follow next. Diaphoretic herbs like cinnamon and ginger in the tonic consisting of bala-root, comfrey root or dashamula can be offered to the vata person. While saunas and dry sweats aggravate vata, adequate liquids and respites safeguard the process such that the native does not dehydrate. Use of tonic and invigorating herbs like garlic, ashwagandha, bala-root, comfrey root and ginseng, along with spices like ginger, fennel, cinnamon and herbal wines[181] follows the sweat treatment. One must be careful with tonic herbs when any tongue-coating persists or if abdominal distention and constipation occur. Sesame seeds, medicated sesame oil or ghee taken as food and treated on the skin for a week may follow through to enema purification. Oil in large amounts internally must be avoided when the digestive fire is weak or there are signs of abdominal distention. Mild physical exercise with comforting yoga postures such as sitting and lying, mahamudra, mild sunbathing sidestepping wind and cold, mild-strengthening breathing exercises, alternate-nostrils-pranayama offer excellent vata-neutralizing capability while steer clear of strenuous exertions. Adequate, nutritious diet is anti-vata, comprising dairy, nuts, grains like rice, wheat or oats, root vegetables, strengthening fruit, meat, with mild spices like ginger, cardamom, cinnamon or fennel. One should try to eat more, improve nutrition and avoid overeating. Short fasting for one to three days with spice tea like ginger and cinnamon helps in many ways. Warm environment and clothing, colors of red, orange and gold with moist colors like white ease the vata levels. Physical relaxation, soft beds and pleasant environment with a good deal of self-care works very well. Physical rest and mental relaxation with no crazy travel, no excess noise or distraction, resorting to daytime-naps when tired, delving in the luxury of a secure and stable lifestyle, with moments of happiness, joy and contentment are suggested for the vata individual. The last part sounds vastly utopian, but the saturnine nature of the vata beast needs appeasing. Optional meditation and prayer, solitary moments subdue the excess levels in vata folks. Palliation for vata has a nutritive or tonic side that is not too reducing, somewhat differing from tonic therapy where more spices and lighter diet are recommended until Ama is eliminated to manageable levels. Tonics taken only in lower dosages get to work better for vata people."

---

[181] Astanga Hridayam, Chapter 5 Dravadravya Vijnana – Knowledge of liquids 5.62 onwards. Madya (wine), Sura (beer), Mardvika (Wine from grapes), Kharjura (From dates), Sarkara (from sugar), Sidhu (from sugarcane), Madhvasava (from honey), Sukta (from jaggery), Asava (from fruits).

"For the pitta person, the palliative techniques begin with light massage with moderate amount of oil. Yes, oil that can be cooling, like coconut, olive or ghee along with bitter and sweet herbs like brahmi, bhringaraj, sandalwood, licorice or shatavari. Brahmi oil works great and so does any gentle, soothing and a little cool human touch. A cold shower, bath or a quick walk up the hill that induces mild perspiration accompanied by cool and dispersing herbs like mint, yarrow or burdock decreases elevated pitta. Surplus perspiration may cause thirst, burning sensation, dizziness or fever. Cooling herbs, bitter and astringent, comprising aloe gel, barberry, dandelion, burdock, red clover, comfrey and coriander help cleanse the blood and bile, while emptying excess heat from the system. Ghee with triphala on the eyes lowers the pitta pressure, complimented by triphala and brahmi taken orally. Moderate workout in cool air and wind, a stroll in a moonlit night, cool the pitta effects. Yoga postures that cool are shoulder-stand and pranayama of 'shitali', lunar-pranayama. Diet must be moderate, consistent, cool and anti-pitta with lots of sweet fruit, raw vegetables, green vegetable juices, cool grains like rice and wheat, mung beans, cool spices like coriander, cumin or fennel, the least amount of spices, salt and vinegar. Moderate fasting accompanied by cooling herbs such dandelion or burdock, green vegetable juices or fruit juices like pineapple or pomegranate keeps the pitta from flaring. Where debility trespasses, dairy products like milk become acceptable. Soothing fragrances that are emitted from sandalwood, vetiver, and rose, applied as oils or inhaled while wearing cool pastel shades of clothing in a pleasant environment, cool colors like blue, green and white; resorting to cool breezes, moonlight and avoidance of sun, heat and fire, is a definite way to skirt pitta problems. Relaxation, diversion, amusement, sports, love and friendship and frequenting places with water and gardens without any doubts ease the pains. It is also worth avoiding any conflict, argument, aggression, ambition, too much strain, striving, work and effort. Meditations involving the positive direction of energy, peace, love, and forgiveness along with artistic visualizations help in lowering pitta. Palliation therapy for pitta results in cooling and calming the person, being neither strongly invigorating nor powerfully reducing. It differs from tonic invigoration, the latter being more nutritive."

"For the kapha person, the palliative techniques entail strong dry massages or deep body workout, which may imbibe a little pain. Light mustard oil with hot herbs like cinnamon, mustard or camphor is very useful. Strong perspiration fetched by dry heat and hot diaphoretic herbs like ginger, sage, thyme or cinnamon can shake the kapha sluggishness. Dry and hot pungent herbs of ginger, cayenne, elecampane, calamus, myrrh, garlic and trikatu or bitter herbs like aloe gel, turmeric or barberry taken orally reduces fat. Such herbs dissolved in honey works even better."

"Internally consuming old, raw honey[182] obtained from spicy flowers like sage added to dry oil like mustard or flaxseed loosens the phlegm. Strong aerobic jogging or running against the wind and sun with heavy physical labor helps tremendously. Physical exercise should raise a healthy sweat and leave the individual feeling tired, but not drained. Light diet of anti kapha with honey, steamed vegetables, diuretic grains and beans with hot spices like cayenne or ginger and less of water and juice, if possible, fasting with lower water intake for a few days are part of the process. Spices and honey are strategic, so is avoiding sugar, dairy, oils, meat and anything complimentary to kapha. Dry, rough clothing, environment, what in essence comprises an austere, rough lifestyle, has a dramatic effect on kapha elevations. The key is to embrace cool and dry, avoid warm and moist. Complimentary to the austerity is physical work and effort, staying up at night till sleep overtakes and not slumber during the day, besides breaking attachments and habits and giving up the past at a psychological level. In giving up unnecessary possessions, kapha types must challenge their need for comfort and try to rough it with long hikes and nature camps. Active meditation, thinking and inquiry, reading scriptures, chanting, dancing or singing bring about the kapha release. The mind when stimulated, activated and well-exercised; again, not to the point of discomfort, besides being on a stimulating and reducing palliation therapy with tonics reduces the negative side of kapha rapidly."

"Stronger purification therapy[183] expels the excess dosha types that can instigate a disease. It signifies not just any kind of reducing, though others are performed along with it. Without proper preparation, the purification fails. Pancha Karma is a therapy for guiding the toxins to their sites of elimination. Mere flushing out from various organs or systems of the body may not be effective unless the toxins are directed to the elimination sites."

"The need for purification arises when aggravated dosha levels strike the gastro intestinal tract. When lodged in the tissues or waste, Ama, the undigested food mass poses a challenge when attempts are made to eliminate. In this process of purification, palliative methods go first, followed by preparatory measures like Snehana and Svedana."

---

[182] Old honey, preferably a n year old, stored well without any preservatives or other herbs.
[183] Purification therapy is 'Shodhana', Pancha Karma. Shodhana is from the root "shudh," to cleanse; is a special form of eliminating therapy.

"Pancha Karma comprises five activities of 'cleansing enemas, flushing nasal build ups, purgation, emesis and bloodletting'. I recommend none of them be tried without proctoring and supervision. I will therefore abstain from talking about them any further. When attempting to do any reducing and cleansing on your own, the palliative techniques pose a much lower risk."

"Whatever be the treatment, Pancha Karma, surgery, other toxin elimination methods; the wellness program as a composite defines a powerful rehabilitation program for restoration of health. Rejuvenation through such techniques comes under the method of 'Rasayana'. Once the excess dosha is pacified, and the toxins eliminated, it is pertinent that the body is restored to its proper functioning. Tonics or supplementation therapy has terrific benefits for the elderly, pregnant women, nursing mothers, young children, and debilitated, emaciated, or convalescent. It works great in conditions of anemia, wasting diseases, malnutrition, sexual debility, impotence or infertility, in states of nerve weakness, emotional collapse, chronic insomnia or nervous exhaustion. A certain amount of Rasayana is helpful for vegetarians and those who do strong physical or mental work or needing more nutrition."

"For vata types and conditions vata imposes, there cannot be a better therapy than tonics, vata being the essential catabolic force instigating tissue depletion, the native welcomes the way the tonics compensate. Tonics are also useful for many pitta conditions, such as fever, bleeding, hepatitis and ulcers, which can in no time reach a state of severe deficiency, largely through high pitta burning the tissues. It may even be useful in kapha conditions, where clogging by kapha may result in blood deficiency, reproductive tissue or nerve tissue scarcities. Tonic invigoration of such tissues may be necessary for kapha types when they are run-down and debilitated, as happens in the chronic conditions of asthma or arthritis."

"The dreaded season of autumn warrants more supplementation, when dry, cold and lightness of vata prevails. Supplement tonics have a definite use in winter when we need more strength and from our ability to digest heavier foods. It is less useful in the summer as its heavy and greasy character can increase toxins in the body, in fact, the process can invigorate the toxins that appear in late spring. What is great about this process is, there is no hard and fast rule on when to start it."

"Recommended are supplements whenever severe debility sets in. Supplement use is more constitutional than seasonal; the treatment may go on for months or years. Older we get, the more we need the extras. Most of us need a certain supplementation and oil massage in late autumn. It gives us the vigor to endure the vicissitudes of winter. Supplementation therapy often gets contraindicated in Ama conditions where the presence of undigested food mass becomes evidenced by a thick tongue coating. Like in the case of obesity or a critical disease, the person has an attack of congestive disorder, fever or infectious disease where all supplements to the long-term ailment will have to give in to onset of a seasonal disorder. All therapeutic applications need proctoring when allergies come into play, especially in allergic diseases like arthritis. Tonic food and herbs may prove hard to digest being heavy, one must check the condition of the digestive fire of the native before suggesting them."

"Ancient texts describe the supplement-technique as one that nourishes the body with 'meat, milk, raw sugar, ghee and honey; sleep and rest, oil massage, special baths and extra comfort'. The main emphasis is on diet, which permits rich, nutritive food, along with strong, tonic herbs, mild oil massage, rest and relaxation. Administered tonic substances are usually sweet or pleasant in taste, where dominates the elements of earth and water. The native is advised to rein in all work, be it physical or mental; set aside worry, strain, anxiety, sex for the duration of the process. One should sleep as much - whenever one likes and hit the bed early. Sexual abstinence, according to the Yoga Sutras, is the best means of regaining energy. Breathing exercises like Pranayama build more energy, followed by moderate breath-increasing exercises."

"It is best to avoid stimulants like coffee, beer, tobacco and all other narcotics. Meditation, contemplation and study of scriptural teachings ensure the supplementation's success. It may not be possible for us to do everything suggested, though tonics remain the most effective in the therapy. A native in supplementation therapy, when in real need of it, should have a nurse or friend to take care of the bare minimum needs and help with cooking. Loving companionship has no substitute. Tonic nourishments are simpler than elimination therapy. This is not just a matter of eating more, but also in other ways of increasing nutrition using other sites in the body such as skin, nose and colon enabling a broader tonic therapy."

Refreshing oil

"Oil application therapy[184] employs medicated oil for external and internal use, nourishing the body through the skin and oral intake. The effects of such nutrients extend to the bones and nerve tissue, allowing a direct penetration into the deeper parts, making oil application therapy useful in tonic supplements."

"External application of oil bypasses the digestive tract where different oil types go into the system that would be difficult to digest internally. An array of nutrient oils includes sesame, almond, olive, coconut and avocado and many medicated sesame oils. Excessive oil intake can depress the digestive fire and the other Agni types such as Bhrajaka Pitta which imparts luster to the skin."

"Ghee, butter, sesame oil, animal fat and meat broth facilitates the internal passages for tonics to be consumed. Warm milk with a teaspoon or two of ghee, ginger, and saffron serves this purpose. Inhaling tonic substances in oil through the nose is also an old practice. Ghee, sesame oil and herbs such as brahmi, calamus and licorice nourish the brain. Calamus ghee works quite well."

Tonics for dosha types

"Strengthening the body defenses with tonics for vata persons can be shrink-wrapped with several palliative schemes, all vigorous, followed by much rest and sleep to bring out the desired effect. Mild oil massage, warm baths with salt and mineral with no perspiration has a strong effect on a native who is not debilitated. As with any convalescence, physical workout needs close monitoring and so does any prolonged exposure to sun[185]."

"Food comprising whole grains like wheat, rice and oats, mung beans, root vegetables, dairy products, nuts, eggs and meat, along with oil, salt and spices speed up the vata tonics. Tonic herbal preparation in a sweet and pungent base, topped with herbs like ashwagandha, ginseng, guggul, kapikacchu, bala, shatavari, marshmallow, comfrey root, astragalus, licorice, triphala, ginger, cinnamon, cloves, long pepper works well with vata folks."

---

[184] Snehana – Oil application therapy
[185] Astanga Hridayam, 2.8 – 2.10. Abhyanga and Vyayama.

"With pitta affected folks, four parts of ashwagandha to one part of calamus taken in a cup of warm milk with little ghee and honey works the best. Tonic fortification for pitta is gentler than vata. Mild massage with no excess oil or heat yields good results. A warm bath, not hot, with no purgatives, no physical workouts, no raw food, minimum cold juices, rich diet, no fasting or skipping meals is used as tonic for pitta. Food may consist of whole grains like wheat, rice and oats, mung beans, tofu, steamed vegetables, sweet dairy products, sugar, but no spices, a little salt or anything that comprises the nutritive side of anti-pitta diet."

"Sweet and bitter tonic prepared with herbs such as amalaki, aloe gel, shatavari, bala, gotu kola, guduchi, brahmi, shankha pushpi, lotus, marshmallow, comfrey root, licorice go a long way for pitta. Four parts of shatavari and two parts of fennel taken in a cup of warm milk with a dash of ghee and raw sugar one to four times a day works well in conditions of severe debility. One can take the Chyavana-Prash jelly alternatively."

"Tonic nourishment for kapha involves a lesser nutritive and more stimulating approach, involving not too strong a massage that may induce mild perspiration, enough to warm, but not so much as to weaken the native. Adequate rest is necessary, but napping during the day is forbidden. Well, literally forbidden. The native must be reminded in avoiding strong physical exercise; even the mind needs the exercise but not the strain. Unlike palliative therapy, there is no room for rigorous, harsh methods. Even raw or light food does not satisfy the kapha. Food may contain whole grains like corn, barley or rice, beans like mung, tofu, chick peas or lentils, but no dairy products, free use of spices, some oils including a little ghee; the nutritive side of the anti kapha diet. Mushrooms like shitaki are helpful and in cases of severe debility, sesame or almond oil supports the system, fortified with adequate spices. Good tonic preparation with tinge of sweetness as base, topped with herbs for kapha include garlic, long pepper, guggul, myrrh, aloe gel with spices, elecampane, cinnamon, ginger and shilajit serves the purpose. It is better to avoid strong bitters such as senna, rhubarb, gentian or barberry. Two parts of aloe gel taken with half of fresh ginger juice and one-part honey, twice a day or every two or three hours in more debilitated conditions is quite a savior."

Rehabilitation

"Different rejuvenating methods are mentioned in the Rasayana supplementary therapy for supporting rehabilitation after a complex medical treatment or surgery. The rehabilitation is mainly herbal and other techniques are also applicable. For different tissues, the herb tonics may be different."

Tissue or organ	Rehabilitation tonic
Plasma	Shatavari, Amalaki, Marshmallow, comfrey root, slippery elm, Irish moss, milk decoctions.
Blood	Amalaki as in Chyavana-Prash, Shatavari, Saffron in milk decoction, Turmeric Ghee, Lyceum berries.
Muscle	Ginseng, bala, Amalaki, Ashwagandha.
Fat	Sesame oil, Ghee with tonic herbs like Ashwagandha or Bala.
Bone	Ashwagandha, Comfrey root, Solomon's seal, Guggul, Myrrh, Coral Bhasma.
Nerve	Calamus Ghee, Brahmi Ghee, Sankha Pushpi, Licorice, Ashwagandha, Haritaki, Sandalwood, Ziziphus seeds.
Reproductive	Ashwagandha, Shatavari, Bala, Garlic, Lotus seeds, Black and White Musali, Saw palmetto.
Lungs	Long pepper, Elecampane, Bibhitaki, Garlic, Fenugreek in milk decoction or with demulcent herbs like Shatavari or Comfrey root.
Heart	Saffron, Arjuna, Cinnamon, Rose, Lotus, Sandalwood, Ginseng, Hawthorn berries, Grape herbal wine[186].
Stomach	Shatavari, Marshmallow, Vamsha Rochana, Licorice for the stomach lining or mucosa.
Small Intestine	Ginger, cinnamon, galangal, cardamom, fennel, wine for Agni.
Liver	Aloe Gel with turmeric, sesame oil; ghee made with bitter herbs like barberry, turmeric or manjishta, and dandelion root.
Spleen	Licorice, Ginseng, Bala, Astragalus.
Colon	Triphala, Haritaki, Asafetida, Basil.
Kidneys	Shilajit, Gokshura, Brahmi Gotu Kola.
Brain	Brahmi Gotu Kola, Calamus, Tulsi, Haritaki, Sankha pushpi, Jatamamsi as medicated ghee.
Uterus	Shatavari, Aloe Gel, Saffron, Kapikacchu.
Testes	Ashwagandha, Bala, Kapikacchu, Black Musali.

---

[186] Astanga Hridayam, Chapter 5.63 Dravadravya Vijnana – Knowledge of liquids – Madya Varga (wines)

"Tonic and rejuvenating herbs need the accompaniment of nutritive diet. Herbs by themselves offer no sustenance, good food does. Herbs taken with food, honey, sugar, ghee, sesame oil, almonds, dates, raisins, wheat flour, lotus seed flour, rice and mung beans provide the right food vehicle for tonic and rejuvenating herbs to work."

Rejuvenating the mind

"Rejuvenation of the mind or 'Brahma Rasayana' is perhaps the oldest and most important part of the wellness therapy. While it is very difficult and demanding to attempt, spreading it over a week or a month, it can prove very effective. If we cannot do all, even a partial treatment can be very helpful. Mind renewal is the key to all disease factors that arise from the mind. In the practice of Yoga, the scriptures state that only 'silence' rejuvenates the mind; silence comes when thought and mental agitation ceases. Some physical or mental activity can also contribute to the silence – music, painting, sculpting or something artistic. To silence the mind, the native must take the stand of the witness, the seer, Cosmic man– a recursive process of self-inquiry tracing the 'I' thought to its origin. Peace-inducing words, music, mantras and prayers are very effective whenever the mind wanders and Pranayama brings the breath to a state of equipoise and peace. The other dimensions are well within reach, where connecting to the cosmic life force by opening to the healing force of nature; the body brought into tranquility through right posture provides the ability to sit for long hours. Any comfortable posture is acceptable, preferable though is the time-tested lotus pose or siddhasana in achieving tranquility without the strain. One must curtail any tendency for the mind to disperse and seek external objects of enjoyment. One must also keep the digestive fire running strong, consume sattvic foods and nothing that can clog the channels. Stimulants, coffee, tea, chocolate, drugs, tobacco, alcohol have no room here, neither do strong colors, but mild shades of blue, green or white, with some gold. Sandalwood incense, sattvic oils and aromas, flowers such as camphor or rose are of tremendous help. The right herb to take is 'Brahmi Rasayana', a jelly prepared with brahmi. Four parts brahmi, one-part calamus, one-part ashwagandha and one-part licorice taken in milk with ghee is the formulation. A natural retreat is essential, winter being a good season when our consciousness gets internalized. Most preferable is the winter solstice. Higher elevated mountainous regions are preferred as the air is clearer and the ether element is dominant."

"It is important to sleep as little as possible from midnight to four in the morning, with no sleep during the day. So, must physical activity and exertion be avoided, except for an occasional stroll, meditation and prayers at sunrise, noon, sunset and midnight. Sleep between midnight and 4 am, or between sunset and midnight in a place of solitude accelerates the rehabilitation process. This is the occasion to set aside the past, worries, anxiety, ambition and striving; and welcome the quiet."

Treat Vikruti safeguard Prakruti

"To treat any condition, you must first uncover the Prakruti, or the primitive constitution of the native and of course the Vikruti, the evolved state of the native and the nature of his disease. It matters not whether the evolved condition stands in good or bad shape. The general rule is 'treat the Vikruti, safeguard the Prakruti', aiming at easing the main symptoms of the disease without worsening the underlying constitution of the native. Practitioners can also observe a constitutional balancing, aiming just at the Prakruti when no significant Vikruti or disease symptoms are evident. This is in line with the general health maintenance and guidance."

"In any wellness program, several not-so-common-sense patterns emerge. One must not take on conditions that become impossible to handle, which implies avoiding most febrile diseases, acute pain conditions, injuries or bleeding conditions; or treating such natives only when such difficult conditions are in abeyance. It is simpler to treat any known pathogenic disorder or externally caused disease first, like common cold, influenza or fever which display their symptoms in earnest. As such, the practitioner can deal with such problems by the symptoms before targeting deeper dosha problems. When vata is disturbed it will not be possible to deal with any other issues, it is imperative that dosha-s that show signs of derangement are dealt with earlier. It is quite important that you as practitioners deal with psychological, emotional, stress, nervous and pain hazards connected with the disease and clear the native's energy fields to begin treating the body. No amount of counseling and herbal supplements can be effective, unless the native is determined to fix his issues. Treatment of Agni and the digestive system comes before dealing with the dosha types at a tissue level or trying to clear Ama from the digestive tract. With the digestive system not functioning, even the herbs and foods good for the native may fail in their mission."

"Agni needs to be rekindled and balanced with proper herbs and spices. Any attempt to cut Ama, taking care in not damaging the constitutional dosha is a welcome start. Along with balancing the Agni, normalizing the elimination process so that Ama gets removed from the body gets to be part of this process. The tongue is an important diagnostic tool to determine the state of Agni and Ama. The sites where dosha types accumulate are an important key to treatment - vata aggregates in the large intestine, pitta in the small intestine and kapha in the stomach. The tissue connection is another important thing to remember – vata's connection to the bone tissue tells you where to look for vata elevated levels; pitta has connections to blood and kapha to the plasma and lymphatic system."

"As one gets closer to prescribing a remedial process, the focus stays strictly on the main dosha derangement, on the sub-dosha types, tissues and systems involved, striving to bring the Ama-Dosha back to the digestive tract for elimination. Close on this activity's heels is a follow-through activity of rebuilding and Rasayana therapy required to restore the tissues and reinstate the native's strength. This usually requires intake of herbal tonics, which also ascertains the rejuvenation is on track. A thing to remember is that restoration can often take much longer than the treatment."

Key Treatment Principles

"Between the native and practitioner, the moment is opportune to reckon a few key points of strategy. While a thorough examination of the native stays in progress, the practitioner must delve deep into the astrology charts, guna and dosha types, chart indications, dasa period and transits, dhatu tissues, sub-dhatu systems, mull excretions and srotamsi along with a perusal of the medical history. Such a deep dive is indispensable whether the practitioner plans to make only life-style recommendations or treat specific diseases. Whatever be the actual outcome, one must build realistic expectations with the native and avoid presenting the program as a quick and magical cure. To the native must be emphasized the long-term changes needed in his lifestyle to accomplish the wellness equilibrium. The native must understand that it generally takes about one month for every year of the disease condition to correct and reverse it - there are no short cuts. Expecting long-standing conditions to correct themselves quickly is setting up for failure. Side effects occur along the way, some even unpredictable in case of vata types."

"Any dietary changes require slow and gradual introduction as deep-seated habits can only flex with time. There is little need to push hard on the native to adapt to a different life-style overnight. Setting up an incremental system of changes that allows them to learn how to manage their health, changing a few key factors at a time ensures greater success in the adaptation. Many natives are unfamiliar with taking herbs, so they might have unusual reactions to even the correct herbs for them. Starting with smaller dosages and increasing them gradually ensures the herb's success with the native. It is always a good idea to bring the client actively into the treatment process, early on."

"A therapist may know and understand the disorders, it is only what the native applies in his or her own daily regimen that can facilitate in bringing about the desired wellness. A well-rounded strategy of diet, herbs, exercise, yoga, meditation and other life-style changes offers options to the client, which he can prioritize and carry out. If there is difficulty with one aspect of the treatment, there is always another that he can fall back on. It is but natural that treatment brings out clues to additional diagnosis completing the wide circle of wellness. As the treatment gets under way, familiarity with the native's constitution and birth-chart increases, reveals more on their condition. Familiarity also breeds contempt and short-sightedness, it's like those mornings when you walk around the whole household looking for the beverage with the mug in your hand! The native must be made aware of the rules of engagement. The first session reveals something but not all. The first prognosis of the native's constitution or even the nature of the disease may require revision in passage of time. Initial assessments are only preliminary. A good rule for wellness is scheduling a timetable that is agreeable to both outlining clearly the responsibilities of the practitioner and the native. Let the native not narrow his health condition as his chief complaint and just seek symptomatic relief; but as a practitioner, you use that to discuss their deeper health problems and the need to tune a life-style that works for his constitution. In summary, native must be offered a process with a realistic assessment of what the practitioner can do for him, how long it takes and what efforts he must make."

"Many a time, there is no cure. While there are treatments for all disorders, there is cure only for some. Sometimes, treatments just make a condition better, but not offer a cure; astrological readings provide deeper insight into this. If such is the case with the native, it is best to tell him of the finding and ask him to try different treatments over a certain period to see which helps him the most."

"Disease usually has a more specific base involving one of the three dosha types. This depends upon the systems affected by the disease. Most respiratory diseases are kapha diseases being in the zone of kapha, but they truly are colored with vata, pitta and kapha essences. Similarly, arthritis is a vata disease being related to the bones, bones being a vata tissue; it is a disease associated with aging and occurring at a vata or kapha stage of life. But it also has shades of vata, pitta and kapha. Learning the art of differential diagnosis of disease according to the dosha types considering both the site and symptoms of the disease is the key to correct analysis and treatment."

"That makes the art of treatment equally complex. Treatment therefore applies to the disorder, its organs, tissues, systems and dosha types and the specific dosha behind the problem. In treating arthritis, disease of the bones, a vata disorder, required are specific herbs for the bones. These include guggul, myrrh, angelica, nirgundi and other herbs that improve the circulation to the bones. On top of this, specific herbs must be added relative to the dosha involved. When vata is behind the problem, what works are tonics like ashwagandha or vidari. For pitta, anti-inflammatory herbs like manjishta or turmeric are a big help and for kapha, hot circulatory stimulants like cayenne or pippali are useful additives."

"Besides a general treatment of the dosha constitution and specific disease, life-style changes can sometimes make or break the treatment. In case of arthritis, life-style and diet recommendations go a long way to reduce the underlying dosha as well as to strengthen the tissues and organs affected. An anti-vata diet for vata arthritis or yoga asana types for strengthening the bones and joints go hand in glove with the dual herb combinations. Final goal lies in successful draining of the dosha from the affected tissue to digestive tract for subsequent elimination from the body. Once eliminated, tonics and rejuvenation therapies are an immediate follow through countering any damages and promoting a higher level of vitality."

"I would like you to recall the six stages of disease, where it states that a specific disease treatment is not an end, but only part of balancing the dosha types and returning to an overall good state of health, which may require rejuvenation practices eventually, besides rebuilding the immune system."

"As in astrology, some events are mundane and affect the population, contagious and infectious diseases like influenza and other epidemics can bypass the subtle dosha types, where the treatment gets to be more symptomatic. Elevated dosha-s can be worked on afterwards."

"Immune system disorders and endocrine troubles are more a problem of Ojas, Tejas or Prana than vata, pitta and kapha. Rebuilding the Ojas, Tejas and Prana is the basis of all rejuvenating and energy-building programs."

Subtle therapy

"Healing modalities in the wellness program come mainly through diet and herbs. These are quick treatments at the physical level, however with the mind involved, there comes a dire need to add subtle and occult healing techniques to such methods. Such treatments work through the mind and senses, correcting our intake of subtle impressions. Aroma, music, color, gem and mantra therapy belong to this curative category. Aromatherapy uses fragrances to promote the restorative process, like incense, flowers and essential oils. Aromas are not only effective in physical diseases treatment; they also have tremendous use in treating psychological, emotional, psychic and spiritual maladies. In addition, aroma aids in meditation, health maintenance, disease prevention, longevity and rejuvenation. Many aromatic oils strengthen the immune system and Ojas, help treat chronic fever and infections and ward off contagious diseases. Aromatic oils comfort both the mind and life-force. They also cleanse and open the channels and chakras, clear and strengthen the aura. They remove pathogens from the air and body, neutralize negative emotions and attitudes and build Sattva."

"Aromatic oils contain their own share of the cosmic life-force or prana, through which they nourish and energize the prana within us. Aromatic oils go well with massage and marma therapy; of course, they are a treatment by themselves. Fragrances from the essential oils of flowers, resins and aromatic plants have a definite objective in aromatherapy."

"Many garden flowers like rose, lily, gardenia, honeysuckle, jasmine and iris are used fresh, dried or oils extracted. Even their colors soothe the eyes, promote perception, awaken the creative imaginations and increase the power of vision and visualization."

"Aromatherapy lets the astral light pervade the physical world. When the heart opens, devotion unfolds, blood is cleansed and toxins dispersed."

"Aromatic tree resins produce a fragrant smoke when burnt. Such are myrrh, frankincense, guggul and the resins of many pine trees. Resins secreted by the tree to heal its wounds and damages to the bark can certainly heal the bones, flesh and skin. Elastic and sticky, they lubricate the tendons and ligaments, strengthening the immune system, cleansing the blood and subtle channels, relieving pain and healing the tissues. Resins with their strong cleansing and antiseptic properties for the body and mind, promote longevity. They offer firmness, strength, stability and flexibility, increase energy levels and streamline movement on physical and psychological levels."

"Many plants like spices and pungent tasting herbs are aromatic; some even carry aromatic oils. Herbaceous plants such as mint, sage, rosemary, lavender, lemon-grass, vetiver, ginger, turmeric, cinnamon and sandalwood also belong to this group. Plants employ these oils as protection from insects and pests. Many oils with antiseptic, antibiotic and cleansing properties remove negative ions, promote circulation and clear the channels, while improving energy."

"Pleasant aromatic oils straighten the mind, being sattvic. While they balance the dosha types, and Ojas, Tejas and Prana, they are light and soothing, flourishing in the element of ether. Fragrance is the sensory quality that is owed to the earth element; however, the subtle part of earth is delivered from its perfumed attributes to the mind and emotions portion. As such, the aromatic oils possess all the five elements, however, in subtle and refined forms. As with all excesses, the aromas invigorate the dosha types when over-consumed. Oils, parched, light with strong smell can vitiate vata, those hot and spicy intensify pitta; cooler and sweet oils worsen the kapha levels. Aromatic oils work against pathogens, refresh the ambience, clear out negative emotions and astral pathogens. Oils contain decent amounts of prana, which enforce the act of healing. They are useful in supporting health, preventing disease and calming the mind and emotions."

"Fragrances delight the heart. While they improve circulation and ease its pumping, they also inspire love, joy and happiness. They open the mind, senses and improve receptivity and discernment; as they work on Prana, they arouse the life- force within. Fragrances through prana can remove the disturbances and obstructions to the life- force that come from diseases."

"Flower that bear fragrances come with a sweet taste and sweet post- digestive effect, besides being a coolant. Few of them act bitter- sweet, like jasmine or chrysanthemum. Flower oils decrease the levels of pitta and vata, but in excess can increase kapha. Elevating the emotions and calmness, gladdening the heart, they help open the heart chakra."

"Flower fragrances increase Ojas, the underlying energy reserve of the body and mind. They are an important part of anti-pitta therapy reducing irritability, anger while clearing heat and fire from the head. Many fragrances bolster the immune system and rinse the ambience of negativism and pathogens. Flower oils normally decrease kapha and vata levels, but can increase pitta. While they clear the head, sinuses and lungs, they stimulate the mind, senses, increasing Tejas-clarity and power of perception. Some are even strong analgesics like camphor and cinnamon."

"Vegetable oils galvanize the circulatory and digestive systems and unblock the channels. An important part of anti-Kapha therapy, pure pungent fragrances like juniper extracts, rosemary, fresh basil, camphor and sage lower the kapha levels. Some oils, which are both pungent and sweet, like cinnamon, mustard, ginger and cardamom work better with elevated vata. Few of the oils that are bitter and spicy such as wormwood, vetiver and henna decrease high pitta levels with their intense-cooling properties. One has to be careful with the fragrant oils - being light, with a strong smell; in excess, they can worsen vata, triggering light-headedness and hypersensitivity. In small doses, they act great for vata disorders."

"Most aromatic oils resemble the herb they are extracted from. In aromatherapy however, the way they are prepared and applied is different from the way the herbs are consumed. Ajwan from wild celery seed is pungent and hot. It keeps vata levels at bay. Ajwan is used as spice, or in tea sometimes as part of steam therapy. Almond essential oil is bitter, sweet and warm. It strengthens the lungs and nerves while reducing vata levels. It eases cough and also helps dissolve congestion and tumors. Aloes wood is another important incense and fragrance, with its pungent, sweet and warm character. It is a stimulant, aphrodisiac and analgesic and has good restorative properties for the kidneys, bones and reproductive system. Basil is pungent and warm; known to calm the mind, nerves and senses and decontaminate the air. It reduces fevers, clears the phlegm and has powerful antiviral action. Basil also cleanses the large intestine and removes Apana, the negative or downward moving life-force. From its cooling, calming and nurturing attributes, Benzoin soothes the nerves, settles the emotions, and brings about higher awareness, promoting meditation."

"Calamus is bitterly pungent and warm and can cleanse the subtle channels of the mind and the nerves. Calamus enriches the act of hearing, strengthens and regenerates the power of speech. Working within, it has positive effects on intelligence and wisdom, while strengthening the Tejas, the fire of the mind."

"Camphor is warmly pungent with lot of energy. Camphor instantly opens the mind, the senses and lungs and increases powers of perception and meditation. Camphor is cleansing, anti-parasitical, antiseptic and a strong analgesic, and for thousands of years taken for headaches and arthritic pain. Health advantages of camphor oil come from its properties as a stimulant, antispasmodic, antiseptic, decongestant, anesthetic, sedative and nerve pacifier, anti-inflammatory, disinfectant, and insecticide and at a higher level, it energizes the power of pure consciousness. Cardamom is pungent, sweet and warm; stimulating the mind, heart, digestive system and circulatory scheme. Cardamom associated with joy, delight and creativity counters the dullness and depression that accompany physical and mental disorders. Intake of cardamom during pregnancy does well for the native with its harmonizing effect."

"Cedar is pungent, bitter, sweet and warm, stimulating, cleansing and antiseptic; reducing the ill effects of arthritis, edema and diabetes, besides strengthening the lungs and heart. The pungent, sweet and warm cinnamon clears the circulation system, besides relieving pain. It strengthens the heart, lowers the sugar levels, fortifies the muscles, and improves fertility and sexual functions."

"Cinnamon empowers the will and muscles. Clove with its pungent, warm, stimulating, strong expectorant, analgesic and a mild aphrodisiac, awakens the senses, acts as the decongestant making us more joyful and alive."

"Eucalyptus with its pungent, warm and stimulating attributes, much like camphor, opens the senses and lungs, redresses the mind, besides working as an analgesic and antiseptic. It works against phlegm, stagnation, toxicity and depression. Eucalyptus cleanses the ambient and the psychic air. Frankincense, like its relative Myrrh, decontaminates the blood, nerves, head and heart, relieving pain and strengthening the joints. Calming the mind, frankincense increases faith and promotes purity, virtue, detachment and devotion. Frankincense is pungent, astringent, bitter, sweet and warm. Gardenia tastes sweet, bitter and cool, cleanses the blood, liver, kidneys and heart and counters infection and fevers of all kinds. Similar to Jasmine, it is milder as an aphrodisiac for women. Gardenia works well in uterine infections."

"Garlic, pungent, hot, unpleasant, is a well-known antibiotic and antiseptic. It emits a grounding effect taken in conditions of hysteria, fright or convulsions. It lowers the blood pressure and works against high pitta conditions."

"Ginger juice pressed out of fresh ginger root retains much of its oils and is pungent, sweet and warm. It is a good stimulant and analgesic for cold, influenza, headache, lung congestion and joint and muscle pain. It also helps improve the pulse and strengthen the appetite. One can prepare a paste from dry ginger. Ginger, even its flower fragrance promotes joy, happiness and creativity. Guggul has similar properties to myrrh and frankincense. It is not quite as specific to the female reproductive system, but is better for the nerves. It balances vata in the deeper tissues for bone, marrow and reproductive."

"Heena, a special warming oil works well for kapha and vata but a pitta promoter, endorses perception and clarity of mind. Honeysuckle tastes sweet, bitter and cool; while combating blood and plasma contamination and strengthening the lungs. Honeysuckle resists common cold and contagious influenza, besides its refrigerant attributes are great for heatstroke, sunstroke and insomnia. Iris has a sweet, bitter and cool side to it. It cleanses the blood, liver and lymphatic, besides being a good laxative, countering infections, and helps in the fight against jealousy, envy, anger and hatred. Jasmine feels seductively sweet, bitter and a little warm. It strengthens the feminine reproductive system and makes the female sex more attractive and alluring. Jasmine may induce a warming action on males. Besides, jasmine is clearing, cleansing and can battle tumors. It has its use in breast and uterine infections, even cancer, purifying the mind and emotions."

"Juniper with its pungent, bitter, sweet and warm, stimulating, cleansing and antiseptic properties works well with arthritis, edema and diabetes disorders. Juniper when burnt clears the air. Lavender offers a pungent, sweet fragrance, calming the emotions and soothing the nerves, promoting contentment, works well with women. It is excellent in downgrading elevated vata. Lemon balm is pungent, sour, sweet and cool. Calming and relaxing, lemon balm is a good coolant for fevers, even calming infants. Lemon grass with its pungent, sour and cool temperament is diuretic, expectorant and refrigerant. It aids in digestion, insomnia, cleansing the lungs and kidneys, providing an overall calmness. Lily has a sweet and cool essence. It calms the heart, soothes the nerves, harmonizes the emotions and works great in reducing irritability, anxiety and insomnia, countering dry cough, nurturing the lungs and stomach, increasing faith, devotion, virtue and purity and contentment. Sweet is lotus, a little bitter and cool; it calms the mind, heart, promoting deep sleep and meditation. It is a natural astringent for the skin and can be safely used on the face. Lotus increases love, faith, devotion and compassion and helps build Ojas. It strengthens the reproductive system and the nerves."

"Mint as oil is menthol, composed from several mints. Mint is pungent, cool and stimulating, it clears the mind and the head, disperses heaviness and dullness while increasing lightness and motility. Peppermint enables digestion and circulation. Spearmint is more calming and relaxing. Catnip is yet more so and stronger of the two. It also helps the native to sleep. Mug wort is bitter, slightly warm. It helps warm and clear the channels, easing menstruation and preventing miscarriage. With musk, I prefer the oil obtained from musk-wood. The act of killing an animal to use its body-parts as fragrance is disgusting and deceitful. Musk from plants offers similar features. Musk is pungent, hot, stimulating and aphrodisiac, a big help in reviving people in near collapse situations. It invigorates the heart, strengthens the reproductive system, and awakens the senses. Myrrh, pungent, bitter, astringent, sweet, slightly warm helps clear the blood of impurities, counters infection and putrefaction and works against tumors. While it strengthens the bones and the nerves, helps cut excess fat, it promotes tissue healing, as with traumatic injuries and post-surgery. It strengthens the heart and the uterus. Neroli oil from bitter orange tree is pungent, bitter, warm, and metallic with a citrus aroma it gets from the plant. It stimulates digestion and circulation and helps open the mind and senses. Patchouli, pungent and warm, is stimulant, diaphoretic and expectorant. It cleanses the digestive system and stimulates the senses, promoting joy and activity; it relieves high kapha."

"Pennyroyal is spicy with a little warmth, used as anti-hysteric, anti-microbial, anti-bacterial, anti-rheumatic, anti-arthritic, antiseptic, astringent, cordial, decongestant, depurative, digestive, emmenagogue, insecticide and stomachic substance oil. Pennyroyal as such is highly toxic; the oil is diluted before using. It cleanses the lungs, clears the liver and improves peripheral circulation. Plumeria or 'frangipani' is a common tropical flowering tree. It bears a sweet and spicy taste that is cool enough to counter heat, infection and agitation. Plumeria clears the mind, calms the emotions and fills the psyche with balance and harmony. It promotes psychological clarity. Prickly Ash is pungent, bitter and warm analgesic. Its oil treats any trauma, toothache, facial nerve pain and arthritis."

"Rose is the unmistakable queen of the garden. Seductive, sweet, cool, refrigerant and alterative; rose cools and cleanses the eyes. It increases love, compassion and devotion. Rose has a balancing and nurturing effect upon the female reproductive system. Rosemary is pungent, bitter and cool. It fortifies the heart, stimulates blood circulation and works well in relieving headaches. It facilitates menstruation and eases emotional tension."

"Saffron, an important but rare fragrance, is pungent, sweet and neutral. It cleanses the blood, clears the emotions and energizes the heart. Saffron strengthens love and devotion and boosts the feelings of faith, forgiveness and compassion. It strengthens Ojas and helps against emotionally influenced disorders. Sandalwood offers the best aroma for the mind, as incense or as oil. Sandalwood targets the upper body – the head, the heart – wherever pitta in blood can be destructive. Sweet, pungent, and cool, diuretic, alterative, antiseptic and sedative, sandalwood nourishes the heart, cleanses the kidneys, soothes the lungs, and brings down fever, irritability and anxiety. Thyme, pungent and warm is a stimulant, diaphoretic and cough relieving. It is also antiseptic and insect repellant, strengthening the immune system. Turmeric, bitter and warm cleanses the blood, lymphatic and the subtle channels. It is hemostatic, analgesic and antiseptic and heals injured muscles and tendons. Turmeric strengthens the skin and improves complexion. Vetiver, also known as khus, bitter, pungent and refrigerant calms the mind and clears heat from the head, great for fever and heatstroke. It is anti-pitta and anti-infection. Wild ginger or Asarum, spicy and warm, is stimulating, diaphoretic and analgesic. It clears the head, opens the senses, and counters headache and nerve pain. Wintergreen[187], pungent, warm and stimulating, great in relieving pain works well for muscle pain, joint pain, headache or nerve pain, provides quick relief from being rubbed on the pain site. It clears and harmonizes the mind and emotions. Wormwood is bitter, pungent and cold. It is a strong bitter aromatic and cleanses the blood, improves digestion and counters parasites. It detoxifies the liver, relieves fever and counters anger and irritability."

"When vata conditions prevail, warm and pleasant oil, which are not too over-stimulating is the better choice. Spicy wood-musk, cinnamon balanced with sweet and calming oils of sandalwood, rose-flower work better in derailing the elevated vata. Recommended oils are sandalwood, aloes wood, lotus, frankincense, cinnamon, basil and camphor. When encountering pitta conditions, cool and pleasant oils give better results, mainly flower essences, though few cooler spices and bitter aromatics are also useful. Recommended oils and pastes are sandalwood, rose, vetiver, lemon grass, lotus, lavender, lily, saffron, gardenia, honeysuckle and iris. In kapha stress conditions, hot spicy oils are best. These include essential oils and resins like mustard, camphor, cinnamon, heena, cloves, sage, thyme, cedar, frankincense and myrrh. Sweet flowers like rose, jasmine and sandalwood generally have no say in lowering elevated kapha."

---

[187] Wintergreen - contains methyl salicylate, from which aspirin is derived.

Perfumery

"Perfumes made from flower essences containing aromatic oils, pleasant and spiced promote general health, good complexion and improved perception. For thousands of years, perfumes have been used to allure and seduce. Flower fragrances from rose, jasmine, saffron, plumeria and gardenia add to a woman's attractiveness. Other fragrances like sandalwood, lavender and cinnamon are as common. Interestingly, most fragrant plants enjoy the company of highly poisonous snakes. The more alluring the smell, the more vicious is their serpentine buddy. Some snakes like the viper coil so well, that an unwary human may think of it as a branch or an ivy."

"Analgesic ointments made from the oils of wintergreen, mint, wild ginger, myrrh, cinnamon and camphor offer relief in trauma. Rubbing alcohol or beeswax forms the base, whereupon they get applied to the site of pain, typically in headaches, neuralgia or arthritis. Decongestant oils made with eucalyptus, camphor, sage, basil or mint help in removing phlegm congestions. Prepared in ethanol base, the oil gets rubbed on the body, while steamed decoctions of the herbs are inhaled."

"Antibiotic oils made of fragrances such as sandalwood, myrrh, jasmine, gardenia, honeysuckle and iris act in acute stages of fevered diseases to counter the fever and infection and protecting the blood. The oils fortify the immune system, countering thirst and delirium that the fever brings. Antiseptic oils made of camphor, eucalyptus, cedar, thyme and pennyroyal even treat parasites, ward off insects, handle insect bites and cleanse the skin, air and the aura."

"Calming oils made with sandalwood, rose, lotus, lily, nutmeg, frankincense and lavender soothe the entire system when placed on the head or the heart. They prevent negative dreams by pacifying worries and mental anxiety. Oils for gynecological disorders made from rose, pennyroyal, rosemary ease and regulate menstruation. Saffron, lotus and jasmine form another group and combining the two groups brings a better-balanced action, which reinforces and enhances feminine energy."

"Digestive stimulants, made from oils of cardamom, cloves, fennel, anise and ginger promote Agni and Samana Vayu, thus stimulating the digestion process."

"Oils for the immune system and invigorating Ojas made from myrrh, frankincense, guggul, saffron, rose, and lotus are often consumed as tonic besides used in combatting chronic fevers and persistent infections. The oils help in a big way when the native is unable to take other therapies. Such oils are an essential part of creating a positive psychic environment where people suffering from devitalized immune disorders are cared for in a clinic."

"Rejuvenating oils can resurrect and breathe new life into the native. Myrrh delivers a powerful rejuvenation of the blood and heart, frankincense does it for the blood and brain, guggul for the brain and bones. Saffron reconditions the blood, heart and uterus, rose works similarly for the heart and uterus. Lily reconstructs the heart and brain, sandalwood does it for the nerves and brain; and lotus works well for the heart and reproductive system. Calamus stays specific to the brain and the nerves while basil caters to the nerves and lungs. Iris finds its use with the liver organ."

Treating tissues and channels

"A multilevel, comprehensive wellness spanning affected tissues and systems of the body, starts with herbs and food involving the digestive process. Herbs work on the plasma or rasa dhatu from the inside such as the gastrointestinal tract and use the plasma as a conduit to reach the other tissues. In the process, some herbs and food augment the affected tissue, there are others that reduce the inflammation or its oversize. Similarly, several of them increase the tissue activity, while others lower or sedate it. Some herbs and food are specific in eliminating one or other dosha that may be the cause of problems to the tissue. Physical exercises and workouts come next that touch the tissues and systems from a different angle. They can stimulate and increase tissue function, offering different ways of removing blockages from within them. Other methods like oil massage work more directly with the tissues through the skin to the plasma from the outside. The ambience, music, fragrance, colors take the subtle route to influence the mind and nerves in stabilizing the tissue."

"Such a treatment of an affected tissue exploits different parts of the body to target the culprits effectively. Once the condition of the dosha and dhatu is known, every phase of the treatment must ensure in unplugging the dosha's penetration into the deep crevices. While treating the tissue, care comes first, then comes the need to have the toxins cleared and finally strengthen the tissue."

"Ingested food, water and herbs start work on the basic tissue, plasma through which their action gets known and communicated to other tissues. Most anti-kapha herbs do their magic well, including stimulants and expectorants. Kapha being the waste material of the plasma, in excess vitiates the tissue, wherein the anti-kapha army of food and herbs promise to cleanse the plasma system. Affected plasma as in edema with fluids in the skin and periphery, an anti-kapha base of warming, pungent expectorants and diaphoretics like elecampane, bayberry, sage, thyme, ginger, cardamom, cinnamon and cloves are very effective. Also useful are bitter and astringent, cooling expectorants, alterative herbs and lymphatic cleansers such as echinacea, yellow dock, mullein, yarrow, burdock and vasa. While few diuretics can be added, their role is secondary. Great results come from juniper berries, cubebs, cinnamon, lemon grass and coriander, which have a diaphoretic action. Food with reduced salt and fluids, devoid of grease and stickiness accompany the herbs. Dry perspiration is also useful as it cleanses and reduces the plasma. Aerobic exercise, like running works quite well, so does any strong exercise that induces perspiration."

"Conversely, when rasa is low or depleted, marked by dehydration, as happens after high fever, application of herbs such as milk, shatavari, licorice and marshmallow come in handy. Fever damages plasma and damages the basic water retention management of the body. Sour herbs such as lemon, lime, amalaki, passion fruit corrects the situation when taken with a small amount of salt. Sweet fruit juices like grape, watermelon, pineapple and coconut also do well. Raw sugar and not honey in the diet is valuable in such conditions. A big help also comes from thick creamy soup and rice gruel. External applications of sesame oil, swimming and frequent showers and wearing white pearl can be helpful. Nights are the times of recovery. Exposure to heavy food such as beans and corn, strong exercise, sun and wind can only worsen it."

"With vata out of control in the plasma, a Rasagata vata situation develops, as seen in dry, itchy skin diseases. Using plasma-increasing demulcents such as milk, shatavari, licorice and marshmallow with small amount of spices like ginger, cinnamon, cardamom or cloves to facilitate their digestion along with sour juices with salt are useful. A mild perspiration therapy with just enough sweat to moisten the skin using fresh ginger or cinnamon eases the skin situation. Oil massage snehana with sesame oil and other medicated oils like mahanarayan applied to the back, head and soles of the feet yield great results. Strong perspiration or workouts are not recommended. Anti-vata diet, sweet and light goes a long way into easing the problem."

"Pitta in the plasma develops as Rasagata pitta, resulting in swollen and inflamed skin, lymphatic infections and sore throat. Herbal expectorants such as echinacea that can cool the pitta overload, act as alterative and lymphatic cleanser comes to the rescue. Shatavari, milk, mint and marshmallow also work well when thirst and dryness show their presence. Pitta inflammation can be brought under control with aloe gel, or bitter decoctions of turmeric or cooling oils like coconut and ghee."

"Kapha's extreme level in the plasma is classified as Rasagata kapha. Swollen glands, damp oozy skin conditions call for plasma-reducing therapy. Pungent plasma-cleansing herbs, along with bitter, astringent herbs work better when fever and infection are quite pronounced. Mustard, horseradish and trikatu along with hot spices like black pepper, ginger, cloves and cinnamon bring in the relief. Strong aromatic oils of camphor, eucalyptus, mint, sage and wintergreen also offer reprieve. The infected area washed with infusions of pungent herbs and a dry powder massage with calamus reduces the infection. Ginger paste and perspiration with strong diaphoretics is recommended along with aerobic exercise. Only mustard oil and flaxseed oil in small amounts are permissible."

"Dealing with Rakta dhatu or blood, many herbs related to pitta get involved in lowering blood's abnormal pitta levels. Pitta happens to be a waste product of blood. In cleaning the blood and in situations where blood infections and inflammation are noticeable, alterative substances are of much use. Typical herbs comprising dandelion, plantain, red clover and manjishta are suggested for such situations. Diet with no red meat, greasy and fried stuff, sugars, pastries, salt, sour articles like pickles and vinegar and alcohol is recommended. Salads, green herbs and vegetables and mung beans expedite the relief."

"To revive a weak heart, where signs of cold extremities are evident, herbs like black pepper, cayenne, cinnamon, ginger, garlic, purified aconite[188], makaradhwaj[189] and camphor are recommended under close supervision. Any hot spice or strong stimulant works well, even the short-term use of coffee. Diet should be light, hot and nourishing."

---

[188] Aconite from Monkshood, a plant grown in cold regions is a dangerous poison. Preparation through dilution is possible, though putting the preparer at risk.

[189] Makaradhwaj like Aconite is a dangerous herbal combination containing mercury and sulfur. Both Aconite and Makaradhwaj must be administered under strict supervision.

"When decreasing the blood flow, as in the case of acute, subcutaneous bleeding the use of vulnerary herbs such as alum, alum root, oak bark, plantain, manjishta, cattail and thistle come to the rescue. These herbs applied as paste along with cooler and light food bring the respite."

"Increasing the blood volume after blood loss as in anemia and debility, tonics such as amalaki, shatavari and lyceum berries give good results. Saffron milk decoctions and iron containing fruit and vegetables are useful. Black grapes, apples, pears, pomegranate, carrots, red beets, yams and aduki beans help in the recovery. Sesame oil or turmeric in ghee facilitate the absorption of iron and other trace elements. Meat can be useful in extreme conditions. Blood having a pitta bias, astrologically Sun and Mars likely are involved in affecting the native. Weak Sun or Mars Dasa or Antara-dasa could bring such trepidations, where Coral, Ruby, Carnelian or Bloodstone gem in gold can offer good relief."

"Vata in the blood as Raktagata vata results into anemia and gout. Blood-increasing measures with amalaki, shatavari work well along with mild or warm alterative fluids like anantamul[190], cinnamon, garlic, saffron, safflower and turmeric to cleanse the blood. The native can pursue any strong anti-vata diet along with seeds and oils of sesame."

"Pitta in the blood is Raktagata pitta giving rise to boils, carbuncles, hepatitis, anemia, bleeding disorders and poor liver function. Standard alterative solutions and antiseptics apply here like echinacea, golden seal, katuka, guduchi, red clover, yellow dock, honeysuckle, manjishta, turmeric, saffron and salvia which work best in acute and febrile conditions. In debilitated conditions combine them with cooling blood tonics like shatavari, amalaki, sarsaparilla and marshmallow. Apply hemostatic herbs like manjishta, plantain or mullein in case of bleeding. Arjuna, salvia and turmeric are particularly good for damaged tissue and promoting healing. Anti-pitta diet should be light and cooling with green drinks made of celery, cilantro, alfalfa and sunflower sprouts or with sour free fruit juices. In debilitated conditions, where there is bleeding, milk finds a good use as blood tonic. Avoid exposure to the sun, heat and fire, and anger and conflict. Pitta emotions aggravate the blood."

"Kapha in the blood is Raktagata kapha indicated by kapha dysbalanced anemia, with mucus or congestion. Circulatory stimulants and expectorants are extremely useful; herbs such as garlic, cayenne, cinnamon, guggul, myrrh, dry ginger, shilajit, and prickly ash improve circulation and clear congestion.

---

[190] Anantamul also known as sarsaparilla.

Aconite or makaradhwaj are useful in extreme conditions. Bitters effectively clear the dampness and dry the pus. Indulging in heavy, greasy and sticky and sweat food only aggravates the condition. Fasting is worth an attempt."

"Good food develops good muscles. Muscles as in Mamsa dhatu can suffer from infections, tumors and inflammation, and different alterative solutions, analgesics and anti-rheumatic herbs rectify such problems. Herbs such as turmeric, guggul, myrrh, cyprus, sarsaparilla, manjishta, brahmi and aloe gel play an important part in muscular recovery. Muscle mass decreased through debility, poor nutrition and diseases, can be managed by tonics of astragalus, ashwagandha, bala, amalaki, licorice, and sesame. Wheat and ghee breads, besides barley, corn, potato, beans, tofu, lentils and nuts help in muscle atrophy. Regular exercise is important."

"Fatigued muscles cause cramps and spasms, either chronic or acute, from overwork or injury. Herbs like valerian, jatamamsi, mustard, quinine, skullcap, brahmi, and licorice come to the rescue. These herbs are recommended internally, applied to the site as a wash or poultice or in an oil base or as oil massage or as mineral salt baths to bring the relief. Mahanarayan oil and Arnica can bring relief from the trauma that follows."

"Vata in the muscular system or Mamsagata vata destroys the muscle tissue, causing loss of flexibility. Herbs like ashwagandha, amalaki and bala revive the muscular atrophy. Tonic induced diet comes of much use with use of whole grains, seeds and nuts, oils, dairy products and mild spices. Relaxing exercises and yoga-asana are helpful, along with gentle massage and external application of oils. Swimming works exceedingly well."

"Pitta in the muscle propagates as Mamsagata pitta. When treating innate muscular infection or its inflammation, herbs like turmeric, manjishta, saffron, safflower, salvia, sarsaparilla, brahmi and red clover offer the means. Treatment is similar to blood therapy where cooling, gentle exercise and workouts add value to the remedy. Cool water or application of cold packs deliver the much-needed relief, so does application of cooling herbs and oils like shatavari, brahmi, sandalwood and coconut oil."

"Kapha in the muscle manifests as Mamsagata kapha, where observed are flabbiness, looseness, even excess muscle tissue and tumors. Spices are a great remedy with the likes of cinnamon, saffron, turmeric, black pepper, and cayenne. Myrrh, guggul and dandelion are helpful."

"An anti-kapha diet for kapha in the muscle is recommended along with strong physical workouts unless the kidneys are weak. When reducing the quantity of fat as in obesity or fatty tumors, pure bitters work the best like katuka, barberry, gentian, golden seal, and dandelion, along with hot spices like cayenne, black pepper, dry ginger, and calamus. Trikatu plus Triphala is another great set of herbs. Resins like guggul and myrrh are specific, stored honey is useful in forming a fat-reducing group called lekhana. Fasting or perhaps light, anti-kapha diet lessen the fat, so does strong perspiration."

"To revive fatty tissue lost from debility, dehydration and emaciation, tonics employed are shatavari, white musali, saw palmetto, licorice and ashwagandha. A modified diet with butter, ghee, sesame oil, or lighter almond oil and sugars and if needed in extreme conditions animal fat and bone marrow serves the immediate needs. The body needs rest and relaxation; mind needs contentment."

"Vata in the fat tissue leads to Medogata vata dryness, translating into fatty tissue wastage where herbal tonics like ashwagandha, shatavari come to the rescue. Food prepared with ghee, or sesame oil and animal fats restore the elevated dosha. Perspiration works negatively, and anxiety or hyperactivity makes it worse."

"Pitta in the fat or Medogata pitta shows pronounced inflammation and infection. Herbs like turmeric, barberry, dandelion and aloe work well."

"Kapha in the fat as Medogata kapha rapidly turns into obesity and fatty tumors, where guggul, myrrh, dry ginger, black pepper and gentian along with laxatives reduce the excess. Perspiration therapy undoubtedly shows good results, it is however dependent on the native's condition. An ambience devoid of attachment, sentimentality and greed, with increased level of physical activity, study and meditation break the fat-progress."

"Problems in bones flexibility and porosity result as stiffness, pain, arthritis, where guggul, myrrh, frankincense, ginseng and ashwagandha give excellent results. Greasy nutritive diet along with cinnamon, turmeric and ginger can accompany the herbs. Oil massages are helpful, especially medicated sesame oil. Rejuvenating the bones with ashwagandha, comfrey root, solomon's seal, triphala, licorice and sesame offer the best results. Dairy products, sesame, wheat and potatoes provide the food content. Mineral supplements like calcium and zinc work well."

"In treating excess bone, like bone spurs, enlarged joints, herbs like guggul, myrrh, gentian and black are excellent supplements. Often this is a circulatory problem, therefore herbs to improve circulation like cinnamon, and cayenne or hawthorn berries come to the rescue."

"When providing analgesics for bone and joint pain, guggul, myrrh, frankincense, ligusticum, angelica, wintergreen, mint or menthol, camphor, kava-kava, cyprus, galangal, ashwagandha, pueraria and brahmi serve the purpose. A variety of herbal preparation such as medicated or essential oils, infusions, baths or plasters provide many alternatives. Balms made from camphor, menthol, eucalyptus and wintergreen are helpful for cold and acute pain. Medicated sesame oils, like mahanarayan oil work better for dry, chronic or stiff pain. Arnica paste offers miraculous effects at sudden onset of pain."

"Vata in the bone as Asthigata vata gets indicated as cold and dry arthritis. Ashwagandha, nirgundi, pueraria and ginseng are specifically useful for increasing flexibility. Triphala along with oil massage of medicated sesame oils like mahanarayan is explicitly targeted in reducing vata levels. Warming anti-rheumatic dry ginger, cinnamon, calamus and galangal along with heat applications work well in easing the condition."

"Pitta in the bone, Asthigata pitta, is indicated by damp and hot arthritis. Cooling and bitter herbs - chaparral, turmeric, willow bark[191], brahmi, white poplar, sandalwood and khus are part of this therapy. Massage with coconut oil or sunflower oil mixed with brahmi cools the fomentations or ice packs. Use aromas like sandalwood and khus."

"Kapha in the bone as Asthigata kapha brings about cold and damp arthritis. Guggul, angelica, dry ginger, cayenne, prickly ash, ajwan and galangal relieve the kapha overload. Dry massage with calamus powder on the severely affected parts also relieves the pain."

"Clearing blocked nerves and channels gets easily achieved with calamus, basil, cardamom, turmeric, camphor, mint, wintergreen, wild ginger and strong aromatics. Boosting the nerve tissue damaged by nervous debility and fatigue, ashwagandha, shatavari, licorice and lotus seeds are of tremendous help. Regarding diet, almonds, walnuts and sesame seeds are useful and so are ghee and milk. The emphasis on positive impressions, avoiding noise levels, sharp colors, stressful environments and conflict is a must."

---

[191] Willow bark contains salicylic acid which is an important ingredient in 'aspirin'

"Nervine combinations of herbs and spices like calamus, basil, camphor, sage, mint, bayberry, and wild ginger get to the rescue, when the mind, senses and nerves turn dull. Most herbs that can clear the nerves are useful here. Herbal sedatives valerian, jatamamsi, brahmi, skullcap, passion flower, sandalwood, ziziphus seeds, lady's slipper and chamomile calm and tranquil the mind. When debility is pronounced, ashwagandha, ziziphus seeds and shatavari acts as the tonic. Tonics for nervous debility and chronic insomnia, one may use ashwagandha, shatavari, lily, ziziphus seeds and licorice, prepared in ghee or sesame oil along with dairy and nuts in the diet, much like the increasing therapy."

"Vata in the nerves as Majjagata vata results in insomnia, tremors, even paralysis. Tonics along with sedatives such as calamus, ashwagandha, guggul, jatamamsi, valerian, basil, ziziphus and chamomile along with prayers, gentle massage and music are helpful. External application of medicated oils works well on the head and back. Burning sandalwood or lotus incense along with silent meditation reduces the anxiety levels."

"Pitta in the nerves, Majjagata pitta results in neuralgia and neuritis. Cooling herbs like brahmi, bhringaraj, skullcap, passion flower, hops, betony, ziziphus and shatavari in medicated oils work very well. Brahmi oil applied to the head, sniffing brahmi ghee through the nose work against the elevated levels of pitta. Sandalwood, rose, gardenia, jasmine and lotus fragrances clear up the pitta as well."

"Kapha in the nerves, Majjagata kapha results in blockage, dullness and even epilepsy where cleansing nervine herbs like calamus, basil, turmeric, ginger, mustard, camphor, eucalyptus, wintergreen, sage and cedar work well. Snuff made of calamus or ginger powder can also reduce the kapha. Guggul, rosemary, myrrh and frankincense act as stimulating fragrances."

"Strengthening the reproductive tissue challenged by sexual debility, infertility, or poor growth instills the use of ashwagandha, shatavari, kapikacchu or atmagupta, black musali, white musali, dioscorea and saw palmetto along with nourishing diet made of milk and ghee, sugar, onions, almonds, sesame, eggs and black gram."

"Lowering the reproductive secretions when faced with excess prostate fluid or vaginal discharge, one may use drying herbs like black pepper, brahmi, gentian, sage and hops. Sidestepping sugar, dairy, nuts, eggs and meat with any anti-kapha diet complements the herbs."

"Stimulating the reproductive system with aphrodisiacs like garlic, onions, pippali, cloves, saffron, cayenne and kapikacchu in case of functional sexual debility. In sedating the reproductive system through an-aphrodisiac agents, for excess or disturbed sexual drive is achieved from nervine sedatives such as brahmi, calamus, sage, skullcap, gentian, nutmeg, passion flower and hops."

"Vata in the reproductive tissue as Shukragata vata directs to impotence, infertility and lack of vitality. This can be easily combated by herbs such as ashwagandha, kapikacchu, bala, white and black musali, gokshura and shatavari. Pitta in the reproductive tissue as Shukragata pitta leads to reproductive system infections. Alterative herbs, diuretics and tonics like sarsaparilla, gentian, uva-ursi, plantain, shatavari, manjishta, marshmallow, gokshura and aloe gel are useful. Flower fragrances work very well such as rose, jasmine, gardenia, saffron, and lotus. Kapha in the reproductive tissue as Shukragata kapha leads to tumors, swellings and cysts. Tonics like garlic, shilajit, stimulants like black pepper, gentian, cloves and long pepper. diuretics are helpful like gokshura, uva-ursi, pipsissewa and parsley go a long way. Diet should avoid dairy, oils, cheese, sugar and diuretic food."

Ojas

"With Ojas level below threshold, the native suffers from weak immune function, sexual debility and exhaustion. Comes to the rescue many herbs like ashwagandha, shatavari, guduchi, astragalus, ginseng and lyceum berries. Food with raw milk, yogurt, ghee, honey, almonds and sesame are of great use. Libra ascendants may be particularly prone to low Ojas."

Herbs and channels

"Herbs can easily fine-tune the flow of energy through channels, working to invigorate the particular system by strengthening the main organ behind it. Increasing the air flow when the breathing gets difficult as in asthma one may resort to herbs such as ginger, mint, sage, basil, cinnamon, cloves, specifically bronchodilators like thyme or ephedra."

"Practicing pranayama methods such as bhastrika[192] or the breath of fire and physical workout in asthmatic conditions is advantageous. Slowing down the flow when the breathing is rapid as in hyperventilation, herbs like oak bark, schizandra, lotus root, ashwagandha and red raspberry along with deep breathing exercises and holding the breath for long duration helps, this being a high vata condition. And, to counter the blockage of flow as with asthma, or severe bronchial congestion, calamus, eucalyptus, mint, thyme, wintergreen, rosemary and camphor in small amounts are the rescue herbs."

"Supplementing a decaying, weak respiratory system recommended are herbs like ginseng, astragalus, shatavari, solomon's seal and elecampane. Nuts and dairy products complement the herbs, along with mild spices like cinnamon, ginger and cardamom. It is worth checking the horoscope for third house afflictions and challenges with the signs - Gemini or Cancer for respiratory issues. A fragile Moon or Mercury may also show weak lungs."

"Vata in the respiratory system shows up as dry cough and decaying lungs. Herbs endorsed for such a condition are ginger, cinnamon, licorice, ashwagandha and astragalus, besides taking food like almonds, sesame, walnuts, dairy products along with spices like ginger, cinnamon, cardamom, cloves. Pitta in the respiratory system suggest lung infections with liver complications. Recommended are alterative herbs[193] and tonics like brahmi, dandelion, echinacea, shatavari and licorice. Brahmi ghee sniffled through the nostrils helps in a big way. Kapha in the respiratory system results in fluid and mucus accumulation in lungs and body. Triphala and bitters, ginger, cloves, cinnamon, bayberry, ephedra, thyme, long pepper and elecampane work zealously to reduce the kapha. Inhalation or external application of camphor, wintergreen, menthol or eucalyptus works well. So, does mustard oil massage and dry massages of calamus powder."

"Weak digestion, poor appetite indicates low agni, where all herbal spices act uniformly well. Ginger, cinnamon, cardamom, cayenne, black pepper, mustard, horseradish, cloves, garlic and asafetida with light and warm diet rekindle the agni. When the reverse occurs with increased Agni and Samana Vayu, resulting in excessive appetite, bitter gourd, gentian, barberry and katuka bitters comes to the rescue. Tea, red raspberry, alum root and lotus seeds, along with cold diet, raw and heavy and lots of fluids ease the raging Agni."

---

[192] Bhastrika or the rapid dragon's breath, the breath of fire
[193] Alterative and depurative substances are known in traditional folk medicine as blood purifiers.

"Supplying tonics to a system where malabsorption and weak digestion are evident, one may use tonics made with ashwagandha or ginseng, astragalus, lotus seeds, bala, spiced with cinnamon, nutmeg, cardamom and ginger in milk decoctions."

"Vata in the digestive system leads to gas, flatus and bloating. Carminatives like orange peel, cardamom, ginger, basil, mint, nutmeg, and asafetida as in hingashtak formula[194] come to the rescue. Complex food combinations can be avoided with the herbs. While pitta in the digestive system results into hyperacidity and burning in the stomach, beside liver heat. Bitter gourd, gentian, barberry, turmeric, golden seal, katuka along with coriander, cumin, fennel and mint are helpful. Licorice, marshmallow and shatavari can also assist. Kapha, when it hits the digestive system, the result is nausea and congestion. Hot spices such as ginger, cayenne, black pepper, cloves, mustard and the trikatu formula along with expectorants and anti-nausea herbs like cardamom, nutmeg and fennel can be helpful."

"Shortage of water flow shows up as thirst, deficiency in salivation and dryness in stomach. Shatavari, marshmallow, licorice, comfrey root, slippery elm, and solomon's seal promote fluids and increase in water intake comes from sour juices, salt, seaweeds and sugar. The treatment is similar to plasma-increasing methods. Rice, gruel, oatmeal and dairy products are also helpful. Excess water and fluids show symptoms of white, greasy tongue covering accompanied by nausea, vomiting, fatigue, high kapha and diabetes. Lowering the fluid flow can be accomplished through gentian, turmeric, black pepper, dry ginger, orange peel and cardamom. Astringents such as fresh leaves and seeds of lotus, red raspberry, beans, barley, diuretic grains and vegetables cut the abnormal flow. However, in weak pancreas function and hypoglycemia ginseng, shatavari, solomon's seal, astragalus and lotus leaves and seeds can correct the disorder. Complex carbohydrates and starches are better than pure sugar."

"Vata in the 'water' system shows up as dehydration and vata type diabetes. Adopting a regimen to increase the flow and nourish the system, similar to vata therapy in plasma goes a long way. So, does licorice, marshmallow, shatavari and lyceum berries."

"Pitta invading the 'water' system brings about signs of thirst, pitta type diabetes and burning sensation in stomach. Here, amalaki, licorice and shatavari, aloe gel, turmeric, gentian, barberry, along with coriander and cilantro work well. Milk and ghee operate to dissuade the problem."

---

[194] Hingashtak formula is Asafetida with 8 other herbs.

"Kapha in the 'water' system is a double dose and results as edema and kapha type diabetes. Any regimen that decreases the flow as with cardamom, calamus, ginger, turmeric, gentian, orange peel, shilajit, gurmar, guggul, myrrh, garlic and bay leaves lower the kapha levels."

"Constipation, infrequent or hard stool can be corrected by rhubarb root, aloe, senna, castor oil, along with ginger, fennel, coriander, cardamom, and orange peel in dosages of one part to four parts of laxative. To decrease diarrhea, or too frequent or soft stool, astringents such as oak bark, alum root, mullein, red raspberry, bayberry, lotus root and strong black tea are helpful. When the condition is infectious, one may contemplate pitta-reducing bitters like bitter gourd, golden seal, katuka, barberry and gentian. If it turns chronic, consider tonics like ashwagandha, ginseng or elecampane. When there is dehydration, add shatavari, licorice or marshmallow."

"Supply of tonics to chronic weak colon, or prolapse of rectum with herbs such as haritaki, triphala, psyllium and flaxseed with anti-vata diet of bulk and greasy food supports the weak condition of colon. Vata in the elimination system shows up as gas, bloating and chronic constipation. Triphala and psyllium act as a laxative. Purgatives like castor oil can be taken whenever necessary. Carminatives such as asafetida, basil, calamus and valerian ease the problem. Sesame oil massage can also be helpful. Pitta in the elimination system gets indicated as colitis, burning sensation, chronic loose stool. Where constipation is dominant, bitters and astringents like rhubarb, senna, aloe[195], and bulk laxatives like psyllium; mild laxatives like rose and cooling diet, avoiding spices and alcohol comes to the rescue. Pitta persons do not require strong laxatives, however, when diarrhea symptoms dominate, the decreasing flow therapy becomes more prevalent besides avoiding hot, greasy and sweet food. Kapha in the elimination system shows as mucus in stool. Hot spices of trikatu, cayenne, black pepper, calamus and basil along with bitter laxatives like rhubarb, aloe, triphala works well for the elderly native, or a person weak from another disorder."

"Poor urination with scanty or difficult flow can be improved with diuretics like gokshura, punarnava, uva-ursi, pipsissewa, cleavers, wild carrot, and burdock seed along with parsley, cilantro, celery, carrots, barley, corn, watercress, asparagus, mushrooms, aduki beans. When urination is in excess, the causes could be many, either infected urinary tract or cold weather. In any case, lotus seeds, ashwagandha and schizandra with plasma-boosting diet of salt, seaweeds, cinnamon, ginger, cubebs or cayenne eases the condition."

---

[195] Aloe should not be taken if there is bleeding

"Blockage in urination can come from urinary stones, where corn silk, Pashana Bheda, gravel root, uva-ursi, white oak bark and turmeric work exceedingly well. When signs of irritation or bleeding are found, marshmallow or licorice along with large amounts of water are recommended. In delivering tonic to the system as in weak kidney function, gokshura, shilajit, ashwagandha, sarsaparilla, marshmallow, shatavari, white musali, and black musali are the herbs of choice."

"Vata in the urination system shows up as dry, scanty urination, pain during urination. Gokshura and ashwagandha invigorate the system and correct the disorder. Pitta in the urination system is indicated by urinary tract infections. Cilantro, coriander, lemon grass, sandalwood, sarsaparilla, uva-ursi, pipsissewa and plantain along with cooling tonics like shatavari and sarsaparilla work their best in debilitated conditions. Fruits and juices of melon, watermelon, pomegranate and cranberry can accompany the herbs. Kapha in the urination system shows up as mucus in urine. Juniper berries, cinnamon, cubebs, shilajit, pippali, guggul and garlic are the chosen herbs for this problem. Higher the perspiration, lesser the load on the kidneys."

"Perspiration along the channels of Svedavaha srotas, related to plasma and prana systems forms the key part of the lung system and the skin. Absence of perspiration is a sign of the first stage of disorder. Proper flow and perspiration can be promoted when common cold, influenza, poor circulation and cold extremities set in. Herbs such as ephedra, cinnamon, ginger, cloves, sage and mint are of tremendous help. Warm bed, warm environment, saunas, steam baths, strong exercise and pranayama can work for the native. When dehydration and night sweats become bothersome, astragalus, schizandra, ashwagandha, hibiscus, red raspberry, strawberry leaf, oak bark, corn silk, gokshura, parsley and cilantro get to be useful."

"Heightened vata in the perspiration system is indicated as vata type cold and external attacks of influenza and poor circulation. Cinnamon, fresh ginger, basil, licorice, marshmallow and ashwagandha are the herbal choice. Pitta has a similar manifestation in the perspiration system indicated by pitta cold and external influenza, herbs like mint, honeysuckle, dandelion, echinacea and burdock come to the rescue. Kapha in the perspiration system manifests as kapha cold, influenza and general congestion. Strong diaphoretics such as angelica, ginger, cloves, ephedra, bayberry, sage, cinnamon, eucalyptus and a perspiration therapy lessens the kapha increase. Anti-cough and lung-opening herbs can be helpful like coltsfoot, mullein, thyme and vasa."

"Regarding the menstruation system, treatment of channels or srotas related to reproductive system and blood get combined in managing its wellness. When delayed, difficult or scanty is the menstruation, turmeric, saffron, safflower, pennyroyal, motherwort, rose, rosemary, myrrh and salvia come to the rescue. Sometimes a simple thing as ginger or cinnamon tea may be sufficient. To decrease flow and stop excess menstruation where indications if excess or painful menstruation are evident, one may use manjishta, mug wort, red raspberry, lodhra, gotu kola, bhringaraj and lotus root as with anti-pitta therapy."

"In supplying tonic to the system indicated in a woman with scanty flow, weakness of the uterus, shatavari, amalaki, lyceum berries, aloe gel or milk decoctions of saffron are all useful. Sticking to the plasma and blood building methods, keeping the diet as anti-vata with much rich, greasy and sweet along with mild spices like ginger, cardamom and turmeric offers the strength to combat the problem. Turmeric ghee in essence works very well. To soothe the flow in the system indicated in counter dysmenorrhea or post menstrual disorder, use antispasmodics like cyprus, valerian, asafetida, pennyroyal, gotu kola, chamomile, mint, bupleurum. Such treatment is similar to elevated vata condition."

"Vata's presence in the menstrual system shows indications of dryness, cramps, painful premenstrual syndrome, use both tonics, sedatives and emmenagogues and also triphala. One may use shatavari and ashwagandha along with cinnamon, saffron or rosemary. Valerian or asafetida reduces cramping, so does cyprus or cramp bark. Applying medicated sesame oil to lower abdomen also eases the symptoms. Pitta's dominance in the menstrual system is revealed through symptoms of excess menstruation or yellow leucorrhea. Manjishta, turmeric, rose or red raspberry with shatavari and aloe gel are useful herbs for this condition. Alterative herbs like sarsaparilla, sandalwood and gotu kola can also bring about desired results. Fragrances like rose, lotus, jasmine and gardenia are helpful. Kapha in the menstrual system shows as white leucorrhea. Turmeric, saffron, ginger, cinnamon and garlic along with bitters like gourd, aloe gel and bayberry can be helpful."

"The lactation system in women, namely the Stanyavaha Srotas has problems similar to disorders of the plasma and the water metabolism system and their treatments can be quite analogous. Calamus, cardamom, ginger, fennel, and cinnamon are the herbs of choice. To increase human milk flow when it is lacking or difficult, fennel, dill, caraway, dandelion root and marshmallow are the herbs of choice. To decrease the flow sage, oak bark and bayberry are excellent choices. Anti-kapha diet with sprouted grains, wheat, rice and barley can accompany the herbs."

"Herbs that rectify deficient production of breast milk and poor development of the breasts are shatavari, licorice, milk, yogurt, ghee, coconut, and sesame balanced with ginger, cinnamon, saffron and turmeric."

"Vata in the lactation system shows as dryness, difficult flow and pain. Ashwagandha, bala, shatavari, licorice accompanied by oil and rich food can fix the problem. Pitta in the lactation system gets indicated from infection and inflammation. Herbs like dandelion, violet, golden seal, turmeric and barberry ease the pitta conditions. Kapha in the lactation system shows up as congestion, swelling, tumors, cysts. Turmeric, calamus, cardamom, sage, cyprus, bupleurum reduce the flow."

"It is amazing how a handful of herbs, food and physical and mental workout can change your lifestyle. Let me introduce you to sub-dosha, which have a slightly different lifecycle, therefore different treatment than their parental dosha-s."

Sub-dosha treatment

"Treating sub-dosha problems requires checks on the dosha out of balance and the subtypes involved. Diagnosis closely considers the sub-dosha types, which is a finer part of pulse diagnosis. Sub-dosha derangement undergoes different treatment depending on their severity. Besides, each sub-dosha may prefer different sites where it manifests the disease. Though I will narrate both the high and low states of sub-dosha types, in most cases, the high state gets treated because it is more likely to cause disease. Recall how sub-dosha types are closely associated. One sub-dosha level going high may cause another to become low. High Sleshaka kapha as in swollen joints can obstruct or make Vyana vayu low. In such cases, the principle turns to targeting the sub-dosha that runs high."

Vata dosha and sub-dosha treatment

"Vata displays two types of symptoms among its sub-dosha types, a little different from the excess and deficient conditions of other dosha-s. There can be too much or too little of the dosha. Vata, formless and mobile gets deranged mainly in terms of movement. It either moves a lot or moves too little."

"These vata conditions run an association because excess movement can lead to deficient movement and the reverse. When the air aspect of vata is high, it moves too much. When the ether aspect of vata is high, it moves too little. However, too much kapha can also impair its movement. Vata is harder to treat and more variable in its symptoms than other two-dosha types. One should not confuse high levels of vata with having much positive energy prana. Prana as such is unstable, not strong in high vata conditions."

"Prana vayu is the inward moving, propulsive force. When in excess, as in high vata, excess movement or agitation is experienced in the head and heart region leading to loss of equilibrium. Symptoms of rapid breathing, hyperventilation, hypersensitivity, dizziness, sensory disorientation, fear, ungrounded feelings, tremors in the head and insomnia runs strong. Herbal treatment comprises calming and invigorating nervine herbs flavored sweet and pungent and warming in energy. Typical herbs used are jatamamsi, valerian, shankha pushpi, ashwagandha, shatavari, nutmeg, garlic; sesame oil massage to the head by means of Shirodhara."

"When Prana vayu is deficient, experienced as high kapha in the head and heart region, symptoms exhibited are shallow and slow breathing, hyposensitivity, congestion in lungs, sinus congestion, and lack of enthusiasm, depression, lethargy and lassitude. Herbal treatment comprises pungent aromatic herbs to stimulate, open and move the prana and dissolve blockages. Typical herbs used in this case are eucalyptus, peppermint, calamus, camphor, sage, thyme, ginger, pippali and honey."

"Apana Vayu, the downward moving, eliminating force; when in excess, surplus movement of vata in the lower abdomen and intestines instigates pain and distention. Symptoms of loose stool, diarrhea, increased peristalsis, undigested food in the stool, and excess menstruation in women are dominant. Herbal treatment comprises astringent herbs to counter excess movement of vata. Typical herbs used are raspberry leaf, alum root, lodhra, bayberry and vidanga."

"Vata makes no movement in lower abdomen when Apana goes deficient. It results in symptoms of constipation, bloating, distention, difficult elimination, and difficult, delayed or painful menstruation in women. Herbal treatment ranges from laxative and purgative herbs depending upon the severity of the condition. Bitter or greasy herbs are the choice. Typical herbs used are triphala, psyllium, flax seed, cascara sagrada, aloe gel, castor oil, sesame oil through basti or enemas."

"Udana vayu is an upward moving, expressive force. When in excess, vata moves in surplus in the throat region symptomatically showing up as cough, dry throat and causing difficulty in swallowing. More symptoms become evident with nausea, possible vomiting, excessive speaking and hyperactivity of all types. Useful herbal treatments recommend antispasmodic, sedative and antitussive and anti-cough herbs made of sweet and pungent tastes and mild warm energy. Typical herbs used are vasa, coltsfoot, calamus, jatamamsi, valerian, licorice, sesame oil and ghee."

"When Udana is deficient, vat movement falls short, blocking energy in the throat region. Symptoms of difficulty in speech, mucus constriction of the throat, lack of motivation, depression, swollen glands in the neck and possible development of tumors become prevalent. Herbal treatment includes herbs to stimulate and strengthen prana in the throat region through flavored pungent and sweet, warm herbs. Typical herbs used are calamus, haritaki, bayberry, peppermint, eucalyptus and ashwagandha."

"Vyana Vayu is the extroverted, expansive force. In excess, when vata runs high, symptoms of superfluous movement, coldness and dryness in the circulatory system and joints and arthritic pain start to appear. Indications often point to palpitations, rapid heartbeat, muscle or joint tremors, lack of muscle-skeletal coordination and coldness in the limbs, besides joint pain. Herbal treatment typically suggests pungent and sweet herbs with pain-relieving action to improve circulation and calm the vata. Typical herbs include ashwagandha, nirgundi, guggul, jatamamsi, valerian, sesame oil; oil therapy or snehana. Deficient Vyana results in kapha levels going high and a slowdown in the circulatory system. Symptoms of poor circulation, high cholesterol, swollen glands and cysts dominate. Herbal treatment with circulatory stimulants of pungent taste and warming behavior such as guggul, myrrh, cinnamon, saffron and angelica ease the condition."

"Samana vayu unveils a consolidating and contracting force. In excess, the high levels of vata agitates the digestive system nervously. Nervous stomach, possible vomiting, variable appetite and digestion, imbalance and malaise appear as symptoms. Mild aromatic spices and carminatives mollify the stomach, where ginger, cardamom, fennel, cloves, basil, jatamamsi, chamomile and lemon juice are the herbs of choice. When Samana is deficient, signs of congestion become apparent with blockages in the digestive system, appetite turning low and poor peristalsis. Symptoms showed are lack of appetite, buildup of Ama or mucus, nausea and headache. Herbal treatment suggests digestive stimulants and aromatics to ease access to the stomach, besides increasing Agni. Typical herbs used are mint, ginger, cardamom, calamus, fennel, cinnamon, basil, bay and curry leaves."

Pitta dosha and sub-dosha treatment

"Pitta sub-dosha types flaunt similar symptoms of high pitta such as fever, inflammation and bleeding. In deficit state, the signs are alike low pitta levels, accompanied by coldness, pallor and loss of acuity. As with kapha, these find a local zone where the sub-dosha can flourish. Overall symptoms of high or low pitta prevail throughout the body. Pitta involving fever, some conditions may become acute and require proctored treatment."

"Pachaka pitta resembling classical pitta problems are the issues of the digestive system. When in excess, high pitta or excess digestive acids affect the fluids and bile in the digestive system and the small intestine. Symptoms of excess production of digestive acids and bile leading to hyperacidity, ulcers, bleeding in the gastrointestinal tract, liver in a jaundiced state and hepatitis are rampant. Herbal treatment uses mainly bitter and sweet tastes to reduce hyperacidity and cool the liver, small intestine and pancreas. Virechana therapy is suggested when Pachaka goes ballistic. Typical herbs employed are shatavari, marshmallow, amalaki, aloe gel, gentian, barberry, coriander, cilantro and licorice. When Pachaka runs deficient, high kapha and vata build up in the digestive system, resulting in low agni and accrual of Ama. Prominent symptoms in deficient Pachaka are lack of digestive secretions, poor appetite and digestion, high Ama production, congestion and coldness in stomach. Herbal treatment for deficient Pachaka comprises spicy digestive stimulants to promote Agni, with greasy food or demulcent herbs to feed it. Typical herbs used are ginger, cayenne, black pepper, basil, cinnamon, cardamom, trikatu and ghee."

"Bhrajaka pitta affects warmth and luster of the skin, the peripheral circulation of skin and joints. When levels are in excess, high pitta or inflammation shows up in the skin, and periphery of the body including the joints, even upsetting the lungs. Symptoms range from intolerance to sunlight, skin rashes, ruddy skin, and burning sensation on skin, bleeding at the skin, subcutaneous bleeding and rheumatoid arthritis. In the herbal treatment of such disorder, often used are alterative herbs or blood purifiers and diuretics, majority being bitter, astringent and sweet in taste, cooling in energy. Typical herbs employed are aloe gel, manjishta, plantain, comfrey leaf, nettles, red clover, chaparral, dandelion leaf and turmeric. When Bhrajaka gets deficient, high kapha and vata take over lowering the circulation in the skin causing coldness, dryness and paleness from lack of skin pigments."

"With Bhrajaka low, symptoms of pallor, coldness of the skin, poor peripheral circulation, and itching, watery cysts beneath the skin, fungal conditions of the skin, kapha or vata type arthritis appear. Herbal treatment includes spiced circulatory stimulants and warm diaphoretics along with Svedana therapy. Typical herbs span cayenne, ginger, cinnamon, bayberry, pippali, nirgundi and angelica."

"Ranjaka pitta disorders stretch to blood, liver and spleen. When in excess, high pitta or heat erupts, turning the blood and liver toxic, producing excessively yellow stool or urine. Symptoms of excess, toxic blood, boils, hepatitis, jaundice, swollen liver and spleen and internal bleeding are prevalent. Herbal treatment starts with those mainly bitter, sweet and cool herbs. Typical herbs used are guduchi, barberry, myrrh, aloe gel, brahmi, manjishta, coriander, cilantro and ghee. When Ranjaka is insufficient, high kapha and vata appear, accompanied by coldness and dryness in the blood and liver. Dearth of color in the blood, underprovided blood, pallor, fainting, anemia and weak immune function show up as symptoms. Treatment suggests sweet-flavored herbs to invigorate and build the blood, along with pungent herbs to kindle the liver function. Typical herbs used are amalaki, shatavari, saffron, chitrak, turmeric, sesame seeds and ghee."

"Alochaka Pitta occurring in excess results in high pitta, heat and inflammation in the eyes and in other sense organs such as ears, nose and throat. The fallout is evident with red, smarting eyes, allergies, sensitivity to light and sunlight, headaches, earaches. Dealing with the problem encompasses herbs to cool and cleanse the eyes and head, primarily sweet or bitter taste and cooling energy. Typical herbs used are triphala-ghee[196], eyebright, golden seal, aloe gel, chrysanthemum, chamomile and sandalwood. When Alochaka is deficient, high kapha and vata become dominant bringing in cold and dryness in the eyes and senses. Symptoms include loss of visual acuity, watery or swollen eyes, frequent tearing, sinus congestion and allergies. Herbal treatment comprises pungent stimulants to improve circulation to the eyes and senses. Typical herbs used are cinnamon, calamus, eucalyptus, barberry, shilajit and sage."

---

[196] Triphala-ghee or Triphala juice with Castor Oil is a great remedy for red and dry eyes. Triphala may sting for a few seconds, but provides instant relief from dry and itchy eyes.

"When Sadhaka Pitta crosses the threshold, the high pitta levels are accompanied by heat and anger leading to nervous and mental imbalance. Symptoms are severe with fever in the head, sensory derangement, anger, irritability, poor judgment, snappiness and insomnia. Therapy comprises cooling nervine herbs and sedatives, mainly sweet or bitter to lower pitta and calm the mind and nerves. Typical herbs used are brahmi, manduka parni, skullcap, passion flower, jatamamsi, ziziphus seeds, licorice and ghee. When Sadhaka runs short, low agni, poor perception and weak functioning of the mind and brain, loss of acuity in nerve function show up. Symptoms range from lack of mental acuity, drowsiness, daydreaming, depression, attachment, fear, anxiety, hallucinations, poor judgment and discrimination. Herbal therapy comprises pungent nervine stimulants, which are heating in energy. Typical herbs used are calamus, bayberry, haritaki, sankha pushpi, shilajit, eucalyptus, peppermint and sage."

Kapha dosha and sub-dosha treatment

"In the case of kapha dosha and its sub-dosha types, all sub-dosha types of kapha tend to demonstrate settings of high kapha in their excess states, like severe congestion, edema, and as low kapha in their deficient states, like dryness and tissue deficiency. Localized by its nature, place and function, the sub-dosha exhibits symptoms of either high or low kapha that prevails throughout the entire body."

"With kapha based arthritis resulting in swollen joints, edema, dull pain and lethargy, an excess of Sleshaka kapha reflects brutal kapha proliferation with obesity, swollen glands and congestion in the lungs. High kapha specializes as a sub-type, sometimes localizes as excess of one of the sub-types. In acute cases, several sub-dosha types may get involved as arthritis and lung congestion occurring simultaneously, namely Sleshaka and Avalambaka kapha."

"Signs of Avalambaka Kapha are seen in the chest, lungs and heart region, the area it serves to cushion and lubricate. Kapha problems of these organs are mostly felt. When in excess, congestion and blockage in the lungs, heart and chest occur, besides lowering their functioning. Symptoms of lung congestion, swollen glands in the neck, excess mucus, productive cough, difficult breathing, tightness in the chest, angina pectoris, high cholesterol and coronary heart disease can be evident."

"Treatment of high levels of Avalambaka Kapha comprises warming and stimulating expectorants, diaphoretics and anti-spasmodic substance, predominantly pungent but secondarily bitter and astringent flavored. Some salty, sweet and sour herbs like licorice, kelp or lemon help in liquefying blocked or hardened kapha. One must remember that such treatment is meant for temporary use only. Aromatic oils application to the chest like eucalyptus, menthol; or massage with pungent oil of mustard can be helpful. Typical herbs are bibhitaki, pippali, elecampane, bayberry, guggul, saffron, thyme, ginger, cayenne, cinnamon, vasa, coltsfoot, licorice, garlic and honey. When deficient is Avalambaka kapha, conditions of vata and pitta affect the lungs and chest, drying out the essential mucus and depleting it, causing nervous heart conditions and emotional unrest. Symptoms suggest dryness of the lungs, showing up as wasting of the lungs, dry throat, thirst, unproductive or dry cough, painful cough, difficult breathing, palpitations, rapid heartbeat, anxiety and insomnia. Treatment uses herbs to increase kapha and cut through the pain and friction; herbs that are predominantly sweet in taste and cooling in energy. Typical herbs used are ashwagandha, shatavari, licorice, marshmallow, vasa, valerian and jatamamsi."

"Kledaka kapha manifests its symptoms as kapha problems in the digestive system. In excess, high kapha in the stomach and digestive system reduces digestion to a sluggish crawl besides the presence of mucus in the stomach. Symptoms show excess production of fluids in the stomach, water or gurgling sound in the area followed by nausea, eructation, vomiting, low appetite, loss of taste, lassitude and possible headache. Treatment exploits pungent herbs and digestive stimulants to drain the stomach, increase Agni and unblock kapha. Typical herbs used are ginger, cinnamon, black pepper, pippali, cayenne, mustard, calamus, cardamom, fennel, bay leaves, orange peel, basil and trikatu. When deficient gets Kledaka kapha, it generates high vata and pitta in the stomach, besides, shortages in kapha digestive secretions, with resultant pain and discomfort and poor digestion. Many symptoms appear, starting with stomach dryness, dry and cracked tongue, stomach ulceration accompanied by pain and loss of appetite, weight-loss and intolerance to dry and light food. Treatment comprises sweet, cool and demulcent herbs to promote kapha and ease digestion. The herbs accompanied by rich and nutritive diet - sweet and greasy, soup, dairy products and mild grains like paddy rice[197] pay rich dividends. Typical herbs used are amalaki, aloe gel, shatavari, licorice, marshmallow, milk decoctions, ghee and coconut juice."

---

[197] Astanga Hridayam, Chapter 6.9-6.10 Paddy rice.

"Bodhaka Kapha confirms its symptoms mainly in the mouth, neck and head. When the levels are in excess, sensed are high kapha and mucus in the mouth and head, blocking most sensory functioning and reducing the senses of taste and smell. Many symptoms get exhibited like salivation, drooling, swollen glands in the neck, allergies, sinus congestion, nasal drainage, watery eyes, loss of sensory acuity, loss of sense of taste and appetite. Treatment extends to using pungent, astringent stimulants and expectorants targeting the mouth and senses. Nasya[198] of a *Virechana* - cleansing base made of calamus oil, where added are aromatic herbs like mint, eucalyptus or camphor can be inhaled to get relief. Several herbs may be used like bayberry, cinnamon, cardamom, ginger, haritaki, peppermint, calamus and sage. When Bodhaka kapha runs short, it generates high vata and pitta in the mouth and head by drying out the mucus membranes of the head, mouth and senses, creating hypersensitivity. Symptoms exhibited are dry mouth, dry tongue and throat, dry sinuses, lack of salivation, difficulty speaking, dry cough, possible dry eyes, ears and scalp. Remedy comprises sweet and demulcent herbs to promote kapha, application of oils like sesame or coconut to the head, mouth and sensory openings. Typical herbs used are shatavari, ginseng, licorice, slippery elm, honey, sesame oil, coconut oil and ghee."

"Sleshaka Kapha occurs largely in the bones and joints. When in excess, high kapha or fluid accumulation in the joints leading to impaired movement and pain resembling kapha-type arthritis. The symptoms are acute encompassing swollen joints, dull pain in the joints, arthritis, lethargy, slow movement, adding extra weight, and weakness of the bones. Treatment comprises pungent and bitter circulatory stimulants, diaphoretics and diuretics to subdue kapha with guggul and myrrh, perspiration through sauna, dry massage with calamus. Typical herbs used are ginger, cayenne, myrrh, guggul, sallaki, nirgundi, angelica, turmeric, chaparral, ginseng and garlic. When Sleshaka turns deficient, it results in insufficient kapha in the joints along with high levels of vata and pitta accompanied by trauma and difficult movement. Prominent symptoms are dry or cracking joints, joint pain, dry skin, vata or pitta type arthritis, and brittleness of the bones. Treatment with demulcent herbs to soothe the joints along with circulatory stimulants to improve blood flow to the region; oil massage or Snehana with sesame oils. Typical herbs used are ashwagandha, vidari, shatavari, nirgundi, guggul, ginseng and sesame oil."

---

[198] Nasya or Nasal inhaling of herbs dissolved in light edible oil.

"Acute are the symptoms of Tarpaka kapha in the brain, nervous system, mind and emotions. When excess is the occurrence, evidenced is surplus kapha, water and mucus in the head, brain and nervous system, accompanied by dullness and rhinocerical heaviness in these zones. Symptoms of allergies, swelling in the head, mental dullness, daydreaming, emotional attachment, grief and depression dominate. As it turns more severe, fluid accumulates in the brain and nervous system. Treatment begins with brain and nervine stimulants and intensely pungent diuretics along with perspiration therapy aimed at the head like inhaling aromatic oils of mustard, horseradish, camphor or mint. Herbs employed are pippali, shilajit, calamus, sankha pushpi, ephedra, haritaki, bibhitaki, brahmi and sage. When Tarpaka is deficient, evidenced is the lack of kapha or lubrication in the brain and nerves, besides vata and pitta emotional imbalances, nervousness and agitation. Symptoms exhibited range from discontentment, mental distress, fear, anxiety and hysteria to mental imbalance and insomnia. Treatment begins with sweet and cool demulcents and tonic herbs for the brain and nerves, along with *Shirodhara* or oil drip on the head. Typical herbs employed are shatavari, licorice, ashwagandha, jatamamsi, valerian, ziziphus seeds, lotus seeds, ghee, almonds and milk."

Treating five prana airs, tissues and channels

"Finer levels of supplementary treatment are achieved through the five prana forces, from the way they affect the tissues and the channel-systems. Prana takes responsibility in fetching nutrition to all the tissues. Opposite in behavior, Apana settles on the accountability in carrying away waste. Samana and Vyana are more internal. Samana governs absorption of the nutrients brought in by prana. Vyana governs circulation both of the digested nutrients and the waste awaiting its release by Prana. Udana governs overall energy and work capacity. Relative to the blood, Prana oversees the quality of air entering the body and Apana supervises the exiting waste air."

"Samana governs the nutrition to the blood cells while Vyana administers blood circulation. Udana oversees the positive energy output of the blood tissue and its effect on the organs and the whole body. In a similar way, Prana governs intake of nutrients through a channel, while Apana administers waste elimination through it. Vyana keeps the channel open and circulating while Samana aids in contraction and protection of its linings. Udana governs the ultimate energy output through the channel."

"Several tissues and channel-systems connect with different prana forces. Apana dominates elimination, urination and reproduction, while the other prana forces continue to work in their zones. Apana governs reproduction rewarding the native with a strong prana result, a newborn child. Agni works on the usual factors and conditions of five-prana-s associated with it. When examining a channel system, it is prudent to check the state of five-prana forces related to the channels. It is important to consider whether to energize the system through prana, detoxify it, or clear the waste through Apana. Whether it needs to be opened, whether to promote circulation through Vyana or close and contract it, improving absorption within it as Samana. Or whether to increase its growth, expression and positive energy output as Udana."

"Naturally, these closely related factors might need to be modified, depending on different conditions. When a channel system suffers from lack of energy, increasing the flow of prana to it raises the energy levels. Similarly, if a channel system suffers from poor absorption, on increasing the flow of Samana through it eases the disorder. When blocked is a channel system, increasing the flow of Vyana using circulatory stimulants for the circulatory system releases the blockages. Channel system suffering from waste accumulation can be resolved by increasing the flow of Apana through it. When the channel system is running on low capacity, by increasing the flow of Udana through it will reduce the issue."

"Prana and Apana work on the body exterior, Prana from above as in the head, Apana from below as in the openings below the navel, providing nutrition and elimination; governing the forces coming in and out of the body from food to ideas. They often call for treatment in order to improve nutrition or facilitate proper elimination. Vyana and Samana work within the body, within the field of Prana and Apana as expansion and contraction, governing the forces working inside the body and internal organs. Treatment mainly consists of improving the digestion and circulation. Work of Prana and Udana complement one another as constructive inputs through nutrition and output of positive energy. Treatment comprises balanced food intake and corresponding work output of life-style and expression. Udana and Apana work opposite one another as Ascending and Descending Forces. Treatment counters the erroneously moving Prana, such as stopping cough by lowering adversely the rising prana, implying balancing Udana with Apana; or stopping diarrhea through adversely lowering prana by balancing Apana with Udana."

Prana diagnosis and therapy

"Treating prana at its different levels is an in-depth treatment, different from the way the physical body gets handled. Without treating the Prana, physical treatment remains incomplete. The essence of all healing is to ascertain prana, the positive energy remains aligned to the cosmic forces, and ensure Apana, the negative life or death energy stays at bay. As such, prana internalizes the ascendance of the consciousness energy, while Apana externalizes the descending of ignorance as energy; these are forces of involution and evolution, forces of true growth and decay."

"Prana promises all diseases, a treatment. Any changes to prana are communicated to the entire body. Dosha levels rise from its dysfunctions. As long as prana is in the body, we live; the more it grows within, we thrive. When it finally leaves the body, our existence on earth ceases."

"Prana incidentally is not just an undirected force. It is the natural and organic intelligence that sustains all the autonomic functions of the body. We can sense prana-intelligence in our unconscious bodily functions, like the marvelous and complex power of digestion, just as we see the cosmic-prana-intelligence in the forces that move the stellar systems. When Prana awakens, it becomes the power of consciousness directing the unfolding of the spiritual evolution. The same intelligence that guides our body and the whole of nature can come to rule our minds. In our normal state, our lives occur according to the unconscious functioning of prana. This is ignorance or the dependent state of the mind, the life of ego, when prana turns the consciousness in us; we transcend beyond the ego. Awakened prana is a force of grace, guiding us. All healing in alternative medicine comes from the power of the life force, true healing through the power of the awakened prana. Prayers, asana, pranayama, meditation, music and fine-arts are the tools to awaken prana. Choose one, choose any."

"Prana based vital sheath known as Pranamaya Kosha envelops the physical or food sheath. It connects to the physical body through the series of channels known as the Pranavaha Srota, the channels that transport prana. Channels have two origins within, the heart and digestive tract. Circulatory and digestive systems pervade the entire body through their mesh - the skin, senses, respiratory and nervous systems. No part of the body is ever without prana."

Prana absorption

"Prana, the way it mingles with the ins and outs of the body, its treatment is different as its absorption is varied through many portions. Prana retained for a short tenure comes through the breath and the lungs, longer duration prana retention happens through food in the colon. The lung system is complex, retaining prana at several sites, taken through the nostrils and the nasal cavity, it sees an immediate ingestion by the brain and senses. Though the senses directly take in prana, like the eyes with the colors they see, prana gets ingested in the lungs and transferred through the blood and plasma, by the heart action to the whole body. Absorbed is prana through the skin, as a longer term or slower respiration that balances prana in the body, regulating the processes of breathing and eating and protecting the body surface from pathogenic attacks. Retained is prana from the food in the large intestine as the final product of digestion."

"Nasal cavity, nostrils and sinuses in the prana absorption are important and often overlooked. Nasal cavity positioned below the brain supplements the brain with a subtle share of prana that comes its way. This subtle serving stimulates the brain, keeping it active and adaptable. In the brain region, the highest of the chakras, the master prana dwells and without its proper stimulation, all the other prana forces get impaired. With the head congested, prana not being absorbed from the nasal passages, the brain becomes dull, thinking gets confused and muddled, memory turns weak, acuity of perception declines and the learning ability suffers."

"With the prana outage, the brain stumbles and then becomes stagnant."

"Meditation becomes very difficult if not impossible. Hence, for the health of the brain and through it the whole nervous system, the right absorption of prana in the head is important. Everything depends upon the right functioning of the nostrils and accurate breathing through them. Through the nasal cavity, prana can reach all the senses using a direct approach. Four of the five senses dwell in the head connected with the nasal passage. Centered here is fifth and general sense of touch. Prana vayu energizes all these."

"When the nostrils and sinuses are challenged, a toxic avalanche hits all the other senses. The nose clogged with the mucus membranes too wet or dry, the sense of smell faces outage. When this impairment extends to the auditory canal, the sense of hearing and equilibrium get adversely affected."

"With sinuses behind the eyes affected, eyesight is disrupted. The nostrils clogged, the head congested, Udana Vayu or the upward moving air becomes impassable, making it worse for our expression, aspiration and enthusiasm. Common cold is the first stage of such diseases, and with it comes a failure of the immune system and defense mechanism. It comes largely through damages to prana, from weakened connection between the Prana based sheath and physical sheath. Maintaining the health and right functioning of the nostrils is important for maintaining the immune system, preventing disease and keeping the physical body under the vitalizing supervision of the prana enforced envelope. Not only does the prana absorbed in the nasal passages clear and energize the brain and senses, purified prana also ensures the lungs can absorb the air better and efficiently extract the life-energy from it. The external air, foreign to the body, remains harmonious to the body in the nasal passages, just as food gets chewed in the mouth. Prana absorbed in the head is the primary and guiding form of all the five-prana forces and directed through it all are the vital processes of the body. Any stagnant or congested space in the nose or sinuses allows the growth of pathogens, which weaken the system and cause Apana Vayu to increase, leading to constipation and digestive disorders."

"Udana's damages relate to cough and nausea. When Samana gets injured, malabsorption becomes rampant not only in the digestive system, but also in the lungs. Vyana's impairment causes poor circulation and body ache. All these symptoms are noticeable in the common cold."

"Remedying prana is the key to the energy and health of the body, which incidentally begins at the nostrils. The nostrils enable the connection with the prana-based sheath that rules over the physical. Therefore, the emphasis on pranayama, nasya and water to clear the sinuses."

"I am not much in favor of the Neti Pot, but sniffing herbs as suggested in nasya or nasal therapy definitely clears the sinuses and feeds the brain. One can snort a pinch of the powder of spicy herbs like calamus, bayberry, brahmi or dry ginger to clear the nostrils; works well with kapha sufferers. For pitta dominant persons, it can cause bleeding. Also, vata people suffer from dryness in the nostrils, which powders can aggravate more. Oil application with the herbs to the nose serves better where dry powders fail. In stimulating the nasal passages and brain, one can apply sesame oil or ghee to the nostrils. It should be remembered that it always requires liquids to absorb prana. When dry conditions prevail in the nasal passages, prana fails to be absorbed. Regular application of oil to the ears, eyes, mouth, nose and skin is important. The oil on our membranes and orifices protects them."

"Nasya is stimulating, reducing and cleansing. Nasya is applying cleansing herbs like spices or bitters to sesame oil. Calamus or other oils with spicy aromas like eucalyptus, camphor or mint are detoxifying, while emollient oils with soothing herbs like licorice as in 'Anu Tel' are medicinal. The texts state, *jivanti, jala, devadaru, jalada, twak, sevya, gopi, hima, darvitwak, madhuka, plava, aguru, vari, pundrahava, bilva, utpala, dhavani, surabhi, sthira, krimihara, patram, truti, renuka, kinjalka, kamala* and *bala* boiled in 100 parts pure water and the decoction added to oil composes the *Anu Tel*. On sniffing the oil regularly through the nasal passages, the skin, shoulders, face and chest thicken, become well developed and gray hair disappears[199]."

"Shirodhara calls for oil application to the forehead and then followed by a head massage. Stream of medicated sesame oil poured drop by drop to the forehead gets directed to the site of the third eye."

"Importance of aroma therapy and essential oils with incense and fragrant herbs comes largely from their profound effect on prana in the head. Aromatic oils work straight on prana and help with the nostrils and through them reach the senses and brain. Many spicy fragrances like mint, camphor, wintergreen or eucalyptus clear the sinuses, stimulating prana. Rose and lotus flower fragrances calm the emotions and enhance creativity."

"In managing prana at its inception in the nostrils, pranayama provides the key techniques. While other treatments tend to stay passive, pranayama is the most active way to treat the prana. Alternate nostril pranayama consists of breathing in through the left nostril and out through the right, then in through the right and out through the left. One can practice it regularly for a few minutes twice a day."

"Connection of prana to the body is the immune system. Immunity suffers when nostrils do not function correctly. Mere taking of good food or herbs may not be enough if prana gets neglected. When the nostrils fail to act, the lungs stop work and activities of the skin come to a grind. Even the colon stops to work right, weakening the entire digestive system."

"Sinuses stay blocked from fear. Fear paralyzes us into not breathing, remaining in a suspended state - an instinct of playing dead. Similar is the expression when life is dreaded. Suppression, often oppression, lack of self-confidence lead people into suffering from this problem. It is often an internalization of our emotional rejection by others."

---

[199] Astanga Hridayam 20.36 – Anu Tel

"Vata accumulates in the nasal passages as blocked air, trapped in its dryness from tissue deficiency in the region. Pitta accumulates as trapped heat or as yellow mucus, with possible inflammation or infection. Kapha accumulates as thick or sticky mucus; trapped dampness or excessively developed tissue and excess secretions. Signs of high vata affecting the head are sensitivity to sound, feeling ungrounded, anxiety, vertigo, dizziness, loss of equilibrium, with possible throbbing headaches and insomnia. Different are signs of high pitta in the head with sensitivity to light, face and eyes turning, bleeding from the nose, inflammatory diseases of the eyes, anger, and irritability, and burning headaches. Signs of high kapha in the head are facial edema, lack of sense of taste, swollen glands, excess or mucoid saliva, with possible dull headaches, heaviness and lethargy. The practitioner must also account for usual dietary and environmental factors that aggravate the dosha types."

"It is also important to clean and massage the ears, mouth and teeth as part of one's daily health routine[200]. This keeps the flow of prana in the senses smooth and steady. Cleaning the eyes through occasional tearing is also helpful. Drop of onion or amalaki juice placed in the eye will burn at first and feel painful, the tears it causes will have a cleansing and clearing effect. Often there will also be the discharge of mucus from the sinuses or another expectoration. When the eyes become inflamed, aloe gel, chrysanthemum, chamomile and eyebright work well. Application of ghee to the eyes is useful, particularly triphala ghee, which helps improve vision and eliminate dry eyes."

"Lungs being the main site for the breath absorption, the breath taken in through the lungs invigorates the circulatory system, energizes the blood, strengthens the body and sustains the flow of energy through all channels. Prana taken in, absorbed by Samana converts into Vyana, the diffusive or circulatory energy, which gets absorbed into the bloodstream. From thereon, the work moves to the motor level through Udana, Vyana and Apana, managing the organs of speech, hands and feet, and the urogenital and reproductive systems. The upper, middle and lower regions of the lungs are important for extracting prana from the breathed air. Should one fail to act, it has a negative impact on the vitality. Stagnant air in the lower lungs, breath not expelled properly, becomes a breeding ground for toxins and for the growth of the negative life-force or Apana Vayu. I give you a list of the three dosha-s on how they work on the different regions of the lungs."

---

[200] Astanga Hridayam, 2.1-2.6. Dantadhavana and Anjana.

Vata accumulates in the upper part of the lungs.	Pitta accumulates in the middle of the lungs	Kapha accumulates at the bottom of the lungs.
High levels of vata manifests as stagnant air in the lungs, dry cough, and rapid or shallow breathing.	High Pitta levels manifest as stagnant heat in the lungs, yellow phlegm, or bleeding in the lungs.	High Kapha levels manifest as fluid accumulation in the lungs, and clear, white or watery phlegm.

"It is important to empty the lungs while exhaling. Exhaling the breath is important; it is more important to learn correctly how to exhale than to inhale. If we learn to exhale fully, a full inhalation will logically occur. If we stress on inhalation alone, we may fail to exhale totally, keeping stagnant air in the lungs. We may even forget to breathe. We hold grief, sorrow and attachment containing kapha emotions in the lungs. The reluctance to 'let go' impedes the breathing process."

"Well established is the role of skin in respiration. While respiration through the skin is not as immediate as is with the nostrils or as evident as through the lungs, it still is significant. When the skin is dirty, or the pores clogged, respiration fails; it also fails absorption when the skin is too dry. Sweat clears the skin, cleansing the plasma and improving peripheral circulation. Svedana or steam therapy works equally well. It maintains this gateway of prana and protects the surface of our body from diseases, making it useful in the winter to ward off common cold and influenza."

Prana in digestive system

"Prana's absorption in the digestive system occurs at all the major sites along the gastro-intestinal tract; first in the mouth and palate, second in the stomach, third in the small intestine, and fourth and final in the large intestine. Degree of prana absorption happens at once from food intake and its taste. Portion of prana taken from food in the mouth energizes the brain and senses. Water sipped during the meal and between meals keeps the taste buds clear to help absorb prana from the food. Another prana portion signals the body to regulate the water content; such is true of the prana we take in through liquid. Third portion goes from the tongue to the digestive fire stimulating its act in digesting food while activating Samana Vayu."

"The tongue runs a close association with the digestive fire. Earth and water elements from the food along with the prana inherent in them get absorbed in the stomach. Also, the Prana absorbed earlier from the mouth and nose energizes the stomach and pancreas to accelerate the absorption. Without enough prana, the body lacks the energy in digesting earth and water elements from food and the undigested food mass remains a stockpile of mucus in the system. One can improve the stomach function with demulcent herbs like shatavari, marshmallow, licorice and amalaki. They aid in producing alkaline secretions in the stomach."

"Absorption of fire elements along with prana occurs at the small intestine. Help comes from the energy of spices and aromatic oils in this extraction. Other fire-containing condiments like salt, vinegar, wine and other sour substances are also helpful. Trikatu has a special place among the other herbs, so does Hingashtak for the small and large intestine."

"Air and ether elements along with main portion of prana from the food enter through the large intestine. Membrane in the colon namely Purishadhara Kala assists in its absorption, transporting prana to the bone or Asti dhatu where it nourishes and energizes the innate bone, marrow, nerve and productive tissues."

"Food lacking in prana or from indigestion, the deeper tissues fail to achieve the quality of nourishment. Especially when colon suffers from toxic gas, the toxins become absorbed instead and damage the deeper tissues, giving rise to many diseases, particularly those of vata as with bone and nervous system disorders. Prana absorbed from the colon is the most concentrated form of prana. It is held dearly in the deeper tissues as energy reserve that sustains life and longevity."

"Triphala facilitates the right absorption of prana in the large intestine. It acts on the colon as a 'restorative', improving the mucus membrane functioning and expelling the toxic gases. Regulating the prana absorption in the large intestine, it can help treat bone, nervous system, sexual and debility type diseases that have their origins in weakness of the deeper tissues of bone, nerve and reproduction. Hingashtak formula comprising asafetida with eight other herbs is equally useful like triphala. Cardamom, basil, cloves, orange peel and fennel do their work well. Hot spices like cayenne and black pepper burn the toxins in the colon."

"Respiratory and digestive systems offer ways and levels of absorbing prana, and the wellness program proposes the means to control them. Short-term and long-term methods allows for a constant streaming of prana through the body. Two main sites to watch for the prana absorption are the nostrils and the colon. Nostrils show the lung system functioning; colon provides the metrics on the digestive system's role in prana absorption. When they function proper, health prospers."

"Mucus lining in the channels extract Prana. The gastro-intestinal tract has mucus lining all over, as do the lungs. The senses also extract prana. All these tissues have aquatic lining; moisture being key in absorbing Prana. In addition, plasma and blood, the liquid tissues of the body carry prana and are part of the prana aqueduct system or Pranamaya Srota. This delicate balance between air and water in the body to facilitate prana, a key balance between dryness and wetness is yet another instance of AquaPisces implementation. Insufficient lubrication, poor hydration of the tissues, or excess lubrication hinders the prana absorption. Prana keeps the mucus membranes dry enough to work satisfactorily, the water in the body keeps them wet enough to function. Blockage of prana builds up mucus. It does not mean that kapha levels are high, but prana is low. Worse, with prana's flow impaired, the water in the body ceases to circulate. Fluids stagnate and create pockets for pathogens to flourish. When water is too high as in many obesity cases, the Prana stays obstructed. Water, a necessary medium for the prana absorption, recursively enables itself namely water to be absorbed along with prana. The brain absorbs portions of prana along with water from the nostrils using an evaporative process. Prana undergoes absorption in the mouth when we taste food; lymph and blood absorb prana with water in the lungs. In the large intestine, absorbed prana and water is navigated to bone tissue. It reaches the nerve tissue within the bones."

"Energized or prana-filled water is the basic tissue element of the body as blood and plasma. Any part of the surface of the body where plasma or rasa related to the skin is present can easily absorb prana. In fact, the entire body experiences different energies with prana-filled water in different zones. People with kapha constitutions may have better prana because they have more water to hold it. In the practice of pranayama, we create such energized water in the system of rasa. Through pranayama, we experience an increase in saliva in the mouth, not the ordinary saliva, but one sweet in taste, a new plasma production of a higher order. Through it, we can build up the plasma of the body to a higher level of energy that prana provides. Such new plasma is food for the deeper tissues and helps balance vata in the system."

"Prana's absorption from the breath may fail when breathing is improper, or the air is stagnant, polluted or impure. Absorption of prana may be unsuccessful from impaired digestion, dead, stale, old or recooked food. From the lung system, lost is prana from too much of conversation, agitated or thoughtless talking, arguments and chatter. Udana Vayu, which governs speech, is the main prana through which energy gets depleted. Strong sound releases like crying, shouting and screaming are even more prana-reducing."

"Perspiration resulting from overwork or physical exertion is another route of the lung system, that of the skin, where prana loss occurs through Vyana Vayu. Initially, perspiration energizes the system and helps dispel toxins, in excess it will sweat out vital fluids and prana. Loss of prana from the digestive system occurs through diarrhea, dysentery and chronic loose stool. Even constipation can cause its loss; similarly, excess urination depletes prana as it increases Apana Vayu. Much prana loss happens from excessive or distorted sexual activity that increases Apana Vayu, especially sex without love, which removes its wellness, emotional force. Body expels prana from excessive exertion of any of the motor organs, from the tongue to the hands, feet and the organs of elimination."

"Just as prana based sheath envelopes the physical sheath, so does mental sheath or Manomaya Kosha envelop the prana and the physical system. The mental sheath connects to the physical body through the brain and senses using the nerve and reproductive tissues of Majja and Shukra. Such a connection involves the nervous system and seven chakras of the subtle body. In this way, the mental sheath takes possession of the sense organs, motor organs and the outer mind. The outer mind runs three functions related to sensation, emotion and thought of an informational or concrete nature. Emotion is the most important of these functions for health."

"With emotions perturbed, there is immediate impact on prana and the physical body gets upset. Negative emotions easily damage the breath. So, does depression lower the breathing. Hysteria at its extreme promotes hyperventilation. Complex thought process, worry, grief and anger are all geared to losing prana. Emotions can be more significant than dietary, environmental, or even structural problems in this aspect of failing to absorb prana. The body waits for the mind to pass into a state of peace before it can exhibit proper functioning. When agitated by emotions, every available energy starts to deal with the distress. Reactions of fear and anger take control when the body feels threatened, shutting down many physical processes to deal with the threat. However, when the emotions remain unresolved, the energies maintain the body in an altered state of suspense, forfeiting its right to function otherwise."

Prana healing

"An aspect of prana infused healing is in transmitting the prana energy from other sources through the medium of the practitioner's hands to the body of the native. This may involve touch, pressure on the Marma points, or the hands held several inches away from the important prana based centers like the forehead, heart or navel. Even while talking and counseling the native, opportunities show up for transmitting prana. Often the prana or healing force of the practitioner is quite powerful in catalyzing the healing process in the native. There are no miracles or magic to learn – proper lifestyle, faith, prayer, mantra, pranayama, yoga can increase the good healing force within the practitioner."

"When the prana infusing healing force turns powerful, many treatments are easy to achieve. Prana healing goes well with other healing modalities and remains a powerful wellness technique."

"Think of that clay doll lying in that corner. A pair of hands used the generic clay found outside and cleaned it of debris. With water and fire, it gave the clay a beautiful form and stature. Our body made of million ingredients, in concert appears as one-whole, with a centralized intelligence in the brain. When the time is up, the doll disappears back into clay as we dissolved into the elements. What remains are the impressions, the prana and the intelligence. Though prana comes from breadth, it is much more than the breath or any physical force. Breath does not convey life, rather to breath is a life-function and when the breath ceases, the body dies. At death, the life-force does not cease, it ends its connection with the physical body. In the process of breathing the inner prana vitalizes the air taken in from the outside. The air from the outside, as subtle matter, acts as fuel and vehicle for the life-force. Prana-filled air does not contain life per-se, it is an energy product set by the inner life-force. What extracts life energy from the air breathed is the primary prana or life-force within us. Through the breath, it projects its life energy into the physical body. Let me tell you about the first three chapters of the Aitareya Upanishad, which is the oldest manuscript that describes the Rig Veda."

> The beginning, there was just the Spirit
> One and without a second
> Nothing else winked
> "Let me create the worlds," he reckoned
>
> 1.1

AQUAPISCES

He created Amba, a world of water-borne clouds
then he built Marichi, the solar world
Mara, the world of mortals
the world of waters, Apah, with his hands he curled

1.2

    'For these worlds
    Let their guardians now come to life'
    From the realms of the deep waters
    he shaped forth a deity with no surgical knife

1.4

As he brooded over the angel
the mouth separated out, just as an egg
From the mouth came speech
the element of Fire was at stake

1.5

    Then as the nostrils flared
    from them arose the organ of breath
    On breath, did he brood again
    the deity of Air thus appeared next

1.6

Then the eyes rolled out
O' from the hazel eyes, the organ of sight
In that sight shone the brilliance of the fire again
He assigned to the Sun, to his rays and might

1.7

    Then the ears sprouted
    from the ears, the organ to hear
    In hearing, the quarters of space
    the etheric deity added to his tier

1.8

Then the skin enveloped
from the skin, came the hairs, organ of touch
From the hairs, plants and trees,
Deity of Air took charge of the whole bunch

1.9

    Then the heart beat aloud
    From the heart thumped the organ of the mind
    O' from the mind, the night was divine
    added was it to the Moon as it shined

1.10

Navel was umbilically out
From the navel, organ of Apana sprang forth
From Apana, came death
Varuna became the deity henceforth

1.11

Then the virile member separated out
from the virile member, same semen
From the semen, what it can produce
the waters teamed with it as a reason

           1.12

These deities thus made
fell into this great ocean
He subjected the creation to hunger and thirst
'Find for us an abode and food therein'

           2.1

    He brought them a cow
    'This is not enough.', they cried
    He brought them a horse
    'This is worse,' they were horrified

           2.2-2.3

He brought them the person
'Ah, this is well done, indeed', the deities clapped
A person is something well done
"Now dwell in your own abodes," He snapped

           2.4

    Fire as the speech organ
    the mouth he chose, he entered
    Air became breath
    the nostrils, he tethered

Sun as sight, he entered the eyes
Ether as sound, he entered the ears
Plants and trees, deity of air
entered the skin and became hairs

    Moon as the mind, he entered the heart
    Death as Apana, he entered the navel
    Water became semen
    It entered the virile member and turned it able

'What about us?', cried hunger and thirst
'Will we have an abode too? O supreme!'
'Hmm.' The great spirit assigned them to the guardians
'When they are pleased, you shall share the joy with them'

           2.5-2.8

    He thought, 'For the worlds and their guardians
    I shall make some food for them'
    He broods over the waters
    from the waters, did emerge the first crumb

           3.1-3.2

AQUAPISCES

But the food from the waters wished to flee
the great spirit sought to grasp it with speech
To utter 'food' and be satisfied, 'that couldn't be'
food he felt was just out of speech's reach

    3.3

    He sought to grasp it with breath
    to smell 'food' and be satisfied, that couldn't be
    He turned to grasp it next with the eye
    one look at food and be satisfied, that was much to see

He sought to grasp it with the ear
to listen of food and be satisfied, that was much to hear
He sought to grasp it with the skin
satisfied with a feel, that was a lot for the skin to bear

    He sought to grasp it with the mind
    Nay. Just the thought of food and be satisfied
    He sought to grasp it with the virile member
    O' to be satisfied with food emitted

    3.4-3.9

He sought to grasp it with Apana
and, he grasped it for good
Grasper of food is vayu, air or prana
this vayu now lives on food

    3.10

    'How could all this exist without me?' He thought
    speech is uttered, smell does the breath
    Eyes do the seeing, hearing by the ears
    touching by the tips, the mind thinks at depth

Apana assists in the eating
semen supported by the virile member
'Then who am I?
Which way shall I enter?'

    3.11

    He pierced the end
    the great spirit entered the opening
    Through the portal of Vidhriti, the cleft
    it became a place of joy, unfailing

    3.12

Spirit embodied has three abodes
three conditions of sleep
Awakened in one abode
dreamt in another, third caught in slumber of deep

    3.13

Born a Jiva, he realized all elements were One
One with him, him with all
At once, he knew the person as all-pervading
'Ah, I have seen it,' he realized the sprawl

3.14

He is Idandra, indeed that is his name.
O' they call Idandra as Indra these days
Gods laugh for they love the code
they are fond of cryptic epithets

3.15

"Food is not just about eating, there are many other subtle implications. Food is prana, digested by the ear, touch, nose, eyes, mouth, mind and other parts. Wellness is not just a chemical balance in the digestive tract, that's where such gross meanings run into limitations. The original prana derives from consciousness. Five-prana forces are modification of the touch Tanmatra[201]. Prana comes from three levels - love, touch and breath. Not only lack of breath, but also absence of touch or dearth of love can bring about prana's loss."

"Goal of pranayama breathing is not just to achieve a deeper and fuller breath or connect better with external sources of energy, it serves to connect with the internal source of energy, the only true source of life - the spirit. Once aligned with nature, essentially the cosmic life-force, the doors fling open to the spirit. On an inner level, the Agni opens the power of nature within us, which is our inner prana or life-force, the heat, energy and fire released - takes us to the realms of the spirit."

"Pranayama achieves the desired objectives when the breath is accompanied by positive intentions, emotions and good thoughts."

"Inhalation relates more to kapha, as kapha plays its hand in absorbing the nutrients. Retention of breath is more pitta like with digestion of nutrients. Exhalation relates more to vata as a major absorption and release of waste-materials. If there is an imbalance in the breathing process, the dosha types will increase depending on the aspect of the breath out of balance. Inhalation is packed with a cooling effect, while exhalation is expressive and warming. Inhalation has more the energy of the left or Lunar Nadi and exhalation the energy of the right or Solar Nadi[202]."

---

[201] Tanmatra - the sensory potential of touch, which exists on a subtle level.
[202] Breathing through the mouth is also cooling and increases kapha but can produce and increase Ama while doing it.

"When the right nostril is used more to inhale, it sets up the heat, conversely, when left nostril is employed more to exhale, the system moves towards cooling. Inhalation relates to Prana Vayu. Retention of the breath relates to Samana Vayu that absorbs and digests air. Exhalation relates to Apana Vayu that eliminates the waste air. These Vayu airs tend to show increase depending on the imbalances in the breathing process. Vyana Vayu supports the breath circulation. Udana Vayu is the ultimate energy of work and expression that comes through the breath. Vyana Vayu connects to retention. Udana Vayu relates to breathing exhalation in a positive sense, as work energy expressed through the motor organs. The voice plays a key role as the organ that expels."

"The breath, made of moist air carries many fragrances, many tones and many energies. Incidentally, the breath also carries thoughts, emotions and sensations; responding to human intentions and motivations."

"How the breath gets energized is more important than the mechanics of breathing. When inhalation is energized with a heating energy, the effect is heat, likewise, when the inhalation gets energized with a cooling energy, the effect is that of cooling. This principle in any pranayama practice clearly means that the mind has to be involved to achieve the right effects. Supplemented with prayers, mantra and visualization creates an effective pranayama."

"Yes, yoga is the inner process that reorients and transmutes our energies to actualize the higher evolutionary potential latent within us; and it begins with breath. Yoga transports us from the planes of generic awareness to a state of self-realization. We transcend the time-space bound personality and its limitations and are awarded with a glimpse of the other dimensional worlds."

"The wellness concepts borrow from the axiomatic principles of the three dosha types; the dosha types being the foundation of energy distribution within. Governing the body tissues to achieve structure and bulk are more kapha-centric, metabolism pertains to pitta and movement to vata. Cosmic energy is also cardinal (hinged), mutable (changeable) and fixed (inert). Three Dosha-s are the basis of different constitutional types of people, as are the characters of the energies for signs and graha-s. Dosha types have a deeper level of function crucial for the practice of yoga. Three subtle counterparts of the dosha types are Prana, Tejas and Ojas - 'three vital essences'. These are the root but subtle forms of vata, pitta and kapha which, if reoriented, unfold the extraordinary potentials of yogic development."

Prana – Primal life-force, the subtle energy of air, the master force and intelligence. Responsible for the coordination of breath, senses, mind and consciousness.	Ojas – Primal vigor, the subtle energy of water, the structure of impressions and thought, the maintenance of sensual and mental health.	Tejas – Inner radiance, the subtle energy of fire - the radiance of vitality through which we digest and express impressions and thoughts.
At the inner level, Prana governs the unfolding of all higher perceptual capacities.	On an inner level, Ojas governs the unfolding of all higher states of awareness.	On an inner level, Tejas takes responsibility in supporting and grounding higher faculties development.

"Prana, tejas and ojas are the essential or positive forms of vata, pitta and kapha. The general rule in treatment is to prevent any of the three-dosha levels from becoming too high because in excess they breed disease. The dosha predominant in our constitution tends towards excess and requires periodical checks to keep it in balance."

"Diet, herbs, exercise and meditation achieve the balance. In the practice of yoga, a new rule comes into play. The yogic seeks to increase levels of all three of the subtle essences of prana, tejas and ojas in a dramatic and sudden manner. Unlike the three-dosha types, the three vital essences when increased do not necessarily bring disorders. They are the purified forms of the dosha types. As subtle forces, they remain close to one another and support each other. Three vital essences only cause problems if only one of them increases in level at the expense of others. The challenge lies in keeping them in equilibrium during the process of their accumulation. Their imbalance will instigate disorders and discomfort, regardless of the degree to which they have accumulated. However, if their accumulation is integral, they can bring a great inner transformation improving health and vitality."

"Prana augmented, delivers enthusiasm, creativity and adaptability – the prime mover to the life divine. Tejas when increased fosters courage, fearlessness, perception and insight to take us along the divine path, without which we will make wrong choices and judgments or fail to be decisive. Increased Ojas brings peace and patience required to keep our development consistent, without which we lack steadiness and balance."

"Any of these factors in error, the subtle growth gets stunted. The same factors increase positive health aspects of the body and mind and are thus helpful in treating all diseases."

"Prana, tejas and ojas contained in the reproductive fluid reach out to the endocrine system. Prana governs equilibrium, adaptability and growth processes. The pineal and pituitary glands are prana predominant. This is why most disorders in the growth process, like people who are unusually tall or short fall under vata disorders. Tejas governs metabolism and digestion. Thyroid and pancreas functions are Tejas-predominant. Most deep-seated metabolic problems are Tejas in nature. Ojas governs reproduction and energy reserve and dominates in the testes, ovary and adrenals. Most problems of the reproductive system concern the Ojas."

"Prana, tejas and ojas galvanize the immune system. Ojas, the basic capacity of immune system, ability to defend against external pathogens, is endurance, resistance and strength to ward off diseases, potential forces set in motion to defend the body. Tejas is the immune system when activated burns and destroys toxins. It generates the fever in the body's fight against the pathogens. It is within everyone's capacity to use ojas and convert it into heat, warmth and vitality, our ability to mobilize our immune systems forces. Prana is the long-term activated form of the immune function to project and develop life-energy, which manifests when dealing with chronic disease. It is the capacity to maneuver all mobilized immune forces."

"Within the nervous system, mainly the nadi, is the 'master system' governing all other body systems. Three vital energies ensure its proper function. Prana monitors the discharge of nerve impulses and takes care of coordination of nerves. When disturbed, hypersensitivity sets in. Tejas provides acuity of nerve activity. Deranged, tejas burns out the nervous system. Ojas gives endurance and stability through the nervous system. It lubricates the nerve channels. Nervous breakdown or nervous exhaustion occurs through low Ojas. The channels of the nervous system are yet subtler channels of the mind and the subtle body, the nadi system. Prana, tejas and ojas govern movement of impulses through these. Ojas is the fluid that lines and lubricates the nadi system. Tejas is the heat working in them. Prana is the energy moving through them."

"In the breath, the three vital essences are present. Prana is the basic energy and movement of the breath. Tejas is the heat produced by the breath. Ojas is the deeper energy absorbed through breath and kept as an energy reserve."

"When disturbed is the prana in the breath, the breathing goes shallow. When Tejas gets unhinged, the heat content of the breath is abnormal. With Ojas deranged, the absorbed energy of the breath is so low that the system cannot hold and consolidate it. In the region belonging to senses, prana establishes the equilibrium and coordination of sensory impulses and stays predominant in the ears, the inner ear, skin and vata dominant etheric and aerial regions. Tejas assumes responsibility of sensory function acuity and the ability to digest sensory impressions. It dominates in the eyes as the pitta or fire-predominant sense. Ojas provides stability to the senses and their lubrication. It dwarfs the others in the tongue and nose in regions which are kapha dominant aquatic and earthy senses."

"Prana, tejas and ojas provide a good deal of metrics on creativity. Ojas denotes latent and hidden creative capacity, the storehouse of creative energy. Tejas signifies creative vision, the ability to see new things and break with the past. Prana represents creative action to bring new things into being and remain in the creative state. Proper ojas is necessary to give us the proper reserve of creative energy. Tejas directs creative energy toward specific goals. Such are suitable functions to keep the creative acumen mobile and transformative. Prana, tejas and ojas are the essence of the nutrients that enter the body as food, heat and water. Ojas provides the essence of the food that comes our way, food that is both nutritious and sattvic. Tejas denotes the essence of the heat and sunlight we absorb through the skin and eyes. Prana serves as the essence of the fluids we take in and the water we drink. Ojas, the underlying fluid-essence, derived from food, supports and stabilizes the mind, senses, will and emotional side of Manas. Within, the reproductive fluid transforms into ojas, which subsequently becomes the substance of the sense mind and emotions. Prana gets transported by blood and plasma, water being the reservoir for the life-energy. Tejas, as the essence of heat is the basis of the speech capacity. Heat and light on entering the body, enables sensory impressions to become expressed, some of which gets articulated as speech. This lets us discern things with the mind."

"Prana, tejas and ojas even exist in subtle levels. A prana force found in the crevices of the mind allows it to move and respond while preserving its balance. Mind has a tejas force that allows it to perceive, digest impressions, ideas and emotions. An ojas force works for the mind to impart patience, endurance and resist disturbances. In similar settings, there is a prana in our deeper consciousness that sustains us through the entire process of rebirth, imparting life to all the different bodies we incarnate through. There is a tejas, the accumulated insight and vitality of our spiritual aspiration. There is an ojas that is the power through which the soul produces all its various bodies."

"On the level of the soul, prana, tejas and ojas offer a glimpse of the original life, light and love. Monitoring the conditions of Prana, Tejas and Ojas within for signs and symptoms of excess and deficiency reveals several functional problems. Inadequate ojas shows up as weak immunity, low sex drive and poor stamina, impatience, difficulty sleeping, unfounded worries and anxiety. Insufficient tejas show as cold extremities, weak digestion, cloudy perception, and indecisiveness and poor judgment. Scarce prana shows in lack of energy and motivation, in attachment and unwillingness to change."

Massage and touch

"The main goal of wellness is in balancing the dosha levels before they lead to disease. Oil and herbs applied during a massage drives the dosha types, Ama, or toxic undigested matter from the deeper connective tissues to the gastro-intestinal tract where it becomes easy to expel them. In this way, massage regularizes all internal energies and brings the dosha types to disease-free state. Oil applied in generous amounts along with certain herbal powders create friction on the skin. Powders applied after the oils absorb the excess oil. Oil lubricates the deeper layers of the skin while the herb in it assists in increasing the passage to stagnant areas where circulation is in wanting. Applying different oils and herbs with varying degrees of pressure, the massage truly meets the native's need. Commonly used oil for all constitutions is sesame, which improves skin texture, luster, and vitality."

"Massages start with a gentle sattvic press, by which the prana gets transferred from practitioner to native. It moves to a Rajasic cycle, immersing the native in a pleasurable feeling and Tamasik, a mechanical massage where feelings matter less. The start with a sattvic workout, then Rajasic, going from a light to mild pressure before attempting anything strong is a recommended practice. This sequence warms up the person, who offers less resistance to the massage. Muscle tissues, inherently elastic, highly receptive to touch welcome the warm-up before any actual massage. All massages go through a human touch of spreading sattvic, then Rajasic and Tamasik love followed by a reverse process before ending."

"Time spent at each massage level depends on the native's condition and aim of the massage. Barring a Marma massage, this guideline stays common to most massages. Marma regions are different having highly sensitive prana induced points where too strong or too quick a massage is uncalled for."

"Tamasik touch and massage works best in non-Marma regions. These three forms of touch also relate to attitude with natives - gentle for vata, moderate for pitta and strong for kapha. As such, massages are two - general body massage of 'Abhyanga[203]', and specific oil therapy of 'Snehana'. Medicinal substances, heavy, cold, mobile, unctuous, dull, thin, soft and liquid are great for Snehana. Those who are weak or obese, under alcoholic intoxication, suffering from diseases of the throat may be exempted from oil therapy[204]."

"Pain has an uncanny way of showing up when vata level runs high. In fact, the most severe forms of pain occur with vata in excess, trauma that is shooting, throbbing, piercing and cutting, and tingling when exposed to cold and wind. Pitta pains are more bearable with burning, sharp, sucking and pulling pain, where pain comes from inflammation within, often accompanied by metallic smell through breath or sweat. Kapha levels in excess brings dull, aching pain, with a sense of heaviness, congestion, or edema, aggravated by cold and dampness."

"Warm sesame oil works well for folks with different constitutions. Especially for vata, sesame counters the cold and dryness. It removes muscular pain and stiffness, benefitting people who suffer from arthritis. It is also helpful for nervous disorders, allaying nerve pain and sensitivity. Almond, mustard, castor and a special preparation of Mahanarayan oil are commonly used for vata conditions of pain and dry skin. Vata folks benefit tremendously from a nurturing oil massage administered gently. Herbs and powders such as calamus, ginger, jyotishmati, dashamula, and licorice in sesame do well for them. External sites associated with vata are the colon, chest and pelvis, hollow and dry cavities in the body. Oil applied generously to these areas can balance and sustain vata."

"Pitta folks who are prone to heat and inflammatory diseases can take a massage with cooling oils such as olive, coconut and sunflower containing lavender, sandalwood and jasmine. These oils treat many conditions of skin eruptions, ulcers, diarrhea and pitta headaches. Most pitta people can also take sesame oil medicated with anti-pitta herbs. Cooling herbs such as brahmi, khus or vetiver, sandalwood and turmeric work well with anyone of such constitution. Main physical sites for pitta are the small intestine, liver and spleen, where pitta accumulates as bile and other toxins. Pitta also collects in the head and eyes. Cooling oils of rose, sandalwood and violet applied to the temples and forehead keep them cool."

---

[203] Astanga Hridayam, 2.8-2.9. Abhyanga
[204] Astanga Hridayam Chapter 16 on Snehavidhi

"For folks with kapha constitutions, heating and drying oils of mustard, almond and sesame increase the circulation and counter the dampness characteristic of such folks. Hot essential oils along with eucalyptus, camphor, musk and heena work well for kapha conditions of sinusitis, cold, obesity and excess mucous. Fast, vigorous and deep pressure applied in the massage works well for kapha people with big frames, large bone structures and thick skin. Heating and drying herbs such as calamus, bala, dashamula, ginger and cinnamon prove effective. The main locations where kapha accumulates as mucus are the stomach, lungs and joints messing up the circulation in these areas. A quick, vigorous oil massage in these areas is good for them. Digestion in kapha people being slow and sluggish, vigorous massage in the abdominal region promotes and increases the digestive fire."

"Regular massage is key to wellness. For the native, starting with three massages a week then tapering down to one a week is optimally energetic. More regular the massage, better the body and mind's deeper perceptions. It is indeed useful to apply sesame or brahmi oil to the soles of the feet, the head and hair at night, or Mahanarayan Oil to back and arms before a warm shower. This promotes deep relaxation, creates calmness in the mind, and enables the muscles to relax, bringing on deep sleep. Such application of oils to the body can becomes a part of daily health regimen."

"In the case of folks with elevated vata, oils of sesame, almond, castor and mustard work the best. In case of pitta, choice of oils is coconut, sunflower, ghee and olive; and for kapha, choice narrows down to mustard, sunflower, safflower, corn, sesame and canola oil."

"Vata afflicted people benefit best with sandalwood, heena, musk, myrrh, wintergreen or rose aroma in oil. Pitta constitutional people benefit from aromatic herbs such as sandalwood, rose, vetiver, lavender and jasmine. For kapha, the aromatic herbs are heena, musk, cedar, myrrh, frankincense and eucalyptus. When vata conditions prevail, herbs and powders used in massage are ginger, cinnamon, licorice, ashwagandha, calamus, jatamamsi, dashamula, jyotishmati and valerian. For pitta they are coriander, violet, licorice, turmeric, brahmi, jatamamsi, shatavari and for kapha they are cinnamon, ginger, juniper, calamus, dashamula and bala."

"When poor circulation persists, use oils of wintergreen and eucalyptus with cinnamon and ginger in them. In case of sprains, cramps or dislocation, treatment with mustard oil, dried arnica, powdered turmeric and myrrh are very effective. Relief from arthritis pain comes from oils of mustard, sesame, olive, mahanarayan and castor with dry ginger, wintergreen, camphor and mint."

"Muscle spasms find relief in pine needle oil, camphor and valerian. Rheumatism finds relief with garlic oil, castor oil, mustard oil, and fenugreek powder."

"Here's how you can make the oil preparations at home. Use herbs, one part each like ashwagandha, dashamula, nirgundi, castor root, punarnava, licorice and bala. For pitta, add brahmi and sandalwood. Oil to use as base is sesame for vata and kapha, coconut for pitta. Take equal parts of powders or the cut forms of the above herbs. Add sixteen times the amount of water. Soak overnight. The next morning, boil the mixture over a low flame for about an hour until only one-fourth of the water remains. Strain the herbs. Then add one-quart the amount of sesame or coconut oil to the remaining decoction. Add fresh ginger, boil for an hour until all the water evaporates and all that is left is the oil."

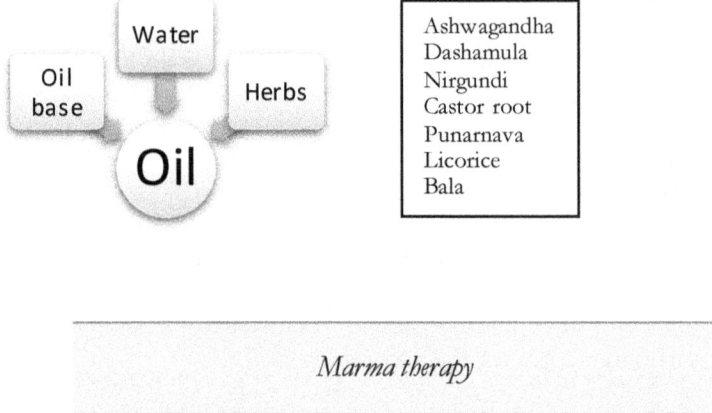

Marma therapy

"Marma[205] regions are special points of energy and vulnerability. There are many Marma points throughout the entire body. Each Marma point relates to different bodily organs and tissues. Marma regions are receptor points on the skin, through which vital energy can stream. Marma regions are the portals in which prana travels and through which the system can direct prana."

"There are references to marma in the ancient texts of Atharva Veda. Knowledge of these sensitive anatomy became essential in combat and surgery. A marma is an anatomical site where flesh, veins, arteries, tendons, bones and joints come together."

---

[205] Marma means secret, hidden, vital energy.

"Practitioners improved their techniques with marma points for stimulating internal organs of the body. Marma points are classified according to the different areas on the body where they occur, the tissue which composes them, and the effects felt if they sustain an injury. Names of Marma regions come from their location and role, their name helps find them."

"Distributed among the hands and legs is the *Talahridaya* or heart or center of the palm of the hand or sole of the foot region. *Kshipra* is quick because of its immediate effects. *Kurccha* is a knot or bundle of muscles or tendons at the base of the thumb or big toe. *Kurcchashira* is the head of *Kurccha*, at the base of the hand or the foot. *Manibanda* - bracelet, as it goes around wrist. *Gulpha* is the ankle joint. *Indrabasti* or Indra's bladder, mid-forearm and mid-calf. *Kurpara* is the elbow joint. *Janu* is the knee joint. *Ani* - the lower region of the upper arm or leg. *Urvi* or 'the wide,' the wide mid-region of the thigh or forearm. *Lohitaksha* the 'red eyed,' the lower frontal-insert of the shoulder joint and leg joint. Kakshadhara or 'what upholds the flanks,' the top of the shoulder joint. *Vitapa* is the perineum where the legs meet the trunk. In the abdominal section is *Guda* the anus, *Basti* the bladder and *Nabhi* the navel."

"Thorax section comprises *Hridaya* the heart, Stanamula, root of the breast, *Stanarohita* the incline or upper region of the breast, *Apastambha*, a point on the upper side of the chest said to carry the Prana or life-force. *Apalapa*, the unguarded armpit or axilla. Back section has *Kukundara*, marking the loins, on either side of the posterior superior iliac spine. *Katikataruna* 'what arises from the sacrum,' the center of the buttocks. *Nitamba*, the upper region of the buttocks. *Parshwasandhi* marking the joint of the sides, the side of the waist. *Brihati* 'the large' or broad region of the back. *Amshaphalaka*, the shoulder blade and *Amsa*, the shoulder."

"Neck section has *Manya*, 'honor,' from its connection with the voice; *Nila* 'dark blue,' from the color of the veins at this point. *Sira Matrika*, 'the mother of the blood vessels,' from the arteries to the head that flow through this region and *Krikatika*, the joint of the neck."

"Head section has *Vidhura*, meaning 'distress,' from its sensitive nature; *Phana*, 'a serpent's hood,' the side of the nostrils; *Apanga*, the outer corner of the eye. *Avarta* or 'calamity,' from its sensitive nature. *Shanka*, 'conch,' comprising the temple. *Utkshepa* or 'what gets thrown upwards,' as it is above the temple. *Sthapani* or 'what gives support'. *Shringatakani*, places where four roads meet, the soft palate of the mouth. *Simanta* or 'the summit,' the skull and surrounding joints. *Adhipati* 'the overlord'."

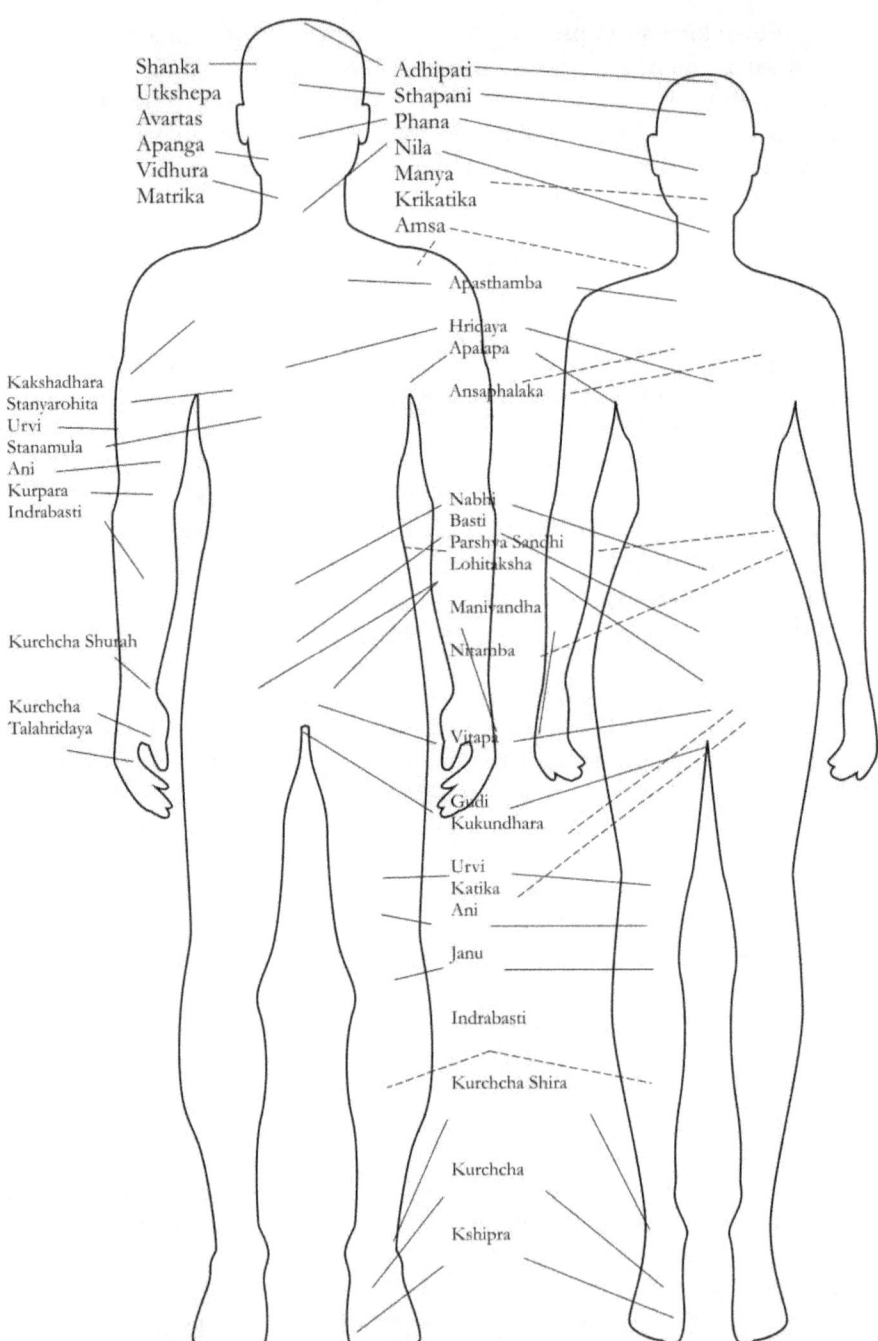

1 - Marma Points (Dotted line shows back of the body; Solid line shows front)

Stimulating Marma regions

"Pressure from the fingers such as the thumb, the index or the middle finger arouses the *Marma* regions. The practitioner may push deep, causing no injury while holding the pressure for a short time, followed by gentle massage. It is best done along with a body massage. Marma points on the head are highly sensitive and should be done gently. Points on the back are harder to reach, while sensitive are the points on the abdomen, whereas the arms and legs, hands and feet are the easiest to work on, yielding great results. Another method is in applying stimulating oils to the Marma site like camphor or eucalyptus. You, the practitioner can focus on Marma to revivify the native or end a valuable life."

Lochan bade the students to their homes, the autumn crisp rain was persistent, steady was its rhythm, and closing his eyes he let the beat of the raindrops entice his solemn face. 'Creation, sustenance and disappearance of the three worlds come from but a rhythm.' He recalled the scriptures, 'from the mere worm to the mighty elephant, all creatures move at its pace. All great work on the terrestrial planet are because of the rhythm. It is by rhythm that the sun and planets move.' He sighed as the tempo of distant drums faded into his ears, 'Yes, the rhythm of mood, of laughter, fear, in wrath as in wonder. The season of fear, where rhythm as 'tala' of death conjoins with the birth of so many, where the music syllable of 'ta' of Cosmic man rapidly unites with the 'la' of Creative-force to mold the flawless rhythm of 'tala' – life, a journey onwards to afterlife! Then why the fear, why dread the rhythmic beat?' Startled he turned to the west, the cry of the last lapwing pierced the twilight 'Did you do it, did you do it right?'

CO-CREATING WELLNESS

Chandrasekhar sat in quiet meditation, submerged was his torso, his chest the color of polished copper a sharp contrast to the dull, cold waters of the river Ganges. Harriet Fergusson sat in the banks, surrounded by oil brushes, charcoal and paint laid out in meticulous preparation in a parchment foil, a stretched canvas lay by the side soaking in the sun, paint and oil. She stifled a yawn, beckoning her orderly to 'wrap up'. She knew better to ask Chandrasekhar for another portrait session that day. 'Was she looking to flatter or to build an impression?' she struggled with the thought as she wondered where Lord Ripon would eventually place the canvas.

"Miss Harriet Ferguson, it is not every day you take a swim in the mighty Ganga. Would you really forego this prospect?", a voice boomed from the waters. Chandrasekhar had emerged from his plunge and she marveled at the copper sheen that still ferried the aging body.

"Hatti. My name's Hatti, mister Nairatna; not even uncle Ripon calls me Harriet." She replied in equal defiance, annoyed at the laughter.

"I know, Ripon warned me how possessive you are of your name and dress." Chandrasekhar swung out of the water and waded the steps towards where she sat. "See the line where the safety rope dints into the river water. Below that is the magical world of Pisces, the treasures of the medicinal water lie in secret. Above stems the stern, crisp and callous Aquarius, the fleeting mind that seeks the gospels from the deep realms."

"Uncle Ripon warned me you would certainly influence my thinking." He stopped at her words, and then the look warmed into a smile.

"He was right. While this curious town is busy viewing a fascinating angel take a stroll with this grandsire, by now, they must have devised many a tale."

"Really? That's such a shame."

"No, it's but natural. You must have noticed how the roads and stairs turn narrow as you leave the city. So, do the minds." His laughter boomed across the narrow corridors as they walked noisily into the cobbled streets. "While the suburbs have retained their aquatic culture, the city goers have lost it to the aerial mandates. Only when the two come together, will the inner fire crackle."

"Aqua-Pisces, what a beautiful thought!" Hatti exclaimed.

"Young lady, in the morning I spoke to you on the factors, herbs, diet, music, aroma that have positive effect on health. Your uncle, Ripon believes in the virtues of health and peace. He believes that the medicinal systems as practiced by the forefathers have lost the original meeting. What we see around us is a degenerated system. I think, Lord Ripon's guidance will give classical medicine a new expression."

"There is the story of a king who in the middle of a war asked the astrologer whether he would win the war. The astrologer paused with his tools and sat on the ground to figure out. The enemy crushed the king's army and then the troops surrounded the astrologer. He exclaimed as he looked at the spears facing him, 'we can never win this war.'" As the giggles subsided, Chandrasekhar continued, "The challenge we have with astrology is that there is no easy way to speed it up, just as the sun will not rush to another day, there is no way you can siphon an exact prophesy. Yes, we get to know it in due course but among the thousands of things that occur in nature, among the many associations an event has with another, it is sometimes a task-behemoth to crack open the answers. As we go deeper into the realms of the Kali-Yuga[206], the human population will increase, so will starvation and death as an aftermath of the evil that surrounds us. The art of predictive accuracy will take a huge hit - so we have to come to a consensus on how to use astrology to its best."

"Being proactive is better than a thousand reactions. Astrology gives us the means to avoid the knee jerk reactions. To stay forewarned is being forearmed. If we know our income will dwindle why not stay prepared for it and open our stored haylofts?"

---

[206] Kali-Yuga coincides with the iron-age

"To merely understand that we are a part of a great cause is the first step to wellness, to comprehend that one has a part in it, is yet another. Ahir Budhnya Samhita illustrates the homeostasis of Saranagati[207] when a passenger desirous of crossing the mighty river of life steps into a boat, his responsibilities end thereafter. Once in the ecosystem, the oarsman decides on the best course to finish the travel, the only thing certain is the destination. Our forefathers spoke of the same immutable fate in varied ways and the several ways to accomplish it."

"I spoke of a Samhita, which suggests a 'compilation'; not any original composition. Samhita condenses many Sastra-s into a unit of text, including details of many subjects written by several authors to expedite that common purpose. Vernaculars of a Samhita prepared for wellness span the subjects of Ayurveda, Jyotish-astrology, Music and Yoga. I have conjoined several Samhita encyclopedias into one such compendium with ancestral learning-s, Atharva Veda, Gandharva Veda, Charaka Samhita, Brighu Samhita, Sushruta Samhita, are the important ones, besides covering advance subjects like Kapil's Samkhya, Parasara's Hora Sastra and Patanjali's Yoga Sutras. Primary view of this study is with human terrestrial life's treasures hidden in the nine planets of a horoscope. I stress on the word 'terrestrial' as it applies to people doing time on this planet only."

"Hear my words well, Hatti; the scriptures offer valuable hints on mind, body and spirit, and the fortunes and misfortunes of every fellowmen. My compilation extends to the Vedas by Brighu sages, or Bhargava clan, descendants of the ancient fire-priest Brighu. On one hand, they compiled the Atharva Veda, on the other they institutionalized the Vedanga and Upanga compositions which disciples reproduced ad-verbatim in the oral tradition of learning. Chyavana, Shukra, Parasara, Brighu, Charaka, Agnivesa are all known sages, each in their own might."

"We are under an onslaught of defects constantly occurring, starting with a three-defect composition that on birth, mark our constitution. A thing to remember Hatti is, our birth is not defective, but born we are with defects. The baseline of three defects or dosha gives us our originality, in a distorted way. Think of a potter who creates many vases from the same wheel. Few are tall, others short, several have more cavities, some have more discoloration, making each of them unique. This balancing Tridosha baseline is the lowest common denominator applicable to health otherwise you cannot take birth. The knowledge of this constitution comes to us also through the eyes of Vedanga Jyotish."

---

[207] Saranagati —Sarana or refuge, gati is the motion.

"As we progress and age, the triad of defects we inherit at birth change in magnitude and direction, persuaded by surroundings, planetary influences, food, diet and numerous such external factors. A close watch on individual and community health divulges how some of the external factors affect life and the psyche. The complexity of the wellness mechanism including astrology makes the subject hard to understand by the wide-ranging public or even the pundits."

"Vata-Pitta-Kapha factors fluctuate during hours, weekdays, seasons, planetary transits and dasa periods; dasa and transits being the astrological variables. While Vedanga-Jyotish astrological factors are more broad-based including social activities, other life events, finance and relationships, coordinates of time and space drive all these systems. If you believe in destiny, then you can fathom the inevitable event occurrence."

"Can you stop or evade the event? Not without divine intervention, but you can lessen the impact. Let's say you get caught in a storm where the nearest shelter, your carriage or house is a mile away. Would you brace yourself and ride the storm out under a large tree or head for the vehicle or house? Aware you are of the possibility of being hit by a lightning or being caught in rising waters. Whatever action you take is not without defects. I will refrain from answering the question as it has many connotations, but you be the judge. Whether you accept being in the fire or the frying pan will not stop the burns. How much you can lessen the impact of the scorching heat or rushing waters gets to matter."

"AquaPisces takes a more pointed slant than mere astrology, psychology or therapy in defining methods that work and exemplify. The methods force an insight into envisioning life as an unabridged integration. It is the same central approach and pyramidal vision as disclosed in the system of Vedas. As a practitioner of this method, we must chaperon the native through the realms of life that spearheads the unfolding of the soul, point to him to look deeper into the intrinsic, Piscean knowledge within that can be harvested by the Aquarian mind; not by giving dogmatic, ritualistic directions or expectations but by pointing out the full scope of capabilities along with applied instruments for using the energies suitably."

"The AquaPisces viewpoint embodies Astrology, Yoga and Ayurveda along with related Vedic subjects proffering an unparalleled approach. It is not essential to major in all of these subjects, but one should gradually learn the fundamentals. Few practitioners enjoy the comprehension intuitively, others stem it from the different teachings that our predecessors have already researched on."

"Wellness practitioner need not have good knowledge or prophetic powers. With a good understanding, the practitioner can easily guide and orient the native to try the higher goals. The practitioner must understand the 'marma' points that subtly traverse one branch of study to another. Nature gave us a seamless universe; we broke it into logical pieces for our convenience. That does not mean nature is a bunch of disparate entities. Well no, it remains as one composition, where everything comes together. Offering genuine service to clients cannot come with a price tag or control over the person. The way I have learned from my teachers in this birth, I offer the same to you augmented with a system that takes you beyond Aquarius or Pisces, it helps in rising above their limitations. I present you many tools, one carpenter to another, helping you to use the transmitted cosmic forces from many a planet, for you to wade through the deep, unfathomed course of the cosmos."

"You get to know the right and wrong powers, you acquire the tools to augment the good and ward off the bad. It is my sincere hope you will be out of the dark shortly. Your inner dweller, the lively spirit transcends time, and it wants to use your potencies in several, positive ways. The approach AquaPisces adopts is more about you managing those energies. Once you have a grasp of the favorable and unfavorable periods, you will know when to use the powers to their maximum."

"To be useful, the practice requires a proactive and a reactive means of fixing and healing. Remember, powers are mere powers; they are atomic units of potencies given to us. For an overall success, we have to control them and use them in a cohesive way. If the powers learn to control us, we become their slaves, which is what happens to the large majority of people. We must go beyond measuring these powerful influences to the point we know how to rein them to a state of harmony. Our method that extends into wellness and healing runs at two levels. In the first

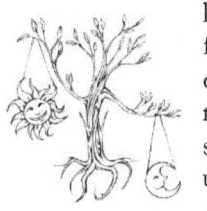

level, it treats our outer nature and, in the second level, it figures out how to treat our inner nature. We can treat the outer nature, our body, senses and conditioned mind, by medical and psychological methods. Our inner nature, our soul, requires occult and yogic methods and ultimately rests upon our own effort to grow spiritually in life. Vedic Astrology is not just a predictive or interpretative system. It is also a remedial system with techniques and methods for balancing planetary influences. These are as essential as the interpretative side. What use is it to tell people what will happen to them if we cannot give them a means of dealing with it?"

"Somewhere in the evolutionary progression, it is hard to say when in a range from 3032 BCE to the last millennium, we lost our talent in communicating with higher dimensions. It could even be later, but certainly not the contemporary period. Our brains, which had from day one coped with nature's wrath in form of climate, wildlife bestial attacks, disasters and diseases had realized the dimensions that surrounded us and helped us react to nature's brute forces. However, the art and science of communication that included visualization of the higher dimensions lost their worth to the passage of time. In today's world, we interpret those as works of magic and miracles, as if they are some esoteric, paranormal mystic happenings. Tigers and carnivores do not pounce from unseen dimensions; they engage in activity in the three-dimensional world. The ancient practiced simple, pure mathematics using the higher dimensional constructs, which became complex approximations when translated to this three-dimensional world. We lost the art of health and wellness; we lost true appreciation of beauty and elegance that nature offers. Unless you are in love with nature's bounty, you will never understand her wrath or her glamor. When you study nature in-depth, you are not looking for useful artifacts to adorn your study, but because she is so intensely beautiful. This practice, now obscure, though I still have access to the originals; happened at a time, an era and situation where collaborating with the higher dimensions were but a matter of fact. While we try to assess it through present day technology and machinery lenses, we end up with no real answers."

"In your excursions to the remote boroughs of the Sunder bans, did you ever watch the Bengal tiger approach its prey? You may think it as ghastly, but imagine the sleek, nimble speed of nature's perfect killing machine in the wild. Now trap and cage the animal. All of a sudden in the confines of the cage, the same tiger no longer exhibits the elegance. Whatever happened? With the original dimensions removed, the setup having moved to a laboratory in a three-dimensional world, the tiger and astrology and wellness become a useless, mundane debacle."

"In today's session, I will introduce you to the simplest of algorithms and mathematical equations to explain the profound working of astrology and ayurveda."

"Concepts in Samkhya[208] include philosophy and deep thinking, and how through the knowledge, some of these dimensions get realized. I use the word 'realized', knowing fully well the language and grammar limitations defining something undecipherable in the semantics of the terrestrials. Think of Sattva, Rajas and Tamas as frequency vectors or degrees of freedom. Whether applying Ramanuja's contribution to string theory, Sattva-Rajas-Tamas theorizes the concepts of creation, aftermath of creation, formation and decay significantly through their degrees of freedom as they permit or decline prana."

"Sattva is one of the three guna vectors translated as a tendency, quality or an attribute in the Samkhya School of philosophy. Sattva is the element or mode of Creative-force associated with virtue, goodness and right. Parasara while explaining to Maitreya in Brihat Hora Shastra, explains the creator in three simple words[209] where he describes the almighty without the three attributes, yet as the purest of Sattva. Which means that above the dimensional plane of the three Guna-s, where absent are the three in their separate manifestations, is the realm of pure Sattva. Sattva at its purest can cross our finite dimensional world to the other dimension where three-Guna-s are but one - Sattva. Other two qualities are 'Rajas' translated as passion and activity, and 'Tamas' translated as destruction and chaos. 'Sight,' or the power of seeing, is an alteration in 'Sattva' unobstructed by 'Rajas' and 'Tamas'. Think of prana as the life-enabling force. Many axioms consider Prana as one that can permeate the space defined by Sattva-Rajas-Tamas, truly three vectors, generalized as mathematical vectors, measurable quantities having direction and magnitude. Such quantities obey the parallelogram law of addition and can transform in a certain way when changes happen in the coordinate system. Prana, the life-giving force is permeable at even the smallest structural construct and either faces obstruction or gets allowed to flow from the direction and cohesion of the three vectors. They exist as potency in pre-creation and manifest as matter in creation."

"Combination of prana with the Sattva-Rajas-Tamas are the regulatory principles of all nature, outspreading to the abstruse Creative-force. Dharma, our set of duties, defined by the many hats we wear, the many roles we play is but an extension to this atomic principle."

---

[208] Author's note – you may read more about Samkhya as poetry in Tepid Blue
[209] Excerpts from Brihat Hora Shastra - suddhsattvo jagatswami nirGuna-strigunanvita – purest of Sattva, one who is lord of the universe, without any Guna-s of the three Guna-s is he.

"Our forefathers defined 'Purushartha', a basic view of life that concedes four selfish but legitimate aims that add meaning to human life, Dharma, Artha, Kama and Moksha. Broadly stated, dharma translates to duties, principles or moral law and refers to the means to fulfill the right purpose. Dharma stands on four pillars or is four-footed. It changes as man cycles between the four yuga-s and ages. What were solemn-duties in Krishna's time is not the same today. Even the natural laws mutate with time. As the sun in its sinusoidal path gets closer to the galactic center, we get to the 'satya' yuga or the golden age. The deterioration begins with its movement away from the galactic center also called the Dharma Navel. Dharma mutates to its worse or to its crudest at the 'kali' yuga and then turns subtle as it returns to the galactic center, the finish cycle is around twenty-five to twenty-six thousand solar years; the complete journey across the galactic band we see in the night sky would be two hundred twenty-five to two hundred fifty million earth years."

"From its present definition, recognition, fame and honor come from partaking in solemn-duties, derived from the broader principles of truth and right action. Artha introduces material gains and monetary achievement of goals, material resources to help fulfill one's solemn-duties in life. It relates to income and wealth. Kama is 'sensual desire' and refers to our need for emotional and sensory happiness. It is enjoyment though I would state it as a sense of achievement that conjoins artha to dharma. You can only titillate the senses for a few moments before they return to normal. Moksha of the other dimension refers to the freedom or liberation that transcends the other three. AquaPisces recognizes the four aims and offers an accelerated program in accomplishing them. Yet, superimposing them into modern living, the first three, career, wealth and enjoyment are by far inferior to spiritual liberation, which is the primary and essential goal. Without the liberating reason, the other goals have no real meaning; it is like oxen on three legs. The first three offer the means and the factor of liberation or salvation defines the end."

"Providing a foundation to the four aims of life, is the need for wellness, branded as 'arogya' or freedom from disease. Without health and wellness, little gets accomplished; wellness is not just physical, it encompasses the mental and spiritual, without which the goals of life are dysfunctional."

"Founded in dharma are axioms and natural laws that govern the atomic particles and the celestial universe. At the individual level, it points to our basic character, inclinations and capacities in life. You may think of solemn-duties as a talent chosen for the native which may have nothing to do with the profession."

"In my younger and more vulnerable years, I received the exact advice I have now been turning over in my mind, yes, true dharma is the soul's vocation, not what human society imposes upon us; the soul being the individualization of the supreme power, our individual solemn-duties reflect in different ways, the universal laws. With dharma incorrectly executed or sabotaged, when actions are damaging to others, without a doubt, it will end up hurting us. Dharma's relationship with artha are objects and goals we seek to acquire a meaningful life, sometimes it is through career one seeks wealth at a certain stage."

"Jupiter, Mercury and the Sun are the core graha-s that rule dharma. Mythological Mercury is the adopted son of Jupiter; Jupiter being the guru of all heavens together with his son is a strong advocate of the natural laws. While the son discloses the way to function and communicate in society, the guru-father reveals the role to adopt, goals to seek, and the guiding principles. Sun confirms our ability to project our character and personality, and how we influence the world."

"Dharma is inherent in the trinal houses of 1-5-9. First house denotes natural laws on us and accountability to self, the fifth, represents solemn-duties towards our species and responsibility of managing offspring, and the ninth shows the dimensional, spiritual and social dharma. Looking at a person's horoscope, the practitioner should mark the first, ninth and tenth houses 1-9-10 and their lords. First tells us who we are; it is the measure of our identity and action in the world, ninth exhibits the goals or profession we aspire. Tenth house measures our capacity to influence the world through the impact of karma, it flashes our personality to the world, showing how dharma achieves artha of 'value' for ourselves and the community."

"Artha or wealth suggests all essential means of physical living and security, not just the pursuit of money. AquaPisces as a tool offers its users on how to better their material potential in life by directing such acts towards dharmic ends, not chasing money for the power or status it may afford. Artha in astrology has connections to Jupiter, Mercury, Venus and Saturn. Jupiter governs our capacity in gains and abundance; Mercury strengthens our ability in commerce and monetary exchange. Venus confers wealth, comfort, love of art and luxury. Saturn refrains from monetary earnings; sometimes pushing us towards poverty though it can bequeath land, and immovable property. Houses that sustain artha are the 2-10-11, their occupants and their lords, where the second house shows how we manage our personal livelihood and our ability to earn through our own labor; tenth shows career success, status and achievement; the eleventh shows how to profit from various sources."

"It is important for the practitioner to consider the fourth, fifth and ninth houses and their lords, which confer wealth. Fourth house gives property and vehicles, fifth gives gain through counseling, advice and speculation, like the stock market; ninth promotes grace and fortunes, like having a sudden windfall. The twelfth, sixth and eighth houses, numerically represented as 6-8-12 along with their lords will limit access to wealth. Twelfth shows loss and expenses; this may not generate poverty if the income-houses are strong. Sixth gives losses through disease, enmity, legal problems, overwork or lack of recognition. Eighth may show difficulties, obstacles, oppression, lack of recognition or bad reputation, but it gives money and wealth through inheritance."

"Kama is enjoyment, not just pleasure in the gross sense but the euphoric feelings that come naturally in the right use of the senses. To enjoy life, to grasp beauty of nature and art; love all creatures is part of our soul's fulfillment. Life gets a fresh meaning in our search of happiness with the right use of the senses. In fact, enjoyment or pleasure in life is largely through relationship. Relationship is the main reason of Kama and its products of love, marriage, partnership and children. Higher strata of Kama or enjoyment gets expressed as sense of art and the highest echelon – the sense of delight that comes from being a devout in divine love."

"Planet that influences Kama is Venus and to a great extent Mars and Moon. According to position of Venus in the chart, the faculty of enjoyment or Kama is revealed. Mars promises success in our quest for right goals. When in line with Venus, it plunges us deeper into the realms of want. Jupiter facilitates enjoyment and happiness of a more general nature while Saturn constrains it. Saturn in line with Mars may push us to seek perverted means of enjoyment. Kama houses are 3-7-12, where the third is the house of talent, hobbies, curiosities, interests and sports culminating as personal Kama. Seventh house is the house of partnership, love, marriage and fulfillment in human relationship, summarized as relationship Kama. Twelfth as the house of secret pleasures and hidden desires is equally relevant, besides, showing 'closure', a big step towards salvation. Fifth is significant as the house of romance, joy and creativity, the happiness that comes from the choice of right dharma."

"Moksha or liberation is the ascent towards self-realization, our efforts at Self-knowledge; whose methods contain tenets of those that unshackle the inner spirit and creative forces. It has nothing to do with organized religion and dogmatic beliefs. The pursuit of knowledge, of philosophy, science and the occult, and creative expression, like art and music, are important pieces of the goal of liberation."

"Allow me to conjure a make-believe situation. A pebble, a nugget, a pearl exists in the depths of aquatic Pisces. We know it exists. Why do we still clamor for them, knowing they exist, because we feel we need to feel them, not just see them. It is such an ironical sensory conflict when seeing is not enough. The mind wants to keep indulging by using one sense over another until all becomes saturated. Then it pounces on another object in a completely distorted way of knowledge acquisition. Liberation aims at redefining this process through quietude, yoga and other balancing acts."

"We seek knowledge or freedom in some form or another. The more we unravel this knowledge, the closer we are to freedom. Lesser knowledge sometimes gives us greater space to operate in the world but it does not free us from the limitations of worldly existence."

"Jupiter, Saturn and Ketu influence this knowledge of Moksha. Jupiter equips us with the right expansion and truth in our search; it works on our objectives and inspires our demand to expand the grow and eventually transcend. Ketu confirms our ability to negate and transcend things, by provoking deep insight, discrimination and perception. Saturn brings in dispassion, renunciation and solitariness. Mercury, an indicator of intellect, shows the level of knowledge we seek. Moksha houses are 4-8-12; fourth house shows our emotional happiness; eighth expresses occult and mental insight and twelfth denotes spiritual liberation. House influences of the ninth and twelfth together are important, along with their lords, with Jupiter the significator of the ninth and Ketu of the twelfth. Ninth house instills a sense of values, goals, principles and aspirations, revealing the dharma and principles directing our pursuit of moksha; twelfth house negates our experiences and allows us to go beyond what we already are as a conditioned being. It discloses the past and the latent impressions in the subconscious that motivates us."

"In the Moksha setting, fifth house is fairly important as a measure of good karma we bring into the present life from past spiritual practices, expressing devotion, form and energy we seek. Ninth house being the fifth from the fifth is the karma culmination, what gets dispelled and what gets carried over and beyond. Eighth house depicts our ability to go beyond death and time, into the gateway to the eternal; besides offering the ability to transcend suffering and deep perception. Venus and Mars often limit our pursuit of Moksha with passion and sexuality, surrounding us with ignorance."

"Saturn offers the detachment needed in liberation, it can also prevent it by darkening the mind, just as Jupiter can fixate us to the material world and ritualism. All graha-s work in dual mode, in the material and spiritual plane; it is important to understand the graha-s, untarnished or posited in houses that promote spirituality. Jupiter, acclaimed as the guru of the deities is the easier and ideal guide to seek the ultimate."

"When Jupiter and Saturn's forces balance each other, they promote the real knowledge. The lunar nodes have a similar role. Rahu, the north node, shows where we are apt to project ourselves in bold into the outer world. Ketu, the south node, specifies where we are prone to contract ourselves deeper into the inner world. When the lords of houses where the nodes are posited are in harmony, our lives function well. When they are in harmony on the higher dimensional level, a wonderful transformation is possible."

"Apt is the time,
To tell you about thousands of things
Of graha-s and aspects and guna vectors
Of beautiful gemstones set on fabulous rings."

"In the mechanics of Vedic astrology are the nine planets or Nava Graha. Energies of the planets influencing us are modulators of the three primary qualities or guna vectors of Sattva, Rajas and Tamas. Sun, Moon and Jupiter induce Sattva, promoting awareness, harmony, intelligence and balance. Mercury and Venus focused more on Rajas endorse action, expression, movement and change. Mars, Saturn, Rahu and Ketu with Tamasik personality develop inertia, resistance, opposition and obstruction."

"The ancestors grouped nine graha-s under five elements of Earth, Water, Fire, Air and Ether. Mercury enjoys a relationship with Earth, Moon and Venus closely associated with Water promotes watery tendencies at physical, emotional and spiritual level. Sun and Mars of the Fire group increase aggression, assertion and perception. Air related to Saturn causes instability, separation and sense of not being grounded. Ether relates to Jupiter, promoting space, expansion, harmony and ascension. Malefic planets tend to be Tamasik on one side, except the Sun. Malefic graha-s have an obverse side also which can be sattvic. All benefic planets are sattvic or Rajasic. The five elements have wellness, psychological and spiritual indications, not just physical connections. The five elements are the basic vibratory levels of all existence of matter, life and mind."

"Few planets comprise the same element but have different guna vectors like the Sun has fire and Sattva, and Mars has fire and Tamas. Sun promotes spiritual knowledge, health and wellbeing, while Mars lean towards impulse, valor and abruptness. Some planets entail same guna vectors but different elements such as Mars and Saturn which are both Tamasik but differ in the fire and air elements. No two planets have similar element and guna combination."

"The system designates planets as benefic or supportive in action; malefic, or obstructive in action, which characterizes their overall influences and functions."

> Supporting life on planets is the malefic Sun
> Leading to pitta, his scorching heat
> Pleasant is Moon's kapha, he[210] nurtures life on earth
> New and waning, he is no longer sweet

Salvation is where Sun shall lead
Materialistic is Moon that's his known feat
Rises the spirit with the ray of the sun
Cool stays the mind in moon's retreat

> Daksha, cosmic progenitor
> Married twenty-seven daughters to prince Moon
> Visited them at their mansions he did by turn
> But to leave Rohini, oh! The day, the night went so soon

Why Rohini? Wept the jealous wives
To their father they went, their tears damped his feet
Enraged Daksha cursed the Moon
Thou shall be childless for this deceit

> No, cried the spouses, arbitrated they in haste
> Pardoned was Moon, but the curse was set
> Only Daksha could regulate it
> Thereafter prince moon, waxes and wanes instead

But elope did the philanderer Moon with Tara
Furious Jupiter waged a war with the fugitive prince
Captive, Moon held her for many a day
Born was Mercury from their love intense

---

[210] All planets and graha-s have a male gender in vedic astrology. They may have feminine attributes however.

AQUAPISCES

    Mercury, no less in talent than Venus
    Compassionate he is, his potency runs divine
    Like the Moon, mind and intellect his playground
    With him, age you shall not with time

Venus, occult, potent with so many secrets
At his best, he is stimulus and instinct
At his lowest, carnal and erotic
Between the poet and the poetry, is he split?

    Pitta-prone Mars of Mangala is of great ambition
    Desires to fathom the unexplored
    Oh! The urge to roam far and experience the new
    Gratifies the Martian urge with his unsheathed sword

Beneficent is thee, O' mighty Jupiter
Provider of cosmic good
The guru embodies the deity Brihaspati
Shows the path of right living from childhood

    Saturn born of Chaya and Sun
    Away from the father he moved, a desolate son
    Limited and constrained
    He learned the hard way, for inheritance he had none

Saturn affects highest and lowest facets
There is no impact you endure when you are real
Saturn spiritualizes different from Jupiter
In causing frustration with the material

    Shadowy are the nodes Rahu and Ketu, not physical matter
    Rahu gets malefic, akin to Saturn
    Dissatisfied with gross and physical
    Frustrated acts the native at every nook and turn

Ketu analyzes the self
Illusory side to material gets revealed
While Rahu frustrates over substance world
Ketu generates the native, spiritually healed

    Bitter enemies of the luminaries, they rule the eclipses
    Even make the moon lose its luster
    A lunar node with full Moon weighs as lunar eclipse
    Nodes with Moon and Sun is the eclipse of solar

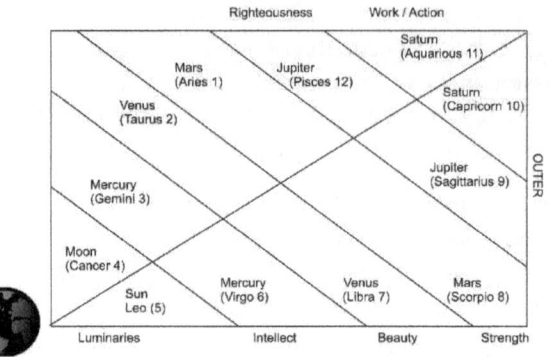

"Hatti, do not even for a moment think benefic graha-s are 'always' favorable in the chart. These graha-s promote the powers of the houses they rule. If the ruled houses are difficult ones like 6, 8 or 12, which bring about loss and destruction, the benefic graha-s act as facilitator and do not oppose the damage. Malefic graha-s are of use in the difficult houses by destroying the adverse impacts. What really matters is the longitudinal position of graha, which can be transposed to a sign and house. Benefic graha-s act favorable in angles and trines like the houses 1, 4, 5, 7, 9, and 10, while malefic graha-s remain useful in Upachaya houses 3, 6, 11 and sometimes 10. This is a basic rule of how location makes all the difference."

"Nine graha-s along with Rahu and Ketu lunar nodes have unique qualities, each comes with a range of offering, each brandishing multiple icons. Graha-s flaunt certain purposes on a lower, mundane level and offer a different set of functionalities at higher, spiritual planes. They symbolize different processes in life and work at all levels of consciousness, distinct by their meaning and different qualities of energy. Sun as the largest and brightest heavenly body embodies authority, acts the king and ruler, the father, showering success, power, prana, will power, soul and the self. Moon signifies the female ruler, queen, mother, public influence, fertility, creativity, mind, emotions and feelings. Mars has a fiery energy similar to the Sun but reduced and specialized as the son, brother, prince, male energy, prowess, aggression, competition, legal and military offerings. Venus as the brightest in the morning or evening has a similar energy to the Moon but reduced and specialized as the daughter, wife, female energy, attraction, beauty, art, and adornment. Jupiter as the bright celestial body in the night sky denotes cosmic energy, law, dharma, spirituality, education, wealth, abundance and health. Mercury, close to the Sun with diminished brightness specifies the child, intellect, perception, prana, speech and communication. Saturn as the slowest of the planets specifies destiny, time, karma, obstruction, inertia, poverty, disease, detachment and renunciation."

"Rahu as the north lunar node expresses illusion, desire, media, Maya, expansion and dissolution. Ketu as the south lunar node directs perception, research, spiritual knowledge and inquiry; also, death, termination, negation. Every graha embodies a set of attributes that may complement or negate other attributes propounding nine unique views of an individual."

"An eighteen-degree highway of Zodiac that spans all destiny has twelve signs from Mesha to Meena, corresponding to the system of Aries, Taurus, Gemini, Cancer, Leo, Virgo, Libra, Scorpio, Sagittarius, Capricorn, Aquarius, and Pisces. Signs decide on the fields of activity for the planets where each has its own characteristics. Planets are moving forces while signs are the static fields of operation. Graha-s rule Signs. For Aries, the ruling graha is Mars, Taurus it is Venus, Gemini's ruler is Mercury, Cancer is ruled by the Moon, Leo by the Sun, Virgo's ruler is Mercury. Libra has Venus as the ruling graha, Scorpio has Mars, for Sagittarius, Jupiter is the ruling graha, Capricorn has Saturn, Aquarius is ruled by Saturn, and Pisces' ruler is Jupiter. Signs are expressions of the planets, twelve windows to life, a blue print for the twelve phases of any aspect of life."

"N-style chart rectangle comprises twelve divisions where the ascendant stays positioned on top, horizontally middle remaining eleven Bhava-s or houses appear counterclockwise and the 'mid-heavens' occupy the vertically middle, on the right."

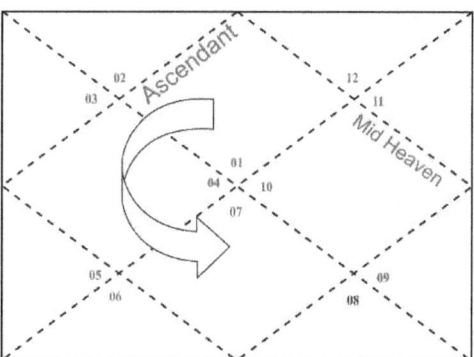

"U-Chart is circular and read in the same way where the ascendant is on the vertical middle, left position. 'Mid-heavens' stays on the top, horizontally middle, coinciding with the sun at mid-day."

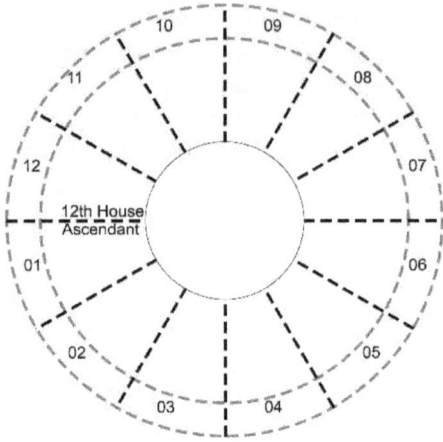

S-Chart is rectangular in shape using a different template. Read are the Bhava-s or houses clockwise. Numbers in the chart depict signs and not houses. The houses are numbered as they occur."

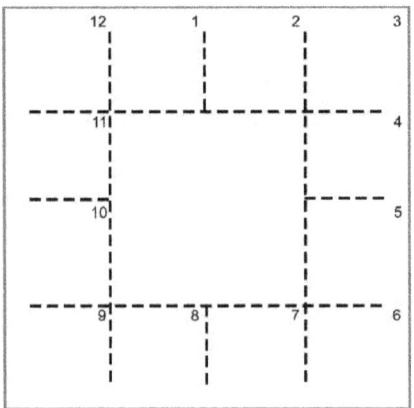

"Similar are the templates for all charts - Divisional Natal, Hora, Decant, Nakshatra and other Horary charts."

Attributes of Signs

"Qualities of the signs define their field of movement. Movements are three - cardinal or moveable, 'chara', which include the signs Aries, Cancer, Libra and Capricorn; fixed or unmoving or 'sthira', including Taurus, Leo, Scorpio and Aquarius; and mutable or dual, 'dvisvabhava' signs including Gemini, Virgo, Sagittarius and Pisces. A high concentration of planets in moveable signs makes a person 'moveable' and active both outwardly and inwardly, but in a focused direction. When a great number of planets are in fixed signs, it will make a person fixed in his personal traits and outer action, providing stability but also inertia. Many planets in mutable or dual signs can turn the native into sensitive, changing and adaptable, but also wavering and vulnerable. As such, planets in moveable signs are more Rajasic, they are willful and assertive; where in fixed signs more Tamasik, steady but conservative; and in dual signs more sattvic in qualities especially being ruled by Jupiter and Mercury that are intelligent but sensitive. When located are Ascendant, Sun and Moon in signs of the same quality, the effects get more pronounced."

"Like the graha-s, signs also have a close connection with the five elements. Earth-element comprises the signs of Taurus, Virgo, and Capricorn, water comprises Cancer, Scorpio, and Pisces. Fire signs are Aries, Leo, and Sagittarius, air group has Gemini, Libra, and Aquarius. Elements are important for delineating the fields of activity for each sign and their different personality characteristics. For example, a person with many planets in earth signs will have a lot of activity in the earth field, body, nature or the physical world. Those who have many planets in watery signs will be emotional, oriented and personal in their interactions. Anyone with many planets in fiery signs are likely willed, aggressive, intelligent and assertive. Natives with many planets in airy signs are changeable, sensitive, expansive and socially driven."

"Signs have connotations as they relate to cosmic evolution and the twelve parts of the cosmic person as time personified[211]. As such, the twelve signs supply a blueprint for the forces working on all levels."

"Signs are odd or even, active and passive, positive and negative. Odd-numbered signs are masculine and assertive, while even-numbered signs are feminine and responsive. Arrayed in a mathematical arrangement, the polarity changes for succeeding sign in the sequence, every sign has a preceding and succeeding sign of opposite polarity. An active sign has passive signs placed on either side. Odd signs are Aries, Gemini, Leo, Libra, Sagittarius, Aquarius; even signs being Taurus, Cancer, Virgo, Scorpio, Capricorn, Pisces."

---

[211] Time personified is Kala Cosmic man

"Mars ruling 1 and 8 shows more hostility in Aries, and more prone to secrets in Scorpio; similarly, Saturn being a ruler of sign 10 and 11, shows restrain in Capricorn where he exhibits more artistic, feminine behavior than in sign 11, where he is more assertive, masculine and aggressive. All graha-s except Sun, Moon, Rahu and Ketu express this duality. Ascendant element from the five colors the chart. Planets gain in strength when posited in signs of similar elements, like the fiery Sun in a fiery sign like Sagittarius, or aerial Saturn in aerial Libra. Planets become fragile in signs ruled by an opposite element, like the fiery Sun in a watery Pisces, or airy Saturn in fiery Leo. Between the fire and water is the worst of turbulence."

"On the energies, you may recall that Ascendant directs its force towards the body, Moon influences the mind and Sun focuses on the spirit."

"Graha-s achieve their best in their signs of exaltation and suffer in their signs of debility. Sun finds exaltation when posited in Aries and gets debilitated in the seventh from Aries, in Libra. Exalted is Moon in Taurus and debilitated in Scorpio. Mars gets exalted in Capricorn and debilitated in Cancer. Exalted is Mercury in Virgo and debilitated in Pisces. Jupiter finds exaltation in Cancer and gets debilitated in Capricorn. Exalted is Saturn in Libra and debilitated in Aries."

"Few authors have incorrectly tried to show longitudinal degrees where lie the exaltation or debilitation. I find their reasoning incorrect, I have recalculated the degrees from where comes a logical correspondence with Nakshatra. Having Sun exalted in 0-10 degrees under Ketu's lordship was incorrect. At 26 degrees 40 minutes in Aries, Sun has a much better room for exaltation."

Num	Nakshatra	Lord	Exalted	Sign	Degrees
1	Ashvini	Ketu	SA--	Aries	0.00
2	Bharani	Venus		Aries	13.33
3	Krittika	Sun	SU++	Ari/Tau	26.66
4	Rohini	Moon	MO++	Taurus	10.00
5	Mrigashira	Mars		Tau/Gem	23.33
6	Ardra	Rahu		Gemini	6.66
7	Punarvasu	Jupiter	JU++	Gem/Cancer	20.00
8	Pushya	Saturn	MA--	Cancer	3.33
9	Aslesha	Mercury		Cancer	16.66

Num	Nakshatra	Lord	Exalted	Sign	Degrees
10	Magha	Ketu		Leo	0.00
11	Purva Phalguni	Venus		Leo	13.33
12	Uttara Phalguni	Sun	ME++	Leo/Virgo	26.66
13	Hasta	Moon		Virgo	10.00
14	Chitra	Mars	VE--	Virgo/Lib	23.33
15	Swati	Rahu	SU--	Libra	6.66
16	Vishakha	Jupiter	SA++	Lib/Scorpio	20.00
17	Anuradha	Saturn	MO--	Scorpio	3.33
18	Jyeshta	Mercury		Scorpio	16.66
19	Moola	Ketu		Sagittarius	0.00
20	Purva Ashada	Venus		Sagittarius	13.33
21	Uttara Ashada	Sun	JU--	Sag/Cap	26.66
22	Sravana	Moon		Capricorn	10.00
23	Dhanistha	Mars	MA++	Cap/Aqua	23.33
24	Shatabhishag	Rahu		Aquarius	6.66
25	Purva Bhadra pada	Jupiter	VE++	Aqua/Pisces	20.00
26	Uttara Bhadra pada	Saturn	ME--	Pisces	3.33
27	Revati	Mercury		Pisces	16.66

"Astrological part of wellness has the special concept of Moolatrikona or root trine, representing other places where graha-s achieve their strength. These are mainly in the odd-numbered or positive sign they rule. Mercury is exceptional in Virgo, ruling it, being exalted and has Moolatrikona in the sign. Sun has Moolatrikona in Leo, Moon in Taurus, Mars in Aries, Mercury in Virgo, Jupiter in Sagittarius and Saturn in Aquarius."

Graha friendship and enmity

"Graha-s turn into friends and enemies through their static and dynamic journey. Static status is their natural one, unchanging and universal to all, despite any chart. Temporal or dynamic status is one that varies in different charts, depending on the ascendant and house positioning."

"Two natural factions emerge, the first being the Deva group comprising Sun, Mars, Moon, and Jupiter and the second Daitya group with Mercury, Venus and Saturn in it. Graha-s in the same camp are natural friends, like Sun and Mars, or Mercury and Venus; and natural enemies when from different camps, like Sun and Mercury, or Mars and Venus."

"A simple rule defines temporal friends and enemies. Graha-s in positions 2, 3, 4, 10, 11, and 12 from a planet's placement are temporal friends. Graha-s conjunct in the same house or in positions 5 through 9 from it are temporal enemies. As in the earlier rule, graha-s fare better in friendly positions and suffer in unfriendly ones."

"Nakshatra-s[212] and their lords, the graha-s decide planetary periods or dasa systems of Vimshottari, Ashtottari, though they can also help in shaping a person's disposition. I have a lot to tell you about the Nakshatra and dasa system."

"Houses or bhava-s are an important reason for us to consider. Signs speak more on the personal nature or character while the houses show more the native's outer manifestation and external life affairs. The first house correlates well with Aries, second with Taurus and the rule applies for the remaining signs. When influenced are the same house and sign number, the result turns more profound."

"On the side of caution, recasting the chart using Moon as the Ascendant applying similar set of rules may reconfirm the results. The moon-chart shows how the planets sanction our mental and personal happiness, while positions on the ascendant show how graha-s dominate our physical world. Extending the same principle to the Sun as the ascendant, we can get a reading on our inner being. As we work with other ascendants, all geometric positions give an insight into the finer aspects of our self."

"Houses have many finer qualities. Houses 1, 4, 7, 10 are treated as Angular or Kendra houses. Planets are usually sturdier when found in Kendra. Trine or Trikona houses 1, 5, 9 are also favorable and powerful. Upachaya or houses on the rise are 3, 6, 10, 11, which work better for malefic graha-s and give powers of competition, endurance and resistance. In the passage of time, Apachaya or houses on fall, 1, 2, 4, 7, 8 cause graha-s to lose their strength and value."

---

[212] Nakshatra whose literal meaning is "by which one wishes to attain" are a cluster of stars or constellations.

"Unhealthy or difficult houses are 6, 8, and 12, also called dusthana, positions, where planets turn weak, particularly the benefic ones. Rulers of 6, 8 and 12 tend to do little good. However, if the ruler of the 8th is in 6 or 12; ruler of 6 in 8 or 12, or ruler of 12 in 6 or 8; then formed is Vipreeta Raj Yoga wherein the negative results get reversed. Also, divided are the houses by the four elements, where Earth houses are 2, 6, 10; Water houses are 4, 8, 12; Fire houses are 1, 5, 9 and Air houses are 3, 7, 11. Taking one house from each of these groups creates a separate group of 'triplicity'. According to Purushartha, the four aims of life, dharma houses are 1, 5, 9; Artha houses are 2, 6, 10; Kama houses are 3, 7, 11 and Moksha houses are 4, 8, 12."

❖ "Dharma houses are contrary to the Kama or desire houses. Kama houses signify what we 'want' to do, the desires. Dharma houses exemplify what we 'need' to do, the purpose."

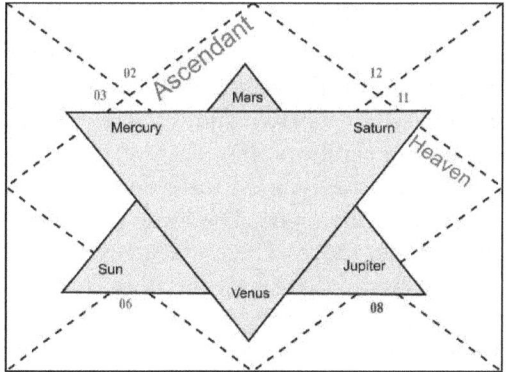

"Every house has an associated graha which becomes a significant contributor or the house Karaka. Think of Karaka as a special worker for the house. Sun is the karaka for the first house, Jupiter for the second, Mars for the third, Moon and the fourth, Jupiter and the fifth, Saturn and Rahu and the sixth, Jupiter and Venus and the seventh, Saturn and the eighth, Jupiter and Sun and ninth, Sun and Mars and the tenth, Jupiter and the eleventh, Saturn and Ketu and the twelfth. Jupiter is the karaka of several houses like 2, 5, 7, 9, and 11. Saturn signifies houses like 6, 8, and 12 implying the difficult or Dusthana houses. If weak is the natural karaka of a house, the house turns fragile."

❖ "Combinations of ruling, friendliness, aspect, and signification are the basis of all interpretations and predictions."

"Where comes the challenge are with graha-s other than Sun and Moon. Remaining five graha-s rule two houses, one house bequeaths good effects, and the other does not. In fact, the graha gives the results of both houses it rules, the results emerge at different times and in diverse ways."

"When a planet rules an angular house or a Kendra comprising houses 1, 4, 7, and 10 and a trinal house like 1, 5, and 9, it signifies a powerful karaka. Such an arrangement gives the native great power, influence and success in life from the graha. Many charts have a yoga karaka graha like Saturn ruling houses 4 and 5, for Libra Ascendant or Venus owning 4 and 9 in Aquarius Ascendant. Extending the principle to two graha-s, where one owns a Kendra, the other a trine; such a combination results into yet another powerful yoga. Raja-Yogas emerge from two such graha combinations of one owning an angular house and the other ruling a trinal house."

"Let me tell you about planetary aspects or dristhi-s. Dristhi means the line of sight, or in this case, planetary light's direction pointed to another graha, a house or a sign. We all know that the graha-s borrow light from the Sun, unlike Sun, which has its own light source. These graha-s reflect the borrowed light to all its neighbors. It's when you come into the triangle, the radiations take a different meaning. Moon being close to our planet provides a soft light that illumines the night. The lunar nodes are geometrical points and have no light source per se. There are many authors who would argue that the nodes have aspects, there may be other definitions of aspects, they do not fall in this definition. Dristhi is largely sign based. All graha-s other than Rahu and Ketu aspect the seventh sign opposite it and its occupants. The word 'aspect' means to influence, if graha-s are opposite one another in a chart, then the influence or aspect is the strongest. Mars has bonus Dristhi on the fourth and eighth signs from its position. Jupiter has extra aspects on the fifth and ninth signs from its location. Saturn has other aspects on the third and tenth signs from itself. These special aspects give special power to these three planets, which relate to fire and Pitta as exhibited by Mars, water and Kapha for Jupiter; and air and Vata in case of Saturn. Having the special Dristhi, they become powerful and influence the fire or Pitta, water or Kapha and air or Vata factors in the chart."

"In the common, seventh house aspect, the Dristhi is mutual. Rules of Dristhi apply to the divisional charts. Sambandha, or association between planets, occurs through conjunction when they live in the same sign, mutual full aspect when they are six houses away, or exchange of signs. Only with Sun, one must examine the differences in longitude of a graha if found in the same house or in neighboring areas. A graha is 'combust', when too close to Sun's longitude, its rays are superseded by the Sun's."

"It is quite a misnomer with graha-s being millions of miles away to be considered combust. 'Combust' denotes the graha when in same line of sight of the Sun, where it has nothing more to offer than the Sun's rays. If the orb or longitudinal difference is less than *8.5* degrees, the graha is too close to the longitude of the Sun who will render it's Dristhi powerless. For inner planets, the orb is even narrower, Venus runs four-degrees orb and Mercury two-degrees. For the Moon, the orb is fifteen-degrees. Moon turns into 'new moon' when alongside Sun's longitude. This rule has an exception where a graha found in a favorable sign or house is excused from the 'combust' rule. On conjunction, yet another rule stumbles into our interpretation when deciding whether a planetary war is at play when longitudinal conjunction between graha-s is less than one degree. When a graha-yuddha or graha war occurs, one of them is a winner. Normally, the one at a higher longitude in the same sign wins. It is important to examine the planets' disposition around any planet, including adjacent signs. Planets or houses with natural malefic planets on either side suffer from being 'hemmed in between malefic graha-s' or Papakartari Yoga, where harm and weakening comes to the graha. Planets or houses with natural benefic planets on either side do well, being 'hemmed in between benefic graha-s' or Shubhakartari Yoga."

"Considered are Sun, Saturn, Rahu, lord of the twelfth house and Mars graha-s responsible for 'separation'. They negate or remove the native from the qualities of the house or planet they influence. Supportive they are in predicting a loss of job, moving away from home, divorces and similar separations. In the wellness program, separations that result in mental anguish are for us practitioners to pay close attention. They may not involve any diseases, but they upset the mental ecosystem."

"The word Yoga is decidedly 'overused' in Vedic literature. While we use Yoga to define physical workout, meditation and postures, astrological-yoga refers to combinations of graha-s, wherein their influence increases by a quantum amount in the chart. Various combinations define yoga, either with a house or sign location, or with house or sign under different ruling or aspects. Maha Purusha Yoga is one such important combination, formed by planets in a Kendra-angle from the Ascendant or Moon, residing in their own sign or exalted. This does not include Sun or Moon."

"Divisional Varga charts supplement the natal chart readings. Each divisional breakup has its own, specific meaning and application. Commonly used are Sapta-Varga or seven different divisional charts. Exact birth time is necessary in smaller divisional charts beyond the Navamsa as it affects the new Lagna position. If calculated well, divisional charts feature an awesome means in fine-tuning chart interpretation."

Drekkana or harmonic third is important for brothers and sisters, friends, prana and vitality, much like the third house in the birth chart. Dasamsa or tenth harmonic chart is much like the tenth house in a birth chart for determining career and success in life. Navamsa or divisional ninth chart is most important for all general indications, for the future, for relationship and for spiritual or ninth house indications. Navamsa acts as a second pair of eyes on a chart analysis. It has a special connection with Nakshatra system, with each Navamsa sign reflecting one-quarter or 'pada' of Navamsa. There is merit in looking at the Navamsa chart along with Rasi chart. Even the Drekkana or third divisional chart offers many clues in unfolding our attributes, besides like all divisional charts, Drekkana and Navamsa show more the subtle characteristics that are not apparent in the basic sign chart."

"A strong ruler of rising Navamsa, Drekkana and Rasi brings happiness to the native. One runs the opportunity to head a community, town or country. In any odd sign, when a graha is within 6° is in its infancy, from 6 - 12° practitioners consider that childhood. Adolescence is at 18° where the graha delivers the maximum it can. Decay and old age occurs at 24°. In an even sign the reverse applies. Infancy is at 24-30° and decay is at 6°. The degrees matter as they affect the personality and maturity of the native."

"Benefic graha-s strong in Varga divisions bring the native wealth, stretching the life span. In a Hora D2 chart malefic graha-s in sun's Hora in an odd sign makes the native strong and sturdy, cruel and wealthy. In Hora chart, benefic graha-s occupying moon's Hora in an even sign gives the person a brilliant appearance, mild speech and pleasant attitude."

"Reversal of the two Hora rules also reverses the results for Sun and Moon Hora. Graha-s if mixed in the Hora chart, give mixed results for both Sun and Moon Hora."

"Decant D3 chart specifies siblings, past life, children, death and disease. Results turn positive if placed are Mars and Sun well and not in 6, 8 and 12 houses. Moon posited in own or friendly house in a Drekkana, D3 chart adds beauty and attractiveness to the native and bestows many good qualities. Chaturthamsa D4 divisional chart deals with fate and destiny. Mars and Venus in 6, 8 or 12 is not positive for the native. Navamsa D9 divisional chart rectifies and verifies many findings and observations in the natal chart. Annulled is the debilitation of a fallen graha when the graha achieves exaltation in Navamsa. Canceled is debilitation through Neecha-Bhanga."

"If the dispositor of the debilitated graha occupies a Kendra or Trine or achieves exaltation or the dispositor aspects the house of descent, then cancelled is the fall or debilitation. Debilitation cancellation brings about a new source of strength. If a debilitated graha gets exalted or is in its own house in Navamsa, the graha becomes very strong. Ruled out is the exaltation if Navamsa shows debilitation. Moon's position in Navamsa describes the person. Moon in the sign of Aries in Navamsa makes the native a warrior, a commandant, having bloodshot eyes; while Moon in Taurus in Navamsa Chart makes the person big and awkward. In Gemini, it makes the native dusky, beautifully formed who loves to scribe. Moon in Cancer in Navamsa Chart makes one dusky, but bereft of father or son. In Leo, in Navamsa chart, it turns one obese, but blessed with wealth and strength. Moon in Virgo in Navamsa makes the native's speech soft and sweet, keeping him lean and good at speculations. Moon in Libra Navamsa gives one glamorous eyes and the adoration by the other sex. When Moon is in Scorpio in Navamsa, it gives the native defective limb and deprives him of stability and wealth. With Moon posited in Sagittarius in Navamsa makes the native lean, liberal, devoted and wealthy. Moon in Capricorn in Navamsa turns one covetous and dusky. The person marries well and begets sons. Moon in Aquarius in Navamsa turns the person into a bigot and a doormat. Moon in Pisces in Navamsa makes one spiritually inclined; the person's speech is soft."

"The 10th house in Navamsa points to profession. When the Navamsa of 10th belongs to Sun, it confers power and authority. If Moon, the profession is agriculture, or food and things from water. Navamsa of 10th if Mars, the person's work hovers around acts of violence. If Mercury becomes the Navamsa of the tenth, the profession and work happens through writing and arts. If Jupiter takes on the tenth Navamsa, the profession revolves around spiritual acts. Navamsa of 10th when Venus, denotes the work is with jewels, beauty and vehicles. Saturn in Navamsa of tenth would yield different results where work gets enacted through wicked acts and underground artifacts or even agriculture or petroleum. When the rising Navamsa is Vargottama and benefic graha-s are in 2nd position from Moon, in addition, Kendra houses are occupied; with such a combination, the sages say, kings take birth. Let me tell you more on Vargottama."

Vargottama is the state when graha
Stays in the same sign as the Amsa division
Association with friendly or exalted house
Strengthens the Varga's position

A Varga score of two confers respect
Score of three Vargottama gives money and power
Four gives intellect, wealth and land
One becomes a friend of the kings, five does empower

> Score of six gives cars and joy
> Seven assures the heaven
> Weak in Vargas does the reverse
> As they assess the lagna lords' strength

"When the ruler of a rising Navamsa is a benefic graha and occupies Kendra houses 1, 4, 7 and 10 then person is likely to get married very early. If the rising Navamsa or Navamsa of the 7th are with malefic graha-s then the marriage is not a happy one. Jupiter in the tenth Navamsa in Sagittarius or Pisces enables one to lead the life of a celebrity. Mercury or Venus Navamsa causes strained relationships with those in authority. In Saturn's Navamsa or in Capricorn one turns into a liar, a cheat. The waxing moon in Sun's Moon's or Jupiter's Navamsa helps the native do deeds of merit, while dismissing all evil. Mars in Moon or Lagna Navamsa with Jupiter's aspects and Moon in Gemini is a lethal combination for a child."

"One who has Aries as ascendant in Navamsa is full of trouble. He is larcenous, his weak eyesight bothers him much, and he shows signs of being lascivious. Worrying are his 12, 25, 50 and 65th years. Incidentally, Taurus Navamsa makes the native intelligent, who knows how to enjoy life; he has a broad belly and long face and walks crooked. The years 10, 22, 32 and 72 are full of trouble. Native born with Gemini rising in Navamsa gets endowed with beauty and a temperamental, fickle-minded nature; he is nevertheless eloquent and joyful, having good knowledge of many sciences. The ages that are troublesome are 16, 24, 34, 40 and 63rd. He whose birth has ascendant as Cancer in Navamsa acts surly and brooding, crooked is his body, malevolent are his looks. He is rich, often travelling to foreign places. Dangerous are his 8, 18, 21, 22 and 72nd years. Leo Navamsa ascendant confines the native to a solitary life. The native is full of himself, suffering from bouts of pride and vanity, possessing a thin waist and weak teeth. Signs of distress accompany him. Years dangerous to him are 10, 20, 30, 60th and 82nd. Virgo as ascendant in Navamsa, turns one happy in early years, where furnished is he with the knowledge of art; he has a few amicable and helpful sons later and spends most of his life in foreign lands. For him, years 20 and 60 are exceptionally bad. The native with Libra ascendant in Navamsa is coquettish and flighty. In addition, native has a lean figure with few sons. He does not get along well with near-relations and suffers from indigestion."

"Unfavorable years for a native with Libra ascendant in Navamsa are 3, 23, 38, 54 and 76th. Person having a Scorpio Navamsa suffers upon the death of father. Though he is intelligent, he is quite a troublemaker, cruel, with weak eyesight. Terrible are 18, 23, 28, 55 and 70th years. A native born in Sagittarius Navamsa, one earns a lot of money; having several good qualities. He has a long neck and speaks incessantly; lazy, but easily satisfied. Years not beneficial are 4, 9, 16, 44th and 72nd. Native with Capricorn Navamsa rising is short limbed, capricious and fickle minded, cruel, nimble and sensual. The native may have married an ill-tempered spouse wherein domestic life turns into living hell. Troublesome years are 19, 27, 34, 49, 54th and 68th. Born in Aquarius Navamsa, the native is possessed of libelous thoughts. Acting without mercy, the native is deceitful, weak and confused. Written is mental misery all over the person. Periods not good are 7, 14, 20, 28th and 61st years. The native born with Pisces Navamsa rising has increased sexual want. Having a slender body, many gains come through water and aquatic resources. The native though learned, in theory may have many spouses or affairs. Dangerous years are 12, 21, 26, 52 and 61."

"Dwadasamsa D12 chart specifies fate intimately connected with blood relatives. Lord of a rising Dwadasamsa occupying the Lagna gives native the same prosperity as that of the father. If the ruler joins Dusthana houses, then the body suffers. Rising Dwadasamsa occupying the eleventh house provides the native with ancestral property. The ruler if debilitated, eclipsed, malefic or in enemy house snatches away the ancestral property."

"Born in Dwadasamsa which has Aries ascendant, turns a person into a troublemaker. At its worst, he is a robber resorting to the evil ways and practices of the worst, vicious class of people. Born in Dwadasamsa of Taurus confers company of the opposite sex to the native. The native suffers from several diseases. Native having Dwadasamsa of Gemini becomes a gambler but is well mannered. When born at the hour where Dwadasamsa has Cancer rising, the native becomes addictive of bad practices. Native with Leo rising in Dwadasamsa has many virtues; he is wealthy, associated with brave men. In Virgo Dwadasamsa, one resorts to gambling, and has uncontrollable attraction for the opposite sex. Libra Dwadasamsa engages the person in matters of trade, which paves the way for increased wealth. Scorpio Dwadasamsa can turn one into a criminal, rogue and robber. Sagittarius Dwadasamsa, one serves the clergy and turns into a highly spiritual person. Capricorn Dwadasamsa, a master with many attendants. Aquarius Dwadasamsa turns one into a troublemaker. Pisces Dwadasamsa gives the native riches and knowledge."

"Trimsamsa D30 chart shows the inherent desires and their fulfillment. A native with Trimsamsa of Mars is fickle minded and has a rough edge. Native with birth in Saturn rising in Trimsamsa has a roaming and depraved mind. Jupiter rising in Trimsamsa, wealth comes in abundance to the native. In Mercury Trimsamsa, the person lives with a lot of respect. The native with Venus rising in Trimsamsa gets endowed with beauty and happiness. Graha in its own Trimsamsa acts like a significator, a Karaka. A weak graha leads to misunderstandings with blood relatives."

"In a chart, the 22nd Drekkana is Khara and its ruler is Kharesh; any graha present in such location becomes considered as death-inflicting for the native. If the Lagna is in first 10°, then the 22nd Drekkana is the eighth house first 10°. When the Lagna is between 11° and 20°, then the 22nd Drekkana is the eighth house in 11° to 20° for the ascendant showing the source and manner of death."

"Whenever Lagna ruler transits the 22nd Drekkana, losses, body discomfort, grief and quarrel result. Transit of 22nd Drekkana ruler in Lagna produces trouble regarding significance of the Lagna."

"Next comes a special set of planetary periods and progressions called dasa. There are many dasa types centered on the Moon's longitude, most important being the Vimshottari or 120-year Dasa system, the basis being the Nakshatra where found is the Moon in the birth chart, and the ruling graha of that Nakshatra[213]. In this system, the Nakshatra lord rules for a number of years as the 'Maha dasa' period, which recursively gets broken into minor planetary periods or 'Bhakti' and sub-minor periods or 'Antara'."

Graha, which transits,
Graha, whose dasa is scheduled,
Denote how the result comes through,
Suggests the 'how' of an event ahead.

Sign and its ruler will show,
To the extent results can be enjoyed,
Contingent on graha's strength,
Suggests the 'what' of the queried.

---

[213] Nakshatra group consist of 27 asterisms or constellations

Lord of an asterism, rules other houses,
Other houses influence the outcome,
Whether it will really manifest,
Suggests the event's 'doing' in turn.

Astrology and Ayurveda

"Wellness is the key means to a wonderful end. Astrology determines the constitution in a different way from Ayurveda. Not just a narrow definition, but determines wellness that spans the body, mind and spirit. Ayurveda is a comprehensive system of wellness that eliminates ailments and rejuvenates the body and mind. Sometimes determining an occult disease or an unknown health problem is outside the premises of Ayurveda or any other medicine system I can think of. Divine help from astrology can suggest pointers in figuring the course of a health problem, what is behind it and where is it headed. Ayurveda could confirm the results through its own methods of introspection and analysis to make better the personal remedy. Treatment methods from both the systems equip an individual with tools to take responsibility of their own health, even self-care. Remember, diseases are nothing but disharmonies associated with negative influences. Several methods exist in harmonizing the influences. If we were to accept the string theory and the three vectors in three different harmonics, then the first key to wellness is through the medium of sound. Sound can harmonize the frequencies in ways that other systems take much longer as sound itself is a product of frequency."

"Herbs expel the unwanted, then as a tonic, they fix and soothe. Sound frequencies like the herbs purge the annoying frequencies at its onset, and the proper harmonics straighten the Sattva-Rajas-Tamas at sub atomic levels smoothening the flow of Prana."

"Ayurveda classifies natives from the basic qualities of the three dosha types or biological humors of Vata, Pitta and Kapha and their planetary connections. Dosha types are similar to the elements in their qualities, having a primary elemental connection."

- Graha-s like Saturn, Mercury, Rahu suggest Vata
- Pitta suggested by Sun, Mars, Ketu
- Kapha suggested by Moon, Venus, Jupiter

"Why is Jupiter included in Kapha when Parasara in his Hora Shastra states Jupiter represents the etheric space? Recall the Puranas which tell you before the creation, Vishnu lay on the Shesha-Naga floating on the celestial waters. I am sure it is an expression of speech, where etheric space is also the metaphorical celestial waters, which puts Jupiter as Kapha. Similar is the categorization for signs."

- Associated is Vata with Gemini, Virgo**, Libra and Aquarius
- Pitta runs an association with Aries, Leo, Sagittarius and Capricorn**
- And Kapha with Taurus**[214], Cancer, Scorpio and Pisces

"Certain planets and houses disrupt all harmony, remarkably the sixth house and sixth sign, Virgo which are both important health indicators. The house to look out for in determining individual constitution and physical discomfort is the ascendant house. Ascendant lord is another strong determining reason. An unblemished Aquarius ascendant will show a Vata person, tall or short, clumsy with irregular eating habits. The lord will specify the prevailing dominant dosha and ailments that span hip problems, heart and respiratory issues. One must not forget to check the occupants in the ascendant and sixth house. Mars in Aquarius ascendant will add to the Pitta nature of problems, suggesting a Vata-Pitta constitution. Other factors that easily come to mind are the depositors of the occupant and the ascendant lord. Third indicator is the Karaka. Sun, signifying the first house reveals from its positional strength and aspects, how resilient is the ascendant."

"Graha-s that are malefic, it matters not if their fiendish nature originates from natural or temporal state, they anyway craft a disease. Sun, Mars, Saturn and Rahu have the natural muscle to cause disease. New Moon and ill-associated Mercury contribute as much. Temporal lords of houses, mainly those of 6th, 8th, 11th and 12th take part in producing illness. Weak graha-s can also act in the disease process. Jupiter being the savior, promotes wellness."

---

[214] ** Signs where Vata Pitta Kapha graha-s become exalted like Moon in Taurus, Mars in Capricorn and Mercury in Virgo.

Astrology and yoga

"Arrangement of graha-s in a person's birth-chart affects the unfolding of the soul, which at the level of particulate matter would in essence work fervently in aligning and balancing Sattva, Rajas and Tamas to a state of equilibrium for Prana to fill up the medium. At the lowest, unrefined level, astrology along with Yoga fosters personal and emotional fulfillment, considering them the real aim of human lives. The systems comprehend the outer nature as a certain formation of cosmic energy and the inner nature as a feature of cosmic consciousness. Inner being subsists at a higher dimension where different are nature's laws from the spatial world we live in; the system of Yoga unravels the workings of the higher dimensions to functioning of the mind. Astrology uses the channel of the higher dimensions to align the body with the spirit. Mind, caught in between as it frequents between the two is the source of disturbance, maintaining the body in a perennial state of confusion until understood is the higher dimension, and the confusion reconciled. In this respect, each graha has different inner impacts."

"Ascendant in a chart symbolizes the physical body, which arouses Rajas and amasses Tamas threefold. I represent the allocation as SR+T++, where in case of lagna, Sattva remains unaffected and the remaining vectors remain unstable. Sun's position in the chart uncovers the inner being, divine self, soul, father, and lineage therein invoking Sattva S++RT. Though unhinged, an increase in Sattva promotes Prana infusion and reveals the knowledge that 'we and the universe' are but 'one'. Moon's position shapes the mind and consciousness, which increases Sattva and Rajas as S++R+T. Mars directs sheer energy and transformation creating a Rajas imbalance of SR++T. Mercury shows judgment, intellect, communication and increases Rajas somewhat as SR+T. Jupiter designates the law of our nature, creative intelligence and expansion, raising S++R+T. Venus specifies love and beauty, bliss invoking S+R+T. Saturn is the power of action, constraint and inertia, its position in the chart invokes S+RT+. Rahu is illusory power which invokes S++RT++ and so does Ketu as illusory power, invoking S++RT++."

"Both Rahu and Ketu are S++, they increase Sattva because they represent Maya, which comes from Cosmic man, the cosmic being. While Maya blocks and veils the Sattva-Rajas-Tamas equilibrium, only Maya reveals the quantum of damage to the balance. At this juncture, when the damage gets revealed, it becomes an easy fix – therapy administered through sound, music, aroma, diet, herbal, massage or workout."

"As I had spoken before, the 'houses' give better cues than 'signs' on specific matters. Think of the signs as generalized representations and the houses using the same signs are specific to a select set of persons. Such are the sign-house laws of universal continuum. Almost all arrangements of graha like yoga gets referred to in terms of the houses, like the effects of a ruler or Karaka of a house positioned in another house. Think of the graha-s as house lords than as sign rulers, and consider the change in numbering of the houses as they get formed from applying different ascendants, such as the lagna, Moon, Sun, Navamsa lagna and others."

"Sun exemplifies the spirit, and by setting the sun as the ascendant brings us closer to accepting the spiritual advance. Ghatika Lagna embodies the Sun and therefore gives us the metrics on the delicate progress of the spirit. While the natal chart ascendant works more at the physical flank, Navamsa works closer to the subtle margin. Similarly, Hora Lagna[215] reveals the subtle side of wealth. The house lords that are formed from the different ascendant types carry the energies of the houses and influence their condition."

"I have chosen many excerpts from the large compilation that Sage Brighu put together, many thousands of years back and his disciples completed it. A foundational astrological thought, you can read the Brighu Samhita translation in its entirety, for most of what I will explain are excerpts on health and wellness and does not cover all the other subjects that have been covered in the ancient scriptures. When you are examining a chart Hatti, please make a mental note of the ascendant and the corresponding graha-s in their signs and assigned houses. Though I shall cover all the possibilities, if you must check for Aquarius ascendant, you can skip the rest to the Aquarius part. Let me start by summarizing what the houses signify - the ascendant implies physique, body, mind, soul, self, ego, health, will-power, fame, figure, physical complex and business; signified by Sun. Second house is about worries, finance, family, bondage and right eye; signified by Jupiter. Third house reveals siblings, energy, Prana, physical work, courage, adventure, enterprise, short foreign travel, right ear and hand, all cognitive and motor sensory organs and skills; Karaka being Mars. Fourth house shows mind, emotions, mother, motherly relations, land and buildings, education at home, peace, happiness, vehicle, fans and friends, mother, partnership and transfer; Karaka is Moon and Mercury. Fifth house is about karma, intelligence, past life influences, education, children, speech and knowledge; Karaka being Jupiter."

---

[215] Author's note – there are many descriptions given on the different geometrical ascendants. The application in Python also reveals the computations. Aquapisces.com is perhaps the best place to know where the ascendants are for the native.

"Sixth house signifies enemies, diseases, diligence, occultism, maternal grandfather, defeats, victories and right foot, struggle and competition; Karaka being Mars and Saturn. Seventh house is on spouse, marriage, diurnal occupation, father-in-law and his family, sexual pleasures, success and happiness; signified by Venus. Eighth house is about death, prison, execution, wealth, age, longevity, daily routine, loss of fame, calamities, old and serious things, help in life, career, troubles and confinement; Karaka is Saturn. Ninth house suggests destiny, dharma, devotion, spirituality, divine power, fame, fortune and wealth; Karaka being Sun and Jupiter. Tenth house is father, government and society, power, reputation, fame, honor, occupation, splendor, sovereignty and heart, Karaka being Mercury, Sun, Jupiter, and Saturn. Eleventh house is about wealth, income and gains, fulfillment of necessities and desires, left ear and hand; significator is Jupiter. Twelfth house shows spending, contact of foreign places, rest, sleep, loss, interest, bankruptcy, short travels, left eye and nose; significator is Saturn."

"Normally, deemed are graha-s as propitious or unfavorable depending on the houses they rule as traversed from different ascendant signs. This gives them a status that is secular and profane, regardless of their natural status. Graha-s work in favor of the affairs of the houses they rule. Even the lord of a harmful house like the eighth, is useful for the house in matters like longevity and inheritance. Ruler of the ascendant is normally good as it supports the native's prosperity. However, if it is a natural malefic or rules another malefic, its benevolent status gets tainted and it may under certain circumstances that give bad results. The ruler of the Second is neutral, though good for wealth and livelihood, which it rules. As a 'Maraka' or death-causing planet, it also has a negative side. Ruler of the third is typically unfavorable, as it harbors an impulsive, impetuous force, works through power and can cause oppress or oppose. It is by and large good for brothers, which the house rules. Fourth house ruler, as an angle or Kendra lord, does good if it is a natural malefic; but wicked if it is a natural benefic. If it is full of strength, it works in favor of the mother and for peace of mind and emotional well-being. Fifth house ruler works well for the native, as the fifth is a trine and gives favorable karma results, festooning the chart with wisdom and positive karma. Sixth house ruler, a house of hostility, disease and injury; it can trigger harm and stimulate enmity. Ruler of the seventh, as an angle, follows the same rules as that of the fourth and works well for the partner. As a 'Maraka', it can cause health problems later in life. Ruler of the eighth, a house of obstacles, opposition and negativity, is inauspicious, though it suggests professional career in the field of medicine, insurance and other likely corporations."

"Ninth house ruler, a trinal house of fortune and solemn-duties, is usually good; giving the native the much-needed grace, good karma, fortune and well-being. Ruler of the tenth follows the same rules as that of any angular ruler and represents the best of angular houses. When strong is the career, overall success to the native comes easy. Ruler of the eleventh provides income and monetary gains. However, it is an overall malefic for the chart from its disruptive, impulsive, anarchic influence and can cause disease and injury like the sixth lord. Eleventh being the sixth from the sixth house is the subtle house of enmity and disease. Ruler of the twelfth is ominous but more often neutral, depending upon the other house it rules. It can cause loss but can also suggest connection with foreign groups and ideas."

"When a graha rules two houses, the results have a mix of the natural status of the planet along with the two houses under its lordship, and its relationship to the ruler of the Ascendant. Let us examine two charts, one having Gemini as Ascendant, where Saturn is the lord of not-so-good eighth and the good ninth house. The second chart has Aquarius as ascendant and Mercury is the lord of not-so-good eighth and the good fifth house. Nice coincidence! In the first chart, Saturn is naturally malefic, but a friend to Mercury, which rules Gemini and its Moolatrikona sign of Aquarius, governs the ninth. Similar is the case with Aquarius ascendant. Considering Saturn is not a temporal enemy of Mercury, it would give reasonably good results; however, if it turns out Saturn and Mercury become temporal enemies, the results would be in the contrary. In the life of a native, all such graha-s that have mixed lordships will give good times and proffer bad times. Saturn in such a case earns a negative trait by its eighth house lordship in the first case and will give few negative effects and not just undergo deactivation by its ownership of the ninth. Saturn in this case will work favorably for few things and not for others, good certain times, evil at other times. Now, consider Venus, a friend of Saturn and Mercury in both the charts. Venus as the lord of the fifth and the twelfth in a Gemini ascendant, gives good results of the fifth lordship and negative results of the twelfth. However, in case of Aquarius ascendant, Venus is a significator owning a trine and an angle. It gives only good results to the native, unless Saturn and Venus turn into temporal enemies. I will even extend this rule for other graha-s - if a graha brings benefit on a specific topic and the other graha-s produce maleficence on the same topic, it is worth remembering both results would take place in the life, though the timing and shape of such an event can change but the effects persist. Also remember, the planet which is the lord of its sign becomes lord of that house also in which placed is that sign. And, not forgetting the Navamsa, the graha posited in good or bad houses in 'Navamsa' imparts its effect through Navamsa positioning."

"There is no so such thing as a 'perfect remedy' with a practitioner. Practitioners like us are ordinary mortals, not miracle workers or sorcerers, who have chosen not to ignore the scriptures and doctrines. Without a doubt, miracles exist, divine interventions happen, but such esoteric matters are clearly outside our scope of studies. When in the horoscope of the householder, the dasa period is favorable; there is an uncanny assurance it is pointing to a progressive one."

"When between spouses, the dasa planetary period of one does good, and the other does not, overall, it is an ordinary period. Similarly, when both have unfavorable dasa times, the period is harmful. When occurs the Antara of the best graha, it marks a fortunate time. In a Sagittarius ascendant, Moon promises longevity and help with the aging process in most positions in the chart, except the twelfth. It may not act favorable in domestic life or earning or spending, or even children. I would not be talking about other matters other than wellness. Sometimes, where there is loss of near and dear, spousal influence, matters regarding mind and mental orientation, I tend to mention them as proper. Similar is Sun in Capricorn ascendant. He provides a long life, except if he is in the tenth and twelfth house, but all this comes with its own price. Another sound example of longevity is Mercury in Aquarius ascendant. It can swing either way depending on its position."

"Graha-s are like humans, having personal likes and dislikes. Based on their friendliness, they fall into two groups. Group of Deva having Sun, Moon, Mars and Jupiter competes with the Daitya group of Venus, Saturn, Rahu, and Ketu. Deva planets are friendly with one another and are adversaries to the planets of the Daitya group. Mercury is a friend to all."

"The planetary combinations and ascendant ownerships that I will now describe to you are from Brighu Samhita compiled in the city of Varanasi. The book publication carries no date, I therefore assume the book's original composition occurred much before my time, but the publication was likely more recent. None of the graha influences are meant to be read as 'general', what gets discussed here relates to wellness only. Graha combinations that have no impact on health or illness, I have skipped them intentionally. In the ancient texts, especially the Astanga Hridayam, which literally means the eight steps to heart's health, our predecessors described the regions where the different dosha types occurred. A common pattern emerged in their research. In chapter twelve, Vagabhatta reveals through the Sloka-s that Pakvasya or the large intestines among other places is the principal Vata seat. Amasaya comprising stomach, small intestine and Nabhi, umbilicus is referred to as the Pitta seat. Amasaya is also the Kapha seat."

"The belly region, containing the heart and the lungs to the genitals was their main concern as all dosha types turn into free radicals in this region. When they wrote of their concerns on health, it was mostly on the belly region. Besides, he said, the Pitta in the Hridaya region is Sadhaka, which meant the 'heart' maintained the mental equilibrium, therefore catered to knowledge, intelligence and self-consciousness."

❖ Aries Ascendant, Graha Sun

"Where the person has Aries ascendant in the natal chart, the Sun[216], as ruler of house 5, becomes a graha of creative intelligence, progeny, counsel and good karma. Sun is very auspicious. Sun in the first house in Aries Sign, in a high Pitta prone region gives the native an expressive physical strength. If the ascendant is Aries, when the Sun transits such a house with no blemishes, it brings a lot of physical prowess and learning. Self-esteem reaches its peak. The person easily changes his focus more towards self-knowledge. Pitta does not give the person much height, rendering the native short and lean, mentally shrewd, with no interest in sex. With Sun positioned in the second house in Taurus in natal chart, in general or in its transit, haunts the native with mental worries. The daily grind, and day-to-day existence and family life become rather turbulent for the person. In the third house in Gemini, the native enjoys power and intellect. The individual gets to express and communicate in a strong and motivating way. This placement of Sun promises the native a lot of physical strength. He works hard, discovers his courage and is outspoken and brave in his communications. Whatever phase of Purushartha the native is in; the month is the best time to make progress when Sun transits the third house. At this hour, even vigor comes from intelligence and fate takes a turn towards the good. Adherence to solemn-duties comes with ease and keeps the native steady on the path to faith. Sun in the fifth house in Leo, makes the native a good speaker and orator, besides, increasing his intellectual level. The position gives him the advantages of farsightedness. While in the seventh house in Libra, the native's discontent with spouse and children is quite apparent. Troubled with family life, he turns more into a workaholic; though his earning means are not always honest. There is a tendency to be corrupt. Unhappy with his sex life, he turns into a man with many secrets. Sun in the eighth house in Scorpio, gives the native a harsh speech, besides his moves are harsh. For the native who has Sun in the ninth house in Sagittarius, the individual's speech is just and honest. Making several wise moves, he gets to a point; he can turn things around and improve his destiny. The person has high morals, and he is never short of energy."

---

[216] Sun – Vidya Buddhi santan - विद्दा बुद्धि संतान

"Sun in the eleventh house in Aquarius, the native goes after intellectual pursuits. He has a selfish side and a harsh speech; overall, he is very ambitious. While in the twelfth house in Pisces, the native struggles with weak eyesight. Being constantly worried, enemies enjoy tormenting him."

- ❖ Aries Ascendant, Graha Moon

"Moon, as ruler of house 4, is the source of emotion, home, happiness, and attachment to the mother. Moon in the first house in Aries festoons the native with happiness and many pleasures. Showing off his good looks, the person indulges in sex and derives pleasures from it. Success seems to follow him around. He earns real respect in occupation and lives in luxury. Moon in the second house in Taurus furnishes the native with a large family. Though he runs into money and wealth, he just does not know how to enjoy it. For the native who has Moon in the third house in Gemini, he is a devout person, he loves and upholds the solemn-duties of dharma. Moon in the fourth house in Cancer, makes the native carefree and emotionally happy, who enjoys many pleasures and luxuries. Moon in the fifth house in Leo, makes the person believe he is intelligent. He speaks well and does not hurt others. He is a deep thinker. While in the sixth house in Virgo, the native finds his happiness dwindle, and he does not find any family joy. His enemies keep him under fear. Moon in the seventh house in Libra, the native enjoys the little pleasure that his family gives. He is strong and handsome and enjoys sex. He is very skilled, and proficient in preserving family relations. Moon in the eighth house in Scorpio maligns the native, thrusting him into an abyss of narrow-mindedness and making him suffer from stomach troubles. The native prone to accidents, faces much penury and troubles. While in the ninth house in Sagittarius, the native is blessed with divine help, which brings him joy and satisfaction and increasing his faith in solemn-duties. Moon in the eleventh house in Aquarius, the native is sweetly rewarded with happiness, though many difficulties accompany; sweet spoken he is, rewarded with many pleasures. Moon in the twelfth house in Pisces, the native bears the loss of his mother. His association with enemies does him no good except add to his mental restlessness."

- ❖ Aries Ascendant, Graha Mars

"Mars, as ruler of houses 1 and 8, is a planet of the self and the body; though auspicious, the fact he is lord of the eighth is a big taint. Mars in the first house in Aries gives the native spiritual powers but makes him restless. In the second house in Taurus, the native's morality is questionable. With Mars in the fourth house in Cancer, the native is short in build and restless. Mars in the sixth house in Virgo, makes the native physically sick with many problems with different parts of the body. The native has the will to win over the ailments without loss of confidence."

"With Mars in the sixth, though somewhat immoral, the native puts on a brave act having occult powers. Mars in the seventh house in Libra, deprives the native of sexual pleasures. Mars in the eighth house in Scorpio, gives the native a lean and petite body. Restlessness inconveniencies him. He earns and gains by restoring life into others; bringing an end to self-identity just like a sage. He ages prematurely. Mars in the ninth house in Sagittarius makes the native fortunate though he remains bereft of any luck. Mars in the tenth house in Capricorn, gives the native significant physical strength, by which he earns dignity and authority in life's daily routine. Capable of doing grand deeds, he displays a remarkable personality. Mars in the eleventh house in Aquarius, gives the native mysterious powers to use in his learning and intelligence. When in the twelfth house in Pisces, Mars makes the native unhappy in sex and domestic work; besides turning him physically weak."

❖ Aries Ascendant, Graha Mercury

"Mercury, as ruler of houses 3 and 6, is a graha of energy, impulse, friendship, injury, disease, egoism, enmity and prowess. Mercury in the first house in Aries, helps the native overcome enemies, win over disputes and hindrances. In the third house in Gemini, the native is endowed with intelligence and perfection. He has good control over enemies. In the fourth house in Cancer, the native turns energetic and industrious, restless, but wins over the enemies. Mercury in the fifth house in Leo, makes the native very careful, judicious and clever. He runs an upper hand over his enemies. In the sixth house in Virgo, the native is influential, courageous and brave. In the seventh house in Libra, Mercury makes the native work hard, enjoy sexual pleasures and offers advances in domestic and worldly affairs. The graha Mercury in the eighth house in Scorpio, the native has faith in occult power, suffers from stomach problems, worries about his daily routine, faces the enemy with courage. While in the ninth house in Sagittarius, the native achieves fame and power, though he is not a strong believer in his solemn-duties, he remains indecisive of right and wrong approaches to better his life. With Mercury in the tenth house in Capricorn, the native becomes more discriminative. Mercury, found in the eleventh house in Aquarius, the native is gifted with an eloquent speech, besides being clever. Mercury in the twelfth house in Pisces showers the native with occult powers."

❖ Aries Ascendant, Graha Jupiter

"Jupiter, as ruler of houses 9 and 12, a spiritual planet of grace, shows the path to renunciation through wisdom. Jupiter in the first house in Aries, makes the native handsome, fortunate and honored, with good health, spiritual inclination, domestic happiness, good forethought and kind-hearted."

"Jupiter in the second house in Taurus, the native is fortunate, blessed with divine help, has spiritual outlook, subdues his enemies and stays happy with what comes his way through daily routine. Jupiter in the fourth house in Cancer, turns the native into a flamboyant, but spiritual and fortunate person. For the native who has Jupiter in the fifth house in Leo, he is prosperous, intelligent and is an authority on Dharma-Sastra, besides being a good orator, he achieves much honor. With Jupiter in the sixth house in Virgo, the native is not very fortunate, traits of immorality are quite evident in such a person. He weathers tough disputes and wins. When in the seventh house in Libra, the native achieves success in daily life, happiness in domestic front, has renewed faith in the almighty, works with energy and has a proper, dharmic outlook. Jupiter in the eighth house in Scorpio, makes the native unlucky and immoral. To compensate, he gets a long life, but parts of his destiny are unpleasant. In the ninth house in Sagittarius, the native is indeed fortunate, achieving success in his activities, blessed with divine help, good intellect and spiritual outlook. In the tenth house in Capricorn, the native lives in peace and happiness; he knows he is fortunate with divine help always around. When in the eleventh house in Aquarius, the native is destined to meet success. He receives the needed help with his activities and spends time in carnal pursuits. Power of speech brings him success. Jupiter in the twelfth house in Pisces, gives the native a spiritual outlook, though he is not very fortunate. He spends for many moral causes, dignified he is, careful about his enemies."

❖ Aries Ascendant, Graha Venus

"Venus, as ruler of houses 2 and 7, is a planet of conjugal relationship, often showing gains through marriage and partnership, or multiple partners. Venus in the first house in Aries, brings sexual pleasures to the native. He is otherwise quite artistic and clever, a competent person, successful in worldly affairs, highly skilled and honorable. Venus in the second house in Taurus, gives the native a large family to enjoy. His relationship with his spouse is a happy one, he indulges quite a bit in sex and knows how to enjoy it. When in the third house in Gemini, Venus infuses morality into the native, in contrast, letting him also enjoy the pleasures of sex. The person learns to care about his dharma-duties and spirituality. A man of standing, he is influential and handsome, stays happy in domestic and worldly affairs. With Venus in the fourth house in Cancer, the native earns happiness and wealth, enjoys material pleasures and uses dexterity in his approach to life. For the native who has Venus in the fifth house in Leo, he indulges in sexual fantasies, mental worries plague him, though he is a good conversationalist and educated. Venus in the sixth house in Virgo, turns the native away from his spouse, unhappy in matters involving sex, secretive in his policies, he suffers ill health."

"Venus in the seventh house in Libra, the native marries and lives well, attractive is his appearance. In the eighth house in Scorpio, the native runs into quite a few problems with health. His unhappiness with spouse and family increases and he turns secretly passionate. When in the ninth house in Sagittarius, the native is fortunate, clever, brave and courageous. He is an ardent executer of his solemn-duties."

❖ Aries Ascendant, Graha Saturn

"Saturn, as ruler of houses 10 and 11, is a planet of power, stature, gains, impulse, injury, disease and conceit. With Saturn in the first house in Aries, the native has a poor, unattractive appearance. He is dependent, and yet very industrious and energetic. The spouse means a lot to the native though he is a trifle lazy. Saturn in the second house in Taurus, restlessness of daily life overcomes the native. In the third house in Gemini, the native is energetic, proud and valorous. He is quite bland about morality. In the seventh house in Libra, the restive native only enjoys sexual pleasures. The person without a doubt has much pride. With Saturn in the eighth house in Scorpio, the native leads a solitary existence. Obstinate at work yet, extremely able, he worries but is under a spell of arrogance. Saturn in the ninth house in Sagittarius, the native is fortunate, and he is spiritual, with no enemies, winning with ease over troubles and hindrances. In the tenth house in Capricorn, the native enjoys the pleasures of the bed. He has tremendous self-pride. When in the eleventh house in Aquarius, the native does deeds of honor, works hard, caring not for comforts, worries a lot on uncertainties about day-to-day matters. Saturn in the twelfth house in Pisces, the native conducts activities that back the solemn-duties, while maintaining a strong impact on enemies."

❖ Aries Ascendant, Graha Rahu

"Rahu in the first house in Aries, the native runs into ill health, especially the face gets weathered through diseases. He musters up enough courage to face the calamities, Rahu brings in. There is also a secret side to him. Rahu in the second house in Taurus separates the native from the family. He has his own share of problems in the domestic front, over and above the family bickering. Even though he stays courageous, restlessness overcomes him. In the third house in Gemini, the native feeds on courage, living a life of no fear. He exerts pressure and control over others and remains influential. When in the fourth house in Cancer, the native faces the loss of his mother. Perpetually unhappy, with no peace, he undergoes much of mental stress. With Rahu in the fifth house in Leo, the native stays under mental duress. He is peevish, his speech is harsh and cutting, with signs of worry written all over him. Being unsympathetic, he has a hard time understanding others."

"In the sixth house in Virgo, the native gets an upper hand over many difficulties and troubles, but remains selfish. When in the seventh house in Libra, the native develops complications with the spouse and much sexual dissatisfaction. He manages things with great difficulty, receiving unauthorized gains from avaricious affairs. In the eighth house in Scorpio, the native has recurrent worries. His face is a perennial frown with loss in livelihood; he gets internal diseases in the abdomen. He is a man of bitter policies. When in the ninth house in Sagittarius, the native is an unhappy person, facing inordinate anxieties. Nervous about his fate and destiny, he resorts to many improper schemes in clandestine. He meets many setbacks in executing his solemn-duties and turns immoral. He loses his fame and stays restless. Rahu in the eleventh house in Aquarius, the native uses many a secret and unauthorized methods to achieve his ends."

❖ Aries Ascendant, Graha Ketu

"Ketu in the first house in Aries, the native is a victim of physical weakness. He is restless and is prone to having a fatal stroke of pain. He has remarkable patience, but is rash and obstinate, lacking self-confidence. Ketu in the second house in Taurus brings untold family miseries. In the fourth house in Cancer, the native experiences separation from the family. Sorrowful and restless, he shoulders grave calamities. Ketu in the sixth house in Virgo, the native is under evil influence and indulges in malicious acts. When in the seventh house in Libra, the native either loses the spouse or gets detached and becomes unhappy with the person in matters of sex. Ketu in the eighth house in Scorpio, the native suffers from weakness in the back and lower part of stomach. Careless in day-to-day matters, he runs into many a problem as he ages. In the ninth house in Sagittarius, the native works hard towards his destiny. Though sacrilegious, he has no ill bearings towards managing his solemn-duties."

❖ Aries Ascendant, Transits

"In making judgments regarding age and other things helping the life course, Mars during its transits, when it occupies either Aquarius, Leo, Scorpio, Capricorn or Aquarius signs in the calendar, or Jupiter when it passes either Cancer or Scorpio signs, or Saturn when it occupies Scorpio, it strengthens the age and the stomach, mid-torso region. Regarding spouse, Venus, during its transit, when it occupies either Aries, Cancer, Libra, Capricorn or Aquarius signs, Jupiter when it occupies either Aries, Leo, Libra or Capricorn, and the Moon when it passes either Libra or Aries, there is congeniality with spouse. Such transits also promise sensual pleasures."

"Regarding physical beauty and countenance, will-power and fame, the physique gets comforts, fame multiplies, the body begets more attractiveness and strength, with the will-power awakening when Mars crosses either Aries, Libra, Capricorn, Aquarius or Gemini, or when Moon, Sun, Venus or Jupiter occupy Aries sign, or when Jupiter dwells in either Leo or Sagittarius. Happiness and peace come by with Moon in either Aries, Taurus, Cancer, Libra, Sagittarius or Capricorn or Aquarius signs, and when Jupiter, Venus and Saturn are in Cancer or one of the two planets are in such a position, then the mother and land bring joy to the native. Native earns honor, prestige, faith, respect, progress and success according to his capacity in the house of father and house of big occupation, when Saturn passes either Sagittarius, Capricorn, Aquarius, Taurus, Cancer or Libra, or when Mars is in Gemini or Libra or Capricorn, or Venus occupies Capricorn."

❖ Taurus Ascendant, Graha Sun

"Sun, as ruler of house 4, is a planet of emotion, home and happiness. Sun in the first house in Taurus, gives the native much needed happiness through spouse and family. Pleasures from sex also come in abundance. In the second house in Gemini, the native faces some restraints in family happiness. When in the third house in Cancer, plagued is the native with unspiritual thoughts and deeds. In the fifth house in Virgo, the native gathers much wisdom. His intelligence goes on the rise. Sun in the sixth house in Libra, the native's enemies bring him anxiety. Feelings of restlessness overwhelm the native and he loses courage. In the seventh house in Scorpio, the native turns unhappy with corporeal problems. Sun in the ninth house in Capricorn, makes the native dharmic and fortunate."

❖ Taurus Ascendant, Graha Moon

"Moon, as ruler of house 3, is a planet of energy, interest, motivation, impulse and enthusiasm. Moon in the first house in Taurus, creates an unhappy rift with the spouse, ending in only sexual indulgence. Restlessness is quite evident in the native in matters regarding the domestic front. In the second house in Gemini, the native stays frail and feeble, dealing with lot of laborious work. When in the third house in Cancer, the native is made to work hard. His mental acumen increases and his belief in God strengthens. Endowed with patience, he is. In the sixth house in Libra, the native gets exhausted quickly, seeking strength in the association of enemies. Moon in the seventh house in Scorpio, pushes the native encounters to loath and feel discontent with everything. When in the ninth house in Capricorn, destiny favors the native. Dharmic in nature, his belief in God is strong; thereupon, he turns joyous and happy. Moon in the twelfth house in Aries, the native stays unharmed by enemies, though he faces a lot of mental unrest."

❖ Taurus Ascendant, Graha Mars

"Mars, as ruler of houses 7 and 12, is a planet of relationship, sexuality and passion. Mars in the first house in Taurus, the native's blood has a high level of impurities. He resorts to wandering; he toils hard and is fairly restless in family matters. When the native has Mars in the fourth house in Leo, he loses his mother, but strong is the happiness in the side of spouse, ineffectual are carnal pleasures. In the fifth house in Virgo, avarice and sexual pleasures are but a thing of anxiety to the native. Mars in the sixth house in Libra, the native has tremendous worries and is likely to suffer from diabetes. When in the seventh house in Scorpio, the native has mixed relations with spouse, often under weakness in sexual pleasures. Mars in the eighth house in Sagittarius, the native runs into diseases below the navel. Some of his organs also face disorders. His lifespan is short. When in the ninth house in Capricorn, the native moves away from executing his solemn-duties. He gets tired and exhausted rapidly. In the tenth house in Aquarius, the native suffers from body disorders, has mixed feelings on sexual pleasures. When in the eleventh house in Pisces, in essence, the native keeps enemies under his thumb. His spouse also makes him unhappy, and sexual pleasures are lacking. In the twelfth house in Aries, the native is incompatible with spouse, but enjoys sex through extra-marital affairs. The affairs weaken him in flesh."

❖ Taurus Ascendant, Graha Mercury

"Mercury, as ruler of houses 2 and 5, is a planet of speech, education, intelligence and creativity. Mercury in the first house in Taurus, the heavenly bodies shower wisdom and education on the native. While his looks are handsome, he has a tremendous appetite for sex. When in the sixth house in Libra, the native faces several shortcomings in family life. He is smart in getting along well with enemies. Mercury in the seventh house in Scorpio brings about conflicts with the spouse leading to unhappiness; though there is no shortage in sexual pleasures. In the eighth house in Sagittarius, mental worries haunt the native. He collaborates with foreign countries many times. In the twelfth house in Aries, worries continue to torment the native, he worries from enemies, from loss and shortages in family."

❖ Taurus Ascendant, Graha Venus

"Venus, as ruler of houses 1 and 6, pushes the native to work with foreigners. Venus in the first house in Taurus, makes the native conceited, though it also helps restrain the challenging enemy camp. Diseases confront the native. He is determined to curb them. When in the second house in Gemini, the native remains in ill health throughout. When the native has Venus in the fourth house in Leo, it negatively affects his physical happiness from losses and disease. The slightest of restlessness irks him, which may originate from his enemies."

"Venus in the fifth house in Virgo, nags the native with worries. Much of the worry comes from enemies. Swathed he is, in weakness. His ideas remain unexpressed, partly a result of his nervous conduct. Diseases prove to be irksome to the native with Venus in the sixth house in Libra, though he wins over many people in spite of opposition. Venus in the seventh house in Scorpio, gives the native a handsome countenance. He indulges in acts that incite his own carnal desires. He runs into problems with the spouse. Venus in the eighth house in Sagittarius produces troubles to the body. The native feels an intense restlessness caused by his enemies. Venus in the ninth house in Capricorn makes the native fortunate; however, he fails to keep a progress tab on dharma. The combination makes him brilliant and a gentleperson. He manages his enemies well. In the tenth house in Aquarius, the native is an unhappy person. When in the eleventh house in Pisces, the native appears attractive and handsome, sharp and shrewd. In the twelfth house in Aries, a cloud of worries hangs over the native who suffers from many diseases. He loses his honor, suffers from pangs of loneliness."

❖ Taurus Ascendant, Graha Jupiter

"Jupiter, as ruler of houses 8 and 11, is a planet of willfulness, violence and destruction. Jupiter in the first house in Taurus turns the native clever, who suffers from health problems. He gets his due importance and dignity in day-to-day matters. In the third house in Cancer, the native turns away from God, unable to fulfill his solemn-duties. When the native has Jupiter in the fourth house in Leo, he lives long with fame having mastered some occult powers. In the sixth house in Libra, the native suffers in health. In the ninth house in Capricorn, the native runs into bottlenecks on his destined journey and in matters of executing his solemn-duties. Health problems irk him, wherein he repeatedly feels restless. He tweaks and manipulates Dharma to meet his gains. Both his faith and monetary income suffer. In the eleventh house in Pisces, the native lives long. He wins unconventionally with the spouse. Unauthorized carnal pleasures go with it. It is likely it comes from some occult strength."

❖ Taurus Ascendant, Graha Saturn

"Saturn, as ruler of houses 9 and 10, confers honor, prestige, power, position and great skill. It shows the enduring drive towards practical achievement in the Taurus nature, which stays weak until old age. When Saturn is too strong, cold and controlling becomes the natives of Taurus, neutralizing their good grace. Saturn is very auspicious giving Raja Yoga. Saturn in the first house in Taurus makes the native influential, however, it builds an enmity against the spouse, leading to deficient sexual pleasures. The native works hard and strenuous work. He is quite obstinate."

"In the second house in Gemini, restlessness engulfs the native. While in the third house in Cancer, the native progresses immensely from sheer hard labor. Being influential and courageous, he achieves success and fame. He sticks to his spiritual duties. When the native has Saturn in the fourth house in Leo, happiness deludes him. The deeds he undertakes are troublesome. However, he is spiritual and a person of faith. In the fifth house in Virgo, the native fulfills his sacred duties and education well. Dissatisfaction comes from spousal relationship. Saturn in the sixth house in Libra, brings respect and honor to the native. He maintains good control over enemies. While in the seventh house in Scorpio, the native drifts towards atheism, away from spirituality. Unhappiness pervades all quarters. Saturn in the eighth house in Sagittarius, the native wins divine powers and succeeds in education. In the ninth house in Capricorn, the native comes out with dignity even after being heckled by enemies. He conducts his work with tremendous energy. He backs solemn-duties winning many an honor. Saturn in the eleventh house in Pisces, the native spends time in holy duties. He works very hard. Saturn in the twelfth house in Aries, the native's involvement in uncaring and miserable activities increases."

❖ Taurus Ascendant, Graha Rahu

"Rahu in the first house in Taurus, plagues the native with a weak constitution. Constant worries and anxieties keep him awake at night. Secretive and clever, he works with courage. When the native has Rahu in the fourth house in Leo, he suffers from losses related to the mother. He incurs losses in land and buildings. All this makes him unhappy. He leaves his birthplace though the move to live away does not help in the situation. There are constant sufferings in life, which has its toll on happiness and peace. In the sixth house in Libra, the native exercises power over enemies. He remains selfish and cautious. Rahu in the seventh house in Scorpio, the native, though selfish encounters many troubles in day-to-day activities. Constant family issues plague him. He finds unique ways to seek sexual pleasures. In the eighth house in Sagittarius age and mortality are perturbed. The native suffers from abdominal troubles in the belly region. Therein results tremendous amount of restlessness and suicidal thoughts. get prevalent when the suffering increases. In the ninth house in Capricorn, the native errs in conducting and fulfilling his solemn-duties and vows. Inflicted by loss of fame or none; the native has no belief in god. In the eleventh house in Pisces, success comes to the native who makes extra efforts to reap more gains, resulting in surplus. A selfish side lurks within the native. While in the twelfth house in Aries, the native lives under a cloud of worries."

❖ Taurus Ascendant, Graha Ketu

"Ketu in the first house in Taurus, gives the native a sense of physical vulnerability. Chances of mental retardation are high. Restlessness overcomes the person. He turns secretive and brave though prejudiced. In the second house in Gemini, the native faces many a trauma, becoming restless. In the fifth house in Virgo, the native feels at a loss when talking to others. Though unconcerned he is about hindrances and falsehood, he continues to work in secret. With Ketu in the sixth house in Libra, the native faces his enemies undaunted. Illness and troubles bother the native, whose approach is rather rash. In the seventh house in Scorpio, the native faces incompatibility in spousal relations. Finding sex as bothersome and inadequate, he turns to secret associations. Ketu in the eighth house in Sagittarius, plagues the native with anxieties. The lifespan of such a native is low. In the ninth house in Capricorn, the native turns unsuccessful in dharma fulfillment and is unable cope with its demands. He continues to live with no fame and little faith in God. Ketu in the twelfth house in Aries, turns the native into an atheist who has no faith in solemn-duties."

❖ Taurus Ascendant, Transits

"Events that favor age, chest health, and other things in life's course are times with Jupiter occupying either Scorpio, Sagittarius, Pisces, Taurus, Gemini or Leo in its transits; or when either Sun, Venus, Mercury or Moon get posited in Sagittarius, it creates strength connected with age and stomach. Physique, attractiveness, will-power and fame change for the better when Venus occupies either Taurus, Cancer, Leo, Scorpio, Capricorn, Aquarius or Pisces and either Moon, Saturn, or Mercury get positioned in Taurus, physical comforts, fame comes to the native. Enhanced are beauty and strength, and the will-power stirs."

❖ Gemini Ascendant, Graha Sun

"Sun, as ruler of house 3, in the first house in Gemini, ensures a strong spousal influence on the native; they both enjoy the nuptial pleasures. When the native has Sun in the third house in Leo, the native possesses great physical strength, but has less faith in god. Sun in the sixth house in Scorpio, the native works using all his strength and energy. With Sun in the seventh house in Sagittarius, the native advances after marriage, the partner's encouragement and carnal pleasures have a positive effect on him. While Sun in the eighth house in Capricorn, weak are the native's energy and strength, and the worries linger in the everyday routine. With Sun in the twelfth house in Taurus, the native runs into facial disorders and in dealings with the enemy. He is lazy and cares little for ill-health."

- ❖ Gemini Ascendant, Graha Moon

"Moon, as ruler of house 2, gives fluency of speech, good education and capacity to earn wealth. Moon in the first house in Gemini, makes the native and his spouse attractive and beautiful. The native drives himself through erotic pleasures, but is of stable mind. Moon in the second house in Cancer, the native follows the dictates of solemn-duties and is respectable. When the native has Moon in the third house in Leo, he earns fame and courage. Moon in the fourth house in Virgo, the native becomes endowed with tons of patience and peace of mind. Moon in the sixth house in Scorpio, makes the native restless. It brings losses in the family. The native worries from enemy side and quarrels. Besides, it brings diseases. Moon in the seventh house in Sagittarius, the native earns honors and dignity. He is compatible with the spouse though decidedly erotic; he still is not short of happiness. Moon in the eighth house in Capricorn, body weakness plagues the native. It brings about losses in the family though his 'Ayu' and age remain untarnished. Moon in the ninth house in Aquarius, the native is behind the goals of solemn-duties and vows. He is fortunate, with tremendous faith in god. Recipient of many honors, he is respectable."

- ❖ Gemini Ascendant, Graha Mars

"Mars, as ruler of houses 6 and 11, in the first house in Gemini, the native is under influence of Pitta diseases and weaknesses. Lacking peace and happiness, the native keeps a strong check on enemies. He and the spouse face anxiety. There is a rash side to him. The positioning has a positive effect on the lifespan. Mars in the second house in Cancer, the native incurs obstacles in dharma. It is easy for the native to indulge in gambling that can lead to his downfall. Native with Mars in the third house in Leo brings victory over enemies. Brave, courageous, he senses lackluster progress in executing solemn-duties and fate. Mars in the fourth house in Virgo, the native has mixed feeling on happiness, cares not for enemies, and in turn exploits them. His relationship with the spouse is just about amicable. With Mars in the fifth house in Libra, the native can easily overrun the enemy, though he faces many anxieties. Mars in the sixth house in Scorpio, the native encounters obstructions in fulfilling solemn-duties, and suffers from diseases. With Mars in the seventh house in Sagittarius, the native runs into family deficiency, gets venereal diseases. Mars in the eighth house in Capricorn, the native enjoys increases in longevity. With Mars in the ninth house in Aquarius, the native is callous and careless. There is a certain extent of blasphemy the native indulges in. Mars in the tenth house in Pisces, the native does activity that is influential, gaining victory over the enemy. With Mars in the eleventh house in Aries, the native has a strong influence on his enemy. Mars in the twelfth house in Taurus, the native feels restless dealing with the spouse, comes down with venereal diseases."

❖ **Gemini Ascendant, Graha Mercury**

"Mercury, as ruler of houses 1 and 4, shows a close alignment to self and mind. Mercury in the first house in Gemini makes the native handsome, with an attractive body. The person receives honors, empowered with self-knowledge. His happiness is profound with his spouse. Native with Mercury in the third house in Leo honors intrinsic duties, wins fame, thinks fair with courage and enthusiasm. Mercury in the fourth house in Virgo, assures the native living in joy, has an impressive physical appearance, though he is careless. Happiness comes to him from spiritual powers. Mercury in the fifth house in Libra, the native enjoys deep educational intellect. He in desperation wants peace, but constant worries torment him. Mercury in the sixth house in Scorpio makes the native unhappy, worried and dependent; even though he imparts joy to others and is a prudent and wise person. Native with Mercury in the seventh house in Sagittarius leads a happy, married life where all his carnal desires get cared for. He has great desires for spiritual progress. Native with Mercury in the eighth house in Capricorn lacks physical powers while he works with force. He feels at ease in foreign countries. Mercury in the ninth house in Aquarius makes the native very fortunate. The person has good physique, follows the dictates of intrinsic duties with immense faith in God. He traverses the path of fate with immense satisfaction, having the power of foresight. Mercury in the tenth house in Pisces, the native receives honors. Constant weakness in the body bothers the native who prefers laziness. He feels many obstructions and hindrances in progress. Mercury in the eleventh house in Aries, showers the native with joy. He receives things and learning that makes him happy and clever. Mercury in the twelfth house in Taurus, deprives the native of physical pleasures. Weakness in the body plagues him, and he goes to other places. The native is a drifter, enjoys wandering."

❖ **Gemini Ascendant, Graha Jupiter**

"Jupiter, as ruler of houses 7 and 10, shows a strong will and idealism, and seeking of power and prestige in relationship. Jupiter in the first house in Gemini, the native enjoys good health, while working hard. Jupiter in the second house in Cancer, overwhelmed is the native by worries. Native with Jupiter in the third house in Leo gives the native special importance; strength and beauty to the spouse. Native enjoys sexual pleasures and uses it as a show of power. There are shortcomings in implementing intrinsic duties. The person is energetic and courageous. Jupiter in the fourth house in Virgo, the native runs his daily livelihood with dignity and sophistication. He is an honorable person. Jupiter in the fifth house in Libra, the native possesses good astute skills with luck on his side. Jupiter in the sixth house in Scorpio, the native has much influence and honor with the enemy. He gets dispassionate in matters on sex."

"Jupiter in the seventh house in Sagittarius, the native portrays a zealous, enthusiastic and very fortunate character. Jupiter in the eighth house in Capricorn, the native runs into problems with foreign countries. Restlessness overcomes him. Jupiter in the ninth house in Aquarius, the native lives on dissatisfaction. Destiny however empowers him. Jupiter in the eleventh house in Aries, the native enjoys good means of erotic pleasures. Jupiter in the twelfth house in Taurus, the native succumbs to losses with spouse. A constant restlessness follows him around. His sex life is up for disruptions."

❖ Gemini Ascendant, Graha Venus

"Venus, as ruler of houses 5 and 12, is a planet of passion and luxury. Venus in the first house in Gemini makes the native healthy and astute. He possesses a strong mind. He brags on the spouse and sexual pleasures. Venus in the second house in Cancer, overwhelmed is the native with mental worries. With Venus in the fourth house in Virgo, the native runs into worries from domestic unhappiness. With Venus in the sixth house in Scorpio, the native faces suffering with enemies. Secretive are his ways. Venus in the tenth house in Pisces, the native faces weakness in every matter. He cares not for pleasures or joy; however, he is clever and influential."

❖ Gemini Ascendant, Graha Saturn

"Saturn, as ruler of houses 8 and 9, can act as a spiritual planet, blessing the native with profound intelligence. Saturn in the first house in Gemini, makes the native fortunate, giving him a long lifespan. Saturn in the second house in Cancer, makes the native laze over the daily chores. Weaknesses in the family side show up as several obstacles. Promised is the native with Saturn in the third house in Leo, a long life. His adherence to solemn-duties has a Tamasik ring to it. He toils hard to earn his wages. Saturn in the fourth house in Virgo, inspires the native who otherwise spends his time in daily routines. Some worries and fortunes come his way. Saturn in the fifth house in Libra, wise is the native who has some problems with monetary income and constantly faces restlessness with the spouse. Saturn in the sixth house in Scorpio, the native uses spiritual strategies to develop a lifestyle, though in reality, he cares not much for morality. Infamous, and an atheist, he still commands over his enemies. Saturn in the seventh house in Sagittarius, gives the native a lengthy lifespan, he is fortunate and enjoys life's many pleasures. With Saturn in the eighth house in Capricorn showered is the native with good longevity though progress and destiny in foreign countries are hindered. Saturn in the ninth house in Aquarius, brings to the native a long, fortunate and progressive life. In adhering to intrinsic duties, he fails quite a lot. Saturn in the twelfth house in Taurus, turns the native restless, weak he is in fulfilling his solemn-duties; being ill-famed and impersonal are his traits."

❖ Gemini Ascendant, Graha Rahu

"Rahu in the first house in Gemini, gives the native a tall stature, he weathers many deep and bitter policy scars in recess of the heart. Strung by self-pride, he does well in attaining fame, pushing his ideas more than necessary crossing all thresholds. The spiritual knowledge he carries, does him well. Native with Rahu in the second house in Cancer feels distressed with the family. Native with Rahu in the third house in Leo, faces many challenges, but acts with courage; he does hard labor, often stays fatigued for many hours. He is timid and selfish, and very courageous. Rahu in the fourth house in Virgo, the native with a serious disposition, stays unhappy in his domestic life. With Rahu in the fifth house in Libra, the native is deprived of wisdom. Rahu in the sixth house in Scorpio, the native is careless in matters of disease and ill health. He does not care for solemn-duties either, committing series of sins and crimes. He is both selfish and brave. Rahu in the seventh house in Sagittarius, the native is incompatible with his spouse, vexed with worries that affect his daily occupation. He cannot enjoy sex, he is lazy and his thoughts drip with perversion. With Rahu in the eighth house in Capricorn, the native worries immensely, running into problems that could easily prove fatal. He has nervous breakdowns, lives in his own secrets, and enjoys little in the daily chores. Stomach troubles bother him a lot. Rahu in the ninth house in Aquarius, pushes the native to not do well with solemn-duties, rendering even his faith in god quite questionable. At a later stage in life comes the relief in his quest for destiny."

❖ Gemini Ascendant, Graha Ketu

"Ketu in the first house in Gemini, makes the native weak and turns him anxious. His looks are not attractive; he gets into accidents and even fatal ones. There is weakness in heart though the native has immense patience. The native lives in moderate secrecy and is an obstinate person. Ketu in the second house in Cancer, the native faces plenty of distress in family. With Ketu in the fifth house in Libra worries bear down on the native. He finds it tough in getting his ideas across to others. Bitter is his speech, selfish are his thoughts with no shred of gentleness. Ketu in the sixth house in Scorpio, makes the native firm, yet rash in dealing with problems and worries. He wins over the problems with little effort though he has a selfish and fearless side to him. Ketu in the seventh house in Sagittarius, the native turns perverted in his quest for normal sex, though his day-to-day activities are notable. There is lack of peace in the domestic front. Ketu in the eighth house in Capricorn, slams the native with restlessness and worries, he labors hard and faces many troubles with no qualms. He runs into complaints around the stomach region. Ketu in the ninth house in Aquarius, the native worries about destiny and fate. He labors very hard. Unable to keep up with the traditions of dharma, he loses all fame and his attempts to revive does not succeed."

❖ Gemini Ascendant, Transits

"Gemini ascendancy promises its natives pleasure, job, enthusiasm, willpower and handsomeness when Mercury occupies either Gemini, Leo, Virgo, Libra, Sagittarius, Aquarius or Aries during its transit; or when Jupiter gets posited in either Gemini, Libra, Sagittarius or Aquarius, or when the Sun occupies Gemini, Leo or Aries; or when Moon occupies Gemini or Sagittarius, or when Mars transits Leo, or when Rahu transits Gemini, or when Saturn crosses Scorpio. The advantage of happiness and peace occurs when Jupiter occupies Virgo or Pisces, or when Mercury occupies Virgo, Gemini, Aquarius, Aries or Sagittarius, or when Moon gets to occupy Virgo or Pisces, or when either Saturn or Mars occupy Virgo. The Sun when it occupies Virgo gives the best results in the matters of happiness connected with buildings, land and mother."

❖ Cancer Ascendant, Graha Sun

"Sun, as ruler of house 2, is a planet of speech, wealth, and education, giving good earning capacity and ruling powers. Sun in the first house in Cancer, gives glory and dignity to the native. There is tedium in matters related to spouse and occupation. In addition, the native feels some other hindrances. Native with Sun in the second house in Leo possesses a big family. There are some anxieties in the daily routine of life. The native is much respected. With Sun in the third house in Virgo, the native makes wonderful progress in matters concerning spirituality. People consider him lucky, possessing the right measures in dominating and influencing others. Sun in the fourth house in Libra, a constant restlessness bothers the native. Sun in the fifth house in Scorpio makes the native wise, supports him with good farsightedness; but also rubs on a hot, pitta temper. Sun in the sixth house in Sagittarius, the native is influential and cares not for enemies and difficult situations. He manages and controls quite well the challenges of ill health and is well respected. With Sun in the eighth house in Aquarius, the native receives ancestral wealth, perhaps the wealth of someone diseased. Sun in the ninth house in Pisces, the native is fortunate and spiritual. With Sun in the tenth house in Aries, denied is the native of any peace, though dignified and influential is the person. Sun in the twelfth house in Gemini, the native escapes from diseases and troubles through hefty expenditure."

❖ Cancer Ascendant, Graha Moon

"Moon, as ruler of house 1, is the planet of self and basic orientation in life. The Moon is auspicious as the lord of the ascendant. Moon in the first house in Cancer, gives the native a fair skin tone and symmetrical body, and control over many desires. His mind is stable; he has self-respect and earns people's respect. He acts according to his own will, lives independent, and is famous and well known."

"Native with Moon in the second house in Leo, gives the native to indulge in aristocracy. Big on maintaining his dignity, he engages in earthly affairs, earns many a respect. Moon in the third house in Virgo, the native is energetic and joyous; has faith in intrinsic duties and is fortunate. Possessing an attractive and handsome physique, he earns lot of fame and works for peace. Endowed he is with strong will power. Moon in the fourth house in Libra, happy and delightful is the native, especially if he continues to live where occurred his birth. Possessing a handsome physique, he makes others cheerful. Earning a name and people's appreciation, he lives in peace and achieves success. With Moon in the fifth house in Scorpio, restlessness bothers the native who has a narrow outlook. He lacks the ability to express himself through speech. He has a short stature and a habit of lying. Moon in the sixth house in Sagittarius, makes the native suffer from weakness and disease. Dependent on others, he feels restless, lives on fear of enemies; though he puts on a calm and courageous front. Moon in the seventh house in Capricorn, the native earns the admiration of others. Passionate he is, with cravings for sexual pleasures, married to a beautiful spouse. Suffering from great troubles, visiting foreign countries, he suffers in health. Moon in the eighth house in Aquarius, the native lacks beauty. With Moon in the ninth house in Pisces, luck favors the native who is spiritual, with much faith in god. He is handsome, happy, and full of energy; lives on fame and virtue. Moon in the tenth house in Aries, the native is stately and imposing, lives with great pomp and show. A happy person, he does good deeds. Moon in the eleventh house in Taurus, makes the native obese, influential, possessing a sharp intelligence, living in much pomp and show. Moon in the twelfth house in Gemini, troubled is the native by weaknesses; even his physical strength dwindles. He moves to foreign places where he earns honors. Under a lot of physical and mental distress, he renews efforts to subdue his enemies."

❖ Cancer Ascendant, Graha Mars

"Mars, as ruler of houses 5 and 10, gives great power. Mars is very auspicious and gives Raja Yoga. Native with Mars in the second house in Leo does great things in life using his wit and wisdom. There is big rise in status, accompanied with sizeable restlessness. Mars in the third house in Virgo, the native is very dignified, keeps a check on the enemy. He has strong nerves and never loses courage. He cares not for solemn-duties, he earns his success, appearing brave and skilled. Mars in the fourth house in Libra, the native acquires enormous knowledge on different subjects. An expert in conducting domestic and earthly affairs, he earns much honor. Mars in the sixth house in Sagittarius makes the native brave and influential, turns him into one who can maintain dignity and glory. He overcomes enemies and diseases; some problems in his body continue to prevail."

"Mars in the seventh house in Capricorn, the native runs into some weakness in his body. The person plays a respected and influential role. Mars in the eighth house in Aquarius, the native lives through falsehoods. His tone is bitter, he is a trifle lazy. Mars in the ninth house in Pisces brings fortunes to the native who has good knowledge of mathematics and accountancy. He is famous and farsighted. Mars in the tenth house in Aries makes the native wise, whose speech is intelligent. He earns many honors and people's respect. The person appears exquisite and attractive. He suffers from significant weaknesses though he is very dignified and influential. Mars in the eleventh house in Taurus makes the native very influential and selfish. Mars in the twelfth house in Gemini, earns the native respect, whose lack of strength in education and intelligence does not deter his courage and energy."

❖ Cancer Ascendant, Graha Mercury

"Mercury, the ruler of houses 3 and 12, shows tendency towards loss of energy and mental power through too much emotion. Mercury in the first house in Cancer, gives the native a robust, physical body and adds courage to his portfolio. He is a respectable person who travels to foreign countries. Native with Mercury in the second house in Leo earns the respect of people. Mercury in the third house in Virgo, makes the native highly energetic and a person with good height. He has little faith in solemn-duties. He possesses courage, ambition and yet comes out modest. Mercury in the fifth house in Scorpio makes the native clever and wise, who attempts to win over people to his side. With Mercury in the sixth house in Sagittarius, the native confronts several predicaments and is intermittently restless. A native with Mercury in the seventh house in Capricorn is a sensation in worldly affairs. Mercury in the eighth house in Aquarius weakens the native in energy and strength. Devoid of foes, he wields hidden power, shows much carelessness and gentleness. Mercury in the ninth house in Pisces, the native has faith in god as can be witnessed from his devotion. However, some inadequacy in performing intrinsic duties come up, the native loses all fame and fortune and his acumen becomes narrow. Mercury in the tenth house in Aries impressively works the native through the power of discrimination, the native enjoying a range of great powers. Mercury in the eleventh house in Taurus, the native earns much using his physical strength. Refined and powerful are his arguments and his speech is stately. Mercury in the twelfth house in Gemini, the native is short on muscle. His medical general upkeep expenses run high."

❖ Cancer Ascendant, Graha Jupiter

"Jupiter, as ruler of houses 6 and 9, highlights the native's ethical nature and sympathy even towards enemies and foreigners. Having Jupiter in the first house in Cancer, makes the native awkward, gracious, fortunate, righteous, brave at heart. The person honors justice and truth, understands the solemn-duties but has a corrupt side to him. He earns immense respect, his golden skin color makes him extremely handsome. The person is very intelligent and has broad forehead, is of tall stature, learned, affectionate and clever. A native with Jupiter in the second house in Leo earns the opportunity to do quite a few influential activities and earn honors. With Jupiter in the third house in Virgo, the native has strength and vigor. He is very considerate of the spouse and has an eye for jollities. Always busy, he still shows his concerns for the family. Jupiter in the fourth house in Libra, influences people into believing the native as lucky. Jupiter in the fifth house in Scorpio gives the native wisdom and virtues. Native is spiritual with adequate knowledge of astrology and has several windfalls. He also plays into politics. With Jupiter in the sixth house in Sagittarius, the native is unable to do a good justice to his solemn-duties. However, he runs an upper hand over his enemies. His influence is powerful, he portrays an image of being progressive. With Jupiter in the seventh house in Capricorn, the native suffers from misapprehension in matters like destiny and marriage. He is unsuccessful in executing his solemn-duties. Restlessness affects marital relationship. Jupiter in the eighth house in Aquarius, the native finds it difficult to manage dharma rules and regulations, leading to loss of fame. Unable to adhere to assigned intrinsic duties, he follows some obscure dharma. Jupiter in the ninth house in Pisces brings fortunes to the native, adding intelligence to his attributes. The person manages his intrinsic duties well and triumphs over his adversaries. With Jupiter in the tenth house in Aries, the native is influential, fortunate, and clever. When found is Jupiter in the eleventh house in Taurus, the native runs surplus energy. However, he is careless and marital relationships suffer, even though the native is clever and intelligent. Jupiter in the twelfth house in Gemini, brings the native turbulence in his destined path, and fame and fortune are difficult to achieve. The lack of happiness makes matters worse."

❖ Cancer Ascendant, Graha Venus

"Venus, as ruler of houses 4 and 11, showers the native with property and home comfort. Venus in the first house in Cancer, keeps the native in shape. Added to that, the graha bestows comfort and happiness in marital sphere. The person has a calm attitude, followed by success in nurturing the family and managing worldly affairs. A native with Venus in the second house in Leo lives a life of nobility earning much respect."

"With Venus in the third house in Virgo, the native delights in the progress his work in dharma brings. He remains lethargic and sluggish. With Venus in the fourth house in Libra, the native finds pleasure in his collection of various objects. Restless, he is, however, he has respect and humility. His involvement in cultured activities is quite intense. Venus in the fifth house in Scorpio gives the native much intelligence. His wisdom fetches gains and respect; honors come his way. Peaceful he is, and adroit. Venus in the sixth house in Sagittarius strikes the native with diseases and increased confrontation with enemies. A brilliant person, he lives in a secret world. Venus in the seventh house in Capricorn, the native pursues his daily occupation with joy, also enjoying a great marital relationship. A brilliant person, success comes to him easy. Venus in the eighth house in Aquarius gives the native the advantage of long life span. He is a bright and shrewd person. With Venus in the ninth house in Pisces, the native is fortunate, but low on energy. He is a devotee and a big believer in the almighty. Venus in the tenth house in Aries makes the native do the right things; makes him adroit and skilled. Venus in the twelfth house in Gemini makes the native callous and careless with his adversaries. The native is restless to a large degree."

❖ Cancer Ascendant, Graha Saturn

"Saturn, as ruler of houses 7 and 8, shows the native's tendency to relationships with those of inferior status, who may be hard-working or harsh in speech. Saturn in the first house in Cancer helps the native pursue his daily occupation with diligence. It promises good longevity. Marital relations are unsatisfactory. The person turns greedy and careless. A native with Saturn in the second house in Leo is promised good longevity. Restlessness comes from marital influences and family. The person leads a life of nobility. His manners are delightful. With Saturn in the third house in Virgo, the native has to exert lot of energy, which he does convincingly well. The person is a control maniac with spouse and in matters of sex. Selfish he is, his speech is bitter. He breaks the rules governing solemn-duties. Saturn in the fourth house in Libra, showers the native with happiness and joy. It promises good longevity. The person learns to enjoy and cherish happiness though such materialistic pleasures affect not his delusions. Much happiness comes from marital relationship and family. Saturn in the fifth house in Scorpio creates confusion in the native, which handicaps his mental acumen. His marital relationship is pleasurable. He treads with care, his speech lined with bitterness. Saturn in the sixth house in Sagittarius strengthens the native's longevity. The person practices the daily occupation with diligence while combating many distresses in marital relationship. Wrath affects him in a negative way."

"Saturn in the seventh house in Capricorn, the promises of good longevity turn true for the native, though he runs into trouble with his physique. Selfish he is, he damages his partake of intrinsic duties. There is a passionate side to him. Saturn in the eighth house in Aquarius, the native is short on honor, but gets help from foreign countries. The person has a bitter speech. With Saturn in the ninth house in Pisces, the native spends the daily routine in a fortunate way. He has the boon for a long life. Dissatisfied with fate, he at times becomes reckless. Saturn in the eleventh house in Taurus increases the native's longevity. He may have a few physical inadequacies with afflictions on his body. Bitter is his speech; he advances in foreign lands."

❖ Cancer Ascendant, Graha Rahu

"Rahu in the first house in Cancer, generates body defects and disorders, and the native suffers from mental distress. Overwhelmed is the person by anxious thoughts, seeking hard to get some happiness. Rahu in the second house in Leo swamps the native with worries and anxiety. With Rahu in the third house in Virgo, the native breaks the law of the land and succumbs to unjust means. He is clever, careful, patient and courageous. Rahu in the fourth house in Libra hinders the native's quest for peace and happiness. Having Rahu in the fifth house in Scorpio brings hardships to the native who fights to stay brave. With Rahu in the sixth house in Sagittarius, the native uses any means, whether just or otherwise in serving his needs. The native remains selfish and cautious. While Rahu in the seventh house in Capricorn, the native stays nervous and selfish, receiving his share of success through hard work. With Rahu in the eighth house in Aquarius, the native runs into several problems in the stomach region. Rahu in the tenth house in Aries helps the native make different artistic schemes."

❖ Cancer Ascendant, Graha Ketu

"Ketu in the first house in Cancer, the native experiences flaws in the body, which makes him skinny, sometimes such extreme emaciation can become fatal. He remains courageous and stubborn. A native who has Ketu in the second house in Leo, has formidable strength and high levels of stamina, besides a convincing level of patience. Ketu in the fifth house in Scorpio gives the native a harsh tongue and makes him suffer from mental anxiety. Ketu in the sixth house in Sagittarius turns the native brave, who in due course forces quite a fierce influence over his enemies. The person violates modesty and cares not for virtues or sin. Such a person can be very dangerous, fearless, dissatisfied and victorious. Ketu in the seventh house in Capricorn, the native is openly passionate about matters regarding sex; he is unsatisfied with one spouse. A native who has Ketu in the eighth house in Aquarius, complains of some integral troubles in stomach region. Otherwise, he is not one to display any anxiety."

"Ketu in the ninth house in Pisces, the native has problems with dharma and destiny, his spiritual nature is just a vogue, laced with hypocrisy."

❖ Cancer Ascendant, Transits

"When graha-s transit certain signs in Cancer ascendant, one can foretell generic happenings on age, health in the belly area, and other life course events. Steady progress and gains occur in matters of age and stomach health, with old and serious things helping the life when Saturn occupies either Capricorn, Aquarius, Leo, Taurus, Cancer, Leo, Virgo, Libra, or Scorpio or when Venus gets to occupy either Aquarius or Scorpio, or when Jupiter is in either Libra or Aquarius, or when Sun transits Aquarius. Regarding physique, attractiveness, will power and fame, the native has to wait until Moon occupies Cancer, Virgo, Libra, Capricorn or Taurus, or when Venus occupies Cancer, Pisces or Scorpio. At such times, comes peace, happiness, handsomeness, will power and physical comforts. When Venus occupies Libra, Capricorn, Aries, Cancer, Pisces or Taurus, or when Saturn is in Libra, Capricorn or Leo signs, or Mars posited in Libra, or Moon in Libra or Aries, or Jupiter occupies Libra or Aries, gains and progress of the matters concerned with mother, land, buildings and happiness occur. When Mars occupies either Taurus, Aries, Virgo, Libra, Capricorn, Leo or Pisces, or Venus sits in Aries or Libra, or Jupiter in Aries, or Moon in Aries or Libra, it creates a big advantage and showers progress in matters regarding father, government and society, business, honor and prestige."

❖ Leo Ascendant, Graha Sun

"Sun, as ruler of first house, denotes character, will power, ego and soul. It is auspicious as the lord of the ascendant. Sun in the first house in Leo, offers dignity and reputation to the native. He is stately, tall, conceited, haughty and brave. Sun in the second house in Virgo, gives the native a long life. Sun in the third house in Libra, brings the native lots of luck. Native has faith in god and gives proper importance to solemn-duties. Weak is his vigor, courage is his strength. With Sun in the fourth house in Scorpio, the native turns fearless, seeking peace, but is haughty. Sun in the seventh house in Aquarius, the native expresses displeasure in marital relations and is overcome by restlessness. With Sun in the eighth house in Pisces, dazed becomes the native with fatigue, experiencing intense seclusion. Sun in the ninth house in Aries, makes the native handsome owning a large forehead. The native earns much respect and fame, attaining a high position at some spiritual place. Sun in the eleventh house in Gemini, gives the native has a robust physique. The native has a good education; and, he shows signs of being contented and farsighted. Sun in the twelfth house in Cancer, gives the native an emaciated body, forcing him to live in a foreign place with weakness in the heart. The person harbors much frailty and prefers life in solitude."

❖ Leo Ascendant, Graha Moon

"Moon, as ruler of house 12, is a graha of spirituality, marking the end of something distraught and the beginning of something new. Moon in the first house in Leo, brings physical weakness to the native, tensions in marital life; he is of weak heart and suspicious mind. With Moon in the third house in Libra, forcefully calm and energetic stays the native. With Moon in the fourth house in Scorpio, the native has problems of peace and happiness, overburdened with mental worries. Moon in the fifth house in Sagittarius, indulges the native with knowledge and wisdom. With Moon in the sixth house in Capricorn, the native runs into mental fatigue, and in general he is a quiet and polite worker. Medical spending runs high. With Moon in the seventh house in Aquarius, the native runs into problems with marital and family life. Driven by anxiety, he perpetrates evil and immorality. With Moon in the eighth house in Pisces, the native constantly worries about his longevity. While Moon in the ninth house in Aries, the native knows he cannot manage dharma, his mind restless, his body pathetically weak, his energy levels run low. Moon in the tenth house in Taurus, makes the native unhappy. Moon in the twelfth house in Cancer, gives the native restlessness but an honorable mind."

❖ Leo Ascendant, Graha Mars

"Mars, as ruler of houses 4 and 9, indicates a strong spirit, energy and zeal, through which the natives can achieve a lot in life. It is a very auspicious Raja Yoga. Mars in the first house in Leo equips the native with easy means to seek happiness. The native is endowed with a good physique. Mars in the second house in Virgo, showers fortunes on the native, it also makes domestic happiness a thing of annoyance. With Mars in the third house in Libra, the native is fortunate. The native achieves success more from physical strength and vigor. He cares little for diseases and problems, does his daily chores with courage and influence. Mars in the fourth house in Scorpio, gives the native luck and fortunes, peace and happiness, and honors. With Mars in the fifth house in Sagittarius, the native has knowledge of many undisclosed secrets and their science. Mars in the sixth house in Capricorn, challenges the native in his quest for peace and happiness. With Mars in the seventh house in Aquarius, the native experiences insufficient domestic happiness. Mars in the eighth house in Pisces, hinders the native from getting any happiness, peace and fame. He has knowledge of many clandestine, secretive methods. With Mars in the ninth house in Aries, the native is fortunate, happy and joyous, having faith in god, winning many admirations. Mars in the tenth house in Taurus, the native possesses good health, and is very influential. Mars in the eleventh house in Gemini, the native is devout and yet selfish."

❖ Leo Ascendant, Graha Mercury

"Mercury, as ruler of houses 2 and 11, shows the capacity to gain from material and work, receive significant income, Mercury being an exponential Karaka of wealth. With Mercury in the first house in Leo, the native earns much respect through his adroit skills. Mercury in the second house in Virgo, gives the native a big family. Though he exhibits callousness, he earns a lot of respect. With Mercury in the third house in Libra, the native shows his faith in god and works in a skilled manner. Mercury in the fourth house in Scorpio helps the native satisfy his every want from his couch. He receives good garments and ornaments throughout. Mercury in the sixth house in Capricorn, the native uses his hard-earned money in paying off medical expenditures. Mercury in the eighth house in Pisces, the native runs into longevity problems. Anxiety in life inconveniences him. With Mercury in the ninth house in Aries, the native earns respect and has immense faith in god. Mercury in the twelfth house in Cancer, the native uses hard-earned money in managing medical expenditures and other problems."

❖ Leo Ascendant, Graha Jupiter

"Jupiter, as ruler of houses 5 and 8, is a graha that bestows profound intelligence and a sense of deep research. With Jupiter in the first house in Leo, the native inherits a long life-span, and gets to spend the daily routine of his life in a distinct style. Challenges exist with his physical features. Jupiter in the second house in Virgo, helps the native pass his hours in a very aristocratic way; some weakness exists though. With Jupiter in the third house in Libra, the native achieves a good life span. Jupiter in the fourth house in Scorpio makes the native happy and joyous. With Jupiter in the fifth house in Sagittarius, the native enjoys awards and honor from exhibitionism and extravagant behavior, though he is full of joy and speaks intricately in traditional way. Jupiter in the eighth house in Pisces, gives the native an increase in life span, but leaves him unhappy. Jupiter in the ninth house in Aries, wins the native respect, intelligence and fortunes. Having Jupiter in the tenth house in Taurus, the native is full of conceit, but skilled he is. With Jupiter in the eleventh house in Gemini, the native gets rewarded with long life. Life to him is a sense of cheer though he is low on stamina. Jupiter in the twelfth house in Cancer, gives the native a good life span, but depriving him of happiness."

❖ Leo Ascendant, Graha Venus

"Venus, as ruler of houses 3 and 10, is a graha that brings power, prestige and egoism. With Venus in the first house in Leo, native works and toils mostly with his strength and energy. He enjoys honor and strength in marital life. Venus in the second house in Virgo, the native faces family problems."

"With Venus in the third house in Libra, the native earns fame doing moral deeds. He works his way in life with courage and skill. Venus in the seventh house in Aquarius, gives the native might and power. Skilled he is besides being equipped with courage. Clever he is, possessing good stamina."

❖ Leo Ascendant, Graha Saturn

"Saturn, as ruler of houses 6 and 7, is a planet of enmity and disease, and relationship. With Saturn in the first house in Leo, native runs into diseases. Saturn in the fourth house in Scorpio, the native is steady in combating life's troubles and diseases. With Saturn in the fifth house in Sagittarius, burdened is the native with mental worries. Saturn in the seventh house in Aquarius, the native goes against the dharma principles, suffers from diseases, and unhappiness. With Saturn in the eighth house in Pisces, the native despairs about his longevity. Saturn in the ninth house in Aries, the native faces many a challenge with his destiny. With Saturn in the tenth house in Taurus, the native faces hindrance in achieving peace and happiness. Saturn in the eleventh house in Gemini brings to the native several diseases though his marital life is enjoyable. With Saturn in the twelfth house in Cancer, the native runs into heavy medical expenditures."

❖ Leo Ascendant, Graha Rahu

"With Rahu in the first house in Leo, native has a frail physique, anxiety and debility in the brain, experiencing some hidden fear. Rahu in the second house in Virgo, the native experiences family problems and a different restlessness. Rahu in the third house in Libra, the native undergoes some painful separation, wherein he turns restless; though patient he is throughout even when the going gets really tough. He pays no heed to troubles and problems. Rahu in the fourth house in Scorpio, keeps the native displeased and distressed with the domestic environment. He finds contentment after a length of time, crossing several hurdles. With Rahu in the fifth house in Sagittarius, mental confusion plagues the native, he lacks the ability to express his views, and even his choice of words is not up to the mark. He is somewhat edgy and impatient. Rahu in the seventh in Aquarius conveys defects in sex organs. Though he desires to quench his unsatisfied passions, he enjoys only perverted sex. The deficiencies disappear at a later stage. With Rahu in the eighth house in Pisces, the native runs into internal suffering in the stomach region. His lifespan suffers."

❖ Leo Ascendant, Graha Ketu

"With Ketu in the first house in Leo, challenged is the native with physical weakness and near-death experiences. With Ketu in the fourth house in Scorpio, the native seeks desperately some happiness."

"Having Ketu in the fifth house in Sagittarius, he feels inhibited in sharing his views and opinion. Ketu in the sixth house in Capricorn, gives the native good control over opponents, resisting diseases and complications with ease. Violating the decorum, the native works in his own selfish way. Ketu in the eighth house in Pisces, makes the native endure confusions in his daily routine; he complains of internal trouble in the stomach region, which if not medically resolved, may prove fatal. Ketu in the ninth house in Aries, the native agonizes from unprecedented troubles with destiny, coupled with shortages in dharma and less faith in god."

❖ Leo Ascendant, Transits

"In the stellar cycle, when Jupiter occupies Pisces, Gemini, Leo, Scorpio, Sagittarius, Aries, or Virgo, or when Mars is in Pisces, Leo, Sagittarius or Virgo, or when Venus occupies Pisces, or Sun is in Virgo, rewarded is the native with useful and improved results in matters connected with age, stomach and serious things helping the life course. Sun getting to occupy Leo, Scorpio, Sagittarius, Aquarius, Aries, Taurus, Gemini or Capricorn, or when Mars gets to occupy Leo or Aquarius, the native experiences enhancement in physique, will power and charm. When Mars occupies Scorpio, Aquarius, Taurus, Leo, Gemini, or when Venus is in Scorpio or Taurus signs, or when Sun occupies either Scorpio or Taurus sign, or when Mercury gets to occupy either Scorpio or Taurus sign, it shows the time as beneficial and fast forwards progress around buildings, land, mother, peace and happiness. Venus transiting Taurus, Gemini, Leo, Libra, Scorpio, Sagittarius, Aquarius, or Pisces, or Mars gets to occupy Taurus, Scorpio, Libra, or Aquarius, or when Mercury occupies Taurus or Scorpio, when Sun is in Taurus or Leo, it increases the luck of the native, showering him with social esteem."

❖ Virgo Ascendant, Graha Sun

"Sun, as ruler of house 12, shows the tendency of Virgo types towards servility and great spiritual work. Sun in the first house in Virgo, makes the native weak and emaciated. He behaves arrogant and haughty. While Sun in the second house in Libra, the native endures losses in the family. With Sun in the third house in Scorpio, the native experiences anxieties. Sun portrays his destiny as weak though he is very industrious. Sun in the fifth house in Capricorn, overwhelms the native with mental worries. From his haughty behavior suffers his expression of ideas. With Sun in the sixth house in Aquarius, the native runs into big medical expenditures. Sun in the seventh house in Pisces, gives the native an emaciated figure. With Sun in the ninth house in Taurus, the native cannot cope with rules his destiny demands, he feels anxious about his fate and loses faith in god. Sun in the eleventh house in Cancer, gives the native a rough speech."

"Sun in the twelfth house in Leo, makes the native incur expenditures in matters of dispute and illness."

❖ Virgo Ascendant, Graha Moon

"Moon, as ruler of house 11, enables the natives to enjoy gains through mental work and social communication. Moon in the first house in Virgo, promises the native all-round happiness. The person is handsome with a cool and calm attitude; he wins a lot of respect from others and has a lively countenance. Desire for sexual pleasures are uncontrollable for the native. With Moon in the second house in Libra, the native gets to live long, remains busy in arcane politics and enjoys a good reputation. Moon in the third house in Scorpio, restores the native's faith in god and dharma. Moon in the fourth house in Sagittarius, captivates the native's emotions with hours of joy. He enjoys many articles of beauty, clothes and adornments. With Moon in the fifth house in Capricorn, the native benefits by the sheer strength of his wisdom. Moon in the sixth house in Aquarius, makes the native endure mental anxieties. He stays preoccupied most of the time and is quite a spendthrift. He is of amiable disposition. Moon in the seventh house in Pisces, makes the native handsome. He flourishes in worldly affairs and is clever. With Moon in the eighth house in Aries, the native endures great mental distress. Moon in the ninth house in Taurus, brings the native many fortunes. The person has distinct faith in god and his intrinsic-duties. With Moon in the tenth house in Gemini, the native lives with great pomp and show. Moon in the eleventh house in Cancer, makes the native wise. Moon in the twelfth house in Leo, gives the native an inconsistent and restless mind. The person incurs large medical expenses."

❖ Virgo Ascendant, Graha Mars

"Mars, as ruler of houses 3 and 8, is double edged being a planet of both death and of longevity. With Mars in the first house in Virgo, the native gets rewarded with a long life, feels intense aches all over. However, this combination makes him powerful. With Mars in the second house in Libra, the native spends his life rolling in wealth, enjoying a long life. Vociferous is his tongue, he in indeed talkative. Having Mars in the fourth house in Sagittarius, the native relishes an extended life, enjoying every bit. With Mars in the fifth house in Capricorn, the native passes his life in magnificence, becoming famous; he is honorable and influential, uses diplomacy with wisdom. He has the gift of speech, but is haughty. With Mars in the sixth house in Aquarius, the native makes the enemies and opponents uneasy, however, lives in stark bondage. Mars in the eighth house in Aries, the native enjoys a long life. Mars in the ninth house in Taurus, the native has a long life, but unhappy facing deep-seated weakness in solemn-duties and destiny, losing his faith in god."

"With Mars in the tenth house in Gemini, the native gets a rough speech. Mars in the twelfth house in Leo brings formidable damage to the side of enemies and spouse."

❖ Virgo Ascendant, Graha Mercury

"Mercury, as ruler of houses 1 and 10, is a graha that influences self and career. Mercury in the first house in Virgo, the native gets to be tall and symmetrical, enjoys royal grandeur, is very influential, clever, wise and skilled, and a great politician, is diligent and has good manners. Mercury in the second house in Libra makes the native rich, with a long life. With Mercury in the third house in Scorpio, makes the native handsome and energetic, deriving success from efficiency. The native enjoys a decent life. Not short of pride, he is a staunch believer in god. Mercury in the fourth house in Sagittarius, the native lives in happiness, decorates his home well, wins respect and honor, and is a good-humored person. Mercury in the fifth house in Capricorn, gives the native self-pride, who is aware of the inherent-duties. He lives surrounded by beauty and nice décor and he is self-conscious. With Mercury in the sixth house in Aquarius, the native lives as a dependent, his progress hindered, overburdened by illness. Overwhelmed by enemies, he has to suffer for past evils. Mercury in the seventh house in Pisces, brings weakness to the native, he still safeguards his honor, but is swamped by worries. With Mercury in the eighth house in Aries, the native suffers physical problems, which makes him unhappy and weak at heart. He moves to other foreign countries. Mercury in the ninth house in Taurus, makes the native fortunate, handsome and attractive. He has faith in god, relishing divine help. Mercury in the tenth house in Gemini, makes the native good-looking and renders him attractive."

❖ Virgo Ascendant, Graha Jupiter

"Jupiter, as ruler of houses 4 and 7, is a planet of emotion, home and relationship. Jupiter in the first house in Virgo ensures the native enjoy domestic happiness. He remains vigilant about his dharma. Suffering from shortage in wisdom and education, his body develops excess fat, but he is clever and happy. With Jupiter in the second house in Libra, the native relishes the joy of life, enjoys a long life and has influence over enemies. Jupiter in the third house in Scorpio, rewards the native with good stature, who has faith in solemn-duties, meets success after marriage, and is fortunate. With Jupiter in the fifth house in Capricorn, the native feels weak and under-provided from all sides; he hesitates a little while speaking. Bliss and harmony are absent; he acts quite a pervert and comes under distress often. With Jupiter in the sixth house in Aquarius, the native feels the dire need of peace and happiness. Jupiter in the eighth house in Aries brings suffering to the native and his family."

"While Jupiter in the ninth house in Taurus, makes the native fortunate, whose speech is barefaced but weak, he is peaceful and farsighted. Jupiter in the tenth house in Gemini gives the native dignity, industriousness and extravagant sexual pleasures. With Jupiter in the twelfth house in Leo, the native enjoys a long life."

❖ Virgo Ascendant, Graha Venus

"Venus, as ruler of houses 2 and 9, brings grace, luck, fortune and success. Venus in the first house in Virgo breeds physical weakness in the native. While Venus in the third house in Scorpio, leads the native to fame, also making the person spiritual, honorable and influential. Having Venus in the fifth house in Capricorn turns the native into a clever and fortunate person, who undertakes solemn-duties undistorted as is. He is a good speaker on matters of spirituality, a learned artist, skilled in astrology and politics. With Venus in the sixth house in Aquarius, the native finds success in politics, even though his performance is poor regarding the dictates of solemn-duties. Venus in the seventh house in Pisces brings fortunes to the native. With Venus in the eighth house in Aries, the native shows vulnerability in matters of family and destiny, not exactly strong in spirituality, finding success in foreign countries. While Venus in the ninth house in Taurus, fortunes get showered on the native. The native is moral, famous, with strong belief in god. Venus in the tenth house in Gemini, the native earns great respect from people around him. Venus in the eleventh house in Cancer makes the native clever and intelligent, who backs intrinsic-duties. With Venus in the twelfth house in Leo, feeble is the native; he runs into family losses and faces challenges with inner-duties."

❖ Virgo Ascendant, Graha Saturn

"Saturn, as ruler of houses 5 and 6, turns the native into a workaholic, which subsequently leads to physical ailments. Saturn in the first house in Virgo makes the person triumphant, who is otherwise serious, involved in deep intricate policies, bearing some enmity, suffering from illnesses. Saturn in the second house in Libra involves the native in grand deeds, who in many ways acts daring and reckless. With Saturn in the third house in Scorpio, wise are the native's activities, laden with energy. Saturn in the fourth house in Sagittarius, gives the native honors, but he loses out on things like peace and happiness. Having Saturn in the fifth house in Capricorn, the native warrants sharp intelligence. With Saturn in the sixth house in Aquarius, the native cares not for quarrels and diseases. Restlessness engulfs him and he talks in a crooked way. Saturn in the eighth house in Aries makes the native talkative, who resorts to tobacco addiction and runs into stomach troubles and anal diseases."

"With Saturn in the ninth house in Taurus, the native is intelligent and shrewd. Like a medical doctor or a surgeon, he is an expert in matters of diseases, he is triumphant over his enemies by the sheer power of intellect power. Profound is his interest in intrinsic-duties."

- ❖ Virgo Ascendant, Graha Rahu

"Rahu in the first house in Virgo gives the native a cunning and clever speech. He learns to endure many physical problems. Rahu in the fourth house in Sagittarius robs the native of happiness. He however, finds strength in the power of the occult. With Rahu in the fifth house in Capricorn, the native gets caught in falsehood and ends up addicted to stimulants like hemp and tobacco. Anger and intuition are also in his character. Rahu in the sixth house in Aquarius gives the native the powers to defeat the enemy, and overcome diseases. A constant weakness he has to endure. Rahu in the eighth house in Aries brings the native troubles and unhappiness. Cut short is his life span, and he suffers from diseases in the stomach region and in the anus. Rahu in the ninth house in Taurus, the native faces hindrances delusions in his quest for destiny."

- ❖ Virgo Ascendant, Graha Ketu

"Ketu in the first house in Virgo, makes the native suffer from conceit. He experiences body weakness but is not seeming outwardly. He is clever, respectable and rash. Ketu in the fourth house in Sagittarius brings the native some pleasures and weakness. Ketu in the sixth house in Aquarius empowers the native with might and energy, and fearlessness. He defeats enemies, overcomes diseases, cares not for justice. Ketu in the eighth house in Aries, makes the native highly restless, who passes his days with many difficulties, experiences disease in the lower parts of stomach below navel or in anus, meets with some major accident now and then. Life to him is full of anxieties. With Ketu in the ninth house in Taurus, the native's destiny turns fragile. He believes in the intrinsic-duties in his own bizarre way."

- ❖ Virgo Ascendant, Transits

"With Mars occupying Aries, Virgo, Scorpio, Capricorn, Sagittarius, Libra, Gemini, Taurus, or Pisces; or Jupiter is in Aries, Scorpio, Libra, or when Moon occupies Aries or Libra, it shows progress and advantages associated with age, stomach and other things helping the life course. Jupiter, when he occupies Cancer, Virgo, Scorpio, Sagittarius, Pisces, or Gemini, or Venus in Pisces or Virgo, or Moon in Pisces or Virgo, it causes progress, happiness and gains from spouse and diurnal occupation."

"Enhancement in physique, handsomeness, will-power and fame occurs during the time Mercury occupies Virgo, Gemini, Sagittarius, Capricorn, Taurus, Cancer, or Scorpio, or when Jupiter occupies Virgo, Pisces, or Taurus, or when Moon occupies Virgo or Pisces. Progress in matters on mother, land and buildings, happiness and peace occur when Jupiter occupies Sagittarius, Pisces, Gemini, Cancer, Virgo, or Taurus, or when Mercury occupies Sagittarius or Gemini, or when Moon occupies Sagittarius or Gemini, or when Ketu occupies Sagittarius. Transiting Mercury in Gemini, Virgo, Sagittarius, Cancer, Taurus, or Libra, or when Jupiter occupies Gemini, Libra, or Sagittarius, or when Moon is in Gemini, or when Mercury occupies longitudinal degrees of Capricorn or Scorpio, are the times when there are marked improvements in honor, prestige, and faith. There is progress in undertakings that include big business, government and society."

❖ Libra Ascendant, Graha Sun

"Sun, as ruler of house 11, promises gains, aspirations and ideals, also impulse, power, prowess, violence, disease and enmity. Sun in the first house in Libra, brings fragility to the native's income and physique. The person possesses a lean and thin body. Sun in the third house in Sagittarius, gives the native power, influence courage and energy. Sun in the sixth house in Pisces, gives the native victory over enemies; influential, brilliant and fearless he is with good manners. Sun in the seventh house in Aries, makes the native easily fatigued. Weakness results from excess sexual indulgence. Sun in the ninth house in Gemini, makes the native fortunate, with destined gains. He is brilliant, influential and carefree. Sun in the eleventh house in Leo, enemies harass the native. The native is insensitive, with tinges of irritation showing up in his conversation. Sun in the twelfth house in Virgo, guides the native into the world of renunciation. He profits from enemies."

❖ Libra Ascendant, Graha Moon

"Moon, as ruler of house 10, assures power, prestige, action and realization. Moon in the first house in Libra guarantees dignity. Native's constitution and countenance is stately, which others respect. With Moon in the second house in Scorpio, the life-span of the native surges and stays well protected. Moon in the third house in Sagittarius, makes the native fortunate and successful. He backs his inherent-duties with undaunted faith in god. Clever and industrious he is. Moon in the fourth house in Capricorn, empowers the native with noble and inventive ideas. He earns respect from government and society. With Moon in the fifth house in Aquarius, education comes to the native, who exhibits creativity and inventive traits. With Moon in the seventh house in Aries, the native enjoys sexual pleasures. He marries someone good-looking, progresses after marriage. His major drawback is his infatuation with sex, which works like a disease."

"With Moon in the eighth house in Taurus, the native suffers a painful death and earns tributes after death. Moon in the ninth house in Gemini, makes the native fortunate, stalwartly supporting inherent-duties. He earns fame and has much faith in the lord. Moon in the tenth house in Cancer, gives the native much pleasure, his respect and honor makes him vane. With Moon in the twelfth house in Virgo, the native fears failing in honor and respect. He influences enemies through his resilient ways, but his mind encounters drawbacks."

❖ Libra Ascendant, Graha Mars

"Mars, as lord of houses 2 and 7, confirms wealth and relationship and hints at the possibility of conflict over finances. Having Mars in the first house in Libra, the native gets an emaciated physique. Married to an able and beautiful person, he enjoys pleasures and happiness. While Mars in the second house in Scorpio, gives the native tremendous power. The native has conflicts with the spouse. Mars in the third house in Sagittarius diminishes the native's power and stamina. While Mars in the fourth house in Capricorn gives the native joy from his marital and maternal side of the family."

❖ Libra Ascendant, Graha Mercury

"Mercury, as ruler of houses 9 and 12, confirms renunciation through wisdom, an idealistic sense of self sacrifice. Having Mercury in the first house in Libra makes the native fortunate, who has no complaints about his strong physique. He possesses a thin and wiry body, enjoys a happy marital life. He is clever and wise, works for the law; besides, he is influential and compassionate. Mercury in the second house in Scorpio makes the native respectable. Mercury in the third house in Sagittarius, the native has a gentle physique and fortunate. He lives on courage and respect and stays reserved. With Mercury in the fourth house in Capricorn, the native enjoys pleasures, backs inherent-duties in a practical way. Mercury in the fifth house in Aquarius gives the native deep and far reaching knowledge on inherent-duties. One may credit his elevation in life to his intellect and speech. He acts like a seasoned politician. Mercury in the sixth house in Pisces gives the native a weak fate, which also marks his doom. Losses to his fortune occur as a result, wherein he uses secret tactics. It brings about restlessness with the enemies. Mercury in the eighth house in Taurus, the native feels distressed with his destiny, gets several confirmations to his increased life span; he dies a peaceful death. Mercury in the ninth house in Gemini brings fortunes to the native. He gets fame and lives with courage. With Mercury in the tenth house in Cancer, the native gets equipped with valor and grandeur, fetching him honors and respect. Mercury in the eleventh house in Leo, fate drives the native to big successes. Besides acting wise and farsighted, he is fortunate and clever."

"Mercury in the twelfth house in Virgo, the native incurs losses from fate, spends on pilgrimages; he is moral, uses his wisdom to cope with enemies."

❖ Libra Ascendant, Graha Jupiter

"Jupiter, as ruler of houses 3 and 6, assures of energy, impulse, gains, ambition, egoism, disease and enmity. With Jupiter in the first house in Libra, the native is careful in exhibiting his faith. With Jupiter in the second house in Scorpio, the native enjoys respect, keeps a steady influence over his enemies and exhibits wisdom. Jupiter in the fourth house in Capricorn deprives the native of any peace. He triumphs over the opposition. With Jupiter in the fifth house in Aquarius, intelligence drives the native into different areas of strength. He is daring, crafty, wise and skilled. Jupiter in the sixth house in Pisces makes the native brave, but careless. He earns his dignity from hard labor. He overthrows his opponents. With Jupiter in the seventh house in Aries, the native turns powerful through the spouse's influence. He routs the enemies and acclaims victory through the sheer power of will. Jupiter in the eighth house in Taurus brings weakness to the native, which has a negative effect on his happiness. Jupiter in the twelfth house in Virgo, deprives the native of strength and energy; though he valiantly stands up against his opponents and eventually wins over them."

❖ Libra Ascendant, Graha Venus

"Venus, as lord of houses 1 and 8, represents self, life and longevity. Venus in the first house in Libra bequeaths a long life on the native. He is respectable, farsighted, diplomatic, influential and famous. Weakness in the body persists. He is a person with good knowledge of the 'self'. Venus in the second house in Scorpio gives the native a long life, along with pleasures and struggles in the family. With Venus in the fourth house in Capricorn, the native spends his life in comfort, happily without moving from his place. He is long lived. He lives a somber existence. Venus in the fifth house in Aquarius gives the native deep insights into self-knowledge. His knowledge runs deep and his life span is long. He is a very farsighted politician, equipped with the acumen to analyze and see through difficult problems. Having Venus in the sixth house in Pisces, gives the native the power to solve many difficult problems in his life, though he is intensely careless. With Venus in the seventh house in Aries, the native lives long; he is handsome, self-sighted, diplomatic and self-centered. Having Venus in the eighth house in Taurus, blessed is the native with a long life, but has to cope with several defects in the body. With Venus in the ninth house in Gemini, the native enjoys the blessings of ample luck and zero anxieties. He may show traits that are fatalistic and industrious, but he is respectable and smart."

"Having Venus in the tenth house in Cancer, the native spends life as royal people do, enjoying tremendous authority, and comforts and pleasures that come with such existence. He runs into hindrances in the progress of honor, but is obstinate. With Venus in the eleventh house in Leo, the native achieves several gains in his life, but laziness distracts him from personal gains, though he is clever. Venus in the twelfth house in Virgo weakens the native making him suffer in his daily chores."

❖ Libra Ascendant, Graha Saturn

"Saturn, as ruler of houses 4 and 5, pledges intelligence and happiness. Saturn is very auspicious, conferring a Raja Yoga. Saturn in the first house in Libra, gives the native a handsome physique, who stays wise, influential, diligent while indulging in self-pride. With Saturn in the third house in Sagittarius, the native has tremendous energy, he is intellectual, talkative, rough and talks freely. Saturn in the fourth house in Capricorn, brings happiness to the native, the combination ensures a sustained joy making the native carefree. With Saturn in the sixth house in Pisces, assured is his longevity. His speech is bitter. Having Saturn in the tenth house in Cancer, the native is verbally abusive towards the spouse and remains happy in his own way. Saturn in the twelfth house in Virgo gives the native a weak intellect. He lacks good education and happiness."

❖ Libra Ascendant, Graha Rahu

"Rahu in the first house in Libra, makes the native over-cautious. He remains physically and mentally worried. He is bright and famous, hurt bodily from blows that make him nervous. Rahu in the third house in Sagittarius, the native uses occult power, somewhat inactive, lazy and suffers from debility. With Rahu in the fourth house in Capricorn, the native is unhappy. Rahu in the sixth house in Pisces gives the native the power to overcome problems like diseases. He knows when to act formidable and when to control his enemies. He stays vigilant, attentive and selfish. With Rahu in the seventh house in Aries, the native's organs have few disorders. Rahu in the eighth house in Taurus, the native faces quite a few distresses in life, he has disorders of stomach, few are constipation related, or complaints in anus section covering the lower part of belly. All these cut his longevity. Rahu in the ninth house in Gemini, the native brags about intrinsic-duties incessantly, though his destiny does not support such ventures."

❖ Libra Ascendant, Graha Ketu

"Ketu in the first house in Libra, burdens the native with physical weakness. He senses 'incompleteness' within himself, lives in a manner dominated by pride and bravery and acts somewhat obstinate. Ketu in the third house in Sagittarius blesses the native with influence, hard work, diligence, craftmanship and fierce strength. With Ketu in the fourth house in Capricorn, the native turns restless and clever. While with Ketu in the fifth house in Aquarius, the native though wise, suffers from anxieties. Ketu in the sixth house in Pisces, helps the native keep a steady influence on enemies. Equipped with immense patience and courage, he makes efforts to become free from diseases. Therein he exhibits his fearless side. Ketu in the eighth house in Taurus, brings to the native significant restlessness accompanied by much weakness. He lacks the strength and motivation to complete his daily tasks besides suffering from illness around the stomach region. Ketu in the ninth house in Gemini increases joy to the native's charter. However, he runs into problems of defamation, intrinsic-duties challenges and loss of faith in god. Ketu in the tenth house in Cancer assures the native of mental anxieties."

❖ Libra Ascendant, Transits

"Regarding age, stomach, and other things that help in the life course, when Venus occupies any sign other than Virgo, or when Saturn occupies Taurus, Leo, Scorpio or Pisces, or when Moon occupies Taurus or Scorpio, or when Mars occupies Libra, Scorpio, Aquarius, or Aries, or when Sun occupies either Taurus or Scorpio, or when Jupiter occupies Taurus, the native experiences increase in life span, decrease in stomach region disorders and other things helping the life course. When Venus occupies Libra, Sagittarius, Capricorn, Aquarius, Pisces, Aries, Gemini, Cancer or Leo, or when Mercury occupies Libra or Aries, or when Saturn occupies either Libra or Capricorn, or when Moon occupies either Libra or Aries sign, or when Jupiter occupies Aquarius or Gemini signs, the native experiences enhancement in physique, handsomeness, will-power and fame. Occasionally, when Saturn occupies Capricorn, Cancer, Scorpio, Leo or Gemini, or when Mars occupies Capricorn, Libra or Gemini, or when Moon gets to occupy Capricorn or Cancer, or when Venus occupies Capricorn, Cancer; or Sun occupying Capricorn or Cancer, the native experiences happiness and peace. In the months when Jupiter occupies Cancer, Scorpio, or Pisces, or when Saturn occupies Cancer, or when Sun will occupy Cancer sign, or when Mercury will occupy Cancer, or when Moon occupy Cancer, Libra, Capricorn or Leo, or when Venus will occupy Cancer sign, the native gains in matters of honor, prestige and faith."

- ❖ Scorpio Ascendant, Graha Sun

"Sun, as ruler of house 10, guarantees power, prestige and position and shows the nature of the individual's life action and realization. With Sun in the first house in Scorpio, the native lives in grandeur, glory and affluence; he lives with pride and is very orderly. Having Sun in the second house in Sagittarius, the native runs into hereditary wealth. He is very industrious and honorable. Sun in the third house in Capricorn, gives the native energy and diligence to be productive, respectful and honorable. The native is fortunate and famous, however complete success is not assured. Sun in the fourth house in Aquarius, brings hindrances to the native. The native, however, is respectable and loyal. With Sun in the fifth house in Pisces, the adroit native always looks to his selfish winnings. Having Sun in the seventh house in Taurus, the native earns honors and is shrewd. Sun in the eighth house in Gemini, the native lacks respect and honor, tries hard to succeed in foreign countries. He gets assured of a long life. Sun in the ninth house in Cancer, makes the native very fortunate, who performs spiritual duties regularly. His pleasure comes from experiencing the divine wonders. The native pursues big business and is influential. Sun in the tenth house in Leo, gives the native great power. He suffers from restlessness. Sun in the eleventh house in Virgo, the native can speak well on political matters. Geared are his activities towards the good; he gains by working quickly. Sun in the twelfth house in Libra, the native loses his respect and honor. He cares not for diseases; he possesses occult power."

- ❖ Scorpio Ascendant, Graha Moon

"Moon, as ruler of house 9, engages the native in performing the intrinsic-duties as a guiding principle, enjoying the grace or fortune that follows it. Moon in the first house in Scorpio, assures the native mental anxieties and a culpable destiny. Lean is his body, difficult are his chances in doing his inherent-duties. While Moon in the second house in Sagittarius, makes the native very fortunate. The person enjoys the pleasures of a family, wins success in worldly affairs, but ages rapidly. Having Moon in the third house in Capricorn, the native, full of enthusiasm, earns much fortunes. Spiritual he is and a true believer, he always works with lofty progressive ideas. Moon in the fourth house in Aquarius, makes the native fortunate. The native is significantly happy, supporting all inherent-duties, a true believer in the lord and is diligent. While Moon in the fifth house in Pisces, helps the native stay intelligent, making him focus on education, giving him the power of farsightedness, equipping him with a sweet speech and deep-seated virtues. With Moon in the sixth house in Aries, the native refuses to believe in intrinsic-duties and the lord."

"While Moon in the eighth house in Gemini, makes the native suffer from mental distress. The native faces many troubles and his perspective[217] on intrinsic-duties suffers. He enjoys a long life. Moon in the ninth house in Cancer, gives the native fortunes and fame. A jovial person, his adoption of the intrinsic-duties makes dharma effective for him. Moon in the tenth house in Leo, makes the native very fortunate. With Moon in the eleventh house in Virgo, the native earns the privilege to receive impressive gains. He is fortunate and kind. Moon in the twelfth house in Libra, confronts the native with a 'weak destiny'[218], where he earns several appeasements from enemies."

❖ Scorpio Ascendant, Graha Mars

"Mars, as ruler of houses 1 and 6, represents self and disease, prosperity and difficulty. Mars in the first house in Scorpio, in his own sign, makes the native short but influential, energetic and proud. He suffers many disorders in the body, yet gains a lot of strength from 'pitta', heat, some of which turn into diseases. Native gains little from parents, encounters challenges in peace and happiness. Mars in the second house in Sagittarius, gives the native many physical problems, however his health stays positive. A person with powerful speech, he adopts duties that are lower than his capabilities. With Mars in the third house in Capricorn, the native turns very influential, though he is plagued with health problems. Having Mars in the fourth house in Aquarius, the native faces the loss of happiness. With Mars in the fifth house in Pisces, the native acts wise, clever and self-sighted. He is a great diplomat; however, his temperament runs high. He suffers from several diseases in the body. Mars in the sixth house in Aries makes the native extremely brave. The person is likely stout, but he faces his enemies with no fear. Honors are credited to his immense will-power, his adoption of intrinsic-duties stays remarkably casual. He suffers from body fatigue, therein his caustic traits show up. Mars in the seventh house in Taurus, challenges the native with enmity, power, struggle and benefits in marital relationship. Conceited and passionate, plagued with several diseases of the body and organs, he still continues to thrive. Mars in the eighth house in Gemini overwhelms the native with diseases. Suffering from an inflammation of the heart, he lives in a foreign place, engulfed in troubles and cares not for slight and insult. He turns a thick skin at abuses hurled at him. Mars in the ninth house in Cancer weakens the native's destiny. Weakness trails him, wherein his body and intrinsic-duties face deterioration. Strained he is in finding happiness."

---

[217] 'Yatharth' – perspective or real. Some words are difficult to interpret as yatharth could also point to a possibility.
[218] 'bhagya ki badi kamjori' – a weak destiny or a weak fate

"Mars in the tenth house in Leo makes the native extremely powerful, bestowing on him, a good, robust physique. The native feeds on lust, though he is clever, diligent, wise and learned. His speech is firm, commanding is his power and fame. Mars in the eleventh house in Virgo, makes the native influential and decent. He triumphs over his enemies. Some weakness in body persists. He acts out of fury but remains cautious. Mars in the twelfth house in Libra inundates the native with physical problems, who with his weak body, spends big in litigations and medicines. He lives in foreign places and travels a lot."

❖ Scorpio Ascendant, Graha Mercury

"Mercury, as ruler of houses 8 and 11, pledges destruction, violence, impulse and aggression, and injury from subconscious emotions. Mercury in the first house in Scorpio imparts in the native a gentle behavior and nature. The native enjoys a long life, taking full responsibility of a rather large and extended family. Mercury in the second house in Sagittarius blesses the native with a long life, who lives in respect and enjoys riches. Mercury in the third house in Capricorn fills the native with tremendous energy to do things in a gentle way. A long life awaits him. He adopts few self-centered plans to adopt and execute the intrinsic-duties. Mercury in the fourth house in Aquarius promises the native a long life, where he finds happiness in 'mystery' ridden plans. Mercury in the fifth house in Pisces weakens the native's intellect and cuts short his education and lifespan. He is anxious about his shortened life span. Sufferings accompany him throughout his life. His speech turns bitter, and he lives a life in privacy. With Mercury in the sixth house in Aries, the native faces many anxieties and is intensely involved with secret schemes. Having Mercury in the seventh house in Taurus, the native is subject to quiet suffering; happiness comes only after marriage. While Mercury in the eighth house in Gemini, gives the native a long life-span. Glory and grandeur comes to him even in his daily routines. He is very careless and hovers between acting stern and tender. With Mercury in the ninth house in Cancer, the native receives hereditary wealth, gets a long life-span with some blemishes in fame. Mercury in the tenth house in Leo, gives native respect and honor and hereditary wealth. He gets to live long and spends most of his life buried in prominent activities. While Mercury in the eleventh house in Virgo, gives the native a long life-span, but his intellect and education remain mediocre. His weak speech turns his conversations rude. Mercury in the twelfth house in Libra makes the native nervous about longevity, suffering some struggles and diseases."

❖ Scorpio Ascendant, Graha Jupiter

"Jupiter, as ruler of houses 2 and 5, confers speech, intelligence, education and wealth. Jupiter in the first house in Scorpio makes the native wise, learned, spiritual and a diplomat. He loves justice and astrology, possessing spiritual knowledge. Being influential, his faith in the lord stays steady throughout. Jupiter in the third house in Capricorn, imbibes in the native a great sense of morality, with immense faith in god. He has a weak heart. Jupiter in the fourth house in Aquarius promises the native a long life-span, but not happiness. Jupiter in the fifth house in Pisces makes the native learned, educated and fortunate, whose speech has poise about it. He has authority and strong knowledge on spiritual matters, besides possessing scientific knowledge. With Jupiter in the sixth house in Aries, the native cannot express his views. With Jupiter in the eighth house in Gemini, restlessness engulfs the native at heart, who enjoys a long life living in riches. While Jupiter in the ninth house in Cancer, makes the native fortunate, intelligent, farsighted and wealthy. He becomes known for his spiritual activities, winning many honors, possessing knowledge of astrology and dharma. Jupiter in the eleventh house in Virgo, makes the native wealthy and respectable. Jupiter in the twelfth house in Libra turns off the native's ability to communicate his ideas. There is shortage of peace and happiness. He spends life in aristocracy."

❖ Scorpio Ascendant, Graha Venus

"Venus, as ruler of houses 7 and 12, confirms passion and shows the potential of loss and sorrow through the marriage partner. With Venus in the first house in Scorpio, the native earns honors; he is clever and skilled, careful and farsighted and enjoys beauty. Having Venus in the fifth house in Pisces, the native is convincingly clever, educated and intelligent. Venus in the tenth house in Leo, makes the native unhappy."

❖ Scorpio Ascendant, Graha Saturn

"Saturn, as ruler of houses 3 and 4, assures strong energy and sometimes violence from too much impulse in the emotional nature. Having Saturn in the first house in Scorpio makes the native energetic, zealous and caustic. While Saturn in the second house in Sagittarius, blesses the native with a long life. He lives happily. Saturn in the third house in Capricorn gives the native ample energy. The native gets involved deeper in several grand schemes and earns joy from other places. Saturn in the fourth house in Aquarius causes defects in the native's body. With Saturn in the fifth house in Pisces, the native possesses a very sharp intellect and his education runs strong. Saturn in the sixth house in Aries, the native lacks power in combating diseases. With Saturn in the seventh house in Taurus, the native finds happiness in domestic life, but gets overcome by fatigue."

"Saturn in the eighth house in Gemini gives the native a long life; he travels to several foreign countries. Saturn in the ninth house in Cancer energizes the native into doing many nice deeds. His devotion to god and intrinsic-duties are his source of happiness. While Saturn in the eleventh house in Virgo, gives the native a long live. He aspires hard to get some happiness. Saturn in the twelfth house in Libra, the native devotes his thoughts to intrinsic-duties and god. He underestimates the enemy."

❖ Scorpio Ascendant, Graha Rahu

"Rahu in the first house in Scorpio makes the native emaciated, suffering blows all his life. His gentle nature turns topsy-turvy. Undertaking many strong measures to fathom the intense divine powers becomes his source of courage and ingenuity. Rahu in the third house in Capricorn gives the native valor, courage and shrewdness. He maintains patience even in the hour of weaknesses, where, despite losing courage sometimes, he eventually emerges triumphant. Rahu in the fourth house in Aquarius makes the native unhappy. While Rahu in the fifth house in Pisces, makes the native wise who puts forth his selfish ideas, caring not for honesty or truth. His conversation is unsweet; he is careless, but believe his views as correct. Rahu in the sixth house in Aries makes the native influential and ever successful over enemies. Being gentle and satisfied is not his character though he works with steady patience. Caring not for troubles or diseases, he acts a daredevil. He is also a good statesman and diplomat. With Rahu in the seventh house in Taurus, the native fears exposure of his weakness and worries. Rahu in the eighth house in Gemini, the native shows signs of force and flirtation. He ponders deep on obscure and mysterious matters. He gets a grant of long life. Rahu in the ninth house in Cancer, engages the native into anxieties about his destiny. He regrets his luck; he has little faith in god and spirituality. Rahu in the tenth house in Leo deprives the native of honor. The person faces many obstacles in his general progress."

❖ Scorpio Ascendant, Graha Ketu

"Ketu in the first house in Scorpio, the native hurts from blemishes and wounds. He is endowed with immense patience. Possessing excessive strength, he trudges on with no heed. Though he acts heroic, he feels and yearns the need for better knowledge. Anxious, he often appears solemn. With Ketu in the second house in Sagittarius, the native sees a virtual collapse in his family. He lives in aristocracy. Ketu in the third house in Capricorn, makes the native heroic. His arms are long; diligent he is, he faces many a separation. With Ketu in the fourth house in Aquarius, the native is short on happiness, faces separation from birthplace. Ketu in the fifth house in Pisces gives the native a rude speech and makes him rather obstinate."

"Ketu in the sixth house in Aries makes the native brave and heroic, enjoying victory over enemies. He cares not about troubles he may have to face, takes care of diseases and difficulties prudently, while remaining alert, he pays attention towards serving his selfishness. With Ketu in the seventh house in Taurus, the native refuses to get nervous and inactive though he faces grave troubles in his occupation, sometimes challenged by troubles connected to his family. He manages the affairs through tact. Sex appeals to him. While Ketu in the eighth house in Gemini, the native experiences great unhappiness and remains disturbed from a weak lifespan. He has a clumsy daily routine, suffers from diseases in anus or stomach. Ketu in the ninth house in Cancer, triggers the native's restlessness with his destiny. The native experiences much hesitation in handling and supporting his inherent duties. He adopts good, strong methods to his advantage, so he can rise above mediocrity and realize his destined fate. With Ketu in the tenth house in Leo, the native faces obstacles in his status, position and standing. Success comes late in life. With courage in his heart, he works patiently. Having Ketu in the eleventh house in Virgo, the native pays attention to only those that serve his selfish needs not caring for what's good or bad."

❖ Scorpio Ascendant, Transits

"As far as age, stomach diseases, and other similar issues, the native must keep an eye on when Mercury occupies Gemini, Virgo, Scorpio, Sagittarius, Capricorn, Aquarius or Taurus, or when Jupiter occupies Gemini, Aquarius, Libra or Sagittarius, or when Saturn occupies Gemini, Virgo or Aries, or when the Sun occupies either Gemini or Sagittarius, or when Rahu occupies Gemini, or when Mars occupies either Pisces or Scorpio or Leo, it accelerates recovery from the stomach diseases, increases longevity and elegance in the daily routine of life. Regarding physique, handsomeness, will-power and fame, the practitioner must keep a watch on when Mars occupies Scorpio, Leo, Taurus, Virgo, Capricorn, Aquarius, Pisces or Aries, or when Jupiter occupies either Scorpio, Pisces, Cancer, or when Saturn transits Scorpio, or when Mercury occupies Gemini, it results in physique enhancement, fame, handsomeness, will-power and honor. When Saturn occupies Aquarius, Taurus, Sagittarius, Virgo, Cancer, Leo, Scorpio or Capricorn, or Moon is in Aquarius or Leo, or Jupiter occupies Leo, or when Mars or Jupiter occupies Aquarius, it facilitates the native to influence the mother's happiness, and enjoy land and buildings. When Sun occupies Leo, Virgo, Scorpio, Sagittarius, Aquarius, Pisces, Cancer, Capricorn, Aries or Taurus, or Jupiter is in Leo, Sagittarius, Aquarius or Aries, or Mars is in Leo, Capricorn, or Taurus, or Moon occupies Leo or Aquarius sign, it raises honor and prestige and accelerates progress of matters connected with government, society, father and big business."

❖ Sagittarius Ascendant, Graha Sun

"Sun, as ruler of house 9, pledges an ethical and spiritual orientation on the Sagittarius native. It is very auspicious. Sun in the first house in Sagittarius, makes the native fortunate and handsome. The person ardently obeys his intrinsic-duties, enjoying the benevolence he gets in return. He possesses an untarnished faith in god, his influence is distinct in the matters connected with spouse and family. Besides, he is very influential and illustrious. Sun in the second house in Capricorn, resolves not the problems faced by the native involving family matters. Blessed with long life, the native negates his solemn-duties, giving more importance to money than to dharma. He spends his life in a civilized manner and is not short of fortunes. With Sun in the third house in Aquarius, the native supports the solemn-duties and works with great courage, but is weak in his diligence. He gets to be famous and fortunate. Sun in the fourth house in Pisces, makes the native highly fortunate. Happiness, he receives from others. He is often involved in doing something nice. Sun in the fifth house in Aries, makes the native wise and learned, equips him with the right knowledge on intrinsic duties. The person is farsighted, learned, clever and fortunate. Sun in the sixth house in Taurus, distresses the native in matters regarding his fate and destiny. He lacks the motivation to abide by his solemn-duties. The combination gives him the power to subdue several mishaps and wrestling back control over diseases. The sign makes him influential. With Sun in the seventh house in Gemini, the native marries a gorgeous and influential partner. Luck favors him. He is powerfully industrious. Having Sun in the eighth house in Cancer, gives the native a weak destiny, though he spends his life in a decent and influential way. The stellar combination increases his longevity. Sun in the ninth house in Leo, makes the native fortunate and illustrious, who backs in a fiery way the solemn-duties. While Sun in the tenth house in Virgo, makes the native fortunate. Great honors and respect come to him much from a predestined fate. The person abides by moral customs. Chances are he is an officer and harbors justice. With Sun in the eleventh house in Libra, the native does not experience much gains. His management of dharma falters. Sun in the twelfth house in Scorpio, does not favor the native's destiny. Fortunes come to him late and after much trepidation. His faith in god stays low, what remains in his possession are a few worldly wisdoms."

❖ Sagittarius Ascendant, Graha Moon

"Moon, as ruler of house 8, brings out the native's profound emotionality that gives them an interest in what transcends death. Moon in the first house in Sagittarius, bequeaths the native with a long life. The person is not striking or handsome."

"Moon in the second house in Capricorn, pledges aristocracy to the native. He incurs family losses, but blessed with a long life, he works through many problems. Moon in the third house in Aquarius, the native confronts some loss in executing solemn-duties. He is a man with many strategies. He lives his life with joy and delight. Moon in the fourth house in Pisces, blesses the native with good longevity. Domestic troubles, and problems with general progress and honor are a setback to his happiness. Once rid of ailments in the belly region, he spends time in a carefree way. With Moon in the fifth house in Aries, the native spends his life in grandeur and dignity. Moon in the seventh house in Gemini, makes the native's domestic life unbearable. He gets a long age with some hidden trouble in the house of spouse. Moon in the eighth house in Cancer, gives the native a long life, and deep knowledge on the concentration techniques. He has the advantage of his heritage. Moon in the ninth house in Leo, the native is unable to manage his solemn-duties. It also bestows on him a long life. He finds a good means of livelihood and opposes troubles and obstacles with money and amassed fortunes. Moon in the tenth house in Virgo, promises the native a long age, who otherwise sticks to obscure methods. In the eleventh house in Libra, Moon gives the native a long life. Moon in the twelfth house in Scorpio, shortens the native's longevity. He wanders much and cannot get over his narrow-mindedness."

❖ Sagittarius Ascendant, Graha Mars

"Mars, as ruler of houses 5 and 12, shows the native's strong passion and creativity which, if afflicted, comes as losses through passion or progeny. Mars in the first house in Sagittarius forces the native to travel extensively though it weakens the native's physique. While other challenges intrigue the native, he still works with tremendous restlessness. Mars in the fourth house in Pisces, the native experiences loss of mother, some losses occur with the spouse. Breaks in his education continue, he settles in foreign places. Mars in the fifth house in Aries instigates the native into implicating others. Even without proper knowledge, he speaks confidently with conceit. Mars in the sixth house in Taurus gives the native a hot temperament and the power to suppress his enemies. Pitta climbs to elevated levels in such a combination. The person is far from modest. Having Mars in the seventh house in Gemini, deprives the native of sufficient education, while introducing body weakness. While Mars in the eighth house in Cancer, cuts short the life of the native. The native lives in secrecy and suffers from disorders in the anus region. Mars in the tenth house in Virgo, makes the native literate and wise, but makes him suffer from physical weakness. Mars in the twelfth house in Scorpio, brings the native tremendous losses from all around, diminishing his wisdom. His influence over enemies stays significant."

- **Sagittarius Ascendant, Graha Mercury**

  "Mercury, as ruler of houses 7 and 10, initiates power, prestige and social preeminence. Mercury in the first house in Sagittarius makes the native immoral, who attains useful knowledge of worldly affairs and achieves success in such materialistic gains. He is honorable, marries an influential person. He is clever and intelligent. Having Mercury in the second house in Capricorn assists the native in receiving large inheritance from the father. While he possesses a big family, he faces several challenges with the spouse and family. Though he craves for carnal pleasures, his wisdom is strong and clever he is. With Mercury in the third house in Aquarius, the native though conceited, is fortunate and wise. With Mercury in the fourth house in Pisces, the native faces dishonors, his family dealings become turbulent, and his relationship with the spouse turns bitter. His wisdom is twisted. Mercury in the fifth house in Aries gives wisdom to the native. With Mercury in the ninth house in Leo, the native is capable of doing well in executing his solemn-duties. Mercury in the twelfth house in Scorpio hinders the native in his quest for progress. He lazes and procrastinates; facing troubles in family."

- **Sagittarius Ascendant, Graha Jupiter**

  "Jupiter, as ruler of houses 1 and 4, is auspicious as the lord of the ascendant. Having Jupiter in the first house in Sagittarius, the native enjoys happiness and receives many honors. His body is bulky; he is a person of respect. The kapha bulk is evident in the person. Lover of peace, he has a strong sweet tooth; he savors the edible delicacies. With a comfortable occupation, he lives in his own place in happiness and comfort. With Jupiter in the second house in Capricorn, makes the native a money-freak, who would even risk his life for it. For him, nothing is more important than money, though he lives with respect. He develops physical weakness and bears family distress. Jupiter in the fourth house in Pisces gives the native a purpose in life, the energy to pursue it and a long life-span. In the fifth house in Aries, Jupiter makes the native wise, conceited, dignified and attractive. Jupiter in the sixth house in Taurus destroys the native's peace and happiness. With Jupiter in the seventh house in Gemini, the native marries someone beautiful and influential. Conceit overruns him. Jupiter in the eighth house in Cancer gives the native unique powers. It promises him elegance and splendor. While Jupiter in the ninth house in Leo, showers the native with fortunes. Possesses scientific knowledge, he still performs rituals. His faith in god is untarnished. The combination promises him attractive looks, wisdom and high success in education. With Jupiter in the tenth house in Virgo, the native is industrious and arrogant. While Jupiter in the eleventh house in Libra, promises the native happiness. He becomes an authority in education and blessed is his marriage with happiness. Jupiter in the twelfth house in Scorpio deprives the native of attractiveness."

❖ Sagittarius Ascendant, Graha Venus

"Venus, as ruler of houses 6 and 11, confirms a tendency towards excessive indulgence and extravagance. Venus in the first house in Sagittarius exposes the native to several diseases. He manages to suppress his enemies, having an uncontrolled passion for ornaments and the joy in acquiring materialistic things. Having Venus in the fifth house in Aries, the native gains much from his own acumen. With Venus in the sixth house in Taurus, the native acts astute, orderly and haughty. Venus in the seventh house in Gemini brings diseases to the native's spouse. He wins many honors; people know him for his astute methods. Venus in the ninth house in Leo brings only obstacles and troubles. The native, courageous and clever, takes advantages in the garb of dharma."

❖ Sagittarius Ascendant, Graha Saturn

"Saturn, as ruler of houses 2 and 3, exhibits a scheming instinct towards wealth. With Saturn in the first house in Sagittarius, the native is energetic and industrious, suffering from restlessness. Saturn in the second house in Capricorn also induces restlessness in the native. Saturn in the third house in Aquarius gives the native a bitter and rude speech. The native works under duress in staying up with intrinsic-duties, though he is industrious, with lots of courage. Saturn in the fourth house in Pisces, the native takes adequate measures to battle his ailments, but is physically restless. Having Saturn in the sixth house in Taurus, the native overturns diseases and problems, though he faces much confusion in his daily chores. Brave and conceited is the native. Saturn in the seventh house in Gemini weakens the native. The person is unable to support his intrinsic-duties. Wild passions run deep in him. With Saturn in the eighth house in Cancer, turns the native unhappy, whose education and intellect remain insufficient, but blessed is the native with a long life. The native possesses secret wisdom. Saturn in the eleventh house in Libra deprives the native of attractiveness. With Saturn in the twelfth house in Scorpio, the native cannot back the intrinsic-duties."

❖ Sagittarius Ascendant, Graha Rahu

"Rahu in the first house in Sagittarius adds to the native's woes, physical distress and worry. He lacks in handsomeness and bears signs and scars of physical blows. Corporeal risk to his body runs high. He often undertakes daring tasks, which all add to the hazard. With Rahu in the third house in Aquarius, the native acts energetic and works with courage. Rahu in the fourth house in Pisces makes the native unhappy. With Rahu in the fifth house in Aries, the native faces shortcomings in education, wherein he resorts to bitterness and secrecy. He showcases truth but cares not for truth."

"Rahu in the sixth house in Taurus makes the native influential. Endowed with adequate strength to suppress enemies, he cares not for hindrances and troubles. With Rahu in the seventh house in Gemini, the native marries an extraordinarily charming spouse and stays immersed in sexual pleasures. Rahu in the eighth house in Cancer, the native complains on stomach and anus, running into problems in the daily walk of life. Rahu in the ninth house in Leo creates anxieties in the native about his destiny. His destiny paved with hindrances, unexpected troubles and losses, he runs into weaknesses in fulfilling intrinsic-duties."

❖ Sagittarius Ascendant, Graha Ketu

"Ketu in the first house in Sagittarius makes the native tall, but not attractive. Vata dosha is predominant here. While brave, diligent, selfish and conceited, he is also superstitious and careless. With Ketu in the fifth house in Aries, the native worries a lot, he runs into several hurdles in acquiring proper education. Forever challenged with trying to make others understand his point of view, his speech gyrates with bitter talks and honest he is not, in fact, he acts selfish and obstinate. Ketu in the sixth house in Taurus, makes the native selfish and conceited, however, he is pleasantly brave. He devises new ways to control opponents and diseases by chalking out secret schemes. Ketu in the seventh house in Gemini debilitates the native who under duress earns his living with effort. With Ketu in the eighth house in Cancer, the native runs into big troubles in his life. He whines of problems with stomach and lower part of the body or anus. Worries haunt him and he acts rude and patient. Ketu in the ninth house in Leo makes the native worry about his destiny. Lacking in fame and respect, his faith in intrinsic-duties diminishes."

❖ Sagittarius Ascendant, Transits

"As far as age and stomach disorders are concerned, when Moon transits the signs of Cancer, Leo, Virgo, Libra, Sagittarius, Capricorn, Pisces, Aries, Taurus or Aquarius, or Sun occupies Cancer or Capricorn, or when Saturn is posited in the signs, or Venus occupies Cancer or Capricorn, it brings improvements to the subjects of age, daily routine and stomach. When Jupiter passes through Sagittarius, Leo, Aries, Gemini, Pisces or Virgo, or Sun occupies Sagittarius, or Mercury visits Sagittarius or Gemini, or when Saturn occupies Sagittarius, or Ketu is found in Sagittarius, or Moon in Cancer or Capricorn, the times are better for the physical body, fame, attractiveness and will-power. Jupiter, when he occupies Pisces, Virgo, Sagittarius or Leo, or Sun in Pisces or Virgo, or Venus visiting Pisces, it helps in matters regarding land, buildings, happiness and mother."

"When Mercury visits the signs Virgo, Libra, Sagittarius, Capricorn, Aquarius, Aries, Gemini or Leo, or Jupiter occupies Virgo or Pisces, or Saturn occupies Virgo or Sagittarius, it gives the native the power and advantage in matters regarding government, society, honor, fame and business."

❖ Capricorn Ascendant, Graha Sun

"Sun, as ruler of house 8, pushes Capricorn types towards excessive willfulness. Sun in the first house in Capricorn, makes the native suffer from physical illnesses. The native suffers from diseases like smallpox and syphilis. Such a combination is not detrimental to longevity, blessed he is with a long life. The combination is more damaging to the native's charm and attractiveness. Sun in the second house in Aquarius, empowers the native with a decent longevity. With Sun in the third house in Pisces, the native enjoys an influential life. He lives long, encountering a few shortcomings that inhibit fulfilling his intrinsic-duties. Having Sun in the fourth house in Aries, the native gets blessed with a long-life span. Pitta influences the age here, and the native spends much of his life in pleasure. He likes to be inactive, and when active, loves to hasten. Sun in the sixth house in Gemini, makes the native influential and arrogant. Blessed with a long life, he lives it with grace. Sun in the seventh house in Cancer, keeps the native worried, who runs into strange and dreadful endeavors. Having Sun in the eighth house in Leo, the native lives long under beneficence. Sun in the eleventh house in Virgo, promises the native a long age, who backs the intrinsic-duties in his own selfish way and lives a gentleman's life. While Sun in the tenth house in Libra, deprives the native of longevity. Sun in the eleventh house in Scorpio, helps the native achieve effective longevity. While Sun in the twelfth house in Sagittarius, has a damaging effect on the native's influence and aging. He also protests of ailments in the lower belly zone."

❖ Capricorn Ascendant, Graha Moon

"Moon, as ruler of house 7, shows the native's dire need for relationship. Moon in the first house in Capricorn, gives the native a pale complexion, but the combination works adversely for the spouse. In the second house Moon in Aquarius, affects the native's spouse in a negative way. Some unpleasantness creeps into the family. With Moon in the sixth house in Gemini, the native faces tremendous medical expenditure. Having Moon in the eighth house in Leo, the native bears mental suffering on account of family. With Moon in the ninth house in Virgo, the native gets married to someone fortunate, and turns towards spirituality. Moon in the eleventh house in Scorpio, gives the native mental restlessness in all dealings with the spouse. He is bitter regarding his education and intellect, which often comes up as anger in conversations."

❖ Capricorn Ascendant, Graha Mars

"Mars, as ruler of houses 4 and 11, shows the native's innate desire for property and income. Mars in the first house in Capricorn makes the native conceited and proud. Mars in the third house in Pisces gives the native honor and prestige and makes him carefree. With Mars in the eighth house in Leo, the native has a happy, long life. Mars in the ninth house in Virgo gives the native fortunate, joy and energy and the ability to enjoy fortunes. Having Mars in the eleventh house in Scorpio, gives the native the prospect to win over diseases and calamities."

❖ Capricorn Ascendant, Graha Mercury

"Mercury, as ruler of houses 6 and 9, shows their ambivalence towards principles and ideals. Mercury in the first house in Capricorn makes the native clever, fortunate, gentle and influential; well-founded is the person's faith in his intrinsic-duties. He suffers from minor ailments, nothing serious. With Mercury in the third house in Pisces, the native suffers from indolence. On a positive side, he considers his destiny as great. Enemies keep him on his toes. While Mercury in the fourth house in Aries, promises the native happiness in his destined route. The stellar combination also settles enmities. With Mercury in the fifth house in Taurus, the native possesses good knowledge of the intrinsic-duties and defuses his enemies. Mercury in the sixth house in Gemini, allows the native to maintain control over diseases, enemies and troubles. With Mercury in the eighth house in Leo, the native makes little progress traversing his rather weak destiny and weaknesses accompany his pursuit of his intrinsic-duties. The combination promises him a long life-span. Mercury in the ninth house in Virgo drapes the native with fortunes. His wisdom is his strength, which he uses to his gamble. He backs the intrinsic-duties well. Mercury in the tenth house in Libra brings the native influence, honor and fortunes. He supports the intrinsic-duties in his own selfish ways. Mercury in the eleventh house in Scorpio promises the native good education and intelligence making him powerful. Mercury in the twelfth house in Sagittarius, the native incurs problems with intrinsic-duties, which manifest as delays and worries in the person's fate."

❖ Capricorn Ascendant, Graha Jupiter

"Jupiter, as ruler of houses 3 and 12, shows the Capricorn tendency towards loss or sorrow that comes from the native's greed and manipulative attitude. Jupiter in the first house in Capricorn brings sufferings to the in form of physical ailments, which he tries to combat with an emaciated body. The spouse makes up a person's physical unattractiveness. Having Jupiter in the fourth house in Aries obstructs the native from getting any peace and happiness, rendering him restless. Jupiter in the fifth house in Taurus makes the native less nice-looking. The native is restless and shrewd."

"Having Jupiter in the seventh house in Cancer, the native suffers from physical weakness. With Jupiter in the eighth house in Leo, weakness engulfs the native. He is low on energy and strength. Jupiter in the ninth house in Virgo weakens the native's destiny and fulfillment of intrinsic-duties. The combination snatches away his attractiveness."

❖ Capricorn Ascendant, Graha Venus

"Venus, as ruler of houses 5 and 10, gives Capricorn much success if they adopt some poise and grace to their strong but often unrefined nature. The graha Venus is very auspicious for the native and forms a Raja Yoga. Venus in the first house in Capricorn transfers wisdom, shrewdness and respect to the native; setting a high bar, the native is involved in wonderful activities. He has an eye for exquisiteness and is a lover of astrology. Having Venus in the second house in Aquarius, the native enjoys good breaks of luck. He receives honors and respects. Venus in the third house in Pisces brings charisma and attractiveness to the native's demeanor. He enjoys the advantages that wisdom and education bring, but loses out on his fulfillment of intrinsic duties. Venus in the fourth house in Aries promises numerous advantages to the native. A lover of beauty and art, the native earns much respect. With Venus in the fifth house in Taurus, the native dives into political knowledge and loves the sarcasm and wit it offers. He loves interior decoration and splendor. Intoxication and substance abuse may corrupt his life. While Venus in the sixth house in Gemini, confers on the native power of education, which he uses to defuse his enemies. He has a handle over diseases. Venus in the seventh house in Cancer generates in the native many mental worries. Having Venus in the eighth house in Leo, the native bears the loss of his father and his education takes a back seat. He becomes very withdrawn. With Venus in the ninth house in Virgo, the native has a weak destiny, but he is privileged otherwise. Venus in the tenth house in Libra destines the native to becoming a judge or an attorney after rewarding him with a powerful education in law. A lover of beauty and art, his speech is dignified, and he carries influence. Vanity and conceit are what he must control. Having Venus in the twelfth house in Sagittarius, the native bears the loss of father and son. He remains lethargic and sluggish."

❖ Capricorn Ascendant, Graha Saturn

"Saturn, as ruler of houses 1 and 2, shows how intimately their self-sense gets bound to work and livelihood, they are often harsh in speech and forced to work hard in life. Saturn is generally auspicious as the lord of the ascendant. Saturn in the first house in Capricorn suggests aristocracy. The native indulges in expensive clothes and the likes. Honorable and having earned a name, he runs into opposition with family members."

"Saturn in the second house in Aquarius can turn the native into megalomaniac, who could risk everything for money. He is unhappy and restless. Saturn in the third house in Pisces makes the native influential and full of energy. He has a strong faith in god. Saturn in the fourth house in Aries affects negatively the happiness and peace of the native. While Saturn in the fifth house in Taurus, makes the native very handsome, wise, clever and learned. Having Saturn in the sixth house in Gemini, the native is influential and wins over enemies. He worries slightly and stays uneasy, which makes him less good-looking. The native has to learn to throw caution to the winds sometimes. With Saturn in the eighth house in Leo, the native gets a long life, but suffers from body ailments, residing in foreign countries. Saturn in the ninth house in Virgo, showers virtues and fortunes on the native who is handsome and spiritual. He knows how to combat diseases and make peace with enemies. Saturn in the tenth house in Libra makes the native very attractive. The person with his impressive looks is very influential, which gets him into trouble with the spouse. Saturn in the twelfth house in Sagittarius deprives the native of health, who with an emaciated body stays unhappy."

❖ Capricorn Ascendant, Graha Rahu

"Rahu in the first house in Capricorn, inflicts the native with physical perplexity, who feels intoxicated from some deficiency in his body. The native determines a secret and cryptic path to progress in an astute way. The native remains steady after going through many uncertainties. Rahu in the second house in Aquarius forces a family separation. Having Rahu in the third house in Pisces, the native becomes very influential and works with courage. Rahu in the fourth house in Aries deprives the native of pleasures and happiness. Disgusted, the native resorts to occult and hidden powers. Rahu in the fifth house in Taurus sways the native with intoxicants. When he is not under influence of substances, there comes tremendous clarity to his speech. However, the native cares little for truth or falsehood. Having Rahu in the sixth house in Gemini, the native becomes influential, winning over enemies. Diplomacy comes naturally to him, possessing wisdom and cleverness. He knows several techniques to combat diseases. Besides, he is egoistic, brave and insolent. With Rahu in the seventh house in Cancer, the native is of unstable mind. Rahu in the eighth house in Leo, keeps the native worried. He suffers from diseases in the lower belly region. Pain and suffering occupies his daily routines, diminished is the longevity. He works against his heritage and damages the bequeathed heirloom. Traveling to foreign countries does not help him the least. Rahu in the ninth house in Virgo, floods the native with anxieties. He faces challenges in his destiny, which causes unfulfilled intrinsic-duties."

❖ Capricorn Ascendant, Graha Ketu

"With Ketu in the first house in Capricorn, the native turns obstinate. He suffers from several wounds. Though he worries, yet cares not for disrepute. Somewhat a daredevil, he works and plays a passionate and selfish game. Ketu in the second house in Aquarius, challenges the native with severe mishaps. Ketu in the third house in Pisces makes the native energetic and a diligent worker. Faced with several failures of high severity, his strength is on the decline. Ketu in the fifth house in Taurus ensures the native stay steady in his wisdom, which he puts to use with some uncanny inner knowledge. He employs several clandestine, unknown methods and cares little for truth or falsehood. While Ketu in the sixth house in Gemini, instills fearlessness into the native. He is tough; fearful are his opponents of his onslaught. Just from his sheer strength and will-power, the native eliminates diseases and problems. Ketu in the eighth house in Leo, makes the native suffer from troubles and disorder in the lower belly region. While the native worries, his life span decelerates. Ketu in the ninth house in Virgo challenges the native's destiny. Something or the other makes him worry. He turns weak as a result. The native has access to secret, unknown powers. He cannot make the adjustments fine-tuned to fulfilling his intrinsic-duties."

❖ Capricorn Ascendant, Transits

"When Sun transits Leo, Virgo, Scorpio, Aquarius, Pisces, Aries, Taurus or Cancer, or when Mars occupies Leo, Capricorn, Taurus or Aquarius, or Mercury resides in Leo or Aquarius, or when Moon occupies Leo or Aquarius, comes a time, useful to matters like age, daily routine and maladies of the stomach. Saturn when it occupies Capricorn, Scorpio, Libra, Pisces, Cancer or Virgo, or when Venus transits Capricorn or Cancer, or Mars occupies Capricorn, Libra or Gemini, or Mercury occupies Cancer, or when Moon occupies Capricorn or Cancer, it ensures progress in matters like attractiveness, will-power and fame. The native progresses and remains happy with land, buildings, mother and happiness when Mars occupies Aries, Virgo, Libra, Scorpio, Capricorn, Pisces or Taurus, or Venus occupies Aries or Libra, or Moon gets posited in Aries or Libra, or Mercury in Aries or Libra, or Sun in Aries. Venus when it occupies Libra, Scorpio, Capricorn, Aries, Pisces, Cancer or Taurus, or Mars is transiting Libra, Pisces or Aries, or Saturn when it occupies Libra or Capricorn, or when Mercury transits Libra or Aries sign, or Moon when it occupies Libra or Aries, or Saturn when occupies either Leo or Aries, it brings in progress in matters concerning the father, positions, inheritance."

- **Aquarius Ascendant, Graha Sun**

"Sun, as ruler of house 7, in the first house in Aquarius, weakens the native. The native wins many an honor and possesses vigor. With Sun in the second house in Pisces, the native does valuable work for the community. While Sun in the third house in Aries, the native labors hard with a weak destiny and remains inefficient in executing his intrinsic-duties. Having Sun in the seventh house in Leo, the native experiences physical distress. Many of the problems manifest from excess sexual pleasures. Sun in the eighth house in Virgo, gives the native noticeable defect in organs. Native faces several challenges with predicaments and separation in the family. Sun in the ninth house in Libra, deprives the native of luck. There are challenges in fulfilling the person's intrinsic-duties. Sun in the eleventh house in Sagittarius, makes the native highly intelligent. Sun in the twelfth house in Capricorn, gives the native mental diseases and problems that delude him."

- **Aquarius Ascendant, Graha Moon**

"Moon, as ruler of house 6, in the first house in Aquarius, confers honors on the native. Moon also equips the native with tremendous power of concentration, and in the process, generates more confusions. It is prudent, the native resides in a warm region away from the freezing. Chances of mental disorders are high. With Moon in the second house in Pisces, the native suffers separation from family. He maintains a dexterous check on opponents and lives life notably. Moon in the third house in Aries, empowers the native with tremendous energy to do good and stay powerful. The power of concentration runs high. He easily suppresses the enemy and performs his intrinsic-duties well. While Moon in the fourth house in Taurus, pushes the native into playing the daredevil, but suffering from scarcities in peace and happiness. With Moon in the fifth house in Gemini, the native struggles from his defective speech, he stammers. Moon in the sixth house in Cancer, emboldens the native into acting brave, dealing with the opponents carefully, caring not for any dangers. He otherwise remains happy and carefree. He is an adversary to resist. Moon in the seventh house in Leo, makes the native suffer from distress. The native lives through some physical oppression. The spouse suffers from problems of the skin. With Moon in the eighth house in Virgo, the native stays stumped by enemies. Stomach troubles plague him. The native is of a disturbed mind. With Moon in the ninth house in Libra, the native remains anxious about his destiny. He is strong, energetic and peaceful. While Moon in the tenth house in Scorpio, brings hardships to the native. Life to him is difficult progress. He repents over all accumulated evils. With Moon in the eleventh house in Sagittarius, the native triumphs by suppressing his opponents. He is somewhat a daredevil and cares little for diseases and afflictions. Moon in the twelfth house in Capricorn, the native runs into heavy medical expenditures."

❖ Aquarius Ascendant, Graha Mars

"Mars, as ruler of houses 3 and 10, tilts the native's energy towards authorities and institutions. Mars in the first house in Aquarius offers the native incredible vigor. He possesses stamina and courage. His reproductive fluid is defective resulting in negative impact on progeny. While Mars in the second house in Pisces, brings the native respect, he is also given the ability to make progress on the path to destiny. Having Mars in the third house in Aries, the native wins over the enemy. The native stays dignified and energetic. With Mars in the sixth house in Cancer, the native is a restless person, possessing hidden powers. He destroys the enemy through acts of deceit. Mars in the eighth house in Virgo takes away the native's honor and respect. While Mars in the ninth house in Libra, makes the native fortunate. Having Mars in the tenth house in Scorpio, the native acts powerful, adorning expensive clothes and acting a legal expert. With Mars in the eleventh house in Sagittarius, the native finds success in the enemies' house and gets to wear fancy clothes and ornaments."

❖ Aquarius Ascendant, Graha Mercury

"Mercury, as ruler of houses 5 and 8, brings out the native's capacity of deep intelligence, philosophical thinking and understanding the mysteries of the psyche. Mercury in the first house in Aquarius gives the native a long life; he also has an easy life, good education and wisdom. While Mercury in the second house in Pisces, gives the native wisdom, whose speech is obstinate, but intellectually logical. Having Mercury in the third house in Aries, the very carefree native's longevity gets augmented. He speaks authoritatively and forcibly on worldly affairs. Mercury in the fourth house in Taurus promises the native an increase in longevity. The native spends a large period of his life intelligently and in comfort. With Mercury in the fifth house in Gemini, the native enjoys a long life, which he relishes with much wealth. He stays slightly baffled and suffers from mental distress. While Mercury in the sixth house in Cancer, has the native worried. He leads a modest, common day-to-day life. Threats on his longevity come intermittently. He faces many hindrances and disturbances in life, suffering from ailments in the stomach region. Positioning of Mercury in the seventh house in Leo, promises the native a good age, where he spends most of his daily routine in worldly and domestic affairs. He receives several honors. Mercury in the eighth house in Virgo gives the native a long age. The person has a shrewd tongue. Mercury in the ninth house in Libra promises the native a long life with lots of luck. Endowed with spiritual knowledge, his anxiety about his destiny does not diminish. Having Mercury in the tenth house in Scorpio, offers the native worldly knowledge. It also promises a good age and long life."

"Mercury in the eleventh house in Sagittarius gives the native advantage of longevity, honors and improvement in his daily chores. While Mercury in the twelfth house in Capricorn, weakens the native's longevity, increasing his restlessness."

❖ Aquarius Ascendant, Graha Jupiter

"Jupiter, as ruler of houses 2 and 11, is a great planet of wealth and income. Jupiter in the first house in Aquarius bequeaths the native with respect and honors of his body; gives him the advantage of education and satisfies his wants. He traverses the destined path. While Jupiter in the second house in Pisces, makes the native rich, respectable and influential. Jupiter in the third house in Aries, the native backs his intrinsic duties well. Fascinated by the human beauty, he indulges in sexual fantasies. He gains in many ways including clothes, ornaments, and wealth. With Jupiter in the fifth house in Gemini, while maintaining the dignity and solemn-duties with a wise, educated native who knows and speaks on things valuable and profits heavily. With Jupiter posited in the ninth house in Libra, the native earns wisdom, education, conceit and cleverness."

❖ Aquarius Ascendant, Graha Venus

"Venus, as ruler of houses 4 and 9, brings out the native's basic sensitive and spiritual nature. Venus is a very auspicious planet and confers a Raja Yoga. With Venus in the first house in Aquarius, the native enjoys happiness fueled by his good fortunes. He backs a proper implementation of his intrinsic duties. Divine support comes to him with ease. The combination packages both fame and enmity. With Venus in the second house in Pisces, the native suffers from a weak life span. Having Venus in the third house in Aries, the native progresses well in his destined path. While Venus in the fourth house in Taurus, ensures happiness for the native as he traverses the destined path and sponsors the rituals. Honor and prestige await him. Venus in the fifth house in Gemini, the farsighted native publishes articles on divinity. While Venus in the sixth house in Cancer, weakens the native's destiny. He faces opposition from others. Many obstacles lie in the path to peace and happiness. He distributes free medicines for specific diseases and helps patients in time of need. Venus in the seventh house in Leo offers the native favors and happiness. The native possesses a good physique. While Venus in the eighth house in Virgo, creates hurdles for the native in his quest for intrinsic duties. There are lapses in joy and happiness, and in fulfilling one's destiny. Success arrives late; he faces immense amount of restlessness in foreign countries."

"Venus in the ninth house in Libra makes the native fortunate, who is able to manage his intrinsic duties well. The person is famous and enjoys divine protection. He is farsighted, learned and clever. With Venus in the eleventh house in Sagittarius, the native acts moral, completes his education, speaks modestly and is farsighted, selfish and virtuous. Venus in the twelfth house in Capricorn deprives the native of happiness and weakens his destiny."

❖ Aquarius Ascendant, Graha Saturn

"Saturn, as ruler of houses 1 and 12, in the first house in Aquarius empowers the native with tremendous will-power and self-respect. The native earns good fame. While Saturn in the third house in Aries, the native tires easily, labors secretly; but is physically weak. He is of a short stature and not attractive. Saturn in the fourth house in Taurus empowers the native's influence, passing spiritual knowledge to him. He has a handsome physique, lives in much luxury. Though the combination negates his joy and happiness. While Saturn in the fifth house in Gemini, gives the native authority but offers little on education. All his knowledge is self-taught. Saturn in the sixth house in Cancer ensures what the native does is significant and earns the rewards of dignified existence. Some of this comes with some sort of dependence. He cares not for enemies. The person often acts selfish and unkind. Saturn in the seventh house in Leo, the native confronts much confusion in domestic life. He is of a short stature. The person is attentive to his solemn-duties. With Saturn in the eighth house in Virgo, the native possesses strength that does not show. He gets a long life. His activities are dangerous and he worries a lot. Saturn in the ninth house in Libra gives the native an attractive body and brings him fortunes. A typical 'Robin Hood', who plays merry, influences the enemies and is fearless. Having Saturn in the tenth house in Scorpio ensures the native does influential work. Respect and fame comes after many problems. Saturn in the eleventh house in Sagittarius brings the native fame along with defects in the physique. The age and life span are both questionable. Saturn in the twelfth house in Capricorn gives the native an emaciated body; he is attentive to his intrinsic duties, which he fosters well. Honors come to him from foreign places."

❖ Aquarius Ascendant, Graha Rahu

"Rahu in the first house in Aquarius is unfortunate to the native, imposing on him mysterious, physical deformities. The native faces many dangers and resorts to using secret methods. Whatever he works with is only intended to satisfy his selfish needs. While Rahu in the third house in Aries, promises the native secret strategies to serve his self-regard. Influential and energetic, he remains alert even when exposed to setbacks."

"Having Rahu in the fourth house in Taurus reduces the native's joy and sense of mirth. The native resorts to secret and perverted means to be happy. Rahu in the fifth house in Gemini poisons the native's mind with cunning and caustic ways. The person tries to fool and cheat others, caring not for truth or falsehood. With Rahu in the eighth house in Virgo, the native suffers from complaints in stomach and lower part of the body. Having Rahu in the ninth house in Libra, the native finds it hard to stay on track with destiny. Missing are any sorts of fame. He leverages the intrinsic duties to meet his selfish needs."

- ❖ Aquarius Ascendant, Graha Ketu

"Ketu here is all about 'secret and occult powers'. With Ketu in the first house in Aquarius, the native suffers from body defects. He acts very callous about doing anything for others. Having Ketu in the second house in Pisces, the native's family relations remain disturbed, with many a separation. While Ketu in the third house in Aries makes the native energetic and gives him courage. His strength suffers, however in the long run. Ketu in the fourth house in Taurus, makes it a challenge for the native to stay happy. He works with patience even in troubled times. With Ketu in the fifth house in Gemini, the native lives through dishonesty. He chalks out secret schemes, but with a weak education and a failing memory, he does not get far. While Ketu in the sixth house in Cancer, showers the native with victory over his opponents. Troubles bother him quite a bit though he remains unconcerned about enemies. When the going gets rough, he uses different schemes in suppressing the enemies. Ketu in the eighth house in Virgo is but a big blow to the native's longevity. He works fearlessly, even in alarming circumstances. Ketu in the ninth house in Libra deprives the native of fame and weakens his destiny. Ketu gives him powers in the secret. The native fails to shape up the intrinsic duties well. Ketu in the tenth house in Scorpio provides the native with secret power, through which he can deliver many things in patience. Even his courage remains hidden and internally stored. He is industrious though. While Ketu in the eleventh house in Sagittarius, gives the native the advantage of using secret powers to win big monetary gains. There is nothing right or wrong in his books as longs as he gets to enjoy the benefits. Having Ketu in the twelfth house in Capricorn, the native runs into large expenditures. This leads to distress and agony. Though endowed with many a secret power, he cannot curtail the spending."

❖ Aquarius Ascendant, Transits

"When Mercury passes over Gemini, Leo, Libra, Scorpio, Sagittarius, Aquarius, Aries or Taurus, or Jupiter transits Gemini, Libra, Aquarius or Sagittarius, or when Mars occupies Gemini, Scorpio, Sagittarius or Pisces, or Sun enters Gemini or Sagittarius, or when Venus occupies Gemini or Sagittarius, or Rahu transits Gemini, or Saturn occupies Gemini, it results in overall happiness. Then again, when Mercury occupies either Leo, Virgo, Scorpio, Aquarius, Libra, Aries, Taurus, Gemini or Sagittarius, or Jupiter gets posited in Virgo, Pisces or Taurus, or when Mars occupies Virgo, Gemini, Aquarius or Pisces, it creates beneficial progress and happiness around matters concerning age and body mid-region. Physique, beauty, will-power and fame are on the rise during Saturn's transit through Aquarius, Scorpio, Libra, Gemini, Sagittarius, Leo or Taurus, or Mars posited in Aquarius, Leo or Scorpio, or Jupiter occupying Aquarius, Gemini, Leo or Libra, or Venus' occupation of Aquarius or Leo, or Sun's occupation of Aquarius or Leo, or Mercury in Virgo. During the time when Venus occupies Libra, Scorpio, Sagittarius, Aquarius, Pisces, Aries, Taurus, Gemini or Leo, or when Mars occupies Libra, Aquarius, Taurus or Scorpio, or when either Moon or Sun occupies Taurus, it promises gains, happiness and peace. During the days and years in the calendar when Mars occupies Gemini, Leo, Libra, Scorpio, Sagittarius, Pisces, Aquarius, Aries or Taurus, or when Jupiter occupies Taurus, Pisces, Scorpio or Cancer, or when Venus occupies Taurus or Scorpio, there comes a rise in honor, prestige, faith, big business and overall paternal happiness."

❖ Pisces Ascendant, Graha Sun

"Sun, as ruler of house 6, in the first house in Pisces, makes the native suffer physical distress; he remains handicapped and shackled. Having Sun in the third house in Taurus, the native is easily fatigued from any physical work. While in the fourth house in Gemini, the native is deprived of happiness. He turns violent. While Sun in the eighth house in Libra, the native suffers from tremendous restlessness that may owe to many hindrances. He complains about disorders in stomach below the navel and encounters severe mishaps at times. Sun in the ninth house in Scorpio, interferes with the native's destiny and his fulfillment of intrinsic duties. While in the tenth house in Sagittarius, the native faces impediments in his strive for peace and happiness. Sun in the twelfth house in Aquarius, makes the native arrogant and prone to bouts of anger."

❖ Pisces Ascendant, Graha Moon

"Moon, as ruler of house 5, brings out its natives' strong creative intelligence. Moon in the first house in Pisces, gives the native the ideal strength of mind, providing depth in his speech and communication. With Moon in the second house in Aries, the native finds happiness in life, stays wealthy and respectable. Moon in the third house in Taurus, dissuades the native from performing his intrinsic duties and makes him stray from his faith in god. Moon in the fifth house in Cancer, makes the native wise and learned, who portrays many convincing ideas and balancing principles. Gentle he is, with a stable mind. Moon in the seventh house in Virgo, brings out the astuteness in the native. He otherwise has a happy disposition. With Moon in the eighth house in Libra, the native suffers from several diseases. Moon in the twelfth house in Aquarius, makes the native suffer defects in the eyes, besides a weak memory. The native suffers restlessness, fears a little and is of unstable mind."

❖ Pisces Ascendant, Graha Mars

"Mars, as ruler of houses 2 and 9, is the native's planet of grace and fortune. Mars is very auspicious in such combination. Mars in the first house in Pisces inculcates in the native the powers to live and abide by his intrinsic duties, wherein fortunes shower on him. He enjoys the pleasures of family life and lives well. With Sun in the second house in Aries, the native renews his faith in god and runs into much fame. While in the third house in Taurus, the native manages his intrinsic duties well. In the fourth house in Gemini, the native fulfills all sacred formalities and grows into being fortunate. While Mars in the fifth house in Cancer, brings to the native weaknesses in his connections to his intrinsic duties. With Mars in the ninth house in Scorpio, the native though fortunate, lives the live of a devotee."

❖ Pisces Ascendant, Graha Mercury

"Mercury, as ruler of houses 4 and 7, in the first house in Pisces, encircles the native with a slim body and helps him progress in occupations which involve hard physical labor. In the second house in Aries, the native finds happiness even in performing his daily chores. While in the third house in Taurus, the native gets to live in comfort. Mars in the fifth house in Cancer, brings physical weakness to the native. While Mars in the eighth house in Libra, deprives the native of happiness, but confers a sustainable life span on him. He finds happiness even in the mundane, daily grind of life. Mars in the twelfth house in Aquarius, the native suffers shortage in happiness and comforts."

❖ Pisces Ascendant, Graha Jupiter

"Jupiter, as ruler of houses 1 and 10, is benefic as the lord of the ascendant. Jupiter in the first house in Pisces provides the native with dignity and a host of both worldly and divine qualities. He has a good physique and lives majestically. Jupiter in the third house in Taurus, the native nurtures the intrinsic duties and values. While Jupiter in the fourth, he remains happy and strong, enjoying a long life. Jupiter in the fifth house promises the native tremendous strength of wisdom. His knowledge runs deep, and he acts learned, being an influential orator, and supporting the intrinsic policies and values. Jupiter in the seventh house in Virgo, makes the native very attractive. Jupiter in the eighth house in Libra gives the native an emaciated body and hurdles in progress. In the ninth house in Scorpio, Jupiter makes the native fortunate, spiritual and just. Soft spoken and attractive, he commands a strong will-power. There is purity in his heart. Jupiter in the twelfth house in Aquarius gives the native an emaciated body and restlessness."

❖ Pisces Ascendant, Graha Venus

"Venus, as ruler of houses 3 and 8 in the first house in Pisces, makes the native tall, diligent and energetic, and adds many years to his long life. With Venus in the second house in Aries, the native lives long and in aristocracy. With Venus in the third house in Taurus, the native lives long, though he differs from all intrinsic values and duties. While with Venus in the fourth house in Gemini, the native enjoys the promise of a long life, but faces difficulties in finding any happiness around him, eventually finds contentment in a foreign country. While with Venus in the fifth house in Cancer, the native receives a long age. Venus in the sixth house in Leo, gives the native diseases of the stomach. In the seventh house in Virgo, the native worries on account of family and spouse, faces mishaps and bears the loss of brothers and sisters. He is rewarded with a long life, but suffers from a poor sex life. Venus in the eighth house in Libra increases the native's longevity, bringing lots of happiness, with it also comes substantial loss of energy. He bears the anguish of the passing of brothers and sisters. In the ninth house in Scorpio, the native attains great joy. In the tenth house in Sagittarius, the native receives an elegance in aging and the honors from undertaking very difficult tasks. Venus in the eleventh house in Capricorn confers on the native, a long life. Venus in the twelfth house in Aquarius, deprives the native of longevity and makes him suffer from restlessness."

❖ Pisces Ascendant, Graha Saturn

"As owner of houses 11 and 12, Saturn in the first house in Pisces, makes the native physically and internally weak, but seem well from the outside. Saturn in the third house in Taurus, the native is highly energetic, but has poor fame and physical strength."

"With Saturn in the fourth house in Gemini, the native experiences exceptional courage. While in the fifth house in Cancer, the native bears separations in the family. Saturn in the seventh house in Virgo gives the native anxieties in executing the intrinsic policies and duties and makes him unhappy. Saturn in the eighth house in Libra, the native spends life happily, enjoying a long life. In the twelfth house in Aquarius, the native turns restless in matters concerning family affairs but is able to overcome such difficulties."

- ❖ Pisces Ascendant, Graha Rahu

"Rahu in the first house in Pisces, overwhelms the native with anxieties and physical deficiency. The body experiences many a shock and wound. In the fourth house in Gemini, the native faces misfortunes and hindrances. While in the fifth house in Cancer, the native faces mental and intellectual worries, unraveling difficult problems with ease. Rahu in the sixth house in Leo, the native cares little about diseases and musters up the courage to face such mishaps. With Rahu in the eighth house in Libra, the native suffers diseases below the stomach and is short on longevity. Rahu in the ninth house in Scorpio, the native confronts many hurdles in destiny, in executing intrinsic policies and duties, in his fate and fame. While in the tenth house in Sagittarius, the native is on the road to deterioration."

- ❖ Pisces Ascendant, Graha Ketu

"Ketu in the first house in Pisces wounds the native quite fatally, subjecting the native through setbacks as he passes through several dangerous times. The native lacks any physical beauty. While Ketu in the second house, the native labors under intense pressure and family duress. Ketu in the third house in Taurus, gives the native an impressive physical strength and the courage to face many misfortunes. While with Ketu in the fourth house in Gemini, the native is short on happiness and constantly heckled by neighbors and colleagues. With Ketu in the fifth house in Cancer, the native faces mental anxieties right from a young age. While Ketu in the sixth house in Leo, the native labors very hard and overcomes many obstacles. His strength is a secret. Besides, he acts selfish and obstinate. While Ketu in the eighth house in Libra, turns the native impatient while dealing with mundane, daily routine. He suffers from stomach disorders where health and longevity get reversed. With Ketu in the ninth house in Scorpio, the native is short on fulfilling intrinsic duties and policies. He works very hard, shows signs of restlessness and has the inclinations of an atheist. In the tenth house in Sagittarius, the native works fearlessly, without reserve. His activities deserve merit, which he executes through secret powers."

❖ Pisces Ascendant, Transits

"Ailments and disorders of the mid-region disappear when Saturn occupies Leo, Libra, Capricorn or Aries or when Mars gets posited in Leo, Libra, Capricorn or Aries, or when Mars occupies Libra, Pisces, Aries or Cancer, or when Mercury moves to Libra or Aries, or when Venus occupies Libra, Aries, Scorpio, Sagittarius, Capricorn, Pisces, Taurus, Gemini or Cancer, or when Jupiter occupies Virgo or Aries, or when Moon gets to occupy Libra or Aries. These are also times when health and longevity are under no duress and stress and any progress towards health improvement turns into success. Physique and beauty, will-power and fame come to fruition during the years and months when Jupiter occupies Pisces, Cancer, Virgo, Scorpio, Sagittarius or Gemini, or when Mars occupies Sagittarius, Pisces or Virgo, or when Moon occupies Pisces or Virgo, or when Venus moves into Pisces, Taurus or Libra. Progress, peace and happiness favor the native when Jupiter occupies Sagittarius or Gemini, or when Mars moves into Gemini or Sagittarius, or when Moon goes through Gemini or Sagittarius, or when Rahu occupies Gemini, Sagittarius, Virgo, Capricorn, Scorpio, Taurus or Cancer. Social progress, happiness, success from authoritarian sources come when Jupiter is in Sagittarius, Pisces, Aries, Gemini, Virgo or Scorpio, or when Mars occupies Sagittarius or Gemini, or when Mercury moves to Sagittarius or Gemini, or when Moon occupies Sagittarius or Gemini, or when Ketu is in Sagittarius."

Graha-s and signs

A graha that rules a sign
rules also the graha-s in the sign.
On the graha ruled,
ruling graha imposes many a guideline.

Dignity is an expression of such leadership,
The graha ruled loses its form to its lord and captor.
where it stays positioned,
the sign ruler becomes the sign's dispositor

When two lords occupy one another's sign,
the exchange is solid and mutual.
Such dispositor-s become very strong,
when the lords are friends and neutral.

"Signs embody the field of activity. Graha-s exemplify the forces in operation within that field. Signs uphold the integrity and their iconic meaning regardless of graha-s resident in them or casting aspect on them. Similarly, the graha-s sustain their meaning, regardless of the field or sign in which they act. Simply put, the character and personality of the graha-s and signs are immutable, but influenceable. Some other graha that may be influencing it does not determine its field of activity. Nor is the nature of the graha determined by the field of activity. It's like a physical house whose curb appeal has nothing to do with a landlord, tenants or visitors. Imagine a person living in a house; the person does not decide the nature of the house, nor is the person determined by the house's nature. They influence one another. While the person may alter, or damage the house, the house may limit the person's activity. The sign shows the field's character while, the house shows its effect on the outer world."

Graha is the source of light in a sign
Promising results from its nature n' lordship
When the occupant rules the fourth house
Gains from mother and property are sure to rip

"First house is the moment of birth, it is the hour of a terrestrial manifestation of something physical - our physical body. The sign marking it shows the field through which we project our energy to the outer world. For example, an Aquarius ascendant projects Aquarius energy, a quiet, expressive, aerial, willful field that marks the field of general life action. If, however, Aquarius is the seventh house, that expressive Aquarius field will mark the sphere of relationship and these traits will more likely occur in the partner or spouse."

"Graha-s that aspect the sign can change the quality of the force working behind it. Remember graha-s or planets aspect by being in a sign, being opposite the sign or for Jupiter, Mars and Saturn from different angles."

"The house provides the fixed coordinates, the sign and graha-s provide the revolving character. In the end, the houses matter as most important."

"Someone may have many strong planets in Aries in their birth chart, like the Sun, Mars and Jupiter, but without being posited in a strong house barring sixth, eighth or twelfth or in signs of debilitation, it will not be possible for them to manifest that strength in the outer world. Graha-s represent the energy the individual manifests within the field of activity represented by the sign."

"There are many discernments the astrologer must make in combining sign, house and planetary influences to arrive at something conclusive. The signs show the nature of the Kshetra[219]; the planets show the quality of energy operating within that Kshetra. Ruler of the sign has the strongest energy to influence it. When the ruler of a sign runs an aspect on its own sign or the placement becomes powerful, the field and force operating within the sign gets the same character and strength. If the nature of the sign and that of planets that aspect it is similar to the ruler of the sign, the sign gains more strength."

"Aries ascendant under aspect of the Sun and Mars or Aquarius ascendant influenced by Saturn and Mercury stays strong because the sets have friends as graha-s. However, if the two sets exchange their aspect to natural and temporal malefic graha-s, there comes the weakening. Of course, this general rule has exceptions. As the ruler of the sign is only one planet among many, other planets jointly overcome its influence. For this reason, individuals may have a quality of energy or body type different from the predominant element of the Ascendant."

"It is better to balance the nature of a sign by the planetary influences on it. The latter possess the power to overcome and change the former. This does not mean we take the character of the signs lightly, but that their capacity to project energy does not have the same unchangeable symptoms as their determination on what field the energy works on."

"This rule has many basic practical considerations. Physical constitution remains influenced by the planets most influencing an aspect on the ascendant, or placed well while associating with it. Whatever planets aspect a sign it still does not lose its nature as determining a specific field of manifestation. Ascendant determines the field of material manifestation, the field of the physical body, but not necessarily the quality of its energy. The Moon sign determines the field of social manifestation, the field of the astral body comprising mind and emotion, namely the memory. However, the practitioner must consider the influences on the Moon and the Moon sign to work out mental and emotional temperament."

"Sun sign determines the field of individual manifestation, the private or inner level, the field of the causal body comprising the power of will and intelligence, ego and self. The practitioner must also consider influences on the Sun and the Sun sign determine the level of development of the soul."

---

[219] Kshetra is a field, representing a system that is bounded. It has distinct borders.

"The practitioner must examine other planets in the same light, discriminating between fields and forces. Planets are usually stronger than signs with their projections. Though the fields the signs represent, they do not get canceled by the planets that aspect them."

Weak ascendants

"Persons with strong ascendants project the sign's energy and the ruling graha's power. A weak ascendant reflects the field of the sign but not the quality of its force. Often when a weak ascendant's influence rubs on to other people in the in the life of the native who may express the untarnished, original qualities. The individual with a feeble ascendant may work with, for or under stronger same-ascendant types. The ascendant would show their field of human communication and self-projection, but not the energy they develop. When examining a chart, many issues come up and all the different factors may confuse and contradict. It is important to proceed gradually, from the primary to the secondary, finding out the general factors, the ascendant, Moon and Sun and see what is obvious in them and then go into greater detail. These major factors do not get altered by minor factors but only adjusted by them. In this way, the mass of planetary data will not confuse you. Nature has set many patterns, patterns show the way out from cluttered data and any anti-patterns thereof."

"In judging the chart, it is best to first work out the relative strengths of the ascendant and the Moon sign. If the chart shows ascendant as unblemished, but the moon in Taurus or Cancer enjoying the glances of Jupiter, Venus and Ketu in Scorpio, then the Moon sign is stronger than the ascendant, and one can safely count the houses from the Moon. Such a person is likely a watery type because of the strength of the Moon sign and the aspect of watery planets upon it. So, the first major choice to make is the relative weights to give the ascendant and Moon signs. Usually the ascendant has more weight but many exceptions exist; the ascendant counts for two-thirds and the Moon sign for one-third of any issue. If the same condition exists from the Moon as from the ascendant, then its results are more likely to manifest."

"As an example, if the seventh from the Moon and the seventh from the ascendant get afflicted by separative planets, then divorce is more likely. It is also prudent that houses get counted from the Sun. In this system, the ascendant counts for one half, the Moon sign for one third, the Sun sign for one sixth. Such a 'Sudarsana[220]' system or 'profound vision' gives a more complete assessment of the native."

Aspects

"Graha-s being together are not as powerful as the glances they get from their fellow graha-s. Yes, such effects from planetary aspects are much stronger. Conjunctions are truly not aspects in Vedic Astrology but associations. Aspects are stronger in determining the resulting good or bad than conjunctions. An aspect can nullify the effect of a conjunction. When three or more planets are conjunct, this creates a powerful concentration of energy, particularly with Sun and Moon involved that can be more significant than any aspect. It becomes another Ascendant, often more important than the rising sign."

"All planets from the four Kendra positions to the Ascendant influence the first house, just like an aspect does. In this regard, planets in the fourth house cast a stronger aspect on the ascendant than graha-s in the first house, those in the seventh even stronger than in the fourth, and those in the tenth the strongest. Planets become stronger when they are in their own signs or with those of their own element or when together with like-minded planets. The closer planets are in degree to exact aspects and conjunctions, the stronger their action."

House and sign positions

"While reiterating the importance of house position over sign position, it is also important to remember that each has its own weight. Good sign position will give many good results, bad house position will give few bad results and vice versa. Regular birth chart, sign chart or Rasi chakra, is a generalized chart."

---

[220] Sudarsana means a higher, explicit vision.

"It remains the same for people born within the same hour or two. Sometimes it even gets repeated for people born the day before or after at the same hour. This is because the Moon stays in the same sign for two and a half days. We cannot rely upon the Rasi chart alone for great accuracy. Those who read specific events from the Rasi chart alone are relying upon intuition because the Rasi chart is common to several thousands of people. Rasi chart is not enough to determine physical constitution. It shows major tendencies, at best 60% accurate. We must, therefore, examine other factors than the basic birth chart before making primary determinations. Birth chart shows us the general field of energies in operation but not their specific manifestations. It is preferable to use the Navamsa along with the basic birth chart. Navamsa Ascendant is an important factor for determining the physical constitution; though with the generally approximate birth times we often have we cannot always be sure of it."

"It is helpful to examine the planet degrees in a chart, the closeness of aspects, and the bhava or house chart along with the positions of the mid-heaven and nadir, which require specific degree positions. Aspects that are almost exact have a special power. Aspects that occur in the Navamsa chart a in the birth chart possess special power. The closer the aspects, the more likely they also occur in different divisional charts. This is true for conjunctions. Examine the Drekkana along with Rasi and Navamsa for all general indications. Two people with the same Rasi but different Drekkana have very different charts. One can be certain of the Drekkana even when the Navamsa itself may be in doubt because of an uncertain birth time. The Drekkana remains same for a period of about forty minutes, while the Navamsa changes every thirteen minutes."

Graha forte

"Practitioner must determine the strength of planets by sign, house and divisional positions, and by directional strength and by aspect. A planet can only give the results it promises, if it has the power to do so. Elaborate calculations to determine exact planetary strength exist, as under Shadbala. Such calculations obscure the obvious. If Moon is under aspect of Mars, Saturn and Rahu and weak in its brightness, it will not yield good results whatever its Shadbala or other strengths. It is important to learn the obvious first and not to consider bewildering calculations, which are only a matter of fine-tuning. Aspect strength overrides positional strength. Mercury in Virgo will not work well if under aspect of several malefic graha-s."

"In addition, house strength overrides sign strength. For example, Jupiter in a bad house, like the twelfth even in its own or exalted sign, will still create few problems. On the other hand, Jupiter debilitated in a good house like the ninth or tenth will still give benefits."

"Readings of charts require synthesizing many factors in order to arrive at any results definite. It is best to ask the native what he really wants to know. If he has too many queries, he needs to prioritize. Explain to the person why it is difficult to arrive at all answers and let him also know what it costs. First comes the sign position of the graha-s. This relates more to the soul or inner dimension. Sign lordship, exaltation and debility in particular, reveal a lot. So, does the house position."

"This shows their outer dimension or potential to manifest in the material world. Most important are benefic graha-s in angles and trines and malefic graha-s in Upachaya houses. Above all, note the groupings of planets and their indications as house lords. Try to find out the main pattern of planetary influences that exists in the chart. Determine the dominating or most characteristic planet, its allies and its opponents. There are no absolute rules of chart interpretation. Everything depends on our capacity to read the pattern of the chart according to the logic of how the main indicators function. Learn the language and the logic of astrology but accept no rules as final. As interpretation depends upon the synthesis of all factors, no rule applied in blind. Do not approach astrology with a sense of awe but one of experiment and creativity. It is a system with much to offer but also with much unwanted inertia that needs clean up. One cannot expect the combinations that produced certain results in ancient times to do the same thing today though a certain energy type may remain the same."

"When cluttered are most graha-s during the day, above the horizon in diurnal zone, the day aspect comes out strong. Houses seven through twelve and portion of the ascending sign represent the daylight zone. This creates an outgoing, materially, political nature because the planets are in the visible half of the chart. The individual will be social or work oriented, communicative but everything stays superficial. They reveal themselves easily and make their lives a public affair. It will be difficult for them to keep secrets or to be uninfluenced by their social environments. Those evolved spiritually express their piety through work or communication. They get drawn into public activity, even though their basic nature as revealed by the signs may be more private."

"In the chart, an uneven distribution of graha-s in house one through seven only, below the horizon in nocturnal zone specifies a nocturnal character. This creates an introverted or inward nature because the planets are in the invisible half of the chart. In the chart, an uneven distribution of graha-s in house the individual stays withdrawn, unexpressive or not revealing of their true feelings or motivations. They hide things, keep things close to themselves and can be hard to understand. More evolved types get drawn towards meditation. While successful in the outer world, they work behind the scenes, sometimes through other people."

"Dispersal of all or majority graha-s in eastern half makes the individual self-motivated, individualistic and self-expressive because planets are in the eastern or personal side of the chart. They may become selfish, egoistic or just individualistic. They talk at length on themselves and act impulsive. Relationships may prove difficult for them. With distribution of all or majority graha-s in western half, implying the predomination of planets in the relationship side of the chart makes the person relationship oriented. They define themselves by the people with whom they are in partnership. Self-identity and self-worth may be difficult to establish. They will find it difficult to stand on their own. However, their aggressiveness in relationships promises to be quite pronounced."

"Duality is the essence of life. One can outline such prime dualities of life in relationship between the houses, between each house and its opposite. Planets in opposite houses reflect these prime issues. Rahu-Ketu axis does this being always in opposite houses."

"First and seventh houses are the first set of opposite Kendra positions. These are the houses of self and other. Planets here show issues in relationship and self-identity. When the planets involved are of harmonious nature, they show harmony of self and partner. When the planets are of conflicting nature, they show conflict between the self and other, between personal drives and relationship needs."

"Second and eighth houses are the houses of personal and collective resources. They show material and financial issues. Gravely disposed, they show the loss of personal resources to groups, organizations or to society at large. Well disposed, they show both personal and collective gains. These are also houses of personal and collective expression. They can show conflict of expression with the partner. They can also show the ability to communicate on both personal and collective levels. Afflicted, they can give health problems because the eighth is the house of death and the second a death-dealing or Maraka house."

"Third and ninth houses are houses of dharma, vocation and motivation. The third shows our basic energy, drive and curiosity, what we like to do of our own accord when not seeking any collective goal. The ninth shows the principles we stand for in the world. It shows what we think is our duty, what we feel a responsibility or calling to do for the benefit of the world. The third is what we like to do and represents following our own personal motivations. Issues between these houses are from a conflict between the personal and social usage of our energies, personal interests and enthusiasms versus collective and spiritual responsibilities. Harmony between these two houses shows a harmony of desire and duty, of personal will and spiritual purpose."

"Fourth and tenth houses are the second set of Kendra opposites - private achievements vs. successes in public. These are houses of the private life versus the public life, of personal identity versus social roles. Here the issues of individual needs versus social responsibility come out. Some of these are similar issues to the third and ninth houses, but for those houses it is a question of values and the usage of energy; for these houses, it is a question of home life and work life. Conflicts between the domestic and the work sphere come into play. Also vivid is the relationship between our hearts desire from fourth house and its public realization in the tenth house. It shows the relationship between desire represented by fourth house and karma from tenth house. Fifth and eleventh house are both houses of gain, expansion and creativity, the former in the personal sphere, the latter in the collective sphere. Issues here are those of creativity and self-expression. The fifth house shows our intelligence and creativity. The eleventh shows how we communicate and share it on a group or collective level. A conflict between these two houses shows a conflict between personal and public aspirations for the person."

"Sixth and twelfth are houses of negation and sorrow. The sixth house shows factors that negate our personal wellbeing; the twelfth house those which negate our social well-being. Issues between these houses relate to disease, enmity, sorrow and loss. On a higher level, these are the issues of service and surrender. This is a highly sensitive axis and malefic influences on this axis can cause much harm though malefic graha-s in the sixth house itself can be beneficial."

"Many graha-s in one sign or one zone shows an unbalanced person. When malefic graha-s get involved, they become stronger in such conditions. Too close a proximity among planets muddies the planetary rays. This combination can cause renunciation or loss regarding the domain of life represented by the house or sign involved. While many graha-s in even signs, implies more feminine, receptive and passive qualities and many planets in odd signs signify more masculine, active and aggressive qualities."

"With majority of planets in the first half of the chart keeps the native constantly changing his personal projection, initiation and manifestation, the first half of the zodiac being the personal sphere. The energy direction is from within to without. However, when the reverse is true and majority of planets are in the second half of the chart, it will keep the native in ever changing motion of completion, universalization and communication as the second half of the zodiac is the collective sphere. The activity direction here comes from outside to within."

"The closer the houses are to the ascendant on the nocturnal side, the more is the emphasis to the introvert side of the self. When majority of grahas occupy the first quarter of the chart as in houses 1 through 3, it indicates a self-motivated but often self-centered person, expressive and dynamic but perhaps lacking the capacity to hesitate or observe himself. The first quarter of the zodiac relates to our personal drives and urges. While most planets in the second quarter of the chart in houses 4 through 6, gives the native a strong sense of self, work and identity. The individual will be prominent in their work and create an issue of their personality. The second quarter of the zodiac relates to our mind and character. Then in the third quarter, with numerous planets clustered in the third quarter of the chart in houses 7 through 9, gives a strong sense of relationship, emotion and principle. The individual projects himself powerfully into relationship and social goals as the third quarter of the zodiac relates to relationship and emotion. Finally, when most planets get posited in the fourth quarter of the chart as in signs 10 through 12, the combination gives a more social or collective orientation but a tendency towards diffusion and loss of self-control. The individual is moving from the collective field toward immersion in himself. The fourth quarter of the zodiac is the collective realm."

"With most planets in moveable or cardinal signs makes a person move and change with ease both inwards and outwards, while maintaining a certain focus and direction, will and motivation. The person here seeks achievement, keeping the bar high. While most planets in fixed signs brings inward and outward fixation, making the person slow to change but persistent in what they wish to do. On the positive side, this gives endurance and stability, on the negative side it can cause stagnation and inertia. With most planets in mutable or dual signs, it makes a person ever changing, indecisive but flexible. They go back and forth and cannot hold to a fixed position or one consistent direction of movement. This works well in adaptability of mind but can create quite a bit of ambivalence and weakness in the character. While the mind is strong, the will turns weak."

"When many graha-s domicile zones dominated by the earth element, the combination keeps the native in the earth manifestation field, namely the body, making things for the practical world, outer achievements, or working with nature and the Earth element, which can extend to the physical body. Dosha factors are less evident than with the other elements. If many planets are in water-dominated signs, it keeps one in a sphere of water, which equates to emotional and intuitive manifestations, a strong feeling nature and regard for others. It can also promote Kapha dosha in body and mind. With many planets in fire signs, it keeps one in the fire field either as outwardly fiery occupations or inwardly as perceptive or willful personality. It can also promote Pitta dosha in body and mind. A person having many planets in air-signs keeps him in the air field, such as communication, intellectual or social activities. It promotes Vata dosha in body and mind."

From graha-s to the stars

"Nakshatra-s are an important part of this learning and a special feature of the system. They imply a 'way of approaching the Divine.' Nakshatra-s reflect the karma and aspiration of our souls and how we reciprocate to the influences of the heavens. As the ancient seers contemplated the heavens, they discovered the Nakshatra-s as our means of communicating with the cosmic influences behind our destiny. The Nakshatra-s known better as 'lunar mansions', 'lunar constellations' and 'asterisms', twenty-seven-Nakshatra-s mark the destination houses of the Moon, as the Moon spends one lunar-day in each. Therefore, they reflect a more intimate relationship with the heavens than the twelve signs. The graha-s in Nakshatra-s are computed from the sidereal zodiac system as they depend upon observable stellar positions. Celtics, Chinese and Arabs used similar systems of lunar mansions. Nakshatra-s are significant in the esoteric and yogic side of astrology as they contain the most ancient Vedic stellar and astrological knowledge. Vivid is their appearance in the Vedas, many deities get associated with them, while the twelve signs occur only in a sketchy manner. In fact, the original deities of the Vedas become identified through the Nakshatra-s. Nakshatra-s are important in mundane astrology, besides used to assess temperamental compatibility, as in marriage, business partnerships, also in determining favorable times to carry out regular activities. Knowledge of Nakshatra-s comprise the key essence of astrology. Nakshatra-s fine-tune and reflect the subtle aspect of planetary meanings. They do not contradict what gets revealed from the signs and houses but clarify it further."

Nakshatra-s

Seven elements manifest the living
On which the soul resides
Annam, prana, manas, vijnana, ananda,
Chit and sat[221] are the different shells

    Moon, deity of Smriti and Prajna, *rules* and *laws*
    Sun, Satyam lord, or *truth*
    Indra rules manas, *mind*; Vayu the Prana, *life-force*
    Mitra, Varuna, Aryaman, Bhaga rule *emotions* and *character strength*

Jupiter rules chit, tapas of knowledge
Brahma of sat, Agni of meditation
Seven graha-s and deities rule the Nakshatra-s
Above attributes decide native's inclination

    First Nakshatra is Ashvini, in line with Aries
    Ketu is the graha ruler, Ashvin is the deity
    The asterism has the basic attribute of Rajas
    Motivated to solemn-duties, principles and integrity

Ashvini natives' feel intense thirst for life
Desire for control and probe overwhelm
Anger, lust, reckless and impulse makes them negative
Quietude is uncharacteristic in them

    In Ashvini, the four quarters get ruled
    By Mars, Venus, Mercury and Moon in entirety
    The motivation is directed to solemn-duties, a male horse
    Symbol is a horse-head, Ashvini Kumar the deity

Ashvins are young, bright as lords of luster
Honey hued, brilliantly golden, beautiful, nimble
Fertility, eyesight, they cure the blind, the sick and maimed
Children are many, many forms in one symbol

---

[221] Annam (gross), prana (vital forces), manas (mind), vijnana (intelligence), Ananda (bliss), chit (awareness) and sat (pure being)

Bharani's basic attribute is Rajas
Focused directed activity, under Yama's rule
The primary motivation is wealth alone
The native, so sensitive, so insightful

Bharani recalls kind acts and help
Also, offenses taken
Restless, pique and stingy are their negative
They create on earth, a heaven

    For Bharani, Venus is the ruler, quarters ruled by
    Sun, Mercury, Venus and Mars
    Motivation is Artha, a female elephant
    Symbol is chalice, Yama is the deity of those stars

Yama, lord of the mountains
Every death is in his paw
Rides a buffalo, holds a staff
Versed in Shastra, he is, in the doctrines and the law

    Krittika shares Aries and Taurus
    Owned by the Sun, Agni presides
    Motivated towards earthly desires, Kama
    Feminine and passive, besides

In Krittika, Sun is ruler, quarters ruled by
Jupiter, Saturn, Saturn and Jupiter
Motivation is Kama, a female sheep
Symbol is a razor, deity Agni is the owner

    Agni is two or four armed,
    In his hand is a rosary, a Raja-Guna, a goat he does ride
    Shakti or intense power is his symbol
    Svaha, the wife seated on his left thigh

Rohini of many myths and stories
Moon owns the aster
Rohini is the consort of Rohit, ruddy Sun
Moon's wife, mistress, favorite paramour

    Rohini heightens indulgence, deity is Prajapati
    Levels above, a procreative force to reckon
    Levels of lower, id and sex
    Whatever Rohini does, imparts a sense of mission

AQUAPISCES

Moon rules Rohini, while Mars, Venus, Mercury, Moon
Quarters they rule, they make
Symbol is a chariot, deity is Brahma
Motivation is Moksha, noted as a male snake

> Brahma with four faces and four arms,
> Seated on a lotus-seat, he rides a goose with his potbelly,
> Holds a pot, a staff, a plate of ghee, four Vedas.
> Attend to him, Savita and Sarasvati

Mrigashira is a beginning, a new experience
Primary motivation is moksha, Rajas is its goal intense
Presiding deity is Soma
Aptitudes hover around sensitive, outward directed intelligence

> Krishna identifies himself with Mrigashira
> Initial point of manifestation
> Good things come to life
> Inertia leads to materialization

Mars rules Mrigashira, quarters ruled by
Sun, Mercury, Venus and Mars of the inner quadrant
Symbol is head of a deer, deity is Soma
Motivation is Moksha, a female serpent

> Soma is ambrosia, sap, blood in arteries
> Plant life and herb, dwelling place of the dead
> Deity of moon, Soma is rarely mortal
> Arrogant, war loving, adulterer is he instead

Ardra presided by Rudra, Rahu is the lord
Primary motive is desire, from a Rajas heritage
Unrestrained activity and fervor
Perceives reality with no foreknowledge

> A female dog is Ardra, symbol a head
> Rudra is so many things, howl and shine are the thrills
> Which is heaven and earth, the Upanishads
> Rudra destroys incest, fierce and feared, he kills

Punarvasu calls for greater action
Logical end to the material, lord Jupiter sets the stage
Provides for the onward journey of the soul,
Deity is Aditi, who rides a cat, symbol is a cottage

Aditi, mother of kings, with excellent sons
Vedic piety and spiritual sense
Brihaspati, guru of gods, holds a staff, lotus and beads
Naga lifts world on shoulders, ragged ascetic in penance

Pushya maps to Cancer, a male sheep
Brihaspati presides, ruled by Saturn, symbol is flower
Jupiter aids expansion, Saturn provides contraction
Combination stabilizes, energies shower

Aslesha is in Cancer, ruled by Mercury; symbol is snake
Presiding deity is Naga of the serpent kingdom
Deeply philosophical, force being solemn-duties
Thoughtful, austere, self-reliant and withdrawn

Ketu rules Magha, deity is Pitris, symbol is Palanquin
Motivation is Artha, a Tamas
Conflicts lead to tensions and frustration
An idealist amidst material affluence

Purva Phalguni ruled by Venus, motivated to Kama
Deity is Bhaga, Vedic god of bliss, a worldly story
Donates riches, affluence and material prosperity
Self-centered, seeks fame and glory

Uttara Phalguni ruled by Sun, motivated to Moksha
Deity is Aryaman, native seeks ambition
Difficulties and righteous struggle
Opportunity for growth and expansion

Pitris, spirits of ancestors, primeval deities who are eternal
Bhaga, wealth, marriage, powers given and taken in entirety
Aryaman, chief of manes[222], witness in a marriage
Savita, power and strength of the Sun, a sky deity

Hasta ruled by Mercury, which gets exalted in the sign
Savita is the deity
Natives face stiff resistance, with power to regenerate
Change, shape and flourish in plenty

---

[222] Chief of manes of the Milky Way

Chitra ruled by Mars, motivated to Kama, ruled by Tvashtar
Sufferings are such common trouble
Sufferings for a cause, for realization of the inner self
An impetus to build, to reach a new level

Swati ruled by Rahu, motivated to Artha
Presided by Vayu, the wind
Self-centeredness, hovers around personal gain
Not knowing what to want, always discontent

    Tvashtar, heaven builder, implementer of special weapons
    Chariot maker, Sukracharya's son ardent
    Vayu, wind god, who knows the way to heaven
    Indra, thunder god, rides the elephant

Vishakha ruled by Jupiter, motivated to Dharma
Two deities preside, Indra and Agni, Saturn exalts
Life's spiritual discontentment
So much infidelity, promises are false

    Anuradha ruled by Saturn, Mitra presides
    Several obstacles and struggles demote
    Latent powers start to manifest
    Endurance is the keynote

Jyeshta ruled by Mercury, presided by Indra
Communication portals with higher powers open
Remorse is none, even under poverty
High status in an elevated plane is proven

    Moola ruled by Ketu, marks the galactic center
    Deity is Nirriti of hidden realm
    Ends the material, begins the chosen path
    Directs the soul, inflicting pain

Purva Ashada ruled by Venus, presided by Apana
Where dwells the spirit in brevity
Intuitive, insight into the Divine Law
A believer, promises charity

    Uttara Ashada ruled by Sun, presided by Vishwadeva-s
    Means and powers for salvation
    There is no dearth of activity
    Humble or self-centered inflexion

Sravana ruled by Moon, presided by Vishnu
Leads one to meditate
Endures pain with an ear for cosmic words
Ready with the Supremes' knowledge

> Dhanistha ruled by Mars, presided by Vasus
> Motivational impulse is dharma
> Provides courage, strength and devotion, Saturn rules
> Patience and protection

Sat Bhishag ruled by Rahu, presided by Varuna
Hardships fulfilling the spiritual mission
Feminine nature, passivity or inertia
Aroused to action, comes speed

> Purva Bhadra ruled by Jupiter, presided by Aja Ekapada
> Independence with no consideration
> Whether for personal advantage or harming others
> Courage, martyrdom, dedication and cruelty, even murder

Uttara Bhadra presided by Ahir Budhnya
Ruled by Saturn, a symbol of wisdom
Growth and expansion in consciousness
While materialistic is careless and dull

> Revati ruled by Mercury, presided by Pushan
> Prepares for a new realization of truth
> Fresh impetus for a meaningful life
> Extra sensitive to external conditions

Every sign has two and quarter asterisms
Rulers are three besides the sign ruler
Any graha is under the sway of two rulers
And the lord of the Asterism Pada

"Deities of the Nakshatra-s appear in the scripts of the Vedas, though some are from the Purana-s. The asters start with Ashvini, which occupies 0 to 13.33 degrees Aries, known as the horse's head. The series of constellations, like that of the signs, begins with the point 0 degrees Aries. An earlier order began with the Krittika, during the age of Taurus some of the observations appear in the Vedas. However, in terms of planetary lordship, the cycle always begins with 0 degrees Aries, marked by the end of Revati and beginning of Ashvini with the star named Revati, identified as one at the end of Pisces."

What the Nakshatra-s mean?

"Every Nakshatra has a special deity that rules it. Originally, the Nakshatra-s received their names after their deities, which show the spiritual energy behind the constellation. These deities are Vedic; their meaning comes from the Vedas. We can use these deities to explore the spiritual issues of life and the energies of our deeper psyche. They represent perhaps the most esoteric side of Vedic Astrology. We therefore relate the deities to the names of the Nakshatra-s, their planetary rulers, the planets exalted or debilitated in them, the signs which harbor them and the sign rulers. While the twelve signs stand for the outer forms of things, the Nakshatra-s are inner energies."

"Ashvins rule Ashvini. Ashvins are twin gods, known as 'the horsemen'. Lords of a journey, they take us on the path of light that leads to the divine. First deities of light, they precede the dawn's appearance in the sky. Ashvini-Kumaras ride a chariot through the air, which encompasses all the worlds; also travel a ship across the sea. Ashvini ruled by Ketu, symbolizes doubts. Ashvini being in the sign Aries, Ketu casts its shadow on Mars - the ruler of Aries, besides the asterism is the place of exaltation for the Sun. The fire element is intensely strong here, Ketu representing smoke, Mars and Sun intense heat, subjecting the native to a massive bout of Pitta. What becomes evident is that the Nakshatra system begins with wellness and healing, Ashvini imparts that power."

"Yama the god of death rules Bharani. He is a resurrection symbol, the divine Son whose sacrifice creates a path to truth for all mankind, derived from a word, it means a 'sense of carrying away'. Yama shows us the path of death leading to immortality. Venus rules Bharani. Shukra is about birth, resurrection, Yama about death, no wonder Venus is so much into art and creativity. In Bharani, Saturn reaches its maximum point of debility. One can experience Saturn's extreme darkness and constraints here. Bharani's ruler Yama has the power to take things away borne by the waters of Bharani. It is the removal of life from the body, transporting the soul to the realm of the ancestors."

"Agni, the god of fire, the messenger rules Krittika. Vedas start and end with the fire of Agni, the spirit or energy hidden in matter. Fire first takes birth as Earth. Krittika is also the place of exaltation for the Moon. Here is an interesting solar and lunar combination of fire and water; Pitta and Kapha forces are at play here."

"You will recall Hatti, that Rig Veda starts with Mantras to Agni and ends with it. Krittika Nakshatra burns up negativity, purifies what is mixed, and prepares the unripe."

"Prajapati, the progenitor rules Rohini. Rohini means 'to rise', it also represents the color 'red' of the 'red cow', or 'red deer'. Prajapati is a demiurge or fashioner of the cosmos. Rohini is very fertile and great for children, houses, land or other materialistic ventures. It can offer much comfort and prosperity though not just materialistic. Moon rules Rohini as his favorite Nakshatra. Rohini gives growth and prosperity. It has loyalty, faith, love and reverence for the Earth. Rohini Nakshatra allows for growth and creation on all levels, bestowing great fertility. Rohini gives the power of creation, including the ability to come together with friends and loved ones."

"Soma, identified with the Moon rules Mrigashira. Mrigashira means 'the head of a deer', the latter related to 'beginning of the year'. Mars is Mrigashira's lord, an active, energetic and goal-seeking planet. Mars gives us the insight into our goal and the means of getting it. In this Nakshatra, the native gets engaged in gaining and enjoying things. Mrigashira's power is in offering fulfillment or 'prinana'. Mrigashira dominates over plants and all matters about them, including healing."

"Rudra, the god of thunder rules Ardra. Ardra gets associated with 'wet and heat', and the asterism's symbol is a gem. Rudra is terrifying whom the rishis propitiate to avoid his wrath and his thunder weapon, which cause sorrow and death. Rudra is also the greatest of the doctors and healers, who cures all forms of fever, and whose hands give life. The ancient seers never called out Rudra's name loud, only whispered it. Ardra means the wet, shows rain and thunder. Rahu rules Ardra as a force of disturbance, eclipse and diffusion. The Nakshatra has a destabilizing effect, the chaos inherent in new formation. Ardra gives lordship over the wilderness it symbolizes."

"Aditi, mother of the Devas, rules Punarvasu, the asterism gets identified with the Earth. From its meaning, Punarvasu 'restores the good'. Aditi is mother of the Deva-s. She embodies the principle of wholeness, the indivisible. She is the source, the origin from which everything good arises, making Punarvasu a place of origins. Punarvasu, ruled by expansive Jupiter, gives knowledge and wisdom, principally the ability to understand duality. Punarvasu's power is the ability to gain wealth or substance. The power is wind or air, and wetness or rain - an AquaPisces plane. These bring about the revitalization of the plants. Punarvasu offers creative powers on herbs and trees. It is a Nakshatra of fertility."

"Brihaspati, guru of the gods, identified with the planet Jupiter rules Pushya. From its meaning, Pushya helps you 'prosper', 'nourish', a flower or a celestial archer. Brihaspati holds all the keys of knowledge as the great teacher. Saturn rules Pushya. To expand we must first contract, it requires discipline and structure to allow our potentials to manifest. Pushya is the Nakshatra wherein Jupiter takes birth, wherein it becomes exalted. It is a very fortunate sign, bequeathing beneficence, creativity and wisdom. Pushya gives spiritual power and authority."

"Sarpa the serpent god rules Aslesha. Aslesha means to 'embrace' and the asterism's symbol is a wheel or serpents. Serpent has a lower status in the Vedas as the force of ignorance that veils our perception of our real nature. Slain it must be, by the power of discrimination if we would discover the real truth of things. Aslesha marks transition and transformation. Mercury rules Aslesha. Aslesha Nakshatra paralyzes the enemy. Aslesha gives the ability to destroy one's opponents, foes, enemies and obstacles."

"Pitris, ancestral fathers rule Magha. Magha's icon is a wheel. Connection with the sages is the deepest aspect of Magha energy. Magha itself means the auspicious, the liberal or the beneficent. Ketu rules Magha. The second cycle of Ketu begins here. Magha grants the favor of one's ancestors and the ability to commune with them inwardly."

"Bhaga, the blissful form of the sun god rules Purva Phalguni. This is the former part of a double asterism, Phalguni. Phalguni means 'red' or 'evil'. The asterisms' representations are fig trees or a bed. Purva Phalguni stays connected to Venus, the planetary significator of beauty and delight. It gives a certain beauty of character. Aryaman governs productive alliances and arranges the wedding festival. Purva Phalguni grants lordship over cattle or wealth"

"Aryaman, the sun god rules Uttara Phalguni as the friend, companion and lover. Uttara Phalguni also gives healing abilities and works well for spiritual, psychic and physical healing. The Asterism stays related to the graha, Sun. Uttara Phalguni brings luck, fortune and glory."

"Savita the sun god of inspiration rules Hasta. The word means the 'hand', viewed as a hand of the huge figure of Prajapati, the lord of the born. Moon and Hasta have a close association. In Hasta, Mercury reaches its exaltation. Savita is the creative will that builds up the universe with all of its beauty. His productions are most wonderful."

"Tvashtar, the craftsman rules Chitra. Chitra means the 'conspicuous' or 'bright', and the asterism's icon is a lamp or a pearl. Tvashtar fashions the forms of things; he is the cosmic demiurge. Like Hasta, Chitra is a Nakshatra of work and craftsmanship but is artistic. Mars influences Chitra. It has a highly spiritual energy and effect. Chitra grants manifold progeny or great creativity."

"Vayu, the God of the wind and life-force rules Swati. Swati means 'fixed', 'good going' or 'sword' and 'an outcast'. Swati's icon is a coral bead, gem, or pearl, visualized as the heart of Prajapati. It gives mobility, velocity and ease of movement and communication. Rahu rules Swati, also an airy influence. Here Saturn reaches its highest exaltation. Swati Nakshatra causes things to move and scatter. Swati gives freedom of motion and travel, literally the ability to do what we want in all the worlds."

"Dual god Indra-Agni rules Vishakha. Vishakha means 'branched'. Vishakha's icon is a decorated arch, visualized as the thighs of Prajapati. Indra and Agni are not opposing god, as fire and lightning, they work together as active agents to further the light and destroy the powers of darkness. Jupiter is the graha lord of Vishakha. It is here that the Moon has no brightness and all light energy returns to the Sun. Indra and Agni here are gods showing the ripening effect of heat, rain and seasonal changes. Vishakha grants glory and pre-eminence among the gods or cosmic powers."

"Mitra, sun god as divine friend rules Anuradha. It shadows the prior asterism, therefore the name 'Anu' and 'Radha'. Romans worshipped Mitra secretly in basements and underground places. Related to Christ is Mitra in his nature and energy. Mitra offers friendship, compassion, devotion and love. Anuradha Nakshatra gives balance in relationship honoring others and us, through which comes fame and recognition. Mitra indicates friendship, compassion, devotion and right relationship."

"Indra, the king of the gods' rules Jyeshta. Jyeshta means 'the eldest' and its symbol is an ear jewel. He is the great god of power, the divine warrior who slays all the demons, particularly the serpent or dragon. Indra is the wielder of the thunderbolt, lightning or sun wheel of direct perception. The issues related to Jyeshta are power, authority, preeminence and independence. Jyeshta is under lordship of Mercury. It allows us to reach the summit of our personal powers but it requires great courage and effort. Jyeshta gives us priority and preeminence over others, the ability to overcome and to achieve our best."

"Nirriti, goddess of calamity, falsehood, death or destruction rules Mula. Mula means 'the root, the basic unit'. Nirriti denotes the abyss or the void but also the foundation, the bottom ground of creation. She is the great emptiness or illusion, goddess of death and destruction. Mula is a Nakshatra of judgment, danger and transition. It is also a sign of negation and transformation. Ketu manages Mula. Mula provides deep powers of perception and the capacity to go beyond things, even to negate the world. Through Mula passes the Galactic Center, the source of light for the solar system. To stay attuned to this center is difficult and places strong demands upon us as a soul. Mula has the power to ruin or destroy. Mula gives the ability to get to the root of things, including connecting with primordial creative powers."

"Apah, the goddess of waters rules Purvashadha. It is the former part of two asterisms known as Ashada, represented by elephant's tusk separately, or as a bed together. Purvashadha shows the cosmic waters or the higher ocean of consciousness, a Nakshatra of cleansing and absolution. Water allows for purification and brings about purification. Water is also about healing and medicine. Venus manages Purvashadha. Purvashadha brings about purification and regeneration. These effects flow from the heavenly waters and provide inner purification. Purvashadha connects us with the ocean."

"Vishwadeva-s, the pantheon of deva-s rule Uttara-Ashada, a host of gods of light that stand for the principle of universality, that all is one and one is all, complex, complete and integrated manifestation of the cosmic powers. It is the Nakshatra of great victory, the universalization of the cosmic being within us and its defeat of the forces of pettiness, ego and limitation. Uttarashadha is under the lordship of Sun, marking the most realization and manifestation of our individuality in the outer world. It brings us to the summit of our power, support and recognition. Uttarashadha gives the supreme victory, never taken away. It helps us gain our highest goals."

"Vishnu, 'one who pervades all', the immanent divine presence or cosmic intelligence that maintains the order and rhythm of the universe rules Sravana. Sravana means the 'ear'. Vishnu's three great strides set up the three worlds and hold the divine space of consciousness within them. The asterism's icon is the 'three footsteps' or a 'trident'. Vishnu, with his Trivrikrama or 'he who with three strides' encompassed the three worlds, relates to his Vamana or dwarf form. Moon governs Sravana. Sravana enables us to link people together by connecting them to their right paths in life. Vishnu's three strides link the three worlds of earth, atmosphere and heaven, connecting all creatures."

"Vasus, the gods of light, particularly the morning light rule Dhanistha. Dhanistha is the 'richest'. Asterism's representation is a drum. Vasus shine when the dawn breaks and dispenses the richness of the plenitude of light. Dhanistha gives abundance and wealth, either that of the materialistic world or that of the greater manifestation of the spirit and its universalization. Mars manages Dhanistha and gets exalted here. Dhanistha allows us to bring the resources of people together. Dhanistha allows us to become the center of attention for our friends and peers."

"Varuna, the lord of the cosmic ocean rules Shatabhishag. Shatabhishag means 'requiring hundred physicians'. Shatabhishag is a sign of healing, articulating well with all kinds of healers, physicians, psychologists, priests, pastors, and ministers, a Nakshatra of catharsis and deliverance. It most typically relates to Aquarius energy. Rahu manages Shatabhishag. It gives the water of wisdom poured forth in Aquarius. While Ashvini gives more immediate cures, Shatabhishag brings about a healing crisis leading to revitalization. Shatabhishag makes us firm and strong and helps us overcome weakness."

"Aja Ekapada, which means 'one-footed' or 'one-horned goat' rules Purva bhadra. These words refer to the former, or Purva of the two asterisms. The base words mean 'auspicious feet' and 'footstool' or 'carp feet' or 'oxen feet'. The asterisms' icons are the bi-faced ones or twins and together as a couch. It is an intuitive Nakshatra imparting deep wisdom, openness, individuality and independence of a spiritual, not a personal order. Jupiter manages Purva Bhadra. It is a Nakshatra of prosperity, auspiciousness, expansion and growth. It denotes creativity, fertility and flowering. Aja Ekapada is the cosmic or celestial form of Agni or the sacred fire. It raises our spiritual aspiration in life. Purva Bhadra gives creative fire and spiritual luster."

"Ahir Budhnya, the snake or dragon dwelling at the bottom of the sea, the dragon of the depths rules Uttara bhadra. It is a Nakshatra of deep, intuitive wisdom, the higher side of the serpent or dragon. It guides us to the core of things, attunes us with the universal life-energy within them. Saturn governs Uttara Bhadra. Uttara Bhadra's power brings rain. Uttara Bhadra grants growth and prosperity in a broad way, benefiting the entire world. This makes it very auspicious. Ahir Budhnya is the benefic serpent that brings the rain, connecting us with the creative powers at the world's foundation."

"Pushan, a sun god who nourishes, the lord of the fields, pastures and earth, the god of fertility rules Revati. For its meaning, Revati describes the 'wealthy'. He is also the lord of the path found at the beginning, pointing the way of light."

"As the last of the Nakshatra-s, it relates to achievement and a closure – or rather, a closure to a beginning. Mercury manages Revati. Here Venus reaches its maximum exaltation as the devotional principle gets integrated into the wisdom principle. Revati creates abundance through providing proper nourishment. Pushan is the lord of cattle and the lord of the paths. He leads, protects and gathers the herd in their movement to newer pastures. In this way, he also protects the soul in its journey to the next world. Revati gives power over cattle, power over sources of nourishment."

"Research on Taittiriya Brahmana book three, an important constituent of Krishna Yajur-Veda, suggests that every Nakshatra has the ingredients of certain wishes or desires for those who take birth under them. In the Vedas, the Nakshatra deity secretly echoes those wishes. Sage Brighu verified the results, many thousands of years back. Incidentally, Brighu had a very impressive lineage, having married Khyati, the daughter of Progenitor Daksha. He had two sons by her, named Dhata and Vidhata. His daughter Bhargavi married Vishnu or Narayan. From his wife Usana, he had another son, Shukra, learned sage and guru of the Asura-s. Sage Chyavana is his son through Puloma. One of his descendants was sage Jamadagni, whose son sage Parasurama, was an avatar of Vishnu."

"Taittiriya Brahmana offers supplementary insight into the Nakshatra-s. Ashvini-Kumar-s wished, 'May we hear better and not be deaf.' This Nakshatra relates to secret knowledge and miraculous powers, especially in the field of medicine. Yama desired, 'May I become the lord of all ancestors.' Those born under Bharani crave for their elders' respect and their peers. Agni desired, 'May I eat the food of the gods.' One whose ideologies and practices match Agni's will cherish the offering given to high mortals. Agni as fire cooks and digests food. Prajapati created creatures but thus created they went way. Of them he thought about Rohini. He desired, 'May she approach me. May we unite as one love!' One who rises to Prajapati's level, his beloved approaches him and he unites with her. Rohini is a Nakshatra of love, passion and sexuality; fertile and creative, but not inclined to abide by limits. Soma wished. 'May I rule the plants!' Those born under Mrigashira act their best with a retinue of friends. Rudra preferred, 'May I become the lord of the animals.' Rudra is the lord of the wild animals and all things wild, strange or disturbing. Aditi desired, 'May I produce herbs and trees.' Punarvasu, produces progeny and cattle. Punarvasu is a creative Nakshatra with the ability to create form and structure. Brihaspati wished, 'May I possess the splendor of spiritual knowledge.' Pushya connects us with higher knowledge and morality. Through it, the good overcomes the evil."

"Once the gods and demons were at war and the gods made Aslesha an offering, which drove away the demons. Through it one gains the poison of the serpent to use on others. Those born under Aslesha make powerful warriors with powerful weapons. The Pitris desired, 'May we thrive in the world of the ancestors.' Magha gives fame that lasts through the generations. Those born under it seek a high reputation for themselves, a king's position or paternal status. Bhaga desired, 'May I partake the best portion of the gods.' One, who takes to Bhaga, gains the best portion among his peers. Those born under Purva Phalguni seek the best portion for themselves. Aryaman preferred, 'May I become the lord of the animals.' Those born under Uttara Phalguni seek colleagues and followers to help them in their noble causes. Savita reckoned, 'May the gods place their faith in me.' It is true, that one who sets his ideologies to match Savita's, other men place their faith in him. He becomes the Sun among his peers. People born under Hasta crave for others to have faith and belief in them. Tvashtar wished, 'May I gain a wonderful progeny.' One, who makes the appropriate offering to Tvashtar, in turn, experiences his rewards of a wonderful progeny. Chitra therefore has great creative powers, giving splendor, multiplicity and abundance. Vayu requested, 'May I have the freedom to move as I wish in the three worlds.' Vayu has free movement in all the worlds. Those born in Vayu's Nakshatra of Swati have a similar desire. They hate being held or tied down. Indra and Agni desired, 'May I gain the greatest splendor among the gods.' One, who matches the characters of Indra and Agni in the true spirit, gains the greatest splendor among his peers. Vishakha is a competitive Nakshatra and has a fiery and lightning like energy and effects."

"Mitra preferred, 'May others regard me as a friend in the three worlds.' Those born under Anuradha want to be friends with everyone. Sensitive to others, they place other's welfare over their own. Indra wanted, 'May I achieve supremacy over the gods.' Those born under Jyeshta seek to be the best on their own, by their own effort, as individuals, not by relying on others. They often do their best when left alone. Prajapati sought, 'May I find the root of progeny.' This gives Mula a more creative energy. It gives the root of progeny or strong creative powers. In the negative sense in the Vedas, Mula ruled by Nirriti takes away the root of one's progeny or causes the loss of one's first child. Apah desired, 'May we gain the sea.' Purvashadha rewards one who seeks connections with water desiring to reach the ocean. It is a creative, nurturing and healing Nakshatra. The Vishwadeva-s hoped, 'May we win a victory and never lose.' Uttarashadha is a competitive Nakshatra that forces us to seek more achievements, but allied with others, in great partnerships, organizations and associations. One succeeds by one's broad connections."

"Vishnu desired, 'May I hear people say good things about me. May I not blemish my reputation!' Those born under Sravana worry about what people say about them and their public reputation. They will strive to keep themselves in good repute. Vasus requested, 'May we revolve around the pantheon of the gods.' The native, whose practices match the Vasus, gains the summit of achievements among his peers. Vasus rule over material and worldly splendors, which their Nakshatra grants. Varuna wished, 'May I be firm and steady.' One whose ideologies match Varuna's becomes firm and steady enjoying the freedom from disease and debility. Shatabhishag is a Nakshatra of healing and energy. Aja Ekapada desire, 'May I gain radiance and the splendor of spiritual knowledge.' Purva Bhadra has a great spiritual potential like Brihaspati ruled Pushya. It can give even more insight, perception and spiritual fire – that of the soul. Ahir Budhnya wished, 'May I begin a foundation.' Uttara Bhadra grants a firm foundation in life, connecting us with the wellsprings of vitality, the serpent that dwells in the middle of the sea. Pushan desired, 'May I become the lord of the animals.' One, who acts like Pushan, becomes lord of the animals. Revati gives lordship over domestic cattle, rich harvests and fertile fields. Those born under this Nakshatra are fond of good things in life but live in harmony with nature."

Nakshatra-s and guna vectors

"Each Nakshatra relates to one of the three guna vectors or primary qualities of nature. While the primary level is more evident in the outer action of the Nakshatra, the secondary and tertiary qualities are more obvious on a deeper level. Three guna vectors divide Nakshatra-s into three groups. First third of the zodiac, 0° Aries – 0° Leo, the Nakshatra-s from Ashvini 1 to Aslesha 9, are under a Rajasic or active influence, concerned with projection, motivation, initiating things, and dynamic movement. They project personality and individuality and relate to the self. Cardinal and Rajasic are similar qualities."

"Second third of the zodiac, 0° Leo – 0° Sagittarius, the Nakshatra-s from 10 Magha to 18 Jyeshta, are under a Tamasik or inertial influence. Their concern is with developing form and substance, with materializing things and creating stability, endurance and structure. They relate to the other or the opposite, the partner, and have a fixed character as they contain two fixed signs, Leo and Scorpio. Fixed and Tamasik are similar qualities."

"The third series, the last third of the zodiac, 0° Sagittarius − 0° Aries, or the Nakshatra-s from 19 Mula to 27 Revati, are under a sattvic or harmonizing influence, concerned with creating balance and harmony, with completing, spiritualizing, universalizing or negating things. This group develops collective, impersonal and universal and relate to the multitudes. They have a mutable character, as they contain two mutable signs, Sagittarius and Pisces. Mutable and sattvic are similar qualities."

"This leads us to secondary guna vectors where each of these three primary guna series of Nakshatra-s gets further subdivided into three groups. Hence, the first third of each group is Rajasic in secondary quality, the second third is Tamasik and the last third is sattvic."

"A further subdivision results in tertiary guna vectors, where each of the secondary guna series gets further subdivided into three once more. Hence, the first Nakshatra of this group is Rajasic, the second is Tamasik, and the third is sattvic. In this way, Rajas, Tamas and Sattva alternate from one Nakshatra to another, starting with Ashvini as Rajasic, Bharani as Tamasik, and the sequence carries on."

"Though some points of commonality exist, it makes the two systems rather distinct – the systems of Graha-s and Nakshatra-s."

Ruler	Nakshatra	Guna	Quality	Element
Ketu	1 Ashvini	Rajas	Cardinal	Fire
	10 Magha	Tamas	Fixed	Fire
	19 Mula	Sattva	Moveable	Fire
Venus	2 Bharani	Rajas	Cardinal	Fire
	11 Purva Phalguni	Tamas	Fixed	Fire
	20 Purvashadha	Sattva	Moveable	Fire
Sun	3 Krittika	Rajas	Cardinal/Fixed	Fire/Earth
	12 Uttara Phalguni	Tamas	Fixed/Moveable	Fire/Earth
	21 Uttarashadha	Sattva	Moveable/Cardinal	Fire/Earth
Moon	4 Rohini	Rajas	Fixed	Earth
	13 Hasta	Tamas	Moveable	Earth
	22 Sravana	Sattva	Cardinal	Earth
Mars	5 Mrigashira	Rajas	Fixed/Moveable	Earth/Air
	14 Chitra	Tamas	Moveable/Cardinal	Earth/Air
	23 Dhanistha	Sattva	Cardinal/Fixed	Earth/Air
Rahu	6 Ardra	Rajas	Moveable	Air
	15 Swati	Tamas	Cardinal	Air

Ruler	Nakshatra	Guna	Quality	Element
	24 Shatabhishag	Sattva	Fixed	Air
Jupiter	7 Punarvasu	Rajas	Moveable/Cardinal	Air/Water
	16 Vishakha	Tamas	Cardinal/Fixed	Air/Water
	25 Purva Bhadra	Sattva	Fixed/Moveable	Air/Water
Saturn	8 Pushya	Rajas	Cardinal	Water
	17 Anuradha	Tamas	Fixed	Water
	26 Uttara Bhadra	Sattva	Moveable	Water
Mercury	9 Aslesha	Rajas	Cardinal	Water
	18 Jyeshta	Tamas	Fixed	Water
	27 Revati	Sattva	Moveable	Water

"Ketu rules Ashvini, Magha and Mula, the Nakshatra-s ruled by the Ashvins, the Fathers and the Nirriti. These are signs of new beginnings, initial problems signifying danger of presumption or impulsiveness. Ketu rules beginnings, representing what gets reprocessed from the end. Venus rules Bharani, Purva Phalguni and Purvashadha, the Nakshatra-s ruled by Yama, Bhaga and Apah. These are Nakshatra-s of growth and gain, warmth, expansion and the movement towards communication. They give pleasure, happiness and abundance. Sun rules Krittika, Uttara Phalguni and Uttara Ashada, whose deities are Agni, Aryaman and the Vishwadeva-s. These are signs of energy, power and fruition. They show work and development and direct us towards self-unfolding. Moon rules Rohini, Hasta and Sravana, ruled by the deities Prajapati, Savita and Vishnu, Nakshatra-s of creativity, receptivity, knowledge and expression. They are productive and formative and bring things into manifestation. They are earthly and solid being located entirely in earth signs. Mars rules Mrigashira, Chitra and Dhanistha, ruled by the deities Soma, Tvashtar and Vasu, Nakshatra-s of power, light, work, search and struggle. They make us seek things to achieve other things and strive for gains. They are restless. In them we move from materialistic resources to mental application. In Dhanistha we become capable of great wealth, affluence and happiness, but it becomes directed towards family, society, or the universal good. We achieve our goals under this Nakshatra but they cease to be anything personal. Rahu rules Ardra, Swati and Shatabhishag, ruled by the deities Rudra, Vayu, and Varuna, Nakshatra-s of change, dispersion, judgment and the storm. They bring fluctuations, danger, challenges, difficulty, and obscuration, volatile and airy, being entirely in air signs as Nakshatra-s of disease and healing. Jupiter rules Punarvasu, Vishakha and Purva Bhadra, ruled by the deities Aditi, Indra-Agni and Aja Ekapada. These are Nakshatra-s of growth, development, joy and expansion. They denote thought movement towards emotional expression."

"Saturn rules Pushya, Anuradha and Uttara Bhadra, ruled by Brihaspati, Mitra and Ahir Budhnya, Nakshatra-s that force discipline and detachment. Found in watery signs, their energy is opposite to Saturn's nature and quality. Saturn creates the banks, the structure, for this water to flow on a deeper level. These deities are open and intuitive, opposite energies than Saturn's. Mercury rules Aslesha, Jyeshta and Revati, governed by the Serpent God, Indra, and Pushan, Nakshatra-s of wisdom, knowledge and profundity. They force not just intellectual facility but discriminating powers of intelligence to deal with their powers appropriately, implying they want the deeper aspects of Mercury energy. Submerged in watery signs, there comes demand for the deeper functioning of superficial Mercury."

Nakshatra gender

"One can classify Nakshatra-s by their sex. Male Nakshatra-s have a more active character. They can manifest their forces rather directly. Female Nakshatra-s exhibit a more passive character. They demand motivation from an outside force like the planets to bring their latent powers into function. They have a more receptive and creative nature. Masculine planets like the Sun, Mars and Jupiter act with more energy in masculine Nakshatra-s. In feminine Nakshatra-s they have a more creative or fructifying effect. Feminine planets, like the Moon and Venus, in masculine Nakshatra-s gain a more active character, while in feminine Nakshatra-s their power remains rather passive, unless activated by other planetary aspects and associations. The Moon in feminine Nakshatra-s, for example, is better for fertility and childbirth."

"In classifying Nakshatra-s, no mathematical patterns are adopted. Masculine Nakshatra-s are 1. Ashvini, 2. Bharani, 8. Pushya, 9. Aslesha, 10. Magha, 12. Uttara Phalguni, 15. Swati, 18. Jyeshta, 19. Mula, 20. Purvashadha, 21. Uttarashadha, 22. Sravana, 25. Purva Bhadra. Feminine Nakshatra-s are 3. Krittika, 4. Rohini, 5. Mrigashira, 6. Ardra, 7. Punarvasu, 11. Purva Phalguni, 13. Hasta, 14. Chitra, 16. Vishakha, 17. Anuradha, 23. Dhanistha, 24. Shatabhishag, 26. Uttara Bhadra, 27. Revati."

Nakshatra and Purushartha

"Grouped are Nakshatra-s also by the four goals of life, dharma, artha, kama and moksha, the motivating forces of principle, directed activity, desire or aspiration, and liberation. Dividing Nakshatra-s this way follows a simple pattern. The first Nakshatra relates to Dharma, the second to Artha, the third to Kama and the fourth to Moksha, with the pattern then reversed, with the fifth Nakshatra governing Moksha, the sixth, Kama, the seventh, Artha and the eighth Dharma. It is best to crosscheck the results with the Dasamsa chart according to the principles laid out by Sage Parasara."

Dharma Nakshatra-s
1. Ashvini, 8. Pushya, 9. Aslesha, 16. Vishakha, 17. Anuradha, 23. Dhanistha, 24. Shatabhishag
Artha Nakshatra-s
2. Bharani, 7. Punarvasu, 10. Magha, 15. Swati, 18. Jyeshta, 22. Sravana, 25. Purva Bhadra
Kama Nakshatra-s
3. Krittika, 6. Ardra, 11. Purva Phalguni, 14. Chitra, 19. Mula, 26. Uttara Bhadra
Moksha Nakshatra-s
4. Rohini, 5. Mrigashira, 12. Uttara Phalguni, 13. Hasta, 20. Purvashadha, 21. Uttarashadha, 27. Revati

Nakshatra Pairs

"Nakshatra-s get paired often with those that share similar qualities, both either auspicious or inauspicious. A few Nakshatra-s, however, appear on their own, apart from these pairs. Purva and Uttara Bhadra are very auspicious, belonging to the Bhadra asterism and work well in spiritual and in materialistic ways. Revati and Ashvini are inauspicious as they are under influence of Gandhanta, transitional periods of fire-water marking the end and beginning of personal endeavors. Bharani and Krittika are inauspicious. The first relates more to the struggle of death, the second to the struggle of birth, but they are somewhat difficult. Rohini and Mrigashira are highly auspicious. Mrigashira offers gains, but it does not come easy. Ardra is inauspicious; it shows struggle and turmoil but can lead to new achievements once difficulties get removed. Punarvasu and Pushya are very auspicious. Punarvasu characterizes the Divine Mother and Pushya represents the Divine Father. Aslesha and Magha are very inauspicious, governing Gandhanta. Both relate to death or ending."

"Aslesha is more the infliction of death, while Magha is moving on to the next world. Purva and Uttara Phalguni are auspicious, somewhat like Purva and Uttara Bhadra. They give gains, alliances and marriage. Hasta and Chitra are auspicious and both give good creative and artistic abilities. Swati is very auspicious but can show changeability. Vishakha and Anuradha are auspicious, more so the latter, with Vishakha being mixed in its results, but they involve some effort. Jyeshta and Mula are the most inauspicious of the Nakshatra-s, governing the worst Gandhanta. Jyeshta, opposite Rohini in the zodiac is a constellation of misfortune. Purva and Uttarashadha are favorable requiring effort for success where victory comes from struggles. Sravana and Dhanistha are auspicious, promising rewards and connections. Dhanistha is superlative of Sravana. Shatabhishag is auspicious once the person is past the initial hurdles, or when rectified are the past misdoings."

Nakshatra-s and Lunar Months

Chaitra	Full Moon in Hasta, Chitra or Swati
Vaisakha	Full Moon in Vishakha or Anuradha
Jyeshta	Full Moon in Jyeshta or Mula
Ashada	Full Moon in Purva or Uttarashadha
Sravana	Full Moon in Sravana, Dhanistha or Shatabhishag
Bhadra	Full Moon in Purva or Uttara Bhadra
Ashvini	Full Moon in Revati or Ashvini
Kartika	Full Moon in Bharani or Krittika
Margashirsha	Full Moon in Rohini, Mrigashira, or Ardra
Pushya	Full Moon in Punarvasu or Pushya
Magha	Full Moon in Aslesha or Magha
Phalguni	Full Moon in Purva or Uttara Phalguni

"This grouping also relates to the lunar months, which get named after the main Nakshatra in which the Moon is full during the month."

"Nakshatra planetary ruler has a more inner meaning, while the sign ruler has a more external connotation. Nakshatra ruler remains colored by nature of the planet ruling the sign in which the Nakshatra dwells, much like a planetary aspect. Ashvini, therefore, gets a Ketu-Mars energy, like a Ketu-Mars conjunction."

"Nakshatra divisions of one hundred eight points to the native. Each division is 3.33 part of the arc. Check for which is stronger, the Lagna or the Moon. Stronger graha posited in the Nakshatra would show the character. Every division 108th part helps determine the physical attributes as twenty-seven-Nakshatra-s have nine graha rulers. Each graha ruler takes up three-Nakshatra-s by turn and rotation. Each Nakshatra has four Padas or divisions. The lordship of each pada follows the same rules as signs. Ketu rules Ashvini, first pada, ruled by Mars and second pada by Venus. Third pada is ruled by Mercury and fourth by Moon. Bharani comes next ruled by Venus, first Pada ruled by Sun, second Pada ruled by Mercury, third by Venus and fourth by Mars. Krittika is next ruled by Sun, first Pada by Jupiter and second by Saturn. Saturn rules third Pada and Jupiter rules the fourth. Repeated is the process for the next three-Nakshatra-s. When completed are nine Nakshatra-s with three cycles of Pada lordship, the sequence repeats for the next nine Nakshatra-s. The Pada kinship marks highlights of the person Ashvini Pada 1 would have Ketu, Mars and Mars as triad. The position grants the native the face of a ram, a male-goat. Ketu mimics Mars conferring the native a fierce voice. Ashvini Pada 2 has Ketu, Venus and Mars as the triad grouping lending the person a dusky complexion. In addition, the speech is pleasing from Venus dominance, the face and nose, upper parts of the body become prevalent. Nakshatra-s provide the means to arrive at a Native from both the Kalachakra and the Manomaya chakra view. The physical and mental characteristics are as described above. Kalachakra view comes from the Dasa progression and the Hora."

"Nakshatra rulers are more of control planets. They dispense the influences of the planets in the Nakshatra through the course of time as in Vimshottari Dasa."

Retrogression and hidden traits

"Any planet that is retrograded in the birth chart shows a return to the past. Mercury retrograde, for example, will show a mind taken over by influences from the past or having insight into the past. This may cause hesitation in speech, or speech defects if afflicted. However, if well-placed, it will give a good knowledge of history. Mars retrograde may show violence carried over from past lives, which may result in injury. Retrograde planets make us deal with unresolved issues from the past. Few or no retrograde planets in the chart show a new karmic cycle beginning."

"The ninth divisional or Navamsa shows the hidden side of our planets and where their secret influence is. Like the two sides of a coin, you get to see one explicitly in the birth chart reading and the other obverse hidden in the Navamsa."

"The two lunar nodes, Rahu and Ketu as they always regress, they tell us what the secrets are – not necessarily the truth."

Quality of time

"Unlike events that need a chart with all graha-s plotted in it, a less complex system using just the moon to figure an auspicious almanac is the system of Panchanga. This system considers five factors in timing events through (1) Tithi, lunar day (2) Vara, solar weekday (3) Nakshatra, lunar constellation (4) Yoga or combinations involving Sun and Moon and (5) Karana or half of the Tithi."

"Panchanga is part of the Muhurta system. Let me introduce the main principles so that one can learn how to choose a favorable time. On such a favorable day from Nakshatra and Tithi the chances of success are high. Panchanga determines a customary, wide-ranging quality of time. In a general chart, ascendant and its lord must be strong for any good actions to succeed. Which implies that even if a day is auspicious, only a few hours defined by the changing ascendant will give the best results. For most ordinary purposes, a favorable day, Nakshatra and Tithi is enough. Nakshatra-s are the most important factor here. Moon occupying different Nakshatra-s turns favorable for different activities. Few Nakshatra-s act favorable for different activities, others have limited offerings. The Nakshatra occupied by the Moon determines what actions are fruitful on that lunar day. Like the graha-s and signs, Nakshatra-s belong to several groups."

Fixed (Dhruva)	Rohini, Uttara Phalguni, Uttarashadha, Uttara Bhadra
Harsh (Tikshna)	Ardra, Aslesha, Mula, Jyeshta
Fierce (Ugra)	Bharani, Magha, Purva Phalguni, Purvashadha, Purva Bhadra
Quick (Kshipra)	Ashvini, Pushya, Hasta, Abhijit
Soft (Mridu)	Mrigashira, Chitra, Anuradha, Revati
Mixed (Mridu-Tikshna)	Krittika, Vishakha
Moveable (Chara)	Punarvasu, Swati, Sravana, Dhanistha, Shatabhishag

"Among Nakshatra-s, Rohini, Uttara Phalguni, Uttarashadha, and Uttara Bhadra having Nakshatra numbers 4, 12, 21, 26 are 'fixed'. With the moon posited in such asterisms, they become favorable for establishing or founding any project expected to be largely enduring, such as building houses, planting trees, wedding and conceiving."

"Nakshatra-s such as Punarvasu, Swati, Sravana, Dhanistha, and Shatabhishag with numbers 7, 15, 22, 23, 24 are mutable or moving Nakshatra-s. They are favorable for actions wherein change and movement are important like education, communication and commerce, travel, buying new vehicles, recreational ventures and influencing the public."

"Among Nakshatra-s, Mrigashira, Chitra, Anuradha and Revati their numbers being 5, 14, 17, 27 are soft Nakshatra-s. When the Moon passes over them, favored they are in issues addressing softness, pliability and sensitivity, like putting on new clothes, artistic ventures, healing, domestic, personal and emotional issues and sexual activity."

"Nakshatra-s such as Ashvini, Pushya and Hasta, numbers being 1, 8, 13 are light unlike other heavy Nakshatra-s. They are favorable for new undertakings as they promote growth, development and movement. With Moon occupying them, they work well in actions of adorning new clothes and gemstones, taking medicines or medical therapies, subtle endeavors such as gaining knowledge, physical activities and sports, and travel."

"Sharp Nakshatra-s, Ardra, Aslesha, Jyeshta and Mula with Nakshatra numbers 6, 9, 18, 19 are unfavorable, though useful for negative, protective, or wrathful actions like countering enemies, warding off evil spirits or dispensing punishment. All actions that are sharp and decisive like arguments, debates, competitive athletics and struggle. They prohibit any new breakthroughs even if we are open to their energy."

"Nakshatra-s such as Bharani, Magha, Purva Phalguni, Purvashadha and Purva Bhadra with numbers 2, 10, 11, 20, 25 are cruel, fierce and dreaded. They are most unfavorable, best for negative actions like the sharp Nakshatra-s. They require that we take a wrathful or harsh mode in our actions. On their days, difficulties, obstructions, enmity, and calamities of various sorts are more likely to happen. However, they can enable us to overcome such difficulties and gain much more power in life. There are two mixed Nakshatra-s, Krittika and Vishakha numbers 3, 16 combining good and bad, harsh and gentle impacts. While performing negative actions to overcome difficulties and gain power, they are suitable for ordinary ventures."

"With Nakshatra-s in AquaPisces zone of Aquarius and Pisces, which are in the last portion of the zodiac, it suggests a time when not to consider establishing any new actions. Starting from last half of Dhanistha to the end of Revati is the period of Nakshatra Panchaka. When the Moon occupies this region, one should avoid journeys going south, repairing or renovation or acquiring new items."

Favorable and unfavorable Nakshatra-s

1 Ashvini	Favorable	15 Swati	Very Favorable
4 Rohini	Very Favorable	17 Anuradha	Favorable
5 Mrigashira	Favorable	21 Uttarashadha	Favorable
7 Punarvasu	Very Favorable	22 Sravana	Favorable
8 Pushya	Most Favorable	23 Dhanistha	Favorable
12 Uttara Phalguni	Favorable	24 Shatabhishag	Favorable
13 Hasta	Favorable	26 Uttara Bhadra	Favorable
14 Chitra	Favorable	27 Revati	Favorable
2 Bharani	Very Unfavorable	16 Vishakha	Mixed
3 Krittika	Mixed	18 Jyeshta	Unfavorable
6 Ardra	Unfavorable	19 Mula	Unfavorable
9 Aslesha	Unfavorable	20 Purvashadha	Very Unfavorable
10 Magha	Very Unfavorable	25 Purva Bhadra	Very Unfavorable
11 Purva Phalguni	Very Unfavorable		

"Specific Nakshatra-s falling on particular days of the week give rise to certain combinations or Yogas, some of which are favorable, others are adverse. Some auspicious combinations of weekdays and Nakshatra-s under Siddha Yoga and Sarvartha Siddhi Yoga are favorable for all pursuits and Amrita Siddhi Yoga ensuring accomplishments in one's endeavors."

Siddha Yoga

1 Sun	19 Mula
2 Mon	22 Sravana
3 Tue	26 Uttara Bhadra
4 Wed	3 Krittika
5 Thu	7 Punarvasu
6 Fri	11 Purva Phalguni
7 Sat	15 Swati

Sarvartha Siddhi Yoga

1 Sun	1, 8, 12, 13, 19, 21, 26
2 Mon	4, 5, 8, 17, 22
3 Tue	1, 3, 9, 26
4 Wed	3, 4, 5, 13, 17
5 Thu	1, 7, 8, 17, 27
6 Fri	1, 7, 17, 22, 27
7 Sat	4, 15, 22

Amrita Siddhi Yoga

1 Sun	13 Hasta
2 Mon	22 Sravana
3 Tue	1 Ashvini
4 Wed	17 Anuradha
5 Thu	8 Pushya
6 Fri	27 Revati
7 Sat	4 Rohini

"It is better to avoid an unfavorable weekday and Nakshatra combination listed under Mrityu Yoga, when possible, in performing important activities, especially travelling."

Mrityu Yoga

1 Sun	17 Anuradha
2 Mon	21 Uttarashadha
3 Tue	24 Shatabhishag
4 Wed	1 Ashvini
5 Thu	5 Mrigashira
6 Fri	9 Aslesha
7 Sat	13 Hasta

Nakshatra-s transits

"Twenty-Seven Nakshatra divisions have their explicit indications, determining whether the period the moon is in them are favorable or unfavorable."

"Ashvini, Nakshatra #1, 0° to 13.33° Aries, as the first Nakshatra, is useful for all good beginnings and for creating higher goals and good intentions in our actions. First quarter of the Nakshatra, however, is not so auspicious as it is a transitional period between the ending and beginning of the zodiac. Bharani, #2, 13.33° to 26.66° Aries is largely unfavorable, ruled by Yama, the god of death, and has an untrusted active, aggressive and sometimes impulsive energy. Krittika, #3, 26.66° Aries to 10° Taurus is also hostile, ruled by fire symbolized as a razor. However, it ensures victory over enemies and obstacles and is therefore suitable for harsh actions. Rohini, #4, 10° to 23.33° Taurus, a favorable Nakshatra recognized for its creativity allows us to manifest our desires in material form. It is the Nakshatra most loved by the Moon. Mrigashira, #5, 23.33° Taurus to 6.66° Gemini is favorable period but can tend toward self-indulgence. Favorable indications are travel, wedding, sexual activity, building temples, consecrating spiritual items or altars; spiritual initiations, adopting a new name, healing and treatment of disease as in case of convalescence; rejuvenation practices, artistic work like in sculpture, buying and building or entering a new house; commencing educational ventures, learning languages, legal matters, excellent for moving or change of residence; spiritually good for developing divine joy or bliss. Ardra, #6, 6.66° to 20° Gemini is unfavorable as it relates to Rudra's wrath and storms. Punarvasu, #7, 20° Gemini to 03.33° Cancer, regarded as very favorable, the last quarter of asterism where the Moon is in its own sign, offers proper time for commencing educational ventures, learning astrology or spoken languages, taking medicines, undergoing healing therapies, putting on gemstones or new clothes, adopting a new name, planting and gardening, buying houses, legal matters, spiritual services, initiations, fasting, building temples and churches, altars or installing deities. Pushya, #8, 3.33° to 16.66° Cancer, considered highly favorable Nakshatra for all auspicious actions, grants fearlessness and success indicative of commencing educational ventures, learning astrology and spoken languages, artistic ventures, taking medicines and therapies, putting on gemstones or new clothes, adopting a new name, planting and gardening, purchasing a building or entering a home, legal matters, spiritual services, installing altars or statues of deities, performing rituals, meditation, spiritual initiation, excellent time for learning spiritual teachings Vedas or the Bible."

"Aslesha, #9, 16.66° to 30° Cancer acts as an unfavorable and unreliable Nakshatra. Deception is more likely to occur under its influence, so is disease, including contagious diseases like cold and influenza. Magha, #10, 00° to 13.33° Leo denotes the Nakshatra of the Pitris, or the fathers works well towards honoring one's ancestors. The period suggests honoring one's father, guru, the rishis, and other ancestors; promoting tradition or family, meeting great personages, assuming positions of authority, wedding and marriage, planting, buying houses, hazardous undertakings, learning music and dancing. It is not good for initiations, lending money, wedding, sexual activity. Purva Phalguni, #11, 13.33° to 26.66° Leo, ruled by Bhaga gets regarded as unfavorable. It facilitates buying houses, hypnotizing and gaining control over others, gaining fame, charisma, or personal power; artistic ventures, like music, painting or dance; business matters, commencing studies; adoration of the divine; devotional practices. It is not good for travel, initiations or sexual activity. Uttara Phalguni, #12, 26.66° Leo to 10° Virgo is favorable and is the best Nakshatra for wedding. It is also favorable for performing rituals, starting new mantras, taking spiritual initiation, taking vows, installing altars or deities, healing and treating diseases, giving advice and good counsel, mediating between hostile parties, legal matters, gaining fame and recognition, beginning studies, learning philosophy, constructing buildings or entering houses, putting on gemstones or new clothes, planting, sexual activity and service ventures. Hasta, #13, 10° to 23.33° Virgo, ruled by Savita, the divine solar creator is a favorable Nakshatra. Indications are travel, starting studies, beginning work ventures, wedding, putting on gemstones or new clothes, adopting a new name, treatment of disease, planting, building a house, manual, artistic and creative ventures, legal matters, learning astrology, learning languages or philosophies, launching educational ventures, mantras, spiritual initiations, chanting, yogic practices, study of the Vedas or the Bible, change of residence and wedding. Chitra, #14, 23.33° Virgo to 6.66° Libra, ruled by Tvashtar, the divine craftsman works consistently well for production activities of all types. It is favorable, indicating a time best for taking medicines, or giving and receiving healing therapies, starting an artistic work, construction work such as building houses, temples, or making statues of deities making or putting on of gemstones or new clothes, housewarming, embarking on educational ventures, artistic activities such as music and dancing, planting and gardening, legal matters, public, social and political issues relating to women or the opposite sex, collecting herbs and preparing medicines; spiritual practices such as visualization. Swati, #15, 06.66° to 20° Libra, ruled by Vayu or the wind, reckoned one of the most favorable Nakshatra-s can be quite unstable. A time to put on gemstones or new clothes, adopt a new name, install altars, treat diseases, garden, gather herbs and prepare medicines; start educational ventures, learn astrology, get involved in social and political activities and wedding."

"Vishakha, #16, 20° Libra to 3.33° Scorpio gets inclined towards Krishna from the asterism's association with Radha, his consort. Radha incidentally is also the highest abode. Vishakha indications are making gemstones, ornaments, arts and crafts; sculpture, architecture, dancing, mechanical work, taking medicines or giving therapies; putting on gemstones or new clothes; buying houses, overcoming enemies. Contra-indications and things to avoid are travel, initiations, sexual activity. Children's health may get affected negatively[223]. Anuradha, #17, 03.33° to 16.66° Scorpio is a favorable Nakshatra. Jyeshta, #18, 16.66° to 30° Scorpio is unfavorable. It requires a strong will and decisive action to cut through the obstacles it may bring us. Mula, #19, 0° to 13.33° Sagittarius is the period for seeding plants, agriculture - Mula means root and the season is great for root based diet. It is also favorable for buying or constructing houses, adopting a new name, wedding, sexual activity, learning astrology and philosophy, harsh actions like surgery, warding off negative influences and avoiding calamities through discretion and protective action. Contra-Indications and things to avoid are spiritual initiations, lending or borrowing money. Purvashadha, #20, 13.33° to 26.66° Sagittarius is unfavorable. Indications are agriculture, preparing medicines, making spiritual objects, reciting mantras, reconciliation, forgiveness and settling debts, issues relating to water, spiritual practices aimed at purification and elimination of sin and negative karma. Uttarashadha, #21, 26.66° Sagittarius to 10° Capricorn is favorable for artistic ventures, wearing new clothes or ornaments, treatment of disease, planting, installing altars, temples or deities, spiritual services and initiation, beginning Vedic or Bible studies, wedding, sexual activity, entering a new house, improving one's home, public and political action, assuming political power or public office, taking positions of authority, gaining success and victory in our endeavors. Some activities are unfavorable like travel. Sravana, #22, 10° to 23.33° Capricorn is auspicious for all favorable activities, including education and administrative actions and travel. It a Nakshatra that specifies great incarnations like Jesus Christ and Vishnu. It supports purchasing new items, adopting a new name, study and teaching; philosophy, learning music, meditation, taking herbs and medicines, influencing the public and political matters, learning spiritual teachings of Vedas and the Bible, spiritual initiations and rituals, gaining space, freedom and understanding."

---

[223] The point between Jyeshta and Mula is considered to be the most unfavorable position for the Moon. It also indicates Fall or Autumn, when death is at its highest. Moon is between signs, between the end of the second third of the zodiac and the start of the last third, and between demonic or Rakshasa Nakshatra-s. It is a particularly dangerous time for children to be born and can cause poor health or early death. This marks the last quarter of Jyeshta and the first two of Mula.

"Dhanistha, #23, 23.33° Capricorn to 06.66° Aquarius, ruled by the Vasus or powers of earthly light and abundance is a favorable aster, with indications of travel, putting on gemstones or new clothes, taking a new name, treating disease, artistic ventures, financial gain and profit Dhanistha means 'the wealthiest'. It also is favorable for beginning educational ventures, learning languages, handling weapons, legal matters, gaining fame and recognition, excellent for learning spiritual teachings like Vedas and Bible; spiritual initiations, learning medicine, gaining of merit. One must not be borrowing money. Shatabhishag, #24, 06.66° to 20° Aquarius, ruled by Varuna who governs debts, karmic retribution and purification gives mixed results in its sphere of influence like medicines and therapies. Shatabhishag supports vehicles, travels, voyages by sea, educational ventures, adopting a new name, learning philosophy, artistic ventures, starting a new business, sexual activity; spiritual practices aimed at purification of the mind and clearing out old karma psychological therapies; longevity and rejuvenation. One should not take part in activities like spiritual initiations, legal issues, visiting spiritual teachers and lending money. Purva Bhadra, #25, 20° Aquarius to 03.33° Pisces is unfavorable. Indications are building and construction, agriculture, business purchases, receiving mantras, installation of spiritual objects, working with water. One must be careful of travel and sexual activity. Uttara Bhadra, #26, 03.33° to 16.66° Pisces is favorable. Indications are artistic ventures, healing and treatment of disease, planting and gardening, sexual activity, wedding, putting on of gemstones, installing altars, temples and churches; spiritual services and initiations, entering a new house, naming of children, establishing deep and solid foundations in life. However, one must avoid travel when moon is under the Nakshatra. Revati, #27, 16.66° to 30° Pisces, last quarter of the Nakshatra system, is inauspicious as it marks the end of the zodiac. Ruled by Pushan who is the solar power of perception, nourishment and transition to a new life. It supports putting on gemstones or new clothes, healing and treatment of disease, wedding, sexual activity, planting and gardening, legal matters, spiritual initiations, learning astrology, languages or philosophy; artistic ventures, music, entering a new house, buying houses, business ventures, exchanges, finances and income - Revati means 'the ultra-wealthy', protection."

Nakshatra daily transits

"Favorability of the daily Nakshatra is computed by examining the relationship with the birth Nakshatra that is the Nakshatra of the Moon at birth. For this, we count from the birth Nakshatra to the daily Nakshatra by counting the birth Nakshatra as one. We subtract multiples of nine from that amount and consider the remainder. If the amount is less than nine, we take that[224]. Difference between the number of Nakshatra-s traveled by the moon from the birth star and mathematically computed would show how the Nakshatra works at a personal level."

1) "Janma" or birth	Specifies danger, threat to the body; unfavorable
2) "Sampat" or gain	Gains and accomplishments; favorable
3) "Vipat" or loss	Losses, dangers and accidents; unfavorable
4) "Kshema" or prosperity	Security and safety; favorable
5) "Pratyak" or opposition	Difficulties and obstacles; unfavorable
6) "Sadhana" or accomplishment	Success, achievement and realization of goals and desires; favorable
7) "Naidhana" or danger	Unfavorable
8) "Mitra" or friend	Help and alliances; favorable
9) "Param-Mitra" or long-lasting friend	Great help; very favorable

"Challenges from the third, fifth and seventh positions is lowered if it occurs at the twelfth, fourteenth and sixteenth Nakshatra-s from the birth Nakshatra; the second division of nine or paryaya from the birth Nakshatra. It is only slight if it occurs at the twenty-first, twenty-third, and twenty-fifth from it; the third division of nine from the birth Nakshatra. Hence, it is better if the daily Nakshatra is behind the birth Nakshatra in the zodiac than in front of it. This system is the general rule and has its variations. In addition, the Nakshatra previous to one's birth Nakshatra, the twenty-seventh, is often not favorable. For example, if the birth Nakshatra is Sravana."

---

[224] For example, if the birth Nakshatra is Uttara Phalguni (12) and the Nakshatra for the day is Sravana (22), the number is 11. Subtracting 9 we get 2.

"Uttarashadha, the previous Nakshatra, is not good for important actions. Hence, even if a Nakshatra is favorable or not, it may not be so if we look at its relationship with the birth star or Nakshatra of a person. Results are best when it falls on a Nakshatra that is favorable from both methods."

Favorable birth Nakshatra

"Days when the Moon is in one's own birth Nakshatra are not favorable for special actions, but prove useful for career advances, planting and gardening, buying and building as in construction, learning and meditation. One's birth Nakshatra is not good for travel, for medical treatment or for sexual activity. For women, however, it is excellent for wedding and marriages. When the Moon is in the eighth house from its natal sign, it is usually not auspicious, regardless of the Nakshatra-s involved. For the Nakshatra to be favorable, moon should not be in the same sign as the Sun or in the sign before or after. With the Sun is in Aries, Moon should not be in Pisces, Aries or Taurus. While Sun is excellent in Aries and so is Moon in Taurus, the constellation does not become fruitful. One should also avoid the new Moon. Nakshatra takes precedence, followed by Tithi in assessing the quality of time."

"Vedic thought states Moon contains sixteen portions or Kala-s. The sixteenth Kala is unchangeable and represents the basic power or energy of the Moon, through which it renews itself in the cycles of time. The number of the other Kala-s increases and decreases with the waxing and waning of the Moon. On the day of the new Moon, the Moon becomes one Kala, the immutable sixteenth. Then it gains one Kala every day approximately until reaching the full sixteen on the day of the full Moon. The increasing and decreasing of the portions of the Moon shows our experience of karma, the cycle of enjoyment of the fruits of our action. It shows the fluctuations of the mind, as the Moon represents the mind or feeling nature."

"Cosmic man or cosmic person as time personified, the individual who is a microcosm of the universe, comprises sixteen parts, five elements of earth, water, fire, air, ether; five organs of action - reproductive organs, organ of elimination, organ of motion or feet, hands, vocal organ; five sense organs of smell, taste, sight, touch, sound. There is mutual correspondence between the three sets. Cosmic man, or mind, is the sixteenth factor, correlates the other fifteen."

"This is all part of standard Samkhya system. The same energy that drives the celestial bodies moves us, taking the corollary higher, the same energy that drives Cosmic man and Creative-force drive the celestial bodies. Moon's movement is a clear reflection of Cosmic Man-Creative-force in the manifestation. After first five-days following the new Moon, the five elements get formed at the terrestrial level as inert or Tamasik type. Another five-days, five-organs of action get formed having Rajasic tendencies. In the next five-days lot, five sense organs get formed, which are pure and sattvic. Then in five-day sequences, the five sense organs, organs of action and the five elements get withdrawn. In the individual, however, these fluctuations are minor, although still important. Mastering these energies through meditation, we gain the energy of bliss. Being dominated by them through the senses, we end up in sorrow and exhaustion. In this way, the portions of the Moon give us a key to our entire spiritual development. They also can act in ordinary actions and in understanding monthly fluctuations of energy."

"Period between two full Moons, or a lunar month, divided into thirty lunar days or 'Tithi-s' measure the Kala-s or portions of the Moon. Moon remains in one Nakshatra per Tithi as both set zodiacal division of around 13 degrees[225]. Period between two full moons is about 29½ days. Each lunar day or Tithi averages a little shorter than one day[226]. There are 371 Tithi-s in a normal year of 365 days. Length of Tithi-s are irregular, the calculation comes from 12-degree movements on a linear scale between the Sun and Moon. Sun moves little less than one degree per day; the Moon moves 13 degrees on the longitudinal scale. Moon's rate of motion is irregular, varying from 11 to 15 degrees in a day."

"This means that an actual Tithi may be a little longer or shorter than a day. The Tithi in effect at sunrise determines Tithi for the day. When the Moons rate of motion is fast, there may be two-Tithi-s in one day. One can skip one such Tithi in the calendar. When the Moons rate is slow, which is rare, the same Tithi may occur on two consecutive days as an increased or 'vriddha' tithi."

---

[225] Each Tithi covers 12-13 degrees of arc between the Sun and Moon. The Purna Tithi-s roughly parallel 60º, 120º and 180º aspects between the Sun or Moon, or trinal aspects. Rikta Tithi-s roughly parallel 45º, 90º and 135º or square and semi-square aspects, malefic aspects

[226] To be exact, each Tithi marks an average period of 23 hours and 37 minutes, or about 23 minutes short of a regular day.

"Tithi of the previous dawn determines what Tithi is in effect during the day for horary astrology. For natal astrology, you can use the Tithi in operation at the birth time. There are 15 types of Tithi-s, divided into two groups relative to the waxing and waning Moon resulting in 30. Bright or waxing half of the Moon is Shukla Paksa. Fifteen-Tithi-s of Shukla Paksa extend from the new Moon at the first Tithi beginning to the full Moon at the end of the fifteenth Tithi. Dark or waning half of the Moons phase is Krishna Paksa. Fifteen-Tithi-s of Krishna Paksa extend from the full Moon at the first Tithi beginning to the new Moon at the end of the fifteenth Tithi. This means there are two days of the full Moon and two days of the new Moon. Purnima ends with the Moon becoming completely full. Hence, it refers to the lunar day culminating with the full Moon. Krishna Pratipat begins with the exact full Moon; it refers to the lunar day that starts with the full Moon. Amavasya similarly ends with the Moon becoming fully new. Hence, it refers to the lunar day culminating with the new Moon. Shukla Pratipat begins with the exact new Moon, it refers to the lunar day that starts with the new Moon."

"Exact new and full Moon occur between the fifteenth and first Tithi-s. Exact half-moon occurs in the middle of the eighth Tithi. These points of the new, full and half-moons are transitional. Such days are somewhat unstable and are better for conserving energy, or practicing meditation than engaging in outside activity. Eighth Tithi or half-moon remains equally unstable and avoided for most auspicious actions."

"At transitional times of dawn and dusk, fluctuations in the energy make the atmosphere unfavorable for initiating outer actions but it becomes favorable for making inner transformations and rising to a higher level of consciousness. The horizontal movement of energy becomes vertical, thus allowing ascension rather than an outer expansion of energies to occur. During transitional Tithi-s, the Prana or vital energy is better able to enter the central channel or Sushumna, making it favorable for meditation. Energy becomes introverted, consolidated and powerful."

"Most even-numbered lunar days, second, fourth, sixth, eighth, and fourteenth are inauspicious, the exception being the tenth, which is excellent. By other accounts the twelfth and the sixth are also good. Odd days are auspicious, except for the day of the New Moon - the fifteenth of the dark half, the first day after the new Moon, which remains in the shadow the new Moon, and the ninth Tithi."

"Tithi-s get divided into five groups of three Tithi-s each."

First, sixth and eleventh. Element: Earth	Joyous. Auspicious for all ventures and in initiating them.
Second, seventh and twelfth. Element: Water	Auspicious.
Third, eighth and thirteenth. Element: Fire	Victorious. Slightly auspicious. Requires more effort on our part to gain good results, but with effort can bring high level of gains.
Fourth, ninth and fourteenth. Element: Air	Discarded. Inauspicious - not used for any important actions.
Fifth, tenth and fifteenth. Element: Ether	'Purna' or full. Very favorable, except the day of the new Moon. They allow maximum development to occur.

"The ancient seers measured lunar energy coming to this planet in certain waves. Each half of the lunar month gets divided into three segments, with the lunar energy having three crests. Tithi just before each of these crests of energy is unstable and unfavorable for most actions. First of the five sets of Tithi-s relate to the earth element, the second to the water element, the third to the fire element, the fourth to the air element, and the fifth to the ether element. One may consider Tithi-s dominated by air as unstable."

Tithi-s for activities

Tithi Group	Shukla Paksa (Bright Half)	Mental Virtue	Krishna Paksa (Dark Half)
1 – 5	Commencing new ventures; establishing foundations, setting things in motion	Low High	Revising, reorganizing, reforming ventures; Internalizing what's gained
6 – 10	Developing and sustaining action and accomplishment	Average	Consolidation and contraction
11 – 15	Developing knowledge, Creative and spiritual ventures	High Low	Bringing things to completion; withdrawal; Evaluation

"Fourth, ninth, fourteenth, the day of the New Moon and the day after the new Moon, the first are unfavorable. Many practitioners also consider the sixth, the eighth in particular, and twelfth days unsuitable for important actions. Tithi-s starting with the twelfth or Dwadashi of the dark half of the Moon get avoided for important actions as practitioners consider them unfavorable."

"Mental power is highest at the time of the full Moon and hence this is the best time for spiritual realization, the awareness of pure being, and the experience of joy and bliss. It is also more favorable for communion, communication and relationship. The mental power is lowest at the time of the New Moon. Each Tithi exhibits certain indications. The hints for the Tithi-s are generally the same, whether they occur in the bright or dark half of the month. Just a general rule prevails that the bright half is more favorable than the dark half. The only exception to this is the first Tithi, in which case the dark half, the sixteenth is better, since on the first Tithi of the bright half, the Moon stays combust. Positive signals from the Tithi-s are more probable in the bright half, and the negative ones in the dark half."

"First day after the full or new moon, is negative for all important activities. The day is still useful for meditation, study, and planning and initiating new directions. Krishna Pratipat or 16, the day after full moon is useful in starting new enterprises, knowledge seeking, installing new items, putting on gemstones, performing ceremonies, meditation, weddings, and unfavorable for travel. Dwitiya, 2 and 17, are moderately promising for travel, wearing gemstones, weddings, house or land rites, installing new items, acquiring new objects or income, starting new ventures, forming new goals, commencing new studies and medical treatment. Tritiya days, 3 and 18 are fortunate for travel, construction, medical treatment, learning, performing spiritual services, giving of gifts and supporting wedding days in the bright half. Chaturthi, 4 and 19 are advantageous for discarding unwanted or excess possessions, cleaning of the house or the mind, internal purification and renunciation, dispensing punishment, preparing medicines, but are not favorable for giving treatment. The days are negative for starting projects and unfavorable for travel, initiations, spiritual services or putting on gemstones as they bring obstacles, delays and obstructions. Panchami days, 5 and 20 are very promising days for travel, gaining wealth and giving gifts, performing spiritual services and devotional practices, putting on gemstones, meditation, study, gaining occult knowledge, fasting, healing and medical treatment, travel, wedding and all other sacraments. Such days are also good for learning, but disadvantageous for negative actions or actions requiring force such as punishment."

"Shashti, 6 and 21 are not good for travel, but otherwise good for putting on gemstones, fasting, construction, house or land rites, study, and for preparing medicines but not for using them in any treatment. Useful for harsh actions or defending oneself against hostile influences. Saptami days, 7 and 22 are promising for travel, use and maintenance or purchase of vehicles, physical activity and exercise, medical treatment, performing spiritual services, and marriage and wedding. Such days are fair but not excellent for putting on gemstones or new clothes. Guard against any tendency towards rash actions on this day. Ashtami, 8 and 23, are great days for studies, physical activity, sports, artistic ventures, construction, best for meditation, also good for healing and rejuvenation practices. Not good for most important projects and decisions, initiations, travel, or sexual activity. Navami, 9 and 24, are auspicious for competitive ventures like sports, debates, exercise and physical activity, and for preparation of medicines but not for giving treatment. There is a danger of excessive use of force on this day. Not good for most important projects like installation of deities or altars, putting on of gemstones, travel, or for sexual activity. Yet, in the bright half, it is one of the best days for meditation, chanting and rituals. Dashami, 10 and 25, are very favorable for travel, putting on gemstones or new clothes, wedding in the bright half, ceremonies and parties, income, vehicles and houses, study and learning, all healing actions, excellent for oil massage, and for visiting important people. The bright Tithi on the tenth is perhaps the most fortunate of all Tithi-s and works well for all expansive ventures. Ekadashi, 11 and 26, are auspicious for travel, learning, ceremonies and meditation, social and career gains, wedding or putting on of gemstones in the bright half, exercise, learning, study and educational ventures. Dwadashi, 12 and 27 are favorable for weddings in the bright half, spiritual services, devotional practices, charity and renunciation. Thrayodashi, 13 and 28, are favorable for medical treatment, spiritual services, meditation, and travel. The days are moderately favorable for wedding or putting on of gemstones only in the bright half. Chaturdashi, 14 and 29, are fortunate for the study of scriptures, chanting and meditation especially in the bright half. Good for preparing medicines but not for giving treatment, and for fasting in the dark half. The days are unfavorable for most actions, including putting on of gemstones, travel or sexual activity. Promotes misunderstandings and negative emotions and provides a good day to preserve one's energy. Purnima, full moon day or 15, is favorable for house construction, putting on of gemstones, and for career gains. The days are better for fasting, contemplation and meditation."

"Purnima or full moon beckons a time when we experience the fruit of our actions during the month, and bring things to completion, but not so useful for starting new ventures. The days are unfavorable for travel. Amavasya, new moon or day 30, is favorable for meditation, study and ascetic practices, tributes to those departed and for giving gifts. Not good for health, but an important time for bringing a new healing energy to those who are sick, the debilitated or suffering from chronic illness. The day is unfavorable for most things, including putting on of gemstones, travel and sexual activity. A favorable day to remain inactive and introverted."

"Results are better in the brighter than darker half of the Moon. Prathama is industrious, with much initiative, inclined to do good. Dwitiya gives wealth, strength, recognition and increase. Tritiya acts good-natured, timid, with powerful speech. Chaturthi gets influenced easily, changeable, accustomed to wandering, yet inclined toward spiritual knowledge. Panchami stays virtuous, spiritual, intelligent, and strong willed, creative, thin. Shashti shows low vitality, prestige, and wrathful or fiery disposition. Saptami gives power over people, firm voice, kapha or watery constitution. Ashtami specifies many desires or greed, attachment to spouse and children, kapha or watery constitution. Navami showers recognition, charisma and charm, along with desires and ambitions and is not good for wedding or children. Dashami directs virtuosity with good marriage and family, prosperity, intelligent. Ekadashi suggests virtuosity, respect, intelligent, wealth and following. Dwadashi engages in good works, acts liberal, fortunate and learned. Thrayodashi fulfills many desires, strengthens the will, and the capacity to gain and hold wealth. Chaturdashi shows passion, ambition, and power with fiery, pitta disposition. Purnima gives popularity, honor, virtue, fame and happiness. Amavasya remains easily influenced, weak vitality, low body fluids, single-minded perceptions."

Lords of Tithi-s

"Like the Nakshatra, a deity rules the tithi[227]. For tithi # 1, the deity is Brahma or Prajapati, the cosmic creator. The tithi approves in initiating all ventures, all sacraments and spiritual actions. It promises a time for planning, not executing. For tithi # 2, the deity is Vidhatar, cosmic designer in establishing structure and order."

---

[227] Nakshatra and Tithi rulings are similar. What is meant by a deity ruling them are the icon, the symbolism and the characteristics.

"Second tithi is better for establishing the broader scope of our endeavors, rationalizing the plans set in first tithi. For tithi # 3, it is Vishnu, the cosmic preserver. This tithi promotes activities meant to last and brings things to a high level of development and recognition. Yama rules Tithi # 4 switching the day to unfavorable status, except for harsh actions and self-discipline. Soma rules Tithi # 5 turning it favorable for most activities involving women, mother and emotions. It marks a period good for preparing or taking herbal medicines, natural healing therapies of both body and mind, devotional meditation. Agni or Skanda, the warlord rules Tithi # 6. Ruled by fire, the tithi works well for harsh or fiery actions, such as surgery, overcoming enemies, disciplining our physical nature or organizing our material resources. Tithi # 7, ruler is Agni, works well for actions aimed at establishing independence, for personal gains and for self-development. It can give great success but requires will and motivation. Vasus, the gods of splendor rule Tithi # 8. It gives success and splendor but with a tendency toward excess, overdevelopment and diffusion of energies. The Serpent rules Tithi # 9, a day generally avoided. It also inclines toward excess and possible deception. Dharma or Brihaspati rules Tithi # 10. This tithi is favorable for all solemn-duties and spiritual actions, for rituals, meditation, and for all sacraments and positive actions in life. It has an energy similar to Pushya in mid-Cancer, also ruled by Brihaspati, which gives the ability to promote all positive ventures. Rudra, lord of thunder rules Tithi # 11. This tithi is very strong and can give success and transformation but its energy can be difficult to deal with, like the fierce Rudra, the ferocious attributes of Vishnu. Sun, Aditya or Savita rules Tithi # 12. This tithi is very auspicious for creative and spiritual actions, for creative work and learning. It has an energy similar to Hasta in mid-Virgo, also ruled by Savita. Bhaga, god of love and charm rules Tithi # 13. This tithi is favorable for matters of pleasure, enjoyment, recreation, friendship, social gains, charm, and charisma and dealing with the mass media."

"Tithi # 14 is strife. This tithi causes conflict and misunderstanding. It caters to harsh actions like administering drugs or performing surgery, or for occult sorcery. Universal Gods, Vishwadeva-s rules Tithi # 15, full moon. This tithi works well for cosmic action and for promoting the future. Pitris, the ancestors rule Tithi # 15 of the new moon. This tithi connects the native to the ancestors, dealing with one's past. It is better for self-examination and for clearing up the past. The first half of the lunar month is better for spiritual actions and for initiating new activities. The second half is better for personal, social or family matters and for finishing actions already started."

"Each day of the week has its characteristic quality based upon the planet's nature that rules it. Astrological day begins at sunrise. The nature of the day is the easiest factor to consider, as it requires neither an ephemeris nor a Panchanga. It is usually the first factor we should consider and the basis for determining the Nakshatra and Tithi. If we choose an auspicious day for our actions, we have already taken a significant step in protecting them."

"Days ruled by graha-s are Sunday, the Sun; Monday, the Moon; Tuesday, Mars; Wednesday, Mercury; Thursday, Jupiter; Friday, Venus and Saturday, Saturn."

"Sunday is favorable for rituals, meditation, self-knowledge, gains in career or status, receiving honors, honoring tradition, authorities, parents or gurus, worship of the divine father. The day is unfavorable for wedding, sexual activity or conception. Not useful for business ventures. Not a good day for outward expansion as much as inner examination and for establishing personal intentions and goals realized during the week. Monday is favorable for affairs relating to the public or society, for gaining popularity, for relating to women or to the mother, including worship of the divine mother, for friends, family and household matters. It promises good weddings, sexual activity and conception of children, medical treatment, contemplation and meditation. The day can bring financial or business gains through friends and social contact. Tuesday gets favored for physical activity, sports and competitive ventures but one must not act reckless. It is important that we use the restless Mars energy of this day and not allow it to become bottled up inside ourselves, good for developing warrior energy. The day is also useful for mechanical work, fixing things, for research, mathematical studies, and scientific pursuits. Tuesday is more favorable in the afternoon than in the morning and is unfavorable for marriage or sexual activity. Unfavorable for travel, legal affairs, relationship and human issues requiring tact or sensitivity."

"Wednesday promises better communication, talking, writing, learning, study, teaching, educational activities, meditation. Better day for business, commerce, and career gains, communication ventures, making money, marriage and sexual activity. Good for all healing practices, using herbs, and preparing medicines. The day is also good for healing the mind and all psychological studies, paying tribute to the divine conservator. Yet more a day for creating the theoretical background for our projects than for trying to begin anything that lasts. Thursday is the most favorable day of the week for all good actions, including spiritual services, ceremonies, meditation, study and worship of the divine, the guru or traditions."

"Wednesday is good for financial gain, speculative ventures, career advancement, and for enjoyment and social interaction. Good for healing practices, workouts of all types, reconciliation and for giving gifts. It is excellent for legal matters. It is favorable for wedding, sexual activity, or conception; it is also good for the affairs of children. The best day for initiating expansive ventures we hope will endure. Friday is a promise of artistic ventures, decorations and ornaments, business ventures, purchasing vehicles, buying gemstones, clothes, or other precious items, for affairs relative to women like marriage, sexual activity, romance; enjoyment and entertainment; it is also good for devotional practices or study of the occult. Saturday is unfavorable for most social or business matters, as it brings loss or opposition, but good for acquiring fixed property and for doing service work. Not good for health, marriage, or for sexual activity, but good for retreat, study, meditation and relaxation. It is also good for self-discipline, yoga, fasting and ascetic practices; a good day to spend time alone. Good for worshipping the dark or wrathful forms of the Divine. Our cultural tendency is to escape the influence of Saturn on Saturday by turning it into a day of self-indulgence but this is not wise, as it keeps our lives out of the control of our deeper nature and spiritual intent. Hence, Saturday is perhaps the most important day of the week for structuring our time wisely."

"These are only general indications. One must consider the graha's position on that day. For example, if Mercury is with Saturn and Rahu, Wednesday may cause loss and difficulties in matters involving communication and business. The effects of the days of the week on an individual's life vary according to the place and strength of the planet within the individual's birth chart. For example, if a person has a strong Mars as a Raja Yoga Karaka, Tuesday would be very favorable for work, career, or starting new ventures."

"It is best to combine favorable days, Tithi-s and Nakshatra-s for the best possible results. When a favorable day of the week, like Thursday or Friday, is under a favorable Tithi, like the fifth or the tenth, it is a good day for auspicious actions. If, in addition, the Moon is in a favorable Nakshatra - like Pushya, Punarvasu, Rohini, Mrigashira, Revati, Uttara Phalguni, Uttara Bhadra or Chitra, then the results are quite excellent. When such a good day is under a favorable Tithi for meditation, like the ninth, fourteenth or fifteenth, then it becomes very strong for that."

Karana

"Each tithi gets divided into two Karana-s or 'instruments'. Karana-s give us the means to fulfill our actions. In total, there are eleven Karana-s."

1. Lion (bava)	2, 9, 16, 23, 30, 37, 45, 51
2. Leopard (balava)	3, 10, 17, 24, 31, 38, 46, 52
1. Pig (kaulava)	4, 11, 18, 25, 32, 39, 47, 53
2. Donkey (taitula)	5, 12, 19, 26, 33, 40, 48, 54
3. Elephant (garija)	6, 13, 20, 27, 34, 41, 49, 55
4. Cow (vanija)	7, 14, 21, 28, 35, 42, 50, 56
5. Vishti	8, 15, 22, 29, 36, 43, 51, 57
6. Pullu (shakuna)	58
7. Cattle (chatuspada)	59
8. Snake (naga)	60
9. Worm (kimstughna)	1

"Karana-s are named after animals. The first and last three denote a fixed character. They relate to the new Moon and show the enduring factor of the Moon's power. Remaining fifty-six Karana-s designate a mutable quality. They show fluctuations of the lunar force. One may avoid activities in Fixed and Vishti Karana-s as they are unfavorable. Fixed Karana-s occur during unfavorable Tithi-s anyway and are therefore hostile. They relate to the latter half of the fourteenth day of the waning Moon, the day of the new Moon, and the first half of the day after the new Moon. Hence, the first half of the first day of the waxing Moon is more unfavorable than the second half. The new Moon, though a Purna or full tithi, becomes unfavorable as both of its Karana-s show the negative aspect. Fixed Karana-s of 58, 59, 60, 1 and Mutable class of the Vishti group of 8, 15, 22, 29, 36, 43, 50, 57 are unfavorable and inauspicious. Fixed Karana-s, occurring once a lunar month as a transition between the two halves or Paksa of the Moon, cover a two-day time period, in lunar terms, four consecutive half-days, or two Tithi-s. For the remaining period, the Karana-s of Vishti and of the other groups occur in alternation eight times each in a lunar month, on every seventh lunar half-day computed as 8 * 7 = 56. Vishti Karana occurs in the bright half of the moon in the first half of the 4th Tithi, excluded as unfavorable, the first half of the 8th tithi also disallowed, the second half of the 11th tithi, and the first half of the full moon tithi. During the dark half of the moon, it occurs on the second half of the 3rd tithi, the first half of the 7th Tithi, the second half of the 10th Tithi, and the first half of the 14th Tithi also rejected. The Karana-s of the lion prove beneficial for starting ventures of an enduring nature, those of the donkey work well for marriages. Some typical classical indications of the Karana-s for birth and activities."

1. Bava	Youthful, childish, valiant
2. Balava	Modest, careful in conduct, respected
3. Kaulava	Impressive, active, dramatic
4. Taitula	Skillful in speech and action, able to influence
5. Garija	Powerful, able to overcome opposition
6. Varija	Clever, passionate, may lack self-control
7. Vishti	Gives opposition, acts contrary to normal order, culpable, self-reliant, honored by his followers
8. Shakuna	Able to read events, psychic perception, intelligence, prosperity
9. Chatuspada	Many obstacles, yet many possibilities, comprehensive
10. Naga	Ambitious, powerful, dangerous
11. Kimstughna	Dependent, changeable, superficial, easy going

Panchanga yogas

"The term 'Yoga' has several usages in the methods used in Muhurta or Electional context of astrology. Like the Nakshatra-s, each-yoga corresponds to a 13.33° section of the zodiac. The calculations are different, adding the longitudes of the Sun and the Moon and dividing the amount by 800, the number of minutes in 13.33° denotes the yoga."

"For example, if the Moon is at 14.33° Gemini, its longitude from the point 0 Aries would be 74.33°. If the Sun is at 20.66° Sagittarius, its longitude would be 260.5°. Adding these together, 74.33° plus 260.5° we would get 334.83°. If we get a number higher than 360, we should subtract 360 from it. This we then turn into minutes by multiplying the degrees by 60, which would be 20,040 plus 50 for the minutes or 20,090. We then divide this amount by 800, which gives us 25.1125. This place us in the twenty-sixth Brahma yoga, as the twenty-fifth has already finished. To determine when a particular yoga ends, multiply the remainder by 24. In the above example 24 x 0.1125 is 2.7 or two houses and forty-two minutes from the particular time in question."

"Some typical indications of Yogas are as given in the table."

1. Vishkambha*	Overcomes obstacles, gains wealth and property
2. Priti*	Easily influenced by attractive objects

3. Ayushman	Good for health and longevity
4. Saubhagya	Gives happiness, is auspicious for action
5. Sobhana	Gives beauty but also sensuality
6. Atiganda*	Destructive and deceptive tendency, clever
7. Sukarma	Good for action, work and accomplishment
8. Dhriti*	Dominates and controls other people
9. Shula*	Gives anger, conflict and pain
10. Ganda*	Gives attachments and addictions
11. Vriddhi	Gives wisdom, speech capacity and increase
12. Dhruva	Gives stability, firmness and wealth
13. Vyaghata*	Dangerous and wrathful, can bring injury
14. Harshana	Exhilarating, gives joy, fame and wisdom
15. Vajra*	Gives will, power, energy and motivation
16. Siddhi	Gives success and protection
17. Vyatipatha*	Deceptive, unclear, moving in many directions
18. Variyan*	Causes one to seek gain, can give greed, ambition
19. Parigha*	Inimical but wealthy and successful
20. Shiva	Auspicious, peaceful, intelligent, loved
21. Siddha	Successful, virtuous, adept, skillful
22. Sadhya	Righteous (virtuous), able to accomplish goals
23. Shubha	Gives beauty and wealth but may give sensuality
24. Shukla	Gives intelligence, powers of speech, virtuosity but changeable in mind and difficult to please
25. Brahma	Gives wisdom, good judgment, honor, secret wealth
26. Aindra	Gives comprehensive intellect, beneficence, wealth, power, honor, prestige
27. Vaidhriti*	Firm, powerful, wealthy but obstinate and inflexible

Less favorable

"Of these Yogas, the first, sixth, ninth, tenth, fifteenth, seventeenth and twenty-seventh are inauspicious. The twenty-first, twenty-fifth and twenty-sixth are auspicious. All other remaining Yogas become favorable, in particular 21 Siddha, 25 Brahma and 26 Aindra, under which permitted are all auspicious undertakings."

Unfavorable yogas

Yoga	Sanskrit Name	Meaning	Time to avoid
1	Vishkambha	Pot filled with poison	First 3 Ghatis or 1 hour and 12 minutes
6	Ati-Ganda	Very strong knot or obstacle	First 6 Ghatis or 2 hours and 24 minutes
9	Shula	Sharp or pointed weapon	First 5 Ghatis 2 hours
10	Ganda	Knot or hindrance	First 6 Ghatis or 2 hours and 24 minutes
13	Vyaghata	Striking against or obstacle	First 9 Ghatis or 3 hours and 36 minutes
15	Vajra	Thunderbolt, lightning	First 3 Ghatis or 1 hour and 12 minutes
17	Vyatipata	Destruction	60 Ghatis - whole time period
19	Parigha	Iron bar / club	30 Ghatis or first half of Yoga
27	Vaidhriti	Division	60 Ghatis - whole time period

Karana and yoga

"Once a favorable day with Tithi and Nakshatra gets determined, it can be further checked to see if an unfavorable Yoga and Karana could bring about any obstruction. If this is not the case, the outcome becomes more favorable. If it is the case, we may look to a part of the day when negative Yogas and Karana-s are not in operation, or we can look to another favorable day, Tithi and Nakshatra that do not have such a negative condition. There is a part of this system, which delineates specific tithi-s coinciding with particular days of the week as being auspicious or inauspicious. Certain combinations of weekdays and lunar days, Vara-s and Tithi-s, give rise to certain qualities during the time in question, according to integration of individual qualities of these two-time factors."

Siddha favorable tithi-s

Tithi Group	Tithi-s	Vara
Nanda	1, 6, 11	Friday
Bhadra	2, 7, 12	Wednesday
Jaya	3, 8, 13	Tuesday
Rikta	4, 9, 14	Saturday
Purna	5, 10, 15	Thursday

Dagdha unfavorable tithi-s

Tithi Group	Vara
Nanda	Sunday, Tuesday
Bhadra	Monday, Friday
Jaya	Wednesday
Rikta	Thursday
Purna	Saturday

Krakacha favorable tithi-s

Tithi	Vara
12 Dwadashi	1 Sunday
11 Ekadashi	2 Monday
10 Dashami	3 Tuesday
9 Navami	4 Wednesday
8 Ashtami	5 Thursday
7 Saptami	6 Friday
6 Shashti	7 Saturday

Sun's travel into new signs

"Suns movement into new signs, at a Sankranti juncture is also a time not favorable for activities. Six hours before and after changing signs are inauspicious, the last fifteen minutes or quarter of longitudinal-degree of one sign and the first fifteen minutes of another. When other planets are in the last or first degree of a sign, this can also cause difficulties."

Equinoctial and Solstice Points

"Days of the equinoxes and solstices are additional important transitional periods. They are more favorable for meditation than for ordinary activities. Most important perhaps is the day of the winter solstice as it allows us to bring in a spiritual energy for the whole year. Like transitional points of sunrise and sunset, the solstices and equinoxes are points at which the mind can more easily become still and the Prana or vital energy can enter the central channel for inner transformation. Hence, these times are important for spiritual rather than ordinary actions."

Northern and Southern Courses of the Sun

"All activities yield better results when done during the northern course of the Sun, Uttarayana, the period between the winter and the summer solstices from December 22 to June 21. It is not that the remaining part of the year is idle. Activities during the southern course of the Sun yield better results during the bright half of the Moon."

"Eclipses are important points of knowledge revelation and energy transformation. They release energy into the central channel and allow the mind to be still, withdrawing it from its ordinary outward actions. Lunar eclipses are important times for purification and negation of the mind. Solar eclipses are important times for self-knowledge and transcendence of the ego."

"Gandhanta Moon is when the Moon occupies the first Navamsa of 3° 20 of fire signs or the last quarter of water signs. These junction points are inauspicious, and dangerous for the birth of children. This position is the first quarter of Ashvini, Magha and Mula Nakshatra-s and the last of Revati, Aslesha and Jyeshta Nakshatra-s. Jyeshta-Mula or Scorpio-Sagittarius Gandhanta gets to be the worst. Aslesha-Magha or Cancer-Leo Gandhanta is second. Revati-Ashvini or Pisces-Aries is not always so bad. The same positions are difficult for other planets but only in the first and last degrees of the respective signs, not through the entire 3.33° section. The full Gandhanta arc of 3.33° applies only to the Moon as it is a fast-moving planet."

Music therapy

"Chinese Emperor Fu-Hsi circa 3000 BCE played a stringed instrument Ch'in or the Veena of Kinnaras. Li Chi wrote thousands of years later, Confucius in 571-578 BCE always had his Ch'in with him when he went for a walk or a journey. In Genesis 4.21, a stringed instrument Kinnor gets played by David. The antiquity of Vedic music was well known to the ancient world. Strabo wrote about the Greek theory and view of music was from melody, rhythm and instruments, which came from Thrace and Asia. Megasthenes in Indika, 7.8 talks about the 153 kings that preceded Chandragupta, 6042 years to Dionysus or Siva who roamed the primeval forests and taught the oldest system of dance and music to the people. The Siva School of music predates the Vedic school; the latter may have adopted much from the music into Gandharva Veda. The study of music in Gandharva extended to physics, medicine and magic."

"Music theory came under language as general science of sound. Same authors such as Vasistha, Yajnavalkya, Narada, Kashyap and Panini amongst others codified spoken language and music. However, the Carnatic music is vastly different school and so are many of the schools that have stayed in the plains of Assam, Bengal and the hills of Himalayas. The southern music is extremely ancient and uninfluenced like its northern counterpart. Styles and Raga-s have been maintained that conform to the scriptures. References in Sama Veda, Gandharva Veda, Purana-s such as Ramayana, Mahabharata, Vishnu-Dharmottara, Markendeya Purana, Vayu Purana and other literature put us in a pre-Buddhism era."

"From an anonymous manuscript, Madhava Krishna Sharma explains the musical sounds on the basis of Mahesvara Sutras, a divine arrangement of syllabic sounds as the basis of all language. The Narada Samhita clearly talks about linkages between Vedic chants and profane music. The main available work is Bharata Natya Sastra which was compiled somewhere between 200 BCE and 300 CE. The word 'Bharata' designates a dance-actor, perhaps related to the Celtic 'Bard'. Adi Bharata, Nandikeswara Bharata, Matanga Bharata were the Vedic Bards. Bharata Natya Sastra possibly meant the 'textbook of a dance-actor', though according to tradition, Bharata had four sons, Sandilya, Vatsya, Kohala and Dattila. In Natya Sastra, chapter 1.26 it states 'I taught my sons Sandilya, Vatsya, Kohala and Dattila music in its perfection.' Matanga who wrote 'Brihaddeshi' is mentioned in the epics Mahabharata and Ramayana and the many Puranas."

"There were several authors of that period including Nandikeswara, Kohala and Dattila. Among the existent works of Sangeeta Ratnakar, Sangeeta Narayana, Bharata Sastra, Raga Mala many author names come up, Bhatta, Soma, Narayana, Damodar."

"Music predates to Sama Veda with Brahma, Prajapati, Kashyap, Brihaspati, Angira, Bharadvaja, Soma, Vasistha, Tumburu as the earliest teachers followed by Agastya, Manu, Valmiki, Bhargava, Durvasa. This is a small representative list. What I wanted to establish was the same sages taught astrology, Ayurveda and music in overall wellness program 6000-7000 years before. A parallel tradition existed with divine-teachers, Sankara, Vignesha, Shashank, Indra, Chandi, Parvati, Gauri, Vallabh and others. In the third tradition, the teachings are passed on to Atri, Kapil, Brighu, Yaksha, Sarasvati, Bali, Yaksha, Daksha, Bhaskara and others. In the Epic Mahabharata, Arjuna who is the expert archer is also expert in Gandharva techniques. Some author names come up in the latter part of history, still thousands of years back like Kohala, Sandilya, and Vasuki. The Buddhism period saw a sharp decline in Vedic music. Some authors flourished in this period Katayana, Datta, Bhatta and several others."

Intelligible sound, joy for the happy
distraction for those who hurt
Win the hearts of many a listener
O' messenger of the god of love

Let there be ease of access
O' nimble beloved of women of passion
May it ever be honored
fifth approach to the eternal wisdom

"True music produces two kinds of sound, one an un-struck vibration in ether, the second vibration in the air. The etheric disturbance, unperceived is the principle of all manifestation. Permanent numerical patterns get created, on which is based the world's existence. The un-struck sound delights the gods. Great minds project their minds into the un-struck sound and attain liberation. The struck sound, audible to our ears gives pleasure. The Narada Purana, Sangeeta Makarand agree to this explanation. Musical sounds have the power to reproduce the first creation of primordial intellect, Mahat. The creation is both a rhythm and a thought. Musical sounds convey ideas, emotions and form harmonious relations. Three main elements are considered in musical sound, intensity, interval and timber. Intensity can be soft or powerful, interval is the relative pitch or Sruti and timber arises from resonance of voices and instruments."

"Music is a relationship of sounds. Modal music sets a sound as fixed and invariable, the tonic 'Sa' or 'C', subsequent to which come other sounds, the notes. The relationship to the tonic determines the meaning of any given sound. The tonic must always be 'heard' - as a drone or repeated at frequent intervals. It is not important that singers use a lower tonic like B flat. If the tonic is noted as C, the modes can be transposed to commence on any note. The note or svara is the sound that generates an expression. Like the seven graha-s, two phantom nodes, in modal music seven-main and two-secondary svara-s form a pure 'Suddha' scale. When they are raised, or lowered to form other scales, they are considered as altered 'vikrita' scale. From twenty-two main intervals come seven notes – Shadja, Rishabha, Gandhara, Madhyama, Panchama, Dhaivata, Nisadha."

"The seven notes relate to seven limbs of Cosmic man, Shadja, Sa, Do or C the tonic note is the spirit, Rishabha, Ri, Re, D is the head, Gandhara, Ga, Mi, E represent the arms, Madhyama, Ma, Fa, F the chest, Panchama, Pa, Sol, G the throat, Dhaivata, Dha, La, A the hips, Nisadha, Ni, Si, B the feet. They originate in the physical body from the seven subtle body chakras. Like the zodiac, the signs correspond to animals, so does the seven notes symbolically become represented by birds and animals. Sa is sounded by the peacock, Ri the chataka bird, Ga the sound emitted by a goat, Ma cries the heron, Pa sung by cuckoo in spring, Dha from a frog in monsoons and Ni by an elephant."

"Musical theory says the ear can perceive sixty-six distinct meaningful intervals. Twenty-two are used in music. Sangeeta-Samayasara states that twenty-two sounds cannot be produced in succession; they must be demonstrated on a stringed instrument. Tumburu says that a sound that is high is harsh and piercing, the wise know it to be born of the wind."

"A low sound, deep and mellow comes from the bile and the attractive, perfect, sweet and tender sound takes birth from the lymph. The high sounds of an instrument have the vata force, the low strings emit the pitta qualities and the middle are kapha natured."

"Each audible sound or Sruti is given a name depicting its character. Sangeeta-Ratnakar defines five families of intervals or jati-s – moderate, keen, broad, tender, compassionate. The expression of a mode is the sum of expressions of its different notes, defined by their relationship to the tonic. Different schools have variations in what some of the note 'expressions' conveyed, but a system has evolved that manages it well. Since all notes cannot have the same kind of expression, there are therefore contrasts. For intense styles or Raga-s, the scale can be pentatonic. In a pentatonic arrangement, it is easier to eliminate those notes that do not support the predominant expression."

"A very sad melody would leave out Pa, fifth as Pa expresses joy and sunshine. Incidentally, even in western music, the fifth is Sol, belongs to the sun. A passionate sequence would leave out fourth Ma, as it is serene and peaceful. Compared to a heptatonic scale which has more contrasts, indecisions and subtleties, the pentatonic offers a more elegant way to approach the wellness."

"When sounds are used to creating ecstasy, hypnotic sessions, treating mental and physical diseases, the number of notes may be further reduced to a few sounds constantly heard to keep it very focused."

	Note	Ratio from C	Expression
1	Sa, C	1/1	Base
2	Sa+, C+	81/80	
3	Rik-, Db-	25/24	Sad, pathetic
4	Rik, Db	256/243	Tender, at peace
5	Rik+, Db+	16/15	Loving, calm
6	Ri++, Db++	27/25	Enterprising
7	Ri-, D-	10/9	Anxious, weak
8	Ri, D	9/8	Strong, confident
9	Ri+, D+	256/225	Fierce
10	Gak-, Eb-	75/64	Sad
11	Gak, Eb	32/27	Loving
12	Gak+, Eb+	6/5	Passionate
13	Ga, E	5/4	Calm, pleasing
14	Ga+, E+	81/64	Awaken, lively

AQUAPISCES

	Note	Ratio from C	Expression
15	Ga++, E++	32/25	Hard, indifferent
16	Ma-, F-	320/243	Doubt
17	Ma, F	4/3	Moonlight, peace
18	Ma+, F+	27/20	Intense
19	Mat-, F#-	25/18	Intense, grief
21	Mat, F#	45/32	Uncertain, doubtful
22	Mat+, F#+	64/45	Intense, active
23	Mat++, F#++	36/25	Acute, interrogative
24	Pa-, G-	27/20	Inexpressive, self-contradictory
25	Pa, G	3/2	Sunlight, joyful
26	Pa+, G+	243/160	Confused, self-contradictory
27	Dhak-, Ab-	25/16	Deep sorrow
28	Dhak, Ab	128/81	Tender
29	Dhak+, Ab+	8/5	Loving, enterprising
30	Dha-, A-	400/243	Uncertainty
31	Dha, A	5/3	Soft, calm
32	Dha+, A+	27/16	Restless, playful
33	Dha++, A++	128/75	Hard, active
34	Nik-, Bb-	225/128	Helpless, subdued
35	Nik, Bb	16/9	Beauty, love
36	Nik+, Bb+	9/5	Desire, anxiety
37	Ni--, B--	729/400	Doubt
38	Ni-, B-	50/27	Anguish, depression
39	Ni, B	15/8	Soft, voluptuous
40	Ni+, B+	243/128	Strong, sensuous
41	Ni++, B++	48/25	Selfish, eager
42	Sa-, C-	160/81	

"Let us take an example of fifths. Pa or G is the fifth from C, fifth is Leo or Sol expressing sunshine and joy. The ratio is 3/2, which means the mathematical progression to this scale would be C, G (3/2), D 9/8 ($3^2/2^3$), A+ 27/16 ($3^3/2^4$), E+ 81/64 ($3^4/2^6$), B+ 243/128 ($3^5/2^7$). The ascending fifths are G D A+ E+ B+ and descending fifths are F Bb Eb Ab Db. The ascending represents sunshine, joy and the descending moonlight, peace. The twenty-two divisions cannot be considered equal, they are chosen from fifty-three or sixty-six possible positions."

"In present day, few other intervals are used, though rarely. Expression conveyed by different classes of intervals is not arbitrary, it is closely related to psycho-physiological facts upon which all music depends. When a note rises by one interval, it reaches a sharp or tivra, another Sruti, it becomes a double sharp. It can go up to four becoming extra extreme sharp. When lowered, it is a flat or komala. Taking consonant intervals, composed of simple ratios involving prime numbers not more than five, the basic harmonic scale is arrived at — C D E F G A B. The alternate scale is C D Eb+ F G A Bb+. The southern scale conforms to a slightly different setting of C Db+ D F G Ab+ A. The division of an octave to twenty-two or sixty-six Sruti-s is an enharmonic division. Three different scales or grama-s correspond to different tunings of a harp. The ancient scale was a Pythagorean one or Shadja grama in the scale of C. Lowering the A+ or Dha+ into A or Dha, known as the Madhyama grama or F scale, second harmonic gets formed. The Shadja grama starts Sa Ri Ga Ma Pa Dha Ni, the Madhyama grama is Ma Pa Dha Ni Sa Ri Ga and Gandhara grama is Pa Dha Ni Sa Ri Ga Ma as stated in Sangeeta Damodar."

"The Gandhara and Madhyama grama are no longer in use. Born of seven notes is the Murchana which gets grouped into (1) heptatonic, pure (2) hexatonic, shadava (3) pentatonic, audava and (4) intercalary, sadharana. Melodies less than five notes are not Raga-s but Tana-s, mere melodic figures. Raga-s may be Suddha or pure, chhaya-laga or shadowed and sankirna or mixed. A Raga gets shadowed borrowing a few notes from another Raga without altering the mood, but enhance it. Mixture of several Raga-s is sankirna. For celebrating battle, charm and beauty or depicting a character the hexatonic class of shadava is recommended. In destroying disease or enemies, dispelling fear or sorrow, in difficulty or in suffering, in forgiveness, when the graha-s are unfavorable, auspicious words must be sung in pentatonic, audava scale as stated in Siva-Tattva-Ratnakar."

"Music gets divided into two tetra chords, first comprising C D E F and higher tetra chord G A B C. Six main types of tetra chords are envisaged in the music system spanned by a perfect fourth and six secondary types by an augmented fourth. Combining possible lower tetra chords with higher ones, the number arrived is thirty-six, replacing F by F#, thirty-six more are obtained, giving a possibility of seventy scales. This classification is a 'mela'. Mela is a group of sounds from which Raga-s modes manifest. Arrangement of svaras-s or notes into scales or mela-s under which Raga-s can be grouped are spoken of as thata-s."

"The first mela is Kalyan, second Bilaval, third Khammaja, fourth Bhairava, fifth Bhairavi, sixth Asavari or Yavanapuri, seventh Todi, eighth Puravi or Sri, the ninth Marava and the tenth Kafi. The chief modes represent the male principle, Raga-s, the secondary modes are Ragini-s, their spouses. The main modes are all pentatonic, considered six in number – Bhairava, Malakosha, Hindola, Dipak, Sri, Megha are male Raga-s as defined in Sangeeta Darpana. Sangeeta-Makarand however states twenty-one-male Raga-s. The note with which a Raga begins is a 'graha' not to be mistaken with planets. 'Nyasa' is the ending note; 'Amsa' is the most often used. Amsa may be the tonic or predominant note. Rhythm, 'tala', comprises an initial beat 'Sama', other beats 'tali' and empty beats 'khali'. The attack of sound can be 'on the beat' or same, 'after the beat' or atita, and 'before the beat', anagata. Played 'after' expresses reluctance, 'on the beat', precision and soberness, and 'before' expresses joy, liveliness and vitality. All forms of melodic forms or variations by which a scale can be developed is 'melodic movement' or Varna. The movement comprises three elements, ascending or aroha, same note or sthayi and descending or avaroha. Tana-s are melodic figures that come from notes combined. A Tana could be pure or Suddha, or kuta, deceitful."

"Today, Tana is often used to ornament the music – alamkara. Many modes are pentatonic ascending and heptatonic descending. Ascending is exploratory whereas descending is precise. Alamkara, often confused with tana adorns the melody, there are no definitions, but musicians play seven to twelve adornments. Graces or gamaka-s are ornaments of notes. A note may rise from its own pitch and move towards another such that the second sound passes over it as a shadow. Graces and adornments are many simulating a whirlpool, flurry, laughter, sobbing, obeisance, shake, overflow and others."

"Many kinds of music get described in the texts, Gita – arrangement of sounds that is pleasing to the ear in form of music. There are two types, Gandharva, which is composed in accordance to the cosmic laws. Physical harmony here is just a reflection. The second is Gana or profane music that is sung in modes of secular music or Desi-Raga."

"That which charms is a Raga. The word comprises two root syllables, 'Ranj', to please and 'Ghan', the act of doing. In the text of Raga Kalpadruma, K Vyasa explains, 'for 16,108 Gopis, did Krishna clone himself and for every Krishna did the Gopis sing a different Raga, a different rhythm and thus 16,108 modes took birth on this terrestrial planet.' In the pentatonic scale, one could describe 'Gunakali' whose 'head is bowed low, lovely tresses disheveled about her, once famous for her looks, now with her lover gone, Gunapriya is in a state of pity."

"*Her reddened eyes desperate, her sorrow shrunken limbs soiled with clay and mud.* The Raga is in the group of Bhairava, pentatonic, sonant is Ab, consonant Db where the expression is sadness, a first step towards renunciation."

"Each Raga has a time of day, a season, and an occasion associated with it. In the time association, an approximate three-hour window gets used for a Raga to be effective. Some are flexible; others are not; when the first rays of the dawn strike the land, Raga Ahir Bhairava comes to the mind. When the lamps are lit in the evening, Raga Purvi sets the mood and well-being."

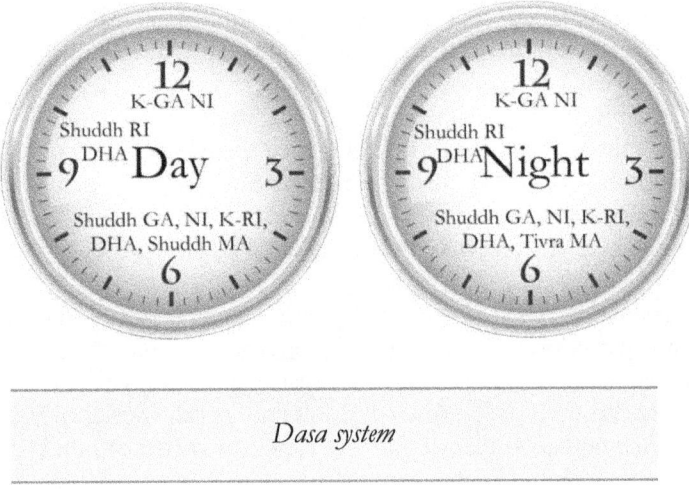

Dasa system

"Dasa system sets a maximum tenure to a human life. The Jiva or the individual soul has a pre-determined agenda on this planet. Astrology does not foretell or change the charter. The individual has the choice to live up to the prescribed charter. Alternatively, face the consequences of an unchartered life. The dasa methods can tell you what the charter is and when certain events may happen. Grasping the dasa system is important, the dasa is like a charter, it does not take into account events that may change the destiny or take a native off course. The transiting graha-s specify events that make our lives unique."

"There are two types of movements of graha-s. One is direct movement such as transits; the other type is a projected or progressed movement. These comprise the dasa system. Some dasa systems come from the Nakshatra system. Vimshottari and Ashtottari are examples of these. Built are others on the Rasi system like Chara Dasa, then there are Dasa systems like Kalachakra that use both Nakshatra and Rasi."

"Some dasa systems Vimshottari, Ashtottari, Kalachakra and Yogini offer the best results. Sage Parasara opines about usage of Nakshatra Dasa. First choice is Vimshottari Dasa unless other conditions prevail at birth, like in case of birth during day in Krishna Paksa, moon waning or at night in Shukla Paksa waxing, Ashtottari Dasa gets advised."

"Ashtottari Dasa applies if Rahu is in quadrant or trine from Lagna ruler the basic premise behind dasa system remains simple and straightforward human life gets segmented into sections, which become progression of graha-s in the Nakshatra-s or the signs."

"Orientation point for the Nakshatra Dasa is the natal Moon, Lagna, Sun or rulers of trines whichever is strongest, considering the Dasa keeper progressing through time as it passes through the different Nakshatra-s, the ruler ship changes."

"Graha ruler is the primary indicator during that period. Vimshottari and Ashtottari have long durations 120 and 108 years and most individuals do not complete the full cycle. Others like Yogini have shorter cycles. The two luminaries, five planets and the lunar nodes play their part in the Vimshottari, ruling between 6 and 20 years Ketu rules for 7 years, Venus 20, Sun 6, Moon 10, and Mars 7, Rahu rules 18 years, Jupiter 16, Saturn 19 and Mercury 17. Each Vimshottari dasa period gets subdivided in the same manner into nine sub-periods called Antara-dasa or bhukti. The dasa ruler directs the first bhukti in any dasa, shadowed by the bhukti of other graha-s in the sequence."

"First bhukti in the dasa of Sun is the Sun, the next in sequence would be Moon, Mars, Rahu, Jupiter, Saturn, Mercury, Ketu, Venus. Each sub-period gets further divided proportionately into Antara, Pratyantara, Sukshma; the sub division rules being the same as the main dasa. Nakshatra lordship and house disposition is important. It is a scheme whereby each planet's association with another like a body or soul relationship, where the guna qualities of a graha gets associated with the sign, house and Nakshatra. During a dasa and to some extent in a bhukti, influences of the graha-s get expressed by the sign's nature in which placed is the planet in the natal chart. Planets in cardinal signs generate restlessness, activity, outwardly directed expression and dynamism. Seen are opposite effects during periods of planets in fixed signs. Mutable signs generate ambiguity, bipolar responses and nervousness. Quadruplicity of the sign must get account for, the way it interacts with the inherent nature of the graha."

"Whenever, any important event happens in the life of a native, the transit of planets plays an important role; particularly the transit of Saturn and Jupiter. When Saturn and Jupiter influence a house and house ruler, activity related to that house happens in the transit, Sun shows the month of event, the Moon specifies the day of event. One can say Saturn approves and Jupiter blesses the event. For predicting an event in any natal chart, one has to study the dasa, and Antara of planets and transit of planets."

"Maha Dasa of a functional malefic with bhukti of a functional malefic can subject the native to many sufferings, however, with the bhukti of a functional benefic graha comes good results. A weak functional benefic can plant the seeds but yields no results. Maha Dasa of a functional benefic with functional benefic bhukti - the results are excellent, and with bhukti of a weak functional benefic, the results are average. Bhukti of functional malefic brings in mild sufferings."

"If the bhukti lord is a functional malefic associated with weak graha-s, then it is of grave concern. Where Sun is a functional malefic, then any planet associated with it will suffer. Nakshatra cusps of 13.33° become critical degrees, they denote cosmic restraints like obstruction and frustration especially in progressions when graha-s other than Moon are at Cusps. These are times when denied is satisfaction, increased is self-reliance."

"Maha Dasa or Bhukti of Lagna ruler's enemies bring forth diseases and troubles. If the Maha Dasa is Aquarius, then Sun and Moon sub-dasa periods will cause troubles and diseases. If a sign has a graha occupant, then the graha is the source of light, it shows the source of a result by its character and ownership. Ascendant ruler in a sign shows gains through own efforts, the third ruler will show gains through siblings and publications. Transiting graha or the dasa graha shows how results get produced. Sign and the ruler signify to what extent one can enjoy, the graha being strong or weak."

"Ruler of the constellation is the one which shows the nature of the result through the houses the ruler is the owner. The matter signified by those houses will be the ones to manifest. If this ruler is evil, it shows difficulties, otherwise success. If it is strong by lordship, position and association, effects during its period get felt. Nature of the effect gets determined by the graha in whose star the dasa or bhukti ruler resides. Asterism sub, which is the angular representation of the duration of bhukti in a dasa, considering the dasa duration to represent an arc of 13d 20m specifies success or failure depending on its relationship with the asterism ruler, indicating the effect during a dasa."

"The ancestors labeled different categories of dasa types based on Nakshatra-s. Sage Parasara in Brihat Hora Shastra in chapter 46 states, 'Beginning with Krittika Nakshatra, the Lords of dasa in Vimshottari system are Surya, Chandra, Mangala, Rahu, Brihaspati, Sani, Budha, Ketu and Shukra. Counting the number of Nakshatra-s from Krittika to the birth star dividing the count by nine, the remainder suggests the lord of the beginning dasa period. Remaining dasa will be of the graha-s in the order. Dasa periods of Surya, Chandra, Mangala, Rahu, Brihaspati, Sani, Budha, Ketu and Shukra in Vimshottari are 6, 10, 7, 18, 16, 19, 17, 7 and 20 years, setting the maximum lifespan to 120 years."

"At first, one must compute the remainder or balance of the start dasa. Begin by calculating the expired portion of the dasa of the concerned graha. If you multiply the dasa period of the graha by the period of the stay of Moon in Janma Nakshatra that has expired and divide that amount by the total period of the stay of Chandra in that Nakshatra. The result in calendar days is the expired period of the dasa. Deducting this amount from the total period of the dasa, we get the Balance of Dasa at the time of birth."

"Consider the cycle of graha-s in a Vimshottari setting as shown in the figure. It is an example of a dasa period starting in the Nakshatra ruled by Mangala."

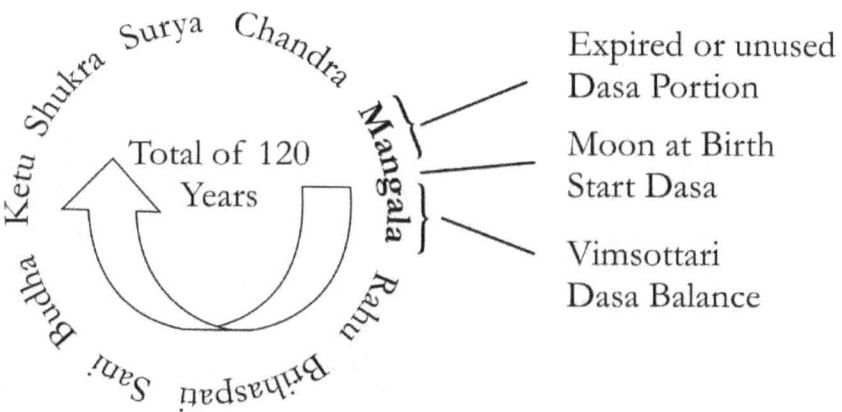

"It is recommended adopting the Ashtottari, when Rahu is not in Lagna, in any other Kendra or Kona to the lord of the Lagna. Four-Nakshatra-s from Ardra constellation starts the dasa of Surya, from three after that begins the dasa of Chandra, four after that will bring the dasa of Mangala."

"Three after that the lord of dasa will be Budha, four there from will have Sani, as the dasa lord, three thereafter the lord will be Brihaspati, Rahu will be the lord of the dasa four Nakshatra-s after that and then Shukra will take over the lordship of the dasa three Nakshatra-s from the last. The lord of the dasa at birth is found by counting in this order up to the Janma Nakshatra."

"The duration of Ashtottari Dasa for Surya, Chandra, Mangala, Budha, Sani, Brihaspati, Rahu and Shukra are 6, 15, 8, 17, 10, 19, 12 and 21. In this dasa system only eight graha-s play the role of dasa lords, Ketu is denied this privilege."

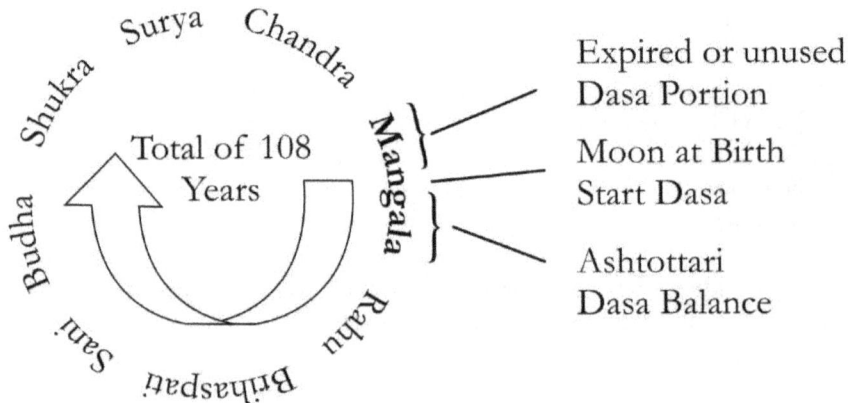

"For Ashtottari Dasa malefic graha-s, the dasa span of one Nakshatra is 1/4 of the graha's dasa. It is 1/3 with benefic graha-s. The expired portion of the dasa gets calculated like that of Vimshottari Dasa, by multiplying the Bhayat, implying the expired period of the stay of Moon in the Janma Nakshatra, by the dasa portion of the Janma Nakshatra and dividing it by Bhabhog, the total period of the stay of Moon in the Janma Nakshatra."

"From this procedure, we can find out the balance of dasa at birth. If Uttara Ashada constellation is the Janma Nakshatra, the duration of its first three pada becomes the Bhabhog and the dasa gets calculated accordingly. One can complete the dasa and calculations for Abhijit Nakshatra by taking the fourth pada of Uttara Ashada plus the one-fifth part of the start portion of Sravana. For Sravana the Bhabhog would be the total of its duration in Ghatika minus the one-one-fifth part of the start of Sravana."

"It is advisable to adopt the Shodashottari, if the birth is in the day in Krishna Paksa or dark half of the lunar fortnight, or if the birth occurs at night in Shukla Paksa or the bright half. Shodashottari Dasa finds its usage when the Lagna is in the Hora of Chandra with birth in the Krishna Paksa or when Lagna is in the Hora of Surya with birth in the Shukla Paksa. Count the number of Nakshatra-s from Pushya to the Janma Nakshatra. Divide this number by 8. The remainder shows the dasa-s of Surya, Mangala, Brihaspati, Sani, Ketu, Chandra, Budha and Shukra. The dasa periods of the above graha-s are of 11, 12, 13, 14, 15, 16, 17 and 18 years."

"Different dasa periods of graha-s give effects from their strength. A graha positioned in first Drekkana will show its effects when the dasa begins. Graha positioned in the second Drekkana of 10-20 degrees, makes its effects felt in the middle of the dasa."

"A graha in the third Drekkana shows its effects at the end of the dasa. Retrograde graha shows its effects in reverse sequence, like Rahu and Ketu. Effects are favorable if at the start of the dasa, the dasa lord is in Lagna, in his exaltation, own or a peaceful Rasi or sign. The results are unfavorable, if the dasa lord is in sixth, eighth or twelfth house, in his debilitation or in an inimical sign."

"Dasa of Sun brings possession of wealth, great felicity and honors from authority, if at the time of birth Sun is in his own sign, in his exaltation sign, in a Kendra, in eleventh, associated with the lord of ninth, or the lord of tenth and strong in his Varga. The dasa blesses the native with a son if Sun is with the lord of fifth. Native gains elephants and other kinds of wealth with Sun's association with the lord of second."

"The native enjoys comforts of conveyances, if Sun associates with the lord of fourth. He attains a high position, like that of Army Chief, by the beneficence of the king and enjoys much happiness. In strong and favorable Sun Dasa, acquisitions of clothes, agricultural products, wealth, honors and conveyances are common. Dasa of Sun brings anxieties, loss of wealth, punishment from authority, defamation, opposition by relations, distress to father, inauspicious happenings at home, distress to paternal and maternal uncles, anxiety and inimical relations with other people without a reason, if Sun is in his sign of debilitation. One witnesses' same results when Sun weakens in sixth, eighth, or twelfth or associates with malefic graha-s, or with the lord of sixth, eighth, or twelfth. There will be some favorable effects occasionally, if in the above situations, Sun receives aspect from benefic graha-s. The effects will always be unfavorable when malefic graha-s offer their aspects to Sun."

"Effects of Vimshottari Dasa of Moon promises from its commencement to the end - opulence and glory, good fortune, gain of wealth, auspicious functions at home, dawn of fortune, attainment of a high position in authority, gaining of conveyances, clothes, birth of children and ownership of cattle. These bargains come to fruition when Moon, exalted, in own sign, in Kendra, in eleventh, ninth, fifth, associates with or receives aspect from benefic graha-s, or associates with the lord of tenth, ninth or fourth. There come extraordinary gains in wealth and luxuries, if such a Moon is in second house. When Moon is waning or in her debilitation sign, there comes loss of wealth in the dasa period. If Moon is in third, there will be happiness off and on."

"When Moon associates with malefic graha-s, there comes stupidity, mental tension, trouble from employees and mother and loss of wealth. If waning Moon occupies sixth, eighth, or twelfth, or associates with malefic graha-s, there come inimical relations with authority, loss of wealth, distress to mother and similar evil effects. When a strong Moon is in sixth, eighth, or twelfth, it cycles between troubles and good times."

"Mars or Mangala in state of exaltation, in his Moola Trikona, in own sign, in Kendra, eleventh, or second house with strength, in a benefic Amsa or Navamsa and associates with a benefic, gives positive results during his dasa. They include ownership of kingdom, rise to a high administrative role, or political position in government, gain of wealth and land, recognition by authority, gain of wealth from foreign countries and custody of conveyances and ornaments. The native will receive happiness and have good relations with siblings. If Mangala with strength gets placed in a Kendra or in third, there will be gain of wealth through valor, victory over enemies, happiness from wife and children."

"There is a possibility of some unfavorable effects at the end of the Mars dasa. Mangala in his debilitation sign, weak in an inauspicious house, associates with or receives aspect from malefic graha-s, there can occur in his dasa loss of wealth, distress and similar unfavorable effects."

"To clarify the effects of the dasa of Rahu, I shall first mention the exaltation and debilitation signs of Rahu and Ketu. These rules apply for dasa system and should not be arbitrarily extended to the natal chart. Exaltation Rasi of Rahu is Taurus and that of Ketu is Scorpio. Moola Trikona of Rahu and Ketu are Gemini and Capricorn. Rahu's own sign is Aquarius, though some sages are of the view that Rahu owns Virgo and Ketu owns Pisces."

"Rahu in his exaltation sign during his dasa brings happiness from acquisition of wealth, agricultural products, ownership of conveyances with the help of friends and authority, construction of a new house, birth of sons, moral inclinations, recognition from government of foreign countries, gain of wealth and clothes. When Rahu associates or receives aspect from benefic graha-s, is in a benefic sign and is in first, fourth, seventh, tenth, eleventh, or third, the dasa period promises all kinds of comforts by the beneficence of government, custody of wealth through a foreign government or sovereignty and felicity at home. Rahu in eighth or twelfth house, the results are painful. If Rahu associates with a malefic, or a Maraka, or is debilitated, there is loss of position, destruction of his residential house, mental agony, trouble to wife and children and misfortune of getting unpalatable food. There will be loss of wealth at the start of dasa, some relief and gain of wealth in his own country and distress and anxieties during the last portion of the dasa."

"Jupiter in exaltation, own sign, Moola Trikona, in tenth, fifth, or ninth house, own Navamsa, or exalted Navamsa, show signs of many positive gains in his dasa. They include owning a kingdom, great felicity, recognition by government, procurement of conveyances and clothes, devotion to deities and wise, happiness regarding his wife, children, and success in performing holy sacrifices and oblations. If Jupiter gets debilitated, combust, associated with malefic graha-s, or in sixth, or eighth, there will be during his dasa loss of residential premises, anxiety, distress to children, loss of cattle and pilgrimage. The dasa will confer unfavorable effects at its commencement only. During the latter part of the dasa, there will come good effects, like gain of wealth, awards from and recognition by government."

"If Saturn or Sani is in his exaltation, in own sign, or in Moola Trikona, or friendly sign, in his own, or exalted Navamsa and in third, or eleventh, there will be during his dasa recognition by government. It will bring opulence and glory, name and fame, success in the educational sphere, ownership of conveyances and ornaments, gain of wealth, favors from authority, attainment of a high position, like Commander of an Army, custody of a kingdom, benevolence of goddess Lakshmi, gain of property and birth of children. With Sani in sixth, eighth, or twelfth, in his debilitation sign or combust there comes during his dasa ill effects from poison, injury from weapons, separation from father, distress to wife and children, disaster, resulting from displeasure of government, imprisonment. When Sani receives aspect, or associates with a benefic graha, dwells in an angle, trine, in Capricorn or Pisces, there will be ownership of kingdom, conveyances and clothes."

"Mercury in exaltation, in own sign, in friendly sign, eleventh, fifth, or ninth, there comes during his dasa much wealth, gain of reputation, improvement in knowledge, compassion from government, auspicious functions, happiness from wife and children, good health, availability of sweetish preparations, profits in business. If Mercury receives aspect from a benefic, is in ninth, or is the lord of tenth, the native experiences beneficial results in full, resulting in great contentment. When Mercury associates with a malefic, there will be during his dasa punishment by government, inimical relations with relations, journey to a foreign country, dependence on others and the possibility of urinary troubles. With Mercury in sixth, eighth, or twelfth, there will be loss of wealth, due to indulgence in lascivious activities, possibility of suffering from rheumatism and jaundice, danger of thefts and malevolence of government, loss of land and cattle. At the start of Mercury dasa, wealth comes easy with improvement in education, birth of children and overall happiness. In the middle of the dasa comes recognition from government. Last part of the dasa is distressful."

"Ketu, who as a headless trunk is a Kabandha[228] among the graha-s. If Ketu is in an angle, trine, or in eleventh, in a benefic sign, in his exaltation, or in his own sign, there will be during his dasa cordial relations with the king, desired headship of a country, or village, comforts of conveyances, happiness from children, gain from foreign countries, happiness from wife and gaining of cattle. If Ketu is in third, sixth, or eleventh, there will be in his dasa possession of a kingdom, good relations with friends and opportunities for the ownership of elephants. At the start of Ketu dasa, there is Raja Yoga. During the middle portion of the dasa, there will be possibilities of fearfulness and in the last part - there will be sufferings from ailments and journeys to distant places. Ketu in second, eighth, or twelfth, or receiving aspect from a malefic, there comes imprisonment, destruction of relations and residential premises and anxieties, company of menials and diseases."

"With Venus in his exaltation, in his own sign, in an angle or trine, there comes during his dasa custody of fancy clothes, ornaments, conveyances, cattle and land, availability of sweet preparations every day, recognition from the sovereign, luxurious functions of songs and dances. Venus in Moolatrikona, during his dasa there come definite custody of a kingdom, possession of a house, birth of children and grandchildren, celebration of marriage in the family, attainment of a high position, like the Commander of an Army, visits by friends, recovery of lost wealth, property, or kingdom."

---

[228] Kabandha – Headless. Who died and was freed of celestial curse or karma.

"If Venus is in sixth, eighth, or twelfth, there will be during his dasa inimical relations with relations, distress to wife, losses in business, destruction of cattle and separation from relations."

"When Venus is in fourth, as lord of ninth, or tenth, there will be during his dasa attainment of lordship of a country, or village, performance of pious deeds, like building of reservoirs and temples and giving grains in charity, availability of sweet preparations every day, vigor in work, name and fame and happiness from spouse and children. Similar are the effects of Venus in his sub-periods. If Venus is lord of second, or seventh, there will be during his dasa physical pains and troubles."

The way forward

"As a practitioner, it is imperative to know what you are doing and telling the native what applies to him. Diseases don't come in good periods, its preparation and recovery does. Just the way the farmer hordes the grain and firewood for the winter, one has to apply the preventives in the times that permit their application. Similarly, remedial actions need graha support for them to act. Besides, it takes a while to understand a chart, as each one of us well knows through examining our own particular chart. Seeing a client briefly may not yield all the intricacies of the chart."

"Man, or machine cannot read everything about a person by mere examination of the birth chart, or a cursory constitutional questionnaire, a pulse read or a tongue check. It's easy to spot similarities, it is extremely arduous to determine the differences. Even if the differences can be spotted, it becomes a bigger challenge in determining what caused those differences and where do they lead. In my opinion, it is the last question which is the most important. I agree that there was a past, there were past lives, there were successes and failures; but what good are they if they cannot determine the future. But, isn't that true? What good is knowing the Prakruti if it cannot determine the Vikriti and other turning points? In knowing an event, its occurrence and course is all good, but such knowledge unless can be turned into productive thinking is a worthless piece of information."

"Success gets measured by how effective we are in aiding our clients to implement a lifestyle in harmony with cosmic laws that astrology, constitution and spiritual makeup can offer corrective actions, not just by mere accurate predictions on an event. The need to help people understand themselves and the world they live in is in big demand and that is the charter of this wellness program."

"Extracting information is always a challenge, besides being extra informed makes the practitioner biased. Questionnaires are helpful along with cross-referencing astrology and Ayurveda we gain much more accuracy in both. Astrology is the proactive prognosis, it tells you the possibilities, it points to events and dates; Ayurveda and Yoga are reactive, they work against indications and symptoms, here is where readings are information comes to use. As conformation, physical information gets revealed by the ascendant and the third, and their lords and depositors. Mental health revelation comes from the Moon, fourth and fifth houses. Spiritual information is revealed by the sun and Navamsa. Afflictions to the first house and the Sun can cause ego and identity problems and color the life. Sun-Saturn conjunctions indicate solitariness, Moon-Saturn conjunctions promote depression or detachment, Sun-Mars conjunctions in emotional signs like Scorpio promote anger or aggression."

"Many people pursue the spiritual life through creative work of various kinds, including artistic pursuits. Here we can consult divisional charts, particularly the Navamsa, and self-indicator, Atmakaraka, along with lunar nodes. Jupiter, the lord of the Ascendant, and the lord of the ninth from the Ascendant and the Moon are important factors to examine."

"Recommended treatments are several and appropriate means of balancing planetary influences can be through herbs and diet, through gemstone, color, mantra, music, meditational, art or whatever is appropriate. When viewing a chart, one may note the angular houses, 1, 4, 7 and 10, succedent houses, 2, 5, 8 and 11, and cadent houses, 3, 6, 9 and 12. The first event in human life is the birth. The first house marking this first event is key to getting the information right. Skin color, the limbs, the logical profession are linked intimately to the first. One must look at other house configurations, the position of dharma through 5 and 9, artha from 6 and 10, kama from 7 and 11, and moksha from 8 and 12 houses."

"Angular houses, 1, 4, 7 and 10 are places of strength. First house indicates color and stature of the body, disease, health, fame, progress, wealth and brain. Fourth indicates the mother, maternal connections, mind, emotions, home, conveyance and masses. Seventh indicates our partner, marriage happiness, sexual organ, courage, trade. The tenth indicates good and bad deeds, career, fame, name, height and knees. Trine houses, 1, 5, and 9 are places of principles and values and all relate to Dharma. They are houses of god or Vishnu Sthana. The first shows the principles of our personal life, our svadharma or natural duty. The fifth indicates our children or family duties on one level, but on a higher level shows our creative and intellectual principles. The ninth shows our education and our spiritual values, solemn-duties in the highest sense."

"What is important is ensuring astrology points to a manageable longevity. Three rules can determine a person's life-span if they all point to a definite number of years. The first rule employs the ascendant and moon. Where ascendant and moon are posited in a movable sign, the life-span indicated is long; if either of them are found in a fixed sign and the other in a common sign, the life-span will remain long. The life-span falls in the middle if one of them fall in a movable sign and the other in a fixed sign or ascendant and moon both fall in a common sign. Life will be short with the ascendant in a movable and moon in a common sign, even if they swap such positions. Life will be short if both ascendant and moon are posited in a fixed sign. The same rule is checked against the ascendant and lord of 8th house. The third combination in this rule comes from the ascendant lord and eighth lord and a fourth one with Hora Lagna and the ascendant."

"In the second rule, one takes the four combinations in rule one and applies the following mathematics of add the number of sign which comes from the ascendant and the moon. This sum is divided by three. If the remainder is 1, then the life will be short, if the remainder is 2, then the life will be long, if the remainder is 0, then the life will be middle. Short life is 32 years, middle is 62 and long-life touches 100."

"Houses 2, 6, 8 and 12 generally cause difficulties, particularly 6, 8 and 12, the well-known Dusthana or bad places. A graha posited in 6, 8 and 12th house without benefic influence either through aspect or association becomes isolated and worse if under malefic influence. Such isolated graha-s can affect the bone, blood, muscle, skin, fat, nervous and reproductive tissues. Bone tissue can come from isolated sun, blood from isolated moon, muscles by Mars, skin from isolated Mercury, fat from isolated Jupiter, reproductive from isolated Venus and nerves from isolated Saturn."

"Where the sixth house lord and eleventh house lord come together or aspect one another with a malefic helping, disease becomes predominant."

"We are what our mind thinks we are. For all mental problems and issues, many graha-s and geometrical positions need to be checked (a) ascendant, (b) its lord, (c) Mercury, (d) fifth house and its occupants, (e) fifth house lord, (f) fourth house, (g) fourth house lord and (h) moon. Eyesight can be judged from 2nd and the 12th house and sun and moon as the light bearers. Diabetes can be judged from Jupiter and Venus. When they are influenced by separative factors like Sun, Saturn and Rahu, their control over sugar, liver and kidney diminishes."

"Timing the disease comes from the Vimshottari dasa. A dasa and antardasha period of graha-s that are enemies to the ascendant and the sixth lord will bring in a disease. If the lords of second or seventh are weak and posited in 6,8 or 12th house, then during their dasa period or even sub-dasa period will prove fatal to the native."

> Any graha in the 10th always influences ascendant
> 2nd, 4th and 11th from the graha causes Argala to dispose
> Argala is obstruction to the graha's strengths
> With malefic positioned there, it will add to the woes

Graha casting aspect on its own sign strengthens the house
Fifth house under aspect by male graha-lord confers son and wealth
When Saturn aspects own house or *Lagna,* comes honor and wealth
Adverse though to life-span and health

> Factors affecting the 'self' are in 1, 3, 10 and 11 and the Sun
> 1st, 3rd, 10th or 11th ruler with Sun is success and conceit
> Fame comes from the Lagna and 10th house
> Their rulers and the Sun's dead heat

Marriages, homemaking hidden in seventh and second
Seventh lord under good aspects and strong
No negative aspects from malefic graha
Results are good, otherwise nuptials go wrong

> Beauty is in the second, skin deep in the face
> Spouse is attractive in second from 7th, namely the eighth
> Education also lurks in the second
> A natural benefic in *Navamsa* would give studies and good grade

Read profession first from ascendant
Check 10th for fame, 11th for gains and success
Sixth house indicates the means of livelihood
Seventh indicates trade and partnership process

> Progeny is a matter of houses 2 and 5, to some extent eleven
> Jupiter, *Putra-karaka*[229] and must be strong
> 5th is progeny, 2nd indicates family
> 5th from the spouse house,[230] the 11th must come along

For Aries, Cancer, Libra, and Capricorn, *Bhadak*[231] is eleventh
Taurus, Leo, Scorpio, Aquarius, *Bhadak* is ninth
Death inflicting are 2nd and 7th and *Bhadak*
Graha-s, constellations and their rulers are behind

Workplace, one needs to look at 8th and 10th rulers
Mental problems at work arise from the Moon
When 7th stronger than 6th, business becomes a better alternative
10th is how your manager and you work in tune

> Change of residence shows up in 3, 10 and 12
> 3rd would indicate change of place, 10th profession
> And 12th the new environment
> Residence suggested by 2, 4, 11 and Mars expression

Judge a native's child from the fifth
And judge the father from the ninth and tenth
Siblings lurk in the third
Mother shows up from the fourth

> "In my younger and more vulnerable years, I received many an advice through which I formulated the 'Wellness Zone'. It is the zone you really want to be in. It is the place you want to set the stakes, it is your retreat, it is a place to regroup, understand, proact and resolve."

| Set the stakes | Retreat | Re-group | Under-stand | Proact | Resolve |

---

[229] Putra Karaka - Child significator
[230] Spouse house is the seventh
[231] Bhadak houses are close to death bearing. They bring in sudden downfall

PIECING IT ALL TOGETHER

I made several attempts earlier at compiling one comprehensive book that repositioned 'Vedic Astrology' and 'Ayurveda' as one subject; from the sheer size and unmanageable translator's expectations, I abandoned the idea. I realized I was getting into the same trap as other authors and translators who could not raise the bar on this wonderful subject. Rise of the Native and Way of the Native are both algorithmic astrology books that has worked in bringing the ancient scriptures to modern technology. Rise of the native compiles the diverse chronicles of Lilly, Raphael and Mihira, Way of the Native stays with Parasara. I extend some of the algorithms and chart judgment methods in an easier logical manner. For readers of this book, I have chosen the computer language of Python to expound the algorithms. The code is available from https://github.com/devbnj/aquapisces

When judging a chart, here are a few rules to adopt. When giving an overall judgment of the chart, the first examination should hover around the house location of the planets in their natural status. The main rule states that natural benefic graha-s run better in angles or trines involving houses 1, 4, 5, 7, 9, 10; natural malefic graha-s prefer Upachaya houses of 3, 6, 11. This rule likewise applies to the divisional charts. Overall health and longevity of the person is something one must bolster first. Every graha fares better in signs they rule, and in signs of their exaltation. A good positioning in a sign becomes insignificant if a difficult house.

Natural benefic graha-s, neither retrograde nor blemished implying Jupiter, Venus, Mercury, Moon offer to give their best in angular houses 4, 7, 10 or in trinal places of 1, 5, 9. Being under malefic aspect and retrogression ruins their chances of being beneficial, where benefic graha-s in Kendra-s are more weakened by retrograde status than are those in trines. Debilitated benefic graha-s in angles and trines show uncertainty but no harm. Moon and Mercury stay sensitive to their associations. While they act extroverted in the presence or aspect of a malefic, Moon and Mercury set the stage for inner search and contemplation.

There are three divisional charts concerned with health. If a person is running the dasa of a planet ill placed in all three charts, they should pay special heed to their health. Shashtamsha of six divisions and Ashtamsha with eight divisions are both Tajik divisional charts, which were added to the Vedic system thousands of years later. The Shashtamsha specifies health issues, more than other divisional charts and Ashtamsha signifies major challenges and crises in a person's chart, including the death of those intimately associated with them. Bhamsha with 27 divisions suggests general vitality, and the ability to rise to the occasion.

Dasa-s time the event. (a) Unless having taken birth in Sagittarius and Pisces ascendants, Venus and Saturn create yogas in other's dasa-s, wherein unfortunate results come by in Saturn-Venus or Venus- Saturn combinations. (b) Where Sun and Mercury associate, Sun's dasa stays ordinary but Mercury's dasa becomes excellent. (c) Jupiter and Saturn in association, Jupiter's dasa becomes ordinary, Saturn's dasa turns excellent. (d) Same with Jupiter and Moon associated, Jupiter's dasa remains ordinary, Moon's dasa excels. (e) Rahu when in a quadrant or trine confers a Raja Yoga during his dasa period. (f) When Sun conjoins other graha-s, Sun's dasa becomes favorable, while the dasa period of other graha-s conjoined with Sun yield ordinary results.

The tenth is MC or midheaven and provides a strong angular position for every graha. For benefic, the tenth is foremost, followed by the seventh, fourth and first. Seventh being a Maraka position may harm the health and decrease the longevity. Angular locations for benefic graha-s may not always confer spiritual benefits, but helps the native in the worldly sense.

For a benefic graha, ninth house is very favorable trinal position. Ninth elevates us, brings favorable luck and future. Fifth foresees intelligence and education. A benefic posited in fifth will confer intelligence, good children and bring luck and fortunes from its aspect on the eleventh.

Fifth house positioned on the nocturnal side of the chart shows the inward, self-achievements in learning, the ninth on the brighter side of the chart shows achievements aided by parents, teachers, gurus, schools, institutions, community and the government.

Benefic graha-s suffer in houses 6, 8, 12, the native succumbs to ill health. Their presence in the sixth increases enemies, pathogens and conflict. Eighth house brings abrupt problems, diseases and accidents. Twelfth induces loss of fame, weakened vitality, being nursed, early retirement. Benefic graha-s in the eighth and twelfth are a blessing for the spirit, particularly unblemished Mercury or Jupiter conjoined with Ketu. The same is true of these planets in the fourth Moksha house. Such positions bring occult and spiritual insight. Benefic graha-s in the twelfth are useful for travel, living overseas and dealing with foreign countries, people and culture. Moon suffers more in these positions and makes the health and constitution suffer.

Benefic graha-s suffer less in the third house and normally do well in the eleventh house where every graha acts favorable. Eleventh gives abundance to whatever planet resides there. It signifies a noble mind and promises financial success, being the house of gain. Benefic graha-s in the second house are great for self-expression and business but not always for health being a Maraka house. Location of a planet in its own sign or sign of exaltation improves the status of benefic graha-s in wicked houses but does not eliminate it. For example, an exalted Jupiter in the sixth house can still cause health problems, though less than otherwise. However, it does well for its own houses, two and eleven in increasing wealth. Location in its own sign or sign of exaltation seriously improves the power of benefic graha-s situated in good houses, of course creating a Maha Purusha Yoga, but the occupation has to be unblemished, otherwise the harm gets doubled. Natural benefic graha-s improve the houses they occupy, even if these are difficult houses, but they weaken the houses they rule. If a graha is a natural benefic but a temporal malefic, such as Jupiter ruling the twelfth and second for Aquarius ascendant, its natural benefic status and influence get compromised, though not totally eliminated.

Natural malefic graha-s comprising Saturn, Mars, Rahu, Ketu, and Sun do far better in Upachaya houses of 3, 6, 11. Here they guard the health of the person and are a source of strength, vitality and motivation, besides giving the native the capacity to work hard. Malefic graha-s in Upachaya houses promise a person steadiness, fearlessness, courage and the ability to make great achievements. Sometimes the tenth house gets counted as an Upachaya house just for Mars, the Sun and Rahu.

The exception comes in when multiple malefic graha-s tenant the sixth, or a malefic in the sixth is under malefic aspect. Such yogas can cause health problems. Eleventh is the best house for malefic graha-s, where their maleficence is pardoned.

Natural malefic graha-s in angles and trines including houses 1, 4, 5, 7, 9, 10 usually cause harm and suffering. With no benefic graha-s in angles and trines to counter their influence, malefic graha-s in these positions can cause great harm to a person, including major health problems or injury. In Kendra positions, malefic graha-s may give success, specifically if they rule good houses or are in a good sign position. Yet they are inclined to make the person harsh, infuse in him a negative character, or make him difficult to deal with. They can generate powerful enemies even if they make a person strong.

For example, Mars in Aries in the tenth house brings success but can invoke enmity or make the native aggressive in temperament. Maha Purusha Yogas strengthen malefic graha-s in bringing power and success but do not always give a better character or morality. Saturn becomes strong in the seventh house and Mars in the tenth because of their aspects to the Ascendant from these positions.

In trines, malefic graha-s are largely harmful, damaging the integrity of the houses. Malefic graha-s situated in trines destroy the good fortunes they promised. For example, in the fifth they harm children or weaken one's intelligence, and in the ninth they injure the father, bring trouble in education or with persons in authority. Malefic graha-s in the fifth weaken the health. But overall, malefic graha-s in trines are less depraved than they are in Kendra-s. When retrograded in Kendra and Kona, malefic graha-s grow more harmful. When debilitated, malefic graha-s cause less harm but also confer less power to the person. In fact, debilitated malefic graha-s can make a person humble and spiritual because the promised pride is missing in a fallen malefic.

In the tenth house, Sun does well and suffers less from being in a Kendra. Sun positioned in the first and tenth house can make a person strong in personality and charisma. In the seventh house, on the other hand, the Sun is particularly difficult in matters regarding relationship though it is better for career. Sun in the seventh can be worse than Mars dosha and can foster other relationships. Sun can delay or deny children being in the fifth house. Mars gains directional strength in the tenth. Saturn gains directional strength in the seventh but only helps career and travel, not relationships. Saturn in the tenth becomes very strong and raises a person, likewise brings his fall. Malefic graha-s in the tenth enforce power leading to excesses that causes harm.

Unblemished temporal lords and malefic graha-s in angles and trines give better results in materialistic matters, more so, if the planets are yoga karakas. For example, Mars in the tenth in Taurus gives success because it is a yoga karaka for Leo Ascendant. However, the well-placed Mars may make the person harsh or obstinate. The effects of planets on houses come from their temporal status as well from their natural status. Effects of malefic graha-s in angles outweigh the benefic graha-s, should both types of planets be present in Kendra-s in the chart. Malefic graha-s in Dusthana houses of 6, 8, 12 become weak, except for the sixth, which as an Upachaya house renders them strong. Saturn in the eighth promises health and longevity but may damage career, finances and relationships. Saturn retrograde or afflicted in the eighth can bring karmic health from the past. Malefic graha such as Saturn in the twelfth can provide spiritual guidance. In Dusthana houses, malefic graha-s weaken the energy and vitality. Malefic graha-s in the second house cause harm to the native's speech and happiness in childhood. Mars posited in the second, however, gives a person sharp, aggressive or pleasant speech; Saturn gives only detachment and poverty.

Rahu and Ketu do well in the six-twelve axis, especially Rahu in the sixth and Ketu in the twelfth. They still cause difficulties in these houses but such difficulties are easily overcome, leading to greater accomplishments. Rahu in an angle associated with a Lord of a trine or in a trine associated with a Lord of an angle gives Raja Yoga and such a position benefits the native big time.

Lords of Kendra and Kona give better results when associated with each other in the chart, giving rise to a Raja Yoga, if their yoga occurs in angular or trine houses. Yet a Raja Yoga occurring in difficult houses 6, 8, 12 will still confer benefits. However, it may require overcoming an obstacle, being first defeated, or undergoing humiliation before one's success. A lord of a trine remains benefic, even if the other house the planet rules is not a favorable house, especially if the other house is second or twelfth such as Venus for Gemini and Virgo Ascendants. If its other house is six or eight, it will also inflict harm on the person, particularly in terms of health, but still act favorable as with Saturn for Gemini and Virgo Ascendants. Generally, the status of a Moolatrikona sign ruled by the planet has more weight in turning it either benefic or malefic.

Maraka or death-bearing graha-s are the lords of the second and seventh houses. Graha-s located in such houses similarly come under the Maraka group. Extending the rule, second and twelfth houses from the Moon likewise get counted as Maraka houses. These houses being twelfth from the houses of longevity - three and eight, negate their life-giving qualities.

Apart from these special Maraka planets, the rulers of the eighth and twelfth houses have a Maraka status, as well as natural malefic graha-s, particularly Saturn and Ketu. Maraka planets can harm health only during the period of life in which their influence ripens, not necessarily bring upon death. When the chart is rendered weak, with poor health written all over it, Maraka negative health will manifest during their Dasa period starting from the time of birth. If the chart indicates average health, the negative effect of Maraka planets will only manifest in their Dasa-s that occur after the age of 32, and can become grave after the age of 64. If the chart promises good health, the negative effect of Maraka planets will only manifest in their Dasa-s that occur after the age of 64, and can become critical after the age of 80. Otherwise Maraka lords will give the ordinary results of the second and seventh houses such as wealth or marriage.

Maraka planets are more likely to injure when posited in a Maraka house of two and seven. Any planets in the second and seventh houses can turn into Maraka graha-s. Natural benefic graha-s can become Maraka lords as well. They cause trouble when in Dusthana houses of 6, 8 and 12.

Graha lords of Upachaya houses - 3, 6 and 11 are more injurious as malefic lords. Lord of the eighth inflicts harm but less so. Twelfth house lord brings the least harm but has a separative influence, removing the native from what it influences. The lords of the eighth and twelfth sometime combine with lordship of a more benefic house, giving them positive influence in other areas relative to the personality of the good houses they rule. If a malefic lord is also an enemy of the Ascendant lord, his malefic powers are amplified. When he is a natural malefic, his malefic power is augmented yet further. If a malefic lord turns out to be a friend of the Ascendant lord, his malefic powers become lessened.

Graha-s fare better placed in friendly signs and act their worst in unfriendly signs. Friendly signs improve their condition if situated in hostile house positions. Considered are sixth and eighth house relationships as most difficult, followed by second and twelfth. Positive or friendly relationships are mainly trinal 5, 9 and 3, 11 relationships. The others fall in between. Relative houses are counted from the house in which a planet resides in the chart like planets in 2-12 house relationships though temporal friends, but brings difficulties by inimical house relationships, particularly during their Dasa-s. This factor similarly comes into play with house lordship. When posited is a planet in a chart in the second, sixth, eighth or twelfth position from any house it rules, the house-results cannot be great (see the chart overleaf). Such a graha, when resident in third, fifth, ninth or eleventh place from the house it rules, the results show marked improvement.

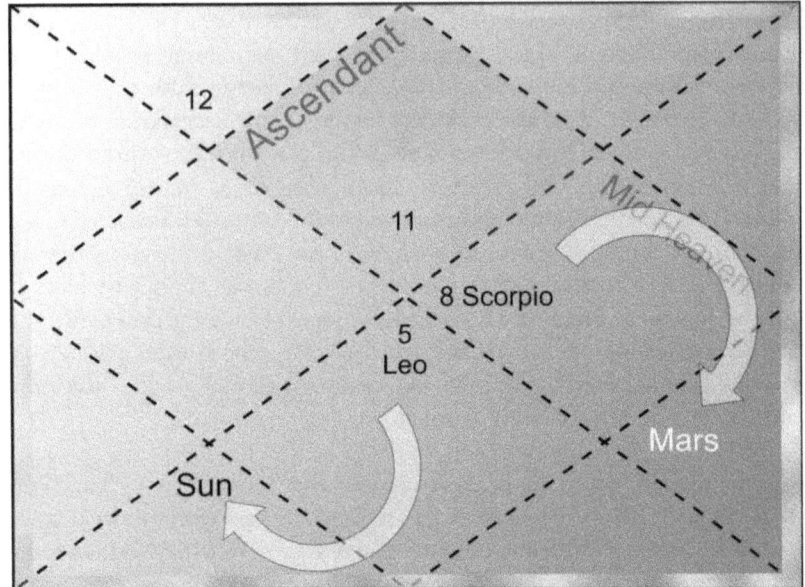

Figure 2 - Lord of a sign posited in 12th house from the sign

House position largely has priority over sign position. A planet placed in its own, exalted or friendly signs but in a difficult house will still cause problems.

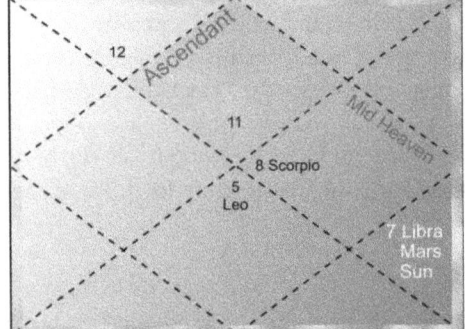

Similarly, a debilitated planet in a favorable house like a trine or Kendra will give beneficial results. For example, a debilitated Sun, Lord of Kendra in Libra in the ninth house will give good effects of the ninth house.

Malefic aspects outweigh both good sign and house positions. Difficult aspects ruin good sign and house positions and can make them twice negative. A benefic in an angle or trine under malefic aspects will not always give decent results but will show the good fortune of a person harmed or destroyed. A benefic in its own sign faces significant weakness from the influence of a malefic aspect.

Benefic aspects do not always outweigh evil sign and house positions. A planet in a wicked house will benefit by good aspects but the blemish of its depraved location is not entirely erased. For example, benefic graha-s in the sixth house will still suffer, even if they have some benefic aspects.

Benefic aspects show relief, such as medical treatment of disease, but may not prevent the complexity from arising. In this regard, one may consider house lordship as well. The aspect of a natural benefic but temporal malefic may not help an ill placed benefic. Natural malefic status is more important for aspects than is temporal malefic status. The aspects of natural malefic graha-s will harm the planets and houses they affect, even if they are temporal benefic graha-s. The effects of graha-s manifest from their temporal status and Dasa periods.

Regarding Dasa-s, it is not always easy to predict what the dasa has in store. Consider an example, a person born under Scorpio with Mercury conjoined with Venus in the seventh house in Taurus, an Atma-Karaka exalted in the Navamsa should have bestowed its best in its dasa period. No, it gave the person an easy bed to sleep and indulge in narcotics and alcohol. In a Moksha position in the seventh, casting its aspect on the ascendant, which was in a dharma position, it was spiritually motivating the person to seek the inner answers, externally, the goals and social needs took a big neglect.

A strong Moon and Mercury may not give a good Dasa, the outer Graha-s are stronger in showing a more consistent behavior on what they offer during their dasa period. When a person has a strong Venus and Saturn in the birth chart, any combination involving Venus' main dasa and Saturn as Antara or Saturn's main dasa with Venus as Antara or even at sub-dasa levels will be a period of fall, severe fall – regarding health, finances, profession.

Navamsa verifies what in the birth chart fully manifest. While the birth chart may show general potential, the Navamsa shows how to activate it. For example, if a person has a strong seventh house in the birth chart, but a severely afflicted seventh house in the Navamsa, promises of marriage or partnership may fail, or after a good beginning, the relationship may turn sour. Similarly, Navamsa finds use in specifying house indications. With Saturn residing in the twelfth in the birth chart, but in the ninth in the Navamsa, the spiritual aspects of the twelfth house are more likely emphasized. If the same Saturn is in the tenth in the Navamsa, it may give honor in foreign lands being twelfth house of the birth chart. If it tenants the eighth house in the Navamsa, the humiliation giving potential of its twelfth house position become enhanced. The Navamsa becomes more important as a person gets older because it takes into consideration more the karma being created in the present life. A close look at the Navamsa offers a deeper insight into the chart. Favorable Navamsa will give the ability to grow in life. Difficult Navamsa may limit the ability of better karmas to manifest.

Perhaps the most confusing thing is in determining what makes natural benefic graha-s become temporal malefic graha-s or natural malefic graha-s turn into temporal benefic graha-s. A graha's natural status reveals the personality of the person, while the temporal status reveals the outward destiny. The basic rules of judging natural benefic and malefic graha-s tell more on the disposition of the person than their destiny, though both impact the native to some degree. Powerfully placed natural malefic graha-s as temporal benefic graha-s still have a malefic influence upon the personality of the person. However, if the malefic is in its own sign its impact on the charisma of the person turns more positive.

Similar to relative status are the 'referred' houses, allowing a somewhat different story to unfold. Graha positions that prove useful for the Ascendant may bring challenges to referred houses such as the fourth for the mother, tenth and ninth for the father, fifth for children. The rule applies to temporal lords similarly.

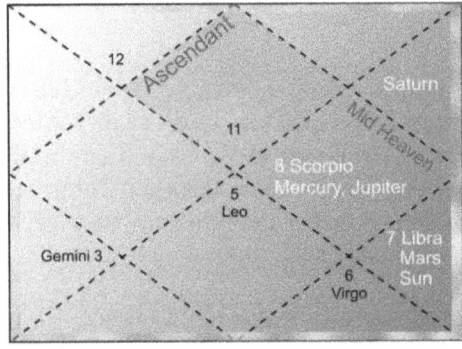

For example, Mercury in the tenth appears well placed, but from Scorpio, Mercury is the relative-eighth lord, besides the ascendant-eighth lord, affecting the father-child relationship. For another example, Saturn in the eleventh is generally good for the native, being an Upachaya house, but as it casts an aspect on the fifth house of children, it can still harm or limit one's children.

Astrological Yogas or combinations are of different types and may include one or more of all the considerations above. Some owe their definition to the natural status of planets alone, others use the temporal status and house lordship. Yet, others get defined by combining both factors.

Combust and retrograde are among the most controversial issues of Vedic Astrology. Here we will examine them in more detail. Combust principally weakens the life, relationship or Jiva aspect of the planets involved. The house lordship plays an important role. First lord combust weakens the health of the person. Third lord combust is damaging for younger siblings, while the eleventh lord combust harms elder siblings. Fourth lord combust makes the mother suffer; ninth lord combust harms the father. Fifth lord combust gives trouble with children or complications having them.

Seventh lord combust gives problems in relationship and marriage. Eighth lord combust weakens longevity. Sixth lord combust weakens immunity and resistance to disease. Evidently, other factors must combine with these indications for them to be significant. Combust distresses our human interactions and negatively affects health and vitality. It interferes not with other significations of houses in matters concerning intelligence, spirituality, wealth and career.

Orbs in determining whether a graha is combust or not is another subject of controversy. Some books refer to them as relatively large, over ten degrees for every planet. Others define them as smaller, particularly for Mercury and Venus, which cannot stray far from the Sun. I have taken the latter position.

Retrogression is yet another factor that carries different interpretations. I will present here my opinion, that every Vedic astrologer may not agree with. Malefic graha-s, Mars and Saturn, when retrograde become stronger inflicting more harm, especially when they occupy Kendra-s. Retrogression increases their ability to cause delays, obstructions and limitations. Benefic graha-s when retrograde turn weak and unreliable, in matters relating to health. Their positive forward energy and their ability to lead us forward get reduced. Mercury and Venus are less weakened by retrograde as it is a more common condition for them. Their retrograde is similarly of two types. They can retrograde towards the Sun, which is towards getting combusted, making it more difficult on themselves. Or, they retrograde away from the Sun, suffering less. When other factors afflict a retrograde graha, it becomes worse. Venus and Mercury can suffer retrogression and combustion, which hits their powers hard. Mars, Jupiter and Saturn retrograde in signs opposite or near opposite to the Sun. They cannot suffer retrogression and combustion.

Retrogression internalizes our energies. Therefore, it can have spiritual benefits. It makes a person hesitant and counter-productive, tending towards reversals. In addition, retrogression has a minor repercussion. It does not outweigh more important factors exhibited by the sign, house or aspect. A well placed benefic retrograde will do much more good than ill placed but not retrograde.

Music Making

The tonic note being 'Sa', when tuning a sitar to the key of 'C', the tonic note 'Sa' becomes the 'C'. When tuning a guitar to play classical instrumental music or accompany a voice rendition, one may tune the six strings in the following manner. The first and second high strings remain as they are E and B, the other strings get tuned lower. Third from G to F#, fourth from D to B, fifth from A to F# and sixth string from E to B. If you play the open strings, you have one power-chord going. Putting a 'capo' on the first fret, the strings become from first to sixth as F C G C G C – a power chord for 'Sa' or 'C'. The guitar offers a drone like a sitar, though there are no extra resonant strings, where lead is mostly played in the first two strings along with a strum with other strings to support the root of 'C'. The capo can be moved between frets to set the root chord.

Patanjali had written in his book on grammar that a word, its meaning and knowledge are entwined so strong, it is impossible to separate them. Once separated, we can even understand the language of birds and animals. In the earlier days, the members of the clan that failed to understand 'sur' became 'asura', though the deities did sometime turn into asura, even the Sarasvati river, now extinct would at times show her Asura tendencies. Sura is melody, which is harmony, a major component of wellness. The Rig Veda sages, Kavi-s or poets understood the cosmic melody.

Gemstones and Colors

Similar to melody and sound, colors have a noteworthy impact on life. Colors are closer to graha-s than dosha-s. Mars, Sun and Rahu prefer red, Jupiter sticks to yellow, Moon and Venus white, Mercury favors white, Ketu likes honey, Saturn dark-blue. With a Vata person, who has dominance of Saturn, Mercury and portions of Venus, not wearing dark colors will qualify Venus and wearing dark would empower Saturn.

For a tall vata person, dark colors bring out the best of Saturn, for a short person with vata constitution, emerald green is preferred. In both cases, the white complements Venus side of things. For a pitta person where Sun and Mars play a pivotal role, colors of red and dark shades of red match their countenance.

The person wearing red does not get effected, but surrounded by much of red increases the warmth around the pitta person and elevates his pitta-dosha. Kapha relates to Moon, Jupiter and Venus; where the white on the wearer suits the personality. Yellow adds to the charm. These colors are for the day, when the body is in motion, at work, at play. When the body gets to rest, the colors must get reversed for the mind to calm and lower the temper. Wearing one's sun-sign gemstone or a Vedic color, it is always better to wear them only during the day and removed from the boy at night.

Herbals

Herbals are truly a handful to have around. In pursuit of health and continued use of herbs, a few of them can fulfill our needs. Honey, ghee or clarified butter and aloe are available at the grocers and act as transporters of the plant herbs to target organs. Ashwagandha is one of those herbs like Gin Seng that stay in the cupboard. For a person concerned about the liver, spleen and heart – Ashwagandha with Arjuna is an excellent choice and can be taken twice a day as tonic for these organs. Ashwagandha, Basil and Brahmi promotes the functioning brain and mind, Ashwagandha and Shatavari supplements the body with cooling, calming and strengthening, acting as a restorative. Ashwagandha, Guggul and Vidari Kanda works against arthritis. For bones, one may increase the intake of pineapple to the diet if there is evidence of bone damage. Ashwagandha and Gokshura supports kidneys and bladder. The combination of Ashwagandha and Bala promises strength to the lungs and muscles. Ashwagandha and Kapikacchu act as an aphrodisiac. Guggul cleanses the blood of cholesterols and LDLs, it also supports arthritic conditions.

Organic and wildly grown herbs found in Northeast, harvested in regions of New Mexico and Florida have tremendous capacity to maintain health. Echinacea, One eyed Susan, Arnica and other Sunflowers increase immunity, so does Dandelion, which are native to the land. The best remedies come from organic and wild grown herbs. As stated before, the herbs are not intended to diagnose, treat, cure or prevent disease, they enable the body to absorb the right nutrients from the food to the organs in ensuring wellness. Herbs steeped in the Ayurveda tradition promote good health and long life.

Throughout Ayurveda, different combinations of these elements form body constitutions of Vata, Pitta and Kapha. The concept of three major constitutional types of Vata, Pitta and Kapha defined as constituents of 'Creative-force'.

A study conducted to correlate genomic variations in classifying the parts of Prakriti had several interesting findings, the study can be found at Nature.COM, the URL being https://www.nature.com/articles/srep15786. A well-known group performed genome-wide SNP or single nucleotide polymorphism analysis known as Affymetrix, 6.0 after screening three thousand odd subjects belonging to three dosha constitutions. They found fifty-two SNPs were significantly different between constitutions. Principal component analysis or PCA of these SNPs classified several individuals into groups of Vata, Pitta and Kapha irrespective of their ancestry, which represent its power in categorization. Subsequently, they found that PGM1 correlates with phenotype of Pitta as described in the ancient text of Charaka Samhita, suggesting that the phenotypic classification of India's traditional medicine had a genetic basis; and its Creative-force-based practice in vogue for many centuries was about personalized medicine.

A quick recap, Vata constitutes air and etheric space, Pitta comes from water and fire, and Kapha owes it to earth and water. In Vedic astrology, signs and divisions are designated as fire, water, earth and air having a graha ruler. Among other commonalities between the two systems are time and the elements as described.

Ayurvedic nascent constitution or "Prakruti" determined from a person's astrological chart, opens a new area of research in medical astrology. A person born of an astrological-mold comes with certain characteristics – the static ones that make a person's character, countenance, morality, the behavioral part determines life's aim and goals.

It is a belief that a person is preset to a prearranged Prakruti at infancy – a set of inherent attributes that in cohesion with natural cosmic laws. The cosmic ecosystem applies to everyone – we are born with a signature, symbiotic to the natural laws, however the karmic or causative principles guide us to a state Vikruti that may diverge from our original state. Prakruti was what nature had planned for us; Vikruti is what we have become.

Body, mind and spirit are the tripod of life; Lagna, Chandra and Surya influence this tripod. Surya, Chandra and Lagna reveals the health perspective. Mental Prakruti comes more from the Chandra.

Important - Specific vitamins, herbs, supplements, scriptures, recommendations or other items or procedures mentioned in the website Aquapisces.com have not been evaluated by USFDA. The information provided in this book and website is not intended as a substitute for advice from a physician or doctor. Please consult a licensed doctor or physician before starting any diet or exercise; especially if you have a medical condition such as diabetes, hypertension, heart problem, arthritis, cancer, addiction, substance-abuse, alcoholism, pregnancy or are nursing.

Herb	Plant Name	Image
Apricot Seed	Prunus armeniaca; Rosaceae meant as lung vitality tonic is used in antitussive, expectorant, laxative, treats cold and coughs, demulcent, dissolves tumors, antispasmodic conditions. The herb is bitter, sweet, heating and pungent. It pacifies Kapha, Pitta and raises Vata.	
Arjuna	Terminalia arjuna is a tree of the genus Terminalia. It is commonly known as arjuna or arjuna tree in English. The arjuna is about 20–25 metres tall; usually has a buttressed trunk, and forms a wide canopy at the crown, from which branches drop downwards. It has oblong, conical leaves which are green on the top and brown below; smooth, grey bark; it has pale yellow flowers which appear between March and June; its glabrous, 2.5 to 5 cm fibrous woody fruit, divided into five wings, appears between September and November.	
Arnica	Arnica is a genus of perennial, herbaceous plants in the sunflower family (Asteraceae). The genus name Arnica may be derived from the Greek arni, 'lamb', in reference to the plants' soft, hairy leaves.	
Ashwagandha	Withania somnifera, known commonly as Ashwagandha, Indian Ginseng, poison gooseberry, or winter cherry, is a plant in the Solanaceae or nightshade family.	

Astragalus	Astragalus membranaceus meant to increase immunity popularly known as influenza buster. The herb is used in antibacterial requirements, supporting the immune system, consolidates defensive energy, detoxification, energy tonic, blood tonic, regulates fluids.	
Atractylodis	Atractylodes macrocephala; Compositae. General body tonic, digestive aid, diuretic, regulates appetite, builds energy, provides tonic to the spleen and stomach. It is sweet and bitter and slightly heating.	
Brahmi Gotu Kola	Centella asiatica, commonly known as centella, is a small, herbaceous, frost-tender perennial plant in the flowering plant family Apiaceous, subfamily Mackinlayoideae. It is native to wetlands in Asia. It is used as a medicinal herb in Ayurvedic medicine, Western Herbal Medicine, traditional African medicine, traditional Chinese medicine and in western orthodox medicine.	
Chaparral	Larrea divaricata; Zygophyllaceae increases immunity. Known as Influenza Buster. Increases immune system, alternative, antiviral, antiseptic, resolvent cleanser, decreases damp heat, stimulates and dredges the liver, promotes cleansing, dissipates tumors. It is bitter, cooling and pungent. Lowers Pitta and Kapha, and raises vata.	
Cherry bark	Prunus virginiana; Rosaceae. Antitussive, antispasmodic, expectorant, alternative, pectoral, carminative, calms respiration, allay cough and asthma, helps stomach disorders. It is bitter, astringent, cooling and sweet. It lowers pitta and kapha.	
Cinnamon	Cinnamon is a spice obtained from the inner bark of several tree species from the genus Cinnamomum. Cinnamon is used in both sweet and savory foods. The term "cinnamon" also refers to its mid-brown color.	

AQUAPISCES

Coconut	The coconut tree (Cocos nucifera) is a member of the family Arecaceae (palm family) and the only species of the genus Cocos. The term coconut can refer to the whole coconut palm or the seed, or the fruit, which, botanically, is a drupe, not a nut.
Chrysanthemum	Chrysanthemum indicum; Compositae. Diaphoretic, antipyretic, antispasmodic, alternative, helps headache, sore throat, heat in upper body, eye infections, nose bleeds, liver diseases, dysmenorrhea, promotes lactation. It affects the systems of digestion, respiratory and nerves. It is bitter, sweet, cooling and pungent. It lowers pitta and kapha, but can elevate vata.
Coltsfoot	Tussilago farfafa. Antitussive, expectorant, demulcent, anti-inflammatory, sedates cough, helps dry cough and shortness of breath, antispasmodic. It is pungent, slightly sweet and heating.
Dandelion	Taraxacum offincinale; Compositae. Alterative, diuretic, laxative, bitter tonic, liver digestion, gall stones, congested lymph, breast sores, breast tumors, diabetes, edema, ulcers, detoxifying tumors and cysts. It works on the circulatory, digestive, urinary, lymphatic systems. It is bitter, sweet and cooling.
Echinacea	Echinacea augustifolia; Compositae. Activates immunity, antiviral, antibacterial, clears toxins, restrains infections, resolves tumors, decreases pain, decreases eruptive fevers, promotes cleansing congested lymph. It is pungent, salty, cooling and dry.

Eucalyptus	Eucalyptus is a diverse genus of flowering trees and shrubs (including a distinct group with a multiple-stem mallee growth habit) in the myrtle family, Myrtaceae. Members of the genus dominate the tree flora of Australia, and include the tallest known flowering plant on Earth. There are more than 700 species of eucalyptus and most are native to Australia; a very small number are found in adjacent areas of New Guinea and Indonesia.	
Fenugreek	Fenugreek is an annual plant in the family Fabaceae, with leaves consisting of three-small obovate to oblong leaflets. It is cultivated worldwide as a semiarid crop, and its seeds are a common ingredient in dishes from South Asia.	
Frankincense	There are four main species of Boswellia that produce true frankincense. Resin from each of the four is available in various grades. The grades depend on the time of harvesting; the resin is hand-sorted for quality.	
Garlic	Garlic (scientific name Allium sativum) is a species in the onion genus, Allium. Its close relatives include the onion, shallot, leek, chive, and Allium chinense. With a history of several thousand years of human consumption and use, garlic is native to the region between the Mediterranean and China, and has long been a common seasoning worldwide.	
Ginger	Ginger (Zingiber officinale) is a flowering plant whose rhizome, ginger root or simply ginger, is used as a spice and herb. It is an herbaceous perennial which grows annual stems about a meter in height bearing narrow green leaves and yellow flowers. Ginger originated in the tropical rainforest in Southern Asia. Although ginger no longer grows wild, it is thought to have originated on the Indian subcontinent because the ginger plants grown in India show the	

	largest amount of genetic variation. Ginger was exported to Europe via India in the first century AD as a result of the lucrative spice trade and was used extensively by the Romans.	
Ginkgo	Ginkgo biloba; Ginkgoaceae. Vitalizes heart blood, restores capillary and coronary circulation, restores brain and nerves, promotes clear thinking, relieves depression, increases memory. It works on cardiovascular, nervous, respiratory, urogenital systems. It is sweet, bitter, astringent.	
Goldenseal	Hydratis Canadensis; Ranunculaceae. Antiseptic, antibiotic, antipyretic, antimicrobial, resolves mucus, decreases inflammation, clears toxins, parasites, decreases heat liver-gallbladder, decongestive. It is bitter, astringent, cooling and pungent. It lowers pitta and kapha, increases vata.	
Hing or Asafetida	Asafetida is the dried latex (gum oleoresin) exuded from the rhizome or tap root of several species of Ferula, a perennial herb that grows 1 to 1.5 meters (3.3 to 4.9 feet) tall. The species is native to the deserts of Iran and mountains of Afghanistan and is mainly cultivated in nearby India	
Jasmine	Jasmine is a genus of shrubs and vines in the olive family (Oleaceae). It contains around 200 species, which are native to tropical and warm temperate regions of Eurasia, Australasia and Oceania.	
Jatamansi, Jatamamsi	Spikenard - Nardostachys Jatamansi is a flowering plant of the Valerian family that grows in the Himalayas. Balances all three dosha-s, sedative though promotes awareness, strengthens mind, insomnia, hysteria, epilepsy, neuralgia. It works on the nervous, digestive, respiratory systems. It is sweet, bitter, astringent, cooling and pungent.	
Khus	Chrysopogon zizanioides, commonly known as vetiver is a perennial bunchgrass of the Poaceae family, native to India. In western and	

	northern India, it is popularly known as khus.	
Lavender	Lavandula (common name lavender) is a genus of 47 known species of flowering plants in the mint family, Lamiaceae. It is native to the Old World and is found from Cape Verde and the Canary Islands, Europe across to northern and eastern Africa, the Mediterranean, southwest Asia to southeast India.	
Lemon Balm	Melissa officinalis. Nervine, carminative, diaphoretic, sedative, antidepressant, Qi tonic, rejuvenation effects, relaxes nervous system, antiviral. It is pungent, sweet, cooling and pungent. It lowers kapha and pitta.	
Licorice	Liquorice, or licorice, is the root of Glycyrrhiza glabra from which a sweet flavor can be extracted. The licorice plant is an herbaceous perennial legume native to southern Europe and parts of Asia, such as India. It is not botanically related to anise, star anise, or fennel, which are sources of similar flavoring compounds. Tonic, demulcent, expectorant, rejuvenation, laxative, provides moisture-relieves dryness, relieves cough and wheezing, clears toxins, decreases infections. Calms mind, nourishes Spirit, Sattvic, nourishes brain, increases cranial and cerebrospinal fluid, dismisses discontentment and disharmony. Systems: digestive, respiratory, nervous, reproduction, excretory. It is sweet, bitter, cooling and sweet. It lowers vata and pitta, may elevate kapha.	
Longan fruit	Euphoria longan. It supplied tonic to the heart and spleen, nourishes blood, calms spirit, supports memory, relieves insomnia, heart palpitations, antifungal. It works on the circulatory, digestive systems. It is sweet and warming.	
Lychee berry	Lycium chinensis. Blood tonic, supports kidney, adrenals, liver, promotes cheerfulness, increases vitality, improves vision, calms heart	

	and nervous system, increases longevity, hyperglycemic, antifungal, hypertension. It is sweet and neutral.	
Marshmallow	The word marshmallow stems from the mallow plant (Althaea officinalis) that is a genus of an herb native to parts of Europe, North Africa, and Asia. The word "marsh" is used, because the mallow plant grows in marshes, and other damp areas. Nutritive tonic, acts to rejuvenate, expectorant, demulcent, emollient, diuretic, laxative, helps cough, bronchitis, whooping cough, decreases kidney and bladder inflammation, decreases infection or bleeding. It works on respiratory, urinary, digestive, nervous systems. It is sweet, cooling.	
Mint	Peppermint (Mentha × piperita, also known as Mentha. balsamea Willd.) is a hybrid mint: a cross between watermint and spearmint. Indigenous to Europe and the Middle East, the plant is now widespread in cultivation in many regions of the world.	
Motherwort	Leonurus cardiac; Labiatae. Emmenagogue, diaphoretic, diuretic, alternative, uterine stimulant, relaxant, cardiac tonic, carminative. It is bitter, pungent, cooling and pungent. It lowers pitta and kapha and raises vata.	
Mullein	verbascum thaspus; Scrophulariaceae. Antispasmodic, anti-tussive, anti-inflammatory, demulcent, expectorant, relieves cough. It is bitter, astringent, sweet, cooling and pungent. It pacifies pitta and kapha and raises vata.	
Mustard	Mustard plants are any of several plant species in the genera Brassica and Sinapis in the family Brassicaceae. Mustard seed is used as a spice.	

Neem	Azadirachta Indica, also known as Neem, Nimtree, and Indian Lilac is a tree in the mahogany family Meliaceae. It is one of two species in the genus Azadirachta, and is native to India and the Indian subcontinent including Nepal, Pakistan, Bangladesh, and Sri Lanka.	
Nirgundi	Vitex negundo, commonly known as the Chinese chastetree, five-leaved chaste tree, or horseshoe vitex, is a large aromatic shrub with quadrangular, densely whitish, tomentose branchlets. It is widely used in folk medicine, particularly in South and Southeast Asia.	
Punarnava	Boerhavia diffusa is a species of flowering plant in the four o'clock family which is commonly known as punarnava (meaning that which rejuvenates or renews the body in Ayurveda), red spiderling, spreading hogweed, or tarvine. It is taken in herbal medicine for pain relief and other uses. The leaves of B. diffusa are often used as a green vegetable in many parts of India.	
Rehmannia	Rehmannia glutinosa; Scrophulariaceae. Nutritive tonic, rejuvenation, sexual debility, weak kidneys, low back pain, irregular menses, anemia, hair loss, cirrhosis, senility, diabetes. It works on reproductive, urinary, digestive, respiratory systems. It is sweet, bitter, cooling and sweet. It lowers pitta and vata and raises kapha	
Rose	Rosa spp.; Rosaceae. Alterative, nervine, emmenagogue, carminative, opens mind and heart, decreases heat in upper body, headache, dizziness, refreshes eyes, removes irritability, promotes peace. It works on circulatory, female reproductive, nervous system. It is sweet, astringent and cooling.	

Sandalwood	Sandalwood is a class of woods from trees in the genus Santalum. The woods are heavy, yellow, and fine-grained, and unlike many other aromatic woods, they retain their fragrance for decades. Sandalwood oil is extracted from the woods for use. Both the wood and the oil produce a distinctive fragrance that has been highly valued for centuries.	
Schizandra	Schizandra chinensis; Magnoliaceae. Yin and Yang tonic, promotes proper liver function, relieves hepatitis, enriches kidney yin, supports lungs, quiets spirit, calms heart, insomnia. It is sour, salty, sweet, pungent, bitter and heating.	
Sesame	Sesame is a flowering plant in the genus Sesamum, also called benne. Numerous wild relatives occur in Africa and a smaller number in India. It is widely naturalized in tropical regions around the world and is cultivated for its edible seeds, which grow in pods or 'buns'.	
Shankhapushpi	Evolvulus alsinoides. Tonic, antidepressant, improves memory, increases intelligence, aids brains function, alternative, antiepileptic, removes addictions, removes evil spirits.	
Shatavari	Asparagus racemosus is a species of asparagus common throughout Nepal, Sri Lanka, India and the Himalayas. It grows one to two metres tall and prefers to take root in gravelly, rocky soils high up in piedmont plains, at 1,300–1,400 metres elevation. Female reproductive tonic, sexual debility, infertility, impotence, menopause, leucorrhea, dehydration, diarrhea, dysentery, stomach ulcers, hyperacidity, lung disorders, hematemesis. It is sweet, bitter, cooling. It lowers pitta and vata and raises kapha.	

Siberian ginseng	Eleuthro senticosus; Araliaceae. Tonic, adrenal support, increase energy, antirheumatic, antispasmodic. It is pungent, sweet, heating. It lowers vata and kapha and raises pitta.	
St. John's Wort	Hypericum perforatum; Hypericaceae. Antispasmodic, expectorant, stimulates lungs, strengthens and restores nervous system, lifts the spirit and rids depression, relieves infection and pain. It is bitter, pungent and cooling. It lowers pitta and kapha and raises vata.	
Tulsi	Ocimum sanctum. Adaptogen, tonic, relieves cold and flu, increases memory and awareness, gives sense of wellbeing, immune stimulant, relieves cough, awakens spiritual insight. It is bitter, sweet, pungent and heating.	
Wintergreen	Wintergreen is a group of aromatic plants. The term "wintergreen" once commonly referred to plants that remain green (continue photosynthesis) throughout the winter.	

Images courtesy Wikipedia.

Healing requires either an external agency or an impetus to recover from deterioration. We think of the obvious happy path and the exceptions that may occur in a process. There is little room for self-healing and that's what matters. The human intervention should slowly disappear and the system or the process should be able to work in its own ecosystem. The more the human intervention, the less the chances of an ecosystem. But, I am so glad that folks are thinking out of the box - out of the cultist-religious box into deciphering and understanding what our forefathers were actually trying to say and not what the latter bards and priests have made us believe. we are all endowed with dharma, karma and kama genes. Some of these genes puff at different times and different situations - the challenge is always re-orienting the proteins back to dharma. I took these words from Swami Vivekananda.

AQUAPISCES

Old man moans at the sight of a steep incline
Oh, Sir, how to cross it
I can walk no more
my chest breaks, my feet are slit

Look down at those feet
the road that is under is the track you traveled
It is the same road before you
it will soon be under your feet, the road so graveled

There is undoubtedly a divine pathway etched with a cosmic brush for all of us. Not the most perfect plan and yet not the least deterrent. You realize you have a shared responsibility with God in creating a better world for yourself, for the next, for the future. Living the life of an ascetic is no answer to salvation. Our ancestors taught us about simple faith and trust that reveal the inner dweller and it does not have to be while cloistered in an ashram and retreat. You have to love the world, align to its movement and live in it. Such alignments are never linear, being a hopeless vassal of the mind-lords. You have encountered the symbols and signposts before; they are sometimes Piscean, other times Aquarian.

INDEX

A

Agni, 5, 50, 61, 62, 63, 70, 82, 83, 84, 85, 86, 99, 142, 143, 157, 169, 192, 193, 211, 213, 215, 226, 250, 253, 383, 384, 387, 389, 392, 394, 395, 399, 420
Alochaka, 61, 62, 63, 64, 245
Aloe, 85, 184, 200, 201, 213, 238
Ama, 86, 87, 91, 93, 107, 113, 130, 141, 142, 143, 151, 153, 154, 157, 158, 159, 167, 169, 174, 175, 183, 184, 195, 205, 206, 208, 210, 215, 243, 244, 269
Ambhuvaha, 88, 91, 94, 99
anger, 4, 42, 48, 73, 92, 97, 100, 110, 112, 116, 127, 129, 131, 147, 171, 221, 223, 225, 230, 246, 255, 259, 358, 368, 383, 425
Annavaha, 88, 91, 94
Anuradha, 295, 387, 392, 399, 400, 401, 402, 404, 405, 406, 407, 410
Apana, 55, 57, 58, 59, 60, 61, 63, 64, 65, 77, 80, 99, 143, 221, 242, 249, 250, 251, 253, 255, 259, 265
appendicitis, 147
AquaPisces, i, ii, 1, 2, 258, 279, 280, 283, 284, 406
Ardra, 294, 385, 390, 398, 399, 400, 401, 402, 404, 405, 406, 408, 439
armor, 169
aroma, 55, 219, 221, 224, 225, 254, 271, 277, 307
Artavaha, 90, 97, 240
Artha, 38, 39, 283, 284, 297, 384, 386, 387, 401
arthritis, 65, 73, 79, 93, 100, 108, 114, 119, 132, 134, 136, 137, 143, 145, 147, 148, 183, 189, 193, 209, 210, 218, 222, 223, 224, 226, 232, 233, 244, 245, 246, 248, 270, 271, 463
Ashtottari, 296, 436, 437, 439, 440
Ashvini, 2, 294, 388, 389, 394, 395, 397, 398, 399, 400, 401, 402, 403, 404, 405, 406, 407, 408, 429
Aslesha, 386, 391, 396, 399, 400, 401, 402, 404, 405, 406, 407, 409, 429

Asthivaha, 89, 92, 96
asthma, 73, 94, 99, 114, 132, 148, 192, 209, 235, 236
astragalus, 28, 211, 231, 235, 236, 237, 239
Astrology, 1, 2, 3, 4, 66, 102, 185, 277, 279, 280, 305, 307, 376, 389, 436, 458
Asura, 395, 460
Avalambaka, 63, 64, 65, 246, 247
Ayurveda, ii, ix, 1, 2, 3, 4, 5, 6, 31, 41, 44, 107, 117, 278, 279, 305, 446, 462

B

Bharani, 294, 384, 389, 398, 399, 400, 401, 402, 403, 404, 405, 406, 408
Bhrajaka, 61, 62, 64, 65, 211, 244
Bhutas, 3, 18
bile, 45, 48, 49, 62, 63, 65, 72, 75, 82, 119, 139, 140, 148, 160, 161, 197, 204, 207, 244, 270
bleeding, 73, 108, 138, 139, 140, 146, 147, 163, 167, 183, 185, 189, 200, 201, 209, 215, 230, 238, 239, 244, 245, 253, 255, 256
Blood, 47, 67, 68, 70, 72, 73, 75, 88, 148, 213, 230
Bodhaka, 63, 64, 248
Boils, 146
Bone, 67, 69, 72, 73, 74, 213
Brighu, 3, 278, 308, 311, 395
Brihat Jataka, 450
bronchitis, 146, 148
Buddhi, 13, 19, 40, 312
bursitis, 147
butter, 76, 93, 211, 232

C

calcium, 76, 232
cancer, 68, 95, 96, 98, 100, 134, 140, 147, 148, 149, 190, 223, 463
carbuncle, 146
Cartilage, 67
Chakras, 18
Charaka, 2, 3, 5, 93, 278, 462
cheese, 76, 93, 174, 177, 183, 195, 235
Chitra, 295, 387, 392, 398, 399, 400, 401, 402, 404, 405, 406, 409, 422
Christ, 392, 410
coconut, 127, 176, 177, 179, 207, 211, 228, 229, 231, 233, 241, 247, 248, 270, 271, 272
colitis, 147, 238
constipation, 46, 49, 80, 86, 94, 98, 107, 113, 119, 131, 132, 138, 140, 141, 142, 163, 164, 189, 193, 194, 196, 197, 206, 238, 242, 253, 259, 270, 345
Constipation, 97, 141
cough, 49, 56, 94, 131, 140, 144, 148, 162, 163, 199, 200, 201, 202, 221, 223, 225, 236, 239, 243, 246, 247, 248, 250, 253, 256

D

Dairy, 76, 176, 177, 179, 183, 232
Damodar, 7, 10, 22, 23, 25, 26, 31, 32, 34, 35, 54, 84, 87, 88, 128
decay, 15, 20, 22, 42, 44, 49, 57, 60, 68, 82, 121, 140, 143, 168, 251, 282, 300
depression, 20, 44, 49, 78, 97, 100, 138, 200, 222, 242, 243, 246, 249
Dhanistha, 388, 394, 398, 399, 400, 401, 402, 404, 405, 406, 411
Dharma, 38, 39, 282, 283, 284, 297, 314, 316, 317, 320, 322, 323, 325, 326, 328, 333, 383, 387, 401, 420, 447
Dhatu, 66, 67, 70, 71, 75, 259
diabetes, 73, 132, 147, 148, 163, 195,

201, 222, 223, 237, 238, 319, 463
Diabetes, 88, 94, 145
diarrhea, 57, 94, 107, 132, 141, 163, 167, 238, 242, 250, 259, 270
Diarrhea, 97, 141
digestion, 45, 47, 56, 57, 58, 61, 62, 63, 68, 70, 73, 84, 85, 86, 92, 99, 103, 111, 127, 130, 140, 149, 159, 161, 162, 165, 167, 173, 181, 182, 184, 185, 192, 193, 195, 196, 197, 199, 200, 201, 202, 205, 211, 224, 225, 226, 228, 237, 243, 247, 250, 251, 252, 259, 264, 267, 269
dogwood, 28
Drekkana, 300, 304, 377, 441
Dusthana, 297, 303, 447, 455
Dwadasamsa, 303

E

Ether, 17, 18, 19, 45, 48, 51, 52, 53, 170, 171, 196, 287, 416

F

Fat, 48, 69, 72, 95, 213
fatigue, 20, 31, 44, 73, 74, 80, 99, 131, 142, 143, 148, 150, 180, 237, 333, 334, 348, 350
fear, 35, 48, 73, 74, 77, 81, 84, 91, 92, 100, 106, 109, 113, 114, 117, 131, 141, 145, 146, 242, 246, 249, 254, 259, 275, 313, 316, 328, 336, 348
Feces, 79, 81, 107, 141
fever, 26, 28, 29, 30, 31, 44, 48, 49, 73, 81, 99, 108, 119, 127, 131, 132, 139, 141, 143, 146, 147, 148, 150, 154, 155, 157, 158, 189, 207, 209, 210, 215, 219, 221, 225, 228, 229, 244, 246, 267, 390
fire, 83, 169
Fire, 84, 169
flame, 84

G

Ganga, 5, 276
garlic, 28, 177, 178, 206, 207, 212, 229, 230, 235, 236, 238, 239, 240, 242, 247, 248, 272
ghee, 76, 78, 179, 187, 199, 206, 207, 210, 211, 212, 213, 214, 229, 230, 232, 233, 234, 235, 236, 237, 240, 241, 243, 244, 245, 246, 247, 248, 249, 253, 255, 271, 385
ginger, 28, 53, 83, 93, 120, 165, 167, 173, 177, 180, 188, 189, 193, 195, 196, 198, 199, 200, 201, 202, 205, 207, 211, 212, 220, 221, 223, 225, 226, 228, 229, 230, 232, 233, 234, 235, 236, 237, 238, 239, 240, 241, 242, 243, 244, 245, 247, 248, 253, 270, 271, 272
glands, 47, 64, 73, 82, 89, 95, 120, 132, 146, 147, 148, 229, 243, 246, 248, 255, 267
gods, 83, 84, 85
Gods, 169
Greece, 5
guitar, 460
Guna, 11, 12, 13, 15, 16, 19, 20, 38, 43, 52, 66, 116, 117, 282, 384, 398

H

Hasta, 295, 386, 391, 392, 398, 399, 400, 401, 402, 404, 405, 406, 407, 409, 420
headache, 98, 101, 131, 147, 195, 223, 225, 243, 247
heart, 25, 28, 48, 55, 56, 59, 61, 63, 64, 68, 74, 77, 78, 88, 91, 98, 99, 112, 116, 121, 131, 132, 134, 137, 145, 147, 148, 149, 155, 157, 158, 162, 163, 189, 191, 192, 219, 220, 222, 223, 224, 225, 227, 229, 242, 246,

247, 251, 252, 260, 273, 306, 309, 311, 326, 330, 333, 334, 339, 348, 350, 370, 392, 463
heart attack, 95, 148
hernia, 94
hypertension, 73, 95, 145, 148, 155, 163, 463

I

immortality, 169
inflammation, 49, 61, 73, 93, 95, 108, 139, 140, 143, 147, 157, 229, 231, 232, 241, 244, 245, 255, 270, 348
influenza, 80, 81, 114, 120, 144, 146, 148, 149, 154, 201, 210, 218, 223, 239, 256, 409
insecurity, 74, 114
insomnia, 49, 63, 96, 99, 100, 102, 110, 113, 119, 125, 131, 141, 145, 155, 163, 189, 193, 200, 209, 223, 234, 242, 246, 247, 249, 255
intestine, 47, 48, 56, 57, 62, 63, 65, 77, 85, 86, 97, 108, 127, 128, 130, 131, 144, 146, 158, 159, 161, 184, 192, 194, 196, 197, 216, 221, 244, 252, 256, 257, 258, 270, 311

J

Jaimini, 3
jaundice, 73, 132, 146, 148, 192, 245, 444
Jehu, 22, 25, 26, 31, 34, 54
joint, 73, 223, 225, 233, 243, 244, 248, 273
Jyeshta, 387, 392, 397, 399, 400, 401, 402, 404, 405, 406, 410, 429
Jyotish, ix, 2, 3, 278, 279

K

Kala, 78, 125, 257, 293, 413

Kalachakra, 403, 436, 437
Kapha, 5, 19, 21, 42, 43, 45, 46, 47, 48, 49, 51, 52, 53, 63, 64, 65, 66, 67, 68, 72, 73, 77, 78, 79, 82, 91, 92, 93, 102, 103, 104, 105, 106, 107, 108, 109, 110, 111, 112, 113, 114, 115, 118, 120, 121, 122, 123, 124, 125, 126, 127, 128, 130, 131, 132, 138, 139, 140, 141, 143, 148, 149, 152, 153, 154, 155, 156, 157, 158, 159, 160, 161, 164, 174, 175, 188, 195, 197, 221, 228, 229, 230, 231, 232, 233, 234, 235, 236, 237, 238, 239, 240, 241, 245, 246, 247, 248, 253, 255, 256, 258, 270, 279, 298, 305, 306, 311, 382, 389, 462
karma, 3, 4, 135, 137, 185, 284, 286, 290, 308, 309, 312, 380, 382, 410, 411, 413, 457
Kledaka, 63, 64, 65, 247
Krishna, 7, 34, 283, 385, 395, 410, 415, 416, 417, 437, 441
Krittika, 294, 384, 388, 389, 398, 399, 400, 401, 402, 403, 404, 405, 406, 407, 408, 439

L

lethargy, 19, 49, 141, 148, 149, 242, 246, 248, 255
Licorice, 53, 161, 194, 213, 468
liver, 56, 62, 63, 65, 73, 85, 86, 88, 95, 100, 108, 112, 140, 146, 148, 155, 157, 158, 164, 192, 194, 195, 198, 200, 201, 222, 223, 224, 225, 227, 236, 237, 244, 245, 270
Lotus, 76, 213, 223, 227
lymph, 47, 146, 192, 204, 258

M

Magha, 295, 386, 391, 397, 398, 399, 400, 401, 402, 404, 405, 406, 409,

429
Mahat, 13, 37, 40
Maitreya, 282
Malla, 8
Mamsavaha, 88, 92, 95
Manovaha, 90, 93, 97
Marrow, 68, 69, 72, 76
meat, 20, 76, 92, 104, 121, 142, 172, 176, 178, 179, 183, 184, 206, 208, 210, 211, 229, 234
medicines, 169
Milk, 76, 78, 183, 237
Mind, 4, 13, 76, 90, 97, 116, 141, 214, 268, 307
Moksha, 38, 39, 283, 285, 286, 297, 385, 386, 401
mortality, 26, 98, 321
Mrigashira, 294, 385, 390, 398, 399, 400, 401, 402, 404, 405, 406, 407, 408, 422
Mula, 393, 398, 399, 400, 401, 402, 404, 405, 406, 407, 410, 429
mull, 71, 79
Muscle, 67, 68, 72, 73, 75, 95, 213, 269, 272
Music, 278, 429, 430, 431, 434, 460, 483
myocarditis, 147

N

Nakshatra, 294, 296, 300, 304, 382, 383, 389, 390, 392, 393, 394, 395, 397, 398, 399, 400, 401, 402, 403, 404, 405, 406, 407, 408, 409, 410, 411, 412, 413, 414, 419, 421, 422, 426, 436, 437, 438, 439, 440, 441
nausea, 49, 73, 85, 99, 100, 128, 131, 191, 195, 237, 243, 247, 253
Nausea, 94, 140, 148
nervous, 45, 47, 48, 55, 56, 61, 64, 74, 78, 81, 84, 89, 90, 98, 99, 108, 109, 113, 118, 137, 138, 149, 151, 155, 168, 192, 194, 196, 209, 215, 233, 234, 246, 247, 249, 251, 252, 257, 259, 267, 270, 320, 326, 332, 345, 349, 352
Nirama, 142, 143, 150, 157, 158, 185

O

obesity, 64, 73, 92, 95, 104, 114, 138, 148, 205, 232, 258, 271
ocean, 83
Ojas, 65, 66, 68, 72, 77, 78, 98, 114, 136, 143, 144, 150, 154, 183, 203, 219, 220, 221, 223, 225, 227, 235, 265, 266, 267, 268, 269
Overeating, 91

P

Pachaka, 61, 62, 63, 64, 65, 244
Pancha, 3, 8, 9, 16, 168, 189, 203, 205, 208, 209
Pancharatha, 8
Pancreatic, 94
Parasara, ix, 2, 3, 278, 282, 306, 401, 437, 439
passion, 48, 66, 73, 75, 165, 228, 234, 235, 246, 282, 286, 319, 325, 350, 354, 395, 419
pepper, 28, 83, 173, 176, 177, 178, 179, 188, 193, 195, 202, 205, 211, 212, 213, 231, 232, 234, 235, 236, 237, 238, 244, 247, 257
Pitta, 5, 19, 42, 45, 46, 47, 48, 49, 51, 52, 53, 61, 62, 63, 64, 65, 66, 67, 72, 75, 77, 78, 79, 82, 84, 85, 86, 92, 93, 102, 103, 104, 105, 106, 107, 108, 109, 110, 111, 112, 115, 118, 119, 121, 122, 123, 124, 125, 126, 127, 128, 130, 131, 132, 134, 138, 139, 140, 141, 146, 147, 152, 153, 154, 155, 156, 157, 158, 159, 160,

174, 175, 182, 184, 192, 194, 197, 201, 204, 211, 229, 230, 231, 232, 233, 234, 235, 236, 237, 238, 239, 240, 241, 244, 245, 246, 255, 256, 270, 271, 279, 289, 298, 305, 306, 311, 312, 323, 354, 358, 382, 389, 462

Plasma, 67, 68, 70, 71, 72, 88, 90, 95, 213, 228

Prakriti, 12, 14, 15, 30, 37, 38, 101, 116, 171, 275, 282, 414, 462

Prakruti, 30, 35, 36, 37, 38, 129, 150, 151, 152, 188, 215, 462

Prana, 4, 5, 11, 12, 16, 19, 37, 43, 55, 57, 58, 59, 60, 61, 63, 64, 65, 66, 77, 79, 80, 81, 82, 88, 91, 98, 99, 109, 117, 150, 194, 196, 197, 219, 220, 242, 243, 250, 251, 252, 253, 255, 256, 257, 258, 260, 265, 266, 267, 268, 269, 273, 282, 305, 307, 308, 383, 415, 428

Pranavaha, 88, 91, 94, 251

pranayama, 58, 78, 134, 143, 206, 207, 239, 251, 253, 254, 258, 260, 264, 265

Pranayama, 55, 65, 93, 210, 214, 236

prostate, 73, 89, 96, 99, 146, 147, 149, 234

Pulse, 109, 151, 152, 154, 155, 156, 194, 195

Punarvasu, 294, 385, 390, 395, 399, 400, 401, 402, 404, 405, 406, 407, 408, 422

Purishavaha, 89, 92, 97

Purusha, 1, 11, 12, 15, 21, 36, 37, 60, 214, 275, 293, 307, 413

Purushartha, 38, 40, 283, 297, 312, 400

Purva Bhadra, 388, 399, 400, 401, 404, 405, 406, 411

Purva Phalguni, 295, 386, 391, 396, 398, 399, 400, 401, 404, 405, 406, 407, 409

Purvashadha, 393, 396, 398, 399, 400, 401, 404, 405, 406, 410

Pushya, 294, 386, 391, 399, 400, 401, 402, 404, 405, 406, 407, 408, 420, 422, 441

R

Radha, 23, 24, 26, 28, 30, 31, 32, 34, 100, 392, 410

Rajas, 11, 12, 13, 14, 15, 16, 19, 20, 38, 39, 43, 44, 52, 104, 116, 117, 118, 187, 282, 305, 307, 383, 384, 385, 398, 399

Raktavaha, 88, 92, 95

Ranjaka, 61, 63, 64, 65, 245

Raphael, 450

Rasavaha, 88, 91, 95

Reproductive, 68, 69, 71, 72, 76, 90, 92, 96, 213

Revati, 295, 388, 394, 397, 398, 399, 400, 401, 402, 404, 405, 406, 407, 411, 422, 429

Rig, 4, 5, 6, 13, 55, 82, 390

Rohini, 288, 294, 384, 385, 390, 392, 395, 398, 399, 400, 401, 402, 404, 405, 406, 407, 408, 422

S

sacrificial, 83

Sadhaka, 61, 64, 65, 66, 246, 312

sages, 84

Sama, 4, 5, 84, 142, 143, 150, 157, 158, 159, 185, 205

Samana, 55, 56, 58, 59, 62, 63, 64, 65, 77, 99, 193, 226, 236, 243, 249, 250, 253, 255, 256, 265

Samkhya, 11, 18, 54, 278, 282, 414

sandalwood, 127, 201, 207, 220, 225, 226, 227, 231, 233, 234, 239, 240, 245, 270, 271, 272

Sankranti, 428

Sarasvati, 5
Sattva, 14, 15, 16, 19, 20, 38, 43, 44, 52, 62, 104, 106, 110, 116, 117, 118, 187, 219, 282, 288, 305, 307, 398, 399
Satva, 11, 12, 13, 40, 307
seeker, 83, 85
sesame, 53, 76, 119, 168, 176, 177, 179, 196, 205, 211, 212, 213, 214, 228, 230, 231, 232, 233, 234, 235, 236, 240, 241, 242, 243, 245, 248, 253, 254, 269, 270, 271, 272
Shatabhishag, 394, 397, 398, 399, 400, 401, 402, 404, 405, 406, 407, 411
Shatavari, 53, 78, 186, 189, 194, 202, 213, 471
Shukravaha, 89, 90, 92, 96
skin, 10, 16, 23, 28, 45, 46, 48, 49, 60, 62, 65, 68, 69, 72, 73, 74, 75, 80, 81, 88, 95, 99, 104, 106, 112, 114, 125, 131, 132, 133, 134, 138, 140, 141, 144, 145, 146, 148, 153, 154, 156, 161, 163, 184, 187, 193, 200, 206, 210, 211, 220, 225, 226, 227, 228, 229, 239, 244, 248, 251, 252, 253, 254, 256, 258, 259, 268, 269, 270, 272, 327, 330, 348, 363
sleeping, 21, 49, 81, 92, 110, 131, 138, 141, 269
Sleshaka, 63, 64, 65, 241, 246, 248
Soma, 6, 32, 50, 77, 169, 385, 390, 395, 399, 420
speech, 49, 56, 59, 61, 76, 109, 138, 150, 221, 255, 259, 268, 290, 300, 301, 306, 308, 312, 314, 315, 316, 319, 323, 326, 327, 328, 329, 331, 337, 338, 340, 341, 343, 345, 347, 348, 349, 350, 351, 357, 360, 361, 369, 403, 419, 424, 425, 454
Spirit, 20, 21, 36
spleen, 56, 63, 73, 74, 88, 95, 145, 146, 148, 153, 157, 159, 163, 201, 245, 270
Sravana, 388, 393, 398, 399, 400, 401, 402, 404, 405, 406, 407, 410, 412, 440
Stanyavaha, 90, 98, 240
stomach, 46, 47, 48, 56, 63, 65, 84, 85, 88, 94, 128, 130, 131, 139, 140, 147, 148, 151, 155, 158, 161, 172, 192, 194, 195, 197, 201, 213, 216, 223, 237, 243, 244, 247, 256, 257, 271, 311, 313, 314, 317, 322, 326, 332, 333, 336, 337, 340, 341, 345, 346, 352, 357, 362, 364, 367, 368, 370, 371
stool, 28, 49, 63, 69, 82, 97, 107, 131, 132, 143, 181, 195, 238, 242, 245, 259
Sun, 169
Sura, 206, 460
Svedavaha, 89, 92, 96
Swati, 295, 387, 392, 398, 399, 400, 401, 402, 404, 405, 406, 407, 409
sweat, 26, 47, 48, 49, 72, 79, 80, 81, 82, 89, 92, 96, 107, 141, 145, 148, 149, 160, 185, 204, 206, 208, 228, 259, 270

T

Tamas, 11, 12, 13, 15, 16, 19, 20, 38, 43, 44, 52, 104, 116, 117, 118, 187, 282, 305, 307, 386, 398, 399
Tanmatra, 14, 16
Tarpaka, 63, 64, 65, 66, 249
Tattvas, 18
TCM, 2
teeth, 72, 73, 74, 76, 105, 121, 145, 148, 255, 302
Terracotta, 9
Tibet, 5, 31
tongue, 16, 28, 29, 47, 63, 75, 141, 142, 143, 149, 150, 157, 158, 168,

185, 193, 194, 195, 205, 206, 210, 216, 237, 247, 248, 256, 259, 268, 332, 364
tonic, 78, 143, 183, 184, 188, 189, 199, 201, 202, 204, 206, 210, 211, 212, 213, 214, 216, 230, 239, 240, 305, 431, 432, 435, 460, 461
tremors, 49, 74, 95, 96, 99, 103, 105, 110, 145, 234, 242, 243
Tridosha, 42
trikatu, 53, 194, 195, 207, 229, 237, 238, 244, 247
Trikatu, 188, 194, 197, 232, 257
truth, 83
tumors, 73, 93, 94, 95, 96, 97, 98, 140, 145, 146, 147, 148, 149, 162, 183, 221, 224, 231, 232, 235, 241, 243

U

Udana, 55, 56, 57, 58, 59, 60, 61, 62, 63, 64, 77, 99, 243, 249, 250, 253, 255, 259, 265
ulcers, 86, 125, 140, 147, 148, 158, 194, 209, 244, 247, 270
Upachaya, 290, 296, 378, 450, 454, 455, 458
Upadhatu', 71
Upaveda, 3
urine, 48, 49, 63, 67, 73, 80, 81, 82, 89, 92, 97, 107, 131, 141, 142, 143, 147, 204, 239, 245
Uttara Bhadra, 388, 394, 399, 400, 401, 402, 404, 405, 406, 407, 411, 422
Uttara Phalguni, 295, 386, 391, 396, 398, 399, 400, 401, 402, 404, 405, 406, 409, 412, 422
Uttarashadha, 393, 396, 398, 400, 401, 402, 404, 405, 406, 407, 410, 413
Uttarayana, 428

V

Varna, 40
Varuna, 10, 383, 388, 394, 397, 399, 411
Vata, 5, 19, 42, 43, 44, 45, 46, 47, 48, 49, 51, 52, 53, 54, 57, 65, 66, 67, 69, 73, 74, 75, 77, 78, 79, 82, 84, 87, 91, 92, 93, 99, 100, 102, 103, 104, 105, 106, 107, 108, 109, 110, 111, 112, 113, 114, 118, 119, 121, 122, 123, 124, 125, 126, 127, 128, 129, 130, 131, 132, 134, 138, 139, 140, 141, 143, 144, 145, 146, 152, 154, 155, 156, 157, 158, 159, 160, 174, 175, 181, 182, 192, 193, 196, 201, 230, 231, 232, 233, 234, 235, 236, 237, 238, 239, 240, 241, 245, 255, 256, 270, 271, 279, 298, 305, 306, 311, 357, 382, 462
Vayu, 5, 10, 55, 56, 57, 60, 62, 63, 64, 65, 66, 80, 99, 143, 193, 226, 236, 242, 243, 253, 255, 256, 259, 265, 383, 387, 392, 396, 399, 409
Veda, 2, 3, 4, 5, 6, 13, 55, 82, 272, 278, 390, 395
Vikruti, 22, 30, 36, 37, 152, 188, 215, 462
Vimshottari, 296, 304, 403, 436, 437, 439, 440, 442
Vishakha, 295, 387, 392, 399, 400, 401, 402, 404, 405, 406, 410
Vishnu, 34, 306, 388, 393, 395, 397, 399, 410, 420, 447
Vyana, 55, 56, 58, 59, 62, 64, 65, 77, 80, 241, 243, 249, 250, 253, 255, 259, 265

W

waters, 83, 169

Y

Yashoda, 34
Yoga, 3, 4, 18, 63, 93, 155, 207, 210, 214, 265, 266, 278, 279, 297, 299, 307, 320, 328, 334, 345, 360, 365, 404, 406, 407, 422, 424, 426, 444, 452, 454

Z

zinc, 76, 232

REFERENCE

The Complete Book of Ayurvedic Home Remedies, by Vasant D. Lad, 1998, Harmony Books, NY.

Ayurveda – Nature's Medicine, by Dr. David Frawley, Dr. Subhash Ranade, 2001, Lotus Press, Twin Lakes, WI USA

Ayurveda: Secrets of Healing, by Bri. Maya Tiwari. 1995, Lotus Press, Twin Lakes, WI USA

Astrology: Understanding the Birth Chart, by Kevin Burke, 2001, Llewellyn Publications, St Paul, MN

Essentials of Medical Astrology, By Dr. K S Charak, 2010, UMA Publications, Delhi, India

The Raga-s of Northern Indian Music, by Alain Danielou, 2014, Munshiram Manoharlal Publishers Pvt. Ltd. New Delhi, India

The Classical Music of North India, by Ali Akbar Khan, George Ruckert, 2015, Munshiram Manoharlal Publishers Pvt. Ltd. New Delhi, India

Vagbhata's Astanga Hrdayam, by Prof. K. R. Srikantha Murthy, 2008, Chowkhamba Krishnadas Academy, Varanasi, India

Charaka Samhita, Volume 1 of 4, Translation by P.V. Sharma, 2014, Chowkhamba Orientalia Varanasi, India

Ayurveda For You, by Vaidya Prof. Suresh Chaturvedi, 2003, Bharitiya Vidya Bhavan, Mumbai, India

---

ABOUT THE AUTHOR

Dev Bhattacharyya like many other authors was indoctrinated into the art of writing. In this book, the author has chosen not to let style rule over content. Dev has written for several journals and periodicals in the past and a book on technology. Dev lives with his wife and children in the northeast United States and is a prolific reader.

The software application illustrated in AquaPisces is available for viewing at www.aquapisces.com/book

www.ingramcontent.com/pod-product-compliance
Lightning Source LLC
Chambersburg PA
CBHW031305150426
43191CB00005B/78